www.wadsworth.com

wadsworth.com is the World Wide Web site for
Wadsworth Publishing Company and is your direct
source to dozens of online resources.

At *wadsworth.com* you can find out about supplements,
demonstration software, and student resources. You can
also send e-mail to many of our authors and preview new
publications and exciting new technologies.

wadsworth.com
Changing the way the world learns®

SOCIAL AND PERSONAL ETHICS

FOURTH EDITION

William H. Shaw
San Jose State University

WADSWORTH

THOMSON LEARNING

Australia • Canada • Mexico • Singapore • Spain • United Kingdom • United States

WADSWORTH

THOMSON LEARNING

Publisher: *Eve Howard*
Philosophy Editor: *Peter Adams*
Assistant Editor: *Kara Kindstrom*
Editorial Assistant: *Chalida Anusasananan*
Development Consultant: *Jake Warde*
Marketing Manager: *Dave Garrison*
Marketing Assistant: *Adam Hofmann*

Print/Media Buyer: *Tandra Jorgenson*
Permissions Editor: *Robert Kauser*
Production Service: *Greg Hubit Bookworks*
Cover Designer: *Yvo Riezebos*
Cover Image: *SuperStock*
Compositor: *Scratchgravel Publishing Services*
Printer: *Von Hoffmann Graphics*

Printed in the United States of America
1 2 3 4 5 6 7 05 04 03 02

For permission to use material from this text, contact us
by **Web:** http://www.thomsonrights.com
Fax: 1-800-730-2215   **Phone:** 1-800-730-2214

ISBN 0-534-56170-5

Wadsworth/Thomson Learning
10 Davis Drive
Belmont, CA 94002-3098
USA

For more information about our products, contact us:
Thomson Learning Academic Resource Center
1-800-423-0563
http://www.wadsworth.com

International Headquarters
Thomson Learning
International Division
290 Harbor Drive, 2nd Floor
Stamford, CT 06902-7477
USA

UK/Europe/Middle East/South Africa
Thomson Learning
Berkshire House
168-173 High Holborn
London WC1V 7AA
United Kingdom

Asia
Thomson Learning
60 Albert Street, #15-01
Albert Complex
Singapore 189969

Canada
Nelson Thomson Learning
1120 Birchmount Road
Toronto, Ontario M1K 5G4
Canada

CONTENTS

11. *Affirmative Action*

12. *Crime and Punishment*

13. *Economic Justice*

14. *Concluding Essay*

For Further Reading

PREFACE

MOST ETHICS COURSES these days, especially at the introductory level, put significant emphasis on contemporary moral issues and problems of applied ethics. *Social and Personal Ethics* is designed for use in such a course. Although a number of "moral issues" anthologies are available, this revised, fourth edition of *Social and Personal Ethics* has several distinguishing features to recommend it.

Ethics: Theoretical and Applied

The first of these distinguishing features is the treatment of ethical theory. *Social and Personal Ethics* begins with two essays that discuss the nature of morality and introduce the major theories and concepts of normative ethics. The first essay is an economical introduction to the relationship between law and morality and between religion and morality, to ethical relativism, to the distinguishing features of moral standards, to the nature of conscience and personal values, and to the potential conflict between morality and self-interest, among other topics. The second essay is a critical overview of egoism, utilitarianism, and Kant's ethics, along with Ross's nonconsequentialism and rights-based approaches to ethics.

Substantial but carefully edited extracts from the works of Aristotle, Kant, and Mill then follow. Part I ends with the rival ethical perspectives of three recent writers. James Rachels puts forward a comprehensive theory integrating the strengths of the Kantian and utilitarian traditions. Julius M. E. Moravcsik rejects this mainstream approach on behalf of a more Aristotelian perspective, which sees ethical issues as inescapably involving questions of human nature, the meaning of human existence, and our overall aims and ideals. Finally, Alison M. Jaggar surveys the main currents of feminist ethics and discusses their implications for the further development of ethical theory and practice.

Depending on instructors' philosophical perspectives and teaching goals, they can use Part I in different ways. They can, of course, work through it systematically. But it is also possible to focus on only some of this material—perhaps, for example, skipping the historical essays in favor of the contemporary ones and assigning the first two essays only as recommended background reading. Some instructors may wish to begin with the applied topics of Part II before turning to the more general questions of ethical theory.

Despite its division into two parts, *Social and Personal Ethics* does not divorce moral theory from the philosophical discussion of applied ethical issues. Questions of ethical theory and of the alternative normative directions that are open to us surface throughout Part II. A number of the essays on applied ethics—for example, those by Rachels, Dworkin, Macklin, Van Wyk, and the writers on capital punishment—explicitly take up the tension between Kantian and utilitarian concerns. Many other essays in Part II respond implicitly to this tension and raise other theoretical issues, such as the nature of rights, the extensiveness of moral obligation, and the meaning of justice.

Ethics: Social and Personal

As the essays by Moravcsik and Jaggar illustrate, many moral philosophers today see ethics as more properly concerned with character, moral education, vices, and virtues than with rules, rights, and public and legal policy. This perspective makes itself felt in Part II. Christina Hoff Sommers, to pick one example, argues that the answers contemporary philosophers have given to Jane English's question, "What Do Grown Children Owe Their Parents?" raise doubts about both the Kantian and utilitarian traditions. And the radical environmentalism of J. Baird Callicott challenges many of the normally unarticulated assumptions of conventional moral theory. Questions of personal value also appear throughout Part II, from Richard B. Brandt's essay on suicide to Derek Bok's advocacy of university-supported programs of community service.

Questions of personal ethics (that is, of personal values and individual moral choice) constantly intermingle with questions of social ethics (that is, of the assessment of social norms, public policy, and the institutional rules of morality). One sees this commingling particularly clearly in the sections on sexuality, on reproduction, on family obligations, and on liberty and paternalism, but it is true of almost every section in the book. Because questions of personal conduct and social policy intertwine in practice, they can and should be taught side by side, and the articles chosen for this collection generally discuss personal or social questions or both without drawing sharp lines between them. Some authors may lean to a virtue-based approach to ethics and others to a rule-based approach, but the essays themselves do not require endorsement of one approach over the other; nor do they presuppose an incompatibility between the two approaches.

The Readings

Because *Social and Personal Ethics* covers a broad range of moral topics and offers a large and diverse collection of articles that lend themselves well to classroom discussion, it should appeal to instructors of various philosophical persuasions. But this fact should not obscure the book's organizational and pedagogical coherence. I have tried to avoid offering simply a grab bag of intriguing essays. The readings of each section are designed to work well together, so that there is a dialogue among the writers on each topic. In addition, the ordering of the various sections and the thematic connections among them make intellectual sense. Taken together with the links between Part I and Part II, these features make for a textbook with about as much unity and coherence as one can expect in this field.

For *Social and Personal Ethics* I have sought essays that are philosophically intelligent yet interesting and accessible to undergraduates and fun to teach. The book contains essays on new issues like date rape, gay rights, racial harassment on campus, gun control, and cloning and surrogate motherhood along with new perspectives on older issues. Women (both feminist and nonfeminist) and people of color speak in their own voice in this book, and space is given to the concerns of those in the environmental movement. *Social and Personal Ethics* reprints a number of "classics," whose classroom effectiveness is well established, but it also includes many recent, previously unanthologized essays. The majority of these selections are by well-known philosophers, but other selections represent important contributions by less well-known philosophers or by other writers with whom philosophers may not be acquainted.

Instructors who have used the previous edition will notice that seven selections are new—on the duty to die, meat eating, cloning, adultery, gun control, punishment, and the welfare system. In addition, the essays by Rachels on moral theory, Boaz on drug prohibition, and Houlgate on divorce have been revised or updated. I have also made some changes in the introductory essays and have improved the editing of a number of the original readings to increase their accessibility and to ensure their relevance to undergraduate ethics courses. As before, the essays are prefaced by short introductions with study questions to guide students in their reading, and they are followed by questions for review and discussion.

Acknowledgments

I am grateful for the assistance of the following reviewers, whose thoughtful suggestions and useful criticisms helped shape this book: Susan Armstrong, Humboldt State University; James Baillie, University of Portland; Joseph Betz, Villanova University; Claudia Card, University of Wisconsin; Ann Davis, University of Colorado, Boulder; Debra DeBruin, University of Illinois, Chicago; James Dreier, Brown University; Randolph Feezell, Creighton University; Sterling Harwood, San Jose City College; Daniel M. Hausman, University of Wisconsin at Madison; John Himelright, Hartnell College; Robert Hollinger, Iowa State University of Science and Technology; Judith Little, State University of New York College at Potsdam; Scott C. Lowe, Bloomsburg University; Don Marietta, Florida Atlantic University; Andrew McLaughlin, City University of New York; John McLaughlin, Elmira College; Lucia Palmer, University of Delaware; Robert E. Reuman, Colby College; Jerome Shaffer, University of Connecticut; Ed Sherline, University of Wyoming; Laurie Shrage, California State Polytechnic University; Caroline J. Simon, Hope College; Sharon Sytsma, Northern Illinois University; Barbara Tucker, Trident Technical College; and Gary Varner, Texas A&M.

PART I

ETHICAL THEORY

AN INTRODUCTION TO ETHICS

The Nature of Morality

In an award-winning television drama, police captain Frank Furillo firmly believes that the two toughs just brought in by his officers are guilty of the rape-murder of a nun earlier that morning inside the parish church. But the evidence is only circumstantial. As word of the crime spreads, the community is aghast and angry. From all sides—the press, local citizens, city hall, the police commissioner—pressure mounts on Furillo and his department for a speedy resolution of the matter. Outside the Hill Street station, a mob grows frenzied, hoping to get their hands on the two young men and administer street justice to them. Someone in the mob has even taken a shot at the suspects inside the police station!

The police, however, have only enough evidence to arraign the suspects on the relatively minor charge of being in possession of goods stolen from the church. Furillo and his colleagues could demand high bail, thus keeping the defendants in custody while the police try to turn up evidence that will convict the men of murder. In a surprise move at the arraignment, the district attorney, acting in conjunction with Furillo, declines to ask the judge for bail. The men are free to go. But they and their outraged public defender, Joyce Davenport, know that their lives will be worthless once they hit the streets: Community members have sworn to avenge the much-loved sister if the police are unable to do their job. To remain in police custody, and thus safe, their only choice is to confess to murder. So the two men confess.

Davenport argues passionately but unsuccessfully against what she considers to be a police-state tactic. Anyone in that circumstance, guilty or innocent, would confess. It is an affront to the very idea of the rule of law, she contends: police coercion by way of mob pressure. No system of justice can permit such conduct from its public officials. Yet the confession allows the police to locate the murder weapon, thus bringing independent confirmation of the culprits' guilt. Furillo's tactic, nevertheless, does not rest easily on his own conscience, and the teleplay closes with him entering the church confessional later that night: "Forgive me, Father, for I have sinned. . . ."

Furillo is understandably worried about whether he did the morally right thing. His action was successful, and it was for a good cause. But does the end always justify the means? Did the police and district attorney behave in a way that accords with due process and the rights of defendants? Should community pressure influence one's professional decisions? Did Furillo act in accordance with some principle that he could defend publicly? In a tough and controversial situation like this, the issue does not concern the moral sincerity of either Furillo or Davenport. Both can be assumed to want to do what is right, but what exactly is the morally justified thing to do? How are we to judge Furillo's tactics?

These are difficult questions. Your answers will depend on the moral principles you accept. Moral principles provide the confirmatory standards for our moral judgments, and any defensible moral judgment must be supportable by a sound moral principle. But what are the appropriate principles to rely on when making moral judgments? Philosophers have given different answers to this question, and the second introductory essay will examine their answers. But first we must look more generally at the nature of morality: what moral standards are, where they come from, and how they fit into our lives. In particular, this essay discusses the following:

- The meaning of ethics
- What distinguishes moral standards from nonmoral standards, such as etiquette, law, and professional codes of conduct
- The relationship between morality and religion
- The doctrine of ethical relativism and its difficulties
- What it means to have moral principles, the nature of conscience, and the relationship between morality and self-interest
- The place of values and ideals in an individual's life

Ethics

"The word *ethics* comes from the Greek word *ethos,* meaning character or custom," writes philosophy professor Robert C. Solomon.[1] Today we use the word *ethos* to refer to the distinguishing disposition, character, or attitude of a specific people, culture, or group (as in, for example, "the American ethos" or "the business ethos"). According to Solomon, the etymology of *ethics* suggests its basic concerns: (1) individual character, including what it means to be "a good person," and (2) the social rules that govern and limit our conduct, especially the ultimate rules concerning right and wrong, which we call *morality.*

Some philosophers like to distinguish ethics from morality. To them *morality* refers to human conduct and values, and *ethics* refers to the study of those areas. *Ethics* does, of course, denote an academic subject, but in everyday parlance we interchange *ethical* and *moral* to describe people we consider good and actions we consider right. And we use *unethical* and *immoral* interchangeably to designate bad people and wrong actions. This essay follows that common usage.

Moral Versus Nonmoral Standards

What falls outside the sphere of moral concern is termed *nonmoral.* Whether your new sports car will top out at 120 or at 130 miles per hour is a nonmoral question. Whether you should top it out on Main Street on a Wednesday at high noon (or even at 3 A.M., for that matter) is a moral question. To see why requires an understanding of the difference between moral standards and other kinds of standards.

Wearing shorts to a formal dinner party is boorish behavior. Murdering the King's English with double negatives violates the basic conventions of proper language usage. Photographing the finish of a horse race with low-speed film is poor photographic technique. In each case a standard is violated—fashion, grammatical, artistic—but the violation does not pose a serious threat to human well-being.

Moral standards are different because they concern behavior that is of serious consequence to human welfare, that can profoundly injure or benefit people.[2] The conventional moral norms against lying, stealing, and murdering deal with actions that can hurt people. And the moral principle that human beings should be treated with dignity and respect uplifts the human personality. Whether products are healthful or harmful, work conditions safe or dangerous, personnel procedures biased or fair, privacy respected or invaded are also matters that seriously affect human well-being. The standards that govern our conduct in these areas are moral standards.

A second characteristic follows from the first. Moral standards take priority over other standards, including self-interest. Something that morality condemns—for instance, the burglary of your neighbor's home—cannot be justified on the nonmoral grounds that it would be a thrill to do it or that it would pay off handsomely. We take moral standards to be more important than other considerations in guiding our actions.

A third characteristic of moral standards is that their soundness depends on the adequacy of the reasons that support or justify them. For the most part, fashion standards are set by clothing designers, merchandisers, and consumers; grammatical standards by grammarians and students of language; technical standards by practioners and experts in the field. Legislators make laws, boards of directors make organizational policy, and licensing boards establish standards for professionals. In every case, some authoritative body is the ultimate validating source of the standards and thus can change the standards if it wishes. Moral standards are not made by such bodies, although they are often endorsed or rejected by them. More precisely, the validity of moral standards depends not on authoritative fiat but on the adequacy of the reasons that support or justify them. Precisely what constitutes adequate reasons for moral standards is problematic and, as we shall see, underlies disagreement about the legitimacy of specific moral principles.

Morality and etiquette

Etiquette refers to any special code of behavior or courtesy. In our society, for example, it is usually considered bad etiquette to chew with one's mouth open or to use obscene language in public; it is considered good etiquette to say "please" when requesting and "thank you" when receiving and to hold a door open for someone entering immediately behind us. Good business etiquette, to take another example, typically calls for writing follow-up letters after meetings, returning phone calls, and dressing appropriately. It is commonplace to judge people's manners as "good" or "bad" and the conduct that reflects them as "right" or "wrong." "Good," "bad," "right," and "wrong" here simply mean socially appropriate or socially inappropriate. In these contexts, such words express judgments about manners, not ethics.

So-called rules of etiquette that you might learn in an etiquette book are prescriptions for socially acceptable behavior. If you want to fit in, get along with others, and be thought well of by them, you should observe common rules of etiquette. If you violate the rules, then you're rightly considered ill mannered, impolite, or even uncivilized—but not necessarily immoral.

Scrupulous observance of rules of etiquette does not make one moral. In fact, it can camouflage moral issues. Not too long ago in some parts of the United States, it was thought bad manners for blacks and whites to eat together. Those who obeyed the convention and were thus judged well mannered certainly had no grounds for feeling moral. The only way to dramatize the injustice underlying this practice was to violate the rule and be judged ill mannered. For those in the civil rights movement of the 1960s, being considered boorish was a small price to pay for exposing the unequal treatment and human degradation that underlay this rule of etiquette.

Morality and law

People sometimes confuse legality and morality, but they are different things. On one hand, breaking the law is not always or necessarily immoral. On the other hand, the legality of an action does not guarantee that it is morally right. Let's consider these points further.

1. An action can be illegal but morally right. For example, helping a Jewish family to hide from the Nazis was against German law in 1939, but it would have been a morally admirable thing to have done. Of course, the Nazi regime was vicious and evil. By contrast, in a democratic society with a basically just legal order, the fact that something is illegal provides a moral consideration against doing it. For example, one moral reason for not burning trash in your back yard is that it violates an ordinance that your community has voted in favor of. Some philosophers believe that sometimes the illegality of an action can make it morally wrong, even if the action would otherwise have been morally acceptable. But even if they are right about this, the fact that something is illegal does not trump all other moral considerations. Nonconformity to law is not always immoral, even in a democratic society. There can be circumstances where, all things considered, violating the law is morally permissible, perhaps even morally required.

Probably no one in the modern era has expressed this point more eloquently than Dr. Martin Luther King, Jr. Confined in the Birmingham, Alabama, city jail on charges of parading without a permit, King penned his now famous "Letter from Birmingham Jail" to eight of his fellow clergymen who had published a statement attacking King's unauthorized protest of racial segregation as unwise and untimely. King wrote:

> All segregation statutes are unjust because segregation distorts the soul and damages the personality. It gives the segregator a false sense of superiority and the segregated a false sense of inferiority. Segregation, to use the terminology of the Jewish philosopher Martin Buber, substitutes an "I–it" relationship for an "I–thou" relationship and ends up relegating persons to the status of things. Hence segregation is not only politically, economically, and sociologically unsound, it is morally wrong and sinful. . . . Thus it is that I can urge men to obey the 1954 decision of the Supreme Court,* for it is morally right; and I can urge them to disobey segregation ordinances, for they are morally wrong.[3]

2. An action that is legal can be morally wrong. For example, it may have been perfectly legal for the chairman of a profitable company to lay off 125 workers and use three-quarters of the money saved to boost his pay and that of the company's other top manager, as recently happened,[4] but the morality of his doing so is open to debate.

Or, to take another example, suppose that you're driving to work one day and see an accident victim sitting on the side of the road, clearly in shock and needing medical assistance. Because you know first aid and are in no great hurry to get to your destination, you could easily stop and assist the person. Legally speaking, though, you are not obligated to stop and render aid. Under common law, the prudent thing would be to drive on, because by stopping you would bind yourself to use reasonable care and thus incur legal liability if you fail to do so and

---

*In *Brown v. Board of Education of Topeka* (1954), the Supreme Court struck down the half-century-old "separate but equal doctrine," which permitted racially segregated schools as long as comparable quality was maintained.

the victim thereby suffers injury. Many states have enacted so-called Good Samaritan laws to provide immunity from damages to those rendering aid (except for gross negligence or serious misconduct). But in most states the law does not oblige people to give such aid or even to call an ambulance. Moral theorists would agree, however, that if you sped away without rendering aid or even calling for help, your action might be perfectly legal but would be morally suspect. Regardless of the law, such conduct would almost certainly be wrong.

What then may we say about the relationship between law and morality? To a significant extent, law codifies a society's customs, ideals, norms, and moral values. Changes in law tend to reflect changes in what a society takes to be right and wrong, but sometimes changes in the law can alter people's ideas about the rightness or wrongness of conduct. However, even if a society's laws are sensible and morally sound, it is a mistake to see them as sufficient to establish the moral standards that should guide us. The law cannot cover the wide variety of possible individual and group conduct, and in many situations it is too blunt an instrument to provide adequate moral guidance. The law generally prohibits egregious affronts to a society's moral standards and in that sense is the "floor" of moral conduct, but breaches of moral conduct can slip through cracks in that floor.

Professional codes

Somewhere between etiquette and law lie *professional codes of ethics*. These are the rules that are supposed to govern the conduct of members of a given profession. Generally speaking, the members of a profession are understood to have agreed to abide by those rules as a condition of their engaging in that profession. Violation of the professional code may result in the disapproval of one's professional peers and, in serious cases, loss of one's license to practice that profession. Sometimes these codes are unwritten

and are part of the common understanding of members of a profession—for example, that professors should not date their students. In other instances, these codes or portions of them may be written down by an authoritative body so they may be better taught and more efficiently enforced.

These written rules are sometimes so vague and general as to be of little value, and often they amount to little more than self-promotion by the professional organization. In other cases—for example with attorneys—professional codes can be very specific and detailed. It is difficult to generalize about the content of professional codes of ethics, however, because they frequently involve a mix of purely moral rules (for example, client confidentiality), of professional etiquette (for example, the billing of services to other professionals), and of restrictions intended to benefit the group's economic interests (for example, limitations on price competition).

Given their nature, professional codes of ethics are neither a complete nor a completely reliable guide to one's moral obligations. First, not all the rules of a professional code are purely moral in character, and even when they are, the fact that a rule is officially enshrined as part of the code of a profession does not guarantee that it is a sound moral principle. As a professional, you must take seriously the injunctions of your profession, but you still have the responsibility to critically assess those rules for yourself.

Where do moral standards come from?

So far you have seen how moral standards are different from various nonmoral standards, but you probably wonder about the source of those moral standards. Most, if not all, people have certain moral principles or a moral code that they explicitly or implicitly accept. Because the moral principles of different people in the same society overlap, at least in part, we can also talk about the moral code of a society, meaning the moral standards shared by its members. How do we come to have certain moral principles and not others? Obviously, many things influence us in the moral principles we accept: our early upbringing, the behavior of those around us, the explicit and implicit standards of our culture, our own experiences, and our critical reflections on those experiences.

For philosophers, though, the important question is not how in fact we came to have the particular principles we have. The philosophical issue is whether the principles we have can be justified. Do we simply take for granted the values of those around us? Or, like Martin Luther King, Jr., are we able to think independently about moral matters? By analogy, we pick up our nonmoral beliefs from all sorts of sources: books, conversations with friends, movies, experiences we've had. The philosopher's concern is not so much with how we actually got the beliefs we have, but whether or to what extent those beliefs—for example, that women are more emotional than men or that telekinesis is possible—can withstand critical scrutiny. Likewise, ethical theories attempt to justify moral standards and ethical beliefs. The second introductory essay examines some of the major theories of normative ethics. That is, it looks at what some of the major thinkers in human history have argued are the best justified standards of right and wrong.

But first we need to consider the relationship between morality and religion on the one hand and that between morality and society on the other. Some people maintain that morality just boils down to religion. Others have argued for the doctrine of *ethical relativism,* which says that right and wrong are only a function of what a particular society takes to be right and wrong. Both these views are mistaken.

Religion and Morality

Any religion provides its believers with a world view, part of which involves certain moral instructions, values, and commitments. The Jew-

ish and Christian traditions, to name just two, offer a view of humans as unique products of a divine intervention that has endowed them with consciousness and an ability to love. Both these traditions posit creatures who stand midway between nature and spirit. On one hand, we are finite and bound to earth, not only capable of wrongdoing but born morally flawed (original sin). On the other, we can transcend nature and realize infinite possibilities.

Primarily because of the influence of Western religion, many Americans and others view themselves as beings with a supernatural destiny, as possessing a life after death, as being immortal. One's purpose in life is found in serving and loving God. For the Christian, the way to serve and love God is by emulating the life of Jesus of Nazareth. In the life of Jesus, Christians find an expression of the highest virtue—love. They love when they perform selfless acts, develop a keen social conscience, and realize that human beings are creatures of God and therefore intrinsically worthwhile. For the Jew, one serves and loves God chiefly through expressions of justice and righteousness. Jews also develop a sense of honor derived from a commitment to truth, humility, fidelity, and kindness. This commitment hones their sense of responsibility to family and community.

Religion, then, involves not only a formal system of worship but also prescriptions for social relationships. One example is the mandate "Do unto others as you would have them do unto you." Termed the "Golden Rule," this injunction represents one of humankind's highest moral ideals and can be found in essence in all the great religions of the world:

• Good people proceed while considering that what is best for others is best for themselves. (*Hitopadesa,* Hinduism)
• Thou shalt love thy neighbor as thyself. (*Leviticus* 19:18, Judaism)
• Therefore all things whatsoever ye would that men should do to you, do ye even so to them. (*Matthew* 7:12, Christianity)

- Hurt not others with that which pains yourself. (*Udanavarga* 5:18, Buddhism)
- What you do not want done to yourself, do not do to others. (*Analects* 15:23, Confucianism)
- No one of you is a believer until he loves for his brother what he loves for himself. (*Traditions,* Islam)

Although inspiring, such religious ideals are very general and can be difficult to translate into precise policy injunctions. Religious bodies, nevertheless, occasionally articulate positions on more specific political, educational, economic, and medical issues, which help mold public opinion on matters as diverse as abortion, euthanasia, nuclear weapons, and national defense.

Morality needn't rest on religion

Many people believe that morality must be based on religion, either in the sense that without religion people would have no incentive to be moral or in the sense that only religion can provide moral guidance. Others contend that morality is based on the commands of God. None of these claims is convincing.

First, although a desire to avoid hell and to go to heaven may prompt some of us to act morally, this is not the only reason or even the most common reason that people behave morally. Often we act morally out of habit or simply because that is the kind of person we are. It would just not occur to most of us to swipe an elderly woman's purse. And if the idea did occur to us, we wouldn't do it because such an act simply doesn't fit with our personal standards or with our concept of ourselves. We are often motivated to do what is morally right out of concern for others or just because it is right. In addition, the approval of our peers, the need to appease our conscience, and the desire to avoid earthly punishment may all motivate us to act morally. Furthermore, atheists generally live lives as moral and upright as believers.

Second, the moral instructions of the world's great religions are general and imprecise: They do not relieve us of the necessity to engage in moral reasoning ourselves. For example, the Bible says, "Thou shalt not kill." Yet Christians disagree among themselves over the morality of fighting in wars, of capital punishment, of killing in self-defense, of slaughtering animals, of abortion and euthanasia, and of allowing foreigners to die from famine because we have not provided them with as much food as we might have. The Bible does not give unambiguous answers to these moral problems. So even believers must engage in moral philosophy if they are to have intelligent answers. On the other hand, there are lots of reasons for believing that, say, a cold-blooded murder motivated by greed is immoral; you do not have to believe in a religion to figure that out.

Third, although some theologians have advocated the *divine command theory*—that if something is wrong (like killing an innocent person for fun), then the only reason it is wrong is that God commands us not to do it—many theologians and certainly most philosophers would reject this view. They would contend that if God commands human beings not to do something, like commit rape, it is because God sees that rape is wrong, but it is not God's forbidding rape that makes it wrong. The fact that rape is wrong is independent of God's decrees.

Most believers think not only that God gives us moral instructions or rules but also that God has moral reasons for giving them to us. According to the divine command theory, this would make no sense. In this view, there is no reason that something is right or wrong, other than it being God's will. All believers, of course, believe that God is good and that He commands us to do what is right and forbids us to do what is wrong. But this doesn't mean, say critics of the divine command theory, that God's saying so makes a thing wrong, any more than your mother's telling you not to steal makes it wrong to steal.

All this is simply to argue that morality is not necessarily based on religion in any of these three senses. That religion influences the moral standards and values of most of us is beyond doubt. But given that religions differ in their moral principles and that even members of the same faith often disagree among themselves on moral matters, practically speaking you cannot justify a moral principle simply by appealing to religion—for that will only persuade those who already agree with your particular interpretation of your particular religion. Besides, most religions hold that human reason is capable of understanding what is right and wrong, so it is human reason to which you will have to appeal in order to support your ethical principle.

Ethical Relativism

Some people do not believe that morality boils down to religion but rather that it is just a function of what a particular society happens to believe. This view is called *ethical relativism,* the theory that what is right is determined by what a culture or society says is right. What is right in one place may be wrong in another, because the only criterion for distinguishing right from wrong—and so the only ethical standard for judging an action—is the moral system of the society in which the act occurs.

Abortion, for example, is condemned as immoral in Catholic Ireland but is practiced as a morally neutral form of birth control in Japan. According to the ethical relativist, then, abortion is wrong in Ireland but morally permissible in Japan. The relativist is not saying merely that the Irish believe abortion is abominable and the Japanese do not; that is acknowledged by everyone. Rather, the ethical relativist contends that abortion is immoral in Ireland because the Irish believe it to be immoral and that it is morally permissible in Japan because the Japanese believe it to be so. Thus, for the ethical relativist there is no absolute ethical standard independent of cultural context, no criteria of right and wrong by which to judge other than those of particular societies. In short, what morality requires is relative to society.

Those who endorse ethical relativism point to the apparent diversity of human values and the multiformity of moral codes to support their case. From our own cultural perspective, some seemingly immoral moralities have been adopted; polygamy, pedophilia, stealing, slavery, infanticide, and cannibalism have all been tolerated or even encouraged by the moral system of one society or another. In light of this fact, the ethical relativist believes that there can be no nonethnocentric standard by which to judge actions.

Contrary to the relativist, some argue that the moral differences among societies are smaller and less significant than they appear. They contend that variations in moral standards reflect differing factual beliefs and differing circumstances rather than fundamental differences in values. But suppose the relativist is right about this matter. His conclusion still does not follow. As Allan Bloom writes, "The fact that there have been different opinions about good and bad in different times and places in no way proves that none is true or superior to others. To say that it does so prove is as absurd as to say that the diversity of points of view expressed in a college bull session proves there is no truth."[5] Disagreement in ethical matters does not imply that all opinions are equally correct.

Moreover, ethical relativism has some unpleasant implications. First, it undermines any moral criticism of the practices of other societies as long as their actions conform to their own standards. We cannot say that slavery in a slave society like that of the American South a hundred and fifty years ago was immoral and unjust as long as that society held it to be morally permissible.

Second, and closely related, is the fact that for the relativist there is no such thing as ethical progress. Although moralities may change, they cannot get better or worse. Thus, we cannot say that our moral standards today are any more enlightened than they were in the Middle Ages.

Third, it makes no sense from the relativist's point of view for people to criticize principles or practices accepted by their own society. People can be censured for not living up to their society's moral code, but that is all. The moral code itself cannot be criticized because whatever a society takes to be right really is right for it. Reformers who identify injustices in their society and campaign against them are only encouraging people to be immoral—that is, to depart from the moral standards of their society—unless or until the majority of the society agrees with the reformers. The minority can never be right in moral matters; to be right it must become the majority.

The ethical relativist is right to emphasize that in viewing other cultures we should keep an open mind and not simply dismiss alien social practices on the basis of our own cultural prejudices. But the relativist's theory of morality doesn't hold up. The more carefully we examine it, the less plausible it becomes. There is no good reason for saying that the majority view on moral issues is automatically right, and the belief that it is automatically right has unacceptable consequences.

Having Moral Principles

Most people at some time in their lives pause to reflect on what moral principles they have or should have and on what moral standards are the best justified. When a person accepts a moral principle, when that principle is part of his or her personal moral code, then naturally the person believes the principle is important and well justified. But there is more to moral principles than that, as the late Richard Brandt of the University of Michigan emphasized. When a principle is part of a person's moral code, that person is strongly motivated toward the conduct required by the principle and against behavior that conflicts with that principle. The person will tend to feel guilty when his or her own conduct violates that principle and to disapprove of others whose behavior conflicts with it. Likewise,

the person will tend to hold in esteem those whose conduct shows an abundance of the motivation required by the principle.[6]

Other philosophers have, in different ways, reinforced Brandt's point. To accept a moral principle is not a purely intellectual act like accepting a scientific hypothesis or a mathematical theorem. Rather, it also involves a desire to follow that principle for its own sake, the likelihood of feeling guilty about not doing so, and a tendency to evaluate the conduct of others according to the principle in question. We would find it very strange, for example, if Sally claimed to be morally opposed to cruelty to animals yet abused her own pets and felt no inclination to protest when some ruffians down the street lit a cat on fire.

Conscience

People can, and unfortunately sometimes do, go against their moral principles. But we would doubt that they sincerely held the principle in question if violating it did not bother their conscience. We have all felt the pangs of conscience, but what exactly is conscience and how reliable a guide is it? Our conscience, of course, is not literally a little voice inside of us. To oversimplify a complex story in developmental psychology, our conscience evolved as we internalized the moral instructions of the parents or other authority figures who raised us as children.

When you were very young, you were probably told to tell the truth and to return something you coveted to its proper owner. If you were caught lying or being dishonest, you were probably punished—scolded, spanked, sent to bed without dinner, denied a privilege. On the other hand, truth telling and honesty were probably rewarded—with approval, praise, maybe even hugs or candy. Seeking reward and avoiding punishment motivate small children to do what is expected of them. Gradually, children come to internalize those parental commands. Thus, they feel vaguely that their parents know what they are doing even when the parents are not around. When children do something forbidden, they experience the same feelings as when scolded by their parents—the first stirrings of guilt. By the same token, even in the absence of explicit parental reward, children feel a sense of self-approval about having done what they were supposed to have done.

As we grow older, of course, our motivations are not so simple and our self-understanding is greater. We are able to reflect on and understand the moral lessons we were taught, as well as to refine and modify those principles. As adults we are morally independent agents. Yet however much our conscience has evolved and however much our adult moral code differs from the moral perspective of our childhood, those pangs of guilt we occasionally feel still stem from that early internalization of parental demands.

The limits of conscience

How reliable a guide is conscience? People often say, "Follow your conscience" or "You should never go against your conscience," but not only is such advice not very helpful, it may sometimes be bad advice. First, when we are genuinely perplexed over what we ought to do, we are trying to figure out what our conscience ought to be saying to us. When it is not possible to do both, should we keep our promise to a colleague or come to the aid of an old friend? To be told that we should follow our conscience is no help at all.

Second, it may not always be good for us to follow our conscience. It all depends on what our conscience says. Our conscience might reflect moral motivations that cannot withstand critical scrutiny. Consider an episode in Chapter 16 of Mark Twain's *The Adventures of Huckleberry Finn*. Huck has taken off down the Mississippi on a raft with his friend, the runaway slave Jim. But as they get nearer to the place where Jim will become legally free, Huck starts feeling guilty about helping him run away:

It hadn't ever come to me before, what this thing was that I was doing. But now it did; and it staid with me, and scorched me more and more. I tried to make out to myself that *I* warn't to blame, because *I* didn't run Jim off from his rightful owner; but it warn't no use, conscience up and says, every time: "But you knowed he was running for his freedom, and you could a paddled ashore and told somebody." That was so—I couldn't get around that, no way. That was where it pinched. Conscience says to me: "What had poor Miss Watson done to you, that you could see her nigger go off right under your eyes and never say one single word? What did that poor old woman do to you, that you could treat her so mean? . . ." I got to feeling so mean and miserable I most wished I was dead.

Here Huck is feeling guilty about doing what we would all agree is the morally right thing to do. But Huck is only a boy, and his pangs of conscience reflect the principles that he has picked up uncritically from the slave-owning society around him. Unable to think independently about matters of right and wrong, Huck in the end decides to disregard his conscience. He follows his instincts and sticks by his friend Jim.

The point here is not that you should ignore your conscience but that the voice of conscience is itself something that can be critically examined. A pang of conscience is like a warning. When you feel one, you should definitely stop and reflect on the rightness of what you are doing. On the other hand, you cannot justify your actions simply by saying you were following your conscience. Terrible crimes have been committed in the name of conscience.

Moral principles and self-interest

Sometimes doing what you believe would be morally right and doing what would best satisfy your own interests may be two different things. Imagine that you are in your car hurrying home along a quiet road, trying hard to get there in time to see the kickoff of an important football game. You pass an acquaintance who is having car trouble. He doesn't recognize you. As a dedicated fan, you would much prefer to keep on going than to stop and help him, thus missing at least part of the game. You might rationalize that someone else will eventually come along and help him if you don't, but deep down you know that you really ought to stop. On the other hand, self-interest seems to say, "Keep going."

Consider another example.[7] You have applied for a new job, and if you land it, it will be an enormous break for you: It is exactly the kind of position you want and have been trying to get for some time. It pays well and will settle you into a desirable career for the rest of your life. The competition has come down to just you and one other person, and you believe correctly that she has a slight edge on you. Now imagine that you could spread a nasty rumor about her that would guarantee she wouldn't get the job and that you could do this in a way that wouldn't come back to you. Presumably, circulating this lie would violate your moral code; on the other hand, doing it would clearly be to your benefit.

Some people argue that moral action and self-interest can never genuinely be in conflict, and some philosophers have gone to great lengths to try to prove this, but they are almost certainly mistaken. They maintain that if you do the wrong thing, then you will be caught, your conscience will bother you, or in some way "what goes around comes around," so that your misdeed will come back to haunt you. This is often correct. But unfortunately—viewed just in terms of personal self-interest—sometimes doing what you know to be wrong may pay off. People sometimes get away with their wrongdoings, and if their conscience bothers them at all, it may not bother them that much. To believe otherwise not only is wishful thinking but also shows a lack of understanding of morality.

Morality serves to restrain our purely self-interested desires so we can all live together.

The moral standards of a society provide the basic guidelines for cooperative social existence and allow conflicts to be resolved by appeal to shared principles of justification. If our interests never came into conflict—that is, if it were never advantageous for one person to deceive or cheat another—then there would be little need for morality. We would already be in heaven. Both a system of law that punishes people for hurting others and a system of morality that encourages people to refrain from pursuing their self-interest at a great expense to others help to make social existence possible.

Usually, following our moral principles is in our best interest. But notice one thing. If you do the right thing only because you think it will pay off, you are not really motivated by moral concerns. Having a moral principle involves having a desire to follow the principle for its own sake—just because it is the right thing to do. If you only do the right thing because you believe it will pay off, you might just as easily not do it if it looks as if it is not going to pay off.

In addition, there is no guarantee that moral behavior will always pay off in strictly selfish terms. As argued earlier, there will be exceptions. From the moral point of view, you ought to stop and help your acquaintance and you shouldn't lie about competitors. From the selfish point of view, you should do exactly the opposite. Should you follow your self-interest or your moral principles? There's no final answer to this question. From the moral point of view, you should, of course, follow your moral principles. But from the selfish point of view, you should look out solely for Number One.

Which option you choose will depend on the strength of your self-interested or self-regarding desires in comparison with the strength of your other-regarding desires (that is, your moral motivations and your concern for others). In other words, your choice will depend on the kind of person you are, which depends in large part on how you were raised. A selfish person will pass by the acquaintance in distress and will spread the rumor, whereas a person who has a stronger concern for others, or a stronger desire to do what is right just because it is right, will not.

Although it may be impossible to prove to selfish people that they should not do the thing that best advances their self-interest (because, if they are selfish, that is all they care about), there are considerations that suggest it is not in a person's overall self-interest to be a selfish person. People who are exclusively concerned with their own interests tend to have less happy and less satisfying lives than those whose desires extend beyond themselves. This is sometimes called the *paradox of hedonism*. Individuals who care only about their own happiness will generally be less happy than those who care about others. Moreover, people often find greater satisfaction in a life lived according to moral principle, and in being the kind of person that entails, than in a life devoted solely to immediate self-interest. Thus, or so many philosophers have argued, people have self-interested reasons not to be so self-interested. How do selfish people make themselves less so? Not overnight, obviously. But by involving themselves in the concerns and cares of others, they can in time come to care sincerely about those people.

Morality and Personal Values

Some philosophers distinguish between morality in a narrow sense and morality in a broad sense. In a narrow sense, morality is the moral code of an individual or a society (insofar as the moral codes of the individuals making up that society overlap). Although the principles that make up our code may not be explicitly formulated, as laws are, they do guide us in our conduct. They function as internal monitors of our own behavior and as a basis for assessing the action of others. Morality in the narrow sense concerns the principles that do or should regulate people's conduct and relations with others. These principles can be debated, however. (Take, for ex-

ample, John Stuart Mill's contention that society ought not to interfere with people's liberty when their actions affect only themselves.) And a large part of moral philosophy involves assessing rival moral principles. This discussion is part of the ongoing development in our moral culture. What is at stake are the basic standards that ought to govern our behavior—that is, the basic framework or ground rules that make coexistence possible. If there were not already fairly widespread agreement about these principles, our social order would not be possible.

But in addition we can talk about our morality in a broader sense, meaning not just the principles of conduct that we embrace but also the values, ideals, and aspirations that shape our lives. Many different ways of living our lives would meet our basic moral obligations. The type of life each of us seeks to live reflects our individual values—whether following a profession, devoting ourselves to community service, raising a family, seeking solitude, pursuing scientific truth, striving for athletic excellence, amassing political power, cultivating glamorous people as friends, or some combination of these and many other possible ways of living. The life that each of us forges and the way we understand that life are part of our morality in the broad sense of the term.

It is important to bear this in mind throughout your study of applied ethics. Although the usual concern is with the principles that ought to govern conduct in certain situations—for example, whether a hiring officer may take the race of applicants into account, whether euthanasia is immoral, or whether surrogate parenting contracts should be permitted—the moral choices you make in your own life will also reflect your other values and ideals—or in other words, the kind of person you are striving to be.

The decisions you make and much of the way you shape your life will depend not just on your moral code but also on the understanding you have of yourself in certain roles and relationships. Your morality—in the sense of your ideals, values, and aspirations—involves, among other things, your understanding of human nature, tradition, and society; of one's proper relationship to the natural environment; and of an individual's place in the cosmos. Professionals in various fields, for example, are invariably guided not just by rules but also by their understanding of what being a professional involves. And a businessperson's conception of the ideal or model relationship to have with clients will greatly influence his or her day-to-day conduct.

There is more to living a morally good life, of course, than being good at your job, as Aristotle (384–322 B.C.E.) argued long ago. He underscored the necessity of trying to achieve virtue or excellence, not just in some particular field of endeavor but as a human being. Aristotle thought that things have functions. The function of a piano, for instance, is to make certain sounds, and a piano that performs this function well is a good or excellent piano. Likewise, we have an idea of what it is for a person to be an excellent athlete, an excellent manager, or an excellent professor—it is to do well the types of things that athletes, managers, or professors are supposed to do.

But Aristotle also thought that, just as there was an ideal of excellence for any particular craft or occupation, similarly there must be an excellence that we can achieve simply as human beings. That is, he thought that we can live our lives as a whole in such a way that they can be judged not just as excellent in this respect or in that occupation, but as excellent, period. Aristotle thought that only when we develop our truly human capacities sufficiently to achieve this human excellence would we have lives blessed with happiness. Philosophers since Aristotle's time have been skeptical of his apparent belief that this human excellence would come in just one form, but many would underscore the importance of developing our various potential capacities and striving to achieve a kind of excellence in our lives. How we understand this excellence is a function of our values, ideals, and world view—our morality in a broad sense.

NOTES

1. Robert C. Solomon, *Morality and the Good Life* (New York: McGraw-Hill, 1984), 3.

2. On the characteristics of moral standards, see Manuel G. Velasquez, *Business Ethics,* 4th ed. (Englewood Cliffs, N.J.: Prentice-Hall, 1998), 10.

3. Martin Luther King, Jr., "Letter from Birmingham Jail," in *Why We Can't Wait* (New York: Harper & Row, 1963), 85.

4. *Newsweek,* May 26, 1997, 54.

5. Allan Bloom, *The Closing of the American Mind* (New York: Simon & Schuster, 1987), 39.

6. Richard B. Brandt, *A Theory of the Good and the Right* (New York: Oxford University Press, 1979), 165–170.

7. Baruch Brody, *Beginning Philosophy* (Englewood Cliffs, N.J.: Prentice-Hall, 1977), 33.

Normative Theories of Ethics

LIKE CAPTAIN FRANK FURILLO in our earlier example, we may sometimes be faced with the problem of deciding what is the right thing to do. How do we go about deciding? Is there a single "right way" to answer moral questions? The scientific method tells us what steps to take if we seek to answer a scientific question, but there is no comparable "moral method" for engaging moral questions. Moral principles are the basis for making moral judgments, but the use of these principles is not a mechanical process in which one cranks in data and out pops an automatic moral judgment. Rather, the principles provide a conceptual framework that guides us in making moral decisions. Careful thought and open-minded reflection are always necessary to work from one's moral principles to a considered moral judgment.

But what are the appropriate principles to rely on when making moral judgments? The truth is that there is no consensus among people who have studied ethics and reflected on these matters. Different theories exist as to the proper standards of right and wrong. As Professor Bernard Williams has put it, we are heirs to a rich and complex ethical tradition, in which a variety of different moral principles and ethical considerations intertwine and sometimes compete.[1]

This essay discusses the normative perspectives and rival ethical principles that are our heritage. After distinguishing between what are called consequentialist and nonconsequentialist normative theories, it looks in detail at several ethical approaches, discussing their pros and cons:

- Egoism, both as an ethical theory and as a psychological theory

- Utilitarianism, the theory that the morally right action is the one that achieves the greatest total amount of happiness for everyone concerned
- Kant's ethics, with his categorical imperative and his emphasis on moral motivation and respect for persons
- Other nonconsequentialist normative themes: duties, moral rights, and prima facie principles

Consequentialist and Nonconsequentialist Theories

In ethics, *normative theories* propose some principle or principles for distinguishing right actions from wrong actions. These theories can, for convenience, be divided into two kinds: consequentialist and nonconsequentialist.

Many philosophers have argued that the moral rightness of an action is determined solely by its results. If its consequences are good, then the act is right; if they are bad, the act is wrong. Moral theorists who adopt this approach are therefore called *consequentialists*. They determine what is right by weighing the ratio of good to bad that an action is likely to produce. The right act is the one that produces, will probably produce, or is intended to produce at least as great a ratio of good to evil as any other course of action.

One question that arises here is, Consequences for whom? Should one consider the consequences only for oneself? Or the consequences for everyone affected? The two most important consequentialist theories, *egoism* and *utilitarianism,* are distinguished by their different answers to this question. Egoism advocates individual self-interest as its guiding principle; utilitarianism holds that one must take into account everyone affected by the action. But both theories agree that rightness and wrongness are solely a function of an action's results.

In contrast, *nonconsequentialist* (or *deontological*) theories contend that right and wrong are determined by more than the likely consequences of an action. Nonconsequentialists do not necessarily deny that consequences are morally significant, but they believe that other factors are also relevant to the moral assessment of an action. For example, a nonconsequentialist would hold that for Kevin to break his promise to Cindy is wrong not simply because it has bad results (Cindy's hurt feelings, Kevin's damaged reputation, and so on) but because of the inherent character of the act itself. Even if more good than bad were to come from Kevin's breaking the promise, a nonconsequentialist might still view it as wrong. What matters is the nature of the act in question, not just its results. This concept will become clearer later in the essay with the discussion of some specific nonconsequentialist theories.

Egoism

The view that associates morality with self-interest is referred to as *egoism*. Egoism contends that an act is morally right if and only if it best promotes the individual's long-term interests. Egoists use their best long-term advantage as the standard for measuring an action's rightness. If an action produces, will probably produce, or is intended to produce for the individual a greater ratio of good to evil in the long run than any other alternative, then that action is the right one to perform. The individual should take that course to be moral.

Moral philosophers distinguish between two kinds of egoism: personal and impersonal. Personal egoists claim they should pursue their own best long-term interests, but they do not say what others should do. Impersonal egoists claim that everyone should follow his or her best long-term interests.

Misconceptions about egoism

Several misconceptions haunt both versions of egoism. One is that egoists do only what they like, that they believe in "eat, drink, and be merry." Not so. Undergoing unpleasant, even painful experience meshes with egoism, provided such temporary sacrifice is necessary for the advancement of our long-term interests.

Another misconception is that all egoists endorse *hedonism,* the view that only pleasure (or happiness) is of intrinsic value, the only good in life worth pursuing. Although some egoists are hedonistic—as was the ancient Greek philosopher Epicurus (341–270 B.C.E.)—other egoists have a broader view of what constitutes self-interest. They identify the good with knowledge, power, or what some modern psychologists call self-actualization. Egoists may, in fact, hold any theory of what is good.

A final but very important misconception is that egoists cannot act honestly, be gracious and helpful to others, or otherwise promote others' interests. Egoism, however, requires us to do whatever will best further our own interests, and doing this sometimes requires us to advance the interests of others. In particular, egoism tells us to benefit others when we expect that doing so will be reciprocated or when the act will bring us pleasure or in some way promote our own good. For example, egoism might discourage a shopkeeper from trying to cheat customers because it is likely to hurt business in the long run. Or egoism might recommend to the chairman of the board that she hire as a vice president her nephew, who is not the best candidate for the job but whom the chairman is very fond of. Hiring the nephew might bring her more satisfaction than any other course of action, even if the nephew doesn't perform his job as well as someone else might.

Psychological egoism

Egoism does not preach that we should never assist others but rather that we have no basic moral duty to do so. The only moral obligation we have is to ourselves. Although you and I are not required to act in the interests of others, we should if that is the only way to promote our own self-interest. In short: Always look out for Number One.

Proponents of the ethical theory of egoism generally attempt to derive their basic moral principle from the alleged fact that humans are by nature selfish creatures. According to this doctrine, termed *psychological egoism*, human beings are, as a matter of fact, so constructed that they must behave selfishly. Psychological egoism asserts that all actions are in fact selfishly motivated and that truly unselfish actions are therefore impossible. Even such apparently self-sacrificial acts as giving up your own life to save the lives of your children or blowing the whistle on your organization's misdeeds at great personal expense are, according to psychological egoism, selfishly motivated. They are done to satisfy the parents' desires to benefit themselves—for example, to perpetuate their family line or avoid unbearable guilt—or the workers' desires for celebrity or revenge.

Problems with egoism

Although egoism as an ethical doctrine has always had its adherents, the theory is open to very strong objections. And it is safe to say that few, if any, philosophers today would advocate it. Consider these objections:

1. Psychological egoism is not a sound theory. Of course, everyone is motivated to some extent by self-interest, and we all know of situations in which someone pretended to be acting altruistically or morally but was really motivated only by self-interest. The theory of psychological egoism contends, however, that people are always motivated only by self-interested concerns.

This claim seems open to many counterexamples. Take the actual case of a man who, while driving a company truck, spotted smoke coming from inside a parked car and a child trying to escape from the vehicle. The man quickly made a U-turn, drove over to the burning vehicle, and found a one-year-old girl trapped in the back seat, restrained by a seat belt. Flames raged in the front seat as heavy smoke billowed from the car. Disregarding his own safety, the man entered the car and removed the infant, who authorities said otherwise would have died from the poisonous fumes and the flames.

Or take a more mundane example. It's Saturday, and you feel like having a beer with a couple of pals and watching the ball game. On the other hand, you believe you ought to take your two children to the zoo, as you had earlier suggested to them you might. Going to the zoo would bring them a lot of pleasure—and besides, you haven't done much with them recently. Of course, you love your children and it will bring you some pleasure to go to the zoo with them, but—let's face it—they've been cranky lately and you'd prefer to watch the ball game. Nonetheless, you feel an obligation and so you go to the zoo.

These appear to be cases in which people are acting for reasons other than self-interested ones. Of course, the reasons that lead you to take your children to the zoo—a sense of obligation, a desire to promote their happiness—are your reasons, but that by itself does not make them self-interested reasons. Still less does it show that you are selfish. Anything that you do is a result of your desires, but that fact doesn't establish what the believer in psychological egoism claims—namely, that the only desires you have, or the only desires that ultimately move you, are self-interested desires.

Psychological egoists (that is, advocates of the theory of psychological egoism) will claim that deep down both the heroic man who saved the girl and the unheroic parent who took the children to the zoo were really motivated by self-interest in some way or another. Maybe the hero was hoping to win praise or the parent to advance his or her own pleasure by enhancing the children's affection for the parent. Or maybe some other self-interested consideration motivated them. Psychological egoists can always claim that some yet-to-be-identified subconscious egoistic motivation is the main impulse behind any action.

At this point, though, the psychological egoists' claims sound a little far fetched, and we may suspect them of trying to make their theory true by definition. Whatever example we come up with, they will simply claim that the person is really motivated by self-interest. One may well wonder how scientific this theory is, or how much content it has, when both the hero and the coward, both the parent who goes to the zoo and the parent who stays home, are equally selfish in their motivations.

A defender of egoism as an ethical doctrine could concede that people are not fully egoistic by nature and yet continue to insist that people morally ought to pursue only their own interests. Yet without the doctrine of psychological egoism, the ethical thesis of egoism becomes less attractive. Other types of ethical principles are possible. We all care about ourselves, but how much sense does it make to see self-interest as the basis of right and wrong? Do we really want to say that someone acting altruistically is behaving immorally?

2. Ethical egoism is not really a moral theory at all. Many critics of egoism as an ethical standard contend that it misunderstands the nature and point of morality: to restrain our purely self-interested desires so we can all live together. If our interests never came into conflict—that is, if it were never advantageous for one person to deceive or cheat another—then we would have no need of morality. The moral standards of a society provide the basic guidelines for cooperative social existence and allow conflicts to be resolved by appeal to shared principles of justification.

It is difficult to see how ethical egoism could perform this function. In a society of egoists, people might publicly agree to follow certain rules so their lives would run more smoothly. But it would be a very unstable world, because people would not hesitate to break the rules if they thought they could get away with it. Nor can egoism provide a means for settling conflicts and disputes, because it simply tells each party to do whatever is necessary to promote effectively his or her interests.

Many moral theorists maintain that moral principles apply equally to the conduct of all persons and that their application requires us to be objective and impartial. Moral agents are seen as those who, despite their own involvement in an issue, can be reasonably disinterested and objective—those who try to see all sides of an issue without being committed to the interests of a particular individual or group, including themselves. If we accept this attitude of detachment and impartiality as at least part of what it means to take a moral point of view, then we must look for it in any proposed moral principle.

Those who make egoism their moral standard are anything but objective, for they seek to guide themselves by their own best interests, regardless of the issue or circumstances. They do not even attempt to be impartial, except insofar as impartiality furthers their own interests. And, according to their theory, any third party offering advice should simply represent his or her own interest.

3. Ethical egoism ignores blatant wrongs. The most common objection to egoism as an ethical doctrine is that by reducing everything to the standard of best long-term self-interest, egoism takes no stand against seemingly outrageous acts like stealing, murder, racial and sexual discrimination, deliberately false advertising, and wanton pollution. All such actions are morally neutral until the test of self-interest is applied.

Of course, the defender of egoism might call this objection a case of begging the question: assuming that such acts are immoral as grounds for repudiating egoism when, in fact, their morality is the very issue that moral principles such as egoism are meant to resolve. Still, egoism must respond to the widely observed human desire to be fair or just, a desire that at least sometimes seems stronger than competing selfish desires. A moral principle that allows the possibility of murder in the cause of self-interest offends our basic intuitions about right and wrong.

Utilitarianism

Utilitarianism is the moral doctrine that we should always act to produce the greatest possible balance of good over bad for everyone affected by our action. By "good," utilitarians understand happiness or pleasure. Thus, they answer the question "What makes a moral act right?" by asserting: the greatest happiness of all. Although the basic theme of utilitarianism is present in the writings of many earlier thinkers, Jeremy Bentham (1748–1832) and John Stuart Mill (1806–1873) were the first to develop the theory explicitly and in detail. Both Bentham and Mill were philosophers with a strong interest in legal and social reform. They used the utilitarian standard to evaluate and criticize the social and political institutions of their day—for example, the prison system. As a result, utilitarianism has long been associated with social improvement.

Bentham viewed a community as no more than the individual persons who compose it. The interests of the community are simply the sum of the interests of its members. An action promotes the interests of an individual when it adds to the individual's pleasure or diminishes the person's pain. Correspondingly, an action augments the happiness of a community only insofar as it increases the total amount of individual happiness. In this way, Bentham argued for the utilitarian principle that actions are right if they promote the greatest human welfare, wrong if they do not.

For Bentham, pleasure and pain are merely types of sensations that differ only in number, intensity, and duration. He offered a "hedonic calculus" of six criteria for evaluating pleasure and pain exclusively by their quantitative differences. This calculus, he believed, makes possible an objective determination of the morality of anyone's conduct, individual or collective, on any occasion.

Bentham rejected any distinctions based on quality of pleasure except insofar as they might indicate differences in quantity. Thus, if equal amounts of pleasure are involved, throwing darts is as good as writing poetry and baking a cake as good as composing a symphony; reading Stephen King is of no less value than reading Shakespeare. Although he himself was an intelligent, cultivated man, Bentham maintained there is nothing intrinsically better about cultivated and intellectual pleasures than about crude and prosaic ones. The only issue is which yields the greater amount of enjoyment.

John Stuart Mill thought Bentham's concept of pleasure was too simple. He viewed human beings as having elevated faculties that allow them to pursue various kinds of pleasure. The pleasures of the intellect and imagination, in particular, have a higher value than those of mere sensation. Thus, for Mill the utility principle allows consideration of the relative quality of pleasure and pain.

Although Bentham and Mill had different conceptions of pleasure, both men identified pleasure and happiness and considered pleasure the ultimate value. In this sense they are hedonists: Pleasure, in their view, is the one thing that is intrinsically good or worthwhile. Anything that is good is good only because it brings about pleasure (or happiness), directly or indirectly. Take education, for example. The learning process itself might be pleasurable to us; reflecting on or working with what we have learned might bring us satisfaction at some later time; or by making possible a career and life that we could not have had otherwise, education might bring us happiness indirectly. In contrast, critics of Bentham and Mill have contended that things other than happiness are or can also be inherently good—for example, knowledge, friendship, and aesthetic satisfaction. The implication is that these things are valuable even if they do not lead to happiness.

Some moral theorists have modified utilitarianism so that it aims at other consequences in addition to happiness. Other utilitarians, wary of trying to compare one person's happiness with another's, have interpreted their theory as requiring us not to maximize happiness but rather to maximize the satisfaction of people's preferences (or desires). The focus here will be utilitarianism in its standard form, in which the good to be aimed at is human happiness or welfare. But what will be said about standard or classical utilitarianism applies, with the appropriate modifications, to other versions as well.

Although this essay will also consider another form of utilitarianism, known as *rule utilitarianism*, utilitarianism in its most basic version, often called *act utilitarianism,* states that we must ask ourselves what the consequences of a particular act in a particular situation will be for all those affected. If its consequences bring more total good than those of any alternative course of action, then this action is the right one and the one we should perform. Thus a utilitarian could defend Frank Furillo's decision not to request bail, thereby coercing a confession from the suspects.

Six points about utilitarianism

Before evaluating utilitarianism, one should understand some points that might lead to confusion and misapplication. First, when a utilitarian like Bentham advocates "the greatest happiness for the greatest number," we must consider unhappiness or pain as well as happiness. Suppose, for example, that an action produces eight units of happiness and four units of unhappiness. Its net worth is four units of happiness. Suppose also that an opposed action produces ten units of happiness and seven units of unhappiness; its net worth is three units. In this case we should choose the first action over the second. In the event that both lead not to happiness but to unhappiness, and there is no third option, we should choose the one that brings fewer units of unhappiness.

Second, actions affect people to different degrees. Your playing the radio loudly might enhance two persons' pleasure a little, cause significant discomfort to two others, and leave a fifth person indifferent. The utilitarian theory is not that each person votes on the basis of his or her pleasure or pain, with the majority ruling, but that we add up the various pleasures and pains, however large or small, and go with the action that brings about the greatest net amount of happiness.

Third, because utilitarians evaluate actions according to their consequences, and actions produce different results in different circumstances, almost anything might in principle be morally right in some particular circumstance. For example, although breaking a promise generally produces unhappiness, there can be circumstances in which, on balance, more happiness would be produced by breaking a promise than by keeping it. In those circumstances, utilitarianism would require us to break the promise.

Fourth, utilitarians wish to maximize happiness not simply immediately but in the long run as well. All the indirect ramifications of an act have to be taken into account. Lying might seem a good way out of a tough situation, but if and when the people we deceive find out, not only will they be unhappy, but our reputation and our relationships with them will be damaged. This is a serious risk that a utilitarian cannot ignore.

Fifth, utilitarians acknowledge that we often do not know with certainty what the future consequences of our actions will be. Accordingly, we must act so that the expected or likely happiness is as great as possible. If I take my friend's money, without his knowledge, and buy lottery tickets with it, there is a chance that we will end up millionaires and that my action will have maximized happiness all around. But the odds are definitely against it; the most likely result is loss of money (and probably of a friendship, too). Therefore, no utilitarian could justify gambling with purloined funds on the grounds that it might maximize happiness.

Sometimes it is difficult to determine the likely results of alternative actions, and no modern utilitarian really believes that we can assign precise units of happiness and unhappiness to people. But as Mill reminds us, we really do have quite a lot of experience as to what typically makes people happy or unhappy. In any case, as utilitarians our duty is to strive to maximize total happiness, even when it may seem difficult to know what action is likely to promote it effectively.

Finally, when choosing among possible actions, utilitarianism does not require us to disregard our own pleasure. Nor should we give it added weight. Rather, our own pleasure and pain enter into the calculus equally with the pleasures and pains of others. Even if we are sincere in our utilitarianism, we must guard against the possibility of being biased in our calculations when our own interests are at stake. For this reason, and because it would be time-consuming to do a utilitarian calculation before every action, utilitarians encourage us to rely on rules of thumb in ordinary moral circumstances. We can make it a rule of thumb, for example, to tell the truth and keep our promises, rather than to calculate possible pleasures and pains in every routine case, because we know that in general telling the truth and keeping promises result in more happiness than lying and breaking promises.

Critical inquiries of utilitarianism

1. Is utilitarianism really workable? Utilitarianism instructs us to maximize happiness, but in hard cases we may be very uncertain about the likely results of the alternative courses of action open to us. Furthermore, comparing your level of happiness or unhappiness with mine is at best tricky, at worst impossible—and when many people are involved, the matter may get hopelessly complex. Even if we assume that it is possible to make comparisons and to calculate the various possible results of each course of action that a person might take (and the odds of each happening), is it realistic to expect people to take the time to make those calculations and, if they do, to make them accurately? Some critics of act utilitarianism have contended that teaching people to follow the basic utilitarian principle would not in fact promote happiness because of the difficulties in applying utilitarianism accurately.

2. Are some actions wrong, even if they produce good? Like egoism, utilitarianism focuses on the results of an action, not on the character of the action itself. For utilitarians, no action is in itself objectionable. It is objectionable only when it leads to a lesser amount of total good than could otherwise have been brought about. Critics of utilitarianism, in contrast, contend that some actions can be immoral and thus are things we must not do, even if doing them would maximize happiness

Suppose a dying woman has asked you to promise to send the $25,000 under her bed to her nephew in another part of the country. She dies without anyone else knowing of the money or of the promise that you made. Now suppose, too, that you know the nephew is a spendthrift and a drunkard and, were the money delivered to him, it would be wasted in a week of outrageous partying. On the other hand, a very fine orphanage in your town needs such a sum to improve and expand its recreational facilities, something that would provide happiness to many children for years to come. It seems clear that on utilitarian grounds you should give the money to the orphanage, because this action would result in more total happiness.

Many people would balk at this conclusion, contending that it would be wrong to break your promise, even if doing so would bring about more good than keeping it. Having made a promise, you have an obligation to keep it, and a deathbed promise is particularly serious. Furthermore, the deceased woman had a right to do with her money as she wished; it is not for you to decide how to spend it. Likewise, having been bequeathed the money, the nephew has a right to it, regardless of how wisely or foolishly he might spend it. Defenders of utilitarianism, however, would insist that promoting happiness is all that really matters and warn you not to be blinded by moral prejudice.

Critics of utilitarianism, on the other hand, maintain that utilitarianism is morally blind in not just permitting, but requiring, immoral actions in order to maximize happiness. Philosopher Richard Brandt states the case against act utilitarianism this way:

> Act-utilitarianism . . . implies that if you have employed a boy to mow your lawn and he has finished the job and asks for his pay, you should pay him what you promised only if you cannot find a better use for your money. . . . It implies that if your father is ill and has no prospect of good in his life, and maintaining him is a drain on the energy and enjoyments of others, then, if you can end his life without provoking any public scandal or setting a bad example, it is your positive duty to take matters into your own hands and bring his life to a close.[2]

In the same vein, ethicist A. C. Ewing concludes that "[act] utilitarian principles, logically carried out, would result in far more cheating, lying, and unfair action than any good man would tolerate."[3]

Defenders of act utilitarianism would reply that these charges are exaggerated. Although it is theoretically possible, for example, that not paying the boy for his work might maximize happiness, this is extremely unlikely. Utilitarians contend that only in very unusual circumstances

will pursuit of the good conflict with our ordinary ideas of right and wrong, and in those cases—like the deathbed promise—we should put aside those ordinary ideas. The antiutilitarian replies that the theoretical possibility of utilitarianism requiring immoral conduct shows it to be an unsatisfactory moral theory.

3. Is utilitarianism unjust? Utilitarianism concerns itself with the sum total of happiness produced, not with how that happiness is distributed. If policy X brings two units of happiness to each of five people and policy Y brings nine units of happiness to one person, one unit each to two others, and none to the remaining two, then Y is to be preferred (eleven units of happiness versus ten), even though it distributes that happiness very unequally.

Worse still from the critic's point of view, utilitarianism may even require that some people's happiness be sacrificed in order to achieve the greatest overall amount of happiness. Sometimes the general utility can be served only at the expense of a single individual or group, but to do so would be unjust.

Consider the Dan River experiment, a part of the long-running controversy over the cause of brown lung disease. Claiming that the disease is caused by the inhalation of microscopic fibers in cotton dust, textile unions fought for years for tough regulations to protect their workers. The Occupational Safety and Health Administration (OSHA) responded by proposing cotton dust standards, which would require many firms to install expensive new equipment. A few months before the deadline for installing the equipment, officials at Dan River textile plants in Virginia asked the state to waive the requirements for a time so the company could conduct an experiment to determine the precise cause of brown lung disease. Both the state and the Department of Labor allowed the extension. In response, the Amalgamated Clothing and Textile Workers Union asked OSHA to stop the proposed project, charging, "It is simply unconscionable to allow hundreds of cotton mill workers to continue to face a high risk of developing brown lung disease."[4]

Suppose that the Dan River project does expose workers to a high risk of contracting lung disease. If so, then a small group of individuals—633 textile workers at ten locations in Danville, Virginia—are being compelled to carry the burden of isolating the cause of brown lung. Is this just?

Although their critics would say no, utilitarians would respond that it is just if the experiment maximizes the total good of society. Does it? If the project succeeds in identifying the exact cause of the disease, then thousands of textile workers across the country and perhaps around the world will benefit. Researchers might also discover a more economical way to ensure worker safety, which in turn would yield a consumer benefit: more economical textiles than the ones produced if the industry installs expensive new equipment. Certainly, utilitarians would introduce the potential negative impact on workers at Dan River, but merely as one effect among many others. After the interests of all affected parties are equally weighed, if extending the deadline would likely yield the greatest net utility, then doing so is just—despite the fact that workers may be injured. (This sketch is not intended to justify the project or to foreclose a fuller utilitarian analysis of the case but merely to illustrate generally the utilitarian approach.)

Kant's Ethics

Most of us find the ideal of promoting human happiness and well-being an attractive one. As a result, we admire greatly people like Mother Teresa (1910–1997), who devoted her life to working with the poor. Despite the attractiveness of this ideal, many moral philosophers are critical of utilitarianism—particularly because, like egoism, it reduces all morality to a concern with consequences. Although nonconsequen-

tialist normative theories vary significantly, adopting different approaches and stressing different themes, the writings of the preeminent German philosopher Immanuel Kant (1724–1804) provide an excellent example of a thoroughly nonconsequentialist approach to ethics. Perhaps few thinkers today would endorse Kant's theory on every point, but his work has greatly influenced philosophers and has helped shape our general moral culture.

Kant sought moral principles that do not rest on contingencies and that define actions as inherently right or wrong apart from any particular circumstances. He believed that moral rules can, in principle, be known as a result of reason alone and are not based on observation (as are, for example, scientific judgments). In contrast to utilitarianism and other consequentialist doctrines, Kant's ethical theory holds that we do not have to know anything about the likely results of, say, my telling a lie to my boss in order to know that it is immoral. "The basis of obligation," Kant wrote, "must not be sought in human nature, [nor] in the circumstances of the world." Rather it is *a priori*, by which he meant that moral reasoning is not based on factual knowledge and that reason by itself can reveal the basic principles of morality.

Good will

The first essay mentioned Good Samaritan laws, which shield from lawsuits those rendering emergency aid. Such laws, in effect, give legal protection to the humanitarian impulse behind emergency interventions. They formally recognize that the interventionist's heart was in the right place, that the person's intention was irreproachable. And because the person acted from right intention, he or she should not be held culpable, except for grievous negligence. The widely observable human tendency to introduce a person's intentions in assigning blame or praise is a good springboard for engaging Kant's ethics.

Nothing, said Kant, is good in itself except a good will. This does not mean that intelligence, courage, self-control, health, happiness, and other things are not good and desirable. But Kant believed that their goodness depends on the will that makes use of them. Intelligence, for instance, is not good when used by an evil person.

By *will* Kant meant the uniquely human capacity to act from principle. Contained in the notion of good will is the concept of duty: Only when we act from duty does our action have moral worth. When we act only out of feeling, inclination, or self-interest, our actions—although they may be otherwise identical with ones that spring from the sense of duty—have no true moral worth.

Suppose that you're a clerk in a small stop-and-go store. Late one night a customer pays for his five-dollar purchase with a twenty-dollar bill, which you mistake for a ten. It's only after the customer leaves that you realize you short-changed him. You race out the front door and find him lingering by a vending machine. You give him the ten dollars with your apologies, and he thanks you profusely.

Can we say with certainty that you acted from a good will? Not necessarily. You may have acted from a desire to promote business or to avoid legal entanglement. If so, you would have acted in accordance with, but not from, duty. Your apparently virtuous gesture just happened to coincide with duty. According to Kant, if you do not will the action from a sense of your duty to be fair and honest, your action does not have true moral worth. Actions have true moral worth only when they spring from a recognition of duty and a choice to discharge it.

But then what determines our duty? How do we know what morality requires of us? Kant answered these questions by formulating what he called the "categorical imperative." This extraordinarily significant moral concept provides Kant's answer to the question "What makes a moral act right?"

The categorical imperative

We have seen that egoists and utilitarians allow factual circumstances or empirical data to determine moral judgments. In contrast, Kant believed that reason alone can yield a moral law. We need not rely on empirical evidence relating to consequences and to similar situations. Just as we know, seemingly through reason alone, such abstract truths as "Every change must have a cause," so we can arrive at absolute moral truth through nonempirical reasoning. And we can thereby discover our duty.

For Kant, an absolute moral truth must be logically consistent, free from internal contradiction. For example, it is a contradiction to say that an effect does not have a cause. Kant aimed to ensure that his absolute moral law would avoid such contradictions. If he could formulate such a rule, he maintained, everyone would be obliged to follow it without exception.

Kant believed that there is just one command (imperative) that is categorical—that is necessarily binding on all rational agents, regardless of any other considerations. From this one categorical imperative, this universal command, we can derive all commands of duty. Kant's *categorical imperative* says that we should always act in such a way that we can will the maxim of our action to become a universal law. So Kant's answer to the question "What makes a moral act right?" is that an act is morally right if and only if we can will it to become a universal law of conduct.

The obvious and crucial question that arises here is, "When are we justified in saying that the maxim of our action can become a universal law of conduct?"

By "maxim," Kant meant the subjective principle of an action, the principle (or rule) that people formulate in determining their conduct. For example, suppose building contractor Martin promises to install a sprinkler system in a project but is willing to break that promise to suit his purposes. His maxim can be expressed this way: "I'll make promises that I'll break whenever keeping them no longer suits my purposes." This is the subjective principle, the maxim, that directs his action.

Kant insisted that the morality of any maxim depends on whether we can logically will it to become a universal law. Could Martin's maxim be universally acted on? That depends on whether the maxim as law would involve a contradiction. The maxim "I'll make promises that I'll break whenever keeping them no longer suits my purposes" could not be universally acted on because it involves a contradiction of will. On the one hand, Martin is willing that it be possible to make promises and have them honored. On the other, if everyone intended to break promises when they so desired, then promises would not be honored in the first place, because it is in the nature of promises that they be believed. A law that allowed promise breaking would contradict the very nature of a promise. Similarly, a law that allowed lying would contradict the very nature of serious communication, for the activity of serious communication (as opposed to joking) requires that participants intend to speak the truth. I cannot, without contradiction, will both serious conversation and lying. In contrast, there is no problem, Kant thinks, in willing promise keeping or truth telling to be universal laws.

Consider, as another example, Kant's account of a man who, in despair after suffering a series of major setbacks, contemplates suicide. While still rational, the man asks whether it would be contrary to his duty to take his own life. Could the maxim of his action become a universal law of nature? Kant thinks not:

> His maxim is: From self-love I adopt it as a principle to shorten my life when its longer duration is likely to bring more evil than satisfaction. It is asked then simply whether this principle founded on self-love can become a universal law of nature. Now we see at once that a system of nature of which it should be a law to destroy life by means of the very feeling whose special nature it is to impel to the improvement of life would contradict itself, and therefore could not exist as a system of nature; hence that maxim cannot possibly exist as a universal law of nature, and consequently would be wholly inconsistent with the supreme principle of all duty.[5]

When Kant insists that a moral rule be consistently universalizable, he is saying that moral rules prescribe categorically, not hypothetically. A hypothetical prescription tells us what to do if we desire a particular outcome. Thus, "If I want people to like me, I should be nice to them" and "If you want to go to medical school, you must take biology" are hypothetical imperatives. They tell us what we must do on the assumption that we have some particular goal. If that is what we want, then this is what we must do. On the other hand, if we don't want to go to medical school, then the command to take biology does not apply to us. In contrast, Kant's imperative is categorical—it commands unconditionally. That is, it is necessarily binding on everyone, regardless of his or her specific goals or desires, regardless of consequences. A categorical imperative takes the form of "Do this" or "Don't do that"—no ifs, ands, or buts.

Universal Acceptability. There is another way of looking at the categorical imperative. Each person, through his or her own acts of will, legislates the moral law. The moral rules that we obey are not imposed on us from the outside. They are self-imposed and self-recognized, fully internalized principles. The sense of duty that we obey comes from within; it is an expression of our own higher selves.

Thus, moral beings give themselves the moral law and accept its demands on themselves. But that is not to say we can prescribe anything we want, for we are bound by reason and its demands. Because reason is the same for all rational beings, we all give ourselves the same moral law. In other words, when you answer the question "What should I do?" you must consider what all rational beings should do. If the moral law is valid for you, it must be valid for all other rational beings.

To see whether a rule or principle is a moral law, we can thus ask if what the rule commands would be acceptable to all rational beings acting rationally. In considering lying, theft, or murder, for example, you must consider the act not only from your own viewpoint but from the perspective of the person lied to, robbed, or murdered. Presumably, rational beings do not want to be lied to, robbed, or murdered. The test of the morality of a rule, then, is not whether people in fact accept it but whether all rational beings thinking rationally would accept it regardless of whether they are the doers or the receivers of the actions. This is an important moral insight, and most philosophers see it as implicit in Kant's discussion of the categorical imperative, even though Kant (whose writings are difficult to understand) did not make the point in this form.

The principle of universal acceptability has important applications. Suppose a man advocates a hiring policy that discriminates against women. For this rule to be universally acceptable, the man would have to be willing to accept it if he were a woman, something he would presumably be unwilling to do. Or suppose the manufacturer of a product decides to market it even though the manufacturer knows that the product is unsafe when used in a certain common way and that consumers are ignorant of this fact. Applying the universal acceptability principle, the company's decision makers would have to be willing to advocate marketing the product even if they were themselves in the position of uninformed consumers. Presumably they would be unwilling to do this. So the rule that would allow the product to be marketed would fail the test of universal acceptability.

Humanity as an End, Never Merely as a Means. In addition to the principle of universal acceptability, Kant explicitly offered another,

very famous way of formulating the core idea of his categorical imperative. According to this formulation, rational creatures should always treat other rational creatures as ends in themselves and never as only means to ends. This formulation underscores Kant's belief that every human being has an inherent worth resulting from the sheer possession of rationality. We must always act in a way that respects this humanity in others and in ourselves.

As rational beings, humans would act inconsistently if they did not treat everyone else the way they themselves would want to be treated. Here we see shades of the Golden Rule. Indeed, Kant's moral philosophy can be viewed as a profound reconsideration of this basic nonconsequentialist principle. Because rational beings recognize their own inner worth, they would never wish to be used as entities possessing worth only as means to an end.

Thus, when brokers encourage unnecessary buying and selling of stocks in order to reap a commission (a practice called churning), they are treating their clients simply as a means and not respecting them as persons, as ends in themselves. Likewise, Kant would object to using patients as subjects in a medical experiment without their consent. Even though great social benefit might result, the researchers would intentionally be using the patients solely as a means to the researchers' own goals and thus failing to respect the patients' basic humanity.

Kant maintained, as explained first, that what makes an action morally right is that we can will it to be a universal law. We now have two ways of reformulating his categorical imperative that may be easier to grasp and apply:

First reformulation:

What makes an action right is that the agent would be willing to be so treated were the positions of the parties reversed.

Second reformulation:

What makes an action right is that the agent treats human beings as ends in themselves.

Critical inquiries of Kant's ethics

1. What has moral worth? According to Kant, the clerk who returns the ten dollars to the customer is doing the right thing. But if his action is motivated by self-interest (perhaps he wants to get a reputation for honesty), then it does not have moral worth. That seems plausible. But Kant also held that if the clerk does the right thing out of instinct, habit, or sympathy for the other person, then the act still does not have moral worth. Only if it is done out of a sense of duty does the clerk's action have moral value. Many moral theorists have felt that Kant was too severe on this point. Do we really want to say that giving money to famine relief efforts has no moral worth if one is emotionally moved to do so by pictures of starving children rather than by a sense of duty? We might, to the contrary, find a person with strong human sympathies a better and more admirable person than someone who gives solely out of an abstract sense of duty.

2. Is the categorical imperative an adequate test of right? Kant said that a moral rule must function without exception. Critics wonder why the prohibition against such actions as lying, breaking a promise, committing suicide, and so on must be exceptionless. They say that Kant failed to distinguish between saying that a person should not except himself or herself from a rule and that the rule itself has no exceptions.

If stealing is wrong, it's wrong for me as well as for you. "Stealing is wrong, except if I do it" is not universalizable, for then stealing would be right for all to do, which contradicts the assertion that stealing is wrong. But just because no one may make of oneself an exception to a rule, it does not follow that the rule itself has no exceptions.

Suppose, for example, that we decide that stealing is sometimes right, perhaps in the case of a person who is starving. Thus the rule becomes "Never steal except when starving." This rule seems just as universalizable as "Never steal." The phrase "except . . ." can be viewed not as justifying a violation of the rule but as building a qualification into it. Critics in effect are asking why a qualified rule is not just as good as an unqualified one. If it is, then we no longer need to state rules in the simple, direct, unqualified manner that Kant did.

In fairness to Kant, it could be argued that his universalization formula can be interpreted flexibly enough to meet commonsense objections. For example, perhaps we could universalize the principle that individuals should steal rather than starve to death or that it is permissible to take one's own life to extinguish unspeakable pain. And yet to qualify the rules against stealing, lying, and taking one's life seems to invite a non-Kantian empirical analysis to morally justify the exceptions. One could, it seems, universalize more than one moral rule in a given situation: "Do not lie unless a life is at stake" versus "Lying is wrong unless necessary to avoid the suffering of innocent people." If so, then the categorical imperative would supply at best a necessary, but not a sufficient, test of right. But once we start choosing among various alternative rules, then we are adopting an approach to ethics that Kant would have rejected.

3. What does it mean to treat people as means? Kant's mandate that individuals must always be considered as ends in themselves and never merely as means expresses our sense of the intrinsic value of the human spirit and has profound moral appeal. Yet it is not always clear when people are being treated as ends and when merely as means. For example, Kant believed that prostitution is immoral because, by selling their sexual services, prostitutes allow themselves to be treated as means. Prostitutes, however, are not the only ones to sell their services. Anyone who works for a wage does so. Does that mean that we are all being treated immorally, because our employers are presumably hiring us as a means to advance their own ends?

Presumably not, because we freely agreed to do the work. But then the prostitute might have freely chosen that line of work too.

Other Nonconsequentialist Perspectives

For Kant, the categorical imperative provides the basic test of right and wrong, and he is resolutely nonconsequentialist in his application of it. You know now what he would say about the case of the deathbed promise: The maxim permitting you to break your promise cannot be universalized, and hence it would be immoral of you to give the money to the orphanage, despite the happiness that doing so would bring. But nonconsequentialists are not necessarily Kantians, and several different nonutilitarian moral concerns emerged in the discussion of the deathbed promise.

Critics of act utilitarianism believe that it is faulty for maintaining that we have one and only one moral duty. A utilitarian might follow various principles as rules of thumb, but they are only calculation substitutes. All that matters morally to utilitarians is the maximization of happiness. Yet this idea, many philosophers think, fails to do justice to the richness and complexity of our moral lives.

Prima facie principles

One influential philosopher who argued this way was the British scholar W. D. Ross (1877–1971).[6] Ross rejected utilitarianism as too simple and as untrue to the way we ordinarily think about morality and about our moral obligations. We see ourselves, Ross and like-minded thinkers contend, as being under various moral duties that cannot be reduced to the single obligation to maximize happiness. Often these obligations grow out of special relationships into which we enter or out of determinate roles that we undertake. Our lives are intertwined with other people's in particular ways, and we have, as a result, certain specific moral obligations.

For example, as a professor, Rodriguez is obligated to assist her students in the learning process and to evaluate their work in a fair and educationally productive way—obligations to the specific people in her classroom that she does not have to other people. As a spouse, Rodriguez must maintain a certain emotional and sexual fidelity to her partner. As a parent, she must provide for the individual human beings who are her children. As a friend to Smith, she may have a moral responsibility to help him out in a time of crisis. Having borrowed money from Chang, Rodriguez is morally obligated to pay it back. Thus, different relationships and different circumstances generate a variety of specific moral obligations.

In addition, we have moral duties that do not arise from our unique interactions and relationships with other people. For example, we ought to treat all people fairly, do what we can to remedy injustices, and make an effort to promote human welfare generally. The latter obligation is important, but for a nonconsequentialist like Ross it is only one among various obligations that people have.

At any given time, we are likely to be under more than one obligation, and sometimes these obligations can conflict. That is, we may have an obligation to do *A* and an obligation to do *B*, where it is not possible for us to do both *A* and *B*. For example, I promise to meet a friend on an urgent matter, and now, as I am hurrying there, I pass an injured person who is obviously in need of assistance. Stopping to aid the person will make it impossible for me to fulfill my promise. What should I do? For moral philosophers like Ross, there is no single answer for all cases. What I ought to do will depend on the circumstances and relative importance of the conflicting obligations. I have an obligation to keep my promise, and I have an obligation to assist people in distress. What I must decide is which of these obligations is, in the given circumstance, the more important. I must weigh the moral significance of the promise against the comparative moral urgency of assisting the injured person.

Ross and many contemporary philosophers believe that all (or at least most) of our moral obligations are prima facie ones. A *prima facie obligation* is an obligation that can be overridden by a more important obligation. For instance, we take the keeping of promises seriously, but almost everyone would agree that in some circumstances—for example, when a life is at stake—it would be not only morally permissible, but morally required, to break a promise. Our obligation to keep a promise is a real one, and if there is no conflicting obligation, then we must keep the promise. But that obligation is not absolute or categorical; it could in principle be outweighed by a more stringent moral obligation. The idea that our obligations are prima facie is foreign to Kant's way of looking at things.

Consider an example that Kant himself discussed.[7] Imagine that a murderer comes to your door, wanting to know where your friend is so that he can kill her. Your friend is in fact hiding in your bedroom closet. Most people would probably agree that your obligation to your friend overrides your general obligation to tell the truth and that the right thing to do would be to lie to the murderer to throw him off your friend's trail. Although you have a genuine obligation to tell the truth, it is a prima facie obligation, one that other moral considerations can outweigh. Kant disagreed. He maintained that you must always tell the truth—that is, in all circumstances and without exception. For him, telling the truth is an absolute or categorical obligation, not a prima facie one.

Ross thought that our various prima facie obligations could be divided into seven basic types: duties of fidelity (that is, to respect explicit and implicit promises), duties of reparation (for previous wrongful acts), duties of gratitude, duties of justice, duties of beneficence (that is, to make the condition of others better), duties of self-

improvement, and duties not to injure others.[8] Unlike utilitarianism, Ross's ethical perspective is pluralistic in recognizing a variety of genuine obligations. But contrary to Kant, Ross does not see these obligations as absolute and exceptionless. On both points, Ross contended that his view of morality more closely fits with our actual moral experience and the way we view our moral obligations.

Ross also saw himself as siding with commonsense morality in maintaining that our prima facie obligations are obvious. He believed that the basic principles of duty are as self-evident as the simplest rules of arithmetic and that any person who has reached the age of reason can discern that it is wrong to lie, to break promises, and to injure people needlessly. However, what we should do, all things considered, when two or more prima facie obligations conflict is often difficult to judge. In deciding what to do in any concrete situation, Ross thought, we are always "taking a moral risk."[9] Even after the fullest reflection, judgments about which of these self-evident rules should govern our conduct are only "more or less probable opinions which are not logically justified conclusions from the general principles that are recognised as self-evident."[10]

Assisting others

Nonconsequentialists believe that utilitarianism presents too simple a picture of our moral world. In addition, they worry that utilitarianism risks making us all slaves to the maximization of total happiness. Stop and think about it: Isn't there something that you could be doing—for instance, volunteering at the local hospital or orphanage, collecting money for Third World development, helping the homeless—that would do more for the general good than what you are doing now or are planning to do tonight or tomorrow? Sure, working with the homeless might not bring you quite as much pleasure as what you would otherwise be doing, but if it would nonetheless maximize total happiness, then you are morally required to do it. However, by following this reasoning, you could end up working around the clock, sacrificing yourself for the greater good. This notion seems mistaken.

Most nonutilitarian philosophers, like Ross, believe that we have some obligation to promote the general welfare, but they typically view this obligation as less stringent than, for example, the obligation not to injure people. They see us as having a much stronger obligation to refrain from violating people's rights than to promote their happiness or well-being.

Many moral philosophers draw a related distinction between actions that are morally required and charitable or *supererogatory* actions—that is, actions that it would be good to do but not immoral not to do. Act utilitarianism does not make this distinction. While we admire Mother Teresa and Albert Schweitzer for devoting their lives to doing good works among the poor, we see them as acting above and beyond the call of duty. We do not expect so much from ordinary people. Yet people who are not moral heroes or who fall short of sainthood may nonetheless be living morally satisfactory lives.

Nonutilitarian theorists see the distinction between morally obligatory actions and supererogatory actions not so much as a realistic concession to human weakness but as a necessary demarcation if we are to avoid becoming enslaved to the maximization of the general welfare. The idea here is that each of us should have a sphere in which to pursue our own plans and goals, to carve out a distinctive life plan. These plans and goals are limited by various moral obligations, in particular by other people's rights, but the demands of morality are not all-encompassing.

Moral rights

What, then, are rights, and what rights do people have? Broadly defined, a *right* is an entitlement to act or have others act in a certain way. The connection between rights and duties is that, generally speaking, if you have a right to do something, then someone else has a correlative duty to act in a certain way. For example, if you claim a right to drive, you mean that you are entitled to drive or that others should—that is, have a duty to—permit you to drive. Your right to drive under certain conditions is derived from our legal system and is thus considered a *legal right.*

In addition to rights that are derived from some specific legal system, we also have *moral rights.* Some of these moral rights derive from special relationships, roles, or circumstances in which we happen to be. For example, if Tom has an obligation to return Bob's car to him on Saturday morning, then Bob has a right to have Tom return his car. If I have agreed to water your plants while you are on vacation, you have a right to expect me to look after them in your absence. As a student, you have a right to be graded fairly, and so on.

Even more important are rights that do not rest on special relationships, roles, or situations. For example, the rights to life, free speech, and unhampered religious affiliation are widely accepted, not just as the entitlements of some specific political or legal system but as fundamental moral rights. More controversial, but often championed as moral rights, are the rights to medical care, decent housing, education, and work. Moral rights that are not the result of particular roles, special relationships, or specific circumstances are called *human rights.* They have several important characteristics.

First, human rights are universal. For instance, if the right to life is a human right, as most of us believe it is, then everyone, everywhere, and at all times, has that right. In contrast, there is nothing universal about your right that I keep my promise to help you move or about my right to drive 65 miles per hour on certain roads.

Second, and closely related, human rights are equal rights. If the right to free speech is a human right, then everyone has this right equally.

No one has a greater right to free speech than anyone else. In contrast, your daughter has a greater right than do the daughters of other people to your emotional and financial support.

Third, human rights are not transferable, nor can they be relinquished. If we have a fundamental human right, we cannot give, lend, or sell it to someone else. That is what is meant in the Declaration of Independence when certain rights—namely, life, liberty, and the pursuit of happiness—are described as "inalienable." By comparison, legal rights can be renounced or transferred, as when one party sells another a house or a business.

Fourth, human rights are natural rights, not in the sense that they can be derived from a study of human nature, but in the sense that they do not depend on human institutions the way legal rights do. If people have human rights, they have them simply because they are human beings. They do not have them because they live under a certain legal system. Human rights rest on the assumption that people have certain basic moral entitlements simply because they are human beings. No authoritative body assigns us human rights. The law may attempt to protect human rights, to make them safe and explicit through codification, but law is not their source.

Rights, and in particular human rights, can be divided into two broad categories: negative rights and positive rights. *Negative rights* reflect the vital interests that human beings have in being free from outside interference. The rights guaranteed in the Bill of Rights—freedom of speech, assembly, religion, and so on—fall within this category, as do the rights to freedom from injury and to privacy. Correlating with these are duties that we all have not to interfere with others' pursuit of these interests and activities. *Positive rights* reflect the vital interests that human beings have in receiving certain benefits. They are rights to have others provide us with certain goods, services, or opportunities. Today, positive rights often are taken to include the rights to education, medical care, a decent neighborhood, equal job opportunity, comparable pay, and so on. Correlating with these are positive duties for appropriate parties to assist individuals in their pursuit of these interests.

Thus a child's right to education implies not just that no one should interfere with the child's education but also that the necessary resources for that education ought to be provided. In the case of some positive rights—for example, the right to a decent standard of living, as proclaimed by the United Nations' 1948 Human Rights Charter—who exactly has the duty to provide the goods and services required to fulfill those rights is unclear. Also, interpreting a right as negative or positive is sometimes controversial. For example, is my right to liberty simply the right not to be interfered with as I live my own life, or does it also imply a duty to provide me with the means to make the exercise of that liberty meaningful?

The significance of positing moral rights is that they provide grounds for making moral judgments that differ radically from utilitarianism's grounds. Once moral rights are asserted, the locus of moral judgment becomes the individual, not society. For example, if every potential human subject has a moral right to be fully informed about the nature of a medical experiment and the moral right to decide freely for himself or herself whether to participate, then it is wrong to violate these rights—even if, by so doing, the common good would be served. Again, if workers have a right to compensation equal to what others receive for doing comparable work, then they cannot be paid less on grounds of the greatest good for the greatest number. And if everyone has a right to equal consideration for a job regardless of color or sex, then sex and color cannot be introduced merely because so doing will result in greater net utility.

Utilitarianism, in effect, treats all such entitlements as subordinate to the general welfare. Thus individuals are entitled to act in a certain way and entitled to have others allow or aid them to so act only insofar as acknowledging this right or entitlement achieves the greatest good. The assertion of moral rights, therefore, decisively sets nonconsequentialists apart from utilitarians.

Critical inquiries of nonconsequentialism

1. How well justified are these nonconsequentialist principles and moral rights? Ross maintained that we have immediate intuitive knowledge of the basic prima facie moral principles, and indeed it would seem absurd to try to deny that it is wrong to cause needless suffering or that making a promise imposes some obligation to keep it. Only someone the moral equivalent of colorblind could fail to see the truth of these statements; to reject them would seem as preposterous as denying some obvious fact of arithmetic—for example, that 12 + 4 = 16. Likewise, it appears obvious—indeed, as Thomas Jefferson wrote, "self-evident"—that human beings have certain basic and inalienable rights, unconditional rights that do not depend on the decrees of any particular government.

Yet we must be careful. What seems obvious, even self-evident, to one culture or at one time in human history may turn out to be not only not self-evident but actually false. That the earth is flat and that heavier objects fall faster than lighter ones were two "truths" taken as obvious in former centuries. Likewise, the inferiority of women and of various nonwhite races was long taken for granted; this supposed fact was so obvious that it was hardly even commented on. The idea that people have a right to practice a religion that the majority "knows" to be false—or, indeed, to practice no religion whatsoever—would have seemed morally scandalous to many of our forebears and is still not embraced in all countries today. Today, many vegetarians eschew meat eating on moral grounds and contend that future generations will consider our treatment of animals, factory farming in particular, to be as morally benighted as slavery. So what seems obvious, self-evident, or simple

common sense may not be the most reliable guide to morally sound principles.

2. Can nonconsequentialists satisfactorily handle conflicting rights and principles? People today disagree among themselves about the correctness of certain moral principles. Claims of right, as we have seen, are often controversial. For example, do employees have a moral right to their jobs—an entitlement to be fired only with just cause? To some of us, it may seem obvious that they do; to others, perhaps not. And how are we to settle various conflicting claims of right? Jones, for instance, claims a right to her property, which she has acquired honestly through her labors; that is, she claims a right to do with it as she wishes. Smith is ill and claims adequate medical care as a human right. Because he cannot afford the care himself, acknowledging his right will probably involve taxing people like Jones and thus limiting their property rights.

To sum up these two points: First, even the deliverances of moral common sense have to be examined critically; and second, nonconsequentialists should not rest content until they find a way of resolving disputes among conflicting prima facie principles or rights. This is not to suggest that nonconsequentialists cannot find deeper and theoretically more satisfactory ways of grounding moral claims and of handling disputes between them. The point to be underscored here is simply the necessity of doing so.

Utilitarianism Once More

Until now, the discussion of utilitarianism has focused on its most classic and straightforward form, called act utilitarianism. According to *act utilitarianism,* we have one and only one moral obligation—the maximization of happiness for everyone concerned—and every action is to be judged according to how well it lives up to this principle. But a different utilitarian approach, called rule utilitarianism, is relevant to the discussion of the moral concerns characteristic of nonconsequentialism—in particular, relevant to the nonconsequentialist's criticisms of act utilitarianism. The rule utilitarian would, in fact, agree with many of these criticisms. (Rule utilitarianism has been formulated in different ways, but this discussion follows the version defended by Richard Brandt.)

Rule utilitarianism maintains that the utilitarian standard should be applied not to individual actions but to moral codes as a whole. The rule utilitarian asks what moral code (that is, what set of moral rules) a society should adopt in order to maximize happiness. The principles that make up that code would then be the basis for distinguishing right actions from wrong actions. As Brandt explains:

> A rule-utilitarian thinks that right actions are the kind permitted by the moral code optimal for the society of which the agent is a member. An optimal code is one designed to maximize welfare or what is good (thus, utility). This leaves open the possibility that a particular right act by itself may not maximize benefit. . . . On the rule-utilitarian view, then, to find what is morally right or wrong we need to find which actions would be permitted by a moral system that is "optimal" for the agent's society.[11]

The "optimal" moral code does not refer to the set of rules that would do the most good if everyone conformed to them all the time. The meaning is more complex. The optimal moral code must take into account what rules can reasonably be taught and obeyed, as well as the costs of inculcating those rules in people. Recall that if a principle or rule is part of a person's moral code, then it will influence the person's behavior. The person will tend to follow that principle, to feel guilty when he or she does not follow it, and to disapprove of others who fail to conform to it. Rule utilitarians must consider not just the benefits of having people motivated to act in certain ways but also the cost of in-

stilling those motivations in them. As Brandt writes:

> The more intense and widespread an aversion to a certain sort of behavior, the less frequent the behavior is apt to be. But the more intense and widespread, the greater the cost of teaching the rule and keeping it alive, the greater the burden on the individual, and so on.[12]

Thus, the optimality of a moral code encompasses both the benefits of reduced objectionable behavior and the long-term costs. Perfect compliance is not a realistic goal. "Like the law," Brandt continues, "the optimal moral code normally will not produce 100 percent compliance with all its rules; that would be too costly."[13]

Elements of the rule-utilitarian approach were clearly suggested by Mill himself, although he did not draw the distinction between act and rule utilitarianism. According to the rule-utilitarian perspective, we should apply the utilitarian standard only to the assessment of alternative moral codes; we should not try to apply it to individual actions. We should seek, that is, to determine the specific set of principles that would in fact best promote total happiness for a society. Those are the rules we should promulgate, instill in ourselves, and teach to the next generation.

What will the optimal code look like?

Rule utilitarians like Brandt argue strenuously that the ideal or optimal moral code for a society will not be the single act-utilitarian command to maximize happiness. They contend that teaching people that their only obligation is to maximize happiness would not in fact maximize happiness.

First, people will make mistakes if they always try to promote total happiness. Second, if all of us were act utilitarians, such practices as keeping promises and telling the truth would be rather shaky, because we would expect others to keep promises or tell the truth only when they believed that doing so would maximize happiness. Third, the act-utilitarian principle is too demanding, because it seems to imply that each person should continually be striving to promote total well being.

For these reasons, rule utilitarians believe that more happiness will come from instilling in people a pluralistic moral code, one with a number of different principles. By analogy, imagine a traffic system with just one rule: Drive your car in a way that maximizes happiness. Such a system would be counterproductive; we do much better in terms of total human well-being to have a variety of traffic regulations—for example, obey stop signs and pass only on the left. In such a pluralistic system we cannot justify cruising through a red light with the argument that doing so maximizes total happiness by getting us home more quickly.

The principles of the optimal code would presumably be prima facie in Ross's sense—that is, capable of being overridden by other principles. Different principles would also have different moral weights. It would make sense, for example, to instill in people an aversion to killing that is stronger than the aversion to telling white lies. In addition, the ideal code would acknowledge moral rights. Teaching people to respect moral rights maximizes human welfare in the long run.

The rules of the optimal code provide the sole basis for determining right and wrong. An action is not necessarily wrong if it fails to maximize happiness; it is wrong only if it conflicts with the ideal moral code. Rule utilitarianism thus gets around many of the problems that plague act utilitarianism. At the same time, it provides a plausible basis for deciding which moral principles and rights we should acknowledge and how much weight we should attach to them. We try to determine those principles and rights that, generally adhered to, would best promote human happiness.

Still, rule utilitarianism has its critics. There are two possible objections. First, act utilitarians maintain that a utilitarian who cares about happiness should be willing to violate rules in order to maximize happiness. Why make a fetish out of the rules?

Second, nonconsequentialists, although presumably viewing rule utilitarianism more favorably than act utilitarianism, still balk at seeing moral principles determined by their consequences. They contend, in particular, that rule utilitarians ultimately subordinate rights to utilitarian calculation and therefore fail to treat rights as fundamental and independent moral factors.

Conclusion

Theoretical controversies permeate the subject of ethics, and as we have seen, philosophers have proposed rival ways of understanding right and wrong. These philosophical differences of perspective, emphasis, and theory are significant and can have profound practical consequences. This essay has surveyed some of these issues, but obviously it cannot settle all of the questions that divide moral philosophers. Fortunately, however, many problems of applied ethics can be intelligently discussed and even resolved by people whose fundamental moral theories differ (or who have not yet worked out their own moral ideas in some systematic way).

In the abstract, it might seem impossible for people to reach agreement on controversial ethical issues, given that ethical theories differ so much and that people themselves place moral value on different things. Yet in practice moral problems are rarely so intractable that open-minded and thoughtful people cannot, by discussing matters calmly, rationally, and thoroughly, make significant progress toward resolving them. Moral judgments should be logical, should be based on facts, and should appeal to sound moral principles. Bearing this in mind can often help, especially when various people are discussing an issue and proposing rival answers.

First, in any moral discussion, make sure participants agree about the relevant facts. Often moral disputes hinge not on matters of moral principle but on differing assessments of what the facts of the situation are, what alternatives are open, and what the probable results of different courses of action will be. For instance, the directors of an international firm might acrimoniously dispute the moral permissibility of a new overseas investment. The conflict might appear to involve some fundamental clash of moral principles and perspectives and yet, in fact, be the result of some underlying disagreement about what effects the proposed investment will have on the lives of the local population. Until this factual disagreement is acknowledged and dealt with, little is likely to be resolved.

Second, once there is general agreement on factual matters, try to spell out the moral principles to which different people are, at least implicitly, appealing. Seeking to determine these principles will often help people clarify their own thinking enough to reach a solution. Sometimes they will agree on what moral principles are relevant and yet disagree over how to balance them. But identifying this discrepancy can itself be useful. Bear in mind, too, that skepticism is in order when someone's moral stance on an issue appears to rest simply on a hunch or intuition and cannot be related to some more general moral principle. As moral decision makers, we are seeking not just an answer to a moral issue but an answer that can be publicly defended. And the public defense of a moral judgment usually requires an appeal to general principle. By analogy, judges do not hand down judgments based simply on what strikes them as fair in a particular case. They must relate their decisions to general legal principles or statutes.

A reluctance to defend our moral decisions in public is almost always a warning sign. If we are unwilling to account for our actions publicly, chances are that we are doing something we cannot really justify morally. In addition, Kant's point that we must be willing to universalize our moral judgments is relevant here. We cannot sincerely endorse a principle if we are not willing to see it applied generally. Unfortunately, we occasionally do make judgments—for example, that Alfred's being late to work is a satisfactory reason for firing him—that rest on a principle we would be unwilling to apply to our own situations. Hence, the moral relevance of the familiar question: "How would you like it if . . . ?" Looking at an issue from the other person's point of view can cure moral myopia.[14]

NOTES

1. Bernard Williams, *Ethics and the Limits of Philosophy* (Cambridge, MA: Harvard University Press, 1985), 16.

2. Richard B. Brandt, "Toward a Credible Form of Utilitarianism," in Hector-Neri Castañeda and George Nakhnikian, eds., *Morality and the Language of Conduct* (Detroit: Wayne State University Press, 1963), 109–110.

3. A. C. Ewing, *Ethics* (New York: Free Press, 1965), 40.

4. Molly Moore, "Did the Experts Really Approve the 'Brown Lung' Experiment?" *The Washington Post National Weekly Edition,* June 4, 1984, 31.

5. Immanuel Kant, *The Foundations of the Metaphysics of Morals,* trans. T. K. Abbott. See p. 48 of this volume.

6. See, in particular, W. D. Ross, *The Right and the Good* (London: Oxford University Press, 1930).

7. Immanuel Kant, *Practical Philosophy,* ed. M. J. Gregor (Cambridge: Cambridge University Press, 1996), 611–615.

8. Ross, *The Right and the Good,* 21.

9. Ibid., 30.

10. Ibid., 31.

11. Richard B. Brandt, "The Real and Alleged Problems of Utilitarianism," *The Hastings Center Report* (April 1983), 38.

12. Ibid., 42.

13. Ibid., 42.

14. This and the previous essay draw on material from William H. Shaw and Vincent Barry, *Moral Issues in Business,* 8th ed. (Belmont, CA: Wadsworth Publishing Co., 2001). I am grateful to Vince for permitting me to use our joint work here.

CLASSICAL THEORIES

Happiness, Function, and Virtue

ARISTOTLE

Aristotle was born in 384 B.C.E. in a town near Macedonia. When he was seventeen years old, he went to Athens and studied with Plato for twenty years. When Plato died, Aristotle left Athens and became a tutor to Alexander, the young heir to the Macedonian throne, who was later to become known as Alexander the Great. In 334 B.C.E. Aristotle returned to Athens and founded his own school, the Lyceum. When Alexander died in 323, there was strong anti-Macedonian feeling in Athens, and Aristotle left the city. He died the next year at the age of sixty-two.

Aristotle studied and wrote about an astonishing range of subjects. His knowledge was encyclopedic and deep. No one person has ever founded and advanced so many fields of learning. Aristotle wrote separate treatises on physics, biology, logic, psychology, politics, metaphysics, aesthetics, literary criticism, and political science. In the Middle Ages, Aristotle was known simply as the Philosopher.

Nicomachean Ethics, from which the following reading selection is drawn, is a classic in the history of philosophy. Thought to have been named after Aristotle's son, *Nicomachean Ethics* appears to have been prepared as a series of lectures. In them Aristotle argues that the good for human beings is happiness and that happiness consists in their fulfilling their function as human beings. He then goes on to describe the nature of virtue, which he sees as a mean between excess and deficiency.

Study Questions

1. What are some of the ordinary views of good or happiness that people have? What does Aristotle have to say about them?

From Nicomachean Ethics, *translated by James E. C. Weldon (1897). Subheadings added.*

2. Why is happiness the supreme or highest good?

3. What is the function of human beings?

4. What is the connection between function and happiness? What other factors influence human happiness?

5. What is Aristotle's theory of virtue as a mean?

Book I: Happiness

All human activities aim at some good

EVERY ART AND EVERY SCIENTIFIC INQUIRY, and similarly every action and purpose, may be said to aim at some good. Hence the good has been well defined as that at which all things aim. But it is clear that there is a difference in ends; for the ends are sometimes activities, and sometimes results beyond the mere activities. Where there are ends beyond the action, the results are naturally superior to the action.

As there are various actions, arts, and sciences, it follows that the ends are also various. Thus health is the end of the medical art, a ship of shipbuilding, victory of strategy, and wealth of economics. It often happens that a number of such arts or sciences combine for a single enterprise, as the art of making bridles and all such other arts as furnish the implements of horsemanship combine for horsemanship, and horsemanship and every military action for strategy; and in the same way, other arts or sciences combine for others. In all these cases, the ends of the master arts or sciences, whatever they may be, are more desirable than those of the subordinate arts or sciences, as it is for the sake of the former that the latter are pursued. . . .

If it is true that in the sphere of action there is some end which we wish for its own sake, and for the sake of which we wish everything else, and if we do not desire everything for the sake of something else (for, if that is so, the process will go on *ad infinitum,* and our desire will be idle and futile), clearly this end will be good and the supreme good. Does it not follow then that

the knowledge of this good is of great importance for the conduct of life? Like archers who have a mark at which to aim, shall we not have a better chance of attaining what we want? If this is so, we must endeavor to comprehend, at least in outline, what this good is. . . .

Ethics is not an exact science

This then is the object at which the present inquiry aims. . . . But our statement of the case will be adequate, if it be made with all such clearness as the subject-matter admits; for it would be as wrong to expect the same degree of accuracy in all reasonings. . . . Things noble and just . . . exhibit so great a diversity and uncertainty that they are sometimes thought to have only a conventional, and not a natural, existence. There is the same sort of uncertainty in regard to good things, as it often happens that injuries result from them; thus there have been cases in which people were ruined by wealth, or again by courage. As our subjects then and our premises are of this nature, we must be content to indicate the truth roughly and in outline; and as our subjects and premises are true generally *but not universally,* we must be content to arrive at conclusions which are only generally true. It is right to receive the particular statements which are made in the same spirit; for an educated person will expect accuracy in each subject only so far as the nature of the subject allows. . . .

Everybody is competent to judge the subjects which he understands, and is a good judge of them. It follows that in particular subjects it is a person of special education, and in general a person of universal education, who is a good judge. Hence the young are not proper students of political science,* as they have no experience of the actions of life which form the premises and subjects of the reasonings. Also it may be added that from their tendency to follow their emotions they will not study the subject to any purpose or profit, as its end is not knowledge but action. It makes no difference whether a person is young in years or youthful in character; for the defect of which I speak is not one of time, but is due to the emotional character of his life and pursuits. Knowledge is as useless to such a person as it is to an intemperate person. But where the desires and actions of people are regulated by reason the knowledge of these subjects will be extremely valuable.

But having said so much by way of preface as to the students of [the subject], the spirit in which it should be studied, and the object which we set before ourselves, let us resume our argument.

Different conceptions of happiness

As every science and undertaking aims at some good, what is in our view . . . the highest of all practical goods? As to its name there is, I may say, a general agreement. The masses and the cultured classes agree in calling it happiness, and conceive that "to live well" or "to do well" is the same thing as "to be happy." But as to what happiness is they do not agree, nor do the masses give the same account of it as the philosophers. The former take it to be something visible and palpable, such as pleasure, wealth, or honor; different people, however, give different definitions of it, and often even the same man gives different definitions at different times. When he is ill, it is health, when he is poor, it is wealth; if he is conscious of his own ignorance, he envies people who use grand language above his own comprehension. . . .

Men's conception of the good or of happiness may be read in the lives they lead. Ordinary or vulgar people conceive it to be a pleasure, and accordingly choose a life of enjoyment. For there are, we may say, three conspicuous types of life, the sensual, the political, and, thirdly, the life of thought. Now the mass of men present an absolutely slavish appearance, choosing the life of brute beasts, but they have ground for so doing because so many persons in authority share the tastes of Sardanapalus.† Cultivated and energetic people, on the other hand, identify happiness with honor, as honor is the general end of political life. But this seems too superficial an idea for our present purpose; for honor depends more upon the people who pay it than upon the person to whom it is paid, and the good we feel is something which is proper to a man himself and cannot be easily taken away from him. Men too appear to seek honor in order to be assured of their own goodness. Accordingly, they seek it at the hands of the sage and of those who know them well, and they seek it on the ground of their virtue; clearly then, in their judgment at any rate, virtue is better than honor. Perhaps then we might look on virtue rather than honor as the end of political life. Yet even this idea appears not quite complete; for a man may possess virtue and yet be asleep or inactive throughout life, and not only so, but he may experience the greatest calamities and misfortunes. Yet no one would call such a life a life of happiness, unless he were maintaining a paradox. . . . The third life is the life of thought, which we will discuss later.‡

The life of money making is a life of constraint; and wealth is obviously not the good of which we are in quest; for it is useful merely as a means to something else. It would be more reasonable to take the things mentioned before—sensual pleasure, honor, and virtue—as ends

---

*Political science as Aristotle understands it includes moral philosophy.—ED.

† A half-legendary ruler whose name to the Greeks stood for extreme luxury and extravagance.—ED.

‡ In Book X of *Nicomachean Ethics*.—ED.

than wealth, since they are things desired on their own account. Yet these too are evidently not ends, although much argument has been employed to show that they are. . . .

Characteristics of the good

But leaving this subject for the present, let us revert to the good of which we are in quest and consider what it may be. For it seems different in different activities or arts; it is one thing in medicine, another in strategy, and so on. What is the good in each of these instances? It is presumably that for the sake of which all else is done. In medicine this is health, in strategy victory, in architecture a house, and so on. In every activity and undertaking it is the end, since it is for the sake of the end that all people do whatever else they do. If then there is an end for all our activity, this will be the good to be accomplished; and if there are several such ends, it will be these.

Our argument has arrived by a different path at the same point as before; but we must endeavor to make it still plainer. Since there are more ends than one, and some of these ends—for example, wealth, flutes, and instruments generally—we desire as means to something else, it is evident that not all are final ends. But the highest good is clearly something final. Hence if there is only one final end, this will be the object of which we are in search; and if there are more than one, it will be the most final. We call that which is sought after for its own sake more final than that which is sought after as a means to something else; we call that which is never desired as a means to something else more final than things that are desired both for themselves and as means to something else. Therefore, we call absolutely final that which is always desired for itself and never as a means to something else. Now happiness more than anything else answers to this description. For happiness we always desire for its own sake and never as a means to something else, whereas honor, pleasure, intelligence, and every virtue we desire partly for their own sakes (for we should desire them independently of what might result from them), but partly also as means to happiness, because we suppose they will prove instruments of happiness. Happiness, on the other hand, nobody desires for the sake of these things, nor indeed as a means to anything else at all. . . .

The function of man

Perhaps, however, it seems a commonplace to say that happiness is the supreme good; what is wanted is to define its nature a little more clearly. The best way of arriving at such a definition will probably be to ascertain the function of man. For, as with a flute player, a sculptor, or any artist, or in fact anybody who has a special function or activity, his goodness and excellence seem to lie in his function, so it would seem to be with man, if indeed he has a special function. Can it be said that, while a carpenter and a cobbler have special functions and activities, man, unlike them, is naturally functionless? Or, as the eye, the hand, the foot, and similarly each part of the body has a special function, so may man be regarded as having a special function apart from all these? What, then, can this function be? It is not life; for life is apparently something that man shares with plants; and we are looking for something peculiar to him. We must exclude therefore the life of nutrition and growth. There is next what may be called the life of sensation. But this too, apparently, is shared by man with horses, cattle, and all other animals. There remains what I may call the active life of the rational part of man's being. . . .

The function of man then is activity of soul in accordance with reason, or not apart from reason. Now, the function of a man of a certain kind, and of a man who is good of that kind—for example, of a harpist and a good harpist—are in our view the same in kind. This is true of all people of all kinds without exception, the superior excellence being only an addition to the function; for it is the function of a harpist to play the harp, and of a good harpist to play the harp well. This being so, if we define the function of man as a kind of life, and this life as an activity of the soul or a course of action in accordance with reason, and if the function of a good man is such activity of a good and noble kind, and if everything is well done when it is done in accordance with its proper excellence, it follows that the good of man is activity of soul in accordance with virtue, or, if there are more virtues than one, in accordance with the best and most complete virtue. But we must add the words "in a complete life." For as one swallow or one day does not make a spring, so one day or a short time does not make a man blessed or happy. . . .

Human happiness

Still it is clear that happiness requires the addition of external goods; for it is impossible, or at least difficult, to do noble deeds with no outside means. For many things can be done only through the aid of friends or wealth or political power; and there are some things the lack of which spoils our felicity, such as good birth, wholesome children, and personal beauty. For a man who is extremely ugly in appearance or low born or solitary and childless can hardly be happy; perhaps still less so, if he has exceedingly bad children or friends, or has had good children or friends and lost them by death. As we said, then, happiness seems to need prosperity of this kind in addition to virtue. For this reason some persons identify happiness with good fortune, though others do so with virtue. . . .

It is reasonable then not to call an ox or a horse or any other animal happy; for none of them is capable of sharing in this activity. For the same reason no child can be happy, since the youth of a child keeps him for the time being from such activity; if a child is ever called happy, the ground of felicitation is his promise, rather than his actual performance. For happiness demands, as we said, a complete virtue and a com-

plete life. And there are all sorts of changes and chances in life, and the most prosperous of men may in his old age fall into extreme calamities, as Priam did in the heroic legends.* And a person who has experienced such chances and died a miserable death, nobody calls happy. . . .

Now the events of chance are numerous and of different magnitudes. Small pieces of good fortune or the reverse do not turn the scale of life in any way, but great and numerous events make life happier if they turn out well, since they naturally give it beauty and the use of them may be noble and good. If, on the other hand, they turn out badly, they mar and mutilate happiness by causing pain and hindrances to many activities. Still, even in these circumstances, nobility shines out when a person bears with calmness the weight of accumulated misfortunes, not from insensibility but from dignity and greatness of spirit.

Then if activities determine the quality of life, as we said, no happy man can become miserable; for he will never do what is hateful and mean. For our idea of the truly good and wise man is that he bears all the chances of life with dignity and always does what is best in the circumstances, as a good general makes the best use of the forces at his command in war, or a good cobbler makes the best shoe with the leather given him, and so on through the whole series of the arts. If this is so, the happy man can never become miserable. I do not say that he will be fortunate if he meets such chances of life as Priam. Yet he will not be variable or constantly changing, for he will not be moved from his happiness easily or by ordinary misfortunes, but only by great and numerous ones; nor after them will he quickly regain his happiness. If he regains it at all, it will be only over a long and complete period of time and after great and notable achievement.

We may safely then define a happy man as one who is active in accord with perfect virtue

---

* The disastrous fate of Priam, King of Troy, was part of the well-known Homeric tales.—ED.

and adequately furnished with external goods, not for some chance period of time but for his whole lifetime. . . .

Inasmuch as happiness is an activity of soul in accordance with complete or perfect virtue, it is necessary to consider virtue, as this will perhaps be the best way of studying happiness. . . .

Book II: Virtue

Virtue and habit

Virtue is twofold, partly intellectual and partly moral, and intellectual virtue is originated and fostered mainly by teaching; it demands therefore experience and time. Moral virtue on the other hand is the outcome of habit. . . . From this fact it is clear that moral virtue is not implanted in us by nature; for nothing that exists by nature can be transformed by habit. It is neither by nature then nor in defiance of nature that virtues grow in us. Nature gives us the capacity to receive them, and that capacity is perfected by habit. . . .

It is by playing the harp that both good and bad harpists are produced; and the case of builders and others is similar, for it is by building well that they become good builders and by building badly that they become bad builders. If it were not so, there would be no need of anybody to teach them; they would all be born good or bad in their several crafts. The case of the virtues is the same. It is by our actions in dealings between man and man that we become either just or unjust. It is by our actions in the face of danger and by our training ourselves to fear or to courage that we become either cowardly or courageous. It is much the same with our appetites and angry passions. People become temperate and gentle, others licentious and passionate, by behaving in one or the other way in particular circumstances. In a word, moral states are the results of activities like the states themselves. It is our duty therefore to keep a certain character in our activities, since our moral states depend on the differences in our activities. So the difference between one and another training in habits in our childhood is not a light matter, but important, or rather, all-important.

Virtues and the mean

Our present study is not, like other studies, purely theoretical in intention; for the object of our inquiry is not to know what virtue is but how to become good, and that is the sole benefit of it. We must, therefore, consider the right way of performing actions, for it is acts, as we have said, that determine the character of the resulting moral states. . . .

The first point to be observed is that in the matters we are now considering deficiency and excess are both fatal. It is so, we see, in questions of health and strength. . . . Too much or too little gymnastic exercise is fatal to strength. Similarly, too much or too little meat and drink is fatal to health, whereas a suitable amount produces, increases, and sustains it. It is the same with temperance, courage, and other moral virtues. A person who avoids and is afraid of everything and faces nothing becomes a coward; a person who is not afraid of anything but is ready to face everything becomes foolhardy. Similarly, he who enjoys every pleasure and abstains from none is licentious; he who refuses all pleasures, like a boor, is an insensible sort of person. For temperance and courage are destroyed by excess and deficiency but preserved by the mean. . . .

Every art then does its work well, if it regards the mean and judges the works it produces by the mean. For this reason we often say of successful works of art that it is impossible to take anything from them or to add anything to them, which implies that excess or deficiency is fatal to excellence but that the mean state ensures it. Good artists too, as we say, have an eye to the mean in their works. Now virtue, like Nature herself, is more accurate and better than any art; virtue, therefore, will aim at the mean. I speak of moral virtue, since it is moral virtue which is concerned with emotions and actions, and it is in these we have excess and deficiency and the mean. Thus it is possible to go too far, or not far enough in fear, pride, desire, anger, pity, and pleasure and pain generally, and the excess and the deficiency are alike wrong; but to feel these emotions at the right times, for the right objects, towards the right persons, for the right motives, and in the right manner, is the mean or the best good, which signifies virtue. Similarly, there may be excess, deficiency, or the mean, in acts. Virtue is concerned with both emotions and actions, wherein excess is an error and deficiency a fault, while the mean is successful and praised, and success and praise are both characteristics of virtue.

It appears then that virtue is a kind of mean because it aims at the mean. . . .

But not every action or every emotion admits of a mean. There are some whose very name implies wickedness, as, for example, malice, shamelessness, and envy among the emotions, and adultery, theft, and murder among the actions. All these and others like them are marked as intrinsically wicked, not merely the excesses or deficiencies of them. It is never possible then to be right in them; they are always sinful. . . .

Practical advice

We have now sufficiently shown that moral virtue is a mean, and in what sense it is so; that it is a mean as lying between two vices, a vice of excess on the one side, and a vice of deficiency on the other, and as aiming at the mean in emotion and action.

That is why it is so hard to be good; for it is always hard to find the mean in anything. . . . Anybody can get angry—that is easy—and anybody can give or spend money, but to give it to the right person, to give the right amount of it, at the right time, for the right cause and in the right way, this is not what anybody can do, nor

---

In *Nicomachean Ethics,* Aristotle went on to work out the means, excesses, and deficiencies for various virtues. The following table summarizes Aristotle's discussion of some of these virtues:

Type of Feeling or Action	Vice (Excess)	Virtue (Mean)	Vice (Deficit)
Fear	Too much fear (i.e., cowardice)	Right amount of fear (i.e., courage)	Too little fear (i.e., foolhardiness)
Confidence	Too much confidence (i.e., recklessness)	Right amount of confidence (i.e., courage)	Too little confidence (i.e., cowardice)
Pleasure	Licentiousness/ self-indulgence	Temperance/ self-control	No name for this state, but it might be called "insensibility"
Giving money	Extravagance	Generosity	Stinginess
Large-scale giving	Vulgarity	Magnificence	Being cheap
Claiming honors	Vanity	Pride	Humility
Anger	Irascibility/short-temperedness	Good temper	Too little anger ("inirascibility"/apathy)
Retribution for wrongdoing	Injustice	Justice	Injustice
Social intercourse	Obsequiousness	Friendliness	Surliness
Giving amusement	Buffoonery	Wittiness	Boorishness

is it easy. That is why goodness is rare and praiseworthy and noble. One then who aims at a mean must begin by departing from the extreme that is more contrary to the mean . . . , for of the two extremes one is more wrong than the other. As it is difficult to hit the mean exactly, we should take the second best course, as the saying is, and choose the lesser of two evils. This we shall best do in the way described, that is, steering clear of the evil which is further from the mean. We must also note the weaknesses to which we are ourselves particularly prone, since different natures tend in different ways; and we may ascertain what our tendency is by observing our feelings of pleasure and pain. Then we must drag ourselves away towards the opposite extreme; for by pulling ourselves as far as possible from what is wrong we shall arrive at the mean, as we do when we pull a crooked stick straight.

In all cases we must especially be on our guard against the pleasant, or pleasure, for we are not impartial judges of pleasure.

Review and Discussion Questions

1. Aristotle believed that ethics is not an exact science and that young people are not proper students of ethics. Why? Are you persuaded by his reasoning?

2. Why did Aristotle believe that happiness is the supreme good? Do you agree?

3. What were Aristotle's reasons for rejecting the view that the pursuit of honor or wealth constitutes the good or happy life?

4. What did Aristotle mean when he talked about our function as human beings? Can you state his viewpoint in your own words?

5. What is the relationship between virtue and habit? How do we come to be virtuous?

6. Discuss Aristotle's theory of virtue with regard to the specific virtues given in the table on page 42.

Good Will, Duty, and the Categorical Imperative

IMMANUEL KANT

Immanuel Kant was born in Königsberg in East Prussia in 1724. He spent his whole life there, eventually becoming a professor at the local university. He remained a bachelor and was reported to have been so regular in his habits that neighbors set their clocks by his afternoon walks. He died at eighty, by which time he had left a lasting mark on the world of philosophy. Today he is considered one of the greatest philosophers of all time.

Kant's ethical theory has been enormously influential. This excerpt from his classic work *The Foundations of the Metaphysics of Morals* presents Kant's account of moral duty. For an action to have moral worth, for it to reflect a good will, Kant

From The Foundations of the Metaphysics of Morals, *translated by T. K. Abbott (1873). Subheadings added.*

stressed that the action must be undertaken for duty's sake—and not for some other reason, such as fear of being caught and punished. Ethics is based on reason alone, Kant thought, and not—as it was for Aristotle—on human nature. The imperatives of morality are, in his famous terminology, not hypothetical but categorical. That is, the moral duty that binds us is unconditional, universally valid, and necessary.

Kant formulated his basic test of right and wrong, his famous categorical imperative, in different ways. But the core idea is that an action is right if and only if we can will it to become a universal law of conduct. That is, we must never perform an action unless we can consistently will that the maxim or principle governing it be one that everyone can follow. Consider, for example, making a promise that you know you cannot keep. Kant believed that it is impossible to will the maxim "Make promises that you know you cannot keep" as a universal law, because if everyone were to act on this maxim, the institution of promising would be impossible. An alternative formulation of the categorical imperative Kant offered is that one should always treat human beings as ends in themselves, never as means alone.

Study Questions

1. Why is a good will the only thing that is good without qualification?
2. When does an action have moral worth?
3. What is the difference between a hypothetical imperative and a categorical imperative?
4. What is the second formulation of the categorical imperative?
5. What did Kant mean by the "kingdom of ends"?

The Good Will

NOTHING CAN POSSIBLY BE CONCEIVED in the world, or even out of it, which can be called good, without qualification, except a Good Will. Intelligence, wit, judgment, and the other *talents* of the mind, however they may be named, or courage, resolution, perseverance, as qualities of temperament, are undoubtedly good and desirable in many respects; but these gifts of nature may also become extremely bad and mischievous if the will which is to make use of them, and which, therefore, constitutes what is called *character*, is not good. It is the same with the *gifts of fortune*. Power, riches, honour, even health, and the general well-being and contentment with one's condition which is called *happiness*, inspire pride, and often presumption, if there is not a good will to correct the influence of these on the mind, and with

this also to rectify the whole principle of acting, and adapt it to its end. The sight of a being who is not adorned with a single feature of a pure and good will, enjoying unbroken prosperity, can never give pleasure to an impartial rational spectator. Thus a good will appears to constitute the indispensable condition even of being worthy of happiness.

There are even some qualities which are of service to this good will itself, and may facilitate its action, yet which have no intrinsic unconditional value, but always presuppose a good will, and this qualifies the esteem that we justly have for them, and does not permit us to regard them as absolutely good. Moderation in the affections and passions, self-control, and calm deliberation are not only good in many respects, but even seem to constitute part of the intrinsic worth of the person; but they are far from deserving to be called good without qualification, although they have been so unconditionally praised by the ancients. For without the principles of a good will, they may become extremely bad; and the coolness of a villain not only makes him far more dangerous, but also directly makes him more abominable in our eyes than he would have been without it.

A good will is good not because of what it performs or effects, not by its aptness for the attainment of some proposed end, but simply by virtue of the volition, that is, it is good in itself, and considered by itself is to be esteemed much higher than all that can be brought about by it in favour of any inclination, nay, even of the sum-total of all inclinations. Even if it should happen that, owing to special disfavour of fortune, or the niggardly provision of a stepmotherly nature, this will should wholly lack power to accomplish its purpose, if with its greatest efforts it should yet achieve nothing, and there should remain only the good will (not, to be sure, a mere wish, but the summoning of all means in our power), then, like a jewel, it would still shine by its own light, as a thing which has its whole value in itself. Its usefulness or fruitlessness can neither add to nor take away anything from this value. It would be, as it were, only the setting to enable us to handle it the more conveniently in common commerce, or to attract to it the attention of those who are not yet connoisseurs, but not to recommend it to true connoisseurs, or to determine its value. . . .

Moral Worth

It is always a matter of duty that a dealer should not overcharge an inexperienced purchaser; and wherever there is much commerce the prudent tradesman does not overcharge, but keeps a fixed price for everyone, so that a child buys of him as well as any other. Men are thus *honestly* served; but this is not enough to make us believe that the tradesman has so acted from duty and from principles of honesty: his own advantage required it; it is out of the question in this case to suppose that he might besides have a direct inclination in favour of the buyers, so that, as it were, from love he should give no advantage to one over another. Accordingly the action was done neither from duty nor from direct inclination, but merely with a selfish view.

On the other hand, it is a duty to maintain one's life; and, in addition, everyone has also a direct inclination to do so. But on this account the often anxious care which most men take for it has no intrinsic worth. . . . They preserve their life *as duty requires,* no doubt, but not *because duty requires.* On the other hand, if adversity and hopeless sorrow have completely taken away the relish for life; if the unfortunate one, strong in mind, indignant at his fate rather than desponding or dejected, wishes for death, and yet preserves his life without loving it—not from inclination or fear, but from duty—then his maxim has a moral worth.

To be beneficent when we can is a duty; and besides this, there are many minds so sympathetically constituted that, without any other motive of vanity or self-interest, they find a pleasure in spreading joy around them, and can take delight in the satisfaction of others so far as it is their own work. But I maintain that in such a case an action of this kind, however proper, however amiable it may be, has nevertheless no true moral worth, but is on a level with other inclinations, *e.g.* the inclination to honour, which, if it is happily directed to that which is in fact of public utility and accordant with duty, and consequently honourable, deserves praise and encouragement, but not esteem. For the maxim lacks the moral import, namely, that such actions be done *from duty,* not from inclination. Put the case that the mind of that philanthropist was clouded by sorrow of his own, extinguishing all sympathy with the lot of others, and that while he still has the power to benefit others in distress, he is not touched by their trouble because he is absorbed with his own; and now suppose that he tears himself out of this dead insensibility, and performs the action without any inclination to it, but simply from duty, then first has his action its genuine moral worth. Further still; if nature has put little sympathy in the heart of this or that man; if he, supposed to be an upright man, is by temperament cold and indifferent to the sufferings of others, perhaps because in respect of his own he is provided with the special gift of patience and fortitude, and supposes, or even requires, that others should have the same—and such a man would certainly not be the meanest product of nature—but if nature had not specially framed him for a philanthropist, would he not still find in himself a source from whence to give himself a far higher worth than that of a good-natured temperament could be? Unquestionably. It is just in this that the moral worth of the character is brought out which is incomparably the highest of all, namely, that he is beneficent, not from inclination, but from duty. . . .

An action done from duty derives its moral worth, *not from the purpose* which is to be attained by it, but from the maxim by which it is determined and therefore does not depend on the realization of the object of the action, but merely on the *principle of volition* by which the action has taken place, without regard to any object of desire. . . . Moral worth . . . cannot lie anywhere but in the *principle of the will*. . . . An action done from duty must wholly exclude the influence of inclination, and with it every object of the will, so that nothing remains which can determine the will except objectively the *law* and subjectively *pure respect* for this practical law, and consequently the maxim that I should follow this law even to the thwarting of all my inclinations.

Thus the moral worth of an action does not lie in the effect expected from it, nor in any principle of action which requires to borrow its motive from this expected effect. For all these effects—agreeableness of one's condition, and even the promotion of the happiness of others—could have been also brought about by other causes, so that for this there would have been no need of the will of a rational being; whereas it is in this alone that the supreme and unconditional

good can be found. The pre-eminent good which we call moral can therefore consist in nothing else than *the conception of law* in itself, *which certainly is only possible in a rational being*, in so far as this conception, and not the expected effect, determines the will. . . .

The Supreme Principle of Morality: The Categorical Imperative

But what sort of law can that be, the conception of which must determine the will, even without paying any regard to the effect expected from it, in order that this will may be called good absolutely and without qualification? As I have deprived the will of every impulse which could arise to it from obedience to any law, there remains nothing but the universal conformity of its actions to law in general, which alone is to serve the will as a principle, *i.e.* I am never to act otherwise than so *that I could also will that my maxim should become a universal law.* Here, now, it is the simple conformity to law in general, without assuming any particular law applicable to certain actions, that serves the will as its principle, and must so serve it, if duty is not to be a vain delusion and a chimerical notion. The common reason of men in its practical judgments perfectly coincides with this, and always has in view the principle here suggested. Let the question be, for example: May I when in distress make a promise with the intention not to keep it? I readily distinguish here between the two significations which the question may have: Whether it is prudent, or whether it is right, to make a false promise? The former may undoubtedly often be the case. I see clearly indeed that it is not enough to extricate myself from a present difficulty by means of this subterfuge, but it must be well considered whether there may not hereafter spring from this lie much greater inconvenience than that from which I now free myself, and as, with all my supposed *cunning,* the consequences cannot be so easily foreseen but that credit once lost may be much more injurious to me than any mischief which I seek to avoid at present, it should be considered whether it would not be more *prudent* to act herein according to a universal maxim, and to make it a habit to promise nothing except with the intention of keeping it. But it is soon clear to me that such a maxim will still only be based on the fear of consequences. Now it is a wholly different thing to be truthful from duty, and to be so from apprehension of injurious consequences. In the first case, the very notion of the action already implies a law for me; in the second case, I must first look about elsewhere to see what results may be combined with it which would affect myself. For to deviate from the principle of duty is beyond all doubt wicked; but to be unfaithful to my maxim of prudence may often be very advantageous to me, although to abide by it is certainly safer. The shortest way, however, and an unerring one, to discover the answer to this question whether a lying promise is consistent with duty, is to ask myself, Should I be content that my maxim (to extricate myself from difficulty by a false promise) should hold good as a universal law, for myself as well as for others? and should I be able to say to myself, "Every one may make a deceitful promise when he finds himself in a difficulty from which he cannot otherwise extricate himself"? Then I presently become aware that while I can will the lie, I can by no means will that lying should be a universal law. For with such a law there would be no promises at all, since it would be in vain to allege my intention in regard to my future actions to those who would not believe this allegation, or if they over-hastily did so, would pay me back in my own coin. Hence my maxim, as soon as it should be made a universal law, would necessarily destroy itself.

I do not, therefore, need any far-reaching penetration to discern what I have to do in order that my will may be morally good. Inexperienced in the course of the world, incapable of being prepared for all its contingencies, I only ask myself: Canst thou also will that thy maxim should be a universal law? If not, then it must be rejected, and that not because of a disadvan-

tage accruing from myself or even to others, but because it cannot enter as a principle into a possible universal legislation, and reason extorts from me immediate respect for such legislation. I do not indeed as yet *discern* on what this respect is based (this the philosopher may inquire), but at least I understand this, that it is an estimation of the worth which far outweighs all worth of what is recommended by inclination, and that the necessity of acting from *pure* respect for the practical law is what constitutes duty, to which every other motive must give place, because it is the condition of a will being good *in itself,* and the worth of such a will is above everything.

Thus, then, without quitting the moral knowledge of common human reason, we have arrived at its principle. And although, no doubt, common men do not conceive it in such an abstract and universal form, yet they always have it really before their eyes, and use it as the standard of their decision. . . .

Imperatives: Hypothetical and Categorical

Everything in nature works according to laws. Rational beings alone have the faculty of acting according *to the conception of laws,* that is according to principles, *i.e.* have a *will.* Since the deduction of actions from principles requires *reason,* the will is nothing but practical reason. If reason infallibly determines the will, then the actions of such a being which are recognized as objectively necessary are subjectively necessary also, *i.e.* the will is a faculty to choose *that only* which reason independent of inclination recognizes as practically necessary, *i.e.* as good. But if reason of itself does not sufficiently determine the will, if the latter is subject also to subjective conditions (particular impulses) which do not always coincide with the objective conditions; in a word, if the will does not *in itself* completely accord with reason (which is actually the case with men), then the actions which objectively are recognized as necessary are subjectively contingent, and the determination of such a will according to objective laws is *obligation,* that is to say, the relation of the objective laws to a will that is not thoroughly good is conceived as the determination of the will of a rational being by principles of reason, but which the will from its nature does not of necessity follow.

The conception of an objective principle, in so far as it is obligatory for a will, is called a command (of reason), and the formula of the command is called an Imperative. . . .

Now all *imperatives* command either *hypothetically* or *categorically.* The former represent the practical necessity of a possible action as means to something else that is willed (or at least which one might possibly will). The categorical imperative would be that which represented an action as necessary of itself without reference to another end, *i.e.,* as objectively necessary. . . .

If now the action is good only as a means *to something else,* then the imperative is *hypothetical;* if it is conceived as good *in itself* and consequently as being necessarily the principle of a will which of itself conforms to reason, then it is *categorical.* . . .

When I conceive a hypothetical imperative, in general I do not know beforehand what it will contain until I am given the condition. But when I conceive a categorical imperative, I know at once what it contains. For as the imperative contains besides the law only the necessity that the maxims shall conform to this law, while the law contains no conditions restricting it, there remains nothing but the general statement that the maxim of the action should conform to a universal law, and it is this conformity alone that the imperative properly represents as necessary.

There is therefore but one categorical imperative, namely, this: *Act only on that maxim whereby thou canst at the same time will that it should become a universal law.*

Now if all imperatives of duty can be deduced from this one imperative as from their principle, then, although it should remain unde-

cided whether what is called duty is not merely a vain notion, yet at least we shall be able to show what we understand by it and what this notion means.

Since the universality of the law according to which effects are produced constitutes what is properly called *nature* in the most general sense (as to form), that is the existence of things so far as it is determined by general laws, the imperative of duty may be expressed thus: *Act as if the maxim of thy action were to become by thy will a universal law of nature.*

Four Illustrations

We shall now enumerate a few duties, adopting the usual division of them into duties to ourselves and to others, and into perfect and imperfect duties.

1. A man reduced to despair by a series of misfortunes feels wearied of life, but is still so far in possession of his reason that he can ask himself whether it would not be contrary to his duty to himself to take his own life. Now he inquires whether the maxim of his action could become a universal law of nature. His maxim is: From self-love I adopt it as a principle to shorten my life when its longer duration is likely to bring more evil than satisfaction. It is asked then simply whether this principle founded on self-love can become a universal law of nature. Now we see at once that a system of nature of which it should be a law to destroy life by means of the very feeling whose special nature it is to impel to the improvement of life would contradict itself, and therefore could not exist as a system of nature; hence that maxim cannot possibly exist as a universal law of nature, and consequently would be wholly inconsistent with the supreme principle of all duty.

2. Another finds himself forced by necessity to borrow money. He knows that he will not be

able to repay it, but sees also that nothing will be lent to him, unless he promises stoutly to repay it in a definite time. He desires to make this promise, but he has still so much conscience as to ask himself: Is it not unlawful and inconsistent with duty to get out of a difficulty in this way? Suppose, however, that he resolves to do so, then the maxim of his action would be expressed thus: When I think myself in want of money, I will borrow money and promise to repay it, although I know that I never can do so. Now this principle of self-love or of one's own advantage may perhaps be consistent with my whole future welfare; but the question now is, Is it right? I change then the suggestion of self-love into a universal law, and state the question thus: How would it be if my maxim were a universal law? Then I see at once that it could never hold as a universal law of nature, but would necessarily contradict itself. For supposing it to be a universal law that everyone when he thinks himself in a difficulty should be able to promise whatever he pleases, with the purpose of not keeping his promise, the promise itself would become impossible, as well as the end that one might have in view in it, since no one would consider that anything was promised to him, but would ridicule all such statements as vain pretences.

3. A third finds in himself a talent which with the help of some culture might make him a useful man in many respects. But he finds himself in comfortable circumstances, and prefers to indulge in pleasure rather than to take pains in enlarging and improving his happy natural capacities. He asks, however, whether his maxim of neglect of his natural gifts, besides agreeing with his inclination to indulgence, agrees also with what is called duty. He sees then that a system of nature could indeed subsist with such a universal law although men (like the South Sea islanders) should let their talents rest, and resolve to devote their lives merely to idleness, amusement, and propagation of their species—in a

word, to enjoyment; but he cannot possibly *will* that this should be a universal law of nature, or be implanted in us as such by a natural instinct. For, as a rational being, he necessarily wills that his faculties be developed, since they serve him, and have been given him, for all sorts of possible purposes.

4. A fourth, who is in prosperity, while he sees that others have to contend with great wretchedness and that he could help them, thinks: What concern is it of mine? Let everyone be as happy as Heaven pleases, or as he can make himself; I will take nothing from him nor even envy him, only I do not wish to contribute anything to his welfare or to his assistance in distress! Now no doubt if such a mode of thinking were a universal law, the human race might very well subsist, and doubtless even better than in a state in which everyone talks of sympathy and good-will, or even takes care occasionally to put it into practice, but, on the other side, also cheats when he can, betrays the rights of men, or otherwise violates them. But although it is possible that a universal law of nature might exist in accordance with that maxim, it is impossible to *will* that such a principle should have the universal validity of a law of nature. For a will which resolved this would contradict itself, inasmuch as many cases might occur in which one would have need of the love and sympathy of others, and in which, by such a law of nature, sprung from his own will, he would deprive himself of all hope of the aid he desires. . . .

Second Formulation of the Categorical Imperative: Humanity as an End in Itself

The will is conceived as a faculty of determining oneself to action *in accordance with the conception of certain laws.* And such a faculty can be found only in rational beings. . . .

Now I say: man and generally any rational being *exists* as an end in himself, *not merely as a means* to be arbitrarily used by this or that will, but in all his actions, whether they concern himself or other rational beings, must be always regarded at the same time as an end. All objects of the inclinations have only a conditional worth; for if the inclinations and the wants founded on them did not exist, then their object would be without value. But the inclinations themselves being sources of want are so far from having an absolute worth for which they should be desired, that, on the contrary, it must be the universal wish of every rational being to be wholly free from them. Thus the worth of any object which is *to be acquired* by our action is always conditional. Beings whose existence depends not on our will but on nature's, have nevertheless, if they are nonrational beings, only a relative value as means, and are therefore called *things;* rational beings, on the contrary, are called *persons,* because their very nature points them out as ends in themselves, that is as something which must not be used merely as means, and so far therefore restricts freedom of action (and is an object of respect). These, therefore, are not merely subjective ends whose existence has a worth *for us* as an effect of our action, but *objective ends,* that is things whose existence is an end in itself: an end moreover for which no other can be substituted, which they should subserve *merely* as means, for otherwise nothing whatever would possess *absolute worth;* but if all worth were conditioned and therefore contingent, then there would be no supreme practical principle of reason whatever.

If then there is a supreme practical principle or, in respect of the human will, a categorical imperative, it must be one which, being drawn from the conception of that which is necessarily an end for everyone because it is *an end in itself,* constitutes an *objective* principle of will, and can therefore serve as a universal practical law. The foundation of this principle is: *rational nature exists as an end in itself.* Man necessarily con-

ceives his own existence as being so: so far then this is a *subjective* principle of human actions. But every other rational being regards its existence similarly, just on the same rational principle that holds for me: so that it is at the same time an objective principle, from which as a supreme practical law all laws of the will must be capable of being deduced. Accordingly the practical imperative will be as follows: *So act as to treat humanity, whether in thine own person or in that of any other, in every case as an end withal, never as means only. . . .*

Looking back now on all previous attempts to discover the principle of morality, we need not wonder why they all failed. It was seen that man was bound to laws by duty, but it was not observed that the laws to which he is subject are *only those of his own giving,* though at the same time they are *universal,* and that he is only bound to act in conformity with his own will; a will, however, which is designed by nature to give universal laws. . . .

The Kingdom of Ends

The conception of every rational being as one which must consider itself as giving in all the maxims of its will universal laws, so as to judge itself and its actions from this point of view— this conception leads to another which depends on it and is very fruitful, namely, that of a *kingdom of ends.*

By a *kingdom* I understand the union of different rational beings in a system by common laws. Now since it is by laws that ends are determined as regards their universal validity, hence, if we abstract from the personal differences of rational beings, and likewise from all the content of their private ends, we shall be able to conceive all ends combined in a systematic whole (including both rational beings as ends in themselves, and also the special ends which each may propose to himself), that is to say, we can conceive a kingdom of ends, which on the preceding principles is possible.

For all rational beings come under the *law* that each of them must treat itself and all others *never merely as means,* but in every case *at the same time as ends in themselves.* Hence results a systematic union of rational beings by common objective laws, *i.e.,* a kingdom which may be called a kingdom of ends, since what these laws have in view is just the relation of these beings to one another as ends and means.

Review and Discussion Questions

1. Consider the case of the philanthropist who lacks sympathy for others. Was Kant correct to maintain that an action has moral worth only if it is done from a sense of duty (and not from inclination)?

2. How exactly does a hypothetical imperative differ from a categorical imperative? Can there really be an imperative that is more than hypothetical?

3. Explain how each of Kant's four examples illustrates the categorical imperative. Do you see any problems with Kant's reasoning?

4. Kant believed that we should always treat people as ends in themselves, never as a means only. What exactly does this imply? How can one square this duty with normal, day-to-day business activity—for example, buying a ticket to a movie?

5. How do you see Kant's approach as differing from that of Aristotle?

Utilitarianism

JOHN STUART MILL

John Stuart Mill (1806–1873) was a leading exponent of utilitarian moral philosophy and probably the most important British philosopher of the nineteenth century. He was educated at home by his father, learning Greek at the age of three and Latin at eight. He was something of a prodigy and as a young man was an active crusader for the utilitarian cause. His autobiography describes very movingly his education and youthful activities and the mental breakdown he suffered when he was twenty years old. Around the time of his recovery, he began a friendship with Harriet Taylor, who became his lifelong companion and intellectual collaborator. Their relationship was viewed as unorthodox, if not scandalous, because Taylor was married. In fact, she continued to live with her husband until his death twenty years later, at which time she and Mill married. Mill spent much of his life working for the East India Company, where he began as a clerk at the age of seventeen and eventually became a company director. He was elected to Parliament in 1865.

Utilitarianism is the moral theory that right and wrong are a function of the consequences of our actions. It holds that we should act so as to produce the greatest

From *John Stuart Mill,* Utilitarianism *(1869).*

possible balance of good over bad for everyone affected by our actions. By "good," utilitarians like Mill understand happiness or pleasure. Mill, however, modified the earlier utilitarian theory of Bentham by arguing that the "higher" pleasures of the intellect are of greater value than other pleasures. This excerpt from Mill's classic work *Utilitarianism* explains the utilitarian principle, defends it against various objections, and argues that happiness is the only thing of intrinsic value. The final section presents a slightly more complicated view of right and wrong and discusses the relationship between utility, on the one hand, and rights and justice, on the other.

Study Questions

1. What is Mill's initial statement of the utilitarian principle?
2. What is Mill's test for distinguishing higher pleasures from lower pleasures?
3. How did Mill answer the objection that utilitarianism is too demanding because it requires us always to act in a way that promotes the general interests of society?
4. What is Mill's proof of the principle of utility? How did he try to establish that the only thing people desire is happiness?
5. What is Mill's final definition of right and wrong, and how does it differ from his initial statement of the utilitarian doctrine?
6. What is the relationship between utility and justice?

Chapter I: General Remarks

THERE ARE FEW CIRCUMSTANCES among those which make up the present condition of human knowledge, more unlike what might have been expected, or more significant of the backward state in which speculation on the most important subjects still lingers, than the little progress which has been made in the decision of the controversy respecting the criterion of right and wrong. . . .

On the present occasion, I shall . . . attempt to contribute something towards the understanding and appreciation of the Utilitarian or Happiness theory, and towards such proof as it is susceptible of. It is evident that this cannot be proof in the ordinary and popular meaning of the term. Questions of ultimate ends are not amenable to direct proof. . . . We are not, however, to infer that its acceptance or rejection must depend on blind impulse, or arbitrary choice. There is a larger meaning of the word

proof. . . . Considerations may be presented capable of determining the intellect either to give or withhold its assent to the doctrine; and this is equivalent to proof. . . .

Chapter II: What Utilitarianism Is

. . . The creed which accepts as the foundation of morals, Utility, or the Greatest Happiness Principle, holds that actions are right in proportion as they tend to promote happiness, wrong as they tend to produce the reverse of happiness. By happiness is intended pleasure, and the absence of pain; by unhappiness, pain, and the privation of pleasure. . . . Pleasure, and freedom from pain, are the only things desirable as ends; and . . . all desirable things (which are as numerous in the utilitarian as in any other scheme) are desirable either for the pleasure inherent in themselves, or as means to the promotion of pleasure and the prevention of pain.

Now, such a theory of life excites in many minds, and among them in some of the most estimable in feeling and purpose, inveterate dislike. To suppose that life has (as they express it) no higher end than pleasure—no better and nobler object of desire and pursuit—they designate as utterly mean and grovelling; as a doctrine worthy only of swine, to whom the followers of Epicurus were, at a very early period, contemptuously likened. . . .

When thus attacked, the Epicureans have always answered, that it is not they, but their accusers, who represent human nature in a degrading light; since the accusation supposes human beings to be capable of no pleasures except those of which swine are capable. . . . The comparison of the Epicurean life to that of beasts is felt as degrading, precisely because a beast's pleasures do not satisfy a human being's conceptions of happiness. Human beings have faculties more elevated than the animal appetites, and when once made conscious of them, do not regard anything as happiness which does not include their gratification. . . . It is quite compatible with the principle of utility to recognize the fact, that some *kinds* of pleasure are more desirable and more valuable than others. It would be absurd that while, in estimating all other things, quality is considered as well as quantity, the estimation of pleasures should be supposed to depend on quantity alone.

If I am asked, what I mean by difference of quality in pleasures, or what makes one pleasure more valuable than another, merely as a pleasure, except its being greater in amount, there is but one possible answer. Of two pleasures, if there be one to which all or almost all who have experience of both give a decided preference, irrespective of any feeling of moral obligation to prefer it, that is the more desirable pleasure. If one of the two is, by those who are competently acquainted with both, placed so far above the other that they prefer it, even though knowing it to be attended with a greater amount of discontent, and would not resign it for any quan-

tity of the other pleasure which their nature is capable of, we are justified in ascribing to the preferred enjoyment a superiority in quality, so far outweighing quantity as to render it, in comparison, of small account.

Now it is an unquestionable fact that those who are equally acquainted with and equally capable of appreciating and enjoying, both, do give a most marked preference to the manner of existence which employs their higher faculties. Few human creatures would consent to be changed into any of the lower animals, for a promise of the fullest allowance of a beast's pleasures; no intelligent human being would consent to be a fool, no instructed person would be an ignoramus, no person of feeling and conscience would be selfish and base, even though they should be persuaded that the fool, the dunce, or the rascal is better satisfied with his lot than they are with theirs. They would not resign what they possess more than he, for the most complete satisfaction of all the desires which they have in common with him. If they ever fancy they would, it is only in cases of unhappiness so extreme, that to escape from it they would exchange their lot for almost any other, however undesirable in their own eyes. A being of higher faculties requires more to make him happy, is capable probably of more acute suffering, and is certainly accessible to it at more points, than one of an inferior type; but in spite of these liabilities, he can never really wish to sink into what he feels to be a lower grade of existence. . . . Whoever supposes that this preference takes place at a sacrifice of happiness—that the superior being, in anything like the equal circumstances, is not happier than the inferior—confounds the two very different ideas, of happiness, and content. It is indisputable that the being whose capacities of enjoyment are low, has the greatest chance of having them fully satisfied; and a highly-endowed being will always feel that any happiness which he can look for, as the world is constituted, is imperfect. But he can learn to bear its imperfections, if they are at all bearable; and they will not make him envy the being who is indeed unconscious of the imperfections, but only because he feels not at all the good which those imperfections qualify. It is better to be a human being dissatisfied than a pig satisfied; better to be Socrates dissatisfied than a fool satisfied. And if the fool, or the pig, is of a different opinion, it is because they only know their own side of the question. The other party to the comparison knows both sides. . . .

From this verdict of the only competent judges, I apprehend there can be no appeal. On a question which is the best worth having of two pleasures, or which of two modes of existence is the most grateful to the feelings, apart from its moral attributes and from its consequences, the judgment of those who are qualified by knowledge of both, or, if they differ, that of the majority among them, must be admitted as final. . . . There is no other tribunal to be referred to even on the question of quantity. What means are there of determining which is the acutest of two pains, or the intensest of two pleasurable sensations, except the general suffrage of those who are familiar with both? . . . When, therefore, those feelings and judgment declare the pleasures derived from the higher faculties to be preferable *in kind,* apart from the question of intensity, to those of which the animal nature, disjoined from the higher faculties, is susceptible, they are entitled on this subject to the same regard. . . .

The assailants of utilitarianism seldom have the justice to acknowledge, that the happiness which forms the utilitarian standard of what is right in conduct, is not the agent's own happiness, but that of all concerned. As between his own happiness and that of others, utilitarianism requires him to be as strictly impartial as a disinterested and benevolent spectator. In the golden rule of Jesus of Nazareth, we read the complete spirit of the ethics of utility. To do as one would be done by, and to love one's neighbour as oneself, constitute the ideal perfection of utilitarian morality. As the means of making the nearest approach to this ideal, utility would enjoin, first,

that laws and social arrangements should place the happiness, or (as speaking practically it may be called) the interest, of every individual, as nearly as possible in harmony with the interest of the whole; and secondly, that education and opinion, which have so vast a power over human character, should so use that power as to establish in the mind of every individual an indissoluble association between his own happiness and the good of the whole; especially between his own happiness and the practice of such modes of conduct, negative and positive, as regard for the universal happiness prescribes. . . .

The objectors to utilitarianism . . . say it is exacting too much to require that people shall always act from the inducement of promoting the general interests of society. But this is to mistake the very meaning of a standard of morals, and to confound the rule of action with the motive of it. It is the business of ethics to tell us what are our duties, or by what test we may know them; but no system of ethics requires that the sole motive of all we do shall be a feeling of duty; on the contrary, ninety-nine hundredths of all our actions are done from other motives, and rightly so done, if the rule of duty does not condemn them. It is the more unjust to utilitarianism that this particular misapprehension should be made a ground of objection to it, inasmuch as utilitarian moralists have gone beyond almost all others in affirming that the motive has nothing to do with the morality of the action, though much with the worth of the agent. He who saves a fellow creature from drowning does what is morally right, whether his motive be duty, or the hope of being paid for his trouble: he who betrays the friend that trusts him, is guilty of a crime, even if his object be to serve another friend to whom he is under greater obligations. But to speak only of actions done from the motive of duty, and in direct obedience to principle: it is a misapprehension of the utilitarian mode of thought, to conceive it as implying that people should fix their minds upon so wide a generality as the world, or society at large. The great majority of good actions are intended, not for the benefit of the world, but for that of individuals, of which the good of the world is made up; and the thoughts of the most virtuous man need not on these occasions travel beyond the particular persons concerned, except so far as is necessary to assure himself that in benefitting them he is not violating the rights—that is, the legitimate and authorized expectations—of any one else. . . . In the case of abstinences indeed—of things which people forbear to do, from moral considerations, though the consequences in the particular case might be beneficial—it would be unworthy of an intelligent agent not to be consciously aware that the action is of a class which, if practised generally, would be generally injurious, and that this is the ground of the obligation to abstain from it. The amount of regard for the public interest implied in this recognition, is no greater than is demanded by every system of morals; for they all enjoin to abstain from whatever is manifestly pernicious to society. . . .

Defenders of utility often find themselves called upon to reply to such objections as this—that there is not time, previous to action, for calculating and weighing the effects of any line of conduct on the general happiness. . . . The answer to the objection is, that there has been ample time, namely, the whole past duration of the human species. During all that time mankind have been learning by experience the tendencies of actions; on which experience all the prudence, as well as all the morality of life, is dependent. People talk as if the commencement of this course of experience had hitherto been put off, and as if, at the moment when some man feels tempted to meddle with the property or life of another, he had to begin considering for the first time whether murder and theft are injurious to human happiness. . . . It is truly a whimsical supposition that if mankind were agreed in considering utility to be the test of morality, they would remain without any agreement as to what *is* useful, and would take no measures for having their notions on the subject taught to the young, and enforced by law and opinion. There is no difficulty in proving any

ethical standard whatever to work ill, if we suppose universal idiocy to be conjoined with it, but on any hypothesis short of that, mankind must by this time have acquired positive beliefs as to the effects of some actions on their happiness. . . . That the received code of ethics is by no means of divine right; and that mankind have still much to learn as to the effects of actions on the general happiness, I admit, or rather, earnestly maintain. The corollaries from the principle of utility, like the precepts of every practical art, admit of indefinite improvement, and, in a progressive state of the human mind, their improvement is perpetually going on. But to consider the rules of morality as improvable, is one thing; to pass over the intermediate generalizations entirely, and endeavour to test each individual action directly by the first principle, is another. It is a strange notion that the acknowledgment of a first principle is inconsistent with the admission of secondary ones. To inform a traveller respecting the place of his ultimate destination, is not to forbid the use of landmarks and direction-posts on the way. The proposition that happiness is the end and aim of morality, does not mean that no road ought to be laid down to that goal, or that persons going thither should not be advised to take one direction rather than another. Men really ought to leave off talking a kind of nonsense on this subject. . . . Whatever we adopt as the fundamental principle of morality, we require subordinate principles to apply it by. . . .

Chapter IV: Of What Sort of Proof the Principle of Utility Is Susceptible

It has already been remarked, that questions of ultimate ends do not admit of proof, in the ordinary acceptation of the term. To be incapable of proof by reasoning is common to all first principles; to the first premises of our knowledge, as well as to those of our conduct. But the former, being matters of fact, may be the subject of a direct appeal to the faculties which judge of fact—namely, our senses, and our internal consciousness. Can an appeal be made to the same faculties on questions of practical ends? Or by what other faculty is cognizance taken of them?

Questions about ends are, in other words, questions [about] what things are desirable. The utilitarian doctrine is, that happiness is desirable, and the only thing desirable, as an end; all other things being only desirable as means to that end. What ought to be required of this doctrine—what conditions is it requisite that the doctrine should fulfil—to make good its claim to be believed?

The only proof capable of being given that an object is visible, is that people actually see it. The only proof that a sound is audible, is that people hear it: and so of the other sources of our experience. In like manner, I apprehend, the sole evidence it is possible to produce that anything is desirable, is that people do actually desire it. If the end which the utilitarian doctrine proposes to itself were not, in theory, and in practice, acknowledged to be an end, nothing could ever convince any person that it was so. No reason can be given why the general happiness is desirable, except that each person, so far as he believes it to be attainable, desires his own happiness. This, however, being a fact, we have not only all the proof which the case admits of, but all which it is possible to require, that happiness is a good: that each person's happiness is a good to that person, and the general happiness, therefore, a good to the aggregate of all persons. Happiness has made out its title as *one* of the ends of conduct, and consequently one of the criteria of morality.

But it has not, by this alone, proved itself to be the sole criterion. To do that, it would seem, by the same rule, necessary to show, not only that people desire happiness, but that they never desire anything else. Now it is palpable that they do desire things which, in common language, are decidedly distinguished from happiness. They desire, for example, virtue, and the absence of vice, no less really than pleasure and the

absence of pain. The desire of virtue is not as universal, but it is as authentic a fact, as the desire of happiness. . . .

The ingredients of happiness are very various, and each of them is desirable in itself, and not merely when considered as swelling an aggregate. The principle of utility does not mean that any given pleasure, as music, for instance, or any given exemption from pain, as for example health, are to be looked upon as a means to a collective something termed happiness, and to be desired on that account. They are desired and desirable in and for themselves; besides being means, they are a part of the end. Virtue, according to the utilitarian doctrine, is not naturally and originally part of the end, but it is capable of becoming so; and in those who love it disinterestedly it has become so, and is desired and cherished, not as a means to happiness, but as a part of their happiness.

To illustrate this farther, we may remember that virtue is not the only thing, originally a means, and which if it were not a means to anything else, would be and remain indifferent, but which by association with what it is a means to, comes to be desired for itself, and that too with the utmost intensity. What, for example, shall we say of the love of money? There is nothing originally more desirable about money than about any heap of glittering pebbles. Its worth is solely that of the things which it will buy; the desires for other things than itself, which it is a means of gratifying. Yet the love of money is not only one of the strongest moving forces of human life, but money is, in many cases, desired in and for itself; the desire to possess it is often stronger than the desire to use it, and goes on increasing when all the desires which point to ends beyond it, to be encompassed by it, are falling off. It may be then said truly, that money is desired not for the sake of an end, but as part of the end. From being a means to happiness, it has come to be itself a principal ingredient of the individual's conception of happiness. The same may be said of the majority of the great objects of human life—

power, for example, or fame; except that to each of these there is a certain amount of immediate pleasure annexed, which has at least the semblance of being naturally inherent in them; a thing which cannot be said of money. Still, however, the strongest natural attraction, both of power and of fame, is the immense aid they give to the attainment of our other wishes; and it is the strong association thus generated between them and all our objects of desire, which gives to the direct desire of them the intensity it often assumes, so as in some characters to surpass in strength all other desires. In these cases the means have become a part of the end, and a more important part of it than any of the things which they are means to. What was once desired as an instrument for the attainment of happiness, has come to be desired for its own sake. In being desired for its own sake it is, however, desired as *part* of happiness. The person is made, or thinks he would be made, happy by its mere possession; and is made unhappy by failure to obtain it. The desire of it is not a different thing from the desire of happiness, any more than the love of music, or the desire of health. They are included in happiness. They are some of the elements of which the desire of happiness is made up. Happiness is not an abstract idea, but a concrete whole; and these are some of its parts. . . .

It results from the preceding considerations, that there is in reality nothing desired except happiness. Whatever is desired otherwise than as a means to some end beyond itself, and ultimately to happiness, is desired as itself a part of happiness, and is not desired for itself until it has become so. . . .

We have now, then, an answer to the question, of what sort of proof the principle of utility is susceptible. If the opinion which I have now stated is psychologically true—if human nature is so constituted as to desire nothing which is not either a part of happiness or a means of happiness, we can have no other proof, and we require no other, that these are the only things desirable. If so, happiness is the sole end of hu-

man action, and the promotion of it the test by which to judge of all human conduct; from whence it necessarily follows that it must be the criterion of morality, since a part is included in the whole. . . .

Chapter V: On the Connexion Between Justice and Utility

. . . We do not call anything wrong, unless we mean to imply that a person ought to be punished in some way or other for doing it; if not by law, by the opinion of his fellow creatures; if not by opinion, by the reproaches of his own conscience. This seems the real turning point of the distinction between morality and simple expediency. It is a part of the notion of Duty in every one of its forms, that a person may rightfully be compelled to fulfil it. Duty is a thing which may be *exacted* from a person, as one exacts a debt. Unless we think that it might be exacted from him, we do not call it his duty. Reasons of prudence, or the interest of other people, may militate against actually exacting it; but the person himself, it is clearly understood, would not be entitled to complain. There are other things, on the contrary, which we wish that people should do, which we like or admire them for doing, perhaps dislike or despise them for not doing, but yet admit that they are not bound to do; it is not a case of moral obligation; we do not blame them, that is, we do not think that they are proper objects of punishment. . . . I think there is no doubt that this distinction lies at the bottom of the notions of right and wrong; that we call any conduct wrong, or employ instead, some other term of dislike or disparagement, according as we think that the person ought, or ought not, to be punished for it; and we say that it would be right to do so and so, or merely that it would be desirable or laudable, according as we would wish to see the person whom it concerns, compelled or only persuaded and exhorted, to act in that manner. . . .

The term [*justice*] appear[s] generally to involve the idea of a personal right—a claim on the part of one or more individuals, like that which the law gives when it confers a proprietary or other legal right. Whether the injustice consists in depriving a person of a possession, or in breaking faith with him, or in treating him worse than he deserves, or worse than other people who have no greater claims, in each case the supposition implies two things—a wrong done, and some assignable person who is wronged. Injustice may also be done by treating a person better than others; but the wrong in this case is to his competitors, who are also assignable persons. It seems to me that this feature in the case—a right in some person, correlative to the moral obligation—constitutes the specific difference between justice, and generosity or beneficence. Justice implies something which it is not only right to do, and wrong not to do, but which some individual person can claim from us as his moral right. No one has a moral right to our generosity or beneficence, because we are not morally bound to practise those virtues towards any given individual. . . .

When we call anything a person's right, we mean that he has a valid claim on society to protect him in the possession of it, either by the force of law, or by that of education and opinion. If he has what we consider a sufficient claim, on whatever account, to have something guaranteed to him by society, we say that he has a right to it. If we desire to prove that anything does not belong to him by right, we think this done as soon as it is admitted that society ought not to take measures for securing it to him, but should leave it to chance, or to his own exertions. . . .

To have a right, then, is, I conceive, to have something which society ought to defend me in the possession of. If the objector goes on to ask why it ought, I can give him no other reason than general utility. . . .

Justice is a name for certain classes of moral rules, which concern the essentials of human well-being more nearly, and are therefore of more absolute obligation, than any other rules for the guidance of life; and the notion which we have found to be of the essence of the idea of justice, that of a right residing in an individual, implies and testifies to this more binding obligation.

The moral rules which forbid mankind to hurt one another (in which we must never forget to include wrongful interference with each other's freedom) are more vital to human well-being than any maxims, however important, which only point out the best mode of managing some department of human affairs.

Review and Discussion Questions

1. Are you persuaded by Mill that some pleasures are higher than others in terms of quality rather than quantity? Do you agree that it is "better to be Socrates dissatisfied than a fool satisfied"? If so, why?

2. How convincing do you find Mill's "proof" of the principle of utility? Are things other than happiness intrinsically desirable? What sort of proof can one expect in ethics?

3. What is significant about Mill's treatment of right and wrong in the final chapter? Do you agree with his theory of justice?

4. Contrast Mill's approach to ethics with those of Kant and Aristotle.

THREE CONTEMPORARY ETHICAL PERSPECTIVES

What Would a Satisfactory Moral Theory Be Like?

JAMES RACHELS

After studying various moral theories, one is bound to be left wondering what to believe. In this revised chapter from a new edition of his book *The Elements of Moral Philosophy,* James Rachels, professor of philosophy at the University of Alabama at Birmingham, sketches what he thinks would be a satisfactory ethical theory. Although his theory has a utilitarian orientation, it takes seriously people's right to choose and the moral importance of treating people as they deserve to be treated. In this way Rachels follows Kant's emphasis on respect for persons.

Study Questions

1. What does Rachels mean by "morality without hubris"?
2. According to Rachels, what important implications does the fact of human rationality have for ethics?
3. How and why does Rachels modify the utilitarian approach? What is "multiple-strategies utilitarianism"?
4. In what three ways does Rachels expand the idea of "moral community"?

Some people believe that there cannot be progress in Ethics, since everything has already been said. . . . I believe the opposite. . . . Compared with the other sciences, Non-Religious Ethics is the youngest and least advanced.

Derek Parfit, *Reasons and Persons* (1984)

Morality Without Hubris

MORAL PHILOSOPHY has a rich and fascinating history. A great many thinkers have approached the subject from a wide variety of perspectives and have produced theories that both attract and repel the thoughtful reader. Almost all the classical theories contain plausible elements, which is hardly surprising, considering that they were devised by philosophers of undoubted genius. Yet the various theories are not consistent with one another, and most are vulnerable to crippling objections. After reviewing them, one is left wondering what to believe. What, in the final analysis, is the truth? Of course, different philosophers would answer this question in different ways. Some might refuse to answer at all, on the grounds that we do not yet know enough to have reached the "final analysis." (In this, moral philosophy is not much worse off than any other subject of human inquiry—we do not know the "final" truth about most things.) But we do know a lot, and it may not be unduly rash to say something about what a satisfactory moral theory might be like.

A modest conception of human beings

A satisfactory theory would, first of all, be sensitive to the facts about human nature, and it would be appropriately modest about the place of human beings in the scheme of things. The universe is some 15 billion years old—that is the time elapsed since the "big bang"—and the earth itself was formed about 4.6 billion years ago. The evolution of life on the planet was a slow process, guided largely by natural selection. The first humans appeared quite recently. The extinction of the great dinosaurs 65 million years ago (possibly as the result of catastrophic collision between the earth and an asteroid) left ecological room for the evolution of the few little mammals that were about, and after 63 or 64 million more years, one line of that evolution finally produced us. In geological time, we arrived only yesterday.

But no sooner did our ancestors arrive than they began to think of themselves as the most important things in all creation. Some of them even imagined that the whole universe had been made for their benefit. Thus, when they began

to develop theories of right and wrong, they held that the protection of their own interests had a kind of ultimate and objective value. The rest of creation, they reasoned, was intended for their use. We now know better. We now know that we exist by evolutionary accident, as one species among many, on a small and insignificant world in one little corner of the cosmos.

How reason gives rise to ethics

Hume, who knew only a little of this story, nevertheless realized that human *hubris* is largely unjustified. "The life of a man," he wrote, "is of no greater importance to the universe than that of an oyster." But he also recognized that our lives are important to *us*. We are creatures with desires, needs, plans, and hopes; even if "the universe" does not care about those things, we do.

Human *hubris* is largely unjustified, but it is not entirely unjustified. Compared to the other creatures on earth, we do have impressive intellectual capacities. We have evolved as rational beings. This fact gives some point to our inflated opinion of ourselves; as it turns out, it is also what makes us capable of having a morality. Because we are rational, we are able to take some facts as reasons for behaving one way rather than another. We can articulate those reasons and think about them. Thus we take the fact that all action would help satisfy our desires, needs, and so on—in short, the fact that all action would *promote our interests*—as a reason in favor of doing it. And of course we take the fact that all action would frustrate our interests as a reason against doing it.

The origin of our concept of "ought" may be found in these facts. If we were not capable of considering reasons for and against actions, we would have no use for such a notion. Like the lower animals, we would simply act from impulse or habit, or as Kant put it, from "inclination." But the consideration of reasons introduces a new factor. Now we find ourselves impelled to act in certain ways as a result of deliberation, as a result of thinking about our behavior and its consequences. We use the word "ought" to mark this new element of the situation: We ought to do the act supported by the weightiest reasons.

Once we consider morality as a matter of acting on reason, another important point emerges. In reasoning about what to do, we can be consistent or inconsistent. One way of being inconsistent is to accept a fact as a reason for action on one occasion, while refusing to accept a similar fact as a reason on another occasion, even though there is no difference between the two occasions that would justify distinguishing them. ([Elsewhere] I referred to this as "Kant's basic idea.") This happens when a person unjustifiably places the interests of his own race or social group above the comparable interests of other races and social groups. Racism means counting the interests of the members of other races as less important than the interests of the members of one's own race, despite the fact that there is no general difference between the races that would justify doing so. It is an offense against morality because it is first an offense against reason. Similar remarks could be made about other doctrines that divide humanity into the morally favored and disfavored, such as egoism, sexism, and (some forms of) nationalism. The upshot is that reason requires impartiality: We ought to act so as to promote the interests of everyone alike.

If Psychological Egoism were true, this would mean that reason demands more of us than we can manage. But Psychological Egoism is not true; it gives an altogether false picture of human nature and the human condition. We have evolved as social creatures, living together in groups, wanting one another's company, needing one another's cooperation, and capable of caring about one another's welfare. So there is a pleasing theoretical "fit" between (a) what reason requires, namely impartiality; (b) the requirements of social living, namely adherence to a set of rules that, if fairly applied, would serve

everyone's interests; and (c) our natural inclination to care about others, at least to a modest degree. All three work together to make morality not only possible, but in an important sense, natural for us.

Treating people as they deserve

The idea that we should "promote the interests of everyone alike," when it is taken as a proscription of bigotry, is appealing; however, it may be objected that such a maxim ignores the fact that people have different merits. At least some of the time, we should treat individuals as they deserve to be treated, rather than dealing with them as if they were only members of the great crowd of humanity.

The idea that people should be treated as they deserve is connected with the idea that they are rational agents with the power of choice—if they were not rational and had no control over their actions, they would not be responsible for their conduct and they would not deserve good or ill on account of it. Rational beings, however, are responsible for what they freely choose to do, and those who choose to behave decently, toward others deserve to be treated well in return, while those who treat others badly deserve to be treated badly in return.

This sounds harsh, but when we consider examples, it seems plausible. Suppose Smith has always been generous, helping you whenever she could, and now she is in trouble and needs your help. There is now a special reason *she* should be helped, beyond the general obligation you have to be helpful to everyone. She is not just another member of the crowd, but a particular person who, by her own previous conduct, has earned your respect and gratitude. But now consider someone with the opposite history: Suppose Jones is your neighbor, and he has always refused to help you when you needed it. One day, for example, your car wouldn't start, and Jones wouldn't give you a lift to work—he had no particular excuse, he just wouldn't be bothered.

Imagine that, after this episode, Jones has car trouble and he has the nerve to ask you for a ride. Perhaps you will think you should help him anyway, despite his own lack of helpfulness. (You might think this will teach him generosity.) Nevertheless, if we concentrate on what he *deserves,* we must conclude that he deserves to be left to fend for himself. Certainly, if circumstances arise in which you must choose between helping Smith and helping Jones, you have good reason to choose Smith.

Adjusting our treatment of individuals to match how they themselves have chosen to treat others is not just a matter of rewarding friends and holding grudges against enemies. It is a matter of treating people as responsible agents, who by their own choices show themselves to be deserving of particular responses, and toward whom such emotions as gratitude and resentment are appropriate. There is an important difference between Smith and Jones; why shouldn't that be reflected in the way we respond to them? What would it be like if we did *not* tailor our responses to people in this way?

For one thing, we would be denying people (including ourselves) the ability to earn good treatment at the hands of others. This is an important matter. Because we live together with other people, how each of us fares depends not only on what we do but on what others do as well. If we are to flourish, we need to obtain the good treatment of others. A system of understandings in which desert is acknowledged gives us a way doing that. Thus, acknowledging deserts is a way of granting people the power to determine their own fates.

Absent this, what are we to do? What are the alternatives? We might imagine a system in which the only way for a person to ensure good treatment by others is somehow to coerce that treatment from them, or we might imagine that good treatment always comes as charity. But the practice of acknowledging deserts is different. The practice of acknowledging deserts gives people control over whether others will treat them well or badly, by saying to them: If you behave well, you will be *entitled* to good treatment from others. You will have earned it. Without this control, people would be impotent. Respecting people's right to choose their own conduct, and then adjusting our treatment of them according to how they choose, is ultimately a matter of "respect for persons" in a sense somewhat like Kant's.

Other motives of action

There are other ways in which the idea of "promoting the interests of everyone alike" apparently falls to capture the whole of moral life. (I say "apparently" because I want to return later to the question of whether the failure is apparent or real.) Certainly, people should sometimes be motivated by an impartial concern for "the interests of everyone alike." But this is not the only morally praiseworthy motive:

- A mother loves and cares for her children: She is not concerned to "promote their interests" simply because they are people she can help. Her attitude toward them is entirely different from her attitude toward other children. While she might feel that she should help other children when she can, that vaguely benevolent feeling is nothing like the love she has for her own.

- A woman is loyal to her friends: Again, she is not concerned with their interests only as part of her benevolent concern for people generally. They are her friends, and friendship makes them special.

Only a philosophical idiot would propose to eliminate love, loyalty, and the like from our understanding of the moral life. If such motives were eliminated, and instead people simply calculated what was for the best, we would all be much worse off. And in any case, who would want to live in a world without love and friendship?

There are, of course, many other valuable sorts of motives that come into play as people go about their lives:

- A composer is concerned, above all else, to finish her symphony. She pursues this even though she might do "more good" by doing something else.

- A teacher devotes great effort to preparing his classes, even though more overall good might be accomplished if he directed part of this energy elsewhere.

While these are not usually considered "moral" motives, they are motives that, from a moral point of view, we should not want to eliminate from human life. The desire to create, pride in doing one's job well, and other such desires, contribute both to personal happiness (think of the joy of having created something beautiful or the satisfaction of having done a job well) and to the general welfare (think how much worse off we would be without music and good teachers). We should no more want to eliminate them than we would want to eliminate love and friendship.

Is there a single moral standard?

To recapitulate: On the basis of some remarks about human nature and reason, we gave a sketchy justification of the principle that "we ought to act so as to promote the interests of everyone alike." This looks very much like a utilitarian principle. But then we noted that this cannot be the whole story concerning our moral obligations because (at least sometimes) we should treat people according to their individual deserts. And then we noted that there are morally important motives that apparently have nothing to do with the impartial promotion of interests.

Yet it may be possible to see these diverse concerns as related to one another. At first blush it seems that treating people according to their individual deserts is quite different from seeking to promote the interests of everyone alike. But when we asked why deserts are important, the answer turned out to be that *we would all be much worse off* if the acknowledgment of deserts

was not part of our moral scheme. And when we ask why love, friendship, artistic creativity, and pride in one's work are important, the answer is that *our lives would be so much poorer* were it not for such things. This suggests that there is a single standard at work in the assessment of all these different things.

Perhaps, then, the single moral standard is human welfare (or perhaps, as Mill put it, the welfare of "the whole of sentient creation"—I will return to this complication in a moment). What is important is that people be as well-off as possible. And this standard is to be used in assessing a wide variety of things including actions, policies, social customs, laws, rules, motives, and traits of character. When we reflect about rules, motives, and the like, we refer to the standard of welfare. But this does not mean that we should always be motivated by that standard in the ordinary course of our lives. Our lives will go better if, instead, we love our children, enjoy our friends, take pride in our work, keep our promises, and so on. An ethic that values "the interests of everyone alike" will endorse this conclusion.

This is not a new idea. Henry Sidgwick, the great utilitarian theorist of the Victorian era, made the same point when he wrote:

> the doctrine that Universal Happiness is the ultimate *standard* must not be understood to imply that Universal Benevolence is the only right or always best *motive* of action . . . it is not necessary that the end which gives the criterion of rightness should always be the end at which we consciously aim: and if experience shows that the general happiness will be more satisfactorily attained if men frequently act from other motives than pure universal philanthropy, it is obvious that these other motives are reasonably to be preferred on Utilitarian principles.

Sidgwick's thought has been cited in support of a view called Motive Utilitarianism, the central idea of which is that we should act from the combination of motives that best promote the general welfare.

Yet the most plausible view of this type does not focus exclusively on motives; nor does it focus entirely on acts or rules, as other varieties of Utilitarianism have done. The most plausible view might be called *Multiple-Strategies Utilitarianism*. The ultimate end is the general welfare, but diverse strategies may be endorsed as means of achieving that end. Sometimes we aim directly at it, as when a legislator enacts laws for the general welfare, or an individual calculates that sending money to UNICEF would do more good than anything else available. But sometimes we don't think of it at all; instead we simply care for our children, work at our jobs, obey the law, and keep our promises.

The Moral Community

From a moral point of view, the interests of everyone are important. In principle, the community with which we should be concerned is limited only by the number of individuals who have interests, and that, as we shall see, is a very large number indeed.

This may seem a pious platitude, but in reality it can be a hard doctrine. In the year between the time I write this and the book is published, about a million children will die of measles. People in the affluent countries could easily prevent this, but of course they will not. People would no doubt feel a greater sense of obligation if it were children in their own neighborhoods that needed vaccinations, rather than strangers in a foreign country. But on the theory we are considering, the location of the children makes no difference: Everyone is included in the community of moral concern. If the interests of children dying of measles were taken seriously, wherever the children lived, it would make an enormous difference in our behavior.

If the moral community is not limited to people in one *place,* neither is it limited to people at any one *time.* Whether people will be affected by our actions now or in the distant future makes no difference. Our obligation is to consider all their interests equally. One consequence of this concerns weapons of mass destruction. With the development of nuclear weapons, we now have the capacity to alter the course of history in an especially dramatic way. If the welfare of future generations is given proper weight, it is difficult to imagine any circumstances in which the large-scale use of nuclear weapons would be justified. The environment is another issue in which the interests of future generations figure prominently: We do not have to think that the environment is important "in itself" to see that its destruction is a moral horror; it is sufficient to consider what will become of people if the rain forests, sea algae, and ozone layer are ruined.

There is one other way in which our conception of the moral community must be expanded. Humans, as we have noted, are only one species of animal inhabiting this planet. Like humans, the other animals also have interests that are affected by what we do. When we kill or torture them, they are harmed, just as humans are harmed when treated in those ways. Bentham and Mill were right to insist that the interests of nonhuman animals must be given weight in our moral calculations. As Bentham pointed out, excluding creatures from moral consideration because of their species is no more justified than excluding them because of race, nationality, or sex. . . . Impartiality requires the expansion of the moral community not only across space and time but across the boundaries of species as well.

Justice and Fairness

Classical Utilitarianism was criticized severely for failing to account for the values of justice and fairness. Can the complications we have introduced help?

Punishment

One criticism had to do with punishment. We can imagine cases in which it promotes the general welfare to frame an innocent person, which is blatantly unjust; yet taking the Principle of Utility as our ultimate standard, it is hard to explain why this is so. More generally, as Kant pointed out, the basic utilitarian "justification" of punishment is in terms of treating individuals as mere "means."

We have argued that a policy of *treating people as they deserve* is justified by the general utilitarian standard. This may permit a somewhat different view of punishment than utilitarians have customarily taken. (In fact, the resulting view of punishment will be very close to Kant's.) In punishing someone, we are treating him differently from the way we treat others— punishment involves a failure of impartiality. But this is justified, on our account, by the person's own past deeds. It is a response to what he has done. That is why it is not right to frame an innocent person; the innocent person has not done anything to deserve being singled out for such treatment.

The theory of punishment, however, is only one part of the subject of justice. Questions of justice arise any time one person is treated differently from another. Suppose an employer must choose which of two employees to promote, when she can promote only one of them. The first candidate has worked hard for the company, taking on extra work when it was needed, giving up her vacation to help out, and so on. The second candidate, on the other hand, has always done only the minimum required of him. (And we will assume he has no excuse; he has simply chosen not to work very hard.) Obviously, the two employees will be treated very differently: One will get the promotion; the other will not. But this is all right, according to our theory, because the first employee deserves to be advanced over the second, considering the past performance of each. The first employee has earned the promotion, the second has not.

Insofar as fairness is concerned, a person's voluntary actions can justify departures from the basic policy of "equal treatment," but nothing else can. This goes against a common view of the matter. Often, people think it is right for individuals to be rewarded for physical beauty, superior intelligence, or other native endowments. (In practice, people often get better jobs and a greater share of life's good things just because they were born with greater natural gifts.) But on reflection, this does not seem right. People do not deserve their native endowments; they have them only as a result of what John Rawls has called "the natural lottery." Suppose the first employee in our example was passed over for the promotion, despite her hard work, because the second employee had some native talent that was more useful in the new position. Even if the employer could justify this decision in terms of the company's needs, the first employee would rightly feel that there is something unfair going on. She has worked harder, yet he is now getting the promotion, and the benefits that go with it, because of something he did nothing to merit. That is not fair. A just society, according to this conception, would be one in which people may improve their positions through work (with the opportunity for work available to everyone), but they would not enjoy superior positions simply because they were born lucky. . . .

What would a satisfactory moral theory be like?

I have outlined the possibility that seems most plausible to me. However, it is instructive to remember that a great many thinkers have tried to devise such a theory, and history has judged them to have been only partially successful. This suggests that it would be wise not to make too grandiose a claim for one's own view, whatever it might be. But there is reason for optimism. As the Oxford philosopher Derek Parfit has observed, the earth will remain habitable for another billion years, and civilization is now only a few thousand years old. If we do not destroy ourselves, moral philosophy, along with all the other human inquiries, may yet have a long way to go.

Review and Discussion Questions

1. Does reason require us to promote the interests of all? Why is it important to treat people as they deserve? Is doing so compatible with the impartiality that, according to Rachels, reason requires?

2. How does Rachels's theory differ from classical utilitarianism? Is his theory still a basically utilitarian theory? Is it a "satisfactory moral theory"?

3. Rachels believes that it is morally acceptable for us to have other motives besides the desire to promote happiness. How can one square this belief with a utilitarian approach to ethics?

4. How would adopting Rachels's perspective on "the moral community" cause people to change their moral attitudes and conduct? In your view, do the practical implications of his theory increase or diminish the theory's plausibility?

5. With regard to the examples of punishment and job promotion, does Rachels's theory do a better job of accounting for our sense of justice and fairness than classical utilitarianism does?

On What We Aim At and How We Live

JULIUS M. E. MORAVCSIK

In the previous essay, James Rachels defended a broadly utilitarian approach to ethics, but one that has been influenced by Kant's ethical ideas. In contrast, in this essay Julius M. E. Moravcsik, professor of philosophy at Stanford University, contends that the dominant modern theories of ethics—in particular, utilitarianism and Kantian ethics—are deficient. He offers an alternative approach to ethics, one that has roots in the classical theories of Plato and Aristotle. In particular, Moravcsik argues that morality is more than a matter of rules and that it inescapably involves questions of meaning in human life, of human nature, and of our overall aims and ideals.

Study Questions

1. Explain the two arguments Moravcsik uses to support his claim that, even if two people agree on the relevant moral rules, they could still disagree on how to handle the predicament of the lonely woman.

2. What are three features of a well-lived life that are more likely to be realized by someone with what Moravcsik calls "overall aims in life"?

Reprinted by permission from David J. Depew, ed., The Greeks and the Good Life. *Copyright © 1980 by California State University, Fullerton. Some notes omitted.*

3. What does Moravcsik see as the shortcomings of utilitarianism and Kantianism?

4. Can rules apply to feelings? What is the connection between rules and sensitivities?

5. What does Moravcsik mean by an "ideal"? Contrast the two patterns of practical reasoning that Moravcsik presents in the final section.

T HE PERILS OF A HUMAN LIFE can be divided into two kinds. On the one hand, we can be harmed by actions and circumstances that work against realizing what is in our interest and what would help fulfill our potentialities. On the other hand, our actions and attitudes can harm or diminish our contributions to the benefit of others. The dominant ethical theories of modern philosophy separate these kinds of perils into matters of what we want to do with our lives and how we find means to carry out such plans, on the one hand, and matters of morality, to be specified in terms of an autonomous set of rules, on the other.

In this paper this conception will be challenged. First a case will be presented to illustrate certain salient facts about our choices and related attitudes. These facts show that moral choices are partly a matter of the exercise of sensitivities that are not rule-governed. The development of these sensitivities is inextricably linked to questions about the over-all aims, or "meaning" in our lives. Adequate consideration of "meaning-of-life" questions turns out to be based on conceptions of human nature. Hence the claim of the autonomy of morality is ill-founded. There is no sharp line between the moral and the non-moral in terms of choices, relevant considerations, and desirable character traits. The structure of this alternative pattern for construing our moral lives will be laid bare. . . . The ethics of Plato and Aristotle fit this alternative, and more adequate, pattern rather than the pattern into which the modern theories of utilitarianism and Kantian ethics fall. The point of this illustration is not merely historical; it is meant as a spur towards a reconsideration and revitalization of thought along the alternative pattern in contemporary philosophy.

I. A Case

On my way to San Francisco I turn on the car-radio. On a "talk-show" a woman is phoning in. She is poor, sick, and without friends or relatives. She cannot pay for her medicine, and at times goes ten to fourteen days without talking to anyone. This radio-show is one of her few links with the outside world.

Having parked my car in Union Square, I pass by Magnin's. They have a fur sale. I see people rushing in and out. They spend thousands of dollars on expensive furs—to be worn to parties or the theater. They are preoccupied with their pleasure in acquiring luxury items and thus possession of goods that will gain them prestige in the community.

I find the situation incongruous. In a world in which we have so many lonely shut-ins, people ought not to be preoccupied so much with luxury and with prestige. A society in which people exhibit that degree of indifference towards the lonely cannot be a morally sound society.

There are, however, many people who, though they regret the predicament of the lonely, disagree with me. They claim that there is nothing incongruous about the scene I described, and that the people rushing to Magnin's are not doing anything unethical. They are not harming anybody, and they are not doing anything that worsens the conditions of the lonely woman who phoned in to the radio station. On the contrary, they might go on, acquiring wealth and luxury often leads to expanded charitable activity; hence in a society in which scenes like the one at Magnin's are allowed, the lonely might get more relief in the long run than they would in a society in which such preoccupation with prestige and luxury is not permitted.

Since the disagreement between me and the hypothetical opponent is about ethical matters, the dominant modern ethical theories would attempt to construe it as one concerning rules or principles.

Can we construe it as a disagreement about the application of the principle of maximizing happiness for the greatest number of people? The difficulty with such a construal is that nothing in the case presented so far indicates that this principle is violated. Furthermore, even if someone should show that everything is being done in our society with regard to the shut-ins that maximizes happiness for the greatest number, this would not assuage my feeling of disapproval and sense of incongruity with respect to the situation. What bothers me is the indifference on the part of the people, and not what is done or not done to the shut-ins.

One might try to construe the disagreement as being about the application of the categorical imperative. But the universalization principle leaves the situation unscathed. If everyone were concerned with luxury, etc. we would not have necessarily a society in which people harm each other or take advantage of each other. It would be a society of self-indulgent people; how does one show on Kantian grounds that this would be a morally reprehensible society?

It is important to see that the problem concerns features of the situation of the lonely that could not be alleviated by more rigorous application of a fair principle of distributing goods. It is not the poverty of the woman but her loneliness that is in the focus of the predicament.

One might think that the disagreement is about some "local" moral rule, rather than about the application of the most general ethical rules. Plausible candidates might be: "Do not neglect lonely people!" or "Do not buy luxury items as long as you could use your time and energy to help those who are shut-ins!"

Are these rules, or are these exhortations? We all agree in general that one ought not to neglect the lonely; but there are serious disagreements about what constitutes, in any given context, neglect of the lonely. Again, nobody would accept the second candidate as a rule of ethics without qualifications. As it stands, it would be difficult to derive it from any of the acknowledged higher moral principles.

The claim of this paper is that even if two people agree on all of the relevant moral rules, they could still disagree on how the predicament of the lonely woman described above should be handled. Two arguments will be advanced to support this claim.

The first argument rests on the fact of "historical moral blindness." People in different historical periods may accept the same set of moral principles and yet one period may have customs that are morally abhorrent to the people of the other period. For example, in earlier periods of history people in the Western world professed the same moral principles as we do today, and yet they thought nothing of impaling their foes on stakes in case of war. In fact, one cannot help but wonder which of our own current practices will be singled out by future generations as abhorrent. It would be easy to find examples of historical periods in which people professed the same principles as I do, and yet found indifference towards the shut-in not morally repugnant. Apparently, we need moral sensitivity in addition to moral rules, and some of these sensitivities are historically conditioned.

The second argument rests on a premise—to be defended in detail later—that rules apply primarily to actions. We can have rules governing how we act, but it makes no sense to talk of rules governing how we should feel. But in the case under consideration a crucial element is feeling. I complain about indifference, and urge more care and kindness exhibited towards the shut-in. Care and kindness are matters of feeling and attitude; not only matters of what we do. Hence what is at issue is the desirability of the development and manifestation of certain feelings and attitudes. But such matters must be regarded as something additional to the formulation of moral rules.

Once we reach the stage at which we discuss the desirability of certain feelings and attitudes, we reach the point at which—in order to justify our preferences—we must appeal to some overall aim and choice of pattern in human life. Such choices involve "meaning-of-life" questions; i.e., questions as to what gives value to certain patterns of human life, and questions concerning worthwhile over-all aims in our lives. An adequate defense of options in this sphere requires as its foundation some conception of human nature. We cannot have an adequate view as to what are human potentialities that are worth developing unless we have some general conception as to what the class of human potentialities is. Why should I be the kind of person who tries to be kind to others and cares for their feelings? On the one hand, this is a matter for choosing as my over-all aim a certain kind of life-pattern and the development of a certain kind of personality. On the other hand, this is also a matter of moral interest, since my developing or not developing certain attitudes such as kindness and care affects the well-being of other humans.

Thus the case presented illustrates the following two facts. First, it shows that in addition to moral rules the possession of certain attitudes and feelings is also relevant to the assessment of the moral congruousness or incongruity of a given situation. Secondly, it shows that through the consideration of personality traits whose possession is not a matter of rules, ethical considerations are inextricably linked to questions of over-all aims in life and "meaning-of-life" issues, and that these, in turn, are linked to questions about human nature. Hence ethical theories, construed as made up of rules governing actions, are not autonomous; their justificatory basis must reach matters of meaning in human life, and questions about human nature.

II. "Meaning-of-Life" Questions

. . . The question: "Why be kind?" leads us to "meaning-of-life" questions, i.e., questions about what our over-all aims in life should be. There are a number of ways of formulating such aims.* Certain formulations yield for the agent self-esteem and self-respect. If I can mould my life into a pattern whose instantiation I can regard as having intrinsic value, then I can have respect for myself as the partial embodiment of something worth while. . . .

There are people who never bother to formulate over-all aims in their lives. They live by a vague principle of minimal coherence. One cannot say that such persons could not live in a morally acceptable way, or that they could not be leading happy lives. But there are three features of a well-lived life that are more likely to be realized by someone with over-all aims than by someone lacking such. One of these is the retaining of *interest* in things. For instance, we talk of people having retained interest or losing interest; "having the will to live," or having lost that will. If one's interest fits into a general pattern, the interest is less likely to be lost. Another such feature is *hope*. If one has over-all aims in life, and thinks that one's life leads up to something, then one can entertain hope even under adverse circumstances in which the prospects of doing well appear dim. Without over-all aims such hope is more difficult to sustain. Finally, an over-all conception of what is worthwhile in a human life enables us to find *acceptance* of conditions beyond our control (e.g. aging, death) without lapsing into phlegmatic inactivity that prevents us from working towards changing what is not inevitable.

One can specify one's over-all aims in life in three ways. Our purpose may involve basically either what one can have or *possess* (wealth,

*The framework may be religious or secular. Again it may be pluralistic or monolithic; it can leave also more or less room for matters of individual difference.

pleasure, etc.) or what one can do or *accomplish* (contributing to economic welfare, gaining prestige, etc.) or what one can *be* (an intelligent, kind, cooperative human being, etc.). The link we saw between ethics and "meaning-of-life" issues assumes that the third of these is the most adequate way of specifying one's over-all aims. . . .

Someone might object at this point by saying that one could form the view according to which any over-all scheme in life is acceptable as long as it leads to enjoyment. This is, however, to put the cart before the horse. For human nature is very plastic with regards to the possible sources of enjoyment. If we enjoy a certain life-pattern, and we decide that another life-pattern would be intrinsically more valuable, then in most cases we can reorient our lives so that the new pattern becomes enjoyable. . . .

III. Utilitarianism and Kantian Ethics

The two most dominant modern ethical theories are utilitarianism and Kantian ethics. How would these theories deal with the case presented earlier? . . .

At the base of these theories concerning what we ought to do lies the distinction between morality and prudence. Morality tells us what our duties and obligations are, regardless of our individual interests, while prudence tells us what we should do if we are to serve our interests.

Theories of duty and obligation are either teleological theories, specifying duty in terms of the maximization of pleasure, utility, happiness, etc. for the greatest number, or they are deontological theories specifying duty in terms of some intrinsic character of the right actions. Kant's theory, basing duty on the universalizability of one's maxims, is a unitarian deontological theory. Those opting for more than one such basic principle are pluralistic deontological theories.

Orthagonal to these distinctions is the one separating ethical theories depending on whether they regard rules or character traits as central and the other element derivative. . . . The ethics of Plato and Aristotle [are] theories dealing with duty that construe traits as primary.

Most versions of utilitarianism and Kantian ethics are rule-oriented, and embrace either some version of the maximization principle or some formulation of the principle of universalizability. . . .

Let us consider first the heavy stress that these modern theories lay on "big rules," be they those of maximization or universalizability. When applied to concrete situations, these rules seem singularly uninformative. My judgment that the scene described in a previous section is morally incongruous is not based either on a maximization rule, or on a rule of universalizability. Even if someone were to demonstrate that the situation involving the lonely woman represents the maximization of pleasure for the greatest number as much as the realization of such a rule is possible for us, I would still be dissatisfied with the situation from a moral point of view. The same holds for deontic principles. After all, the situation described is neither logically inconsistent, when generalized, nor one that could not be regarded as satisfactory by a completely rational being. But assurances of this sort will not assuage my sense of moral dissatisfaction.

Perhaps the criticism of our indifference towards the shut-ins can be based on the claim that some less general rule—possibly derivable from the "big rules"—is violated. We saw, however, that at the heart of my criticism of the status of the shut-in is not simply what people do, but what they feel. And, as we will see in the next section, there can be no rules about what attitudes we should have and how we should feel.

The situation can be summed in the following way. The ethical is concerned with how we affect other humans. Ethical rules, however, can only regulate actions. We do, however, affect others not only through what we do, but also through what we feel and what attitudes we adopt towards them. But feelings and attitudes cannot be regulated exclusively by rules. Hence there are ethically relevant matters that cannot be settled simply by invoking the rule-systems of either utilitarianism [or] that of Kantian ethics.

Thus these dominant modern theories do not do justice to the role that certain sensitivities play in moral contexts. This shortcoming leads to the central weakness in the claim that ethics is autonomous. Apparently it is ethically relevant what feelings and attitudes I have. But this, in turn, is tied to questions about over-all aims and purpose in life. It is a question of what *to be* and not simply a question of what *to do*. Neither the utilitarian principles nor Kant's principles tell us what sort of a person we should be.

Finally, neither utilitarian nor Kantian ethics can explain what was called above the phenomenon of "historical moral blindness." For this phenomenon does not involve changes in the rules of ethics. Rather, it involves shifts in the sensitivities that affect how we construe certain situations involving interpersonal relations. The conflict between those who see nothing wrong in impaling a foe on a stake and the rest of us cannot be a matter of our being able to deduce an injunction against such a practice from one of the "big rules," while the others fail to see this consequence. The conflict is one of differences in sensitivity and not one of differences in logical acumen. . . .

IV. Rules and Sensitivity

. . . We can choose, decide on, reject, or deliberate upon plans of action. Hence these plans can be formulated with reference to rules. But can we decide or deliberate upon how and what we should feel? Can we decide what personality traits we are to have? We can, of course, decide to adopt a rule according to which we should do everything in our power so that we will be-

come such-and-such a person, e.g., a courageous individual. Or we can try to do everything in our power so that we will develop into kind persons. But one cannot decide to be kind, or to become kind; and one cannot decide to be courageous or to become courageous. What we feel and what we are is not a matter of decisions, or mere actions; and if rules govern solely actions, then there can be no rule governing feelings or character traits. There can be rules of the kind: "Do everything you can in order to become a kind person!" But a statement like: "Be kind!" is not a rule; it is an exhortation.*

Similar considerations hold for states of character or bodily states. We can have rules telling us everything that we can do to restore or maintain health. But we cannot have a rule saying: "Be healthy!"; for to be healthy is a state. It makes no sense to say that someone is (in a state) in accordance with a rule, or that someone is (in a state) by following a rule, though it does make sense to say that someone got himself to be in a state by following a rule. What can one say to someone who is not healthy? If you say: "Do not be unhealthy!," this is not a command or the formulation of a rule; this is an exhortation.

Thus rules do not cover states and feelings; yet—as we saw—some of our states and feelings affect the welfare of other human beings; hence they are within the sphere of the ethical. . . .

What the rules do not cover has been described so far as feelings and sensitivities. It is time to look at the notion of sensitivity in more detail.

A certain kind of sensitivity is needed in applying rules of conduct or laws. A good judge, whether he ranks individuals on a scale, or delivers judgments in accordance with the law,

---

*This has implications for institutions like marriage in which both feelings and actions are important factors. If the argument presented here is sound, then it makes no sense to promise how we will feel for the rest of our lives; we can only promise to do everything within our power to maintain certain feelings.

must be sensitive. He or she must be aware of special circumstances that might surround a case, special interpretations placed on certain kinds of conduct by people from certain socio-economic groups, etc. Though this kind of sensitivity too is not a matter of following rules, it is not a matter of feelings either.

The sensitivities relevant to our topic are exemplified by capacities such as kindness, forgiveness, or care. Each of these has feelings as well as actions as components of their manifestations. What is ethically relevant is not the mere possession of these capacities, but the creating of contexts which facilitate the manifestations of these capacities, or dispositions.

Still, one might reply that this cannot be all that we want. One can "kill" with too much kindness, and forgiving too easily and too often can harm rather than help a child or partner. Do we not need moral rules to tell us what the proper objects of kindness and forgiveness are, and what the appropriate ways and modes of expressing these feelings are?

Certainly, merely being kind or forgiving is not sufficient for leading a successful life. One needs good sense and judgment in developing the appropriate dispositions for the expressing of the relevant feelings. But this "good sense" is not a matter of rules either. The "rule" telling us how to manifest kindness is at best saying that kindness should be manifested in the appropriate way, in the appropriate circumstances, towards the appropriate person; which is to say that it is not a rule at all, moral or otherwise. Rather, it involves skill in interpreting concrete situations, in perceiving correctly the needs of others, etc. As we saw above, this is—as Aristotle would emphasize—a matter of practice and habit, and not a matter of rules. . . .

V. An Alternative Account

In this section an account will be sketched that offers a radical alternative to utilitarianism and Kantian ethics. According to this account we start by forming a conception of human nature. We saw above that this is necessitated already by what was called the "plasticity" of human nature with regards to possible objects and sources of enjoyment. This "plasticity" has its limits. Hence a conception of human nature should reveal the basic human potentialities, the limits of what humans can do and can expect of themselves, and the sources of what can keep humans going as purposeful creatures. Such a conception will be no more "value-free" than the analogous conception of physical health.

In the light of such a conception of human nature we formulate a conception of the type of person we should want to be. In this paper such a conception will be called an *ideal*. Adequate ideals cannot be deduced from conceptions of human nature; but they must be consistent with and grounded in such conceptions. Thus the general form of the arguments spelling out adequate ideals will be the following: "Given that humans have the following (unique?) potentialities G, H, K, etc., our ideal should be to become a person with characteristics $C_1, C_2 \ldots C_n$."

If the ideal is adequate, then a part of it must be concerned with our relationships with others. At this point, considerations of the ideal and ethical considerations become inextricably intertwined. Thus ethics is construed by this pattern as having essential relationships to the over-all aims that we set for ourselves, and thus to "meaning-of-life" questions.

For example, the development of intellectual capacities, our sense of beauty, and our ability to cooperate and to feel kindness and sympathy towards others might fit into the specification of an adequate ideal. Given the "plasticity" of human nature with regards to enjoyment, we are forced to form an ideal for ourselves, tacitly or consciously.

If the ideal we form includes the characteristics listed above, then it also goes a long way to determine our relationships with others. Hence there is no need for a system of independent rules spelling out what our conduct towards others should be. There are, however, other types of ideals that require supplementary ethical principles. Suppose that the ideal-specification emphasizes meditation and self-searching. If it says nothing about our relations and attitudes towards others, then there is a need for additional independent principles to govern one's relations to others. Again, to take another case, if the ideal specifies a tough warrior as the desirable character to be emulated—as in Homer—then there will be a need for additional principles governing one's relations to others, in order to curb the egocentricity and competitiveness of the warrior-type.

Ideal-formation and ethics-formation are most intimately related in those cases in which the ideal involves being kind, cooperative, etc. The notions of "interest," "benefit," etc. can be defined only once we have formed an ideal. The situation is analogous to that of bodily well-being. We can talk of what is beneficial to the body only after we have formed a conception of what a healthy body is.

Thus if we have the right kind of ideal, we will want to do what the ethical rules tell us. These rules, then, function at best as a means to help us to achieve our end. Depending on the ideal formed, much or little of what we call "ethical" falls out of the conception of the ideal.* This alternative pattern does not deny, however, that for certain areas of inter-personal relations we might need rules not derivable from any ideal.

Having an ideal pattern of life gives one interests, and the maintaining of these will shape our capacities for enjoyment. Most of modern ethics seems to have this backwards. It asks: "What do we enjoy?" and then attempts to characterize what is valuable. But with adequate ideals, a human can try to shape life in such a way that embodying the ideal should be also enjoyable. Human nature is very flexible with respect to what we can enjoy.

Given what was said above about rules, we can see why these do not play such a crucial role

in the alternative pattern. One cannot define an ideal in terms of rules, since the ideals are in terms of what we are and feel, and not only in terms of what we do. Having over-all aims and thus interest, hope, and acceptance is a matter of having the required capacities, and not a matter of merely following rules. . . .

The rational and objective character of ideal-formation is compatible with a pluralistic approach to desirable patterns of life. Given individual differences, within certain parameters, we cannot expect all humans to be suited for the same kind of life. But this pluralism is no more or less extensive than the corresponding pluralism in our concept of bodily health. The fact that different types of people and different age-groups realize bodily health in different ways does not show medicine to be a subjectivistic or relativistic science.

Understanding these variations in human nature should enable us to incorporate tolerance into an adequate ideal. For example, this understanding would enable a rational and cooperative person to understand why less gifted and less privileged persons might have more difficulties forming an ideal that is not self-centered and leaves room for capacities to feel for others.

But such tolerance has its limits. The limits are set by the extent to which those opting for different ideals possess characteristics that are the grounds for our respect for them. It will not do to say that the mere fact that someone belongs to the biological species *homo sapiens* should suffice for the eliciting of respect, unless it is assumed that by merely being a human biologically entails having at all times capacities for reason, cooperativeness, kindness, etc. And even on this assumption, the *latter* characteristics serve as the grounds for respect, and not the mere biological classification.

. . . Let us sketch what the alternative pattern has to say about practical reasoning. . . . We saw already that the first step is the formation of an ideal, i.e., a characterization of an ideal personality pattern or patterns. This is grounded in, but not deductively derivable from, a concep-

---

* Much of what is a matter of distributing goods, and other parts of social and political philosophy, will require independent foundations, not based solely on ideal-formation.

tion of human nature. The ideal will yield—to the extent that it specifies our relations to others—capacities for forming attitudes and feeling, and rules for conduct towards others. The extent to which ethics thus "falls out of" the ideals is dependent on the nature of the ideal. . . .

Looking at it in reverse order, actions and feelings are justified in terms of the constituents of the ideal. The ideal itself does not admit of further justification but is subject to rational criticism. For instance, it might be in conflict with assumptions about human nature, or be incomplete, incoherent, etc. . . .

The alternative pattern leaves only a small role for the "big rules" of modern ethics to play. Their role is merely that of a couple of items on a long check-list. Having utilized our conception of an adequate ideal, and having allowed a variety of capacities to be exercised, we come to a tentative conclusion of what we should do, or what attitude we should adopt. At this point we add: "And it should be done as fairly as possible, and in such a way as to make it as enjoyable for people as possible." Thus the big rules do not really specify the substance of how to react. They merely help at the end of a deliberative process, in case we have several equally viable alternatives, to narrow things down to a choice to be made. They have no priority over kindness, care, the development of intelligence, etc.

The difference between the modern patterns and the alternative sketched here can be shown also in terms of charts representing cognitive processes involved in practical reasoning. According to the modern frameworks, practical reasoning is basically a matter of rule-application, with sensitivity being relegated at most to the role of facilitating the application of rules to concrete situations (Figure 1).

Figure 1

According to the alternative pattern, the input is already affected by the exercise of sensitivities. Our perception of a morally tainted situation depends partly on our inner cognitive-perceptual structure. For example, it takes sensitivity to perceive cruelty, abuse, etc. in all circumstances. The output is a judgment, action, or feeling. (The sound agent need not go through the justificatory procedure in any conscious way prior to reacting to a situation in an appropriate way.) Finally, what the mind contributes to the formation of the output is not merely a set of ethical rules, but also a conception of what we called an *ideal,* i.e. a set of capacities, dispositions to feel, etc. (Figure 2).

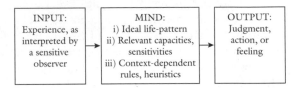

Figure 2

. . . The alternative pattern can also account for the facts mentioned at the outset that utilitarianism and deontic ethics have problems with. First, it can account for the important role that sensitivities such as kindness play in our "moral" reaction to others. For it can represent differences between humans which do not center on disagreements about rules but on lack of uniformity of kinds and degrees of sensitivity and feelings.

Thus it can also account for what was called "historical moral blindness." For it can represent the salient difference between us and those who impaled their foes on stakes as not a difference in rules to be followed, but a difference in sensitivities.

Finally, the alternative pattern can account for the case presented in the first section more adequately than utilitarianism and deontic ethics. For it can represent the difference between those who find the scene described incongruous and those who do not as a difference in sensitivity rather than in rule-systems, and it can explain how critiques of each other's sensitivities lead to comparisons of ideals, rather than to comparisons of rule-hierarchies. The fact that according to this approach, the resolution of the conflict requires a reorientation of how we should feel, and hence not merely deductive reasoning, does not make conflict-resolution any less rational.

Review and Discussion Questions

1. In your view, how well does the case of the lonely woman support Moravcsik's argument that the dominant modern ethical theories are deficient? What do you see as their shortcomings, if any? Support your position with reference to Rachels's theory in the previous reading.

2. Would you agree that any satisfactory moral theory has to deal with questions about the meaning of life? Is Moravcsik correct to claim that questions about what kind of person we should be and what kinds of things we should do are inextricably interwoven? To what extent will reasonable people agree or disagree in their conception of human nature and in the ideals they accept?

3. Describe the basic features of Moravcsik's alternative account of ethics. In what ways, if any, is it an improvement over the more standard approaches to ethics?

Feminist Ethics: Some Central Issues

ALISON M. JAGGAR

In the previous essay, Julius Moravcsik criticized many of the assumptions of mainstream ethical theory from a perspective that, like Aristotle's, sees questions of character traits, ideals, human nature, and the meaning of life as of the utmost importance for ethics. Perhaps, however, the most significant challenge to conventional ethical theory to emerge in recent years has been from feminism. In this essay, Alison M. Jaggar, professor of philosophy at the University of Colorado and author of *Feminist Politics and Human Nature,* surveys the main currents of feminist ethics, focusing on four issues that have been at the center of feminist discussions in ethics.

Study Questions

1. What are Jaggar's three "minimum conditions" for characterizing an approach to ethics as feminist?

2. What is the difference between sex and gender? How have feminism's insights into gender complicated discussions of equality?

Reprinted by permission from Journal of Social Philosophy, *vol. 20, nos. 1–2 (Spring/Fall 1989). Copyright © 1989* Journal of Social Philosophy. *Some notes and references omitted.*

3. Ethical theorists have traditionally seen impartiality as a fundamental value. Why have feminist writers in ethics tended to play down the importance of impartiality?

4. In what ways have contemporary feminists had a mixed response to the ideal of moral autonomy?

5. Jaggar writes that feminist discussions of moral epistemology (that is, of the theory of moral knowledge) can be divided into two main categories. What are they?

FEMINIST APPROACHES TO ETHICS are distinguished by their explicit commitment to rethinking ethics with a view to correcting whatever forms of male bias it may contain. Feminist ethics, as these approaches are often called collectively, seeks to identify and challenge all those ways, overt but more often and more perniciously covert, in which western ethics has excluded women or rationalized their subordination. Its goal is to offer both practical guides to action and theoretical understandings of the nature of morality that do not, overtly or covertly, subordinate the interests of any woman or group of women to the interests of any other individual or group.

While those who practice feminist ethics are united by a shared project, they diverge widely in their views as to how this project may be accomplished. These divergences result from a variety of philosophical differences, including differing conceptions of feminism itself, a perennially contested concept. The inevitability of such disagreement means that feminist ethics cannot be identified in terms of a specific range of topics, methods or orthodoxies. For example, it is a mistake, though one to which even some feminists occasionally have succumbed, to identify feminist ethics with any of the following: putting women's interests first; focusing exclusively on so-called women's issues; accepting women (or feminists) as moral experts or authorities; substituting "female" (or "feminine") for "male" (or "masculine") values; or extrapolating directly from women's experience.

Even though my initial characterization of feminist ethics is quite loose, it does suggest certain minimum conditions of adequacy for any approach to ethics that purports to be feminist.

1. Within the present social context, in which women remain systematically subordinated, a feminist approach to ethics must offer a guide to action that will tend to subvert rather than reinforce this subordination. Thus, such an approach must be practical, transitional and non-utopian, an extension of politics rather than a retreat from it. It must be sensitive, for instance, to the symbolic meanings as well as the practical consequences of any actions that we take as gendered subjects in a male dominated society, and it must also provide the conceptual resources for identifying and evaluating the varieties of resistance and struggle in which women, particularly, have tended to engage. It must recognize the often unnoticed ways in which women and other members of the underclass have refused co-operation and opposed domination, while acknowledging the inevitability of collusion and the impossibility of totally clean hands.

2. Since so much of women's struggle has been in the kitchen and the bedroom, as well as in the parliamentary chamber and on the factory floor, a second requirement for feminist ethics is that it should be equipped to handle moral issues in both the so-called public and private domains. It must be able to provide guidance on issues of intimate relations, such as affection and sexuality, which, until quite recently, were largely ignored by modern moral theory. In so doing, it cannot assume that moral concepts developed originally for application to the public

realm, concepts such as impartiality or exploitation, are automatically applicable to the private realm. Similarly, an approach to ethics that is adequate for feminism must also provide appropriate guidance for activity in the public realm, for dealing with large numbers of people, including strangers.

3. Finally, feminist ethics must take the moral experience of all women seriously, though not, of course, uncritically. Though what is *feminist* will often turn out to be very different from what is *feminine,* a basic respect for women's moral experience is necessary to acknowledging women's capacities as moralists and to countering traditional stereotypes of women as less than full moral agents, as childlike or "natural." Furthermore, as Okin [1987], among others, has argued, empirical claims about differences in the moral experience of women and men make it impossible to assume that any approach to ethics will be unanimously accepted if it fails to consult the moral experience of women. Additionally, it seems plausible to suppose that women's distinctive social experience may make them especially perceptive regarding the implications of domination, especially gender domination, and especially well equipped to detect the male bias that has been shown to pervade so much of male-authored western moral theory.

On the surface, at least, these conditions of adequacy for feminist ethics are quite minimal—although I believe that fulfilling them would have radical consequences for ethics. I think most feminist, and perhaps even many nonfeminist,* philosophers would be likely to find the general statement of these conditions relatively uncontroversial, but that inevitably there will be sharp disagreement over when the conditions have been met. Even feminists are likely to differ

* "Nonfeminist" here refers to philosophers who do not make their feminist concerns explicit in their philosophical work; it is not intended to imply that such philosophers do not demonstrate feminist concern in other ways.

over, for instance, just what are women's interests and when they have been neglected, what is resistance to domination and which aspects of which women's moral experience are worth developing and in which directions.

I shall now go on to outline some of these differences as they have arisen in feminist discussions of [four] ethical and meta-ethical issues....

1. Equality and Difference

The central insight of contemporary feminism without doubt has been the recognition of gender as a sometimes contradictory but always pervasive system of social norms that regulates the activity of individuals according to their biological sex. Thus individuals whose sex is male are expected to conform to prevailing norms of masculinity, while female individuals are expected to conform to prevailing norms of femininity. In 1970, Shulamith Firestone began her classic *The Dialectic of Sex* with the words "Sex class is so deep as to be invisible" and, for the first decade of the contemporary women's movement, feminists devoted themselves to rendering "sex-class" or gender visible; to exploring (and denouncing) the depth and extent of gender regulation in the life of every individual. Norms of gender were shown to influence not only dress, occupation and sexuality, but also bodily comportment, patterns of speech, eating habits and intellectual, emotional, moral and even physical development—mostly in ways that, practically and/or symbolically, reinforced the domination of men over women.

The conceptual distinction between sex and gender enabled feminists to articulate a variety of important insights. These included recognizing that the superficially nondiscriminatory acceptance of exceptional, i.e., "masculine," women is not only compatible with but actually presupposes a devaluation of "the feminine." The sex/gender distinction also enabled feminists to separate critical reflection on cultural norms of masculinity from antagonism towards actual men.

Useful as the concept of gender has been to feminism, however, more recent feminist reflection has shown that it is neither as simple nor as unproblematic as it seemed when feminists first articulated it. Some feminists have challenged the initially sharp distinction between sex and gender, noting that, just as sex differences have influenced (though not ineluctably determined) the development of gender norms, so gender arrangements may well have influenced the biological evolution of certain secondary sexual characteristics and even of that defining criterion of sex, procreation itself. Other feminists have challenged the distinction between gender and other social categories such as race and class. Recognizing that feminist claims about "women" often had generalized illicitly from the experience of a relatively small group of middle-class white women, feminists in the last ten years have emphasized that gender is a variable rather than a constant, since norms of gender vary not only between but also within cultures, along dimensions such as class, race, age, marital status, sexual preference and so on. Moreover, since every woman is a woman of some determinate age, race, class and marital status, gender is not even an independent variable; there is no concept of pure or abstract gender that can be isolated theoretically and studied independently of class, race, age or marital status. Neither, of course, can these other social categories be understood independently of gender.

Their increasingly sophisticated understandings of gender have complicated feminists' discussions of many moral and social issues. One of these is sexual equality. At the beginning of the contemporary women's movement, in the late 1960s, this seemed to be a relatively straightforward issue. The nineteenth century feminist preference for "separate spheres" for men and women had been replaced by demands for identity of legal rights for men and women or, as it came to be called, equality before the law. By the end of the 1960s, most feminists in the United States had come to believe that the legal system should be sex-blind, that it should not differentiate in any way between women and men. This belief was expressed in the struggle for an Equal Rights Amendment to the U.S. Constitution, an amendment that, had it passed, would have made any sex-specific law unconstitutional.

By the late 1970s and early 1980s, however, it was becoming apparent that the assimilationist goal of strict equality before the law does not always benefit women, at least in the short term. One notorious example was "no fault" divorce settlements that divided family property equally between husband and wife but invariably left wives in a far worse economic situation than they did husbands. In one study, for instance, ex-husbands' standard of living was found to have risen by 42% a year after divorce, whereas ex-wives' standard of living declined by 73%. This huge discrepancy in the outcome of divorce resulted from a variety of factors, including the fact that women and men typically are differently situated in the job market, with women usually having much lower job qualifications and less work experience. In this sort of case, equality (construed as identity) in the treatment of the sexes appears to produce an outcome in which sexual inequality is increased.

The obvious alternative of seeking equality by providing women with special legal protection continues, however, to be as fraught with dangers for women as it was earlier in the century when the existence of protective legislation was used as an excuse for excluding women from many of the more prestigious and better paid occupations. For instance, mandating special leaves for disability on account of pregnancy or childbirth promotes the perception that women are less reliable workers than men; recognizing "premenstrual syndrome" or postpartum depression as periodically disabling conditions encourages the perception that women are less responsible than men; while attempts to protect women's sexuality through legislation restricting pornography or excluding women from employment in male institutions such as prisons, perpetuate the dangerous stereotypes that women are by nature the sexual prey of men. This cultural myth serves as an implicit legitimation for the prostitution, sexual harassment and rape of women, because it implies that such activities are in some sense natural. In all these cases, attempts to achieve equality between the sexes by responding to perceived differences between men and women seem likely to reinforce rather than reduce existing differences, even differences that are acknowledged to be social rather than biological in origin.

Furthermore, a "sex-responsive," as opposed to "sex-blind," conception of equality ignores differences *between* women, separating all women into a single homogenous category and possibly penalizing one group of women by forcing them to accept protection that another group genuinely may need.

Sooner or later, most feminist attempts to formulate an adequate conception of sexual equality run up against the recognition that the baseline for discussions of equality typically has been a male standard. In Catharine MacKinnon's inimitable words:

> Men's physiology defines most sports, their needs define auto and health insurance coverage, their socially designed biographies define workplace expectations and successful career patterns, their perspectives and concerns define quality in scholarship, their experiences and obsessions define merit, their objectification of life defines art, their military service defines citizenship, their presence defines family, their inability to get along with each other—their wars and rulerships—defines history, their image defines god, and their genitals define sex [MacKinnon 1987:36].

Having once reached this recognition, some feminist theorists have turned away from debating the pros and cons of what MacKinnon calls the "single" versus the "double standard" and begun speculating about the kinds of far-reaching social transformation that would make sex differences "costless." In discussions elaborating such notions as that of "equality as acceptance," feminists seem to be moving towards a radical construal of equality as similarity of individual outcome, equality of condition or effect, a conception quite at odds with traditional liberal understandings of equality as equality of procedure or opportunity.

While some feminists struggle to formulate a conception of sexual equality that is adequate for feminism, others have suggested that the enterprise is hopeless. For them, equality is an integral part of an "ethic of justice" that is characteristically masculine insofar as it obscures human difference by abstracting from the particularity and uniqueness of concrete people in their specific situations and seeks to resolve conflicting interests by applying an abstract rule rather than by responding directly to needs that are immediately perceived. Such feminists suggest that a discourse of responsibility or care may offer a more appropriate model for feminist ethics—even including feminist jurisprudence. Both of these suggestions remain to be worked out in detail.

The tangled debate over equality and difference provides an excellent illustration of one characteristic feature of contemporary feminist ethics, namely, its insistence that gender is often, if not invariably, a morally relevant difference between individuals. Given this insistence, the starting point of much feminist ethics may be different from that of modern moral theory: instead of assuming that all individuals should be treated alike until morally relevant grounds for difference in treatment can be identified, feminist theorists may shift the traditional burden of moral proof by assuming, until shown otherwise, that contemporary men and women are rarely "similarly situated." This leads into a related and equally crucial question for feminist ethics in the nineties, namely, how to characterize and evaluate impartiality.

2. Impartiality

In the modern western tradition, impartiality typically has been recognized as a fundamental value, perhaps even a defining characteristic of morality, distinguishing true morality from tribalism. Impartiality is said to require weighing the interests of each individual equally, permitting differentiation only on the basis of differences that can be shown to be morally relevant. Impartiality thus is linked conceptually with equality and also with rationality and objectivity, insofar as bias often has been defined as the absence of impartiality.

In the last few years, the preeminence traditionally ascribed to impartiality has been challenged both by feminist and nonfeminist philosophers. Nonfeminists have charged that an insistence on impartiality disregards our particular identities, constituted by reference to our particular projects and our unchosen relationships with others; and that it substitutes abstract "variables" for real human agents and patients. . . .

Nell Noddings [1984] is one of the most extreme opponents of impartiality and her work has been influential with a number of feminists, even though the sub-title of her book makes it clear that she takes herself to be elaborating a feminine rather than a feminist approach to ethics. Noddings views the emotion of caring as the natural basis of morality, a view that would require impartiality to be expressed in universal caring. Noddings claims, however, that we are psychologically able to care only for particular others with whom we are in actual relationships, i.e., relationships that can be "completed" by the cared-for's acknowledgment of our caring. She concludes that pretensions to care for humanity at large are not only hypocritical but self-defeating, undermining true caring for those with whom we are in actual relationship. Noddings' arguments, if valid, of course would apply indifferently to caring practised either by men or by women, and so the distinctively feminist interest of Noddings' work might seem to reside solely in her obviously debatable claim that women are "better equipped for caring than men" (97) and therefore less likely to be impartial. As we have noted already, however, feminist ethics is not committed to reproducing the moral practice even of most women and so feminist (and nonfeminist) moral theorists need to evaluate critically all of Noddings' arguments against impartiality, independently of whether her claims about "feminine" morality can be empirically confirmed.

A different criticism of impartiality has been made by those feminist philosophers who assert that, while impartiality is associated historically with individualism, it paradoxically undermines respect for individuality because it treats individuals as morally interchangeable [Code 1988; Sherwin 1987]. Many, though certainly not all, feminists claim that women are less likely than men to commit this alleged moral error because they are more likely to appreciate the special characteristics of particular individuals; again, however, feminist estimates of the soundness or otherwise of Code's and Sherwin's argument must be independent of this empirical claim.

Finally, at least one feminist has extended the claim that women need special protection in the law by recommending that feminist ethics should promote a double standard of morality, limiting moral communities on the basis of gender or perhaps gender solidarity. Susan Sherwin writes that feminists feel a special responsibility to reduce the suffering of women in particular; thus, "(b)y acknowledging the relevance of differences among people as a basis for a difference in sympathy and concern, feminism denies the legitimacy of a central premise of traditional moral theories, namely that all persons should be seen as morally equivalent by us" [Sherwin 1987:26 . . .]. However, since women and even feminists are not homogenous groups, as we have seen, this kind of reasoning seems to push the suggested double standard towards becoming a multiple moral standard—which Enlightenment theorists might well interpret as the total abandonment of impartiality and thus of morality itself.

A variety of responses seems to be available to the foregoing criticisms of impartiality. One alternative is to argue that the criticisms are unwarranted, depending on misrepresentation, misunderstanding and caricature of the impartialist position. If this response can be sustained, it may be possible to show that there is no real conflict between "masculine" impartialism and "feminine" particularism, "masculine" justice and "feminine" care. Another alternative is to bite the bullet of direct moral confrontation, providing arguments to challenge the intuitions of those who criticize impartiality as requiring courses of action that are morally repugnant or politically dangerous. Yet a third alternative may be to reconceive the concept of impartiality and the considerations appropriate for determining our responsibilities toward various individuals and groups. Feminist ethics must find a way of choosing between those or other options and evaluating the proper place of impartiality in ethics. . . .

It is [also] evident that a central concern for feminist ethics . . . must be to develop ways of thinking about moral subjects that are sensitive *both* to their concreteness, inevitable particularity and unique specificity, expressed in part through their relations with specific historical communities, *and* to their intrinsic and common value, the ideal expressed in Enlightenment claims about common humanity, equality and impartiality.

3. Autonomy

One aspect of this task is the rethinking of autonomy which, like impartiality (to which it is often conceptually connected), has been a continuing ideal of modern moral theory. . . . The core intuition of autonomy is that of indepen-

dence or self legislation, the self as the ultimate authority in matters of morality or truth. In the Kantian tradition, where the ideal of autonomy is particularly prominent, moral autonomy has been elaborated in terms of disinterest, detachment from particular attachments and interests, and freedom from prejudice and self-deception [Hill 1987].

Contemporary feminists have had a mixed response to the modern ideal of moral autonomy. On the one hand, they have insisted that women are as autonomous in the moral and intellectual sense as men—as rational, as capable of a sense of justice, and so on; and they have also demanded political, social and economic autonomy for women through political representation, the abolition of sex discrimination and respect for women's choices on issues such as abortion. On the other hand, however, some feminists have questioned traditional interpretations of autonomy as masculine fantasies. For instance, they have explored some of the ways in which "choice" is socialized and "consent" manipulated. In addition, they have questioned the possibility of separating ourselves from particular attachments and still retaining our personal identity, and they have suggested that freeing ourselves from particular attachments might result in a cold, rigid, moralistic rather than a truly moral response [Noddings 1984]. Rather than guaranteeing a response that is purely moral, freeing ourselves from particular attachments might instead make us *incapable* of morality if an ineliminable part of morality consists in responding emotionally to particular others.

Feminist ethics . . . must find ways of conceptualizing moral agency, choice and consent that are compatible with the feminist recognition of the gradual process of moral development, the gendered social construction of the psyche, and the historical constraints on our options. This is one area in which some promising work by feminists exists already.

4. Moral Epistemology and Anti-Epistemology

Enlightenment moral theory characteristically assumed that morality was universal—that, if moral claims held, they were valid at all times and in all places. However, the modern abandonment of belief in a teleological and sacred universe rendered the justification of such claims constantly problematic, and much moral theory for the last three centuries has consisted in attempts to provide a rational grounding for morality. At the present time, both the continental European tradition, especially but not only in the form of post-modernism, and the Anglo-American tradition, especially but not only in the form of communitarianism, have developed powerful challenges to the very possibility of the view that morality consists in universally valid rules grounded in universal reason. The inevitable result of these sceptical challenges has been to reinforce normative and meta-ethical relativism.

Feminists are ambivalent about these challenges. On the one hand, many of the feminist criticisms of modern moral theory parallel the criticisms made by communitarianism and post-modernism. On the other hand, however, feminists are understandably concerned that their critique of male dominance should not be dismissed as just one point of view. It is therefore crucial for feminist ethics to develop some ways of justifying feminist moral claims. However, moral epistemology is an area in which feminists' critiques are better developed than their alternatives.

Feminist discussions of moral epistemology may be divided into two categories, each distinguished by a somewhat different view of the nature of morality. Feminists in the first category do not explicitly challenge the modern conception of morality as consisting primarily in an impartial system of rationally justified rules or principles, though few feminists would assert that it is possible to identify rules that are substantive, specific and hold in all circumstances. Those in the second category, by contrast, deny that morality is reducible to rules and emphasize the impossibility of justifying the claims of ethics by appeal to a universal, impartial reason. The contrast between these two groups of feminists is not as sharp as this initial characterization might suggest: for instance, both share several criticisms of existing decision procedures in ethics. But feminists in the former group are more hopeful of repairing those procedures, while feminists in the latter group seem ready to abandon them entirely.

Feminists in the latter group frequently claim to be reflecting on a moral experience that is distinctively feminine. . . . They . . . reject the view attributed to modern moral theorists that the right course of action can be discovered by consulting a list of moral rules, charging that undue emphasis on the epistemological importance of rules obscures the crucial role of moral insight, virtue and character in determining what should be done. A feminist twist is given to this essentially Aristotelian criticism when claims are made that excessive reliance on rules reflects a juridical-administrative interest that is characteristic of modern masculinity [Blum 1982] while contemporary women, by contrast, are alleged to be more likely to disregard conventionally accepted moral rules because such rules are insensitive to the specificities of particular situations [Gilligan 1982; Noddings 1984]. A morality of rule, therefore, is alleged to devalue the moral wisdom of women, as well as to give insufficient weight to such supposedly feminine virtues as kindness, generosity, helpfulness and sympathy.

Some feminists have claimed that "feminine" approaches to morality contrast with supposedly masculine rule-governed approaches in that they characteristically consist in immediate responses to particular others, responses based on supposedly natural feelings of empathy, care and compassion [Gilligan 1982; Noddings 1984] or loving attention [Murdoch 1970; Ruddick

1989]. However, . . . attempts to develop a moral epistemology based on such responses face a variety of problems. First, they confront the familiar, though perhaps not insuperable, problems common to all moral epistemologies that take emotion as a guide to right action, namely, the frequent inconsistency, unavailability or plain inappropriateness of emotions. In other words, they face the danger of degenerating into a "do what feels good" kind of subjective relativism. In addition, it is not clear that even our emotional responses to others are not responses to them under some universal description and so in this sense general rather than particular—or, if indeed particular and therefore nonconceptual, then perhaps closer to animal than to distinctively human responses. It is further uncertain how these sorts of particular responses can guide our actions towards large numbers of people, most of whom we shall never meet. Finally, the feminist emphasis on the need for "contextual" reasoning opens up the obvious dangers of *ad hoc*ism, special pleading and partiality.

Not all feminists, of course, are committed to a particularist moral epistemology. Even some of those who take emotions as a proper guide to morality emphasize the intentionality of emotions and discuss the need for their moral education. Additionally, while most feminists criticize certain aspects of the decision procedures developed by modern moral theory, some believe it may be possible to revise and reappropriate some of these procedures. The main candidates for such revision are the methods developed by Rawls and Habermas, each of whom believes that an idealized situation of dialogue (which each describes differently) will both generate and justify morally valid principles. . . .

One possible alternative both to an unwelcome relativism and to what many feminists see as the pretensions of moral rationalism may be the development of a moral standpoint that is distinctively feminist. Sara Ruddick claims that such a standpoint can be found in maternal thinking [1989], but her work has been criticized by some feminists as ethnocentric and overvaluing motherhood. . . .

The controversy in feminist moral epistemology currently is so sharp that Held [1984] has suggested abandoning the search for a "unified field theory" covering all domains of life activity. However, other authors have pointed to the danger that, if a supposedly feminine "ethic of care" were limited to the realm of personal life, as Kohlberg, for instance has suggested, it would be perceived as subordinate to the supposedly masculine "ethic of justice," just as, in contemporary society, the private is subordinate to the public.

Conclusion

Even such a limited survey as this should make it evident that feminist ethics, far from being a rigid orthodoxy, instead is a ferment of ideas and controversy, many of them echoing and deepening debates in nonfeminist ethics. The centrality of the issues and the liveliness of the on-going discussions suggest that the [future] will be a fruitful period for feminist ethics—and thus for ethics generally.

References

Blum, Lawrence, "Kant's and Hegel's Moral Rationalism: A Feminist Perspective," *Canadian Journal of Philosophy* 12:2 (June 1982)

Code, Lorraine, "Experience, Knowledge and Responsibility," *Feminist Perspectives in Philosophy,* eds. Morwenna Griffiths and Margaret Whitford, Bloomington & Indianapolis: Indiana University Press, 1988

Gilligan, Carol, *In a Different Voice: Psychological Theory and Women's Development,* Cambridge, MA: Harvard University Press, 1982

Held, Virginia, *Rights and Goods,* New York: The Free Press, 1984

Hill, Thomas E., Jr., "The Importance of Autonomy," *Women and Moral Theory,* eds. Eva Feder

Kittay and Diana T. Meyers, Totowa, NJ: Rowman and Littlefield, 1987

MacKinnon, Catharine A., *Feminism Unmodified: Discourses on Life and Law,* Cambridge, MA: Harvard University Press, 1987

Murdoch, Iris, *The Sovereignty of Good,* London: Routledge & Kegan Paul, 1970

Noddings, Nell, *Caring: A Feminine Approach to Ethics and Moral Education,* Berkeley: University of California Press, 1984

Okin, Susan Moller, "Justice and Gender," *Philosophy and Public Affairs* 16:1 (Winter 1987)

Ruddick, Sara, *Maternal Thinking: Toward a Politics of Peace,* Boston: Beacon Press, 1989

Sherwin, Susan, "A Feminist Approach to Ethics," *Resources for Feminist Research* 16:3, 1987. (Special issue on "Women and Philosophy")

Review and Discussion Questions

1. Given that there is much controversy and significant disagreement among feminist writers in ethics, do you think there is such a thing as "feminist ethics"? If so, what do you see as its basic or defining features? What distinguishes feminist from nonfeminist ethics?

2. What do you see as the most important and relevant insights of feminism for ethics? Can these insights be accommodated by more traditional ethical approaches?

3. Discuss the pros and cons of a "sex-responsive," as opposed to a "sex-blind," conception of equality.

4. Assess feminist criticisms of impartiality. Do they have merit?

5. Do you see any similarities or connections between the issues under debate in feminist ethics and Moravcsik's disagreements with conventional ethical theory? Explain.

PART II

ISSUES IN APPLIED ETHICS

SUICIDE AND EUTHANASIA

The Morality and Rationality of Suicide

RICHARD B. BRANDT

Richard B. Brandt was professor of philosophy at the University of Michigan for many years and author of *Ethical Theory, A Theory of the Good and the Right,* and *Facts, Values, and Morality.* Elsewhere, he defines suicide "as doing something that results in one's death, from the intention either of ending one's life or to bring about some other state of affairs (such as relief from pain) that one thinks it certain or highly probable can be achieved only by means of death or that will produce death." In this essay, he examines the conditions under which suicide would be morally blameworthy, the moral arguments for and against suicide, the question of when suicide would be rational from the individual's point of view, and the moral obligations of others toward someone contemplating suicide.

Study Questions

1. What is Brandt's definition of "moral blameworthiness," and how does it apply to the case of suicide?

2. What are three types of suicide that can be morally excused even if they are objectively wrong?

3. Explain what Brandt means when he says that there are things we can have some moral obligation to avoid doing even though in particular situations they may be right or even obligatory. How does this principle apply to the analysis of suicide?

4. Restate the theological, the natural law, and the harm-to-others arguments against suicide.

5. What are some of the errors a person must avoid if his or her decision to commit suicide is to be a rational one?

FROM THE POINT OF VIEW of contemporary philosophy, suicide raises the following distinct questions: whether a person who commits suicide (assuming that there is suicide if and only if there is intentional termination of one's own life) is morally blameworthy, reprehensible, sinful in all circumstances; whether suicide is objectively right or wrong, and in what circumstances it is right or wrong, from a moral point of view; and whether, or in which circumstances, suicide is the best or the rational thing to do from the point of view of the agent's personal welfare.

The Moral Blameworthiness of Suicide

In former times the question of whether suicide is sinful was of great interest because the answer to it was considered relevant to how the agent would spend eternity. At present the practical issue is not as great, although a normal funeral service may be denied a person judged to have committed suicide sinfully. The chief practical issue now seems to be that persons may disapprove of a decedent for having committed suicide, and his friends or relatives may wish to defend his memory against moral charges.

The question of whether an act of suicide was sinful or morally blameworthy is not apt to arise unless it is already believed that the agent morally ought not to have done it: for instance, if he really had very poor reason for doing so, and his act foreseeably had catastrophic consequences for his wife and children. But, even if a given suicide is morally wrong, it does not follow that it is morally reprehensible. For, while asserting that a given act of suicide was wrong, we may still think that the act was hardly morally blameworthy or sinful if, say, the agent was in a state of great emotional turmoil at the time. We might then say that, although what he did was wrong, his action is *excusable,* just as in the criminal law it may be decided that, although a person broke the law, he should not be punished because he was *not responsible,* that is, was temporarily insane, did what he did inadvertently, and so on.

The foregoing remarks assume that to be morally blameworthy (or sinful) on account of an act is one thing, and for the act to be wrong is another. But, if we say this, what after all does it *mean* to say that a person is morally blameworthy on account of an action? We cannot say there is agreement among philosophers on this matter, but I suggest the following account as being safe from serious objection: "*X* is morally blameworthy on account of an action *A*" may be taken to mean "*X* did *A,* and *X* would not have done *A* had not his character been in some respect below standard; and in view of this it is fitting or justified for *X* to have some disapproving attitudes including remorse toward himself, and for some other persons *Y* to have some disapproving attitudes toward *X* and to express them in behavior." . . .

In case the foregoing definition does not seem obviously correct, it is worthwhile pointing out that it is usually thought that an agent is not blameworthy or sinful for an action unless it is a *reflection on him;* the definition brings this fact out and makes clear why.

If someone charges that a suicide was sinful, we may now properly ask, "What defect of character did it show?" Some writers have claimed that suicide is blameworthy because it is *cowardly;* and since being cowardly is generally conceded to be a defect of character, if an act of suicide is admitted to be both objectively wrong and also cowardly, the claim to blameworthiness might be warranted in terms of the above definition. Of course, many people would hesitate to call taking one's own life a cowardly act, and there will certainly be controversy about which acts are cowardly and which are not. But at least we can see part of what has to be done to make a charge of blameworthiness valid.

The most interesting question is the general one: which types of suicide in general are ones that, even if objectively wrong (in a sense to be explained below), are not sinful or blameworthy? Or, in other words, when is a suicide *morally excused* even if it is objectively wrong? We can at least identify some types that are morally excusable.

1. Suppose I *think* I am morally bound to commit suicide because I have a terminal illness and continued medical care will ruin my family financially. Suppose, however, that I am mistaken in this belief, and that suicide in such circumstances is not right. But surely I am not morally blameworthy; for I may be doing, out of a sense of duty to my family, what I would personally prefer not to do and is hard for me to do. What defect of character might my action show? Suicide from a genuine sense of duty is not blameworthy, even when the moral conviction in question is mistaken.

2. Suppose that I commit suicide when I am temporarily of unsound mind, either in the sense of the M'Naghten rule that I do not know that what I am doing is wrong, or of the Durham rule that, owing to a mental defect, I am substantially unable to do what is right. Surely, any suicide in an unsound state of mind is morally excused.

3. Suppose I commit suicide when I could not be said to be temporarily of unsound mind, but simply because I am not myself. For instance, I may be in an extremely depressed mood. Now a person may be in a very depressed mood, and commit suicide on account of being in that mood, when there is nothing the matter with his character—or, in other words, his character is not in any relevant way below standard. What are other examples of being "not myself," of emotional states that might be respon-

sible for a person's committing suicide, and that might render the suicide excusable even if wrong? Being frightened; being distraught; being in almost any highly emotional frame of mind (anger, frustration, disappointment in love); perhaps just being terribly fatigued.

So there are at least three types of suicide which can be morally excused even if they are objectively wrong. The main point is this: Mr. X may commit suicide and it may be conceded that he ought not to have done so, but it is another step to show that he is sinful, or morally blameworthy, for having done so. To make out that further point, it must be shown that his act is attributable to some substandard trait of character. So, Mrs. X after the suicide can concede that her husband ought not to have done what he did, but she can also point out that it is no reflection on his character. . . .

The Moral Reasons For and Against Suicide

Persons who say suicide is morally wrong must be asked which of two positions they are affirming: Are they saying that *every* act of suicide is wrong, *everything considered;* or are they merely saying that there is always *some* moral obligation—doubtless of serious weight—not to commit suicide, so that very often suicide is wrong, although it is possible that there are *countervailing considerations* which in particular situations make it right or even a moral duty? It is quite evident that the first position is absurd; only the second has a chance of being defensible.

In order to make clear what is wrong with the first view, we may begin with an example. Suppose an army pilot's single-seater plane goes out of control over a heavily populated area; he has the choice of staying in the plane and bringing it down where it will do little damage but at the cost of certain death for himself, and of bailing out and letting the plane fall where it will, very possibly killing a good many civilians. Suppose he chooses to do the former, and so, by our definition, commits suicide. Does anyone want to say that his action is morally wrong? Even Immanuel Kant, who opposed suicide in all circumstances, apparently would not wish to say that it is; he would, in fact, judge that this act is not one of suicide, for he says, "It is no suicide to risk one's life against one's enemies, and even to sacrifice it, in order to preserve one's duties towards oneself."[1] . . .

In general . . . there are things [we have] some moral obligation to avoid which, on account of other morally relevant considerations, it is sometimes right or even morally obligatory to do. There may be some obligation to tell the truth on every occasion, but surely in many cases the consequences of telling the truth would be so dire that one is obligated to lie. The same goes for promises. There is some moral obligation to do what one has promised (with a few exceptions); but, if one can keep a trivial promise only at serious cost to another person (i.e., keep an appointment only by failing to give aid to someone injured in an accident), it is surely obligatory to break the promise.

The most that the moral critic of suicide can hold, then, is that there is *some* moral obligation not to do what one knows will cause one's death; but he surely cannot deny that circumstances exist in which there are obligations to do things which, in fact, will result in one's death. If so, then in principle it would be possible to argue, for instance, that in order to meet my obligation to my family, it might be right for me to take my own life as the only way to avoid catastrophic hospital expenses in a terminal illness. Possibly the main point that critics of suicide on moral grounds would wish to make is that it is never right to take one's own life *for reasons of one's own personal welfare*, of any kind whatsoever. Some of the arguments used to support the immorality of suicide, however, are so framed that if they were supportable at all, they would prove that suicide is *never* moral.

One well-known type of argument against suicide may be classified as *theological*. St. Augustine and others urged that the Sixth Commandment ("Thou shalt not kill") prohibits suicide, and that we are bound to obey a divine commandment. To this reasoning one might first reply that it is arbitrary exegesis of the Sixth Commandment to assert that it was intended to prohibit suicide. The second reply is that if there is not some consideration which shows on the merits of the case that suicide is morally wrong, God has no business prohibiting it. It is true that some will object to this point, and I must refer them elsewhere for my detailed comments on the divine-will theory of morality.[2]

Another theological argument with wide support was accepted by John Locke, who wrote: ". . . Men being all the workmanship of one omnipotent and infinitely wise Maker; all the servants of one sovereign Master, sent into the world by His order and about His business; they are His property, whose workmanship they are made to last during His, not one another's pleasure. . . . Every one . . . is bound to preserve himself, and not to quit his station wilfully. . . ."[3] And Kant: "We have been placed in this world under certain conditions and for specific purposes. But a suicide opposes the purpose of his Creator; he arrives in the other world as one who has deserted his post; he must be looked upon as a rebel against God. So long as we remember the truth that it is God's intention to preserve life, we are bound to regulate our activities in conformity with it. This duty is upon us until the time comes when God expressly commands us to leave this life. Human beings are sentinels on earth and may not leave their posts until relieved by another beneficent hand."[4] Unfortunately, however, even if we grant that it is the duty of human beings to do what God commands or intends them to do, more argument is required to show that God does *not* permit human beings to quit this life when their own personal welfare would be maximized by so doing. How does one draw the requisite inference about the intentions of God?

The difficulties and contradictions in arguments to reach such a conclusion are discussed at length and perspicaciously by David Hume in his essay "On Suicide," and in view of the unlikelihood that readers will need to be persuaded about these, I shall merely refer those interested to that essay.[5]

A second group of arguments may be classed as arguments *from natural law*. St. Thomas says: "It is altogether unlawful to kill oneself, for three reasons. First, because everything naturally loves itself, the result being that everything naturally keeps itself in being, and resists corruptions as far as it can. Wherefore suicide is contrary to the inclination of nature, and to charity whereby every man should love himself. Hence suicide is always a mortal sin, as being contrary to the natural law and to charity."[6] Here St. Thomas ignores two obvious points. First, it is not obvious why a human being is morally bound to do what he or she has some inclination to do. (St. Thomas did not criticize chastity.) Second, while it is true that most human beings do feel a strong urge to live, the human being who commits suicide obviously feels a stronger inclination to do something else. It is as natural for a human being to dislike, and to take steps to avoid, say, great pain, as it is to cling to life.

A somewhat similar argument by Immanuel Kant may seem better. In a famous passage Kant writes that the maxim of a person who commits suicide is "From self-love I make it my principle to shorten my life if its continuance threatens more evil than it promises pleasure. The only further question to ask is whether this principle of self-love can become a universal law of nature. It is then seen at once that a system of nature by whose law the very same feeling whose function is to stimulate the furtherance of life should actually destroy life would contradict itself and consequently would not subsist as a system of nature. Hence this maxim cannot possibly hold as a universal law of nature and is therefore entirely opposed to the supreme prin-

ciple of all duty."[7] What Kant finds contradictory is that the motive of self-love (interest in one's own long-range welfare) should sometimes lead one to struggle to preserve one's life, but at other times to end it. But where is the contradiction? One's circumstances change, and, if the argument of the following section in this chapter is correct, one sometimes maximizes one's own long-range welfare by trying to stay alive, but at other times by bringing about one's demise.

A third group of arguments, a form of which goes back at least to Aristotle, has a more modern and convincing ring. These are arguments to show that, in one way or another, a suicide necessarily does harm to other persons, or to society at large. Aristotle says that the suicide treats the *state* unjustly.[8] Partly following Aristotle, St. Thomas says: "Every man is part of the community, and so, as such, he belongs to the community. Hence by killing himself he injures the community."[9] Blackstone held that a suicide is an offense against the king "who hath an interest in the preservation of all his subjects," perhaps following Judge Brown in 1563, who argued that suicide cost the king a subject—"he being the head has lost one of his mystical members."[10] The premise of such arguments is, as Hume pointed out, obviously mistaken in many instances. It is true that Freud would perhaps have injured society had he, instead of finishing his last book, committed suicide to escape the pain of throat cancer. But surely there have been many suicides whose demise was not a noticeable loss to society; an honest man could only say that in some instances society was better off without them.

It need not be denied that suicide is often injurious to other persons, especially the family of a suicide. Clearly it sometimes is. But, we should notice what this fact establishes. Suppose we admit, as generally would be done, that there is some obligation not to perform any action which will probably or certainly be injurious to other people, the strength of the obligation being dependent on various factors, notably the seriousness of the expected injury. Then there is *some* obligation not to commit suicide, when that act would probably or certainly be injurious to other people. But, as we have already seen, many cases of *some* obligation to do something nevertheless are *not* cases of a duty to do that thing, *everything considered*. So it could sometimes be morally justified to commit suicide, even if the act will harm someone. Must a man with a terminal illness undergo excruciating pain because his death will cause his wife sorrow—when she will be caused sorrow a month later anyway, when he is dead of natural causes? Moreover, to repeat, the fact that an individual has some obligation not to commit suicide when that act will probably injure other persons does not imply that, everything considered, it is wrong for him to do it [or] that in all circumstances suicide *as such* is something there is some obligation to avoid.

Is there any sound argument, convincing to the modern mind, to establish that there is (or is not) *some moral obligation* to avoid suicide *as such,* an obligation, of course, which might be overridden by other obligations in some or many cases? . . .

To present all the arguments necessary to answer this question convincingly would take a great deal of space. I shall, therefore, simply state one answer to it which seems plausible to some contemporary philosophers. Suppose it could be shown that it would maximize the long-run welfare of everybody affected if people were taught that there is a moral obligation to avoid suicide—so that people would be motivated to avoid suicide just because they thought it wrong (would have anticipatory guilt feelings at the very idea), and so that other people would be inclined to disapprove of persons who commit suicide unless there were some excuse (such as those mentioned in the first section). One might ask: how could it maximize utility to mold the conceptual and motivational structure of persons in this way? To which the answer

might be: feeling in this way might make persons who are impulsively inclined to commit suicide in a bad mood, or a fit of anger or jealousy, take more time to deliberate; hence, some suicides that have bad effects generally might be prevented. In other words, it might be a good thing in its effects for people to feel about suicide in the way they feel about breach of promise or injuring others, just as it might be a good thing for people to feel a moral obligation not to smoke, or to wear seat belts. However, it might be that negative moral feelings about suicide as such would stand in the way of action by those persons whose welfare really is best served by suicide and whose suicide is the best thing for everybody concerned.

When a Decision to Commit Suicide Is Rational from the Person's Point of View

The person who is contemplating suicide is obviously making a choice between future world-courses: the world-course that includes his demise, say, an hour from now, and several possible ones that contain his demise at a later point. One cannot have precise knowledge about many features of the latter group of world-courses, but it is certain that they will all end with death some (possibly short) finite time from now.

Why do I say the choice is between *world-*courses and not just a choice between future life-courses of the prospective suicide, the one shorter than the other? The reason is that one's suicide has some impact on the world (and one's continued life has some impact on the world), and that conditions in the rest of the world will often make a difference in one's evaluation of the possibilities. One *is* interested in things in the world other than just oneself and one's own happiness.

The basic question a person must answer, in order to determine which world-course is best or rational for him to choose, is which he *would* choose under conditions of optimal use of information, when *all* of his desires are taken into account. It is not just a question of what we prefer *now*, with some clarification of all the possibilities being considered. Our preferences change, and the preferences of tomorrow (assuming we can know something about them) are just as legitimately taken into account in deciding what to do now as the preferences of today. Since any reason that can be given today for weighting heavily today's preference can be given tomorrow for weighting heavily tomorrow's preference, the preferences of any time- stretch have a rational claim to an equal vote. Now the importance of that fact is this: we often know quite well that our desires, aversions, and preferences may change after a short while. When a person is in a state of despair—perhaps brought about by a rejection in love or discharge from a long-held position—nothing but the thing he cannot have seems desirable; everything else is turned to ashes. Yet we know quite well that the passage of time is likely to reverse all this; replacements may be found or other types of things that are available to us may begin to look attractive. So, if we were to act on the preferences of today alone, when the emotion of despair seems more than we can stand, we might find death preferable to life; but if we allow for the preferences of the weeks and years ahead, when many goals will be enjoyable and attractive, we might find life much preferable to death. So, if a choice of what is best is to be determined by what we want not only now but later (and later desires on an equal basis with the present ones)—as it should be—then what is the best or preferable world-course will often be quite different from what it would be if the choice, or what is best for one, were fixed by one's desires and preferences now.

Of course, if one commits suicide there are no future desires or aversions that may be compared with present ones and that should be allowed an equal vote in deciding what is best. In that respect the course of action that results in

death is different from any other course of action we may undertake. I do not wish to suggest the rosy possibility that it is often or always reasonable to believe that next week "I shall be more interested in living than I am today, if today I take a dim view of continued existence." On the contrary, when a person is seriously ill, for instance, he may have no reason to think that the preference-order will be reversed—it may be that tomorrow he will prefer death to life more strongly.

The argument is often used that one can never be *certain* what is going to happen, and hence one is never rationally justified in doing anything as drastic as committing suicide. But we always have to live by probabilities and make our estimates as best we can. As soon as it is clear beyond reasonable doubt not only that death is now preferable to life, but also that it will be every day from now until the end, the rational thing is to act promptly.

Let us not pursue the question of whether it is rational for a person with a painful terminal illness to commit suicide; it is. However, the issue seldom arises, and few terminally ill patients do commit suicide. With such patients matters usually get worse slowly so that no particular time seems to call for action. They are often so heavily sedated that it is impossible for the mental processes of decision leading to action to occur; or else they are incapacitated in a hospital and the very physical possibility of ending their lives is not available. Let us leave this grim topic and turn to a practically more important problem: whether it is rational for persons to commit suicide for some reason other than painful terminal physical illness. Most persons who commit suicide do so, apparently, because they face a nonphysical problem that depresses them beyond their ability to bear.

Among the problems that have been regarded as good and sufficient reasons for ending life, we find (in addition to serious illness) the following: some event that has made a person feel ashamed or lose his prestige and status; reduction from affluence to poverty; the loss of a limb or of physical beauty; the loss of sexual capacity; some event that makes it seem impossible to achieve things by which one sets store; loss of a loved one; disappointment in love; the infirmities of increasing age. It is not to be denied that such things can be serious blows to a person's prospects of happiness.

Whatever the nature of an individual's problem, there are various plain errors to be avoided —errors to which a person is especially prone when he is depressed—in deciding whether, everything considered, he prefers a world-course containing his early demise to one in which his life continues to its natural terminus. Let us forget for a moment the relevance to the decision of preferences that he may have tomorrow, and concentrate on some errors that may infect his preference as of today, and for which correction or allowance must be made.

In the first place, depression, like any severe emotional experience, tends to primitivize one's intellectual processes. It restricts the range of one's survey of the possibilities. One thing that a rational person would do is compare the world-course containing his suicide with his *best* alternative. But his best alternative is precisely a possibility he may overlook if, in a depressed mood, he thinks only of how badly off he is and cannot imagine any way of improving his situation. If a person is disappointed in love, it is possible to adopt a vigorous plan of action that carries a good chance of acquainting him with someone he likes at least as well; and if old age prevents a person from continuing the tennis game with his favorite partner, it is possible to learn some other game that provides the joys of competition without the physical demands.

Depression has another insidious influence on one's planning; it seriously affects one's judgment about probabilities. A person disappointed in love is very likely to take a dim view of himself, his prospects, and his attractiveness; he thinks that because he has been rejected by one person he will probably be rejected by any-

one who looks desirable to him. In a less gloomy frame of mind he would make different estimates. Part of the reason for such gloomy probability estimates is that depression tends to repress one's memory of evidence that supports a nongloomy prediction. Thus, a rejected lover tends to forget any cases in which he has elicited enthusiastic response from ladies in relation to whom he has been the one who has done the rejecting. Thus his pessimistic self-image is based upon a highly selected, and pessimistically selected, set of data. Even when he is reminded of the data, moreover, he is apt to resist an optimistic inference.

Another kind of distortion of the look of future prospects is not a result of depression, but is quite normal. Events distant in the future feel small, just as objects distant in space look small. Their prospect does not have the effect on motivational processes that it would have if it were of an event in the immediate future. Psychologists call this the "goal-gradient" phenomenon; a rat, for instance, will run faster toward a perceived food box than a distant unseen one. In the case of a person who has suffered some misfortune, and whose situation now is an unpleasant one, this reduction of the motivational influence of events distant in time has the effect that present unpleasant states weigh far more heavily than probable future pleasant ones in any choice of world-courses.

If we are trying to determine whether we now prefer, or shall later prefer, the outcome of one world-course to that of another (and this is leaving aside the questions of the weight of the votes of preferences at a later date), we must take into account these and other infirmities of our "sensing" machinery. Since knowing that the machinery is out of order will not tell us what results it would give if it were working, the best recourse might be to refrain from making any decision in a stressful frame of mind. If decisions have to be made, one must recall past reactions, in a normal frame of mind, to outcomes like those under assessment. But many suicides seem to occur in moments of despair. What should be clear from the above is that a moment of despair, if one is seriously contemplating suicide, ought to be a moment of reassessment of one's goals and values, a reassessment which the individual must realize is very difficult to make objectively, because of the very quality of his depressed frame of mind.

A decision to commit suicide may in certain circumstances be a rational one. But a person who wants to act rationally must take into account the various possible "errors" and make appropriate rectification of his initial evaluations.

The Role of Other Persons

What is the moral obligation of other persons toward those who are contemplating suicide? The question of their moral blameworthiness may be ignored and what is rational for them to do from the point of view of personal welfare may be considered as being of secondary concern. Laws make it dangerous to aid or encourage a suicide. The risk of running afoul of the law may partly determine moral obligation, since moral obligation to do something may be reduced by the fact that it is personally dangerous.

The moral obligation of other persons toward one who is contemplating suicide is an instance of a general obligation to render aid to those in serious distress, at least when this can be done at no great cost to one's self. I do not think this general principle is seriously questioned by anyone, whatever his moral theory; so I feel free to assume it as a premise. Obviously the person contemplating suicide is in great distress of some sort; if he were not, he would not be seriously considering terminating his life.

How great a person's obligation is to one in distress depends on a number of factors. Obviously family and friends have special obligations to devote time to helping the prospective suicide—which others do not have. But anyone in this kind of distress has a moral claim on the

time of any person who knows the situation (unless there are others more responsible who are already doing what should be done).

What is the obligation? It depends, of course, on the situation, and how much the second person knows about the situation. If the individual has decided to terminate his life if he can, and it is clear that he is right in this decision, then, if he needs help in executing the decision, there is a moral obligation to give him help. On this matter a patient's physician has a special obligation, from which any talk about the Hippocratic oath does not absolve him. It is true that there are some damages one cannot be expected to absorb, and some risks which one cannot be expected to take, on account of the obligation to render aid.

On the other hand, if it is clear that the individual should not commit suicide, from the point of view of his own welfare, or if there is a presumption that he should not (when the only evidence is that a person is discovered unconscious, with the gas turned on), it would seem to be the individual's obligation to intervene, prevent the successful execution of the decision, and see to the availability of competent psychiatric advice and temporary hospitalization, if necessary. Whether one has a right to take such steps when a clearly sane person, after careful reflection over a period of time, comes to the conclusion that an end to his life is what is best for him and what he wants, is very doubtful, even when one thinks his conclusion a mistaken one; it would seem that a man's own considered decision about whether he wants to live must command respect, although one must concede that this could be debated.

The more interesting role in which a person may be cast, however, is that of adviser. It is often important to one who is contemplating suicide to go over his thinking with another, and to feel that a conclusion, one way or the other, has the support of a respected mind. One thing one can obviously do, in rendering the service of advice, is to discuss with the person the various types of issues discussed above, made more specific by the concrete circumstances of his case, and help him find whether, in view, say, of the damage his suicide would do to others, he has a moral obligation to refrain, and whether it is rational or best for him, from the point of view of his own welfare, to take this step or adopt some other plan instead.

To get a person to see what is the rational thing to do is no small job. Even to get a person, in a frame of mind when he is seriously contemplating (or perhaps has already unsuccessfully attempted) suicide, to recognize a plain truth of fact may be a major operation. If a man insists, "I am a complete failure," when it is obvious that by any reasonable standard he is far from that, it may be tremendously difficult to get him to see the fact. But there is another job beyond that of getting a person to see what is the rational thing to do; that is to help him *act* rationally, or *be* rational, when he has conceded what would be the rational thing.

How either of these tasks may be accomplished effectively may be discussed more competently by an experienced psychiatrist than by a philosopher. Loneliness and the absence of human affection are states which exacerbate any other problems; disappointment, reduction to poverty, and so forth, seem less impossible to bear in the presence of the affection of another.

Hence simply to be a friend, or to find someone a friend, may be the largest contribution one can make either to helping a person be rational or see clearly what is rational for him to do; this service may make one who was contemplating suicide feel that there is a future for him which it is possible to face.

NOTES

1. Immanuel Kant, *Lectures on Ethics* (New York: Harper Torchbook, 1963), p. 150.
2. R. B. Brandt, *Ethical Theory* (Englewood Cliffs, N.J.: Prentice-Hall, 1959), pp. 61–82.
3. John Locke, *Two Treatises of Government*, ch. 2.
4. Kant, *Lectures on Ethics,* p. 154.
5. This essay appears in collections of Hume's works.
6. For an argument similar to Kant's, see also St. Thomas Aquinas, *Summa Theologica,* II, II, Q. 64, Art. 5.
7. Immanuel Kant, *The Fundamental Principles of the Metaphysic of Morals,* trans. H. J. Paton (London: The Hutchinson Group, 1948), ch. 2.
8. Aristotle, *Nicomachean Ethics,* Bk. 5, Ch. 10, p. 1138a.
9. St. Thomas Aquinas, *Summa Theologica,* II, II, Q. 64, Art. 5.
10. Sir William Blackstone, *Commentaries,* 4:189; Brown in *Hales v. Petit,* I Plow 253, 75 E.R. 387 (C.B. 1563). Both cited by Norman St. John-Stevas, *Life, Death and the Law* (Bloomington, Ind.: Indiana University Press, 1961), p. 235.

Review and Discussion Questions

1. Assess Brandt's definition of suicide. Does the pilot who stays in the plane commit suicide?

2. Are there suicides that, in your view, show some defect of character and are thus morally blameworthy?

3. Are you persuaded by Brandt's responses to the arguments intended to show that we have some moral obligation to avoid suicide as such? Are there arguments against suicide that Brandt has overlooked?

4. Would it maximize the long-run welfare of everyone affected if people were taught that there is a moral obligation to avoid suicide? Explain your answer.

5. Under what circumstances, if any, would it be rational for a person to commit suicide? Given Brandt's discussion of the decisional errors that people contemplating suicide are

prone to make, how likely is it that the average suicide attempt reflects a rational decision? What implications does this have for our policy toward suicide?

6. Suppose you learned that a friend, acquaintance, or colleague were contemplating suicide. What would you do? What difference would believing that the person's suicide would be rational or irrational make to your actions? Do we ever have a moral obligation to help someone commit suicide?

The Wrongfulness of Euthanasia

J. GAY-WILLIAMS

J. Gay-Williams defines euthanasia as intentionally taking the life of a person who is suffering from some illness or injury from which recovery cannot reasonably be expected. Although ceasing to treat a dying person when the treatment has little hope of success is frequently called "passive euthanasia," Gay-Williams argues that it is not euthanasia at all, because the person is not killed nor is the death of the person intended. He argues, however, that euthanasia, understood as the intentional killing of a person whose condition is hopeless, is both inherently wrong and wrong from the standpoint of self-interest and practical effects.

Study Questions

1. How does Gay-Williams's definition of euthanasia imply that so-called "passive euthanasia" is not really euthanasia at all?

2. What is the "argument from nature" against euthanasia? Why does Gay-Williams believe that euthanasia "sets us against our own nature" and "does violence to our dignity"?

3. In what ways would a policy that permitted euthanasia work against the self-interest of patients?

4. How might such a policy have a corrupting influence on medical practice? Why does Gay-Williams believe that euthanasia as a policy is a "slippery slope"?

MY IMPRESSION IS THAT EUTHANASIA— the idea, if not the practice—is slowly gaining acceptance within our society. Cynics might attribute this to an increasing tendency to de- value human life, but I do not believe this is the major factor. The acceptance is much more likely to be the result of unthinking sympathy and benevolence. Well-publicized, tragic stories like that of Karen Quinlan elicit from us deep feelings of compassion. We think to ourselves, "She and her family would be better off if she were dead." It is an easy step from this very human response to the view that if someone (and others) would be better off dead, then it must be all right to kill that person.[1] Although I respect the compassion that leads to this conclusion, I believe the conclusion is wrong. I want to show that euthanasia is wrong. It is inherently wrong, but it is also wrong judged from the standpoints of self-interest and of practical effects.

Before presenting my arguments to support this claim, it would be well to define "euthanasia." An essential aspect of euthanasia is that it involves taking a human life, either one's own or that of another. Also, the person whose life is taken must be someone who is believed to be suffering from some disease or injury from which recovery cannot reasonably be expected. Finally, the action must be deliberate and intentional. Thus, euthanasia is intentionally taking the life of a presumably hopeless person. Whether the life is one's own or that of another, the taking of it is still euthanasia.

It is important to be clear about the deliberate and intentional aspect of the killing. If a hopeless person is given an injection of the wrong drug by mistake and this causes his death, this is wrongful killing but not euthanasia. The killing cannot be the result of accident. Furthermore, if the person is given an injection of a drug that is believed to be necessary to treat his disease or better his condition and the person dies as a result, then this is neither wrongful killing nor euthanasia. The intention was to make the patient well, not kill him. Similarly, when a patient's condition is such that it is not reasonable to hope that any medical procedures or treatments will save his life, a failure to implement the procedures or treatments is not euthanasia. If the person dies, this will be as a result of his injuries or disease and not because of his failure to receive treatment.

The failure to continue treatment after it has been realized that the patient has little chance of benefitting from it has been characterized by some as "passive euthanasia." This phrase is misleading and mistaken.[2] In such cases, the person involved is not killed (the first essential aspect of euthanasia), nor is the death of the person intended by the withholding of additional treatment (the third essential aspect of euthanasia). The aim may be to spare the person additional and unjustifiable pain, to save him from the indignities of hopeless manipulations, and to avoid increasing the financial and emotional burden on his family. When I buy a pencil it is so that I can use it to write, not to contribute to an increase in the gross national product. This may be the unintended consequence of my action, but it is not the aim of my action. So it is with failing to continue the treatment of a dying person. I intend his death no more than I intend to reduce the GNP by not using medical supplies. His is an unintended dying, and so-called "passive euthanasia" is not euthanasia at all.

1. The Argument from Nature

Every human being has a natural inclination to continue living. Our reflexes and responses fit us to fight attackers, flee wild animals, and dodge out of the way of trucks. In our daily lives we exercise the caution and care necessary to protect ourselves. Our bodies are similarly structured for survival right down to the molecular level. When we are cut, our capillaries seal shut, our blood clots, and fibrogen is produced to start the process of healing the wound. When we are invaded by bacteria, antibodies are produced to fight against the alien organisms, and their remains are swept out of the body by special cells designed for clean-up work.

Euthanasia does violence to this natural goal of survival. It is literally acting against nature because all the processes of nature are bent towards the end of bodily survival. Euthanasia defeats these subtle mechanisms in a way that, in a particular case, disease and injury might not.

It is possible, but not necessary, to make an appeal to revealed religion in this connection.[3]

Man as trustee of his body acts against God, its rightful possessor, when he takes his own life. He also violates the commandment to hold life sacred and never to take it without just and compelling cause. But since this appeal will persuade only those who are prepared to accept that religion has access to revealed truths, I shall not employ this line of argument.

It is enough, I believe, to recognize that the organization of the human body and our patterns of behavioral response make the continuation of life a natural goal. By reason alone, then, we can recognize that euthanasia sets us against our own nature.[4] Furthermore, in doing so, euthanasia does violence to our dignity. Our dignity comes from seeking our ends. When one of our goals is survival, and actions are taken that eliminate that goal, then our natural dignity suffers. Unlike animals, we are conscious through reason of our nature and our ends. Euthanasia involves acting as if this dual nature—inclination towards survival and awareness of this as an end—did not exist. Thus, euthanasia denies our basic human character and requires that we regard ourselves or others as something less than fully human.

2. The Argument from Self-Interest

The above arguments are, I believe, sufficient to show that euthanasia is inherently wrong. But there are reasons for considering it wrong when judged by standards other than reason. Because death is final and irreversible, euthanasia contains within it the possibility that we will work against our own interest if we practice it or allow it to be practiced on us.

Contemporary medicine has high standards of excellence and a proven record of accomplishment, but it does not possess perfect and complete knowledge. A mistaken diagnosis is possible, and so is a mistaken prognosis. Consequently, we may believe that we are dying of a disease when, as a matter of fact, we may not be. We may think that we have no hope of recovery when, as a matter of fact, our chances are quite

good. In such circumstances, if euthanasia were permitted, we would die needlessly. Death is final and the chance of error too great to approve the practice of euthanasia.

Also, there is always the possibility that an experimental procedure or a hitherto untried technique will pull us through. We should at least keep this option open, but euthanasia closes it off. Furthermore, spontaneous remission does occur in many cases. For no apparent reason, a patient simply recovers when those all around him, including his physicians, expected him to die. Euthanasia would just guarantee their expectations and leave no room for the "miraculous" recoveries that frequently occur.

Finally, knowing that we can take our life at any time (or ask another to take it) might well incline us to give up too easily. The will to live is strong in all of us, but it can be weakened by pain and suffering and feelings of hopelessness. If during a bad time we allow ourselves to be killed, we never have a chance to reconsider. Recovery from a serious illness requires that we fight for it, and anything that weakens our determination by suggesting that there is an easy way out is ultimately against our own interest. Also, we may be inclined towards euthanasia because of our concern for others. If we see our sickness and suffering as an emotional and financial burden on our family, we may feel that to leave our life is to make their lives easier.[5] The very presence of the possibility of euthanasia may keep us from surviving when we might.

3. The Argument from Practical Effects

Doctors and nurses are, for the most part, totally committed to saving lives. A life lost is, for them, almost a personal failure, an insult to their skills and knowledge. Euthanasia as a practice might well alter this. It could have a corrupting influence so that in any case that is severe doctors and nurses might not try hard enough to save the patient. They might decide that the patient would simply be "better off dead" and take the steps necessary to make that come about. This attitude could then carry over to their dealings with patients less seriously ill. The result would be an overall decline in the quality of medical care.

Finally, euthanasia as a policy is a slippery slope. A person apparently hopelessly ill may be allowed to take his own life. Then he may be permitted to deputize others to do it for him should he no longer be able to act. The judgment of others then becomes the ruling factor. Already at this point euthanasia is not personal and voluntary, for others are acting "on behalf of" the patient as they see fit. This may well incline them to act on behalf of other patients who have not authorized them to exercise their judgment. It is only a short step, then, from voluntary euthanasia (self-inflicted or authorized), to directed euthanasia administered to a patient who has given no authorization, to involuntary euthanasia conducted as part of a social policy.[6] Recently many psychiatrists and sociologists have argued that we define as "mental illness" those forms of behavior that we disapprove of.[7] This gives us license then to lock up those who display the behavior. The category of the "hopelessly ill" provides the possibility of even worse abuse. Embedded in a social policy, it would give society or its representatives the authority to eliminate all those who might be considered too "ill" to function normally any longer. The dangers of euthanasia are too great to all to run the risk of approving it in any form. The first slippery step may well lead to a serious and harmful fall.

I hope that I have succeeded in showing why the benevolence that inclines us to give approval of euthanasia is misplaced. Euthanasia is inherently wrong because it violates the nature and dignity of human beings. But even those who

are not convinced by this must be persuaded that the potential personal and social dangers inherent in euthanasia are sufficient to forbid our approving it either as a personal practice or as a public policy.

Suffering is surely a terrible thing, and we have a clear duty to comfort those in need and to ease their suffering when we can. But suffering is also a natural part of life with values for the individual and for others that we should not overlook. We may legitimately seek for others and for ourselves an easeful death, as Arthur Dyck has pointed out.[8] Euthanasia, however, is not just an easeful death. It is a wrongful death. Euthanasia is not just dying. It is killing.

NOTES

1. For a sophisticated defense of this position see Philippa Foot, "Euthanasia," *Philosophy and Public Affairs,* vol. 6 (1977), pp. 85–112. Foot does not endorse the radical conclusion that euthanasia, voluntary and involuntary, is always right.

2. James Rachels rejects the distinction between active and passive euthanasia as morally irrelevant in his "Active and Passive Euthanasia," *New England Journal of Medicine,* vol. 292, pp. 78-80. [Reprinted, this volume, pp. 102–106.] But see the criticism by Foot, pp. 100–103.

3. For a defense of this view see J. V. Sullivan, "The Immorality of Euthanasia," in *Beneficent Euthanasia,* ed. Marvin Kohl (Buffalo, New York: Prometheus Books, 1975), pp. 34–44.

4. This point is made by Ray V. McIntyre in "Voluntary Euthanasia: The Ultimate Perversion," *Medical Counterpoint,* vol. 2, 26–29.

5. See McIntyre, p. 28.

6. See Sullivan, "Immorality of Euthanasia," pp. 34–44, for a fuller argument in support of this view.

7. See, for example, Thomas S. Szasz, *The Myth of Mental Illness,* rev. ed. (New York: Harper & Row, 1974).

8. Arthur Dyck, "Beneficent Euthanasia and Benemortasia," in Kohl, op. cit., pp. 117–129.

Review and Discussion Questions

1. Do you agree with Gay-Williams that so-called passive euthanasia is not really euthanasia at all? How would you define euthanasia?

2. Gay-Williams argues that human beings have a natural inclination to continue living and that this urge provides a moral argument against euthanasia. Do you agree? Assess his claim that "euthanasia denies our basic human character and requires that we regard ourselves or others as something less than fully human."

3. How convincing do you find the argument from self-interest? Is Gay-Williams saying that euthanasia can never be rational from the patient's point of view?

4. In your view, how strong is the slippery-slope argument against euthanasia?

5. Can any of Gay-Williams's arguments be used against passive euthanasia as well?

Active and Passive Euthanasia

JAMES RACHELS

The distinction between active and passive euthanasia is widely thought to be of great moral importance. For instance, most doctors believe that, although it may sometimes be permissible to withhold treatment and let a patient die, it can never be permissible to directly kill the patient. In this essay, Professor James Rachels challenges this doctrine. He argues that active euthanasia may be more humane than passive euthanasia, that the conventional doctrine leads one to make life-or-death decisions on morally irrelevant grounds, and that the distinction between killing and letting die makes no moral difference.

Study Questions

1. What is the policy of the American Medical Association, as explained by Rachels?

2. How does Rachels support the contention that active euthanasia can be more humane than passive euthanasia?

3. How does the example about infants with Down's syndrome illustrate the claim that acceptance of the conventional doctrine results in decisions concerning life and death being made on irrelevant grounds?

4. How does Rachels use the hypothetical cases of Smith and Jones to support his argument?

5. How does Rachels explain the generally held feeling that it is worse to kill than to allow to die?

6. What are the implications of Rachels's discussion for the overall morality of euthanasia (whether active or passive)?

Reprinted by permission from The New England Journal of Medicine, *vol. 292, no. 2 (January 9, 1975), pp. 78–80.*

T HE DISTINCTION BETWEEN active and passive euthanasia is thought to be crucial for medical ethics. The idea is that it is permissible, at least in some cases, to withhold treatment and allow a patient to die, but it is never permissible to take any direct action designed to kill the patient. This doctrine seems to be accepted by most doctors, and it is endorsed in a statement adopted by the House of Delegates of the American Medical Association on December 4, 1973:

> The intentional termination of the life of one human being by another—mercy killing—is contrary to that for which the medical profession stands and is contrary to the policy of the American Medical Association.
>
> The cessation of the employment of extraordinary means to prolong the life of the body when there is irrefutable evidence that biological death is imminent is the decision of the patient and/or his immediate family. The advice and judgment of the physician should be freely available to the patient and/or his immediate family.

However, a strong case can be made against this doctrine. In what follows I will set out some of the relevant arguments, and urge doctors to reconsider their views on this matter.

To begin with a familiar type of situation, a patient who is dying of incurable cancer of the throat is in terrible pain, which can no longer be satisfactorily alleviated. He is certain to die within a few days, even if present treatment is continued, but he does not want to go on living for those days since the pain is unbearable. So he asks the doctor for an end to it, and his family joins in the request.

Suppose the doctor agrees to withhold treatment, as the conventional doctrine says he may. The justification for his doing so is that the patient is in terrible agony, and since he is going to die anyway, it would be wrong to prolong his suffering needlessly. But now notice this. If one simply withholds treatment, it may take the pa-

tient longer to die, and so he may suffer more than he would if more direct action were taken and a lethal injection given. This fact provides strong reason for thinking that, once the initial decision not to prolong his agony has been made, active euthanasia is actually preferable to passive euthanasia, rather than the reverse. To say otherwise is to endorse the option that leads to more suffering rather than less, and is contrary to the humanitarian impulse that prompts the decision not to prolong his life in the first place.

Part of my point is that the process of being "allowed to die" can be relatively slow and painful, whereas being given a lethal injection is relatively quick and painless. Let me give a different sort of example. In the United States about one in 600 babies is born with Down's syndrome. Most of these babies are otherwise healthy—that is, with only the usual pediatric care, they will proceed to an otherwise normal infancy. Some, however, are born with congenital defects such as intestinal obstructions that require operations if they are to live. Sometimes, the patients and the doctor will decide not to operate, and let the infant die. Anthony Shaw describes what happens then:

> . . . When surgery is denied [the doctor] must try to keep the infant from suffering while natural forces sap the baby's life away. As a surgeon whose natural inclination is to use the scalpel to fight off death, standing by and watching a salvageable baby die is the most emotionally exhausting experience I know. It is easy at a conference, in a theoretical discussion, to decide that such infants should be allowed to die. It is altogether different to stand by in the nursery and watch as dehydration and infection wither a tiny being over hours and days. This is a terrible ordeal for me and the hospital staff—much more so than for the parents who never set foot in the nursery.[1]

I can understand why some people are opposed to all euthanasia, and insist that such infants must be allowed to live. I think I can also understand why other people favor destroying these babies quickly and painlessly. But why should anyone favor letting "dehydration and infection wither a tiny being over hours and days"? The doctrine that says that a baby may be allowed to dehydrate and wither, but may not be given an injection that would end its life without suffering, seems so patently cruel as to require no further refutation. The strong language is not intended to offend, but only to put the point in the clearest possible way.

My second argument is that the conventional doctrine leads to decisions concerning life and death made on irrelevant grounds.

Consider again the case of the infants with Down's syndrome who need operations for congenital defects unrelated to the syndrome to live. Sometimes, there is no operation, and the baby dies, but when there is no such defect, the baby lives on. Now, an operation such as that to remove an intestinal obstruction is not prohibitively difficult. The reason why such operations are not performed in these cases is, clearly, that the child has Down's syndrome and the parents and the doctor judge that because of that fact it is better for the child to die.

But notice that this situation is absurd, no matter what view one takes of the lives and potentials of such babies. If the life of such an infant is worth preserving, what does it matter if it needs a simple operation? Or, if one thinks it better that such a baby should not live on, what difference does it make that it happens to have an unobstructed intestinal tract? In either case, the matter of life and death is being decided on irrelevant grounds. It is the Down's syndrome, and not the intestines, that is the issue. The matter should be decided, if at all, on that basis, and not be allowed to depend on the essentially irrelevant question of whether the intestinal tract is blocked.

What makes this situation possible, of course, is the idea that when there is an intestinal blockage, one can "let the baby die," but when there is no such defect there is nothing that can be done, for one must not "kill" it. The fact that this idea leads to such results as deciding life or death on irrelevant grounds is another good reason why the doctrine should be rejected.

One reason why so many people think that there is an important moral difference between active and passive euthanasia is that they think killing someone is morally worse than letting someone die. But is it? Is killing, in itself, worse than letting die? To investigate this issue, two cases may be considered that are exactly alike except that one involves killing whereas the other involves letting someone die. Then, it can be asked whether this difference makes any difference to the moral assessments. It is important that the cases be exactly alike, except for this one difference, since otherwise one cannot be confident that it is this difference and not some other that accounts for any variation in the assessments of the two cases. So, let us consider this pair of cases:

In the first, Smith stands to gain a large inheritance if anything should happen to his six-year-old cousin. One evening while the child is taking his bath, Smith sneaks into the bathroom and drowns the child, and then arranges things so that it will look like an accident.

In the second, Jones also stands to gain if anything should happen to his six-year-old cousin. Like Smith, Jones sneaks in planning to drown the child in his bath. However, just as he enters the bathroom Jones sees the child slip and hit his head, and fall face down in the water. Jones is delighted; he stands by, ready to push the child's head back under if it is necessary, but it is not necessary. With only a little thrashing about, the child drowns all by himself, "accidentally," as Jones watches and does nothing.

Now Smith killed the child, whereas Jones "merely" let the child die. That is the only difference between them. Did either man behave better, from a moral point of view? If the difference between killing and letting die were in itself a morally important matter, one should say that Jones's behavior was less reprehensible than

Smith's. But does one really want to say that? I think not. In the first place, both men acted from the same motive, personal gain, and both had exactly the same end in view when they acted. It may be inferred from Smith's conduct that he is a bad man, although that judgment may be withdrawn or modified if certain further facts are learned about him—for example, that he is mentally deranged. But would not the very same thing be inferred about Jones from his conduct? And would not the same further considerations also be relevant to any modification of this judgment? Moreover, suppose Jones pleaded, in his own defense, "After all, I didn't do anything except just stand there and watch the child drown. I didn't kill him; I only let him die." Again, if letting die were in itself less bad than killing, this defense should have at least some weight. But it does not. Such a "defense" can only be regarded as a grotesque perversion of moral reasoning. Morally speaking, it is no defense at all.

Now, it may be pointed out, quite properly, that the cases of euthanasia with which doctors are concerned are not like this at all. They do not involve personal gain or the destruction of normal healthy children. Doctors are concerned only with cases in which the patient's life is of no further use to him, or in which the patient's life has become or will soon become a terrible burden. However, the point is the same in these cases: The bare difference between killing and letting die does not, in itself, make a moral difference. If a doctor lets a patient die, for humane reasons, he is in the same moral position as if he had given the patient a lethal injection for humane reasons. If his decision was wrong—if, for example, the patient's illness was in fact curable—the decision would be equally regrettable no matter which method was used to carry it out. And if the doctor's decision was the right one, the method used is not in itself important.

The AMA policy statement isolates the crucial issue very well: The crucial issue is "the intentional termination of the life of one human being by another." But after identifying this issue, and forbidding "mercy killing," the statement goes on to deny that the cessation of treatment is the intentional termination of a life. This is where the mistake comes in, for what is the cessation of treatment, in these circumstances, if it is not "the intentional termination of the life of one human being by another"? Of course it is exactly that, and if it were not, there would be no point to it.

Many people will find this judgment hard to accept. One reason, I think, is that it is very easy to conflate the question of whether killing is, in itself, worse than letting die, with the very different question of whether most actual cases of killing are more reprehensible than most actual cases of letting die. Most actual cases of killing are clearly terrible (think, for example, of all the murders reported in the newspapers), and one hears of such cases everyday. On the other hand, one hardly ever hears of a case of letting die, except for the actions of doctors who are motivated by humanitarian reasons. So one learns to think of killing in a much worse light than of letting die. But this does not mean that there is something about killing that makes it in itself worse than letting die, for it is not the bare difference between killing and letting die that makes the difference in these cases. Rather, the other factors—the murderer's motive of personal gain, for example, contrasted with the doctor's humanitarian motivation—account for different reactions to the different cases.

I have argued that killing is not in itself any worse than letting die; if my contention is right, it follows that active euthanasia is not any worse than passive euthanasia. What arguments can be given on the other side? The most common, I believe, is the following:

"The important difference between active and passive euthanasia is that in passive euthanasia, the doctor does not do anything to bring about the patient's death. The doctor does nothing, and the patient dies of whatever ills already afflict him. In active euthanasia, however, the doctor does something to bring about the patient's death. He kills him. The doctor who gives the patient with cancer a lethal injection has himself caused his patient's death; whereas if he merely ceases treatment, the cancer is the cause of death."

A number of points need to be made here. The first is that it is not exactly correct to say that in passive euthanasia the doctor does nothing, for he does do one thing that is very important: He lets the patient die. "Letting someone die" is certainly different, in some respects, from other types of action—mainly in that it is a kind of action that one may perform by way of not performing certain other actions. For example, one may let a patient die by way of not giving medication, just as one may insult someone by way of not shaking his hand. But for any purpose of moral assessment, it is a type of action nonetheless. The decision to let a patient die is subject to moral appraisal in the same way that a decision to kill him would be subject to moral appraisal: It may be assessed as wise or unwise, compassionate or sadistic, right or wrong. If a doctor deliberately let a patient die who was suffering from a routinely curable illness, the doctor would certainly be to blame for what he had done, just as he would be to blame if he had needlessly killed the patient. Charges against him would then be appropriate. If so, it would be no defense at all for him to insist that he didn't "do anything." He would have done something very serious indeed, for he let his patient die.

Fixing the cause of death may be very important from a legal point of view, for it may determine whether criminal charges are brought against the doctor. But I do not think that this notion can be used to show a moral difference between active and passive euthanasia. The reason why it is considered bad to be the cause of someone's death is that death is regarded as a great evil—and so it is. However, if it has been decided that euthanasia—even passive euthanasia—is desirable in a given case, it has also been decided that in this instance death is no greater

an evil than the patient's continued existence. And if this is true, the usual reason for not wanting to be the cause of someone's death simply does not apply.

Finally, doctors may think that all of this is only of academic interest—the sort of thing that philosophers may worry about but that has no practical bearing on their own work. After all, doctors must be concerned about the legal consequences of what they do, and active euthanasia is clearly forbidden by the law. But even so, doctors should also be concerned with the fact that the law is forcing upon them a moral doctrine that may well be indefensible, and has a considerable effect on their practices. Of course, most doctors are not now in the position of being coerced in this matter, for they do not regard themselves as merely going along with what the law requires. Rather, in statements such as the AMA policy statement that I have quoted, they are endorsing this doctrine as a central point of medical ethics. In that statement, active euthanasia is condemned not merely as illegal but as "contrary to that for which the medical profession stands," whereas passive euthanasia is approved. However, the preceding considerations suggest that there is really no moral difference between the two, considered in themselves (there may be important moral differences in some cases in their *consequences*, but, as I pointed out, these differences may make active euthanasia, and not passive euthanasia, the morally preferable option). So, whereas doctors may have to discriminate between active and passive euthanasia to satisfy the law, they should not do any more than that. In particular, they should not give the distinction any added authority and weight by writing it into official statements of medical ethics.

NOTE

1. A. Shaw, "Doctor, Do We Have a Choice?" *The New York Times Magazine,* January 30, 1972, p. 54.

Review and Discussion Questions

1. Has Rachels fairly interpreted the American Medical Association's statement? Does that policy statement support the handling of the infants with Down's syndrome described by Rachels?

2. Has Rachels overlooked or failed to deal adequately with any arguments in support of the conventional doctrine?

3. Are there any arguments that might be given against Rachels's view that "killing is not in itself any worse than letting die"?

4. Would you agree with Rachels that, "if a doctor lets a patient die, for humane reasons, he is in the same moral position as if he had given the patient a lethal injection for humane reasons"? Explain why or why not.

5. How would a critic of euthanasia like Gay-Williams respond to Rachels's arguments?

Active and Passive Euthanasia: An Impertinent Distinction?

THOMAS D. SULLIVAN

In this essay, Professor Thomas D. Sullivan of the College of St. Thomas in St. Paul, Minnesota, responds directly to James Rachels's previous article. Sullivan upholds what he calls the traditional doctrine that it is impermissible to terminate intentionally the life of a patient, although it may be permissible in some cases to cease the employment of "extraordinary means" of preserving life. Sullivan argues that Rachels has misinterpreted this view, which does not, according to Sullivan, depend on the distinction between killing and letting die. Rather, the doctrine forbids the intentional termination of life, whether by killing or letting die. The withdrawal of extraordinary means of life support, however, need not involve the intention to terminate life, even if death is foreseen.

Study Questions

1. What is the central objection of writers like Rachels to the position adopted by the American Medical Association (AMA)?

2. According to Sullivan, how has Rachels misinterpreted the AMA statement? How does Sullivan interpret the traditional doctrine?

From Human Life Review, *vol. III, no. 3 (Summer 1977), pp. 40–46. Reprinted with permission from The Human Life Foundation, Inc., 150 East 35th Street, New York, N.Y. 10016.*

3. According to the traditional view, why is it not automatically wrong to withhold extraordinary life support from a patient even though one can foresee that the decision to withhold it will hasten death? What does the traditional doctrine say about withholding ordinary means of life support?

Because of recent advances in medical technology, it is today possible to save or prolong the lives of many persons who in an earlier era would have quickly perished. Unhappily, however, it often is impossible to do so without committing the patient and his or her family to a future filled with sorrows. Modern methods of neurosurgery can successfully close the opening at the base of the spine of a baby born with severe myelomeningocele, but do nothing to relieve the paralysis that afflicts it from the waist down or to remedy the patient's incontinence of stool and urine. Antibiotics and skin grafts can spare the life of a victim of severe and massive burns, but fail to eliminate the immobilizing contractions of arms and legs, the extreme pain, and the hideous disfigurement of the face. It is not surprising, therefore, that physicians and moralists in increasing number recommend that assistance should not be given to such patients, and that some have even begun to advocate the deliberate hastening of death by medical means, provided informed consent has been given by the appropriate parties.

The latter recommendation consciously and directly conflicts with what might be called the "traditional" view of the physician's role. The traditional view, as articulated, for example, by the House of Delegates of the American Medical Association in 1973, declared:

> The intentional termination of the life of one human being by another—mercy killing—is contrary to that for which the medical profession stands and is contrary to the policy of the American Medical Association.
>
> The cessation of the employment of extraordinary means to prolong the life of the body when there is irrefutable evidence that biological death is imminent is the decision of the patient and/or his immediate family. The advice and judgment of the physician should be freely available to the patient and/or his immediate family.

Basically this view involves two points: (1) that it is impermissible for the doctor or anyone else to terminate intentionally the life of a patient, but (2) that it is permissible in some cases to cease the employment of "extraordinary means" of preserving life, even though the death of the patient is a foreseeable consequence.

Does this position really make sense? Recent criticism charges that it does not. The heart of the complaint is that the traditional view arbitrarily rules out all cases of intentionally acting to terminate life, but permits what is in fact the moral equivalent, letting patients die. This accusation has been clearly articulated by James Rachels in a widely-read article . . . entitled "Active and Passive Euthanasia."[1] . . .

In essence . . . the objection to the position adopted by the A.M.A. of Rachels and those who argue like him is that it endorses a highly questionable moral distinction between killing and letting die, which, if accepted, leads to indefensible medical decisions. Nowhere does Rachels quite come out and say that he favors active euthanasia in some cases, but the implication is clear. Nearly everyone holds that it is sometimes pointless to prolong the process of dying and that in those cases it is morally permissible to let a patient die even though a few hours or days could be salvaged by procedures that would also increase the agonies of the dying. But if it is impossible to defend a general distinction between letting people die and acting to terminate their lives directly, then it would seem that active euthanasia also may be morally permissible.

Now what shall we make of all this? It *is* cruel to stand by and watch a Down's baby die an agonizing death when a simple operation would remove the intestinal obstruction, but to offer the excuse that in failing to operate we didn't *do* anything to bring about death is an example of moral evasiveness comparable to the excuse Jones would offer for his action of "merely" letting his cousin die. Furthermore, it is true that if someone is trying to bring about the death of another human being, then it makes little difference from the moral point of view if his purpose is achieved by action or by malevolent omission, as in the cases of Jones and Smith.

But if we acknowledge this, are we obliged to give up the traditional view expressed by the A.M.A. statement? Of course not. To begin with, we are hardly obliged to assume the Jones-like role Rachels assigns the defender of the traditional view. We have the option of operating on the Down's baby and saving its life. Rachels mentions that possibility only to hurry past it as if that is not what his opposition would do. But, of course, that is precisely the course of action most defenders of the traditional position would choose.

Secondly, while it may be that the reason some rather confused people give for upholding the traditional view is that they think killing someone is always worse than letting them die, nobody who gives the matter much thought puts it that way. Rather they say that killing someone is clearly morally worse than not killing them, and killing them can be done by acting to bring about their death or by refusing ordinary means to keep them alive in order to bring about the same goal.

What I am suggesting is that Rachels' objections leave the position he sets out to criticize untouched. It is worth noting that the jargon of active and passive euthanasia—and it is jargon—does not appear in the resolution. Nor does the resolution state or imply the distinction Rachels

attacks, a distinction that puts a moral premium on overt behavior—moving or not moving one's parts—while totally ignoring the intentions of the agent. That no such distinction is being drawn seems clear from the fact that the A.M.A. resolution speaks approvingly of ceasing to use extraordinary means in certain cases, and such withdrawals might easily involve bodily movement, for example unplugging an oxygen machine.

In addition to saddling his opposition with an indefensible distinction it doesn't make, Rachels proceeds to ignore one that it does make—one that is crucial to a just interpretation of the view. Recall the A.M.A. allows the withdrawal of what it calls extra-ordinary means of preserving life; clearly the contrast here is with ordinary means. Though in its short statement those expressions are not defined, the definition Paul Ramsey refers to as standard in his book, *The Patient as Person,* seems to fit.

> Ordinary means of preserving life are all medicines, treatments, and operations, which offer a reasonable hope of benefit for the patient and which can be obtained and used without excessive expense, pain, and other inconveniences.
>
> Extra-ordinary means of preserving life are all those medicines, treatments, and operations which cannot be obtained without excessive expense, pain, or other inconvenience, or which, if used, would not offer a reasonable hope of benefit.[2]

Now with this distinction in mind, we can see how the traditional view differs from the position Rachels mistakes for it. The traditional view is that the intentional termination of human life is impermissible, irrespective of whether this goal is brought about by action or inaction. Is the action or refraining *aimed at* producing a death? Is the termination of life *sought, chosen or planned*? Is the intention deadly? If so, the act or omission is wrong.

But we all know it is entirely possible that the unwillingness of a physician to use extraordinary means for preserving life may be prompted not by a determination to bring about death, but by other motives. For example, he may realize that further treatment may offer little hope of reversing the dying process and/or be excruciating, as in the case when a massively necrotic bowel condition in a neonate is out of control. The doctor who does what he can to comfort the infant but does not submit it to further treatment or surgery may foresee that the decision will hasten death, but it certainly doesn't follow from that fact that he intends to bring about its death. It is, after all, entirely possible to foresee that something will come about as a result of one's conduct without intending the consequence or side effect. If I drive downtown, I can foresee that I'll wear out my tires a little, but I don't drive downtown with the intention of wearing out my tires. And if I choose to forgo my exercises for a few days, I may think that as a result my physical condition will deteriorate a little, but I don't omit my exercise with a view to running myself down. And if you have to fill a position and select Green, who is better qualified for the post than her rival Brown, you needn't appoint Mrs. Green with the intention of hurting Mr. Brown, though you may foresee that Mr. Brown will feel hurt. And if a country extends its general education programs to its illiterate masses, it is predictable the suicide rate will go up, but even if the public officials are aware of this fact, it doesn't follow that they initiate the program with a view to making the suicide rate go up. In general, then, it is not the case that all the foreseeable consequences and side effects of our conduct are necessarily intended. And it is because the physician's withdrawal of extraordinary means can be otherwise motivated than by a desire to bring about the predictable death of the patient that such action cannot categorically be ruled out as wrong.

But the refusal to use ordinary means is an altogether different matter. After all, what is the point of refusing assistance which offers reasonable hope of benefit to the patient without involving excessive pain or other inconvenience?

How could it be plausibly maintained that the refusal is not motivated by a desire to bring about the death of the patient? The traditional position, therefore, rules out not only direct actions to bring about death, such as giving a patient a lethal injection, but malevolent omissions as well, such as not providing minimum care for the newborn.

The reason the A.M.A. position sounds so silly when one listens to arguments such as Rachels' is that he slights the distinction between ordinary and extra-ordinary means and then drums on cases where *ordinary* means are refused. The impression is thereby conveyed that the traditional doctrine sanctions omissions that are morally indistinguishable in a substantive way from direct killings, but then incomprehensibly refuses to permit quick and painless termination of life. If the traditional doctrine would approve of Jones' standing by with a grin on his face while his young cousin drowned in a tub, or letting a Down's baby wither and die when ordinary means are available to preserve its life, it would indeed be difficult to see how anyone could defend it. But so to conceive the traditional doctrine is simply to misunderstand it. It is not a doctrine that rests on some supposed distinction between "active" and "passive euthanasia," whatever those words are supposed to mean, nor on a distinction between moving and not moving our bodies. It is simply a prohibition against intentional killing, which includes both direct actions and malevolent omissions.

To summarize—the traditional position represented by the A.M.A. statement is not incoherent. It acknowledges, or more accurately, insists upon the fact that withholding ordinary means to sustain life may be tantamount to killing. The traditional position can be made to appear incoherent only by imposing upon it a crude idea of killing held by none of its more articulate advocates.

Thus the criticism of Rachels and other reformers, misapprehending its target, leaves the traditional position untouched. That position is simply a prohibition of murder. . . .

I fully realize that there are times when those who have the noble duty to tend the sick and the dying are deeply moved by the sufferings of their patients, especially of the very young and the very old, and desperately wish they could do more than comfort and companion them. Then, perhaps, it seems that universal moral principles are mere abstractions having little to do with the agony of the dying. But of course we do not see best when our eyes are filled with tears.

NOTES

1. *New England Journal of Medicine*, 292; 78–80. Jan. 9, 1975. [Reprinted, this volume, pp. 100–104.]

2. Paul Ramsey, *The Patient as Person* (New Haven and London: Yale University Press, 1970), p. 122. . . .

Review and Discussion Questions

1. Do you agree that Rachels has misinterpreted the traditional view as expressed by the AMA statement? Explain. Does Sullivan's account of the traditional doctrine make it more plausible?

2. Can one uphold the traditional doctrine and yet give up the position that killing is worse than letting die?

3. Sullivan writes that the traditional doctrine is "simply a prohibition of murder." Is it fair to say that active euthanasia is murder but that a refusal to use extraordinary means of life support is not? What about the withdrawal of means of life support that are not extraordinary?

4. How plausible do you find the traditional doctrine as defended by Sullivan? Can a moral argument be made in defense of active or intentional euthanasia?

More Impertinent Distinctions and a Defense of Active Euthanasia

JAMES RACHELS

In this essay, James Rachels responds to Thomas D. Sullivan's criticisms in the previous article. Rachels rejects the idea, which is at the heart of the traditional doctrine upheld by Sullivan, that a person's intention is relevant to determining whether the person's action is right or wrong, and he argues that the distinction between ordinary and extraordinary means of treatment does not furnish a sound ethical guide. Rachels then advances two arguments—the argument from mercy and the Golden Rule argument—in support of active euthanasia.

Reprinted by permission of the author from Thomas A. Mappes and Jane S. Zembaty, eds., Biomedical Ethics, *3rd ed. (1991).*

Study Questions

1. What are Rachels's reasons for arguing that intention is irrelevant for assessing the rightness or wrongness of an action?

2. Explain Rachels's argument that the distinction between ordinary and extraordinary means of support does not have the significance traditionally attributed to it. Why is he critical of the definitions of *ordinary* and *extraordinary* that Sullivan gives?

3. What are Rachels's reservations about the utilitarian version of the argument from mercy? How does he modify that argument?

4. What is the Golden Rule argument in defense of active euthanasia?

MANY THINKERS, including almost all orthodox Catholics, believe that euthanasia is immoral. They oppose killing patients in any circumstances whatever. However, they think it is all right, in some special circumstances, to allow patients to die by withholding treatment. The American Medical Association's policy statement on mercy killing supports this traditional view. In my paper "Active and Passive Euthanasia,"[1] I argued, against the traditional view, that there is in fact no moral difference between killing and letting die—if one is permissible, then so is the other.

Professor Sullivan[2] does not dispute my argument; instead he dismisses it as irrelevant. The traditional doctrine, he says, does not appeal to or depend on the distinction between killing and letting die. Therefore, arguments against that distinction "leave the traditional position untouched."

Is my argument really irrelevant? I don't see how it can be. As Sullivan himself points out,

> Nearly everyone holds that it is sometimes pointless to prolong the process of dying and that in those cases it is morally permissible to let a patient die even though a few hours or days could be salvaged by procedures that would also increase the agonies of the dying. But if it is impossible to defend a general distinction between letting people die and acting to terminate their lives directly, then it would seem that active euthanasia also may be morally permissible. [pp. 106–107]

But traditionalists like Professor Sullivan hold that active euthanasia—the direct killing of patients—is *not* morally permissible; so, if my argument is sound, their view must be mistaken. I cannot agree, then, that my argument "leaves the traditional position untouched."

However, I shall not press this point. Instead I shall present some further arguments against the traditional position, concentrating on those elements of the position which Professor Sullivan himself thinks most important. According to him, what is important is, first, that we should never *intentionally* terminate the life of a patient, either by action or omission, and second, that we may cease or omit treatment of a patient, knowing that this will result in death, only if the means of treatment involved are *extraordinary*.

Intentional and Nonintentional Termination of Life

We can, of course, distinguish between what a person does and the intention with which he does it. But what is the significance of this distinction for ethics?

> The traditional view [says Sullivan] is that the intentional termination of human life is impermissible, irrespective of whether this goal is brought about by action or inaction. Is the action of refraining *aimed at* producing a death?

Is the termination of life *sought, chosen or planned*? Is the intention deadly? If so, the act or omission is wrong. [p. 107]

Thus on the traditional view there is a very definite sort of moral relation between act and intention. An act which is otherwise permissible may become impermissible if it is accompanied by a bad intention. The intention makes the act wrong.

There is reason to think that this view of the relation between act and intention is mistaken. Consider the following example. Jack visits his sick and lonely grandmother, and entertains her for the afternoon. He loves her and his only intention is to cheer her up. Jill also visits the grandmother, and provides an afternoon's cheer. But Jill's concern is that the old lady will soon be making her will; Jill wants to be included among the heirs. Jack also knows that his visit might influence the making of the will, in his favor, but that is not part of his plan. Thus Jack and Jill do the very same thing—they both spend an afternoon cheering up their sick grandmother—and what they do may lead to the same consequences, namely influencing the will. But their intentions are quite different.

Jack's intention was honorable and Jill's was not. Could we say on that account that what Jack did was right, but what Jill did was wrong? No; for Jack and Jill did the very same thing, and if they did the same thing, we cannot say that one acted rightly and the other wrongly.* Consistency requires that we assess similar actions similarly. Thus if we are trying to evaluate their *actions*, we must say about one what we say about the other.

---

* It might be objected that they did not "do the same thing," for Jill manipulated and deceived her grandmother, while Jack did not. If their actions are described in this way, then it may seem that "what Jill did" was wrong, while "what Jack did" was not. However, this description of what Jill did incorporates her intention into the description of the act. In the present context we must keep the act and the intention separate, in order to discuss the relation between them. If they *cannot* be held separate, then the traditional view makes no sense.

However, if we are trying to assess Jack's *character*, or Jill's, things are very different. Even though their actions were similar, Jack seems admirable for what he did, while Jill does not. What Jill did—comforting an elderly sick relative—was a morally good thing, but we would not think well of her for it since she was only scheming after the old lady's money. Jack, on the other hand, did a good thing *and* he did it with an admirable intention. Thus we think well, not only of what Jack did, but of Jack.

The traditional view, as presented by Professor Sullivan, says that the intention with which an act is done is relevant to determining whether the act is right. The example of Jack and Jill suggests that, on the contrary, the intention is not relevant to deciding whether the *act* is right or wrong, but instead it is relevant to assessing the character of the person who does the act, which is very different.

Now let us turn to an example that concerns more important matters of life and death. This example is adapted from one used by Sullivan himself (p. 108). A massively necrotic bowel condition in a neonate is out of control. Dr. White realizes that further treatment offers little hope of reversing the dying process and will only increase the suffering; so, he does not submit the infant to further treatment—even though he knows that this decision will hasten death. However, Dr. White does not seek, choose, or plan that death, so it is not part of his intention that the baby dies.

Dr. Black is faced with a similar case. A massively necrotic bowel condition in a neonate is out of control. He realizes that further treatment offers little hope of saving the baby and will only increase its suffering. He decides that it is better for the baby to die a bit sooner than to go on suffering pointlessly; so, with the intention of letting the baby die, he ceases treatment.

According to the traditional position, Dr. White's action was acceptable, but Dr. Black acted wrongly. However, this assessment faces the same problem we encountered before. Dr.

White and Dr. Black did *the very same thing:* their handling of the cases was identical. Both doctors ceased treatment, knowing that the baby would die sooner, and both did so because they regarded continued treatment as pointless, given the infants' prospects. So how could one's action be acceptable and the other's not? There was, of course, a subtle difference in their *attitudes* toward what they did. Dr. Black said to himself, "I want this baby to die now, rather than later, so that it won't suffer more; so I won't continue the treatment." A defender of the traditional view might choose to condemn Dr. Black for this, and say that his character is defective (although I would not say that); but the traditionalist should not say that Dr. Black's *action* was wrong on that account, at least not if he wants to go on saying that Dr. White's action was right. A pure heart cannot make a wrong act right; neither can an impure heart make a right act wrong. As in the case of Jack and Jill, the intention is relevant, not to determining the rightness of actions, but to assessing the character of the people who act.

There is a general lesson to be learned here. The rightness or wrongness of an act is determined by the reasons for or against it. Suppose you are trying to decide, in this example, whether treatment should be continued. What are the reasons for and against this course of action? On the one hand, if treatment is ceased the baby will die very soon. On the other hand, the baby will die eventually anyway, even if treatment is continued. It has no chance of growing up. Moreover, if its life is prolonged, its suffering will be prolonged as well, and the medical resources used will be unavailable to others who would have a better chance of a satisfactory cure. In light of all this, you may well decide against continued treatment. But notice that there is no mention here of anybody's intentions. The intention you would have, if you decided to cease treatment, is not one of the things you need to consider. It is not among the reasons either for or against the action. That is

why it is irrelevant to determining whether the action is right.

In short, a person's intention is relevant to an assessment of his character. The fact that a person intended so-and-so by his action may be a reason for thinking him a good or a bad person. But the intention is not relevant to determining whether the act itself is morally right. The rightness of the act must be decided on the basis of the objective reasons for or against it. It is permissible to let the baby die, in Sullivan's example, because of the facts about the baby's condition and its prospects—not because of anything having to do with anyone's intentions. Thus the traditional view is mistaken on this point.

Ordinary and Extraordinary Means of Treatment

The American Medical Association policy statement says that life-sustaining treatment may sometimes be stopped if the means of treatment are "extraordinary"; the implication is that "ordinary" means of treatment may not be withheld. The distinction between ordinary and extraordinary treatments is crucial to orthodox Catholic thought in this area, and Professor Sullivan reemphasizes its importance: he says that, while a physician may sometimes rightly refuse to use extraordinary means to prolong life, "the refusal to use ordinary means is an altogether different matter." [p. 108]

However, upon reflection it is clear that it is sometimes permissible to omit even very ordinary sorts of treatments.

> Suppose that a diabetic patient long accustomed to self-administration of insulin falls victim to terminal cancer, or suppose that a terminal cancer patient suddenly develops diabetes. Is he in the first case obliged to continue, and in the second case obliged to begin, insulin treatment and die painfully of cancer, or in either or both cases may the patient choose rather to pass into diabetic coma and an earlier

death? . . . What of the conscious patient suffering from painful incurable disease who suddenly gets pneumonia? Or an old man slowly deteriorating who from simply being inactive and recumbent gets pneumonia: Are we to use antibiotics in a likely successful attack upon this disease which from time immemorial has been called "the old man's friend"?[3]

These examples are provided by Paul Ramsey, a leading theological ethicist. Even so conservative a thinker as Ramsey is sympathetic with the idea that, in such cases, life-prolonging treatment is not mandatory: the insulin and the antibiotics need not be used. Yet surely insulin and antibiotics are "ordinary" treatments by today's medical standards. They are common, easily administered, and cheap. There is nothing exotic about them. So it appears that the distinction between ordinary and extraordinary means does not have the significance traditionally attributed to it.

But what of the *definitions* of "ordinary" and "extraordinary" means which Sullivan provides? Quoting Ramsey, he says that

> Ordinary means of preserving life are all medicines, treatments, and operations, which offer a reasonable hope of benefit for the patient and which can be obtained and used without excessive expense, pain, and other inconveniences.
>
> Extra-ordinary means of preserving life are all those medicines, treatments, and operations which cannot be obtained without excessive expense, pain, or other inconvenience, or which, if used, would not offer a reasonable hope of benefit. [p. 107]

Do these definitions provide us with a useful distinction—one that can be used in determining when a treatment is mandatory and when it is not?

The first thing to notice is the way the word "excessive" functions in these definitions. It is said that a treatment is extraordinary if it cannot be obtained without *excessive* expense or pain. But when is an expense "excessive"? Is a cost of $10,000 excessive? If it would save the life of a young woman and restore her to perfect health, $10,000 does not seem excessive. But if it would only prolong the life of Ramsey's cancer-stricken diabetic a short while, perhaps $10,000 is excessive. The point is not merely that what is excessive changes from case to case. The point is that what is excessive *depends on* whether it would be a good thing for the life in question to be prolonged.

Second, we should notice the use of the word "benefit" in the definitions. It is said that ordinary treatments offer a reasonable hope of *benefit* for the patient; and that treatments are extraordinary if they will not benefit the patient. But how do we tell if a treatment will benefit the patient? Remember that we are talking about life-prolonging treatments; the "benefit," if any, is the continuation of life. Whether continued life is a benefit depends on the details of the particular case. For a person with a painful terminal illness, a temporarily continued life may not be a benefit. For a person in irreversible coma, such as Karen Quinlan, continued biological existence is almost certainly not a benefit. On the other hand, for a person who can be cured and resume a normal life, life-sustaining treatment definitely is a benefit. Again, the point is that in order to decide whether life-sustaining treatment is a benefit we must *first* decide whether it would be a good thing for the life in question to be prolonged.

Therefore, these definitions do not mark out a distinction that can be used to help us decide when treatment may be omitted. We cannot by using the definitions identify which treatments are extraordinary, and then use that information to determine whether the treatment may be omitted. For the definitions require that we must *already* have decided the moral questions of life and death *before* we can answer the question of which treatments are extraordinary!

We are brought, then, to this conclusion about the distinction between ordinary and extraordinary means. If we apply the distinction in a straightforward, commonsense way, the traditional doctrine is false, for it is clear that it is sometimes permissible to omit ordinary treatments. On the other hand, if we define the terms as suggested by Ramsey and Sullivan, the distinction is useless in practical decision-making. In either case, the distinction provides no help in formulating an acceptable ethic of letting die.

To summarize what has been said so far, the distinction between killing and letting die has no moral importance; on that Professor Sullivan and I agree. He, however, contends that the distinctions between intentional and nonintentional termination of life, and ordinary and extraordinary means, must be at the heart of a correct moral view. I believe that the arguments given above refute this view. Those distinctions are no better than the first one. The traditional view is mistaken.

In my original paper I did not argue in favor of active euthanasia. I merely argued that active and passive euthanasia are equivalent: *if* one is acceptable, so is the other. However, Professor Sullivan correctly inferred that I do endorse active euthanasia. I believe that it is morally justified in some instances and that at least two strong arguments support this position. The first is the argument from mercy; the second is the argument from the Golden Rule.

The Argument from Mercy

Preliminary statement of the argument

The single most powerful argument in support of euthanasia is the argument from mercy. It is also an exceptionally simple argument, at least in its main idea, which makes one uncomplicated point. Terminal patients sometimes suffer pain so horrible that it is beyond the comprehension of those who have not actually experienced it. Their suffering can be so terrible that we do not like even to read about it or think about it; we recoil even from the descriptions of

such agony. The argument from mercy says: Euthanasia is justified because it provides an end to *that*.

The great Irish satirist Jonathan Swift took eight years to die, while, in the words of Joseph Fletcher, "His mind crumbled to pieces."[4] At times the pain in his blinded eyes was so intense he had to be restrained from tearing them out with his own hands. Knives and other potential instruments of suicide had to be kept from him. For the last three years of his life, he could do nothing but sit and drool; and when he finally died it was only after convulsions that lasted thirty-six hours.

Swift died in 1745. Since then, doctors have learned how to eliminate much of the pain that accompanies terminal illness, but the victory has been far from complete. So, here is a more modern example.

Stewart Alsop was a respected journalist who died in 1975 of a rare form of cancer. Before he died, he wrote movingly of his experiences as a terminal patient. Although he had not thought much about euthanasia before, he came to approve of it after rooming briefly with someone he called Jack:

> The third night I roomed with Jack in our tiny double room in the solid-tumor ward of the cancer clinic of the National Institutes of Health in Bethesda, Md., a terrible thought occurred to me.
>
> Jack had a melanoma in his belly, a malignant solid tumor that the doctors guessed was about the size of a softball. The cancer had started a few months before with a small tumor in his left shoulder, and there had been several operations since. The doctors planned to remove the softball-sized tumor, but they knew Jack would soon die. The cancer had metastasized—it had spread beyond control.
>
> Jack was good-looking, about 28, and brave. He was in constant pain, and his doctor had prescribed an intravenous shot of a synthetic opiate—a pain-killer, or analgesic—every four hours. His wife spent many of the daylight hours with him, and she would sit or lie on his

bed and pat him all over, as one pats a child, only more methodically, and this seemed to help control the pain. But at night, when his pretty wife had left (wives cannot stay overnight at the NIH clinic) and darkness fell, the pain would attack without pity.

At the prescribed hour, a nurse would give Jack a shot of the synthetic analgesic, and this would control the pain for perhaps two hours or a bit more. Then he would begin to moan, or whimper, very low, as though he didn't want to wake me. Then he would begin to howl, like a dog.

When this happened, either he or I would ring for a nurse, and ask for a pain-killer. She would give him some codeine or the like by mouth, but it never did any real good—it affected him no more than half an aspirin might affect a man who had just broken his arm. Always the nurse would explain as encouragingly as she could that there was not long to go before the next intravenous shot—"Only about 50 minutes now." And always poor Jack's whimpers and howls would become more loud and frequent until at last the blessed relief came.

The third night of this routine, the terrible thought occurred to me: "If Jack were a dog," I thought, "what would be done with him?" The answer was obvious: the pound, and chloroform. No human being with a spark of pity could let a living thing suffer so, to no good end.[5]

The NIH clinic is, of course, one of the most modern and best-equipped hospitals we have. Jack's suffering was not the result of poor treatment in some backward rural facility; it was the inevitable product of his disease, which medical science was powerless to prevent.

I have quoted Alsop at length not for the sake of indulging in gory details but to give a clear idea of the kind of suffering we are talking about. We should not gloss over these facts with euphemistic language, or squeamishly avert our eyes from them. For only by keeping them firmly and vividly in mind can we appreciate the full force of the argument from mercy: If a person prefers—and even begs for—death as the only alternative to lingering on *in this kind of torment,* only to die anyway after a while, then surely it is not immoral to help this person die sooner. As Alsop put it, "No human being with a spark of pity could let a living thing suffer so, to no good end."

The utilitarian version of the argument

In connection with this argument, the utilitarians should be mentioned. They argue that actions and social policies should be judged right or wrong *exclusively* according to whether they cause happiness or misery; and they argue that when judged by this standard, euthanasia turns out to be morally acceptable. The utilitarian argument may be elaborated as follows:

1. Any action or social policy is morally right if it serves to increase the amount of happiness in the world or to decrease the amount of misery. Conversely, an action or social policy is morally wrong if it serves to decrease happiness or to increase misery.
2. The policy of killing, at their own request, hopelessly ill patients who are suffering great pain, would decrease the amount of misery in the world. (An example could be Alsop's friend Jack.)
3. Therefore, such a policy would be morally right.

The first premise of this argument, (1), states the Principle of Utility, which is the basic utilitarian assumption. Today most philosophers think that this principle is wrong, because they think that the promotion of happiness and the avoidance of misery are not the *only* morally important things. Happiness, they say, is only one among many values that should be promoted: freedom, justice, and a respect for people's rights are also important. To take one example: People *might* be happier if there were no freedom of religion; for, if everyone adhered to the same religious beliefs, there would be greater harmony among people. There would be no unhappiness caused within families by Jewish girls marrying Catholic boys, and so forth. Moreover, if people were brainwashed well enough, no one would mind not having freedom of choice. Thus happiness would be increased. But, the argument continues, even if happiness *could* be increased this way, it would not be right to deny people freedom of religion, because people have a right to make their own choices. Therefore, the first premise of the utilitarian argument is unacceptable.

There is a related difficulty for utilitarianism, which connects more directly with the topic of euthanasia. Suppose a person is leading a miserable life—full of more unhappiness than happiness—but does *not* want to die. This person thinks that a miserable life is better than none at all. Now I assume that we would all agree that the person should not be killed; that would be plain, unjustifiable murder. Yet it *would* decrease the amount of misery in the world if we killed this person—it would lead to an increase in the balance of happiness over unhappiness—and so it is hard to see how, on strictly utilitarian grounds, it could be wrong. Again, the Principle of Utility seems to be an inadequate guide for determining right and wrong. So we are on shaky ground if we rely on *this* version of the argument from mercy for a defense of euthanasia.

Doing what is in everyone's best interests

Although the foregoing utilitarian argument is faulty, it is nevertheless based on a sound idea. For even if the promotion of happiness and avoidance of misery are not the *only* morally important things, they are still very important. So, when an action or a social policy would decrease misery, that is *a* very strong reason in its favor. In the cases of voluntary euthanasia we are now considering, great suffering is eliminated, and since the patient requests it, there is no question of violating individual rights. That is why, re-

gardless of the difficulties of the Principle of Utility, the utilitarian version of the argument still retains considerable force.

I want now to present a somewhat different version of the argument from mercy, which is inspired by utilitarianism but which avoids the difficulties of the foregoing version by not making the Principle of Utility a premise of the argument. I believe that the following argument is sound and proves that active euthanasia *can* be justified:

1. If an action promotes the best interests of *everyone* concerned, and violates *no one's* rights, then that action is morally acceptable.
2. In at least some cases, active euthanasia promotes the best interests of everyone concerned and violates no one's rights.
3. Therefore, in at least some cases active euthanasia is morally acceptable.

It would have been in everyone's best interests if active euthanasia had been employed in the case of Stewart Alsop's friend, Jack. First, and most important, it would have been in Jack's own interests, since it would have provided him with an easier, better death, without pain. (Who among us would choose Jack's death, if we had a choice, rather than a quick painless death?) Second, it would have been in the best interests of Jack's wife. Her misery, helplessly watching him suffer, must have been almost equal to his. Third, the hospital staff's best interests would have been served, since if Jack's dying had not been prolonged, they could have turned their attention to other patients whom they could have helped. Fourth, other patients would have benefited since medical resources would no longer have been used in the sad, pointless maintenance of Jack's physical existence. Finally, if Jack himself requested to be killed, the act would not have violated his rights. Considering all this, how can active euthanasia in this case be wrong? How can it be wrong to do an action that is merciful, that benefits everyone concerned, and that violates no one's rights?

The Argument from the Golden Rule

"Do unto others as you would have them do unto you" is one of the oldest and most familiar moral maxims. Stated in just that way, it is not a very good maxim: Suppose a sexual pervert started treating others as he would like to be treated himself; we might not be happy with the results. Nevertheless, the basic idea behind the Golden Rule is a good one. The basic idea is that moral rules apply impartially to everyone alike; therefore, you cannot say that you are justified in treating someone else in a certain way unless you are willing to admit that that person would also be justified in treating you in that way if your positions were reversed.

Kant and the Golden Rule

The great German philosopher Immanuel Kant (1724–1804) incorporated the basic idea of the Golden Rule into his system of ethics. Kant argued that we should act only on rules that we are willing to have applied universally; that is, we should behave as we would be willing to have *everyone* behave. He held that there is one supreme principle of morality, which he called "the Categorical Imperative." The Categorical Imperative says:

> Act only according to that maxim by which you can at the same time will that it should become a universal law.[6]

Let us discuss what this means. When we are trying to decide whether we ought to do a certain action, we must first ask what general rule or principle we would be following if we did it. Then, we ask whether we would be willing for everyone to follow that rule, in similar circumstances. (This determines whether "the maxim of the act"—the rule we would be following— can be "willed" to be "a universal law.") If we would not be willing for the rule to be followed universally, then we should not follow it ourselves. Thus, if we are not willing for others to

apply the rule to *us*, we ought not apply it to *them*.

In the eighteenth chapter of St. Matthew's gospel there is a story that perfectly illustrates this point. A man is owed money by another, who cannot pay, and so he has the debtor thrown into prison. But he himself owes money to the king and begs that *his* debt be forgiven. At first the king forgives the debt. However, when the king hears how this man has treated the one who owed him, he changes his mind and "delivers him unto the tormentors" until he can pay. The moral is clear: If you do not think that others should apply the rule "Don't forgive debts!" to *you*, then you should not apply it to others.

The application of all this to the question of euthanasia is fairly obvious. Each of us is going to die someday, although most of us do not know when or how. But suppose you were told that you would die in one of two ways, and you were asked to choose between them. First, you could die quietly, and without pain, from a fatal injection. Or second, you could choose to die of an affliction so painful that for several days before death you would be reduced to howling like a dog, with your family standing by helplessly, trying to comfort you, but going through its own psychological hell. It is hard to believe that any sane person, when confronted by these possibilities, would choose to have a rule applied that would force upon him or her the second option. And if we would not want such a rule, which excludes euthanasia, applied to us, then we should not apply such a rule to others.

Implications for Christians

There is considerable irony here. Kant [himself] was personally opposed to active euthanasia, yet his own Categorical Imperative seems to sanction it. The larger irony, however, is for those in the Christian Church who have for centuries opposed active euthanasia. According to the New Testament accounts, Jesus himself promulgated the Golden Rule as the supreme moral principle—"This is the Law and the Prophets," he said. But if this is the supreme principle of morality, then how can active euthanasia be always wrong? If I would have it done to me, how can it be wrong for me to do likewise to others?

R. M. Hare has made this point with great force. A Christian as well as a leading contemporary moral philosopher, Hare has long argued that "universalizability" is one of the central characteristics of moral judgment. ("Universalizability" is the name he gives to the basic idea embodied in both the Golden Rule and the Categorical Imperative. It means that a moral judgment must conform to universal principles, which apply to everyone alike, if it is to be acceptable.) In an article called "Euthanasia: A Christian View," Hare argues that Christians, if they took Christ's teachings about the Golden Rule seriously, would not think that euthanasia is always wrong. He gives this (true) example:

> The driver of a petrol lorry [i.e., a gas truck] was in an accident in which his tanker overturned and immediately caught fire. He himself was trapped in the cab and could not be freed. He therefore besought the bystanders to kill him by hitting him on the head, so that he would not roast to death. I think that somebody did this, but I do not know what happened in court afterwards.
>
> Now will you please all ask yourselves, as I have many times asked myself, what you wish that men should do to you if you were in the situation of that driver. I cannot believe that anybody who considered the matter seriously,

as if he himself were going to be in that situation and had now to give instructions as to what rule the bystanders should follow, would say that the rule should be one ruling out euthanasia absolutely.[7]

We might note that *active* euthanasia is the only option here; the concept of passive euthanasia, in these circumstances, has no application. . . .

Professor Sullivan finds my position pernicious. In his penultimate paragraph he says that the traditional doctrine "is simply a prohibition of murder," and that those of us who think otherwise are confused, teary-eyed sentimentalists. But the traditional doctrine is not that. It is a muddle of indefensible claims, backed by tradition but not by reason.

NOTES

1. "Active and Passive Euthanasia," *The New England Journal of Medicine,* vol. 292 (Jan. 9, 1975), pp. 78–80. [Reprinted, this volume, pp. 102–106.]

2. "Active and Passive Euthanasia: An Impertinent Distinction?" *The Human Life Review,* vol. III (1977), pp. 40–46. Parenthetical references in the text are to this article [as reprinted in this volume, pp. 107–111].

3. *The Patient as Person* (New Haven: Yale University Press, 1970), pp. 115–116.

4. *Morals and Medicine* (Boston: Beacon Press, 1960), p. 174.

5. "The Right to Die with Dignity," *Good Housekeeping,* August 1974, pp. 69, 130.

6. *Foundations of the Metaphysics of Morals,* p. 422.

7. *Philosophical Exchange* (Brockport, New York), II: 1 (Summer 1975), p. 45.

Review and Discussion Questions

1. Sullivan claims that Rachels's original argument—that there is no moral difference between killing and letting die—is irrelevant and that it leaves "the traditional position untouched." Rachels claims the opposite. Who is right about this point?

2. Sullivan and Rachels disagree about the role of intention in determining whether an action is right or wrong. Restate their positions as you understand them. With which writer do you agree?

3. Rachels is critical of the traditional doctrine's reliance on the distinction between ordinary and extraordinary means of support. Can his arguments be answered? Does the distinction have any value?

4. How might a critic of euthanasia like J. Gay-Williams or Sullivan respond to the final version of the argument from mercy?

5. Assess Rachels's use of the Golden Rule to defend euthanasia. How persuasive is it?

6. Rachels presents two arguments in defense of active euthanasia. Are there important arguments against euthanasia that he needs to answer?

Is There a Duty to Die?

JOHN HARDWIG

Earlier Richard B. Brandt considered situations in which suicide might be rational from the point of view of the person contemplating it, and in the previous reading James Rachels defended active euthanasia in cases where the patient seeks to avoid horrible suffering. In this essay, John Hardwig, professor of philosophy at East Tennessee State University, supports the more radical view that people can have a duty to die—indeed, that they can sometimes have this duty even when they would prefer to go on living. He is particularly concerned with situations in which modern medical technology makes it possible for an elderly person to extend his or her life for a short time but only at a very high cost to his or her loved ones, and he argues that medical ethics is wrong to focus exclusively on the well-being and autonomy of the patient while ignoring the burden that life-prolonging treatment can sometimes place on one's family.

Study Questions

1. Why does modern medicine raise the question of whether one can have a duty to die?
2. What is the "individualistic fantasy" that Hardwig criticizes?
3. What are the three objections to the idea of a duty to die that he considers?
4. What are the main factors that Hardwig identifies as influencing whether one has a duty to die?
5. Hardwig believes that "we fear death too much." What does he see as the implications of our fear of death?

From the Hastings Center Report, *vol. 27, no. 2 (1997). Reproduced by permission.* © *The Hastings Center.*

FOR ME THE QUESTION IS REAL and very important. I feel strongly that I may very well some day have a duty to die. I do not believe that I am idiosyncratic, morbid, mentally ill, or morally perverse in thinking this. I think many of us will eventually face precisely this duty. But I am first of all concerned with my own duty. . . .

Circumstances and a Duty to Die

Do many of us really believe that no one ever has a duty to die? I suspect not. I think most of us probably believe that there is such a duty, but it is very uncommon. Consider Captain Oates, a member of Admiral Scott's expedition to the South Pole. Oates became too ill to continue. If the rest of the team stayed with him, they would all perish. After this had become clear, Oates left his tent one night, walked out into a raging blizzard, and was never seen again. That may have been a heroic thing to do, but we might be able to agree that it was also no more than his duty. It would have been wrong for him to urge—or even to allow—the rest to stay and care for him.

This is a very unusual circumstance—a "lifeboat case"—and lifeboat cases make for bad ethics. But I expect that most of us would also agree that there have been cultures in which what we would call a duty to die has been fairly common. These are relatively poor, technologically simple, and especially nomadic cultures. In such societies, everyone knows that if you manage to live long enough, you will become old and debilitated. Then you will need to take steps to end your life. The old people in these societies regularly did precisely that. Their cultures prepared and supported them in doing so.

Those cultures could be dismissed as irrelevant to contemporary bioethics; their circumstances are so different from ours. But if that is our response, it is instructive. It suggests that we assume a duty to die is irrelevant to us because our wealth and technological sophistication have purchased exemption for us . . . except under very unusual circumstances like Captain Oates's.

But have wealth and technology really exempted us? We like to think of modern medicine as all triumph with no dark side. Our medicine saves many lives and enables us to live longer. That is wonderful, indeed. We are all glad to have access to this medicine. But our medicine also delivers most of us over to chronic illnesses and it enables many of us to survive longer that we can take care of ourselves, longer than we know what to do with ourselves, longer than we even are ourselves.

The costs—and these are not merely monetary—of prolonging our lives when we are no longer able to care for ourselves are often staggering. If further medical advances wipe out many of today's "killer diseases"—cancer, heart attacks, strokes, ALS, AIDS, and the rest—then one day most of us will survive long enough to become demented or debilitated. These developments could generate a fairly widespread duty to die. A fairly common duty to die might turn out to be only the dark side of our life-prolonging medicine and the uses we choose to make of it.

Let me be clear. I certainly believe that there is a duty to refuse life-prolonging medical treatment and also a duty to complete advance directives refusing life-prolonging treatment. But a duty to die can go well beyond that. There can be a duty to die before one's illnesses would cause death, even if treated only with palliative measures. In fact, there may be a fairly common responsibility to end one's life in the absence of any terminal illness at all. Finally, there can be a duty to die when one would prefer to live. Granted, many of the conditions that can generate a duty to die also seriously undermine the quality of life. Some prefer not to live under such conditions. But even those who want to live can face a duty to die. These will clearly be the most controversial and troubling cases; I will, accordingly, focus my reflections on them.

The Individualistic Fantasy

Because a duty to die seems such a real possibility to me, I wonder why contemporary bioethics has dismissed it without serious consideration. I believe that most bioethics still shares in one of our deeply embedded American dreams: the individualistic fantasy. This fantasy leads us to imagine that lives are separate and unconnected, or that they could be so if we chose. If lives were unconnected, things that happened in my life would not or need not affect others. And if others were not (much) affected by my life, I would have no duty to consider the impact of my decisions on others. I would then be free morally to live my life however I please, choosing whatever life or death I prefer for myself. The way I live would be nobody's business but my own. I certainly would have no duty to die if I preferred to live.

Within a health care context, the individualistic fantasy leads us to assume that the patient is the only one affected by decisions about her medical treatment. If only the patient were affected, the relevant questions when making treatment decisions would be precisely those we ask: What will benefit the patient? Who can best decide that? The pivotal issue would always be simply whether the patient wants to live like this and whether she would consider herself better off dead. "Whose life is it, anyway?" we ask rhetorically.

But this is morally obtuse. We are not a race of hermits. Illness and death do not come only to those who are all alone. Nor is it much better to think in terms of the bald dichotomy between "the interests of the patient" and "the interests of society" (or a third-party payer), as if we were isolated individuals connected only

to "society" in the abstract or to the other, faceless members of our health maintenance organization.

Most of us are affiliated with particular others and most deeply, with family and loved ones. Families and loved ones are bound together by ties of care and affection, by legal relations and obligations, by inhabiting shared spaces and living units, by interlocking finances and economic prospects, by common projects and also commitments to support the different life projects of other family members, by shared histories, by ties of loyalty. This life together of family and loved ones is what defines and sustains us; it is what gives meaning to most of our lives. We would not have it any other way. We would not want to be all alone, especially when we are seriously ill, as we age, and when we are dying.

But the fact of deeply interwoven lives debars us from making exclusively self-regarding decisions, as the decisions of one member of a family may dramatically affect the lives of all the rest. The impact of my decisions upon my family and loved ones is the source of many of my strongest obligations and also the most plausible and likeliest basis of a duty to die. "Society," after all, is only very marginally affected by how I live, or by whether I live or die.

A Burden to My Loved Ones

Many older people report that their one remaining goal in life is not to be a burden to their loved ones. Young people feel this, too: when I ask my undergraduate students to think about whether their death could come too late, one of their very first responses always is, "Yes, when I become a burden to my family or loved ones." Tragically, there are situations in which my loved ones would be much better off—all things considered, the loss of a loved one notwithstanding—if I were dead.

The lives of our loved ones can be seriously compromised by caring for us. The burdens of providing care or even just supervision twenty-four hours a day, seven days a week are often overwhelming. When this kind of caregiving goes on for years, it leaves the caregiver exhausted, with no time for herself or life of her own. Ultimately, even her health is often destroyed. But it can also be emotionally devastating simply to live with a spouse who is increasingly distant, uncommunicative, unresponsive, foreign, and unreachable. Other family members' needs often go unmet as the caring capacity of the family is exceeded. Social life and friendships evaporate, as there is no opportunity to go out to see friends and the home is no longer a place suitable for having friends in.

We must also acknowledge that the lives of our loved ones can be devastated just by having to pay for health care for us. One part of the recent SUPPORT study documented the financial aspects of caring for a dying member of a family. Only those who had illnesses severe enough to give them less than a 50 percent chance to live six more months were included in this study. When these patients survived their initial hospitalization and were discharged about one-third required considerable caregiving from their families; in 20 percent of the cases a family member had to quit work or make some other major lifestyle change; almost one-third of these families lost all of their savings; and just under 30 percent lost a major source of income.

If talking about money sounds venal or trivial, remember that much more than money is normally at stake here. When someone has to quit work, she may well lose her career. Savings decimated late in life cannot be recouped in the few remaining years of employability, so the loss comprises the quality of the rest of the caregiver's life. For a young person, the chance to go to college may be lost to the attempt to pay debts due to an illness in the family, and this decisively shapes an entire life. . . .

I am not advocating a crass, quasi-economic conception of burdens and benefits, nor a shallow, hedonistic view of life. Given a suitably rich understanding of benefits, family members sometimes do benefit from suffering through the long illness of a loved one. Caring for the sick or aged can foster growth, even as it makes daily life immeasurably harder and the prospects for the future much bleaker. Chronic illness or drawn-out death can also pull a family together, making the care for each other stronger and more evident. If my loved ones are truly benefiting from coping with my illness or debility, I have no duty to die based on burdens to them.

But it would also be irresponsible to blithely assume that this always happens, that it will happen in my family, or that it will be the fault of my family if they cannot manage to turn my illness into a positive experience. Perhaps the opposite is more common: a hospital chaplain once told me that he could not think of a single case in which a family was strengthened or brought together by what happened at the hospital.

Our families and loved ones also have obligations, of course—they have the responsibility to stand by us and to support us through debilitating illness and death. They must be prepared to make significant sacrifices to respond to an illness in the family. I am far from denying that. Most of us are aware of this responsibility and most families meet it rather well. In fact, families deliver more than 80 percent of the long-term care in this country, almost always at great personal cost. Most of us who are part of a family can expect to be sustained in our time of need by family members and those who love us.

But most discussions of an illness in the family sound as if responsibility were a one-way street. It is not, of course. When we become seriously ill or debilitated, we too may have to make sacrifices. To think that my loved ones must bear whatever burdens my illness, debility, or dying process might impose upon them is to reduce them to means of my well-being. And that would be immoral. Family solidarity, altruism, bearing the burden of a loved one's misfortune, and loyalty are all important virtues of families as well. But they are all also two-way streets.

Objections to a Duty to Die

To my mind, the most serious objections to the idea of a duty to die lie in the effects on my loved ones of ending my life. But to most others, the important objections have little or nothing to do with family and loved ones. Perhaps the most common objections are: (1) there is a higher duty that always takes precedence over a duty to die; (2) a duty to end one's own life would be incompatible with a recognition of human dignity or the intrinsic value of a person; and (3) seriously ill, debilitated, or dying people are already bearing the harshest burdens and so it would be wrong to ask them to bear the burden of ending their own lives. . . .

An example of the first line of argument would be the claim that a duty to God, the giver of life, forbids that anyone take her own life. It could be argued that this duty always supersedes whatever obligations we might have to our families. But what convinces us that we always have such a religious duty in the first place? And what guarantees that it always supercedes our obligations to try to protect our loved ones?

Certainly, the view that death is the ultimate evil cannot be squared with Christian theology. It does not reflect the actions of Jesus or those of his early followers. Nor is it clear that the belief that life is sacred requires that we never take it. . . .

Secondly, religious considerations aside, the claim could be made that an obligation to end one's own life would be incompatible with human dignity or would embody a failure to recognize the intrinsic value of a person. But I do not see that in thinking I had a duty to die I would necessarily be failing to respect myself or appreciate my dignity or worth. Nor would I necessar-

ily be failing to respect you in thinking that you had a similar duty. There is surely also a sense in which we fail to respect ourselves if in the face of illness or death, we stoop to choosing just what is best for ourselves. Indeed, Kant held that the very best core of human dignity is the ability to act on a self-imposed moral law, regardless of whether it is in our interest to do so. We shall return to the notion of human dignity.

A third objection appeals to the relative weight of burdens and thus, ultimately, to considerations of fairness or justice. The burdens that an illness creates for the family could not possible be great enough to justify an obligation to end one's life—the sacrifice of life itself would be a far greater burden than any involved in caring for a chronically ill family member.

But is this true? Consider the following case:

> An 87-year-old woman was dying of congestive heart failure. Her APACHE score predicted that she had less than a 50 percent chance to live for another six months. She was lucid, assertive, and terrified of death. She very much wanted to live and kept opting for rehospitalization and the most aggressive life-prolonging treatment possible. That treatment successfully prolonged her life (though with increasing debility) for nearly two years. Her 55-year-old daughter was her only remaining family, her caregiver, and the main source of her financial support. The daughter duly cared for her mother. But before her mother died, her illness had cost the daughter all of her savings, her home, her job, and her career.

This is by no means an uncommon sort of case. Thousands of similar cases occur each year. Now, ask yourself which is the greater burden:

a) To lose a 50 percent chance of six more months of life at age 87?

b) To lose all your savings, your home, and your career at age 55?

Which burden would you prefer to bear? Do we really believe the former is the greater burden? . . .

I think most of us would agree that (b) is a greater burden. That is the evil we would more hope to avoid in our lives. If we are tempted to say that the mother's disease and impending death are the greater evil, I believe it is because we are taking a "slice of time" perspective rather than a "lifetime perspective." But surely the lifetime perspective is the appropriate perspective when weighing burdens. If (b) is the greater burden, then we must admit that we have been promulgating an ethics that advocates imposing greater burdens on some people in order to provide smaller benefits for others just because they are ill and thus gain our professional attention and advocacy.

A whole range of cases like this one could easily be generated. In some, the answer about which burden is greater will not be clear. But in many it is. Death—or ending your own life—is simply not the greatest evil or the greatest burden.

This point does not depend on a utilitarian calculus. Even if death were the greatest burden (thus disposing of any simple utilitarian argument), serious questions would remain about the moral justifiability of choosing to impose crushing burdens on loved ones in order to avoid having to bear this burden oneself. . . .

I can readily imagine that, through cowardice, rationalization, or failure of resolve, I will fail in this obligation to protect my loved ones. If so, I think I would need to be excused or forgiven for what I did. But I cannot imagine it would be morally permissible to ruin the rest of my partner's life to sustain mine or to cut off my sons' careers, impoverish them, or compromise the quality of their children's lives simply because I wish to live a little longer. This is what leads me to believe in a duty to die.

Who Has a Duty to Die?

Suppose, then, that there can be a duty to die. Who has a duty to die? And when? To my mind, these are the right questions, the questions we should be asking. Many of us may one day badly need answers to just these questions. . . .

I cannot say when someone has a duty to die. Still, I can suggest a few features of one's illness, history, and circumstances that make it more likely that one has duty to die. I present them here without much elaboration or explanation.

1. A duty to die is more likely when continuing to live will impose significant burdens—emotional burdens, extensive caregiving, destruction of life plans, and, yes, financial hardship—on your family and loved ones. This is the fundamental insight underlying a duty to die.
2. A duty to die becomes greater as you grow older. As we age, we will be giving up less by giving up our lives, if only because we will sacrifice fewer remaining years of life and a smaller portion of our life plans. . . .
3. A duty to die is more likely when you have already lived a full and rich life. You have already had a full share of the good things life offers.
4. There is greater duty to die if your loved ones' lives have already been difficult or impoverished, if they have had only a small share of the good things that life has to offer (especially if through no fault of their own).
5. A duty to die is more likely when your loved ones have already made great contributions—perhaps even sacrifices—to make your life a good one. Especially if you have not made similar sacrifices for their well-being or for the well-being of other members of your family.
6. To the extent that you can make a good adjustment to your illness or handicapping condition, there is less likely to be a duty to die. A good adjustment means that smaller sacrifices will be required of loved ones and there is more compensating interaction for them. . . .

7. There is less likely to be a duty to die if you can still make significant contributions to the lives of others, especially your family.

8. A duty to die is more likely when the part of you that is loved will soon be gone or seriously compromised. Or when you soon will no longer be capable of giving love. Part of the horror of dementing disease is that it destroys the capacity to nurture and sustain relationships, taking away a person's agency and the emotions that bind her to others.

9. There is a greater duty to die to the extent that you have lived a relatively lavish lifestyle instead of saving for illness or old age. Like most upper middle-class Americans, I could easily have saved more. It is a greater wrong to come to your family for assistance if your need is the result of having chosen leisure or a spendthrift lifestyle. . . .

These, then, are some of the considerations that give shape and definition to the duty to die. If we can agree that these considerations are all relevant, we can see that the correct course of action will often be difficult to discern. A decision about when I should end my life will sometimes prove to be every bit as difficult as the decision about whether I want treatment for myself.

Can the Incompentent Have a Duty to Die?

Severe mental deterioration springs readily to mind as one of the situations in which I believe I could have a duty to die. But can incompetent people have duties at all? We can have moral duties we do not recognize or acknowledge, including duties that we never recognized. But can we have duties we are unable to recognize? Duties when we are unable to understand the concept of morality at all? If so, do others have a moral obligation to help us carry out this duty? These are extremely difficult theoretical questions. The reach of moral agency is severely strained by mental incompetence.

I am tempted to simply bypass the entire question by saying that I am talking only about competent persons. But the idea of a duty to die clearly raises the specter of one person claiming that another—one who cannot speak for herself—has such a duty. So I need to say that I can make no sense of the claim that someone has a duty to die if the person has never been able to understand moral obligation at all. To my mind, only those who were formerly capable of making moral decisions could have such a duty.

But the case of formerly competent persons is almost as troubling. Perhaps we should simply stipulate that no incompetent person can have a duty to die, not even if she affirmed belief in such a duty in an advance directive. If we take the view that formerly competent people may have such a duty, we should surely exercise extreme caution when claiming a formerly competent person would have acknowledged a duty to die or that any formerly competent person has an unacknowledged duty to die. Moral dangers loom regardless of which way we decide to resolve such issues.

But for me personally, very urgent practical matters turn on their resolution. If a formerly competent person can no longer have a duty to die (or if other people are not likely to help her carry out this duty), I believe that my obligation may be to die while I am still competent, before I become unable to make and carry out that decision for myself. Surely it would be irresponsible to evade my moral duties by temporizing until I escape into incompetence. And so I must die sooner than I otherwise would have to. On the other hand, if I could count on others to end my life after I become incompetent, I might be able to fulfill my responsibilities while also living out all my competent or semi-competent days. Given our society's reluctance to permit physicians, let alone family members, to perform aid-in-dying, I believe I may well have a duty to end my life when I can see mental incapacity on the horizon.

There is also the very real problem of sudden incompetence—due to a serious stroke or automobile accident, for example. For me, that is the real nightmare. If I suddenly become incompetent, I will fall into the hands of a medical-legal system that will conscientiously disregard my moral beliefs and do what is best for me, regardless of the consequences for my loved ones. And that is not at all what I would have wanted!

Social Policies and a Duty to Die

The claim that there is a duty to die will seem to some a misplaced response to social negligence. If our society were providing for the debilitated, the chronically ill, and the elderly as it should be, there would only be very rare cases of a duty to die. . . .

This much is surely true: there are a number of social policies we could pursue that would dramatically reduce the incidence of such a duty. Most obviously, we could decide to pay for facilities that provide excellent long-term care (not just health care!) for all chronically ill, debilitated, mentally ill, or demented people in this country. We probably could still afford to do this. . . . The duty to die would then be virtually eliminated.

I cannot claim to know whether in some abstract sense a society like ours should provide care for all who are chronically ill or debilitated. But the fact is that we Americans seem to be unwilling to pay for this kind of long-term care, except for ourselves and our own. In fact, we are moving in precisely the opposite direction—we are trying to shift the burdens of caring for the seriously and chronically ill onto families in order to save costs for our health care systems. As we shift the burdens of care onto families, we also dramatically increase the number of Americans who will have a duty to die.

I must not, then, live my life and make my plans on the assumption that social institutions will protect my family from my infirmity and debility. To do so would be irresponsible. More likely, it will be up to me to protect my loved ones.

A Duty to Die and the Meaning of Life

A duty to die seems very harsh, and often in would be. It is one of the tragedies of our lives that someone who wants very much to live can nevertheless have a duty to die. It is both tragic and ironic that it is precisely the very real good of family and loved ones that gives rise to this duty. Indeed, the genuine love, closeness, and supportiveness of family members is a major source of this duty: we could not be such a burden if they did not care for us. Finally, there is deep irony in the fact that the very successes of our life-prolonging medicine help to create a widespread duty to die.

We fear death too much. Our fear of death has led to a massive assault on it. We still crave after virtually any life-prolonging technology that we might conceivably be able to produce. We still too often feel morally impelled to prolong life—virtually any form of life—as long as possible. As if the best death is the one that can be put off longest.

We do not even ask about meaning in death, so busy are we with trying to postpone it. But we will not conquer death by one day developing a technology so magnificent that no one will have to die. Nor can we conquer death by postponing it ever longer. We can conquer death only by finding meaning in it.

Although the existence of a duty to die does not hinge on this, recognizing such a duty would go some way toward recovering meaning in death. Paradoxically, it would restore dignity to those who are seriously ill or dying. It would also reaffirm the connections required to give life (and death) meaning. I close now with a few words about both of these points.

First, recognizing a duty to die affirms my agency and also my moral agency. I can still do things that make an important difference in the lives of my loved ones. Moreover, the fact that I still have responsibilities keeps me within the community of moral agents. My illness or debility has not reduced me to a mere moral patient (to use the language of the philosophers). Though it may not be the whole story, surely Kant was onto something important when he claimed that human dignity rests on the capacity for moral agency within a community of those who respect the demands of morality. . . .

Second, recovering meaning in death requires an affirmation of connections. If I end my life to spare the futures of my loved ones, I testify in my death that I am connected to them. It is because I love and care for precisely these people (and I know they care for me) that I wish not to be such a burden on them. By contrast, a life in which I am free to choose whatever I want for myself is a life unconnected to others. A bioethics that would treat me as if I had no serious moral responsibilities does what it can to marginalize, weaken, or even destroy my connections with others.

But life without connections is meaningless. The individualistic fantasy, though occasionally liberating, is deeply destructive. When life is good and vitality seems unending, life itself and life lived for yourself may seem quite sufficient.

But if not life, certainly death without connection is meaningless. If you are only for yourself, all you have to care about as your life draws to a close is yourself and your life. Everything that you care about will then perish in your death. And that—the end of everything you care about—is precisely the total collapses of meaning. We can, then, find meaning in death only through a sense of connection with something that will survive our death. . . .

If I am correct, death is so difficult for us partly because our sense of community is so weak. Death seems to wipe out everything when we can't fit it into the lives of those who live on. A death motivated by the desire to spare the futures of my loved ones might well be a better death for me than the one I would get as a result of opting to continue my life as long as there is any pleasure in it for me. Pleasure is nice, but meaning is what matters.

I don't know about others, but these reflections have helped me. I am now more at peace about facing a duty to die. Ending my life if my duty required it might still be difficult. But for me, a far greater horror would be dying all alone or stealing the futures of my loved ones in order to buy a little more time for myself. I hope that if the time comes when I have a duty to die, I will recognize it, encourage my loved ones to recognize it too, and carry it out bravely.

Review and Discussion Questions

1. Has Hardwig exaggerated the possible burden that life-prolonging treatment can impose on a patient's loved ones? What about the point that a family can be pulled together and grow by suffering through the drawn-out death of a loved one?

2. Do you agree with Hardwig that one can have a duty to die? If so, why does one have this duty, and under what circumstances does one have it?

3. Does Hardwig successfully answer the three objections to his position that he considers? Are there objections that he overlooks?

4. Does Hardwig's position presuppose a utilitarian approach to ethics? Is he correct to say that he is not advocating a "crass, quasi-economic" approach or a "shallow, hedonistic view of life"?

5. How would you respond to the point that if society were willing to spend the resources necessary for life-prolonging medical care for the elderly, then one would rarely, if ever, have a duty to die?

6. Can a person who is no longer mentally competent have a duty to die? Explain why or why not.

7. Do you agree with Hardwig that we fear death too much? Is it possible to find meaning in death? If so, how? Would recognizing the existence of a duty to die help make death meaningful?

8. Assess the following argument: If society were to acknowledge a duty to die, the consequences would be bad because elderly people would inevitably be pressured (implicitly or explicitly) by family members and others to terminate their lives when they wish to go on living.

ABORTION

An Almost Absolute Value in History

JOHN T. NOONAN, JR.

In this essay, John T. Noonan, Jr., professor of law at the University of California, Berkeley, presents the case against abortion based on the humanity of the fetus. His basic argument is that humanity begins at the moment of conception, when a new being is created with a unique, human genetic code. Noonan argues against attempts to draw a distinction between human and nonhuman life at some later point in fetal development. He specifically rejects arguments that the fetus is not fully human until it is viable, until it has had certain experiences, unless its parents can feel it or would mourn its death, or until it achieves social visibility at birth. All these attempts to distinguish between the human and nonhuman, Noonan argues, fail to mark some morally relevant difference. He argues, furthermore, that a change in biological probabilities supports the position that humanity begins at conception.

Study Questions

1. What does *viability* mean, and why does Noonan reject the idea that it marks the difference between human and nonhuman life (so that abortion would be permissible prior to, but not after, viability)?

2. What are the other attempted distinctions between the human and nonhuman that Noonan criticizes, and what are his criticisms of them?

3. Explain how Noonan appeals to biological probabilities to support his position.

4. Under what circumstances would Noonan permit abortion?

Reprinted by permission from John T. Noonan, Jr., ed., The Morality of Abortion: Legal and Historical Perspectives *(1970). Section titles added.*

I. The Criterion for Humanity

THE MOST FUNDAMENTAL QUESTION involved in the long history of thought on abortion is: How do you determine the humanity of a being? To phrase the question that way is to put in comprehensive humanistic terms what the theologians . . . dealt with as an explicitly theological question under the heading of "ensoulment." . . . But the theological notion of ensoulment could easily be translated into humanistic language by substituting "human" for "rational soul"; the problem of knowing when a man is a man is common to theology and humanism.

If one steps outside the specific categories used by the theologians, the answer they gave can be analyzed as a refusal to discriminate among human beings on the basis of their varying potentialities. Once conceived, the being was recognized as man because he had man's potential. The criterion for humanity, thus, was simple and all-embracing: If you are conceived by human parents, you are human.

II. The Humanity of the Fetus

The strength of this position may be tested by a review of some of the other distinctions offered in the contemporary controversy over legalizing abortion. Perhaps the most popular distinction is in terms of viability. Before an age of so many months, the fetus is not viable, that is, it cannot be removed from the mother's womb and live apart from her. To that extent, the life of the fetus is absolutely dependent on the life of the mother. This dependence is made the basis of denying recognition to its humanity.

There are difficulties with this distinction. One is that the perfection of artificial incubation may make the fetus viable at any time: It may be removed and artificially sustained. Experiments with animals already show that such a procedure is possible. This hypothetical extreme case relates to an actual difficulty: There is considerable elasticity to the idea of viability. Mere

length of life is not an exact measure. The viability of the fetus depends on the extent of its anatomical and functional development. The weight and length of the fetus are better guides to the state of its development than age, but weight and length vary. Moreover, different racial groups have different ages at which their fetuses are viable. Some evidence, for example, suggests that Negro fetuses mature more quickly than white fetuses. If viability is the norm, the standard would vary with race and with many individual circumstances.

The most important objection to this approach is that dependence is not ended by viability. The fetus is still absolutely dependent on someone's care in order to continue existence; indeed a child of one or three or even five years of age is absolutely dependent on another's care for existence; uncared for, the older fetus or the younger child will die as surely as the early fetus detached from the mother. The unsubstantial lessening in dependence at viability does not seem to signify any special acquisition of humanity.

A second distinction has been attempted in terms of experience. A being who has had experience, has lived and suffered, who possesses memories, is more human than one who has not. Humanity depends on formation by experience. The fetus is thus "unformed" in the most basic human sense.

This distinction is not serviceable for the embryo, which is already experiencing and reacting. The embryo is responsive to touch after eight weeks and at least at that point is experiencing. At an earlier stage the zygote is certainly alive and responding to its environment. The distinction may also be challenged by the rare case where aphasia has erased adult memory: Has it erased humanity? More fundamentally, this distinction leaves even the older fetus or the younger child to be treated as an unformed inhuman thing. Finally, it is not clear why experience as such confers humanity. It could be argued that certain central experiences such as loving or learning are necessary to make a man human. But then human beings who have failed to love or to learn might be excluded from the class called man.

A third distinction is made by appeal to the sentiments of adults. If a fetus dies, the grief of the parents is not the grief they would have for a living child. The fetus is an unnamed "it" till birth, and is not perceived as personality until at least the fourth month of existence, when movements in the womb manifest a vigorous presence demanding joyful recognition by the parents.

Yet feeling is notoriously an unsure guide to the humanity of others. Many groups of humans have had difficulty in feeling that persons of another tongue, color, religion, sex, are as human as they. Apart from reactions to alien groups, we mourn the loss of a ten-year-old boy more than the loss of his one-day-old brother or his 90-year-old grandfather. The difference felt and the grief expressed vary with the potentialities extinguished, or the experience wiped out; they do not seem to point to any substantial difference in the humanity of baby, boy, or grandfather.

Distinctions are also made in terms of sensation by the parents. The embryo is felt within the womb only after about the fourth month. The embryo is seen only at birth. What can be neither seen nor felt is different from what is tangible. If the fetus cannot be seen or touched at all, it cannot be perceived as man.

Yet experience shows that sight is even more untrustworthy than feeling in determining humanity. By sight, color became an appropriate index for saying who was a man, and the evil of racial discrimination was given foundation. Nor can touch provide the test; a being confined by sickness, "out of touch" with others, does not thereby seem to lose his humanity. . . .

Finally, a distinction is sought in social visibility. The fetus is not socially perceived as human. It cannot communicate with others. Thus, both subjectively and objectively, it is not a member of society. As moral rules are rules

for the behavior of members of society to each other, they cannot be made for behavior toward what is not yet a member. Excluded from the society of men, the fetus is excluded from the humanity of men.

By force of the argument from the consequences, this distinction is to be rejected. It is more subtle than that founded on an appeal to physical sensation, but it is equally dangerous in its implications. If humanity depends on social recognition, individuals or whole groups may be dehumanized by being denied any status in their society. Such a fate is fictionally portrayed in *1984* and has actually been the lot of many men in many societies. In the Roman empire, for example, condemnation to slavery meant the practical denial of most human rights; in the Chinese Communist world, landlords have been classified as enemies of the people and so treated as nonpersons by the state. Humanity does not depend on social recognition, though often the failure of society to recognize the prisoner, the alien, the heterodox as human has led to the destruction of human beings. Anyone conceived by a man and a woman is human. Recognition of this condition by society follows a real event in the objective order, however imperfect and halting the recognition. Any attempt to limit humanity to exclude some group runs the risk of furnishing authority and precedent for excluding other groups in the name of the consciousness or perception of the controlling group in the society.

A philosopher may reject the appeal to the humanity of the fetus because he views "humanity" as a secular view of the soul and because he doubts the existence of anything real and objective which can be identified as humanity. One answer to such a philosopher is to ask how he reasons about moral questions without supposing that there is a sense in which he and the others of whom he speaks are human. Whatever group is taken as the society which determines who may be killed is thereby taken as human. A second answer is to ask if he does not believe that there is a right and wrong way of deciding moral questions. If there is such a difference, experience may be appealed to: To decide who is human on the basis of the sentiment of a given society has led to consequences which rational men would characterize as monstrous.

III. Biological Probabilities

The rejection of the attempted distinctions based on viability and visibility, experience and feeling, may be buttressed by the following considerations: Moral judgments often rest on distinctions, but if the distinctions are not to appear arbitrary fiat, they should relate to some real difference in probabilities. There is a kind of continuity in all life, but the earlier stages of the elements of human life possess tiny probabilities of development. Consider, for example, the spermatozoa in any normal ejaculate: There are about 200,000,000 in any single ejaculate, of which one has a chance of developing into a zygote. Consider the oocytes which may become ova: There are 100,000 to 1,000,000 oocytes in a female infant, of which a maximum of 390 are ovulated. But once spermatozoon and ovum meet and the conceptus is formed, such studies as have been made show that roughly in only 20 percent of the cases will spontaneous abortion occur. In other words, the chances are about 4 out of 5 that this new being will develop. At this stage in the life of the being there is a sharp shift in probabilities, an immense jump in potentialities. To make a distinction between the rights of spermatozoa and the rights of the fertilized ovum is to respond to an enormous shift in possibilities. For about twenty days after conception, the egg may split to form twins or combine with another egg to form a chimera, but the probability of either event happening is very small.

It may be asked, What does a change in biological probabilities have to do with establishing humanity? The argument from probabilities is not aimed at establishing humanity but at establishing an objective discontinuity which may be taken into account in moral discourse. As life itself is a matter of probabilities, as most moral reasoning is an estimate of probabilities, so it seems in accord with the structure of reality and the nature of moral thought to found a moral judgment on the change in probabilities at conception. The appeal to probabilities is the most commonsensical of arguments; to a greater or smaller degree all of us base our actions on probabilities, and in morals, as in law, prudence and negligence are often measured by the account one has taken of the probabilities. If the chance is 200,000,000 to 1 that the movement in the bushes into which you shoot is a man's, I doubt if many persons would hold you careless in shooting; but if the chances are 4 out of 5 that the movement is a human being's, few would acquit you of blame. Would the argument be different if only one out of ten children conceived came to term? Of course this argument would be different. This argument is an appeal to probabilities that actually exist, not to any and all states of affairs which may be imagined.

The probabilities as they do exist do not show the humanity of the embryo in the sense of a demonstration in logic any more than the probabilities of the movement in the bush being a man demonstrate beyond all doubt that the being is a man. The appeal is a "buttressing" consideration, showing the plausibility of the standard adopted. The argument focuses on the decisional factor in any moral judgment and assumes that part of the business of a moralist is drawing lines. One evidence of the nonarbitrary character of the line drawn is the difference of probabilities on either side of it. If a spermatozoon is destroyed, one destroys a being which had a chance of far less than 1 in 200,000,000 of developing into a reasonable being, possessed of the genetic code, a heart, and other organs, and capable of pain. If a fetus is destroyed, one destroys a being already possessed of the genetic code, organs, and sensitivity to pain, and one which had an 80 percent chance of developing further into a baby, outside the womb, who, in time, would reason.

The positive argument for conception as the decisive moment of humanization is that at conception the new being receives the genetic code. It is this genetic information which determines his characteristics, which is the biological carrier of the possibility of human wisdom, which makes him a self-evolving being. A being with a human genetic code is man.

IV. Conclusion

This review of current controversy over the humanity of the fetus emphasizes what a fundamental question the theologians resolved in asserting the inviolability of the fetus. To regard the fetus as possessed of equal rights with other humans was not, however, to decide every case where abortion might be employed. It did decide the case where the argument was that the fetus should be aborted for its own good. To say a being was human was to say it had a destiny to decide for itself which could not be taken from it by another man's decision. But human beings with equal rights often come in conflict with each other, and some decision must be made as to whose claims are to prevail. Cases of conflict involving the fetus are different only in two respects: the total inability of the fetus to speak for itself and the fact that the right of the fetus regularly at stake is the right to life itself.

. . . In Catholic moral theology, as it developed, life even of the innocent was not taken as an absolute. Judgments on acts affecting life issued from a process of weighing. In the weighing, the fetus was always given a value greater than zero, always a value separate and independent from its parents. This valuation was crucial and fundamental in all Christian thought on the subject and marked it off from any approach which considered that only the parents' interests needed to be considered.

Even with the fetus weighed as human, one interest could be weighed as equal or superior: that of the mother in her own life. . . .

The perception of the humanity of the fetus and the weighing of fetal rights against other human rights constituted the work of the moral analysts. But what spirit animated their abstract judgments? For the Christian community it was the injunction of Scripture to love your neighbor as yourself. The fetus as human was a neighbor; his life had parity with one's own. The commandment gave life to what otherwise would have been only rational calculation.

The commandment could be put in humanistic as well as theological terms. Do not injure your fellow man without reason. In these terms, once the humanity of the fetus is perceived, abortion is never right except in self-defense. When life must be taken to save life, reason alone cannot say that a mother must prefer a child's life to her own. With this exception, now of great rarity, abortion violates the rational humanist tenet of the equality of human lives.

Review and Discussion Questions

1. Assess Noonan's arguments against each of the five attempts (criticized by him) to distinguish between human and nonhuman at some point in development after conception. How strong are his arguments? Can you think of considerations in favor of any of the "distinctions" that he has ignored? Has Noonan overlooked some other way of distinguishing between human and nonhuman at a later point in development?

2. Are you persuaded that one becomes fully human, with a right to life, at conception? Explain your answer.

3. How relevant and how persuasive do you find Noonan's appeal to biological probabilities?

4. Noonan believes that, even if the fetus is seen as human, its life does not have absolute value—in other words, abortion is not necessarily prohibited in every case. Assuming that the fetus is human, when, if ever, would abortion be permissible?

5. Assume that abortion is immoral except to save the life of the mother. Should it therefore be illegal?

The Moral Status of Abortion

MARY ANNE WARREN

In this essay, Mary Anne Warren, professor of philosophy at San Francisco State University and author of *Moral Status*, defends abortion. She distinguishes between two senses of the term "human being": a genetic sense and a moral sense. An entity is human in the genetic sense if it is a member of our biological species; it is human in the moral sense if it is a person, that is, a member of the moral community with full and equal moral rights. She argues that genetic humanity is neither necessary nor sufficient for personhood and that although fetuses are genetically human, they are not persons in the moral sense because they lack the characteristics that are central to personhood. Although it is possible to extend moral rights to beings that have few or none of these characteristics, Warren argues against doing so in the case of fetuses. She also argues that a fetus's potential to develop into a person does not give it a right to life strong enough to outweigh the moral rights of actual persons.

Study Questions

1. Explain the two senses of "human being" that Noonan and other defenders of abortion confuse. What connection, if any, is there between the senses?

2. According to Warren, what are the six characteristics that are central to the concept of personhood?

3. Why does Warren reject the idea that we should extend moral rights to fetuses even though they lack the morally significant characteristics of persons?

4. In the normal course of events, a fetus will ultimately develop into a person with a right to life; it is thus a potential person. Explain the example that Warren uses to argue that potential persons do not have a significant right to life.

5. A critic of Warren might object that her argument entails that infanticide is morally justifiable. What is her response to this objection?

FOR OUR PURPOSES, abortion may be defined as the act a woman performs in deliberately terminating her pregnancy before it comes to term, or in allowing another person to terminate it. Abortion usually entails the death of a fetus.[1] Nevertheless, I will argue that it is morally permissible, and should be neither legally prohibited nor made needlessly difficult to obtain, e.g., by obstructive legal regulations.

Some philosophers have argued that the moral status of abortion cannot be resolved by rational means.[2] If this is so then liberty should prevail; for it is not a proper function of the law to enforce prohibitions upon personal behavior that cannot clearly be shown to be morally objectionable, and seriously so. But the advocates of prohibition believe that their position is objectively correct, and not merely a result of religious beliefs or personal prejudices. They argue that the humanity of the fetus is a matter of scientific fact, and that abortion is therefore the moral equivalent of murder, and must be prohibited in all or most cases. (Some would make an exception when the woman's life is in danger, or when the pregnancy is due to rape or incest; others would prohibit abortion even in these cases.)

In response, advocates of a right to choose abortion point to the terrible consequences of prohibiting it, especially while contraception is still unreliable, and is financially beyond the reach of much of the world's population. Worldwide, hundreds of thousands of women die each year from illegal abortions, and many more suffer from complications that may leave them injured or infertile. Women who are poor, under-age, disabled, or otherwise vulnerable, suffer most from the absence of safe and legal abortion. Advocates of choice also argue that to deny a woman access to abortion is to deprive her of the right to control her own body—a right so fundamental that without it other rights are often all but meaningless.

These arguments do not convince abortion opponents. The tragic consequences of prohibition leave them unmoved, because they regard the deliberate killing of fetuses as even more tragic. Nor do appeals to the right to control one's own body impress them, since they deny that this right includes the right to destroy a fetus. We cannot hope to persuade those who equate abortion with murder that they are mistaken, unless we can refute the standard anti-abortion argument: that because fetuses are human beings, they have a right to life equal to that of any other human being. Unfortunately, confusion has prevailed with respect to the two important questions which that argument raises: (1) Is a human fetus really a human being at all stages of prenatal development? and (2) If so, what (if anything) follows about the moral and legal status of abortion?

John Noonan says that "the fundamental question in the long history of abortion is: How do you determine the humanity of a being?"[3] His anti-abortion argument is essentially that of the Roman Catholic Church. In his words,

> . . . it is wrong to kill humans, however poor, weak, defenseless, and lacking in opportunity to develop their potential they may be. It is therefore morally wrong to kill Biafrans. Similarly, it is morally wrong to kill embryos.[4]

Noonan bases his claim that fetuses are human beings from the time of conception upon what he calls the theologians' criterion of humanity: that whoever is conceived of human beings is a human being. . . .

I argue . . . that a fetus is not a member of the moral community—the set of beings with full and equal moral rights. The reason that a fetus is not a member of the moral community is that it is not yet a person, nor is it enough like a person in the morally relevant respects to be regarded the equal of those human beings who are persons. I argue that it is personhood, and not genetic humanity, which is the fundamental basis for membership in the moral community. A fetus, especially in the early stages of its development, satisfies none of the criteria of personhood. Consequently, it makes no sense to grant it moral rights strong enough to override the woman's moral rights to liberty, bodily integrity, and sometimes life itself. Unlike an infant who has already been born, a fetus cannot be granted full and equal moral rights without severely threatening the rights and well-being of women. Nor, as we will see, is a fetus's *potential* personhood a threat to the moral permissibility of abortion, since merely potential persons do not have a moral right to become actual—or none that is strong enough to override the fundamental moral rights of actual persons. . .

The question we must answer in order to determine the moral status of abortion is: How are we to define the moral community, the set of beings with full and equal moral rights? What sort of entity has the inalienable moral rights to life, liberty, and the pursuit of happiness? Thomas Jefferson attributed these rights to all *men,* and he may have intended to attribute them *only* to men. Perhaps he ought to have attributed them to all human beings. If so, then we arrive, first, at Noonan's problem of defining what makes an entity a human being, and second, at the question which Noonan does not consider: What reason is there for identifying the moral community with the set of all human beings, in whatever way we have chosen to define that term?

On the Definition of "Human"

The term "human being" has two distinct, but not often distinguished, senses. This results in a slide of meaning, which serves to conceal the fallacy in the traditional argument that, since (1) it is wrong to kill innocent human beings, and (2) fetuses are innocent human beings, therefore (3) it is wrong to kill fetuses. For if "human being" is used in the same sense in both (1) and (2), then whichever of the two senses is meant, one of these premises is question-begging. And if it is used in different senses then the conclusion does not follow.

Thus, (1) is a generally accepted moral truth, and one that does not beg the question about abortion, only if "human being" is used to mean something like "a full-fledged member of the moral community, who is also a member of the human species." I will call this the *moral* sense of "human being." It is not to be confused with what I will call the *genetic* sense, i.e., the sense in which any individual entity that belongs to the human species is a human being, regardless of whether or not it is rightly considered to be an equal member of the moral community. Premise (1) avoids begging the question only if the moral sense is intended; while premise (2) avoids it only if what is intended is the genetic sense.

Noonan argues for the classification of fetuses with human beings by pointing, first, to the presence of the human genome in the cell nuclei of the human conceptus from conception onwards; and secondly, to the potential capacity for rational thought.[5] But what he needs to show, in order to support his version of the traditional anti-abortion argument, is that fetuses are human beings in the moral sense—the sense in which all human beings have full and equal moral rights. In the absence of any argument showing that whatever is genetically human is also morally human—and he gives none—nothing more than genetic humanity can be demonstrated by the presence of human chromosomes in the fetus's cell nuclei. And, as we will see, the strictly potential capacity for rational thought can at most show that the fetus may later become human in the moral sense.

Defining the Moral Community

Is genetic humanity sufficient for moral humanity? There are good reasons for not defining the moral community in this way. I would suggest that the moral community consists, in the first instance, of all *persons,* rather than all genetically human entities.[6] It is persons who invent moral rights, and who are (sometimes) capable of respecting them. It does not follow from this that only persons can have moral rights. However, persons are wise not to ascribe to entities that clearly are not persons moral rights that cannot in practice be respected without severely undercutting the fundamental moral rights of those who clearly are.

What characteristics entitle an entity to be considered a person? This is not the place to attempt a complete analysis of the concept of personhood; but we do not need such an analysis to explain why a fetus is not a person. All we need is an approximate list of the most basic criteria of personhood. In searching for these criteria, it is useful to look beyond the set of people with whom we are acquainted, all of whom are human. Imagine, then, a space traveler who lands on a new planet, and encounters organisms unlike any she has ever seen or heard of. If she wants to behave morally toward these organisms, she has somehow to determine whether they are people and thus have full moral rights, or whether they are things that she

need not feel guilty about treating, for instance, as a source of food.

How should she go about making this determination? If she has some anthropological background, she might look for signs of religion, art, and the manufacturing of tools, weapons, or shelters, since these cultural traits have frequently been used to distinguish our human ancestors from prehuman beings, in what seems to be closer to the moral than the genetic sense of "human being." She would be right to take the presence of such traits as evidence that the extraterrestrials were persons. It would, however, be anthropocentric of her to take the absence of these traits as proof that they were not, since they could be people who have progressed beyond, or who have never needed, these particular cultural traits.

I suggest that among the characteristics which are central to the concept of personhood are the following:

1. *sentience*—the capacity to have conscious experiences, usually including the capacity to experience pain and pleasure;
2. *emotionality*—the capacity to feel happy, sad, angry, loving, etc.;
3. *reason*—the capacity to solve new and relatively complex problems;
4. *the capacity to communicate,* by whatever means, messages of an indefinite variety of types; that is, not just with an indefinite number of possible contents, but on indefinitely many possible topics;
5. *self-awareness*—having a concept of oneself, as an individual and/or as a member of a social group; and finally
6. *moral agency*—the capacity to regulate one's own actions through moral principles or ideals.

It is difficult to produce precise definitions of these traits, let alone to specify universally valid behavioral indications that these traits are present. But let us assume that our explorer knows approximately what these six character-istics mean, and that she is able to observe whether or not the extraterrestrials possess these mental and behavioral capacities. How should she use her findings to decide whether or not they are persons?

An entity need not have *all* of these at-tributes to be a person. And perhaps none of them is absolutely necessary. For instance, the absence of emotion would not disqualify a be-ing that was personlike in all other ways. Think, for instance, of two of the *Star Trek* characters, Mr. Spock (who is half human and half alien), and Data (who is an android). Both are de-picted as lacking the capacity to feel emotion; yet both are sentient, reasoning, communica-tive, self-aware moral agents, and unquestion-ably persons. Some people are unemotional; some cannot communicate well; some lack self-awareness; and some are not moral agents. It should not surprise us that many people do not meet all of the criteria of personhood. Crite-ria for the applicability of complex concepts are often like this: none may be logically necessary, but the more criteria that are satisfied, the more confident we are that the concept is applicable. Conversely, the fewer criteria are satisfied, the less plausible it is to hold that the concept ap-plies. And if none of the relevant criteria are met, then we may be confident that it does not.

Thus, to demonstrate that a fetus is not a person, all I need to claim is that an entity that has *none* of these six characteristics is not a per-son. Sentience is the most basic mental capacity, and the one that may have the best claim to be-ing a necessary (though not sufficient) condi-tion for personhood. Sentience can establish a claim to moral considerability, since sentient be-ings can be harmed in ways that matter to them; for instance, they can be caused to feel pain, or deprived of the continuation of a life that is pleasant to them. It is unlikely that an entirely insentient organism could develop the other mental and behavioral capacities that are charac-teristic of persons. Consequently, it is odd to

claim that an entity that is not sentient, and that has never been sentient, is nevertheless a person. Persons who have permanently and irreparably lost all capacity for sentience, but who remain biologically alive, arguably still have strong moral rights by virtue of what they have been in the past. But small fetuses, which have not yet begun to have experiences, are not persons yet and do not have the rights that persons do.

The presumption that all persons have full and equal basic moral rights may be part of the very concept of a person. If this is so, then the concept of a person is in part a moral one; once we have admitted that X is a person, we have im-plicitly committed ourselves to recognizing X's right to be treated as a member of the moral community. The claim that X is a *human being* may also be voiced as an appeal to treat X de-cently; but this is usually either because "human being" is used in the moral sense, or because of a confusion between genetic and moral humanity.

If (1)–(6) are the primary criteria of person-hood, then genetic humanity is neither neces-sary nor sufficient for personhood. Some ge-netically human entities are not persons, and there may be persons who belong to other spe-cies. A man or woman whose consciousness has been permanently obliterated but who remains biologically alive is a human entity who may no longer be a person; and some unfortunate hu-mans, who have never had any sensory or cogni-tive capacities at all, may not be people either. Similarly, an early fetus is a human entity which is not yet a person. It is not even minimally sen-tient, let alone capable of emotion, reason, so-phisticated communication, self-awareness, or moral agency.[7] Thus, while it may be greatly val-ued as a future child, it does not yet have the claim to moral consideration that it may come to have later.

Moral agency matters to moral status, be-cause it is moral agents who invent moral rights, and who can be obliged to respect them. Hu-man beings have become moral agents from so-cial necessity. Most social animals exist well enough, with no evident notion of a moral right. But human beings need moral rights, because we are not only highly social, but also sufficiently clever and self-interested to be capable of undermining our societies through violence and duplicity. For human persons, moral rights are essential for peaceful and mutually beneficial social life. So long as some moral agents are denied basic rights, peaceful existence is difficult, since moral agents justly resent being treated as something less. If animals of some terrestrial species are found to be persons, or if alien persons come from other worlds, or if human beings someday invent machines whose mental and behavioral capacities make them persons, then we will be morally obliged to respect the moral rights of these nonhuman persons—at least to the extent that they are willing and able to respect ours in turn.

Although only those persons who are moral agents can participate directly in the shaping and enforcement of moral rights, they need not and usually do not ascribe moral rights only to themselves and other moral agents. Human beings are social creatures who naturally care for small children, and other members of the social community who are not currently capable of moral agency. Moreover, we are all vulnerable to the temporary or permanent loss of the mental capacities necessary for moral agency. Thus, we have self-interested as well as altruistic reasons for extending basic moral rights to infants and other sentient human beings who have already been born, but who currently lack some of these other mental capacities. These human beings, despite their current disabilities, are persons and members of the moral community.

But in extending moral rights to beings (human or otherwise) that have few or none of the morally significant characteristics of persons, we need to be careful not to burden human moral agents with obligations that they cannot possibly fulfill, except at unacceptably great cost to their own well-being and that of those they care about. Women often cannot complete unwanted

pregnancies, except at intolerable mental, physical, and economic cost to themselves and their families. And heterosexual intercourse is too important a part of the social lives of most men and women to be reserved for times when pregnancy is an acceptable outcome. Furthermore, the world cannot afford the continued rapid population growth which is the inevitable consequence of prohibiting abortion, so long as contraception is neither very reliable nor available to everyone. If fetuses were persons, then they would have rights that must be respected, even at great social or personal cost. But given that early fetuses, at least, are unlike persons in the morally relevant respects, it is unreasonable to insist that they be accorded exactly the same moral and legal status.

Fetal Development and the Right to Life

Two questions arise regarding the application of these suggestions to the moral status of the fetus. First, if indeed fetuses are not yet persons, then might they nevertheless have strong moral rights based upon the degree to which they *resemble* persons? Secondly, to what extent, if any, does a fetus's potential to *become* a person imply that we ought to accord to it some of the same moral rights? Each of these questions requires comment.

It is reasonable to suggest that the more like a person something is—the more it appears to meet at least some of the criteria of personhood—the stronger is the case for according it a right to life, and perhaps the stronger its right to life is. That being the case, perhaps the fetus gradually gains a stronger right to life as it develops. We should take seriously the suggestion that, just as "the human individual develops biologically in a continuous fashion . . . the rights of a human person . . . develop in the same way."[8]

A seven-month fetus can apparently feel pain, and can respond to such stimuli as light and sound. Thus, it may have a rudimentary form of consciousness. Nevertheless, it is probably not as conscious, or as capable of emotion, as even a very young infant is; and it has as yet little or no capacity for reason, sophisticated intentional communication, or self-awareness. In these respects, even a late-term fetus is arguably less like a person than are many nonhuman animals. Many animals (e.g., large-brained mammals such as elephants, cetaceans, or apes) are not only sentient, but clearly possessed of a degree of reason, and perhaps even of self-awareness. Thus, on the basis of its resemblance to a person, even a late-term fetus can have no more right to life than do these animals.

Animals may, indeed, plausibly be held to have some moral rights, and perhaps rather strong ones. But it is impossible in practice to accord full and equal moral rights to all animals. When an animal poses a serious threat to the life or well-being of a person, we do not, as a rule, greatly blame the person for killing it; and there are good reasons for this species-based discrimination. Animals, however intelligent in their own domains, are generally not beings with whom we can reason; we cannot persuade mice not to invade our dwellings or consume our food. That is why their rights are necessarily weaker than those of a being who can understand and respect the rights of other beings.

But the probable sentience of late-term fetuses is not the only argument in favor of treating late abortion as a morally more serious matter than early abortion. Many—perhaps most—people are repulsed by the thought of needlessly aborting a late-term fetus. The late-term fetus has features which cause it to arouse in us almost the same powerful protective instinct as does a small infant.

This response needs to be taken seriously. If it were impossible to perform abortions early in pregnancy, then we might have to tolerate the mental and physical trauma that would be occasioned by the routine resort to late abortion. But where early abortion is safe, legal, and readily available to all women, it is not unreasonable to expect most women who wish to end a pregnancy to do so prior to the third trimester. Most women strongly prefer early to late abortion, because it is far less physically painful and emotionally traumatic. Other things being equal, it is better for all concerned that pregnancies that are not to be completed should be ended as early as possible. Few women would consider ending a pregnancy in the seventh month in order to take a trip to Europe. If, however, a woman's own life or health is at stake, or if the fetus has been found to be so severely abnormal as to be unlikely to survive or to have a life worth living, then late abortion may be the morally best choice. For even a late-term fetus is not a person yet, and its rights must yield to those of the woman whenever it is impossible for both to be respected.

Potential Personhood and the Right to Life

We have seen that a presentient fetus does not yet resemble a person in ways which support the claim that it has strong moral rights. But what about its *potential*, the fact that if nurtured and allowed to develop it may eventually become a person? Doesn't that potential give it at least some right to life? The fact that something is a potential person may be a reason for not destroying it; but we need not conclude from this that potential people have a strong right to life. It may be that the feeling that it is better not to destroy a potential person is largely due to the fact that potential people are felt to be an invaluable resource, not to be lightly squandered. If every speck of dust were a potential person, we would be less apt to suppose that all potential persons have a right to become actual.

We do not need to insist that a potential person has no right to life whatever. There may be something immoral, and not just imprudent, about wantonly destroying potential people, when doing so isn't necessary. But even if a potential person does have some right to life, that right could not outweigh the right of a woman to obtain an abortion; for the basic moral rights of an actual person outweigh the rights of a merely potential person, whenever the two conflict. Since this may not be immediately obvious in the case of a human fetus, let us look at another case.

Suppose that our space explorer falls into the hands of an extraterrestrial civilization, whose scientists decide to create a few thousand new human beings by killing her and using some of her cells to create clones. We may imagine that each of these newly created women will have all of the original woman's abilities, skills, knowledge, and so on, and will also have an individual self-concept; in short, that each of them will be a bona fide (though not genetically unique) person. Imagine, further, that our explorer knows all of this, and knows that these people will be treated kindly and fairly. I maintain that in such a situation she would have the right to escape if she could, thus depriving all of these potential people of their potential lives. For her right to life outweighs all of theirs put together, even though they are all genetically human, and have a high probability of becoming people, if only she refrains from acting.

Indeed, I think that our space traveler would have a right to escape even if it were not her life which the aliens planned to take, but only a year of her freedom, or only a day. She would not be obliged to stay, even if she had been captured because of her own lack of caution—or even if she had done so deliberately, knowing the possible consequences. Regardless of why she was captured, she is not obliged to remain in captivity for *any* period of time in order to permit merely potential people to become actual people. By the same token, a woman's rights to liberty and the control of her own body outweigh whatever right to life a fetus may have merely by virtue of its potential personhood.

The Objection from Infanticide

One objection to my argument is that it appears to justify not only abortion, but also infanticide. A newborn infant is not much more personlike than a nine-month fetus, and thus it might appear that if late-term abortion is sometimes justified, then infanticide must also sometimes be justified. Yet most people believe that infanticide is a form of murder, and virtually never justified.

This objection is less telling than it may seem. There are many reasons why infanticide is more difficult to justify than abortion, even though neither fetuses nor newborn infants are clearly persons. In this period of history, the deliberate killing of newborns is virtually never justified. This is in part because newborns are so close to being persons that to kill them requires a very strong moral justification—as does the killing of dolphins, chimpanzees, and other highly personlike creatures. It is certainly wrong to kill such beings for the sake of convenience, or financial profit, or "sport." Only the most vital human needs, such as the need to defend one's own life and physical integrity, can provide a plausible justification for killing such beings.

In the case of an infant, there is no such vital need, since in the contemporary world there are usually other people who are eager to provide a good home for an infant whose own parents are unable or unwilling to care for it. Many people wait years for the opportunity to adopt a child, and some are unable to do so, even though there is every reason to believe that they would be good parents. The needless destruction of a viable infant not only deprives a sentient human being of life, but also deprives other persons of a source of great satisfaction, perhaps severely impoverishing their lives.

Even if an infant is unadoptable (e.g., because of some severe physical disability), it is still wrong to kill it. For most of us value the lives of infants, and would greatly prefer to pay taxes to support foster care and state institutions for disabled children, rather than to allow them to be killed or abandoned. So long as most people feel this way, and so long as it is possible to provide care for infants who are unwanted, or who have special needs that their parents cannot meet without assistance, it is wrong to let any infant die who has a chance of living a reasonably good life.

If these arguments show that infanticide is wrong, at least in today's world, then why don't they also show that late-term abortion is always wrong? After all, third-trimester fetuses are almost as personlike as infants, and many people value them and would prefer that they be preserved. As a potential source of pleasure to some family, a fetus is just as valuable as an infant. But there is an important difference between these two cases: once the infant is born, its continued life cannot pose any serious threat to the woman's life or health, since she is free to put it up for adoption or to place it in foster care. While she might, in rare cases, prefer that the child die rather than be raised by others, such a preference would not establish a right on her part.

In contrast, a pregnant woman's right to protect her own life and health outweighs other people's desire that the fetus be preserved—just as, when a person's life or health is threatened by an animal, and when the threat cannot be removed without killing the animal, that person's right to self-defense outweighs the desires of those who would prefer that the animal not be killed. Thus, while the moment of birth may mark no sharp discontinuity in the degree to which an infant resembles a person, it does mark the end of the mother's right to determine its fate. Indeed, if a late abortion can be safely performed without harming the fetus, she has in most cases no right to insist upon its death, for the same reason that she has no right to insist that a viable infant be killed or allowed to die.

It remains true that, on my view, neither abortion nor the killing of newborns is obviously a form of murder. Perhaps our legal sys-

tem is correct in its classification of infanticide as murder, since no other legal category adequately expresses the force of our disapproval of this action. But some moral distinction remains, and it has important consequences. When a society cannot possibly care for all of the children who are born, without endangering the survival of adults and older children, allowing some infants to die may be the best of a bad set of options. Throughout history, most societies—from those that lived by gathering and hunting to the highly civilized Chinese, Japanese, Greeks, and Romans—have permitted infanticide under such unfortunate circumstances, regarding it as a necessary evil. It shows a lack of understanding to condemn these societies as morally benighted for this reason alone, since in the absence of safe and effective means of contraception and abortion, parents must sometimes have had no morally better options.

Conclusion

I have argued that fetuses are neither persons nor members of the moral community. Furthermore, neither a fetus's resemblance to a person, nor its potential for becoming a person, provides an adequate basis for the claim that it has a full and equal right to life. At the same time, there are medical as well as moral reasons for preferring early to late abortion when the pregnancy is unwanted.

Women, unlike fetuses, are undeniably persons and members of the human moral community. If unwanted or medically dangerous pregnancies never occurred, then it might be possible to respect women's basic moral rights, while at the same time extending the same basic rights to fetuses. But in the real world such pregnancies do occur—often despite the woman's best efforts to prevent them. Even if the perfect contraceptive were universally available, the continued occurrence of rape and incest would make access to abortion a vital human need. Because women are persons, and fetuses are not, women's rights to life, liberty, and physical integrity morally override whatever right to life it may be appropriate to ascribe to a fetus. Consequently, laws that deny women the right to obtain abortions, or that make safe early abortions difficult or impossible for some women to obtain, are an unjustified violation of basic moral and constitutional rights.

NOTES

1. Strictly speaking, a human conceptus does not become a fetus until the primary organ systems have formed, at about six to eight weeks gestational age. However, for simplicity I shall refer to the conceptus as a fetus at every stage of its prenatal development.

2. For example, Roger Wertheimer argues, in "Understanding the Abortion Argument," *Philosophy and Public Affairs, 1* (Fall, 1971), that the moral status of abortion is not a question of fact, but only of how one responds to the facts.

3. John Noonan, "Abortion and the Catholic Church: A Summary History," *Natural Law Forum,* 12 (1967), 125.

4. John Noonan, "Deciding Who is Human," *Natural Law Forum,* 13 (1968), 134.

5. Noonan, "Deciding Who is Human," 135.

6. From here on, I will use "human" to mean "genetically human," since the moral sense of the term seems closely connected to, and perhaps derived from, the assumption that genetic humanity is both necessary and sufficient for membership in the moral community.

7. Fetal sentience is impossible prior to the development of neurological connections between the sense organs and the brain, and between the various parts of the brain involved in the processing of conscious experience. This stage of neurological development is currently thought to occur at some point in the late second or early third trimester.

8. Thomas L. Hayes, "A Biological View," *Commonweal,* 85 (March 17,1967), 677–678; cited by Daniel Callahan, in *Abortion: Law, Choice, and Morality* (London: Macmillan, 1970).

Review and Discussion Questions

1. Warren rejects the principle, which Noonan appears to accept, that all and only biological human beings are persons. With whom do you agree—Warren or Noonan? Explain why.

2. Does Warren correctly identify the characteristics that are central to the concept of personhood, or should her list be modified in some way? Do you agree that a fetus has none of the characteristics she mentions? Give an example of a being that is genetically human but not a person in the moral sense and an example of a being that is a person but not a human being.

3. Even if a fetus is not a person, we could still choose to extend moral rights to it. Are there sound reasons for doing so, or do you agree with Warren that the consequences of doing so would be unacceptable?

4. Warren concedes that late-term fetuses may be sentient, yet she holds that they are not yet persons. Do you agree, or do all sentient beings have a right to life?

5. Many people have thought that the potential of a fetus to develop full human capacities is of great moral importance, but Warren disagrees. What moral weight, if any, should we place on the fetus's potential for development? How persuasive do you find her argument about the space traveler escaping cloning?

6. Warren argues that even though newborn infants are not persons, infanticide is still wrong. Assess her reasoning. Can infanticide be seriously wrong, as most people believe, if newborn infants lack a right to life?

An Argument That Abortion Is Wrong

DON MARQUIS

Don Marquis, professor of philosophy at the University of Kansas, argues that the debate over whether the fetus has a right to life has reached an impasse and that there are problems with both the standard anti-abortion position (as represented by Noonan) and the standard pro-choice position (as represented by Warren). Turning to the issue of why killing is wrong in the first place, Marquis argues that what makes killing an adult human being wrong is the loss of his or her future. However, because a fetus has a future like ours, killing it would be wrong for the same reason that it would be wrong to kill an adult human being. Accordingly, abortion is seriously wrong (except in rare cases). Marquis goes on to present four arguments in support of his theory and to rebut several objections to it.

Study Questions

1. On what grounds does Marquis criticize the anti-abortion argument that the fetus has a right to life because it is human? Why is he critical of the pro-choice position that the fetus lacks a right to life because it is not a person?

2. What is the Future Like Ours (FLO) account of the wrongness of killing and how does it apply to abortion?

3. Marquis contends that the FLO account yields correct answers to certain life-and-death cases. What examples does he give?

4. Explain the analogy Marquis draws between his anti-abortion argument and the reason it is wrong to cause animals to suffer.

5. How does Marquis respond to the objection that his argument entails that contraception is immoral?

THE PURPOSE OF THIS ESSAY is to set out an argument for the claim that abortion, except perhaps in rare instances, is seriously wrong.[1] One reason for these exceptions is to eliminate from consideration cases whose ethical analysis should be controversial and detailed for clear-headed opponents of abortion. Such cases include abortion after rape and abortion during the first fourteen days after conception when there is an argument that the fetus is not definitely an individual. Another reason for making these exceptions is to allow for those cases in which the permissibility of abortion is compatible with the argument of this essay. Such cases

Reprinted by permission from Hugh LaFollette, ed., Ethics in Practice. *Copyright © 1997 Blackwell Publishers.*

include abortion when continuation of a pregnancy endangers a woman's life and abortion when the fetus is anencephalic. When I speak of the wrongness of abortion in this essay, a reader should presume the above qualifications. I mean by an abortion an action intended to bring about the death of a fetus for the sake of the woman who carries it. (Thus, as is standard on the literature on this subject, I eliminate spontaneous abortions from consideration.) I mean by a fetus a developing human being from the time of conception to the time of birth. (Thus, as is standard, I call embryos and zygotes, fetuses.)

The argument of this essay will establish that abortion is wrong for the same reason as killing a reader of this essay is wrong. I shall just assume, rather than establish, that killing you is seriously wrong. I shall make no attempt to offer a complete ethics of killing. Finally, I shall make no attempt to resolve some very fundamental and difficult general philosophical issues into which this analysis of the ethics of abortion might lead.

Why the Debate over Abortion Seems Intractable

Symmetries that emerge from the analysis of the major arguments on either side of the abortion debate may explain why the abortion debate seems intractable. Consider the following standard anti-abortion argument: Fetuses are both human and alive. Humans have the right to life. Therefore, fetuses have the right to life. Of course, women have the right to control their own bodies, but the right to life overrides the right of a woman to control her own body. Therefore, abortion is wrong. . . .

Do fetuses have the right to life?

. . . An argument that fetuses either have or lack the right to life must be based upon some general criterion for having or lacking the right to life. Opponents of abortion, on the one hand, look around for the broadest possible plausible criterion, so that fetuses will fall under it. This explains why classic arguments against abortion appeal to the criterion of being human (Noonan, 1970 . . .). This criterion appears plausible: The claim that all humans, whatever their race, gender, religion or *age,* have the right to life seems evident enough. In addition, because the fetuses we are concerned with do not, after all, belong to another species, they are clearly human. Thus, the syllogism that generates the conclusion that fetuses have the right to life is apparently sound.

On the other hand, those who believe abortion is morally permissible wish to find a narrow, but plausible, criterion for possession of the right to life so that fetuses will fall outside of it. This explains, in part, why the standard pro-choice arguments in the philosophical literature appeal to the criterion of being a person (Warren, 1973 . . .). This criterion appears plausible: The claim that only persons have the right to life seems evident enough. Furthermore, because fetuses neither are rational nor possess the capacity to communicate in complex ways nor possess a concept of self that continues through time, no fetus is a person. Thus, the syllogism needed to generate the conclusion that no fetus possesses the right to life is apparently sound. Given that no fetus possesses the right to life, a woman's right to control her own body easily generates the general right to abortion. The existence of two apparently defensible syllogisms which support contrary conclusions helps to explain why partisans on both sides of the abortion dispute often regard their opponents as either morally depraved or mentally deficient.

Which syllogism should we reject? The anti-abortion syllogism is usually attacked by attacking its major premise: the claim that whatever is biologically human has the right to life. This premise is subject to scope problems because the class of the biologically human includes too

much: human cancer-cell cultures are biologically human, but they do not have the right to
life. Moreover, this premise also is subject to
moral-relevance problems: the connection between the biological and the moral is merely assumed. It is hard to think of a good *argument*
for such a connection. If one wishes to consider
the category of "human" a moral category, as
some people find it plausible to do in other
contexts, then one is left with no way of showing that the fetus is fully human without
begging the question. Thus, the classic anti-
abortion argument appears subject to fatal
difficulties.

These difficulties with the classic anti-
abortion argument are well known and thought
by many to be conclusive. The symmetrical difficulties with the classic pro-choice syllogism are
not as well recognized. The pro-choice syllogism
can be attacked by attacking its major premise:
Only persons have the right to life. This premise
is subject to scope problems because the class of
persons includes too little: infants, the severely
retarded, and some of the mentally ill seem to
fall outside the class of persons as the supporter
of choice understands the concept. The premise
is also subject to moral-relevance problems: Being a person is understood by the pro-choicer as
having certain psychological attributes. If the
pro-choicer questions the connection between
the biological and the moral, the opponent of
abortion can question the connection between
the psychological and the moral. If one wishes to
consider "person" a moral category, as is often
done, then one is left with no way of showing
that the fetus is not a person without begging
the question. . . .

The argument of this section has attempted
to establish, albeit briefly, that the classic
anti-abortion argument and the pro-choice argument favored by most philosophers both face
problems that are mirror images of one another.
A stand-off results. The abortion debate requires a different strategy.

The "Future Like Ours" Account of the Wrongness of Killing

Why do the standard arguments in the abortion
debate fail to resolve the issue? The general
principles to which partisans in the debate appeal are either truisms most persons would affirm in the absence of much reflection, or very
general moral theories. All are subject to major
problems. A different approach is needed.

Opponents of abortion claim that abortion is
wrong because abortion involves killing someone like us, a human being who just happens to
be very young. Supporters of choice claim that
ending the life of a fetus is not in the same moral
category as ending the life of an adult human being. Surely this controversy cannot be resolved
in the absence of an account of what it is about
killing us that makes killing us wrong. On the
one hand, if we know what property we possess
that makes killing us wrong, then we can ask
whether fetuses have the same property. On the
other hand, suppose that we do not know what
it is about us that makes killing us wrong. If this
is so, we do not understand even easy cases in
which killing is wrong. Surely, we will not understand the ethics of killing fetuses, for if we do
not understand easy cases, then we will not understand hard cases. Both pro-choicer and
anti-abortionist agree that it is obvious that it is
wrong to kill us. Thus, a discussion of what it is
about us that makes killing us not only wrong,
but seriously wrong, seems to be the right place
to begin a discussion of the abortion issue.

Who is primarily wronged by a killing? The
wrong of killing is not primarily explained in
terms of the loss to the family and friends of the
victim. Perhaps the victim is a hermit. Perhaps
one's friends find it easy to make new friends.
The wrong of killing is not primarily explained
in terms of the brutalization of the killer. The
great wrong to the victim explains the brutalization, not the other way around. The wrongness of killing us is understood in terms of what

killing does to us. Killing us imposes on us the misfortune of premature death. That misfortune underlies the wrongness.

Premature death is a misfortune because when one is dead, one has been deprived of life. This misfortune can be more precisely specified. Premature death cannot deprive me of my past life. That part of my life is already gone. If I die tomorrow or if I live thirty more years my past life will be no different. It has occurred on either alternative. Rather than my past, my death deprives me of my future, of the life that I would have lived if I had lived out my natural life span.

The loss of a future biological life does not explain the misfortune of death. Compare two scenarios: In the former I now fall into a coma from which I do not recover until my death in thirty years. In the latter I die now. The latter scenario does not seem to describe a greater misfortune than the former.

The loss of our future conscious life is what underlies the misfortune of premature death. Not any future conscious life qualifies, however. Suppose that I am terminally ill with cancer. Suppose also that pain and suffering would dominate my future conscious life. If so, then death would not be a misfortune for me.

Thus, the misfortune of premature death consists of the loss to us of the future goods of consciousness. What are these goods? Much can be said about this issue, but a simple answer will do for the purposes of this essay. The goods of life are whatever we get out of life. The goods of life are those items toward which we take a "pro" attitude. They are completed projects of which we are proud, the pursuit of our goals, aesthetic enjoyments, friendships, intellectual pursuits, and physical pleasures of various sorts. The goods of life are what makes life worth living. In general, what makes life worth living for one person will not be the same as what makes life worth living for another. Nevertheless, the list of goods in each of our lives will overlap.

The lists are usually different in different stages of our lives.

What makes the goods of my future good for me? One possible, but wrong, answer is my desire for those goods now. This answer does not account for those aspects of my future life that I now believe I will later value, but about which I am wrong. Neither does it account for those aspects of my future that I will come to value, but which I don't value now. What is valuable to the young may not be valuable to the middle-aged. What is valuable to the middle-aged may not be valuable to the old. Some of life's values for the elderly are best appreciated by the elderly. Thus it is wrong to say that the value of my future to me is just what I value now. What makes my future valuable to me are those aspects of my future that I will (or would) value when I will (or would) experience them, whether I value them now or not.

It follows that a person can believe that she will have a valuable future and be wrong. Furthermore, a person can believe that he will not have a valuable future and also be wrong. This is confirmed by our attitude toward many of the suicidal. We attempt to save the lives of the suicidal and to convince them that they have made an error in judgment. This does not mean that the future of an individual obtains value from the value that others confer on it. It means that, in some cases, others can make a clearer judgment of the value of a person's future *to that person* than the person herself. This often happens when one's judgment concerning the value of one's own future is clouded by personal tragedy. . . .

Thus, what is sufficient to make killing us wrong, in general, is that it causes premature death. Premature death is a misfortune. Premature death is a misfortune, in general, because it deprives an individual of a future of value. An individual's future will be valuable to that individual if that individual will come, or would come, to value it. We know that killing us is wrong. What makes killing us wrong, in general, is that it deprives us of a future of value. Thus, killing someone is wrong, in general, when it deprives her of a future like ours. I shall call this "an FLO."

Arguments in Favor of the FLO Theory

At least four arguments support this FLO account of the wrongness of killing.

The considered judgment argument

The FLO account of the wrongness of killing is correct because it fits with our considered judgment concerning the nature of the misfortune of death. The analysis of the previous section is an exposition of the nature of this considered judgment. This judgment can be confirmed. If one were to ask individuals with AIDS or with incurable cancer about the nature of their misfortune, I believe that they would say or imply that their impending loss of an FLO makes their premature death a misfortune. If they would not, then the FLO account would plainly be wrong.

The worst of crimes argument

The FLO account of the wrongness of killing is correct because it explains why we believe that killing is one of the worst of crimes. My being killed deprives me of more than does my being robbed or beaten or harmed in some other way because my being killed deprives me of all of the value of my future, not merely part of it. This explains why we make the penalty for murder greater than the penalty for other crimes.

As a corollary the FLO account of the wrongness of killing also explains why killing an adult human being is justified only in the most extreme circumstances, only in circumstances in which the loss of life to an individual is outweighed by a worse outcome if that life is not taken. Thus, we are willing to justify killing in self-defense, killing in order to save one's own life, because one's loss if one does not kill in that situation is so very great. We justify killing in a just war for similar reasons. We believe that capital punishment would be justified if, by having such an institution, fewer premature deaths would occur. The FLO account of the wrongness of killing does not entail that killing is always wrong. Nevertheless, the FLO account explains both why killing is one of the worst of crimes and, as a corollary, why the exceptions to the wrongness of killing are so very rare. A correct theory of the wrongness of killing should have these features.

The appeal to cases argument

The FLO account of the wrongness of killing is correct because it yields the correct answers in many life-and-death cases that arise in medicine and have interested philosophers.

Consider medicine first. Most people believe that it is not wrong deliberately to end the life of a person who is permanently unconscious. Thus we believe that it is not wrong to remove a feeding tube or a ventilator from a permanently comatose patient, knowing that such a removal will cause death. The FLO account of the wrongness of killing explains why this is so. A patient who is permanently unconscious cannot have a future that she would come to value, whatever her values. Therefore, according to the FLO theory of the wrongness of killing, death could not, *ceteris paribus,* be a misfortune to her. Therefore, removing the feeding tube or ventilator does not wrong her.

By contrast, almost all people believe that it is wrong, *ceteris paribus,* to withdraw medical treatment from patients who are temporarily unconscious. The FLO account of the wrongness of killing also explains why this is so. Furthermore, these two unconsciousness cases explain why the FLO account of the wrongness of killing does not include present consciousness as a necessary condition for the wrongness of killing.

Consider now the issue of the morality of legalizing active euthanasia. Proponents of active euthanasia argue that if a patient faces a future of intractable pain and wants to die, then, *ceteris paribus,* it would not be wrong for a physician to give him medicine that she knows would result in his death. This view is so universally accepted that even the strongest *opponents* of active euthanasia hold it. The official Vatican view . . . is that it is permissible for a physician to administer to a patient morphine sufficient (although no more than sufficient) to control his pain even if she foresees that the morphine will result in his death. Notice how nicely the FLO account of the wrongness of killing explains this unanimity of opinion. A patient known to be in severe intractable pain is presumed to have a future without positive value. Accordingly, death would not be a misfortune for him and an action that would (foreseeably) end his life would not be wrong.

Contrast this with the standard emergency medical treatment of the suicidal. Even though the suicidal have indicated that they want to die, medical personnel will act to save their lives. This supports the view that it is not the mere *desire* to enjoy an FLO which is crucial to our understanding of the wrongness of killing. *Having* an FLO is what is crucial to the account, although one would, of course, want to make an exception in the case of fully autonomous people who refuse life-saving medical treatment. Opponents of abortion can, of course, be willing to make an exception for fully autonomous fetuses who refuse life support.

The FLO theory of the wrongness of killing also deals correctly with issues that have concerned philosophers. It implies that it would be wrong to kill (peaceful) persons from outer space who come to visit our planet even though they are biologically utterly unlike us. Presumably, if they are persons, then they will have fu-

tures that are sufficiently like ours so that it would be wrong to kill them. The FLO account of the wrongness of killing shares this feature with the personhood views of the supporters of choice. Classical opponents of abortion who locate the wrongness of abortion somehow in the biological humanity of a fetus cannot explain this.

The FLO account does not entail that there is another species of animals whose members ought not to be killed. Neither does it entail that it is permissible to kill any non-human animal. On the one hand, a supporter of animals' rights might argue that since some nonhuman animals have a future of value, it is wrong to kill them also, or at least it is wrong to kill them without a far better reason than we usually have for killing non-human animals. On the other hand, one might argue that the futures of non-human animals are not sufficiently like ours for the FLO account to entail that it is wrong to kill them. Since the FLO account does not specify which properties a future of another individual must possess so that killing that individual is wrong, the FLO account is indeterminate with respect to this issue. The fact that the FLO account of the wrongness of killing does not give a determinate answer to this question is not a flaw in the theory. A sound ethical account should yield the right answers in the obvious cases; it should not be required to resolve every disputed question.

A major respect in which the FLO account is superior to accounts that appeal to the concept of person is the explanation the FLO account provides of the wrongness of killing infants. There was a class of infants who had futures that included a class of events that were identical to the futures of the readers of this essay. Thus, reader, the FLO account explains why it was as wrong to kill you when you were an infant as it is to kill you now. This account can be generalized to almost all infants. Notice that the wrongness of killing infants can be explained in the absence of an account of what makes the future of an individual sufficiently valuable so that it is wrong to kill that individual. The absence of such an account explains why the FLO account is indeterminate with respect to the wrongness of killing non-human animals.

If the FLO account is the correct theory of the wrongness of killing, then because abortion involves killing fetuses and fetuses have FLOs for exactly the same reasons that infants have FLOs, abortion is presumptively seriously immoral. This inference lays the necessary groundwork for a fourth argument in favor of the FLO account that shows that abortion is wrong.

The analogy with animals argument

Why do we believe it is wrong to cause animals suffering? We believe that, in our own case and in the case of other adults and children, suffering is a misfortune. It would be as morally arbitrary to refuse to acknowledge that animal suffering is wrong as it would be to refuse to acknowledge that the suffering of persons of another race is wrong. It is, on reflection, suffering that is a misfortune, not the suffering of white males or the suffering of humans. Therefore, infliction of suffering is presumptively wrong no matter on whom it is inflicted and whether it is inflicted on persons or nonpersons. Arbitrary restrictions on the wrongness of suffering count as racism or speciesism. Not only is this argument convincing on its own, but it is the only way of justifying the wrongness of animal cruelty. Cruelty toward animals is clearly wrong. (This famous argument is due to Singer, 1979.)

The FLO account of the wrongness of abortion is analogous. We believe that, in our own case and the cases of other adults and children, the loss of a future of value is a misfortune. It would be . . . morally arbitrary to refuse to acknowledge that the loss of a future of value to a fetus is wrong. . . . To deprive someone of a future of value is wrong no matter on whom the deprivation is inflicted and no matter whether the deprivation is inflicted on persons or non-

persons. Arbitrary restrictions on the wrongness of this deprivation count as racism, genocide, or ageism. Therefore, abortion is wrong. This argument that abortion is wrong should be convincing because it has the same form as the argument for the claim that causing pain and suffering to non-human animals is wrong. Since the latter argument is convincing, the former argument should be also. Thus, an analogy with animals supports the thesis that abortion is wrong.

Replies to Objections

The four arguments in the previous section establish that abortion is, except in rare cases, seriously immoral. Not surprisingly, there are objections to this view. There are replies to the [three] most important objections to the FLO argument for the immorality of abortion.

The potentiality objection

The FLO account of the wrongness of abortion is a potentiality argument. To claim that a fetus has an FLO is to claim that a fetus now has the potential to be in a state of a certain kind in the future. It is not to claim that all ordinary fetuses will have FLOs. Fetuses who are aborted, of course, will not. To say that a standard fetus has an FLO is to say that a standard fetus either will have or would have a life it will or would value. To say that a standard fetus would have a life it would value is to say that it will have a life it will value if it does not die prematurely. The truth of this conditional is based upon the nature of fetuses (including the fact that they naturally age) and this nature concerns their potential.

Some appeals to potentiality in the abortion debate rest on unsound inferences. For example, one may try to generate an argument against abortion by arguing that because persons have the right to life, potential persons also have the right to life. Such an argument is plainly invalid as it stands. The premise one needs to add to make it valid would have to be something like: "If Xs have the right to Y, then potential Xs have the right to Y." This premise is plainly false. Potential presidents don't have the rights of the presidency; potential voters don't have the right to vote.

In the FLO argument potentiality is not used in order to bridge the gap between adults and fetuses as is done in the argument in the above paragraph. The FLO theory of the wrongness of killing adults is based upon the adult's potentiality to have a future of value. Potentiality is in the argument from the very beginning. Thus, the plainly false premise is not required. Accordingly, the use of potentiality in the FLO theory is not a sign of an illegitimate inference.

The argument from interests

A second objection to the FLO account of the immorality of abortion involves arguing that even though fetuses have FLOs, nonsentient fetuses do not meet the minimum conditions for having any moral standing at all because they lack interests. Steinbock (1992, p. 5) has presented this argument clearly:

> Beings that have moral status must be capable of caring about what is done to them. They must be capable of being made, if only in a rudimentary sense, happy or miserable, comfortable or distressed. Whatever reasons we may have for preserving or protecting nonsentient beings, these reasons do not refer to their own interests. For without conscious awareness, beings cannot have interests. Without interests, they cannot have a welfare of their own. Without a welfare of their own, nothing can be done for their sake. Hence, they lack moral standing or status.

Medical researchers have argued that fetuses do not become sentient until after 22 weeks of gestation (Steinbock, 1992, p. 50). If they are correct, and if Steinbock's argument is sound, then we have both an objection to the FLO account of the wrongness of abortion and a basis for a view on abortion minimally acceptable to most supporters of choice.

Steinbock's conclusion conflicts with our settled moral beliefs. Temporarily unconscious human beings are nonsentient, yet no one believes that they lack either interests or moral standing. Accordingly, neither conscious awareness nor the capacity for conscious awareness is a necessary condition for having interests.

The counter-example of the temporarily unconscious human being shows that there is something internally wrong with Steinbock's argument. The difficulty stems from an ambiguity. One cannot *take* an interest in something without being capable of caring about what is done to it. However, something can be *in* someone's interest without that individual being capable of caring about it, or about anything. Thus, life support can be *in* the interests of a temporarily unconscious patient even though the temporarily unconscious patient is incapable of *taking* an interest in that life support. If this can be so for the temporarily unconscious patient, then it is hard to see why it cannot be so for the temporarily unconscious (that is, nonsentient) fetus who requires placental life support. Thus the objection based on interests fails. . . .

The contraception objection

The strongest objection to the FLO argument for the immorality of abortion is based on the claim that, because contraception results in one less FLO, the FLO argument entails that contraception, indeed, abstention from sex when conception is possible, is immoral. Because neither contraception nor abstention from sex when conception is possible is immoral, the FLO account is flawed.

There is a cogent reply to this objection. If the argument of the early part of this essay is correct, then the central issue concerning the morality of abortion is the problem of whether fetuses are individuals who are members of the class of individuals whom it is seriously presumptively wrong to kill. The properties of being human and alive, of being a person, and of having an FLO are criteria that participants in the abortion debate have offered to mark off the relevant class of individuals. The central claim of this essay is that having an FLO marks off the relevant class of individuals. A defender of the FLO view could, therefore, reply that since, at the time of contraception, there is no individual to have an FLO, the FLO account does not entail that contraception is wrong. The wrong of killing is primarily a wrong to the individual who is killed; at the time of contraception there is no individual to be wronged.

However, someone who presses the contraception objection might have an answer to this reply. She might say that the sperm and egg are the individuals deprived of an FLO at the time of contraception. Thus, there are individuals whom contraception deprives of an FLO and if depriving an individual of an FLO is what makes killing wrong, then the FLO theory entails that contraception is wrong.

There is also a reply to this move. In the case of abortion, an objectively determinate individual is the subject of harm caused by the loss of an FLO. This individual is a fetus. In the case of contraception, there are far more candidates (see Norcross, 1990). Let us consider some possible candidates in order of the increasing number of individuals harmed: (1) The single harmed individual might be the combination of the particular sperm and the particular egg that would have united to form a zygote if contraception had not been used. (2) The two harmed individuals might be the particular sperm itself, and, in addition, the ovum itself that would have physically combined to form the zygote. (This is modeled on the double homicide of two persons who would otherwise in a short time fuse. (1) is modeled on harm to a single entity some of whose parts are not physically contiguous, such as a university.) (3) The many harmed individuals might be the millions of *combinations* of

sperm and the released ovum whose (small) chances of having an FLO were reduced by the successful contraception. (4) The even larger class of harmed individuals (larger by one) might be the class consisting of all of the individual sperm in an ejaculate and, in addition, the individual ovum released at the time of the successful contraception. (1) through (4) are all candidates for being the subject(s) of harm in the case of successful contraception or abstinence from sex. Which should be chosen? Should we hold a lottery? There seems to be no non-arbitrarily determinate subject of harm in the case of successful contraception. But if there is no such subject of harm, then no determinate thing was harmed. If no determinate thing was harmed, then (in the case of contraception) no wrong has been done. Thus, the FLO account of the wrongness of abortion does not entail that contraception is wrong.

Conclusion

This essay contains an argument for the view that, except in unusual circumstances, abortion is seriously wrong. Deprivation of an FLO explains why killing adults and children is wrong. Abortion deprives fetuses of FLOs. Therefore, abortion is wrong. This argument is based on an account of the wrongness of killing that is a result of our considered judgment of the nature of the misfortune of premature death. It accounts for why we regard killing as one of the worst of crimes. It is superior to alternative accounts of the wrongness of killing that are intended to provide insight into the ethics of abortion. This account of the wrongness of killing is supported by the way it handles cases in which our moral judgments are settled. This account has an analogue in the most plausible account of the wrongness of causing animals to suffer. This account makes no appeal to religion. Therefore, the FLO account shows that abortion, except in rare instances, is seriously wrong.

NOTE

1. This essay is an updated version of a view that first appeared in the *Journal of Philosophy* (1989). This essay incorporates attempts to deal with the objections of McInerney (1990), Norcross (1990), Shirley (1995), Steinbock (1992), and Paske (1994) to the original version of the view.

References

Marquis, D. B., "A Future Like Ours and the Concept of Person: A Reply to McInerney and Paske," *The Abortion Controversy: A Reader*, ed. L. P. Pojman and F. J. Beckwith, Boston: Jones and Bartlett, 1994, 354–68.
———, "Fetuses, Futures and Values: A Reply to Shirley," *Southwest Philosophy Review*, 11 (1995): 263–5.
———, "Why Abortion Is Immoral," *Journal of Philosophy*, 86 (1989): 183–202.
McInerney, P., "Does a Fetus Already Have a Future Like Ours?" *Journal of Philosophy*, 97 (1990): 264–8.

Noonan, J., "An Almost Absolute Value in History" [see this volume, pp. 129–133].
Norcross, A., "Killing, Abortion, and Contraception: A Reply to Marquis," *Journal of Philosophy*, 87 (1990): 268–77.
Paske, G., "Abortion and the Neo-Natal Right to Life: A Critique of Marquis's Futurist Argument," *The Abortion Controversy: A Reader*, ed. L. P. Pojman and F. J. Beckwith, Boston: Jones and Bartlett, 1994, pp. 343–53.
Shirley, E. S., "Marquis' Argument against Abortion: A Critique," *Southwest Philosophy Review*, 11 (1995): 79–89.
Singer, P., "Not for Humans Only: The Place of Nonhumans in Environmental Issues," *Ethics and Problems of the 21st Century*, ed. K. E. Goodpaster and K. M. Sayre, South Bend: Notre Dame University Press, 1979.
Steinbock, B., *Life Before Birth: The Moral and Legal Status of Embryos and Fetuses*, New York: Oxford University Press, 1992.
Warren, M. A., "On the Moral and Legal Status of Abortion," *Monist*, 57 (1973): 43–61.

Review and Discussion Questions

1. Is the debate over whether the fetus has a right to life deadlocked, as Marquis argues? How persuasive are his arguments against Noonan's anti-abortion position and Warren's pro-choice stance? Is his approach to the abortion issue superior to theirs?

2. Why is it wrong to kill an adult human being? Are there any plausible accounts of why killing is wrong other than Marquis's FLO account?

3. Restate and assess the four arguments that Marquis advances in support of the FLO theory. How persuasive are they? Which argument do you find the most convincing?

4. Assuming that Marquis's account of the wrongness of killing is correct, does it show that abortion is immoral? Assess the following argument: Although fetuses have a FLO, they lack moral standing because, not being sentient, they cannot meaningfully be said to have interests; therefore, abortion is morally permissible.

5. Marquis's position would be implausible if it entailed, as some critics claim it does, that contraception is wrong. Is his defense of his position on this issue successful?

A Defense of Abortion

JUDITH JARVIS THOMSON

The moral debate over abortion has tended to focus on the moral status of the fetus. In this famous article, Judith Jarvis Thomson, professor of philosophy at the Massachusetts Institute of Technology, takes another approach. Conceding for the sake of argument that the fetus is a person with a right to life from the moment of conception, Thomson argues that abortion still is not necessarily wrong. Her essay uses several memorable analogies to make her point that, even if a fetus has a right to life, it may still lack a right to use the mother's body.

Study Questions

1. Explain the example of the kidnapped violinist. How does Thomson use it to challenge the standard anti-abortion argument?

2. What is the extreme anti-abortion view, and what is Thomson's response to it?

3. What is the case of Jones, Smith, and the coat intended to show?

4. What does the Henry Fonda example tell us about the right to life?

5. What argument is Thomson trying to answer with the burglar and people-seeds examples?

6. What is the difference between a Good Samaritan and a Minimally Decent Samaritan? How does this distinction fit into Thomson's defense of abortion?

MOST OPPOSITION TO ABORTION relies on the premise that the fetus is a human being, a person, from the moment of conception. The premise is argued for, but, as I think, not well. Take, for example, the most common argument. We are asked to notice that the development of a human being from conception through birth into childhood is continuous; then it is said that to draw a line, to choose a point in this development and say "before this point the thing is not a person, after this point it is a person" is to make an arbitrary choice, a choice for which in the nature of things no good reason can be given. It is concluded that the fetus is, or any-way that we had better say it is, a person from the moment of conception. But this conclusion does not follow. Similar things might be said about the development of an acorn into an oak tree, and it does not follow that acorns are oak trees, or that we had better say they are. Arguments of this form are sometimes called "slippery slope arguments"—the phrase is perhaps self-explanatory—and it is dismaying that opponents of abortion rely on them so heavily and uncritically.

I am inclined to agree, however, that the prospects for "drawing a line" in the development of the fetus look dim. I am inclined to think also that we shall probably have to agree that the fetus has already become a human person well before birth. Indeed, it comes as a surprise when one first learns how early in its life it begins to acquire human characteristics. By the tenth week, for example, it already has a face, arms and legs, fingers and toes; it has internal organs, and brain activity is detectable. On the other hand, I think that the premise is false, that the fetus is not a person from the moment of conception. A newly fertilized ovum, a newly implanted clump of cells, is no more a person than an acorn is an oak tree. But I shall not discuss any of this. For it seems to me to be of great interest to ask what happens if, for the sake of argument, we allow the premise. How, precisely, are we supposed to get from there to the conclusion that abortion is morally impermissible? Opponents of abortion commonly spend most of their time establishing that the fetus is a person, and hardly any time explaining the step from there to the impermissibility of abortion. Perhaps they think the step too simple and obvious to require much comment. . . . Whatever the explanation, I suggest that the step they take is neither easy nor obvious, that it calls for closer examination than is commonly given, and that when we do give it this closer examination we shall feel inclined to reject it.

I propose, then, that we grant that the fetus is a person from the moment of conception. How does the argument go from here? Something like this, I take it. Every person has a right to life. So the fetus has a right to life. No doubt the mother has a right to decide what shall happen in and to her body; everyone would grant that. But surely a person's right to life is stronger and more stringent than the mother's right to decide what happens in and to her body, and so outweighs it. So the fetus may not be killed; an abortion may not be performed.

It sounds plausible. But now let me ask you to imagine this. You wake up in the morning and find yourself back to back in bed with an unconscious violinist. A famous unconscious violinist. He has been found to have a fatal kidney ailment, and the Society of Music Lovers has canvassed all the available medical records and found that you alone have the right blood type to help. They have therefore kidnapped you, and last night the violinist's circulatory system was plugged into yours, so that your kidneys can be used to extract poisons from his blood as well as your own. The director of the hospital now tells you, "Look, we're sorry the Society of Music Lovers did this to you—we would never have permitted it if we had known. But still, they did it, and the violinist now is plugged into you. To unplug you would be to kill him. But never mind, it's only for nine months. By then he will have recovered from his ailment, and can safely be unplugged from you." Is it morally incumbent on you to accede to this situation? No doubt it would be very nice of you if you did, a great kindness. But do you *have* to accede to it? What if it were not nine months, but nine years? Or longer still? What if the director of the hospital says, "Tough luck, I agree, but you've now got to stay in bed, with the violinist plugged into you, for the rest of your life. Because remember this. All persons have a right to life, and violinists are persons. Granted you have a right to decide what happens in and to your body, but a person's right to life outweighs your right to decide what happens in and to your body. So you cannot ever be unplugged from him." I imagine you would regard this as outrageous, which suggests that something really is wrong with that plausible-sounding argument I mentioned a moment ago.

In this case, of course, you were kidnapped; you didn't volunteer for the operation that plugged the violinist into your kidneys. Can those who oppose abortion on the ground I mentioned make an exception for a pregnancy due to rape? Certainly. They can say that persons have a right to life only if they didn't come into existence because of rape; or they can say that all persons have a right to life, but that some have less of a right to life than others, in particular, that those who come into existence because of rape have less. But these statements have a rather unpleasant sound. Surely the question of whether you have a right to life at all, or how much of it you have, shouldn't turn on the question of whether or not you are the product of a rape. And in fact the people who oppose abortion on the ground I mentioned do not make this distinction, and hence do not make an exception in case of rape.

Nor do they make an exception for a case in which the mother has to spend the nine months of her pregnancy in bed. They would agree that would be a great pity, and hard on the mother; but all the same, all persons have a right to life, the fetus is a person, and so on. I suspect, in fact, that they would not make an exception for a case in which, miraculously enough, the pregnancy went on for nine years, or even the rest of the mother's life.

Some won't even make an exception for a case in which continuation of the pregnancy is likely to shorten the mother's life; they regard abortion as impermissible even to save the mother's life. Such cases are nowadays very rare, and many opponents of abortion do not accept this extreme view. All the same, it is a good place to begin: a number of points of interest come out in respect to it.

1. The Extreme Anti-Abortion View

Let us call the view that abortion is impermissible even to save the mother's life "the extreme view." I want to suggest first that it does not issue from the argument I mentioned earlier without the addition of some fairly powerful premises. Suppose a woman has become pregnant, and now learns that she has a cardiac condition such that she will die if she carries the baby to term. What may be done for her? The fetus, being a person, has a right to life, but as the mother is a person too, so has she a right to life. Presumably they have an equal right to life.

How is it supposed to come out that an abortion may not be performed? If mother and child have an equal right to life, shouldn't we perhaps flip a coin? Or should we add to the mother's right to life her right to decide what happens in and to her body, which everybody seems to be ready to grant—the sum of her rights now outweighing the fetus' right to life?

The most familiar argument here is the following. We are told that performing the abortion would be directly killing the child, whereas doing nothing would not be killing the mother, but only letting her die. Moreover, in killing the child, one would be killing an innocent person, for the child has committed no crime, and is not aiming at his mother's death. . . . If directly killing an innocent person is murder, and thus is impermissible, then the mother's directly killing the innocent person inside her is murder, and thus is impermissible. But it cannot seriously be thought to be murder if the mother performs an abortion on herself to save her life. It cannot seriously be said that she *must* refrain, that she *must* sit passively by and wait for her death. Let us look again at the case of you and the violinist. There you are, in bed with the violinist, and the director of the hospital says to you, "It's all most distressing, and I deeply sympathize, but you see this is putting an additional strain on your kidneys, and you'll be dead within the month. But you *have* to stay where you are all the same. Because unplugging you would be directly killing an innocent violinist, and that's murder, and that's impermissible." If anything in the world is true, it is that you do not commit murder, you do not do what is impermissible, if you reach around to your back and unplug yourself from that violinist to save your life.

The main focus of attention in writings on abortion has been on what a third party may or may not do in answer to a request from a woman for an abortion. This is in a way understandable. Things being as they are, there isn't much a woman can safely do to abort herself. So the question asked is what a third party may do, and what the mother may do, if it is mentioned at all, is deduced, almost as an afterthought, from what it is concluded that third parties may do. But it seems to me that to treat the matter in this way is to refuse to grant to the mother that very status of person which is so firmly insisted on for the fetus. For we cannot simply read off what a person may do from what a third party may do. Suppose you find yourself trapped in a tiny house with a growing child. I mean a very tiny house, and a rapidly growing child—you are already up against the wall of the house and in a few minutes you'll be crushed to death. The child on the other hand won't be crushed to death; if nothing is done to stop him from growing he'll be hurt, but in the end he'll simply burst open the house and walk out a free man. Now I could well understand it if a bystander were to say, "There's nothing we can do for you. We cannot choose between your life and his, we cannot be the ones to decide who is to live, we cannot intervene." But it cannot be concluded that you too can do nothing, that you cannot attack it to save your life. However innocent the child may be, you do not have to wait passively while it crushes you to death. Perhaps a pregnant woman is vaguely felt to have the status of [a] house, to which we don't allow the right of self-defense. But if the woman houses the child, it should be remembered that she is a person who houses it.

I should perhaps stop to say explicitly that I am not claiming that people have a right to do anything whatever to save their lives. I think, rather, that there are drastic limits to the right of self-defense. If someone threatens you with death unless you torture someone else to death, I think you have not the right, even to save your life, to do so. But the case under consideration here is very different. In our case there are only two people involved, one whose life is threatened, and one who threatens it. Both are innocent: the one who is threatened is not threatened because of any fault, the one who threatens does not threaten because of any fault. For this reason

we may feel that we bystanders cannot intervene. But the person threatened can.

In sum, a woman surely can defend her life against the threat to it posed by the unborn child, even if doing so involves its death. And this shows . . . that the extreme view of abortion is false. . . .

The extreme view could of course be weakened to say that while abortion is permissible to save the mother's life, it may not be performed by a third party, but only by the mother herself. But this cannot be right either. For what we have to keep in mind is that the mother and the unborn child are not like two tenants in a small house which has, by an unfortunate mistake, been rented to both; the mother *owns* the house. The fact that she does adds to the offensiveness of deducing that the mother can do nothing from the supposition that third parties can do nothing. But it does more than this: it casts a bright light on the supposition that third parties can do nothing. Certainly it lets us see that a third party who says "I cannot choose between you" is fooling himself if he thinks this is impartiality. If Jones has found and fastened on a certain coat, which he needs to keep from freezing, but which Smith also needs to keep him from freezing, then it is not impartiality that says "I cannot choose between you" when Smith owns the coat. Women have said again and again, "This body is *my* body!" and they have reason to feel angry, reason to feel that it has been like shouting into the wind. Smith, after all, is hardly likely to bless us if we say to him, "Of course it's your coat, anybody would grant that it is. But no one may choose between you and Jones who is to have it."

We should really ask what it is that says "no one may choose" in the face of the fact that the body that houses the child is the mother's body. It may be simply a failure to appreciate this fact. But it may be something more interesting, namely the sense that one has a right to refuse to lay hands on people, even where it would be just and fair to do so, even where justice seems to require that somebody do so. Thus justice might call for somebody to get Smith's coat back from Jones, and yet you have a right to refuse to be the one to lay hands on Jones, a right to refuse to do physical violence to him. This, I think, must be granted. But then what should be said is not "no one may choose," but only "*I* cannot choose," and indeed not even this, but "*I* will not *act*," leaving it open that somebody else can or should, and in particular that anyone in a position of authority, with the job of securing people's rights, both can and should. So this is no difficulty. I have not been arguing that any given third party must accede to the mother's request that he perform an abortion to save her life, but only that he may. . . .

2. The Right to Life

Where the mother's life is not at stake, the argument I mentioned at the outset seems to have a much stronger pull. "Everyone has a right to life, so the unborn person has a right to life." And isn't the child's right to life weightier than anything other than the mother's own right to life, which she might put forward as ground for an abortion?

This argument treats the right to life as if it were unproblematic. It is not, and this seems to me to be precisely the source of the mistake.

For we should now, at long last, ask what it comes to, to have a right to life. In some views having a right to life includes having a right to be given at least the bare minimum one needs for continued life. But suppose that what in fact *is* the bare minimum a man needs for continued life is something he has no right at all to be given? If I am sick unto death, and the only thing that will save my life is the touch of Henry Fonda's cool hand on my fevered brow, then all the same, I have no right to be given the touch of Henry Fonda's cool hand on my fevered brow. It would be frightfully nice of him to fly in from the West Coast to provide it. It would be less nice, though no doubt well meaning, if my

friends flew out to the West Coast and carried Henry Fonda back with them. But I have no right at all against anybody that he should do this for me. Or again, to return to the story I told earlier, the fact that for continued life that violinist needs the continued use of your kidneys does not establish that he has a right to be given the continued use of your kidneys. He certainly has no right against you that *you* should give him continued use of your kidneys. For nobody has any right to use your kidneys unless you give him such a right; and nobody has the right against you that you shall give him this right—if you do allow him to go on using your kidneys, this is a kindness on your part, and not something he can claim from you as his due. Nor has he any right against anybody else that *they* should give him continued use of your kidneys. Certainly he had no right against the Society of Music Lovers that they should plug him into you in the first place. And if you now start to unplug yourself, having learned that you will otherwise have to spend nine years in bed with him, there is nobody in the world who must try to prevent you, in order to see to it that he is given something he has a right to be given.

Some people are rather stricter about the right to life. In their view, it does not include the right to be given anything, but amounts to, and only to, the right not to be killed by anybody. But here a related difficulty arises. If everybody is to refrain from killing that violinist, then everybody must refrain from doing a great many different sorts of things. Everybody must refrain from slitting his throat, everybody must refrain from shooting him—and everybody must refrain from unplugging you from him. But does he have a right against everybody that they shall refrain from unplugging you from him? To refrain from doing this is to allow him to continue to use your kidneys. It could be argued that he has a right against us that we should allow him to continue to use your kidneys. That is, while he had no right against us that we should give him the use of your kidneys, it might be argued that he anyway has a right against us that we shall not now intervene and deprive him of the use of your kidneys. I shall come back to third-party interventions later. But certainly the violinist has no right against you that *you* shall allow him to continue to use your kidneys. As I said, if you do allow him to use them, it is a kindness on your part, and not something you owe him. . . .

I would stress that I am not arguing that people do not have a right to life—quite to the contrary. . . . I am arguing only that having a right to life does not guarantee having either a right to be given the use of or a right to be allowed continued use of another person's body—even if one needs it for life itself. So the right to life will not serve the opponents of abortion in the very simple and clear way in which they seem to have thought it would.

3. The Right to Use the Mother's Body

There is another way to bring out the difficulty. In the most ordinary sort of case, to deprive someone of what he has a right to is to treat him unjustly. Suppose a boy and his small brother are jointly given a box of chocolates for Christmas. If the older boy takes the box and refuses to give his brother any of the chocolates, he is unjust to him, for the brother has been given a right to half of them. But suppose that, having learned that otherwise it means nine years in bed with that violinist, you unplug yourself from him. You surely are not being unjust to him for you gave him no right to use your kidneys, and no one else can have given him any such right. But we have to notice that in unplugging yourself, you are killing him; and violinists, like everybody else, have a right to life, and thus in the view we were considering just now, the right not to be killed. So here you do what he supposedly has a right you shall not do, but you do not act unjustly to him in doing it.

The emendation which may be made at this point is this: the right to life consists not in the right not to be killed, but rather in the right not to be killed unjustly. This runs a risk of circularity, but never mind; it would enable us to square the fact that the violinist has a right to life with the fact that you do not act unjustly toward him in unplugging yourself, thereby killing him. For if you do not kill him unjustly, you do not violate his right to life, and so it is no wonder you do him no injustice.

But if this emendation is accepted, the gap in the argument against abortion stares us plainly in the face: it is by no means enough to show that the fetus is a person, and to remind us that all persons have a right to life—we need to be shown also that killing the fetus violates its right to life, i.e., that abortion is unjust killing. And is it?

I suppose we may take it as a datum that in a case of pregnancy due to rape the mother has not given the unborn person a right to the use of her body for food and shelter. Indeed, in what pregnancy could it be supposed that the mother has given the unborn person such a right? It is not as if there were unborn persons drifting about the world, to whom a woman who wants a child says, "I invite you in."

But it might be argued that there are other ways one can have acquired a right to the use of another person's body than by having been invited to use it by that person. Suppose a woman voluntarily indulges in intercourse, knowing of the chance it will issue in pregnancy, and then she does become pregnant; is she not in part responsible for the presence, in fact the very existence, of the unborn person inside her? No doubt she did not invite it in. But doesn't her partial responsibility for its being there itself give it a right to the use of her body? If so, then her aborting it would be more like the boy's taking away the chocolates, and less like your unplugging yourself from the violinist —doing so would be depriving it of what it does have a right to, and thus would be doing it an injustice.

. . . This argument would give the unborn person a right to its mother's body only if her pregnancy resulted from a voluntary act, undertaken in full knowledge of the chance a pregnancy might result from it. It would leave out entirely the unborn person whose existence is due to rape. Pending the availability of some further argument, then, we would be left with the conclusion that unborn persons whose existence is due to rape have no right to the use of their mothers' bodies, and thus that aborting them is not depriving them of anything they have a right to and hence is not unjust killing.

And we should also notice that it is not at all plain that this argument really does go even as far as it purports to. For there are cases and cases, and the details make a difference. If the room is stuffy, and I therefore open a window to air it, and a burglar climbs in, it would be absurd to say, "Ah, now he can stay, she's given him a right to the use of her house—for she is partially responsible for his presence there, having voluntarily done what enabled him to get in, in full knowledge that there are such things as burglars, and that burglars burgle." It would be still more absurd to say this if I had had bars installed outside my windows, precisely to prevent burglars from getting in, and a burglar got in only because of a defect in the bars. It remains equally absurd if we imagine it is not a burglar who climbs in, but an innocent person who blunders or falls in. Again, suppose it were like this: people-seeds drift about in the air like pollen, and if you open your windows, one may drift in and take root in your carpets or upholstery. You don't want children, so you fix up your windows with fine mesh screens, the very best you can buy. As can happen, however, and on very, very rare occasions does happen, one of the screens is defective; and a seed drifts in and takes root. Does the person-plant who now develops have a right to the use of your house? Surely not—despite the fact that you voluntarily opened your windows, you knowingly kept carpets and upholstered furniture, and you knew that screens were sometimes defective. Someone may argue that you are responsible for its rooting, that it does have a right to your house, because after all you *could* have lived out your life with bare floors and furniture, or with sealed windows and doors. But this won't do—for by the same token anyone can avoid a pregnancy due to rape by having a hysterectomy, or anyway by never leaving home without a (reliable!) army.

It seems to me that the argument we are looking at can establish at most that there are *some* cases in which the unborn person has a right to the use of its mother's body, and therefore *some* cases in which abortion is unjust killing. There is room for much discussion and argument as to precisely which, if any. But I think we should sidestep this issue and leave it open, for at any rate the argument certainly does not establish that all abortion is unjust killing.

4. Rights and Sacrifices

There is room for yet another argument here, however. We surely must all grant that there may be cases in which it would be morally indecent to detach a person from your body at the cost of his life. Suppose you learn that what the violinist needs is not nine years of your life, but only one hour: all you need do to save his life is to spend one hour in that bed with him. Suppose also that letting him use your kidneys for that one hour would not affect your health in the slightest. Admittedly you were kidnapped. Admittedly you did not give anyone permission to plug him into you. Nevertheless it seems to me plain you *ought* to allow him to use your kidneys for that hour—it would be indecent to refuse.

Again, suppose pregnancy lasted only an hour, and constituted no threat to life or health. And suppose that a woman becomes pregnant as a result of rape. Admittedly she did not voluntarily do anything to bring about the existence of a child. Admittedly she did nothing at all which would give the unborn person a right to the use of her body. All the same it might well be said, as in the newly emended violinist story, that she *ought* to allow it to remain for that hour—that it would be indecent in her to refuse.

Now some people are inclined to use the term "right" in such a way that it follows from the fact that you ought to allow a person to use your body for the hour he needs, that he has a right to use your body for the hour he needs, even though he has not been given that right by any person or act. They may say that it follows also that if you refuse, you act unjustly toward him. This use of the term is perhaps so common that it cannot be called wrong; nevertheless it seems to me to be an unfortunate loosening of what we would do better to keep a tight rein on. Suppose that that box of chocolates I mentioned earlier had not been given to both boys jointly, but was given only to the older boy. There he sits, stolidly eating his way through the box, his small brother watching enviously. Here we are likely to say "You ought not to be so mean. You ought to give your brother some of those chocolates." My own view is that it just does not follow from the truth of this that the brother has any right to any of the chocolates. If the boy refuses to give his brother any, he is greedy, stingy, callous—but not unjust. I suppose that the people I have in mind will say it does follow that the brother has a right to some of the chocolates, and thus that the boy does act unjustly if he refuses to give his brother any. But the effect of saying this is to obscure what we should keep distinct, namely the difference between the boy's refusal in this case and the boy's refusal in the earlier case, in which the box was given to both boys jointly, and in which the small brother thus had what was from any point of view clear title to half.

A further objection to so using the term "right," that from the fact that A ought to do a thing for B, it follows that B has a right against A that A do it for him, is that it is going to make the question of whether or not a man has a right to a thing turn on how easy it is to provide him

with it; and this seems not merely unfortunate, but morally unacceptable. Take the case of Henry Fonda again. I said earlier that I had no right to the touch of his cool hand on my fevered brow, even though I needed it to save my life. I said it would be frightfully nice of him to fly in from the West Coast to provide me with it, but that I had no right against him that he should do so. But suppose he isn't on the West Coast. Suppose he has only to walk across the room, place a hand briefly on my brow—and lo, my life is saved. Then surely he ought to do it, it would be indecent to refuse. Is it to be said, "Ah, well, it follows that in this case she has a right to the touch of his hand on her brow, and so it would be an unjustice in him to refuse"? So that I have a right to it when it is easy for him to provide it, though no right when it's hard? It's rather a shocking idea that anyone's rights should fade away and disappear as it gets harder and harder to accord them to him.

So my own view is that even though you ought to let the violinist use your kidneys for the one hour he needs, we should not conclude that he has a right to do so—we should say that if you refuse, you are, like the boy who owns all the chocolates and will give none away, self-centered and callous, indecent in fact, but not unjust. And similarly, that even supposing a case in which a woman pregnant due to rape ought to allow the unborn person to use her body for the hour he needs, we should not conclude that he has a right to do so; we should conclude that she is self-centered, callous, indecent, but not unjust, if she refuses. The complaints are no less grave; they are just different. However, there is no need to insist on this point. If anyone does wish to deduce "he has a right" from "you ought," then all the same he must surely grant that there are cases in which it is not morally required of you that you allow that violinist to use your kidneys, and in which he does not have a right to use them, and in which you do not do him an injustice if you refuse. And so also for mother and unborn child. Except in such cases as the unborn person has a right to demand it—and we were leaving open the possibility that there may be such cases—nobody is morally *required* to make large sacrifices, of health, of all other interests and concerns, of all other duties and commitments, for nine years, or even for nine months, in order to keep another person alive.

5. Good Samaritans

We have in fact to distinguish between two kinds of Samaritan: the Good Samaritan and what we might call the Minimally Decent Samaritan. The story of the Good Samaritan, you will remember, goes like this:

> A certain man went down from Jerusalem to Jericho, and fell among thieves, which stripped him of his raiment, and wounded him, and departed, leaving him half dead.
>
> And by chance there came down a certain priest that way; and when he saw him, he passed by on the other side.
>
> And likewise a Levite, when he was at the place, came and looked on him, and passed by on the other side.
>
> But a certain Samaritan, as he journeyed, came where he was; and when he saw him he had compassion on him.
>
> And went to him, and bound up his wounds, pouring in oil and wine, and set him on his own beast, and brought him to an inn, and took care of him.
>
> And on the morrow, when he departed, he took out two pence, and gave them to the host, and said unto him, "Take care of him; and whatsoever thou spendest more, when I come again, I will repay thee."
>
> Luke 10:30–35

The Good Samaritan went out of his way, at some cost to himself, to help one in need of it. We are not told what the options were, that is, whether or not the priest and the Levite could have helped by doing less than the Good Samaritan did, but assuming they could have, then the fact they did nothing at all shows they were not even Minimally Decent Samaritans, not because they were not Samaritans, but because they were not even minimally decent.

These things are a matter of degree, of course, but there is a difference, and it comes out perhaps most clearly in the story of Kitty Genovese, who, as you will remember, was murdered while thirty-eight people watched or listened, and did nothing at all to help her. A Good Samaritan would have rushed out to give direct assistance against the murderer. Or perhaps we had better allow that it would have been a Splendid Samaritan who did this, on the ground that it would have involved a risk of death for himself. But the thirty-eight not only did not do this, they did not even trouble to pick up a phone to call the police. Minimally Decent Samaritanism would call for doing at least that, and their not having done it was monstrous.

After telling the story of the Good Samaritan, Jesus said, "Go, and do thou likewise." Perhaps he meant that we are morally required to act as the Good Samaritan did. Perhaps he was urging people to do more than is morally required of them. At all events it seems plain that it was not morally required of any of the thirty-eight that he rush out to give direct assistance at the risk of his own life, and that it is not morally required of anyone that he give long stretches of his life—nine years or nine months—to sustaining the life of a person who has no special right (we were leaving open the possibility of this) to demand it.

. . . What we should ask is not whether anybody should be compelled by law to be a Good Samaritan, but whether we must accede to a situation in which somebody is being compelled—by nature, perhaps—to be a Good Samaritan. We have, in other words, to look now at third-party interventions. I have been arguing that no person is morally required to make large sacrifices to sustain the life of another who has no right to demand them, and this even where the sacrifices do not include life itself; we are not morally required to be Good Samaritans or anyway Very Good Samaritans to one another. But what if a man cannot extricate himself from such a situation? What if he appeals to us to extricate him? It seems to me plain that there are cases in which we can, cases in which a Good Samaritan would extricate him. There you are, you were kidnapped, and nine years in bed with that violinist lie ahead of you. You have your own life to lead. You are sorry, but you simply cannot see giving up so much of your life to the sustaining of his. You cannot extricate yourself, and ask us to do so. I should have thought that—in light of his having no right to the use of your body—it was obvious that we do not have to accede to your being forced to give up so much. We can do what you ask. There is no injustice to the violinist in our doing so.

6. Parental Responsibility

Following the lead of the opponents of abortion, I have throughout been speaking of the fetus merely as a person, and what I have been asking is whether or not the argument we began with, which proceeds only from the fetus' being a person, really does establish its conclusion. I have argued that it does not.

But of course there are arguments and arguments, and it may be said that I have simply fastened on the wrong one. It may be said that what is important is not merely the fact that the fetus is a person, but that it is a person for whom the woman has a special kind of responsibility issuing from the fact that she is its mother. And it might be argued that all my analogies are therefore irrelevant—for you do not have that special kind of responsibility for that violinist. Henry Fonda does not have that special kind of responsibility for me. And our attention might be drawn to the fact that men and women both *are* compelled by law to provide support for their children.

I have in effect dealt (briefly) with this argument . . . above; but a (still briefer) recapitula-

tion now may be in order. Surely we do not have any such "special responsibility" for a person unless we have assumed it, explicitly or implicitly. If a set of parents do not try to prevent pregnancy, do not obtain an abortion, but rather take it home with them, then they have assumed responsibility for it, they have given it rights, and they cannot *now* withdraw support from it at the cost of its life because they now find it difficult to go on providing for it. But if they have taken all reasonable precautions against having a child, they do not simply by virtue of their biological relationship to the child who comes into existence have a special responsibility for it. They may wish to assume responsibility for it, or they may not wish to. And I am suggesting that if assuming responsibility for it would require large sacrifices, then they may refuse. . . .

7. Conclusion

My argument will be found unsatisfactory on two counts by many of those who want to regard abortion as morally permissible. First, while I do argue that abortion is not impermissible, I do not argue that it is always permissible. There may well be cases in which carrying the child to term requires only Minimally Decent Samaritanism of the mother, and this is a standard we must not fall below. I am inclined to think it a merit of my account precisely that it does *not* give a general yes or a general no. It allows for and supports our sense that, for example, a sick and desperately frightened fourteen-year-old schoolgirl, pregnant due to rape, may *of course* choose abortion, and that any law which rules this out is an insane law. And it also allows for and supports our sense that in other cases resort to abortion is even positively indecent. It would be indecent in the woman to request an abortion, and indecent in a doctor to perform it, if she is in her seventh month, and wants the abortion just to avoid the nuisance of postponing a trip abroad. The very fact that the arguments I have been drawing attention to treat all cases of abortion, or even all cases of abortion in which the mother's life is not at stake, as morally on a par ought to have made them suspect at the outset.

Secondly, while I am arguing for the permissibility of abortion in some cases, I am not arguing for the right to secure the death of the unborn child. It is easy to confuse these two things in that up to a certain point in the life of the fetus it is not able to survive outside the mother's body; hence removing it from her body guarantees its death. But they are importantly different. I have argued that you are not morally required to spend nine months in bed, sustaining the life of that violinist; but to say this is by no means to say that if, when you unplug yourself, there is a miracle and he survives, you then have a right to turn around and slit his throat. You may detach yourself even if this costs him his life; you have no right to be guaranteed his death, by some other means, if unplugging yourself does not kill him. There are some people who will feel dissatisfied by this feature of my argument. A woman may be utterly devastated by the thought of a child, a bit of herself, put out for adoption and never seen or heard of again. She may therefore want not merely that the child be detached from her, but more, that it die. Some opponents of abortion are inclined to regard this as beneath contempt—thereby showing insensitivity to what is surely a powerful source of despair. All the same, I agree that the desire for the child's death is not one which anybody may gratify, should it turn out to be possible to detach the child alive.

At this place, however, it should be remembered that we have only been pretending throughout that the fetus is a human being from the moment of conception. A very early abortion is surely not the killing of a person, and so is not dealt with by anything I have said here.

Review and Discussion Questions

1. Some writers have criticized Thomson's vivid analogies for being too bizarre and fanciful. Would you agree, or are her analogies useful and illuminating? Could she have made her case without using analogies?

2. Thomson's criticism of the extreme anti-abortion view assumes that the right to self-defense permits us to kill an innocent person if that person threatens our life. Do you agree? Can you imagine such a case outside of the context of abortion?

3. Thomson writes that "the right to life consists not in the right not to be killed, but rather in the right not to be killed unjustly." Do you agree? Assuming that the fetus has a right to life, under what circumstances would it be unjust to abort it? Under what circumstances just?

4. Assess the following argument: If you as a woman have sex, then you know that, even if you do use birth control, there is a chance you may become pregnant. Therefore, knowing this, if you have sex and do become pregnant, then you must assume responsibility for the fetus and not abort it.

5. Thomson maintains that we are not obligated to make large sacrifices to keep other people alive unless they have a right that we do so. Give examples of when we would and would not be obligated to make such sacrifices. Do you find Thomson's principle morally acceptable? Is Thomson correct in arguing that morality does not require us to be Good Samaritans?

Abortion and the "Feminine Voice"

CELIA WOLF-DEVINE

Following the pioneering work of Carol Gilligan, a number of feminist writers have argued that women bring a distinctive perspective to ethical reasoning and that this "feminine voice" represents a superior mode of moral response. They reject what they see as the traditional masculine emphasis in ethics on impartiality, autonomy, justice, and rights in favor of an ethic of care that focuses on relationships, interconnectedness, and our responsibilities to care for others. Yet, feminists who favor the feminine voice and an ethic of care also typically support a woman's unqualified right to abortion. In this essay, Celia Wolf-Devine, professor of philosophy at Stonehill College in Massachusetts, challenges their position. She contends that abortion is a masculine response to unwanted pregnancy and argues that the feminine voice generates a strong presumption against abortion.

Study Questions

1. Describe the differences that Gilligan sees between masculine and feminine perspectives in ethics.
2. What is the masculine bias that some feminists see in traditional thinking about the mind and the body? In what ways, according to them, do male and female attitudes toward social life differ?
3. According to Wolf-Devine, what typically masculine attitudes and values favor abortion?
4. On what grounds does she reject the argument that denying women access to abortion reflects male dominance and violence against women?
5. What aspects of Carol Gilligan's ethical approach does Wolf-Devine see as arguing against abortion?
6. On what grounds does Nel Noddings argue that a fetus has no claim upon our care?

A GROWING NUMBER of feminists now seek to articulate the "feminine voice," to draw attention to women's special strengths, and to correct the systematic devaluation of these by our male-dominated society. Carol Gilligan's book, *In a Different Voice*, was especially important to the emergence of this strain of feminist thought. It was her intention to help women identify more positively with their own distinctive style of reasoning about ethics, instead of feeling that there is something wrong with them because they do not think like men (as Kohlberg's and Freud's theories would imply). Inspired by her work, feminists . . . have tried to articulate further the feminine voice in moral reasoning. . . . When properly transformed by a

Reprinted by permission from Public Affairs Quarterly, *vol. 3, no. 3 (July 1989). Copyright © 1989 Public Affairs Quarterly. Some notes omitted, and one section title modified.*

feminist consciousness, women's different characteristics can, they suggest, be productive of new social visions.

Similar work is also being done by feminists who try to correct for masculine bias in other areas such as our conception of human nature, the way we view the relationship between people and nature, and the kinds of paradigms we employ in thinking about society.

Some of those engaged in this enterprise hold that women *by nature* possess certain valuable traits that men do not, but more frequently, they espouse the weaker position that, on the whole, the traits they label "feminine" are more common among women (for reasons which are at least partly cultural), but that they also can be found in men, and that they should be encouraged as good traits for a human being to have, regardless of sex.

Virtually all of those feminists who are trying to reassert the value of the feminine voice, also express the sort of unqualified support for free access to abortion which has come to be regarded as a central tenet of feminist "orthodoxy." What I wish to argue in this paper is that: (1) abortion is, by their own accounts, clearly a masculine response to the problems posed by an unwanted pregnancy, and is thus highly problematic for those who seek to articulate and defend the "feminine voice" as the proper mode of moral response, and that (2) on the contrary the "feminine voice" as it has been articulated generates a strong presumption against abortion as a way of responding to an unwanted pregnancy.[1]

These conclusions, I believe, can be argued without relying on a precise determination of the moral status of the fetus. A case at least can be made that the fetus is a person since it is biologically a member of the human species and will, in time, develop normal human abilities. Whether the burden of proof rests on those who defend the personhood of the fetus, or on those who deny it, is a matter of moral methodology, and for that reason will depend in part on whether one adopts a masculine or feminine approach to moral issues.

I. Masculine Voice/Feminine Voice

A. Moral reasoning

According to Gilligan, girls, being brought up by mothers, identify with them, while males must define themselves through separation from their mothers. As a result, girls have "a basis for empathy built into their primary definition of self in a way that boys do not."[2] Thus while masculinity is defined by separation and threatened by intimacy, femininity is defined through attachment and threatened by separation; girls come to understand themselves as imbedded within a network of personal relationships.

A second difference concerns attitudes toward general rules and principles. Boys tend to play in larger groups than girls, and become "increasingly fascinated with the legal elaboration of rules, and the development of fair procedures for adjudicating conflicts."[3] We thus find men conceiving of morality largely in terms of adjudicating fairly between the conflicting rights of self-assertive individuals.

Girls play in smaller groups, and accord a greater importance to relationships than to following rules. They are especially sensitive to the needs of the particular other, instead of emphasizing impartiality, which is more characteristic of the masculine perspective. They think of morality more in terms of having responsibilities for taking care of others, and place a high priority upon preserving the network of relationships which makes this possible. While the masculine justice perspective requires detachment, the feminine care perspective sees detachment and separation as themselves the moral problem. . . .

The feminine voice in ethics attends to the particular other, thinks in terms of responsibilities to care for others, is sensitive to our interconnectedness, and strives to preserve relationships. It contrasts with the masculine voice, which speaks in terms of justice and rights, stresses consistency and principles, and emphasizes the autonomy of the individual and impartiality in one's dealings with others.

B. *Mind, body, and nature*

Feminist writers have also discovered a masculine bias in the way we think of mind and body and the relationship between them. A large number of feminists, for example, regard radical mind-body dualism as a masculine way of understanding human nature. Alison Jaggar, for example, criticizes what she calls "normative dualism" for being "male biased,"[4] and defines "normative dualism" as "the belief that what is especially valuable about human beings is a particular 'mental' capacity, the capacity for rationality."[5] . . .

Many feminists hold that mind-body dualism which sees mind as transcendent to and superior to the body, leads to the devaluation of both women and nature. For the transcendent mind is conceived as masculine, and women, the body and nature assigned an inferior and subservient status. As Rosemary Radford Reuther puts it:

> The woman, the body and the world are the lower half of a dualism that must be declared posterior to, created by, subject to, and ultimately alien to the nature of (male) consciousness in whose image man made his God.[6]

Women are to be subject to men, and nature may be used by man in any way he chooses. Thus the male ideology of transcendent dualism sanctions unlimited technological manipulation of nature; nature is an alien object to be conquered. . . .

Feminists who stress the deep affinities between feminism and the ecology movement are often called "ecofeminists." Stephanie Leland, radical feminist and co-editor of a recent collection of ecofeminist writings, has explained that:

> Ecology is universally defined as the study of the balance and interrelationship of all life on earth. The motivating force behind feminism is the expression of the feminine principle. As the essential impulse of the feminine principle is the striving towards balance and interrelationship, it follows that feminism and ecology are inextricably connected.[7]

The masculine urge is, she says, to "separate, discriminate and control," while the feminine impulse is "towards belonging, relationship and letting be."[8] The urge to discriminate leads, she thinks, to the need to dominate "in order to feel secure in the choice of a particular set of differences."[9] The feminine attitude springs from a more holistic view of the human person and sees us as imbedded in nature rather than standing over and above it. It entails a more egalitarian attitude, regarding the needs of other creatures as important and deserving of consideration. It seeks to "let be" rather than to control, and maintains a pervasive awareness of the interconnectedness of all things and the need to preserve this if all are to flourish.

Interconnectedness, which we found to be an important theme in feminist ethics, thus reappears in the writings of the ecofeminists as one of the central aspects of the feminine attitude toward nature.

C. *Paradigms of social life*

Feminists' descriptions of characteristically masculine and feminine paradigms of social life center around two different focusses. Those influenced by Gilligan tend to stress the contrast between individualism (which they take to be characteristic of the masculine "justice tradition") and the view of society as "a web of relationships sustained by a process of communication" (which they take to characterize the feminine "care perspective"). According to them, the masculine paradigm sees society as a collection of self-assertive individuals seeking rules which will allow them to pursue their own goals without interfering with each other. The whole contractarian tradition from Locke and Hobbes through Rawls is thus seen as a masculine paradigm of social life; we are only connected to others and responsible to them through our own choice to relinquish part of our autonomy in favor of the state. The feminine care perspective guides us to think about societal problems in a different way. We are already imbedded in a network of relationships, and must never exploit or hurt the other. We must strive to preserve those relationships as much as possible without sacrificing the integrity of the self.

The ecofeminists, pacifist feminists, and those whose starting point is a rejection of dualism, tend to focus more on the contrast between viewing social relationships in terms of hierarchy, power, and domination (the masculine paradigm) and viewing them in a more egalitarian and nonviolent manner (the feminine one). Feminists taking this position range from the moderate ones who believe that masculine social thought tends to be more hierarchical than feminine thought, to the extreme radicals who believe males are irredeemably aggressive and dominating, and prone to violence in order to preserve their domination.

The more moderate characterization of masculine social thought would claim that men tend to prefer a clear structure of authority; they want to know who is in control and have a clear set of procedures or rules for resolving difficult cases. The more extreme view, common among ecofeminists and a large number of radical feminists, is that males seek to establish and maintain patriarchy (systematic domination by males) and use violence to maintain their control. These feminists thus see an affinity between feminism (which combats male violence against women) and the pacifist movement (which does so on a more global scale). . . .

II. Abortion

A person who had characteristically masculine traits, attitudes and values as defined above would very naturally choose abortion, and justify it ethically in the same way in which most feminists do. Conversely, a person manifesting feminine traits, attitudes and values would not make such a choice, or justify it in that way.

According to the ecofeminists, the masculine principle is insensitive to the interconnectedness of all life; it strives to discriminate, separate and control. It does not respect the natural cycles of nature, but objectifies it, and imposes its will upon it through unrestrained technological manipulation. Such a way of thinking would naturally lead to abortion. If the woman does not *want* to be pregnant, she has recourse to an operation involving highly sophisticated technology in order to defend her control of her body. This fits the characterization of the masculine principle perfectly.

Abortion is a separation—a severing of a life-preserving connection between the woman and the fetus. It thus fails to respect the interconnectedness of all life. Nor does it respect the natural cycles of nature. The mother and the developing child together form a delicately balanced egosystem with the woman's entire hormonal system geared towards sustaining the pregnancy. The abortionist forces the cervical muscles (which have become thick and hard in order to hold in the developing fetus) open and disrupts her hormonal system by removing it.

Abortion has something further in common with the behavior ecofeminists and pacifist feminists take to be characteristically masculine; it shows a willingness to use violence in order to maintain control. The fetus is destroyed by being pulled apart by suction, cut in pieces, or poisoned. It is not merely killed inadvertently as fish might be by toxic wastes, but it is deliberately targeted for destruction. . . . This point was recently brought home to me by a Quaker woman who had reached the conclusion that the abortion she had had was contrary to her pacifist principles. She said, "we must seek peaceableness both within and without."

In terms of social thought, again, it is the masculine models which are most frequently employed in thinking about abortion. If masculine thought is naturally hierarchical and oriented towards power and control, then the interests of the fetus (who has no power) would naturally be suppressed in favor of the interests of the mother. But to the extent that feminist social thought is egalitarian, the question must be raised of why the mother's interests should prevail over the child's.

Feminist thought about abortion has, in addition, been deeply pervaded by the individualism which they so ardently criticize. The woman is supposed to have the sole authority to decide the outcome of the pregnancy. But what of her interconnectedness with the child and with others? Both she and the unborn child already exist within a network of relationships ranging from the closest ones—the father, grandparents, siblings, uncles and aunts, and so on—to ones with the broader society—including the mother's friends, employer, employees, potential adoptive parents, taxpayers who may be asked to fund the abortion or subsidize the child, and all the numerous other people affected by her choice. To dismiss this already existing network of relationships as irrelevant to the mother's decision is to manifest the sort of social atomism which feminist thinkers condemn as characteristically masculine.

Those feminists who are seeking to articulate the feminine voice in ethics also face a *prima facie* inconsistency between an ethics of care and abortion. Quite simply, abortion is a failure to care for one living being who exists in a particularly intimate relationship to oneself. If empathy, nurturance, and taking responsibility for caring for others are characteristic of the feminine voice, then abortion does not appear to be a feminine response to an unwanted pregnancy. If, as Gilligan says, "an ethic of care rests on the premise of non-violence—that no one should be hurt,"[10] then surely the feminine response to an unwanted pregnancy would be to try to find a solution which does not involve injury to anyone, including the unborn.

"Rights" have been invoked in the abortion controversy in a bewildering variety of ways, ranging from the "right to life" to the "right to control one's body." But clearly those who defend unrestricted access to abortion in terms of such things as the woman's right to privacy or her right to control her body are speaking the language of an ethics of justice rather than an ethics of care. For example, Judith Jarvis Thomson's widely read article "A Defense of Abortion"[11] treats the moral issue involved in abortion as a conflict between the rights of the fetus and the mother's rights over her own body. Mary Anne Warren also sees the issue in terms of a conflict of rights, but since the fetus does not meet her criteria for being a person, she weighs the woman's rights to "freedom, happiness and self-determination" against the rights of other people in the society who would like to see the fetus preserved for whatever reason.[12] And, insofar as she appeals to consciousness, reasoning, self-motivated activity, the capacity to communicate, and the presence of self-concepts and self-awareness as criteria of personhood, she relies on the kind of opposition between mind and nature criticized by many feminists as masculine. In particular, she is committed to what Jaggar calls "normative dualism"—the view that what is especially valuable about humans is their mental capacity for rational thought.

It is rather striking that feminists defending abortion lapse so quickly into speaking in the masculine voice. Is it because they feel they must do so in order to be heard in our male dominated society, or is it because no persuasive defense of abortion can be constructed from within the ethics of care tradition? We now consider several possible "feminine voice" defenses of abortion.

III. Possible Responses and Replies

Among the feminists seeking to articulate and defend the value of the feminine voice, very few have made any serious attempt to grapple with abortion. The writings of the ecofeminists and the pacifist feminists abound with impassioned defenses of such values as non-violence, a democratic attitude towards the needs of all living things, letting others be and nurturing them, and so on, existing side by side with impassioned defenses of "reproductive rights." They see denying women access to abortion as just another aspect of male domination and violence against women.

This will not do for several reasons. First, it is not true that males are the chief opponents of abortion. Many women are strongly opposed to it. The pro-life movement at every level is largely composed of women. . . . [and] cannot be dismissed as representing male concerns and desires only. Granted, a pro-choice feminist could argue that women involved in the pro-life movement suffer from "colonized minds," but this sort of argument clearly can be made to cut both directions. After all, many of the strongest supporters of "reproductive rights" have been men—ranging from the Supreme Court in *Roe v. Wade* to the Playboy Philosopher.

Secondly, terms like violence and domination are used far too loosely by those who condemn anti-abortion laws. If there are laws against wife abuse, does this mean that abusive husbands are being subjected to domination and violence? One does not exercise violence against someone merely by crossing his or her will, or even by crossing his or her will and backing this up by threats of legal retribution.

Finally, those who see violence and domination in laws against abortion, but not in abortion itself, generally fail to look at the nature of the act itself, and thus fail to judge that act in light of their professed values and principles. This is not surprising; abortion is a bloody and distressing thing to contemplate. But one cannot talk about it intelligently without being willing to look concretely at the act itself.

One line of thought is suggested by Gilligan, who holds that at the highest level of moral development, we must balance our responsibility to care for others against our need to care for ourselves. Perhaps we could, then, see the woman who has an abortion as still being caring and nurturing in that she is acting out of a legitimate care for herself. This is an implausible view of the actual feelings of women who undergo abortions. They may believe they are "doing something for themselves" in the sense of doing what they must do to safeguard their legitimate interests. But the operation is more naturally regarded as a violation of oneself than as a nurturing of oneself. This has been noted, even by feminists who support permissive abortion laws. For example, Carolyn Whitbeck speaks of "the unappealing prospect of having someone scraping away at one's core," and Adrienne Rich says that "Abortion is violence: a deep, desperate violence inflicted by a woman upon, first of all, herself."

We here come up against the problem that a directive to care, to nurture, to take responsibility for others, and so on, provides a moral orientation, but leaves unanswered many important questions and hence provides little guidance in problem situations. What do we do when caring for one person involves being uncaring toward another? How widely must we extend our circle of care? Are some kinds of not caring worse than others? Is it caring to give someone what they want even though it may be bad for them?

Thinking in terms of preserving relationships suggests another possible "feminine" defense of abortion—namely that the woman is striving to preserve her interconnectedness with her family, husband, or boyfriend. Or perhaps she is concerned to strengthen her relationship with her other children by having enough time and resources to devote to their care. To simply tell a woman to preserve *all* her existing relationships is not the answer. Besides the fact that it may not be possible (women *do* sometimes have to sever relationships), it is not clear that it would be desirable even if it were possible. Attempting to preserve our existing relationships has conservative tendencies in several unfortunate ways. It fails to invite us to reflect critically on whether those relationships are good, healthy or worthy of preservation. It also puts the unborn at a particular disadvantage, since the mother's relationship with him or her is just beginning, while her relationships with others have had time to develop. And not only the unborn, but any needy stranger who shows up at our door can be excluded on the grounds that caring for them would disrupt our existing pattern of relationships. Thus the care perspective could degenerate into a rationalization for a purely tribal morality; I take care of myself and my friends.

But how are decisions about severing relationships to be made? One possibility is suggested by Gilligan in a recent article. She looks at the network of connections within which the woman who is considering abortion finds herself entangled, and says "to ask what actions constitute care or are more caring directs attention to the parameters of connection and the *costs of detachment* . . . (emphasis added)."[13] Thus, the woman considering abortion should reflect upon the comparative costs of severing various relationships. This method of decision, however, makes her vulnerable to emotional and psychological pressure from others, by encouraging her to sever whichever connection is easiest to break (the squeaky wheel principle).*

But perhaps we can lay out some guidelines (or, at least, rules of thumb) for making these difficult decisions. One way we might reason, from the point of view of the feminine voice, is that since preserving interconnectedness is good, we should prefer a short term estrangement to an irremediable severing of relationship. And we should choose an action which *may* cause an irremediable break in relationship over one which is certain to cause such a break. By either of these criteria, abortion is clearly to be avoided.†

Another consideration suggested by Gilligan's work is that since avoiding hurt to others

(or non-violence) is integral to an ethics of care, severing a relationship where the other person will be only slightly hurt would be preferable to severing one where deep or lasting injury will be inflicted by our action. But on this criterion, again, it would seem she should avoid abortion, since loss of life is clearly a graver harm than emotional distress.

Two other possible criteria which would also tell against abortion are: (1) that it is permissible to cut ties with someone who behaves unjustly and oppressively toward one, but not with someone who is innocent of any wrong against one, or (2) we have special obligations to our own offspring, and thus should not sever relationship with them. . . .

It seems that the only way open to the person who seeks to defend abortion from the point of view of the feminine voice is to deny that a relationship (or at least any morally significant relationship) exists between the embryo/fetus and the mother. The question of how to tell when a relationship (or a morally significant relationship) exists is a deep and important one, which has, as yet, received insufficient attention from those who are trying to articulate the feminine voice in moral reasoning. The whole eco-feminist position relies on the assumption that our relationship with nature and with other species is a real and morally significant one. They, thus, have no basis at all for excluding the unborn from moral consideration.

There are those, however, who wish to define morally significant relationships more narrowly—thus effectively limiting our obligation to extend care. While many philosophers within the "justice tradition" (for example, Kant) have seen moral significance only where there is some impact upon rational beings, Nel Noddings, coming from the "care perspective," tries to limit our obligation to extend care in terms of the possibility of "completion" or "reciprocity" in a caring relationship. Since she takes the mother-child relationship to be paradigmatic of caring, it comes as something of a surprise that

* This was evident in the reasoning of the women in Gilligan's case studies, many of whom had abortions in order to please or placate other significant persons in their lives.

† Some post-abortion counsellors find the sense of irremediable break in relationship to be one of the most painful aspects of the post-abortion experience, and try to urge the woman to imaginatively re-create a relationship with the baby in order to be better able to complete the necessary grieving process. . . .

she regards abortion as a permissible response to an unwanted pregnancy.[14]

There are, on Noddings' view, two different ways in which we may be bound, as caring persons, to extend our care to one for whom we do not already have the sort of feelings of love and affection which would lead us to do the caring action naturally. One is by virtue of being connected with our "inner circle" of caring (which is formed by natural relations of love and friendship) through "chains" of "personal or formal relations."[15] As an example of a person appropriately linked to the inner circle, she cites her daughter's fiancé. It would certainly *seem* that the embryo in one's womb would belong to one's "inner circle" (via natural caring), or at least be connected to it by a "formal relation" (that is, that of parenthood). But Noddings does not concede this. Who is part of my inner circle, and who is connected to it in such a way that I am obligated to extend care to him or her seems to be, for Noddings, largely a matter of my feelings towards the person and/or my choice to include him or her. Thus the mother *may* "confer sacredness" upon the "information speck" in her womb, but need not if, for example, her relationship with the father is not a stable and loving one. During pregnancy "many women recognize the relation as established when the fetus begins to move about. It is not a question of when life begins, but of when relation begins."

But making the existence of a relation between the unborn and the mother a matter of her choice or feelings, seems to run contrary to one of the most central insights of the feminine perspective in moral reasoning—namely that we already *are* interconnected with others, and thus have responsibilities to them. The view that we are connected with others only when we choose to be or when we *feel* we are, presupposes the kind of individualism and social atomism which Noddings and other feminists criticize as masculine.

Noddings also claims that we sometimes are obligated to care for "the proximate stranger." She says:

> We cannot refuse obligation in human affairs by merely refusing to enter relation; we are, by virtue of our mutual humanity, already and perpetually in potential relation.

Why, then, are we not obligated to extend care to the unborn? She gives two criteria for when we have an obligation to extend care: there must be "the existence of or potential for present relation" and the "dynamic potential for growth in relation, including the potential for increased reciprocity. . . ." Animals are, she believes, excluded by this second criterion since their response is nearly static (unlike a human infant).

She regards the embryo/fetus as not having the potential for present relationships of caring and reciprocity, and thus as having no claim upon our care. As the fetus matures, he or she develops increasing potential for caring relationships, and thus our obligation increases also. There are problems with her position, however.

First of all, the only relationships which can be relevant to *my* obligation to extend care, for Noddings, must be relationships with *me*. Whatever the criteria for having a relationship are, it must be that at a given time, an entity either has a relationship with me or it does not. If it does not, it may either have no potential for a morally significant relationship with me (for example, my word processor), or it may have such potential in several ways: (1) The relationship may become actual at the will of one or both parties (for example, the stranger sitting next to me on the bus). (2) The relationship may become actual only after a change in relative spatial locations which will take time, and thus can occur only in the future (for example, walking several blocks to meet a new neighbor, or traveling to Tibet to meet a specific Tibetan). Or (3) The relationship may become actual only after some internal change occurs within the other (for example by waiting for a sleeping drug to wear off, for a deep but reversible coma to pass, or for the embryo to mature more fully) and thus can also happen only in the future.

In all three of these cases there is present now in the other the potential for relations of a caring and reciprocal sort. In cases (1) and (2) this is uncontroversial, but (3) requires some defense in the case of the unborn. The human embryo differs now from a rabbit embryo in that it possesses potential for these kinds of relationships although neither of them is presently able to enter into relationships of any sort. That potential becomes actualized only over time, but it can become actualized only because it is there to be actualized (as it is not in the rabbit embryo). Noddings fails to give any reason why the necessity for some internal change to occur in the other before relation can become actual has such moral importance that we are entitled to kill the other in case (3), but not in the others, especially since my refraining from killing it is a sufficient condition for the actualization of the embryo's potential for caring relationships. Her criterion as it stands would also seem to imply that we may kill persons in deep but predictably reversible comas.

Whichever strand of Noddings thought we choose, then, it is hard to see how the unborn can be excluded from being ones for whom we ought to care. If we focus on the narrow, tribal morality of "inner circles" and "chains," then an objective connection exists tying the unborn to the mother and other relatives. If we are to be open to the needy stranger because of the real potential for relationship and reciprocity, then we should be open to the unborn because he or she also has the real and present potential for a relationship of reciprocity and mutuality which comes with species membership.

Many feminists will object to my argument so far on the grounds that they do not, after all, consider abortion to be a *good* thing. They aren't pro-abortion in the sense that they encourage women to have abortions. They merely regard it as something which must be available as a kind of "grim option"—something a woman would choose only when the other alternatives are all immeasurably worse. . . .

Feminists standardly hold that absolutely no restrictions may be placed on a woman's right to choose abortion. This position cannot be supported by the grim options argument. One who believes something is a grim option will be inclined to try to avoid or prevent it, and thus be willing, at least in principle, to place some restrictions on what counts as a grim option. Granted, practical problems exist about how such decisions are to be made and by whom. But someone who refuses in principle to allow any restrictions on women's right to abort, cannot in good faith claim that they regard abortion only as a grim option.

Some feminists will say: yes, feminine virtues are a good thing for any person to have, and yes, abortion is a characteristically masculine way of dealing with an unwanted pregnancy, but in the current state of things we live in a male dominated society, and we must be willing to use now weapons which, ideally, in a good, matriarchal society, we would not use. But there are no indications that an ideal utopian society is just around the corner; thus we are condemned to a constant violation of our own deepest commitments. If the traits, values and attitudes characteristic of the "feminine voice" are asserted to be good ones, we ought to act according to them. And such values and attitudes simply do not lend support to either the choice of abortion as a way of dealing with an unwanted pregnancy in individual cases, or to the political demand for unrestricted[16] access to abortion which has become so entrenched in the feminist movement. Quite the contrary.

NOTES

1. A strong presumption against abortion is not, of course, the same thing as an absolute ban on all abortions. I do not attempt here to resolve the really hard cases; it is not clear that the feminine voice (at least as it has been articulated so far) is sufficiently fine-grained to tell us exactly where to draw the line in such cases.

2. See Carol Gilligan, *In a Different Voice* (Cambridge, MA: Harvard University Press, 1982), p. 8.

3. *Ibid.*, p. 10.

4. Alison Jaggar, *Feminist Politics and Human Nature* (Totowa, N.J.: Rowman & Alanheld, 1983), p. 46.

5. *Ibid.*, p. 28.

6. Rosemary Radford Reuther, *New Woman, New Earth* (New York: The Seabury Press, 1975), p. 195.

7. Stephanie Leland and Leonie Caldecott, (eds.) *Reclaim the Earth: Women Speak out for Life on Earth* (London: The Women's Press, 1983), p. 72. . . .

8. *Ibid.*, p. 71.

9. *Ibid.*, p. 69.

10. Gilligan, *op. cit.*, p. 174.

11. Judith Jarvis Thomson, "A Defense of Abortion" [see this volume, pp. 154–164].

12. Mary Anne Warren, "On the Moral and Legal Status of Abortion," *The Monist*, vol. 57 (January, 1973), reprinted in Wasserstrom, *Today's Moral Problems* (New York: Macmillan, 1985), p. 448.

13. Carol Gilligan "Moral Orientation and Moral Development" in Kittay and Meyers, (eds.) *Women and Moral Theory* (Minneapolis: University of Minnesota, 1987), p. 24.

14. Noddings' discussion of abortion occurs on pp. 87–90 of *Caring: A Feminine Approach to Ethics* (Berkeley: University of California Press, 1984), and all quotes are from these pages unless otherwise noted.

15. *Ibid.*, p. 47.

16. Restrictions can take many forms, including laws against abortion, mandatory counselling which includes information about the facts of fetal development and encourages the woman to choose other options, obligatory waiting periods, legal requirements to notify (and/or obtain the consent of) the father, or in the case of a minor the girl's parents, etc. To defend the appropriateness of any particular sort of restrictions goes beyond the scope of this paper.

Review and Discussion Questions

1. In your experience, do men and women think about moral questions (a) in fundamentally different ways, (b) in somewhat different ways, or (c) in basically the same way? Do men and women differ in their views of social life and of the relation between the mind and body?

2. Assess Wolf-Devine's statement that "a person who had characteristically masculine traits, attitudes, and values . . . would very naturally choose abortion. . . . Conversely, a person manifesting feminine traits, attitudes, and values would not make such a choice."

3. Wolf-Devine argues that feminist defenders of abortion like Judith Thomson and Mary Anne Warren tend to speak in a masculine voice. Do you agree? Why or why not?

4. What strong and weak points do you see in an ethic of care?

5. Do you agree that Carol Gilligan's ethical approach argues against a permissive attitude toward abortion? Is there a contradiction between advocating a feminist care perspective in ethics, on the one hand, and being pro-choice and supporting a woman's right to abortion, on the other?

6. Assess Wolf-Devine's response to Nel Noddings's efforts to square her ethic of care with support for a woman's right to abortion.

6

ANIMALS AND ENVIRONMENTAL ETHICS

The Place of Nonhumans in Environmental Issues

PETER SINGER

Peter Singer, professor of bioethics at Princeton University, is the author of *Animal Liberation,* a work that has stimulated much of today's interest in and debate over our treatment of animals. In the following essay, Singer argues that the effects of our environmental actions on nonhumans should figure directly in our deliberations about what we ought to do. Because animals can feel pleasure and pain and have the capacity for subjective experience, they can therefore be said to have interests, interests that we must not ignore. Singer contends that we must extend the moral principle of "equal consideration of interests" to include the interests of nonhumans, and he sketches the implications of our doing so—including the necessity of abandoning our present practice of rearing and killing other animals for food.

Study Questions

1. What are the two ways that Singer distinguishes of taking into account the effects of our actions on nonhuman animals?
2. What does Singer mean by "speciesism"?
3. Why does Singer maintain that birds and mammals have interests but plants do not?

The first six sections of this essay are reprinted from Peter Singer, "Not for Humans Only: The Place of Nonhumans in Environmental Issues," Ethics and Problems of the 21st Century, *edited by K. M. Sayre and K. F. Goodpaster.* © 1979 by University of Notre Dame Press. Reprinted by permission of the publisher. *The final section is reprinted by permission from Peter Singer, "All Animals Are Equal,"* Philosophic Exchange, *vol. 1, no. 5 (Summer 1974). Copyright © 1974 the Center for Philosophic Exchange. Section headings added.*

4. Why is giving equal consideration to the interests of two different beings not the same as treating them alike or holding their lives to be of equal value?

5. Why is Singer against raising and killing animals for food?

I. Humans and Nonhumans

WHEN WE HUMANS change the environment in which we live, we often harm ourselves. If we discharge cadmium into a bay and eat shellfish from that bay, we become ill and may die. When our industries and automobiles pour noxious fumes into the atmosphere, we find a displeasing smell in the air, the long-term results of which may be every bit as deadly as cadmium poisoning. The harm that humans do the environment, however, does not rebound solely, or even chiefly, on humans. It is nonhumans who bear the most direct burden of human interference with nature.

By "nonhumans" I mean to refer to all living things other than human beings, though for reasons to be given later, it is with nonhuman animals, rather than plants, that I am chiefly concerned. It is also important, in the context of environmental issues, to note that living things may be regarded either collectively or as individuals. In debates about the environment the most important way of regarding living things collectively has been to regard them as species. Thus, when environmentalists worry about the future of the blue whale, they usually are thinking of the blue whale as a species, rather than of individual blue whales. But this is not, of course, the only way in which one can think of blue whales, or other animals, and one of the topics I shall discuss is whether we should be concerned about what we are doing to the environment primarily insofar as it threatens entire species of nonhumans, or primarily insofar as it affects individual nonhuman animals.

The general question, then, is how the effects of our actions on the environment of nonhuman beings should figure in our deliberations about what we ought to do. There is an unlimited variety of contexts in which this issue could arise. To take just one: Suppose that it is considered necessary to build a new power station, and there are two sites, A and B, under consideration. In most respects the sites are equally suitable, but building the power station on site A would be more expensive because the greater depth of shifting soil at that site will require deeper foundations; on the other hand to build on site B will destroy a favored breeding ground for thousands of wildfowl. Should the presence of the wildfowl enter into the decision as to where to build? And if so, in what manner should it enter, and how heavily should it weigh?

In a case like this the effects of our actions on nonhuman animals could be taken into account in two quite different ways: directly, giving the lives and welfare of nonhuman animals an intrinsic significance which must count in any moral calculation; or indirectly, so that the effects of our actions on nonhumans are morally significant only if they have consequences for humans. . . .

II. Speciesism

The view that the effects of our actions on other animals have no direct moral significance is not as likely to be openly advocated today as it was in the past; yet it is likely to be accepted implicitly and acted upon. When planners perform cost-benefit studies on new projects, the costs and benefits are costs and benefits for human beings only. This does not mean that the impact of [a] power station or highway on wildlife is ignored altogether, but it is included only indirectly. That a new reservoir would drown a valley teeming with wildlife is taken into account only under some such heading as the value of the facilities for recreation that the valley affords. In calculating this value, the cost-benefit study will be neutral between forms of recreation like hunting and shooting and those like bird watching and bush walking—in fact hunting and shooting are likely to contribute more to the benefit side of the calculations because larger sums of money are spent on them, and they therefore benefit manufacturers and retailers of firearms as well as the hunters and shooters themselves. The suffering experienced by the animals whose habitat is flooded is not reckoned into the costs of the operation; nor is the recreational value obtained by the hunters and shooters offset by the cost to the animals that their recreation involves.

Despite its venerable origin, the view that the effects of our actions on nonhuman animals have no intrinsic moral significance can be shown to be arbitrary and morally indefensible. If a being suffers, the fact that it is not a member of our own species cannot be a moral reason for failing to take its suffering into account. This becomes obvious if we consider the analogous attempt by white slaveowners to deny consideration to the interests of blacks. These white racists limited their moral concern to their own race, so the suffering of a black did not have the same moral significance as the suffering of a white. We now recognize that in doing so they were making an arbitrary distinction, and that the existence of suffering, rather than the race of the sufferer, is what is really morally significant. The point remains true if "species" is substituted for "race." The logic of racism and the logic of the position we have been discussing, which I have elsewhere referred to as "speciesism," are indistinguishable; and if we reject the former then consistency demands that we reject the latter too.[1]

It should be clearly understood that the rejection of speciesism does not imply that the different species are in fact equal in respect of such characteristics as intelligence, physical strength, ability to communicate, capacity to suffer, ability to damage the environment, or anything else. After all, the moral principle of human equality cannot be taken as implying that all humans are equal in these respects either—if it did, we would have to give up the idea of human equality. That one being is more intelligent than another does not entitle him to enslave, exploit, or disregard the interests of the less intelligent being. The moral basis of equality among humans is not equality in fact, but the principle of equal consideration of interests, and it is this principle that, in consistency, must be extended to any nonhumans who have interests.

III. Nonhumans Have Interests

There may be some doubt about whether any nonhuman beings have interests. This doubt may arise because of uncertainty about what it is to have an interest, or because of uncertainty about the nature of some nonhuman beings. So far as the concept of "interest" is the cause of doubt, I take the view that only a being with subjective experiences, such as the experience of pleasure or the experience of pain, can have interests in the full sense of the term; and that any being with such experiences does have at least one interest, namely, the interest in experiencing pleasure and avoiding pain. Thus consciousness, or the capacity for subjective experience, is both a necessary and a sufficient condition for having an interest. While there may be a loose sense of the term in which we can say that it is in the interests of a tree to be watered, this attenuated sense of the term is not the sense covered by the principle of equal consideration of interests. All we mean when we say that it is in the interests of a tree to be watered is that the tree needs water if it is to continue to live and grow normally; if we regard this as evidence that the tree has interests, we might almost as well say that it is in the interests of a car to be lubricated regularly because the car needs lubrication if it is to run properly. In neither case can we really mean (unless we impute consciousness to trees or cars) that the tree or car has any preference about the matter.

The remaining doubt about whether nonhuman beings have interests is, then, a doubt about whether nonhuman beings have subjective experiences like the experience of pain. I have argued elsewhere that the commonsense view that birds and mammals feel pain is well founded,[2] but more serious doubts arise as we move down the evolutionary scale. Vertebrate animals have nervous systems broadly similar to our own and behave in ways that resemble our own pain behavior when subjected to stimuli that we would find painful; so the inference that vertebrates are capable of feeling pain is a reasonable one, though not as strong as it is if limited to mammals and birds. When we go beyond vertebrates to insects, crustaceans, mollusks and so on, the existence of subjective states becomes more dubious, and with very simple organisms it is difficult to believe that they could be conscious. As for plants, though there have been sensational claims that plants are not only conscious, but even psychic, there is no hard evidence that supports even the more modest claim.[3]

The boundary of beings who may be taken as having interests is therefore not an abrupt boundary, but a broad range in which the assumption that the being has interests shifts from being so strong as to be virtually certain to being so weak as to be highly improbable. The principle of equal consideration of interests must be applied with this in mind, so that where there is a clash between a virtually certain interest and highly doubtful one, it is the virtually certain interest that ought to prevail.

In this manner our moral concern ought to extend to all beings who have interests. . . .

IV. Equal Consideration of Interests

Giving equal consideration to the interests of two different beings does not mean treating them alike or holding their lives to be of equal value. We may recognize that the interests of one being are greater than those of another, and equal consideration will then lead us to sacrifice the being with lesser interests, if one or the other must be sacrificed. For instance, if for some reason a choice has to be made between saving the life of a normal human being and that of a dog, we might well decide to save the human because he, with his greater awareness of what is going to happen, will suffer more before he dies; we may also take into account the likelihood that it is the family and friends of the human who will suffer more; and finally, it would be the human who had the greater potential for future happiness. This decision would be in accordance with the principle of equal consideration of interests, for the interests of the dog get the same consideration as those of the human, and the loss to the dog is not discounted because the dog is not a member of our species. The outcome is as it is because the balance of interests favors the human. In a different situation—say, if the human were grossly mentally defective and without family or anyone else who would grieve for it—the balance of interests might favor the nonhuman.[4]

The more positive side of the principle of equal consideration is this: Where interests are equal, they must be given equal weight. So where human and nonhuman animals share an interest—as in the case of the interest in avoiding physical pain—we must give as much weight to violations of the interest of the nonhumans as we do to similar violations of the human's interest. This does not mean, of course, that it is as bad to hit a horse with a stick as it is to hit a human being, for the same blow would cause less pain to the animal with the tougher skin. The principle holds between similar amounts of felt pain, and what this is will vary from case to case.

It may be objected that we cannot tell exactly how much pain another animal is suffering, and that therefore the principle is impossible to apply. While I do not deny the difficulty and even, so far as precise measurement is concerned, the impossibility of comparing the subjective experiences of members of different species, I do not think that the problem is different in kind from the problem of comparing the subjective experiences of two members of our own species. Yet this is something we do all the time, for instance when we judge that a wealthy person will suffer less by being taxed at a higher rate than a poor person will gain from the welfare benefits paid for by the tax; or when we decide to take our two children to the beach instead of to a fair, because although the older one would prefer the fair, the younger one has a stronger preference the other way. These comparisons may be very rough, but since there is nothing better, we must use them; it would be irrational to refuse to do so simply because they are rough. Moreover, rough as they are, there are many situations in which we can be reasonably sure which way the balance of interests lies. While a difference of species may make comparisons rougher still, the basic problem is the same, and the comparisons are still often good enough to use, in the absence of anything more precise.

V. Animal Rights

The principle of equal consideration of interests and the indefensibility of limiting this principle to members of our own species means that we cannot deny, as Aquinas and Kant denied, that we have direct duties to members of other species. It may be asked whether this means that members of other species have rights against us. This is an issue on which there has been a certain amount of dispute, but it is, I believe, more a dispute about words than about substantive issues. In one sense of "right," we may say that it follows immediately from the fact that animals come within the scope of the principle of equal consideration of interests that they have at least one right, namely, the right to equal consideration. That is, admittedly, an odd kind of right—it is really a necessary foundation for having rights, rather than a right in itself. But some other rights could be derived from it without

difficulty: the right not to have gratuitous pain inflicted would be one such right. There is, however, another sense of "right," according to which rights exist only among those who are part of a community, all members of whom have rights and in turn are capable of respecting the rights of others. On this view, rights are essentially contractual, and hence cannot exist unless both parties are capable of honoring the contract. It would follow that most, if not all, nonhuman animals have no rights. It should be noted, though, that this is a narrower notion of rights than that commonly used in America today; for it follows from this notion of rights that not only nonhuman animals, but also human infants and young children, as well as mentally defective humans, have no rights. Those who put forward this view of rights do not believe that we may do what we like with young or mentally defective humans or nonhuman animals; rather they would say that moral rights are only one kind of constraint on our conduct, and not necessarily the most important. They might, for instance, take account of utilitarian considerations which would apply to all beings capable of pleasure or pain. Thus actions which proponents of the former, broader view of rights may condemn as violations of the rights of animals could also be condemned by those who hold the narrower view, though they would not classify such actions as infringing rights. Seen in this light the question of whether animals have rights becomes less important than it might otherwise appear, for what matters is how we think animals ought to be treated, and not how we employ the concept of a right. Those who deny animal rights will not be likely to refuse to consider their interests, as long as they are reminded that the denial of rights to nonhuman animals does no more than place animals in the same moral category as human infants. Hence I doubt if the claim that animals have rights is worth the effort required in its defense; it is a claim which invites replies which, whatever their philosophical merits, serve as a distraction from the central practical question.

VI. Examples

We can now draw at least one conclusion as to how the existence of nonhuman living things should enter into our deliberations about actions affecting the environment: Where our actions are likely to make animals suffer, that suffering must count in our deliberations, and it should count equally with a like amount of suffering by human beings, insofar as rough comparisons can be made.

The difficulty of making the required comparison will mean that the application of this conclusion is controversial in many cases, but there will be some situations in which it is clear enough. Take, for instance, the wholesale poisoning of animals that is euphemistically known as "pest control." The authorities who conduct these campaigns give no consideration to the suffering they inflict on the "pests," and invariably use the method of slaughter they believe to be cheapest and most effective. The result is that hundreds of millions of rabbits have died agonizing deaths from the artificially introduced disease, myxomatosis, or from poisons like "ten-eighty"; coyotes and other wild dogs have died painfully from cyanide poisoning; and all manner of wild animals have endured days of thirst, hunger, and fear with a mangled limb caught in a leg-hold trap.[5] Granting, for the sake of argument, the necessity for pest control—though this has rightly been questioned—the fact remains that no serious attempts have been made to introduce alternative means of control and thereby reduce the incalculable amount of suffering caused by present methods. It would not, presumably, be beyond modern science to produce a substance which, when eaten by rabbits or coyotes, produced sterility instead of a drawn-out death. Such methods might be more expensive, but can anyone doubt that if a similar amount of human suffering were at stake, the expense would be borne?

Another clear instance in which the principle of equal consideration of interests would indicate methods different from those presently used is in the timber industry. There are two basic methods of obtaining timber from forests. One is to cut only selected mature or dead trees, leaving the forest substantially intact. The other, known as clear-cutting, involves chopping down everything that grows in a given area, and then reseeding. Obviously when a large area is clear-cut, wild animals find their whole living area destroyed in a few days, whereas selected felling makes a relatively minor disturbance. But clear-cutting is cheaper, and timber companies therefore use this method and will continue to do so unless forced to do otherwise.[6] . . .

VII. The Meat Industry

For the great majority of human beings, especially in urban, industrialized societies, the most direct form of contact with members of other species is at meal-times: We eat them. In doing so we treat them purely as means to our ends. We regard their life and well-being as subordinate to our taste for a particular kind of dish. I say "taste" deliberately—this is purely a matter of pleasing our palate. There can be no defence of eating flesh in terms of satisfying nutritional needs, since it has been established beyond doubt that we could satisfy our need for protein and other essential nutrients far more efficiently with a diet that replaced animal flesh by soy beans, or products derived from soy beans, and other high-protein vegetable products.*

It is not merely the act of killing that indicates what we are ready to do to other species in order to gratify our tastes. The suffering we inflict on

---

* In order to produce 1 lb. of protein in the form of beef or veal, we must feed 21 lbs. of protein to the animal. Other forms of livestock are slightly less inefficient, but the average ratio in the U.S. is still 1:8. It has been estimated that the amount of protein lost to humans in this way is equivalent to 90% of the annual world protein deficit. For a brief account, see Frances Moore Lappé, *Diet for a Small Planet* (Friends of The Earth/Ballantine, New York 1971), pp. 4–11.

the animals while they are alive is perhaps an even clearer indication of our speciesism than the fact that we are prepared to kill them.* In order to have meat on the table at a price that people can afford, our society tolerates methods of meat production that confine sentient animals in cramped, unsuitable conditions for the entire durations of their lives. Animals are treated like machines that convert fodder into flesh, and any innovation that results in a higher "conversion ratio" is liable to be adopted. As one authority on the subject has said, "cruelty is acknowledged only when profitability ceases."[7] So hens are crowded four or five to a cage with a floor area of twenty inches by eighteen inches, or around the size of a single page of the *New York Times*. The cages have wire floors, since this reduces cleaning costs, though wire is unsuitable for the hens' feet; the floors slope, since this makes the eggs roll down for easy collection, although this makes it difficult for the hens to rest comfortably. In these conditions all the birds' natural instincts are thwarted: They cannot stretch their wings fully, walk freely, dust-bathe, scratch the ground, or build a nest. Although they have never known other conditions, observers have noticed that the birds vainly try to perform these actions. Frustrated at their inability to do so, they often develop what farmers call "vices," and peck each other to death. To prevent this, the beaks of young birds are often cut off.

This kind of treatment is not limited to poultry. Pigs are now also being reared in cages inside sheds. These animals are comparable to dogs in intelligence, and need a varied, stimulating environment if they are not to suffer from stress and boredom. Anyone who kept a dog in the way in which pigs are frequently kept would be liable to prosecution, in England at least, but because our interest in exploiting pigs is greater than our interest in exploiting dogs, we object to cruelty to dogs while consuming the produce of cruelty to pigs. Of the other animals, the condition of veal calves is perhaps worst of all, since these animals are so closely confined that they cannot even turn around or get up and lie down freely. In this way they do not develop unpalatable muscle. They are also made anaemic and kept short of roughage, to keep their flesh pale, since white veal fetches a higher price; as a result they develop a craving for iron and roughage, and have been observed to gnaw wood off the sides of their stalls, and lick greedily at any rusty hinge that is within reach.

Since, as I have said, none of these practices cater to anything more than our pleasures of taste, our practice of rearing and killing other animals in order to eat them is a clear instance of the sacrifice of the most important interests of other beings in order to satisfy trivial interests of our own. To avoid speciesism we must stop this practice, and each of us has a moral obligation to cease supporting the practice. Our custom is all the support that the meat industry needs. The decision to cease giving it that support may be difficult, but it is no more difficult than it would have been for a white Southerner to go against the traditions of his society and free his slaves; if we do not change our dietary habits, how can we censure those slaveholders who would not change their own way of living?

---

*Although one might think that killing a being is obviously the ultimate wrong one can do to it, I think that the infliction of suffering is a clearer indication of speciesism because it might be argued that at least part of what is wrong with killing a human is that most humans are conscious of their existence over time, and have desires and purposes that extend into the future—see, for instance, M. Tooley, "Abortion and Infanticide," *Philosophy and Public Affairs*, vol. 2, no. 1 (1972). Of course, if one took this view one would have to hold—as Tooley does—that killing a human infant or mental defective is not in itself wrong, and is less serious than killing certain higher mammals that probably do have a sense of their own existence over time.

NOTES

1. For a fuller statement of this argument, see my *Animal Liberation* (New York: A New York Review Book, 1975), especially ch. 1.
    2. *Ibid.*

3. See, for instance, the comments by Arthur Galston in *Natural History,* 83, no. 3 (March 1974): 18, on the "evidence" cited in such books as *The Secret Life of Plants.*

4. Singer, *Animal Liberation,* pp. 20–23.

5. See J. Olsen, *Slaughter the Animals, Poison the Earth* (New York: Simon and Schuster, 1971), especially pp. 153–164.

6. See R. and V. Routley, *The Fight for the Forests* (Canberra: Australian National University Press, 1974); for a thoroughly documented indictment of clear-cutting in America, see *Time,* May 17, 1976.

7. Ruth Harrison, *Animal Machines* (London: Stuart, 1964). This book provides an eye-opening account of intensive farming methods for those unfamiliar with the subject.

Review and Discussion Questions

1. Describe the human practices that most clearly demonstrate speciesism.

2. What does the principle of "equal consideration of interests" imply for our treatment of animals? What does it not imply?

3. Do you agree that animals can have interests that human beings must take into account? If so, which animals and what interests? What about plants?

4. Give examples of how adherence to the principle of equal consideration would change the conduct of human beings.

5. Most people take for granted that there is nothing immoral about eating meat. What are Singer's reasons for challenging this assumption? How compelling is his reasoning? Do you think that meat eating can be morally justified?

Do Animals Have Rights?

TIBOR R. MACHAN

In the previous essay, Peter Singer argued that the moral principle of equal consideration of interests should be extended to animals—that is, that animal interests should be weighed equally with human interests in our moral deliberations. Other moral philosophers have put the point in terms of rights, arguing that animals have certain basic moral rights that humans must respect. In this essay Tibor R. Machan, professor of philosophy at Auburn University, rejects these arguments, contending that animals have no rights and that their interests do not count equally with those of human beings.

Study Questions

1. What is it to have a right, according to Machan? What is the argument for extending rights to animals?

2. Explain why, according to Machan, human beings may use animals for their own purposes.

Reprinted by permission from Public Affairs Quarterly, *vol. 5, no. 2 (April 1991). Copyright © 1991 Public Affairs Quarterly.*

3. Why are human rights important? How does the answer to this question imply that there is no room for animal rights?

4. Does Machan believe that we are morally permitted to do whatever we want to animals?

I N RECENT YEARS the doctrine of animals' rights has found champions in important circles where the general doctrine of rights is itself well respected. For example, Professor Tom Regan, in his important book *The Case For Animal Rights* (UC Press, 1983), finds the idea of natural rights intellectually congenial but then extends this idea to cover animals near humans on the evolutionary scale. The tradition from within which Regan works is clearly Lockean, only he does not agree that human nature is distinctive enough, in relevant respects, to restrict the scope of natural rights to human beings alone.

Following a different tradition, namely, utilitarianism, the idea of animal liberation has emerged. And this idea comes to roughly the same thing, practically speaking. Only the argument is different because for utilitarians what is important is not that someone or something must have a specific sphere of dominion but that they be well off in their lives. So long as the bulk of the relevant creatures enjoy a reasonably high living standard, the moral and political objectives for us will have been met. But if this goal is neglected, moral and political steps are required to improve on the situation. Animal liberation is such a step.

This essay will maintain that animals have no rights and need no liberation. I will argue that to think they do is a category mistake—it is, to be blunt, to unjustifiably anthropomorphize animals, to treat them as if they were what they are not, namely, human beings. Rights and liberty are political concepts applicable to human beings because human beings are moral agents, in need of what Harvard philosopher Robert Nozick calls "moral space," that is, a definite sphere of moral jurisdiction where their authority to act is respected and protected so it is they,

not intruders, who govern themselves and either succeed or fail in their moral tasks.

Oddly, it is clearly admitted by most animal rights or liberation theorists that only human beings are moral agents—for example, they never urge animals to behave morally (by, e.g., standing up for their rights, by leading a political revolution). No animal rights theorist proposes that animals be tried for crimes and blamed for moral wrongs.

If it is true that the moral nature of human beings gives rise to the conception of basic rights and liberties, then by this alone animal rights and liberation theorists have made an admission fatal to their case.

Before getting under way I want to note that rights and liberty are certainly not the whole of moral concern to us. There are innumerable other moral issues one can raise, including about the way human beings relate to animals. In particular, there is the question how should people treat animals. Should they be hunted even when this does not serve any vital human purpose? Should they be utilized in hurtful—indeed, evidently agonizing—fashion even for trivial human purposes? Should their pain and suffering be ignored in the process of being made use of for admittedly vital human purposes?

It is clear that once one has answered the question of whether animals have rights (or ought to be liberated from human beings) in the negative, one has by no means disposed of these other issues. In this essay I will be dealing mostly with the issue of animal rights and liberation. Yet I will also touch briefly on the other moral issues just raised. I will indicate why they may all be answered in the negative without it being the case that animals have rights or should be liberated—i.e., without raising any serious political issues.

Why Might Animals Have Rights?

To have a right amounts to having those around one who have the choice to abstain from intruding on one within a given sphere of jurisdiction. If I have the right to the use of our community swimming pool, no one may prevent me from making the decision as to whether I do or do not use the pool. Someone's having a right is a kind of freedom from the unavoidable interference of moral agents, beings who are capable of choosing whether they will interfere or not interfere with the rights holder.

When a right is considered natural, the freedom involved in having this right is supposed to be justified by reference to the kind of being one is, one's nature as a certain kind of entity. The idea of natural rights was formulated in connection with the issue of the proper relationship between human beings, especially citizens and governments. The idea goes back many centuries. . . .

The major political thinker with an influential doctrine of natural rights was John Locke. In his *Second Treatise on Government* he argued that each human being is responsible to follow the Law of Nature, the source of morality. But to do so, each also requires a sphere of personal authority, which is identified by the principle of the natural right to property—including one's person and estate. In other words, to be a morally responsible being in the company of other persons one needs what Robert Nozick has called "moral space," i.e., a sphere of sovereignty or personal jurisdiction so that one can engage in self-government—for better or for worse. . . .

In our time numerous philosophers and social commentators have made the attempt to demonstrate that if we are able to ascribe basic rights to life, liberty and property to human beings, we can do the same for many of the higher animals. In essentials their arguments can be broken down into two parts. First, they subscribe to Darwin's thesis that no difference of kind, only a difference of degree, can be found between other animals and human beings.[1] Second, even if there were a difference in kind between other animals—especially mammals—and human beings, since they both can be shown to have interests (e.g., the avoidance of pain or suffering), for certain moral and legal purposes the difference does not matter, only the similarity does. In connection with both of these arguments the central conclusion is that if human beings can be said to have certain basic rights—e.g., to life, liberty or consideration for their capacity to suffer—then so do (higher) animals.*

Now I do not wish to give the impression that no diversity exists among those who defend animal rights. Some do so from the viewpoint of natural rights, treating animals' rights as basic limiting principles which may not be ignored except when it would also make sense to disregard the rights of human beings. Even on this matter there are serious differences among defenders of animals' rights—some do not allow any special regard for human beings,[†] some hold that when it comes to a choice between a person and a dog, it is ordinarily the person who should be given protection.[‡] But others choose to defend animal rights on utilitarian grounds—to the extent that it amounts to furthering overall pleasure or happiness in the world, animals must be given equal consideration to what hu-

---

*On these points both the deontologically oriented Tom Regan and the utilitarian Peter Singer tend to agree, although they differ considerably in their arguments.

†Peter Singer holds that "we would be on shaky grounds if we were to demand equality for blacks, women, and other groups of oppressed humans while denying equal consideration to nonhumans." "All Animals Are Equal," *op. cit.,* Regan & Singer, *Animal Rights,* p. 150.

‡Tom Regan contends that "[it] is not to say that practices that involve taking the lives of animals cannot possibly be justified . . . in order to seriously consider approving such a practice [it] would [have to] prevent, reduce, or eliminate a much greater amount of evil . . . there is no other way to bring about these consequences . . . and . . . we have very good reason to believe that these consequences will obtain." "Do Animals Have a Right to Life?" *op. cit.,* Regan & Singer, *Animal Rights,* pp. 204–5.

man beings receive. Thus only if there really is demonstrable contribution to the overall pleasure or happiness on earth may an animal capable of experiencing pleasure or happiness be sacrificed for the sake of some human purpose. Barring such demonstrable contribution, animals and humans enjoy equal rights.*

At times the argument for animal rights begins with the rather mild point that "reason requires that other animals are as much within the scope of moral concern as are men" but then moves on to the more radical claim that therefore "we must view our entire history as well as all aspects of our daily lives from a new perspective."[2]

Of course, people have generally invoked some moral considerations as they treated animals—I can recall living on a farm in Hungary when I was 11 and getting all kinds of lectures about how I ought to treat the animals, receiving severe rebuke when I mistreated a cat and lots of praise when I took the favorite cow grazing every day and established a close bond with it over time. Hardly anyone can have escaped one or another moral lecture from parents or neighbors concerning the treatment of pets, household animals, or birds. When a young boy once tried out an air gun by shooting a pigeon sitting on a telephone wire before the apartment house in which he lived, I recall that there was no end of rebuke in response to his wanton callousness. Yet none of those who engaged in the moralizing ever entertained the need to "view our entire history as well as all aspects of our daily lives from a new perspective." Rather they seemed to have understood that reckless disregard for the life or well being of animals shows a defect of character, lack of sensitivity, callousness—realizing, at the same time, that numerous human purposes justify our killing and using animals in the various ways most of us use them.

*This is the gist of Singer's thesis.

And this really is the crux of the matter. But why? Why is it more reasonable to think of animals as available for our sensible use rather than owed the kind of respect and consideration we ought to extend to other human beings? It is one thing to have this as a common sense conviction, it is another to know it as a sound viewpoint, in terms of which we may confidently conduct ourselves.

Why We May Use Animals

While I will return to the arguments for animal rights, let me first place on record the case for the use of animals for human purposes. Without this case reasonably well established, it will not be possible to critically assess the case for animal rights. After all, this is a comparative matter—which viewpoint makes better sense, which is, in other words, more likely to be true?

One reason for the propriety of our use of animals is that we are more important or valuable than other animals and some of our projects may require animals for them to be successful. Notice that this is different from saying that human beings are "uniquely important," a position avidly ridiculed by Stephen R. L. Clark, who claims that "there seems no decent ground in reason or revelation to suppose that man is uniquely important or significant."[3] If man were uniquely important, that would mean that one could not assign any value to plants or non-human animals apart from their relationship to human beings. That is not the position I am defending. I argue that there is a scale of importance in nature, and among all the various kinds of being, human beings are the most important—even while it is true that some members of the human species may indeed prove themselves to be the most vile and worthless, as well.

How do we establish that we are more important or valuable? By considering whether the idea of lesser or greater importance or value in the nature of things makes clear sense and applying it to an understanding of whether human beings or other animals are more important. If it turns out that ranking things in nature as more or less important makes sense, and if we qualify as more important than other animals, there is at least the beginning of a reason why we may make use of other animals for our purposes.

That there are things of different degree of value in nature is admitted by animal rights advocates, so there is no great need here to argue about that. When they insist that we treat animals differently from the way we treat, say, rocks or iron ore—so that while we may not use the former as we choose, we may use the latter—they testify, at least by implication, that animals are more important than, say, iron ore. Certainly they invoke some measure of importance or value and place animals higher in line with this measure than they place other aspects of nature. They happen, also, to deny that human beings rank higher than animals, or at least they do not admit that human beings' higher ranking warrants their using animals for their purposes. But that is a distinct issue which we can consider later.

Quite independently of the implicit acknowledgment by animal rights advocates of the hierarchy of nature, there simply is evidence through the natural world of the existence of beings of greater complexity and of higher value. For example, while it makes no sense to evaluate as good or bad such things as planets or rocks or pebbles—except as they may relate to human purposes—when it comes to plants and animals the process of evaluation commences very naturally indeed. We can speak of better or worse trees, oaks, redwoods, or zebras, foxes or chimps. While at this point we confine our evaluation to the condition or behavior of such beings without any intimation of their responsibility for being better or worse, when we start discussing human beings our

evaluation takes on a moral component. Indeed, none are more ready to testify to this than animal rights advocates who, after all, do not demand any change of behavior on the part of non-human animals and yet insist that human beings conform to certain moral edicts as a matter of their own choice. This means that even animal rights advocates admit outright that to the best of our knowledge it is with human beings that the idea of moral goodness and moral responsibility enters the universe.

Clearly this shows a hierarchical structure in nature: some things do not invite evaluations at all—it is a matter of no significance or of indifference whether they are or are not or what they are or how they behave. Some things invite evaluation but without implying any moral standing with reference to whether they do well or badly. And some things—namely, human beings—invite moral evaluation. The level of importance or value may be noted to move from the inanimate to the animate world, culminating, as far as we now know, with human life. Normal human life involves moral tasks, and that is why we are more important than other beings in nature—we are subject to moral appraisal, it is a matter of our doing whether we succeed or fail in our lives.

Now when it comes to our moral task, namely, to succeed as human beings, we are dependent upon reaching sensible conclusions about what we should do. We can fail to do this and too often do so. But we can also succeed. The process that leads to our success involves learning, among other things, what it is that nature avails us with to achieve our highly varied tasks in life. Clearly among these highly varied tasks could be some that make judicious use of animals—for example, to find out whether some medicine is safe for human use, we might wish to use animals. To do this is the rational thing for us to do, so as to make the best use of nature for our success in living our lives. That does not mean there need be no guidelines involved in how we might make use of animals—any more than there need be no guidelines involved in how we use anything else.

Why Individual Human Rights?

Where do individual *human* rights come into this picture? The rights being talked of in connection with human beings have as their source, as we have noted earlier, the human capacity to make moral choices. We have the right to life, liberty and property—as well as more specialized rights connected with politics, the press, religion—because we have as our central task in life to act morally. And in order to be able to do this throughout the scope of our lives, we require a reasonably clear sphere of personal jurisdiction—a dominion where we are sovereign and can either succeed or fail to live well, to do right, to act properly.

If we did not have rights, we would not have such a sphere of personal jurisdiction and there would be no clear idea as to whether we are acting in our own behalf or those of other persons. No one could be blamed or praised for we would not know clearly enough whether what the person is doing is in his or her authority to do or in someone else's. This is precisely the problem that arises in communal living and, especially, in totalitarian countries where everything is under forced collective governance. The reason moral distinctions are still possible to make under such circumstances is that in fact—as distinct from law— there is always some sphere of personal jurisdiction wherein people may exhibit courage, prudence, justice, honesty and other virtues. But where collectivism has been successfully enforced, there is no individual responsibility at play and people's morality and immorality is submerged within the group.

Indeed the main reason for governments has for some time been recognized to be nothing other than that our individual human rights should be protected. . . .

Where Is There Room for Animal Rights?

We have seen that the most sensible and influential doctrine of human rights rests on the fact that human beings are indeed members of a discernibly different species—the members of which have a moral life to aspire to and must have principles upheld for them in communities that make their aspiration possible. Now there is plainly no valid intellectual place for rights in the nonhuman world, the world in which moral responsibility is for all practical purposes absent. Some would want to argue that some measure of morality can be found within the world of at least higher animals—e.g., dogs. For example, Rollin holds that "In actual fact, some animals even seem to exhibit behavior that bespeaks something like moral agency or moral agreement."[4] His argument for this is rather anecdotal but it is worth considering:

> Canids, including the domesticated dog, do not attack another when the vanquished bares its throat, showing a sign of submission. Animals typically do not prey upon members of their own species. Elephants and porpoises will and do feed injured members of their species. Porpoises will help humans, even at risk to themselves. Some animals will adopt orphaned young of other species. (Such cross-species "morality" would certainly not be explainable by simple appeal to mechanical evolution, since there is no advantage whatever to one's own species.) Dogs will act "guilty" when they break a rule such as one against stealing food from a table and will, for the most part, learn not to take it.[5]

Animal rights advocates such as Rollin maintain that it is impossible to clearly distinguish between human and non-human animals, including on the grounds of the former's characteristic as a moral agent. Yet what they do to defend this point is to invoke borderline cases, imaginary hypothesis, and anecdotes.

In contrast, in his book *The Difference of Man and the Difference It Makes*, Mortimer Adler undertakes the painstaking task of showing that even with the full acknowledgment of the merits of Darwinian and, especially, post-Darwinian evolutionary theory, there is ample reason to uphold the doctrine of species-distinction—a distinction, incidentally, that is actually presupposed within Darwin's own work.[6] Adler shows that although the theistic doctrine of radical species differences is incompatible with current evolutionary theory, the more naturalistic view that species are superficially (but non-negligibly) different is indeed necessary to it. The fact of occasional borderline cases is simply irrelevant—what is crucial is that the generalization is true that human beings are basically different from other animals—by virtue of "a crucial threshold in a continuum of degrees." As Adler explains:

> . . . distinct species are genetically isolated populations between which interbreeding is impossible, arising (except in the case of polyploidy) from varieties between which interbreeding was not impossible, but between which it was prevented. Modern theorists, with more assurance than Darwin could manage, treat distinct species as natural kinds, not as man-made class distinctions.[7]

Adler adds that "Without the critical insight provided by the distinction between superficial and radical differences in kind, biologists [as well as animal rights advocates, one should add] might be tempted to follow Darwin in thinking that all differences in kind must be apparent, not real."[8]

Since Locke's admittedly incomplete—sometimes even confusing—theory had gained respect and, especially, practical import (e.g., in British and American political history), it became clear enough that the only justification for the exercise of state power—namely the force of the law—is that the rights of individuals are being or have been violated. But as with all successful doctrines, Locke's idea became corrupted by innumerable efforts to concoct rights that government must protect, rights that were actually disguised special interest objectives—values that some people, perhaps quite legitimately, wanted very badly to have secured for them.

While it is no doubt true that many animal rights advocates sincerely believe that they have found a justification for the actual existence of animal rights, it is equally likely that if the Lockean doctrine of rights had not become so influential, they would now be putting their point differently—in a way, namely, that would secure for them what they, as a special interest group, want: the protection of animals they have such love and sympathy for.

Closing Reflections

As with most issues on the minds of many intelligent people as well as innumerable crackpots, a discussion of whether there are animal rights and how we ought to treat animals cannot be concluded with dogmatic certainty one way or the other. Even though those who defend animal rights are certain almost beyond a shadow of doubt, all I can claim is to being certain beyond a reasonable doubt. Animals are not the sort of beings with basic rights to life, liberty and property, whereas human beings, in the main, are just such beings. Yet we know that animals can feel pain and can enjoy themselves and this must give us pause when we consider using them for our legitimate purposes. We ought to be humane, we ought to kill them and rear them and train them and hunt them in a fashion consistent with such care about them as sentient beings.

NOTES

1. Charles Darwin, *The Descent of Man*, Chpts. 3 and 4. Reprinted in Tom Regan and Peter Singer, eds., *Animal Rights and Human Obligations* (Englewood Cliffs, NJ: Prentice-Hall, 1976), pp. 72–81.

2. Bernard E. Rollin, *Animal Rights and Human Morality* (Buffalo, NY: Prometheus Books, 1981), p. 4.

3. Stephen R. L. Clark, *The Moral Status of Animals* (Oxford, England: Clarendon Press, 1977), p. 13.

4. Rollin, *Animal Rights*, p. 14.

5. *Ibid.*

6. See a discussion of this in Mortimer Adler, *The Difference of Man and the Difference It Makes* (New York: World Publishing Co., 1968), pp. 73ff.

7. *Ibid.*

8. *Ibid.*, p. 75.

Review and Discussion Questions

1. Contrast the practical implications of Machan's essay and those of Singer's essay for our treatment of animals, in particular for meat eating and animal experimentation.

2. Do you agree with Machan that human beings are more important or valuable than animals? How could this conclusion be established? Would our being more valuable show that we are morally permitted to use animals for our own purposes?

3. Most people would agree that animals cannot make moral decisions and therefore are not moral agents. If not, does it follow that animals cannot have rights or that their interests count less than human interests?

4. Machan believes that moral considerations still govern our treatment of animals, even if they lack rights and even if we are not obligated to give equal consideration to their interests. Assuming Machan is correct, what are the moral limits on our treatment of animals, and why?

5. How would you respond to Machan's argument if you were Singer? Is Machan guilty of "speciesism"?

Should Trees Have Standing?
Toward Legal Rights for Natural Objects

CHRISTOPHER D. STONE

Professor of law Christopher D. Stone argues that we should extend legal rights to forests, oceans, rivers, and other natural objects. Although the proposal may sound absurd, so did earlier proposals to extend rights, for example, to blacks and women. Stone discusses what it means to be a holder of legal rights and how extending rights

Excerpted from Christopher D. Stone, "Should Trees Have Standing? Toward Legal Rights for Natural Objects," 45 Southern California Law Review *450–501 (1972). Reprinted with the permission of the* Southern California Law Review.

to natural objects would dramatically change our approach to environmental protection. Stone's proposal is in part pragmatic: a legal move to enable environmentalists to better protect the environment. But it also reflects the view that nature deserves to be protected for its own sake.

Study Questions

1. Why does the extension of rights to some new entity always sound absurd?
2. What three criteria must something satisfy to be a "holder of legal rights"?
3. How does the example of the pollution of a stream illustrate the fact that natural objects lack legal rights?
4. How does Stone address the problem that natural objects like forests cannot speak for themselves or claim their rights?
5. What is the new conception advocated by Stone of the relationship of human beings to the rest of nature?

THROUGHOUT LEGAL HISTORY, each successive extension of rights to some new entity has been, theretofore, a bit unthinkable. We are inclined to suppose the rightlessness of rightless "things" to be a decree of Nature, not a legal convention acting in support of some status quo. It is thus that we defer considering the choices involved in all their moral, social, and economic dimensions. And so the United States Supreme Court could straightfacedly tell us in *Dred Scott* that Blacks had been denied the rights of citizenship "as a subordinate and inferior class of beings, who had been subjugated by the dominant race. . . ."[1] In the nineteenth century, the highest court in California explained that Chinese had not the right to testify against white men in criminal matters because they were "a race of people whom nature has marked as inferior, and who are incapable of progress or intellectual development beyond a certain point . . . between whom and ourselves nature has placed an impassable difference."[2] The popular conception of the Jew in the thirteenth century contributed to a law which treated them as "men *ferae naturae,* protected by a quasi-forest law. Like the roe and the deer, they form an order apart."[3] Recall, too, that it was not so long ago that the foetus

was "like the roe and the deer." In an early suit attempting to establish a wrongful death action on behalf of a negligently killed foetus (now widely accepted practice), Holmes, then on the Massachusetts Supreme Court, seems to have thought it simply inconceivable "that a man might owe a civil duty and incur a conditional prospective liability in tort to one not yet in being."[4] The first woman in Wisconsin who thought she might have a right to practice law was told that she did not, in the following terms:

> The law of nature destines and qualifies the female sex for the bearing and nurture of the children of our race and for the custody of the homes of the world. . . . [A]ll life-long callings of women, inconsistent with these radical and sacred duties of their sex, as is the profession of the law, are departures from the order of nature; and when voluntary, treason against it. . . . The peculiar qualities of womanhood, its gentle graces, its quick sensibility, its tender susceptibility, its purity, its delicacy, its emotional impulses, its subordination of hard reason to sympathetic feeling, are surely not qualifications for forensic strife. Nature has tempered woman as little for the juridical conflicts of the court room, as for the physical conflicts of the battle field. . . .[5]

The fact is, that each time there is a movement to confer rights onto some new "entity," the proposal is bound to sound odd or frightening or laughable. This is partly because until the rightless thing receives its rights, we cannot see it as anything but a *thing* for the use of "us"—those who are holding rights at the time. In this vein, what is striking about the Wisconsin case above is that the court, for all its talk about women, so clearly was never able to see women as they are (and might become). All it could see was the popular "idealized" version of *an object it needed.* Such is the way the slave South looked upon the Black. There is something of a seamless web involved; there will be resistance to giving the thing "rights" until it can be seen and valued for itself; yet, it is hard to see it and value it for itself until we can bring ourselves to give it "rights"—which is almost inevitably going to sound inconceivable to a large group of people.

The reason for this little discourse on the unthinkable, the reader must know by now, if only from the title of the paper. I am quite seriously proposing that we give legal rights to forests, oceans, rivers, and other so-called "natural objects" in the environment—indeed, to the natural environment as a whole. . . .

Toward Rights for the Environment

Now, to say that the natural environment should have rights is not to say anything as silly as that no one should be allowed to cut down a tree. We say human beings have rights, but—at least as of the time of this writing—they can be executed. Corporations have rights, but they cannot plead the fifth amendment; *In re Gault* gave fifteen-year-olds certain rights in juvenile proceedings, but it did not give them the right to vote. Thus, to say that the environment should have rights is not to say that it should have every right we can imagine, or even the same body of rights as human beings have. Nor is it to say that everything in the environment should have the same rights as every other thing in the environment. . . .

For a thing to be *a holder of legal rights* something more is needed than that some authoritative body will review the actions and processes of those who threaten it. As I shall use the term, "holder of legal rights," each of three additional criteria must be satisfied. All three, one will observe, go towards making a thing *count* jurally—to have a legally recognized worth and dignity in its own right, and not merely to serve as a means to benefit "us" (whoever the contemporary group of rights-holders may be). They are, first, that the thing can institute legal actions *at its behest;* second, that in determining the granting of legal relief, the court must take *injury to it* into account; and, third, that relief must run to the *benefit of it.* . . .

The Rightlessness of Natural Objects at Common Law

Consider, for example, the common law's posture toward the pollution of a stream. True, courts have always been able, in some circumstances, to issue orders that will stop the pollution. . . . But the stream itself is fundamentally rightless, with implications that deserve careful reconsideration.

The first sense in which the stream is not a rights-holder has to do with standing. The stream itself has none. So far as the common law is concerned, there is in general no way to challenge the polluter's actions save at the behest of a lower riparian—another human being—able to show an invasion of *his* rights. . . .

The second sense in which the common law denies "rights" to natural objects has to do with the way in which the merits are decided in those cases in which someone is competent and willing to establish standing. At its more primitive levels, the system protected the "rights" of the property owning human with minimal weighting of any values. . . . Today we have come more and more to make balances—but only such as will adjust the economic best interests of identifiable humans. . . .

Thus, we find the highest court of Pennsylvania refusing to stop a coal company from discharging polluted mine water into a tributary of the Lackawana River because a plaintiff's "grievance is for a mere personal inconvenience; and . . . mere private personal inconveniences . . . must yield to the necessities of a great public industry, which although in the hands of a private corporation, subserves a great public interest."[6] The stream itself is lost sight of in "a quantitative compromise between *two* conflicting interests."[7]

The third way in which the common law makes natural objects rightless has to do with who is regarded as the beneficiary of a favorable judgment. Here, too, it makes a considerable difference that it is not the natural object that counts in its own right. To illustrate this point let me begin by observing that it makes perfectly good sense to speak of, and ascertain, the legal damage to a natural object, if only in the sense of "making it whole" with respect to the most obvious factors. The costs of making a forest whole, for example, would include the costs of reseeding, repairing watersheds, restocking wildlife—the sorts of costs the Forest Service undergoes after a fire. Making a polluted stream whole would include the costs of restocking with fish, water-fowl, and other animal and vegetable life, dredging, washing out impurities, establishing natural and/or artificial aerating agents, and so forth. Now, what is important to note is that, under our present system, even if a plaintiff riparian wins a water pollution suit for damages, no money goes to the benefit of the stream itself to repair *its* damages. . . .

None of the natural objects, whether held in common or situated on private land, has any of the three criteria of a rights-holder. They have no standing in their own right; their unique damages do not count in determining outcome; and they are not the beneficiaries of awards. In such a fashion, these objects have traditionally been regarded by the common law, and even by all but the most recent legislation, as objects for man to conquer and master and use—in such a way as the law once looked upon "man's" relationships to African Negroes. Even where special measures have been taken to conserve them, as by seasons on game and limits on timber cutting, the dominant motive has been to conserve them *for us*—for the greatest good of the greatest number of human beings. Conservationists, so far as I am aware, are generally reluctant to maintain otherwise. As the name implies, they want to conserve and guarantee *our* consumption and *our* enjoyment of these other living things. In their own right, natural objects have counted for little, in law as in popular movements.

As I mentioned at the outset, however, the rightlessness of the natural environment can and should change; it already shows some signs of doing so.

Toward Having Standing in Its Own Right

It is not inevitable, nor is it wise, that natural objects should have no rights to seek redress in their own behalf. It is no answer to say that streams and forests cannot have standing because streams and forests cannot speak. Corporations cannot speak either; nor can states, estates, infants, incompetents, municipalities, or universities. Lawyers speak for them, as they customarily do for the ordinary citizen with legal problems. One ought, I think, to handle the legal problems of natural objects as one does the problems of legal incompetents—human beings who have become vegetable. If a human being shows signs of becoming senile and has affairs that he is de jure incompetent to manage, those concerned with his well being make such a showing to the court, and someone is designated by the court with the authority to manage the incompetent's affairs. . . .

On a parity of reasoning we should have a system in which, when a friend of a natural object perceives it to be endangered, he can apply to a court for the creation of a guardianship. . . .

The potential "friends" that such a statutory scheme would require will hardly be lacking. The Sierra Club, Environmental Defense Fund, Friends of the Earth, Natural Resources Defense Counsel, and the Izaak Walton League are just some of the many groups which have manifested unflagging dedication to the environment and which are becoming increasingly capable of marshalling the requisite technical experts and lawyers. If, for example, the Environmental Defense Fund should have reason to believe that some company's strip mining operations might be irreparably destroying the ecological balance of large tracts of land, it could, under this procedure, apply to the court in which the lands were situated to be appointed guardian. As guardian, it might be given rights of inspection (or visitation) to determine and bring to the court's attention a fuller finding on the land's condition. If there were indications that under the substantive law some redress might be available on the land's behalf, then the guardian would be entitled to raise the land's rights in the land's name, *i.e.,* without having to make the roundabout and often unavailing demonstration . . . that the "rights" of the club's members were being invaded. . . .

One reason for making the environment itself the beneficiary of a judgment is to prevent it from being "sold out" in a negotiation among private litigants who agree not to enforce rights that have been established among themselves. Protection from this will be advanced by making the natural object a party to an injunctive settlement. Even more importantly, we should make it a beneficiary of money awards. . . .

The idea of assessing damages as best we can and placing them in a trust fund is far more realistic than a hope that a total "freeze" can be put on the environmental status quo. Nature is a continuous theatre in which things and species (eventually man) are destined to enter and exit. In the meantime, co-existence of man and his environment means that *each* is going to have to

compromise for the better of both. Some pollution of streams, for example, will probably be inevitable for some time. Instead of setting an unrealizable goal of enjoining absolutely the discharge of all such pollutants, the trust fund concept would (a) help assure that pollution would occur only in those instances where the social need for the pollutant's product (via his present method of production) was so high as to enable the polluter to cover *all* homocentric costs, plus some estimated costs to the environment *per se,* and (b) would be a corpus for preserving monies, if necessary, while the technology developed to a point where repairing the damaged portion of the environment was feasible. Such a fund might even finance the requisite research and development. . . .

A radical new conception of man's relationship to the rest of nature would not only be a step towards solving the material planetary problems; there are strong reasons for such a changed consciousness from the point of making us far better humans. If we only stop for a moment and look at the underlying human qualities that our present attitudes toward property and nature draw upon and reinforce, we have to be struck by how stultifying of our own personal growth and satisfaction they can become when they take rein of us. Hegel, in "justifying" private property, unwittingly reflects the tone and quality of some of the needs that are played upon:

> A person has as his substantive end the right of putting his will into any and every thing and thereby making it his, because it has no such end in itself and derives its destiny and soul from his will. This is the absolute right of appropriation which man has over all "things."[8]

What is it within us that gives us this need not just to satisfy basic biological wants, but to extend our wills over things, to object-ify them, to make them ours, to manipulate them, to keep them at a psychic distance? Can it all be explained on "rational" bases? Should we not be suspect of such needs within us, cautious as to why we wish to gratify them? When I first read that passage of Hegel, I immediately thought not only of the emotional contrast with Spinoza, but of the passage in Carson McCullers' "A Tree, a Rock, a Cloud," in which an old derelict has collared a twelve-year-old boy in a streetcar cafe. The old man asks whether the boy knows "how love should be begun."

> The old man leaned closer and whispered:
> "A tree. A rock. A cloud."
> "The weather was like this in Portland," he said. "At the time my science was begun. I meditated and I started very cautious. I would pick up something from the street and take it home with me. I bought a goldfish and I concentrated on the goldfish and I loved it. I graduated from one thing to another. Day by day I was getting this technique.
> . . . "For six years now I have gone around by myself and built up my science. And now I am a master. Son, I can love anything. No longer do I have to think about it even. I see a street full of people and a beautiful light comes in me. I watch a bird in the sky. Or I meet a traveler on the road. Everything, Son. And anybody. All stranger and all loved! Do you realize what a science like mine can mean?"[9]

To be able to get away from the view that Nature is a collection of useful senseless objects is, as McCullers' "madman" suggests, deeply involved in the development of our abilities to love—or, if that is putting it too strongly, to be able to reach a heightened awareness of our own, and others' capacities in their mutual interplay. To do so, we have to give up some psychic investment in our sense of separateness and specialness in the universe. And this, in turn, is hard giving indeed, because it involves us in a fight backwards, into earlier stages of civilization and childhood in which we had to trust (and perhaps fear) our environment, for we had not then the power to master it. Yet, in doing so, we—as persons—gradually free ourselves of needs for supportive illusions. Is not this one of the triumphs for "us" of our giving legal rights to (or acknowledging the legal rights of) the Blacks and women? . . .

The time may be on hand when these sentiments, and the early stirrings of the law, can be coalesced into a radical new theory or myth—felt as well as intellectualized—of man's relationships to the rest of nature. I do not mean "myth" in a demeaning sense of the term, but in the sense in which, at different times in history, our social "facts" and relationships have been comprehended and integrated by reference to the "myths" that we are co-signers of a social contract, that the Pope is God's agent, and that all men are created equal. Pantheism, Shinto, and Tao all have myths to offer. But they are all, each in its own fashion, quaint, primitive, and archaic. What is needed is a myth that can fit our growing body of knowledge of geophysics, biology, and the cosmos. In this vein, I do not think it too remote that we may come to regard the Earth, as some have suggested, as one organism, of which Mankind is a functional part—the mind, perhaps: different from the rest of nature, but different as a man's brain is from his lungs.

NOTES

1. *Dred Scott v. Sanford,* 60 U.S. (19 How.) 396, 404–05 (1856).
2. *People v. Hall,* 4 Cal. 399, 405 (1854).
3. Schechter, "The Rightlessness of Medieval English Jewry," 45 *Jewish Q. Rev.* 121, 135 (1954) quoting from M. Bateson, *Medieval England* 139 (1904).
4. *Dietrich v. Inhabitants of Northampton,* 138 Mass. 14, 16 (1884).
5. *In re Goddell,* 39 Wisc. 232, 245 (1875).
6. *Pennsylvania Coal Co. v. Sanderson,* 113 Pa. 126, 149, 6 A. 453, 459 (1886).
7. Hand, J., in *Smith v. Staso Milling Co.,* 18 F.2d 736, 738 (2d Cir. 1927) (emphasis added).
8. G. Hegel, *Hegel's Philosophy of Right,* 41 (T. Knox transl. 1945).
9. C. McCullers, *The Ballad of the Sad Cafe and Other Stories,* 150–51 (1958).

Review and Discussion Questions

1. Do you think the idea of granting legal rights to natural objects is workable? What would be the practical results of doing so? Would it significantly strengthen efforts to preserve the natural environment?

2. Assess Stone's argument in light of the previous essay by Tibor Machan. How do their positions contrast, and whose viewpoint seems more persuasive? Can natural objects have either legal, political, or moral rights? If so, which natural objects and what rights?

3. Peter Singer states that "consciousness, or the capacity for subjective experience, is both a necessary and a sufficient condition for having an interest." This suggests that he would disagree with Stone's talk of protecting the "interests" of nature. Whose point of view is more plausible?

4. Would embracing Stone's proposal lead to a change in our conception of our relationship to nature? Does our conception need to be radically changed, as Stone suggests?

People or Penguins

WILLIAM F. BAXTER

In contrast to Christopher D. Stone, William F. Baxter defends a more traditional, human-centered, cost-benefit approach to environmental issues. According to him, the impact of our actions on, for example, penguins, sugar pines, or geological marvels is irrelevant except insofar as it affects human interests. Baxter argues that this is the only realistic approach to take and that, in any case, what is good for humans is in many respects good for plant and animal life as well. He also rejects the claim that we have an obligation to respect the "balance of nature" or to "preserve the environment." No natural or morally correct state of nature exists, and even pollution is only defined by reference to the needs of human beings. For Baxter, the goal is not pure air and water but the "optimal state of pollution"—that is, the level of pollution that yields the greatest amount of human satisfaction.

Study Questions

1. How does the example of DDT and penguins illustrate Baxter's position?

2. For what reasons does Baxter believe that his position is the only tenable starting place for analysis?

3. Why does Baxter reject the notion that there is a "right" or "morally correct" state of nature to which we should return?

4. What does Baxter mean when he writes that our objective is "not pure air or water but rather some optimal state of pollution"? How are we to determine that optimal state?

I START WITH THE MODEST PROPOSITION that, in dealing with pollution, or indeed with any problem, it is helpful to know what one is attempting to accomplish. Agreement on how and whether to pursue a particular objective, such as pollution control, is not possible unless some more general objective has been identified and stated with reasonable precision. We talk loosely of having clean air and clean water, of preserving our wilderness areas, and so forth. But none of these is a sufficiently general objective: each is more accurately viewed as a means rather than as an end.

With regard to clean air, for example, one may ask, "how clean?" and "what does clean mean?" It is even reasonable to ask, "why have clean air?" Each of these questions is an implicit demand that a more general community goal be stated—a goal sufficiently general in its scope and enjoying sufficiently general assent among the community of actors that such "why" questions no longer seem admissible with respect to that goal.

If, for example, one states as a goal the proposition that "every person should be free to do whatever he wishes in contexts where his actions do not interfere with the interests of other human beings," the speaker is unlikely to be met with a response of "why." The goal may be criticized as uncertain in its implications or difficult to implement, but it is so basic a tenet of our civilization—it reflects a cultural value so broadly shared, at least in the abstract—that the question of "why" is seen as impertinent or imponderable or both. . . .

Without any expectation of obtaining unanimous consent to them, let me set forth four goals that I generally use as ultimate testing criteria in attempting to frame solutions to problems of human organization. My position regarding pollution stems from these four criteria. . . .

My criteria are as follows:

1. The spheres of freedom criterion stated above.

2. Waste is a bad thing. The dominant feature of human existence is scarcity—our available resources, our aggregate labors, and our skill in employing both have always been, and will continue for some time to be, inadequate to yield to every man all the tangible and intangible satisfactions he would like to have. Hence, none of those resources, or labors, or skills, should be wasted—that is, employed so as to yield less than they might yield in human satisfactions.

3. Every human being should be regarded as an end rather than as a means to be used for the betterment of another. Each should be afforded dignity and regarded as having an absolute claim to an evenhanded application of such rules as the community may adopt for its governance.

4. Both the incentive and the opportunity to improve his share of satisfactions should be preserved to every individual. Preservation of incentive is dictated by the "no-waste" criterion and enjoins against the continuous, totally egalitarian redistribution of satisfactions, or wealth; but subject to that constraint, everyone should receive, by continuous redistribution if necessary, some minimal share of aggregate wealth so as to avoid a level of privation from which the opportunity to improve his situation becomes illusory.

The relationship of these highly general goals to the more specific environmental issues at hand may not be readily apparent, and I am not yet ready to demonstrate their pervasive implications. Recently scientists have informed us that use of DDT in food production is causing damage to the penguin population. For the present purposes let us accept that assertion as an indisputable scientific fact. The scientific fact is often asserted as if the correct implication—

that we must stop agricultural use of DDT—followed from the mere statement of the fact of penguin damage. But plainly it does not follow if my criteria are employed.

My criteria are oriented to people, not penguins. Damage to penguins, or sugar pines, or geological marvels is, without more, simply irrelevant. One must go further, by my criteria, and say: Penguins are important because people enjoy seeing them walk about rocks; and furthermore, the well-being of people would be less impaired by halting use of DDT than by giving up penguins. In short, my observations about environmental problems will be people-oriented, as are my criteria. I have no interest in preserving penguins for their own sake.

It may be said by way of objection to this position that it is very selfish of people to act as if each person represented one unit of importance and nothing else was of any importance. It is undeniably selfish. Nevertheless I think it is the only tenable starting place for analysis for several reasons. First, no other position corresponds to the way most people really think and act—i.e., corresponds to reality.

Second, this attitude does not portend any massive destruction of nonhuman flora and fauna, for people depend on them in many obvious ways, and they will be preserved because and to the degree that humans do depend on them.

Third, what is good for humans is, in many respects, good for penguins and pine trees—clean air for example. So that humans are, in these respects, surrogates for plant and animal life.

Fourth, I do not know how we could administer any other system. Our decisions are either private or collective. Insofar as Mr. Jones is free to act privately, he may give such preferences as he wishes to other forms of life: he may feed birds in winter and do with less himself, and he may even decline to resist an advancing polar bear on the ground that the bear's appetite is more important than those portions of himself that the bear may choose to eat. In short my basic premise does not rule out private altruism to competing life-forms. It does rule out, however, Mr. Jones' inclination to feed Mr. Smith to the bear, however hungry the bear, however despicable Mr. Smith.

Insofar as we act collectively, on the other hand, only humans can be afforded an opportunity to participate in the collective decisions. Penguins cannot vote now and are unlikely subjects for the franchise—pine trees more unlikely still. Again each individual is free to cast his vote so as to benefit sugar pines if that is his inclination. But many of the more extreme assertions that one hears from some conservationists amount to tacit assertions that they are specially appointed representatives of sugar pines, and hence that their preferences should be weighted more heavily than the preferences of other humans who do not enjoy equal rapport with "nature." The simplistic assertion that agricultural use of DDT must stop at once because it is harmful to penguins is of that type.

Fifth, if polar bears or pine trees or penguins, like men, are to be regarded as ends rather than means, if they are to count in our calculus of social organization, someone must tell me how much each one counts, and someone must tell me how these life-forms are to be permitted to express their preferences, for I do not know either answer. If the answer is that certain people are to hold their proxies, then I want to know how those proxy-holders are to be selected: self-appointment does not seem workable to me.

Sixth, and by way of summary of all the foregoing, let me point out that the set of environmental issues under discussion—although they raise very complex technical questions of how to achieve any objective—ultimately raise a normative question: what *ought* we to do? Questions of *ought* are unique to the human mind and world—they are meaningless as applied to a nonhuman situation.

I reject the proposition that we *ought* to respect the "balance of nature" or to "preserve the environment" unless the reason for doing so, express or implied, is the benefit of man.

I reject the idea that there is a "right" or "morally correct" state of nature to which we should return. The word "nature" has no normative connotation. Was it "right" or "wrong" for the earth's crust to heave in contortion and create mountains and seas? Was it "right" for the first amphibian to crawl up out of the primordial ooze? Was it "wrong" for plants to reproduce themselves and alter the atmospheric composition in favor of oxygen? For animals to alter the atmosphere in favor of carbon dioxide both by breathing oxygen and eating plants? No answers can be given to these questions because they are meaningless questions.

All this may seem obvious to the point of being tedious, but much of the present controversy over environment and pollution rests on tacit normative assumptions about just such nonnormative phenomena: that it is "wrong" to impair penguins with DDT, but not to slaughter cattle for prime rib roasts. That it is wrong to kill stands of sugar pines with industrial fumes, but not to cut sugar pines and build housing for the poor. Every man is entitled to his own preferred definition of Walden Pond, but there is no definition that has any moral superiority over another, except by reference to the selfish needs of the human race.

From the fact that there is no normative definition of the natural state, it follows that there is no normative definition of clean air or pure water—hence no definition of polluted air—or of pollution—except by reference to the needs of man. The "right" composition of the atmosphere is one which has some dust in it and some lead in it and some hydrogen sulfide in it—just those amounts that attend a sensibly organized society thoughtfully and knowledgeably pursuing the greatest possible satisfaction for its human members.

The first and most fundamental step toward solution of our environmental problems is a clear recognition that our objective is not pure air or water but rather some optimal state of pollution. That step immediately suggests the question: How do we define and attain the level of pollution that will yield the maximum possible amount of human satisfaction?

Low levels of pollution contribute to human satisfaction but so do food and shelter and education and music. To attain ever lower levels of pollution, we must pay the cost of having less of these other things. I contrast that view of the cost of pollution control with the more popular statement that pollution control will "cost" very large numbers of dollars. The popular statement is true in some senses, false in others; sorting out the true and false senses is of some importance. The first step in that sorting process is to achieve a clear understanding of the difference between dollars and resources. Resources are the wealth of our nation; dollars are merely claim checks upon those resources. Resources are of vital importance; dollars are comparatively trivial.

Four categories of resources are sufficient for our purposes: at any given time a nation, or a planet if you prefer, has a stock of labor, of technological skill, of capital goods, and of natural resources (such as mineral deposits, timber, water, land, etc.). These resources can be used in various combinations to yield goods and services of all kinds—in some limited quantity. The quantity will be larger if they are combined efficiently, smaller if combined inefficiently. But in either event the resource stock is limited, the goods and services that they can be made to yield are limited; even the most efficient use of them will yield less than our population, in the aggregate, would like to have.

If one considers building a new dam, it is appropriate to say that it will be costly in the sense that it will require x hours of labor, y tons of steel and concrete, and z amount of capital goods. If these resources are devoted to the dam, then they cannot be used to build hospitals, fishing rods, schools, or electric can openers. That is the meaningful sense in which the dam is costly.

Quite apart from the very important question of how wisely we can combine our resources to produce goods and services is the very different question of how they get distributed—who gets how many goods? Dollars constitute the claim checks which are distributed among people and which control their share of national output. Dollars are nearly valueless pieces of paper except to the extent that they do represent claim checks to some fraction of the output of goods and services. Viewed as claim checks, all the dollars outstanding during any period of time are worth, in the aggregate, the goods and services that are available to be claimed with them during that period—neither more nor less.

It is far easier to increase the supply of dollars than to increase the production of goods and services—printing dollars is easy. But printing more dollars doesn't help because each dollar then simply becomes a claim to fewer goods, i.e., becomes worth less.

The point is this: many people fall into error upon hearing the statement that the decision to build a dam, or to clean up a river, will cost $X million. It is regrettably easy to say: "It's only money. This is a wealthy country, and we have lots of money." But you cannot build a dam or clean a river with $X million—unless you also have a match, you can't even make a fire. One builds a dam or cleans a river by diverting labor and steel and trucks and factories from making one kind of goods to making another. The cost in dollars is merely a shorthand way of describing the extent of the diversion necessary. If we build a dam for $X million, then we must recognize that we will have $X million less housing and food and medical care and electric can openers as a result.

Similarly, the costs of controlling pollution are best expressed in terms of the other goods we will have to give up to do the job. This is not to say the job should not be done. Badly as we need more housing, more medical care, and more can openers, and more symphony orches-

tras, we could do with somewhat less of them, in my judgment at least, in exchange for somewhat cleaner air and rivers. But that is the nature of the trade-off, and analysis of the problem is advanced if that unpleasant reality is kept in mind. Once the trade-off relationship is clearly perceived, it is possible to state in a very general way what the optimal level of pollution is. I would state it as follows:

People enjoy watching penguins. They enjoy relatively clean air and smog-free vistas. Their health is improved by relatively clean water and air. Each of these benefits is a type of good or service. As a society we would be well advised to give up one washing machine if the resources that would have gone into that washing machine can yield greater human satisfaction when diverted into pollution control. We should give up one hospital if the resources thereby freed would yield more human satisfaction when devoted to elimination of noise in our cities. And so on, trade-off by trade-off, we should divert our productive capacities from the production of existing goods and services to the production of a cleaner, quieter, more pastoral nation up to—and no further than—the point at which we value more highly the next washing machine or hospital that we would have to do without than we value the next unit of environmental improvement that the diverted resources would create.

Now this proposition seems to me unassailable but so general and abstract as to be unhelpful—at least unadministerable in the form stated. It assumes we can measure in some way the incremental units of human satisfaction yielded by very different types of goods. The proposition must remain a pious abstraction until I can explain how this measurement process can occur. . . . But I insist that the proposition stated describes the result for which we should be striving—and again, that it is always useful to know what your target is even if your weapons are too crude to score a bull's eye.

Review and Discussion Questions

1. What are the practical implications of Baxter's human-centered, cost-benefit approach to environmental issues? How sympathetic are you to his approach? What do you see as its strong points? Its weak points?

2. Assess each of Baxter's six reasons for claiming that his is the best starting point for examining environmental issues.

3. What exactly does Baxter mean by saying that "questions of *ought* are unique to the human mind and world—they are meaningless as applied to a nonhuman situation"? Does the fact that only human beings are moral agents imply that human beings can have moral responsibilities only to other human beings?

4. Is Baxter right in arguing that there is no right or wrong level of pollution independent of human needs?

5. How would Peter Singer reply to Baxter's arguments? How does Stone's perspective contrast with Baxter's?

6. Does the idea of an optimal level of pollution make sense? If so, how do we determine that level? Is it possible to calculate it or to reach agreement on trade-offs between environmental goods and other goods?

The Search for an Environmental Ethic

J. BAIRD CALLICOTT

J. Baird Callicott, professor of philosophy at the University of Wisconsin, Stevens Point, and author of *In Defense of the Land Ethic,* rejects traditional human-centered approaches to environmental ethics like William F. Baxter's and is also critical of attempts like Peter Singer's to extend traditional morality to include nonhuman sentient beings. Instead, Callicott advocates a holistic or ecocentric environmental ethic based on the "land ethic" of environmentalist Aldo Leopold. Central to an ecosystemic or holistic environmental ethic is the concept of the global ecosystem or biotic community, of which all forms of life on our planet are fellow members. Human beings are members of this community, not the conquerors of nature. Such a perspective, Callicott insists, implies respect for fellow members of the community and for the biotic community as a whole. Callicott defends an ecocentric environmental ethic against the charge that it is antihuman and concludes by discussing what living in accord with such an ethic would mean for our lives.

Study Questions

1. What is the traditional humanistic approach to environmental ethics? On what basis does Callicott criticize it?

2. What is "extensionism"? What are Callicott's reasons for rejecting it as an adequate environmental ethic?

3. What does Callicott mean by describing his ethic as "holistic," "ecocentric," and "ecosystemic"?

4. How do some traditional American Indian cultures illustrate the ethical perspective Callicott advocates?

5. What are the implications of Callicott's ethic for our treatment of animals?

Three Secular Approaches to Environmental Ethics

Since the emergence of a broad awareness of the environmental crisis and an evolutionary-ecological world view, professional philosophers have attempted to construct a logically coherent, adequate, and practicable *theory* of environmental ethics without reference to God or to his "creation." Three main secular theoretical approaches have, in this interval, clearly emerged. They are as follows:

1. *Traditional and protracted humanism:* business-as-usual Western human-centered ethics, in which moral standing is sometimes accorded to human beings of future generations.

2. *Extensionism:* the extension of moral standing and/or moral rights from human beings inclusively to wider and wider classes of *individual* nonhuman natural entities.

3. *Ecocentrism:* moral consideration for the ecosystem *as a whole* and for its various subsystems as well as for human and nonhuman natural entities severally.

I shall argue that the third approach, ecocentrism, is the best approach to environmental ethics. It is, I think, by far the most coherent in both senses, viz., that it is (1) self-consistent and, just as important, (2) consistent with the larger pattern of ideas that gave rise to environ-

mental awareness and concern in the first place. It is, I also think, the most adequate: it *directly* and *effectively* addresses the moral problems that it is supposed to help us resolve. And finally, of the three secular approaches to environmental ethics so far developed, I think it is the most practicable—in the sense that the limitations it would impose on human behavior vis-à-vis the environment are limitations that will help the environment to prosper *and* human beings to live and live well.

Traditional and Protracted Humanism

The traditional humanistic approach to environmental ethics treats the environment merely as a "pool" of "resources" and as an "arena" of human interaction and potential conflict that the science of ecology has recently revealed to be much more complex than previously supposed. The adverse effects human beings may have upon other human beings *indirectly* through things they may do *directly* to the environment—like "developing" and consuming it and treating it as a sink for wastes—have recently become amplified, moreover, by ballooning human numbers and more powerful and/or more toxic technologies. According to philosopher Kristin Shrader-Frechette, a leading advocate of this approach, it is difficult to think of an action which would do irreparable damage to the environment or ecosystem, but which would not also threaten human well-being. . . . if a polluter dumps toxic wastes in a river, this action could be said to be wrong . . . because the "interests" of the river are violated, but also . . . because there are human interests in having clean water (e.g. for recreation and for drinking).[1]

Therefore, we don't need a *new* environmental ethic to set out what human beings may and may not do to nonhuman natural entities and nature as a whole. Our old ethics of equal moral consideration and/or justice for all human beings are quite adequate—especially if by "all" we intend future as well as presently existing human beings, as in protracted humanism.

A Critique of the Traditional and Protracted Humanism Approach

. . . Environmental philosophers Richard Sylvan and Val Plumwood have vigorously challenged the contention that the *practical* implications of an environmental ethic based upon humanism (which they unflatteringly call "human chauvinism") would be equivalent to the *practical* implications of an environmental ethic that accorded intrinsic value to nonhuman natural entities and to nature as a whole: "There is an enormous *felt* or *emotional* difference between feeling that a place should be valued or respected for itself . . . ," they point out, "and feeling that it should not be defaced because it is valued by one's fellow humans. . . . These differences in emotional presentation are accompanied by or expressed by an enormous range of behavioral differences."[2]

I too doubt that a human-centered ethic for the use of the environment would in fact prohibit human harms to the environment as strictly as any other ethic. To take Shrader-Frechette's own example, a polluting industry might generously compensate the affected *people* for the loss of the recreational amenity afforded by a clean river and provide them an alternative source of drinking water. Upon this approach to environmental ethics, the industry could then ethically go on using the river as a dump for its toxic wastes. Although fish, birds, and the river itself would continue to suffer disease, death, and degradation, the "interests" of the affected human parties would be fairly balanced.

However, *even if Shrader-Frechette is right* that "existing utilitarian and egalitarian ethical theories [are adequate] to safeguard the environment," an inconsistency . . . lies at the core of this approach to environmental ethics. Its advocates seem at once ecologically well informed and ecologically unenlightened. According to both the traditional and protracted humanistic approaches to environmental ethics, ecology only complicates human-to-human intercourse, both in the present and across generations; it does not transform our vision of what it means to be human.

Norwegian philosopher Arne Naess and his American exponents Bill Devall and George Sessions call these approaches to environmental ethics "shallow" as opposed to "deep" ecology.[3] Ecology is acknowledged or intellectually affirmed in one area or at one level of thought—relations of cause and effect in the nonhuman natural environment—but it is ignored or denied at another level or area of thought—the general structure of nature and the embeddedness of people within that structure. From an evolutionary-ecological point of view, we are "kin" to the fellow members of the biotic community. Our actions in respect to these fellow members should somehow be *directly* morally accountable, and the integrity of this community per se, the health of the planetary organism, should somehow be of *direct* moral concern. . . .

Extensionism

A second approach to environmental ethics attempts conceptually to articulate and theoretically to ground moral concern *directly* for the environment by extending or stretching traditional Western humanistic moral theory so that it recognizes the moral standing of some nonhuman natural entities. It was first developed, most notably by Peter Singer, as a theory which would extend moral considerability to fellow *sentient* beings (beings capable of experiencing pleasure and pain) without reference to the environment at large or environmental problems per se.[4] . . .

Peter Singer's criterion of sentiency for equal consideration or equal moral standing is not an adequate basis for an ethical theory to address the major moral issues of animal welfare, let alone an adequate basis for a theory of environmental ethics. Singer himself considers meat eating immoral and, throughout his book *Animal Liberation,* insists that people ought, *morally* ought, to become vegetarians. Bentham, the original advocate of sentiency as a criterion for moral considerability, however, recognized that it is perfectly possible to raise animals in comfort and to slaughter them painlessly; thus he would support the view that human carnivorousness is perfectly consistent with a sentiency-based animal welfare ethic. If everyone were a vegetarian, many fewer cows, pigs, chickens, and other domestic livestock would be raised and thus many fewer animals would have the opportunity, for an allotted time, to pursue happiness. One might therefore argue, on Singer's own grounds, that people have a positive moral obligation to eat meat *provided that the animals raised for human consumption were raised in comfort and given the opportunity to live happily.* Even sport hunting—long regarded by some concerned about animal welfare to be the most odious because the most gratuitous abuse of animals—would be permissible on Singer's grounds *provided that hunters deliver a clean kill and by so doing preserve animals from greater suffering from the vicissitudes of life in the wild,* while as a bonus benefit also giving themselves pleasure.

Recognizing these (and other) inadequacies of Singer's moral theory in relation to the moral problems of the treatment of animals, Tom Regan has advocated a "rights" approach to ad-

dress them.[5] Regan postulates that some individual animals have "inherent worth" because they are, like ourselves, not only sentient but *subjects of a life* that from their point of view can be better or worse. Inherent worth, in turn, may be the grounds of basic moral rights. I am persuaded that Regan's representation of animal rights in his book *The Case for Animal Rights* adequately supports the basic moral agenda of those concerned primarily for individual animal welfare: an end to (1) meat eating, (2) the use of animals in "scientific" experimentation, and (3) hunting and trapping.

A Critique of Extensionism in Relation to Environmental Problems

Clearly, however, neither Singer's theory of animal liberation nor Regan's theory of animal rights will do double duty as an environmental ethic. For one thing, most obviously neither animal liberation nor animal rights provides for direct moral consideration of plants and all the many animals that may not be either sentient or, more restrictively still, "subjects of a life." But the brunt of environmental destruction is borne by plants helplessly in the path of chain saws and bulldozers, and the bulk of rare and endangered species are neither sentient nor subjects of a life as Regan defines this concept. . . .

A *sentiency centered* and/or *subject-of-a-life centered* environmental ethic would result, no less than traditional and protracted humanism, in a mere management ethic, an ethic for using the environment by sentient or subject-of-a-life animals (including humans, of course) for their own sake. While not an anthropocentric ethic, it would nonetheless be a management ethic. Animal liberation/rights broaden the base class of morally considerable beings (the former more widely than the latter), but not by very much relative to the millions of plant and invertebrate forms of life making up earth's biotic community. So plants and invertebrate animals, the vast majority of earth's living denizens, remain mere means to be managed for the good of the morally privileged class of sentient or subject-of-a-life animals. . . .

Animal liberation/animal rights seems very well informed by one of modern biology's two great theoretical cornerstones, the theory of evolution, while not at all by the other, ecology. Animal liberation/rights rests in part on the basic notion that there is no essential *morally relevant* difference between mankind and mankind's closest kin in the phylogenetic scale. But the *ecological* order of nature is premised on one fundamental principle—all life (even plant life, for plant nutrients must be recycled) depends upon death. Death and often pain are at the heart of nature's economy. To the extent that the animal liberation/animal rights ethics condemn the taking of life (as a violation of the rights of a subject of life) or the infliction of pain on a sentient being, they are irreconcilably at odds with the ecological "facts of life."

To develop this point more particularly, a ruthlessly consistent deduction of the consequences of both the Singerian and Reganic ethics *might* imply a program of humane predator extermination. For sound ecological reasons, the conservation and reintroduction of predators are among the highest priorities on the agenda of current environmental goals. Predatory fishes, reptiles, birds, and mammals, however, cause a great deal of suffering to other innocent animals. If carnivorous animals could be rounded up, housed comfortably in zoos, fed soyburgers, sterilized, and allowed to die natural deaths, then only herbivorous animals would remain in nature and the total amount of pain and suffering might be vastly reduced. Singer clearly recognizes this implication of his own ethical principles but, inconsistently, turns aside from it:

> It must be admitted that the existence of carnivorous animals does pose one problem for the ethics of Animal Liberation. . . . Assuming humans could eliminate carnivorous species from the earth and that the total amount of

suffering among animals in the world were thereby reduced, should we do it? . . . We cannot and should not try to police all of nature. We do enough if we eliminate our own unnecessary killing and cruelty to other animals.[6]

. . . If the animal welfare ethics of Singer and Regan require the (humane) phasing out of predators from nature, as possibly they may, then they would not only be inadequate but, from an ecological point of view, actually nightmarish. I wish to emphasize that the predator policy required by both the animal liberation and animal rights ethics is controversial, if for no other reason than that their principal advocates, Singer and Regan, respectively, do not themselves admit, what *seem* to me to be, the ecologically untoward implications of both theories.

Both Singer and Regan, however, quite openly admit that rare and endangered species are provided no special, preemptory status by their respective theories.[7] And yet species extirpation and extinction is today widely recognized as the single most pressing problem among the spectrum of problems collectively called the environmental crisis. The specimens of most endangered species, moreover, are neither sentient nor subjects of a life. They are, rather, plants and invertebrates. Hence, if there were a mortal conflict between, say, an endangered plant *species* and *individual* sentient or subject-of-a-life animals, there could be no *moral* reason to choose to save the plant species at the expense of the lives of plentiful individual animals, according to animal liberation/rights. Environmental philosopher Holmes Rolston III reports with approval an action of the National Park Service in which hundreds of rabbits on Santa Barbara Island were killed "to protect a few plants . . . once thought extinct and curiously called the Santa Barbara Live Forever."[8] Since in this and similar cases, the animal liberation/rights ethics would give preference to the sentient/subject-of-a-life animals, the environmental problem of species extinction would be not merely ignored; it would be aggravated, at least for the vast majority of threatened species.

Animal liberation/rights, finally, does not discriminate between the value of domestic and wild animals, since both are equally sentient and/or subjects of a life. However, most environmentalists regard the intrusion of domestic animals into natural ecosystems as very destructive and therefore prima facie contrary to an environmental ethic. . . . Since domestic livestock and wild animals are equally sentient and/or equally subjects of a life and a pasture can support more cows than deer in a woods of the same size, the animal liberation/animal rights ethic cannot, as an environmentalist would prefer, condemn the former and commend the latter.

An ecologically well-informed environmental ethic would draw a moral distinction among animals along another axis than that drawn by animal liberation/rights. Rather than providing moral standing or rights to animals that are sentient or subjects of a life and withholding standing or rights from those that are not, an ecologically oriented environmental ethic would provide preferred moral consideration (and possibly rights) to wild animals, whether or not sentient or subjects of a life, and regard domestic animals as, for all practical purposes, a kind of human technology to be evaluated, like all other technologies, in terms of environmental impact. The environmental impact of domestic animals might be benign—as, for example, that of domestic bees—but from the ecological point of view, environmental impact should be the *primary* consideration governing the treatment of man-made animals originally designed for human utility. . . .

A Plea for a Holistic Approach to Environmental Ethics

. . . A holistic or ecocentric environmental ethic was outlined in *A Sand County Almanac*, the widely read and admired "gospel" of environmental philosophy by Aldo Leopold. For the most part, contemporary moral philosophers searching for a coherent, adequate, and practicable environmental ethic have failed to explore and develop Leopold's "land ethic" to the extent that they have, for example, Bentham's even briefer remarks about the moral considerability of sentient animals. This is, in large measure, because a holistic approach to ethics is so unfamiliar and represents such a radical departure from long-established modern traditions of Western moral philosophy. One prominent moral philosopher has even called Aldo Leopold's land ethic "environmental fascism," because of its holistic characteristics.[9] This impression has unfortunately been invited and abetted by Leopold's few philosophical partisans who have imprudently emphasized the holistic aspects of the land ethic at the expense of its provisions for the moral consideration of individuals.[10] Nevertheless, Leopold's land ethic remains the only holistic or ecosystemic game in town. I shall accordingly first explore and develop its conceptual foundations and moral precepts, and then show how it does not, in fact, lead to the untoward moral consequences its critics have thought that it must. . . .

Transition from Humanistic to Environmental Ethics

According to Aldo Leopold, "All ethics so far evolved rest upon a single premise: that the individual is a member of a community of interdependent parts. . . . The land ethic simply enlarges the boundaries of the community to include soils, waters, plants, and animals, or collectively: the land."[11] . . .

Now, the general world view of the modern life sciences *represents* all forms of life on the planet Earth both as *kin* and as fellow members of a social unit— *the biotic community*. The Earth may now be *perceived* not, as once it was, the unique physical center of the universe but rather a mere planet orbiting around an ordinary star at the edge of a galaxy containing billions of similar stars in a universe containing billions of such galaxies. In the context of this universal spatial-temporal frame of reference, the planet Earth is very small and very local indeed, an island paradise in a vast desert of largely empty space containing physically hostile foreign bodies separated from Earth by immense distances. All the denizens of this cosmic island paradise evolved into their myriad contemporary forms from a simple, single-cell common ancestor. All contemporary forms of life thus are represented to be *kin, relatives, members of one extended family*. And all are equally members in good standing of one *society* or *community*, the biotic community or global ecosystem.

This cosmic/evolutionary/ecological picture of the Earth and its biota can actuate the moral sentiments of affection, respect, love, and sympathy with which we human mammals are genetically endowed. It also actuates the special sentiment or feeling (call it "patriotism"), noticed by both Hume and Darwin, that we have for the *group as a whole* to which we belong, the *family* per se, the *tribe*, and the *country* or *nation*. From the point of view of modern biology, the earth with its living mantle is our tribe and each of its myriad species is, as it were, a separate clan.

Thus the land ethic—in sharp contrast to traditional Western humanism and its protracted and extended variations—provides moral standing for both environmental *individuals* and for the environment *as a whole*. In Leopold's words, "a land ethic changes the role of *Homo sapiens* from conqueror of the land community to plain member and citizen of it. It implies respect for fellow-members *and also* respect for the community as such."[12]

Holism

Respect for wholes, for the community as such and its various subsystems, is a theoretical possibility for the land ethic because it is conceptually and historically related to the Humean-Darwinian theoretical complex. Both individual members of society and the community as such, the social whole (together with its component divisions), are the objects of certain special, naturally selected moral sentiments. Beauty may be in the eye of the beholder, but it does not follow from this that only the eye of the beholder is beautiful. Similarly, there may be no value without valuers, but it does not follow from this that only valuers are valuable. Both beauty and intrinsic value are bivalent concepts; that is, both involve subjective and objective factors. *Intrinsic value* is, as it were, "projected" onto appropriate objects by virtue of certain naturally selected and inherited *intentional* feelings, some of which (patriotism, or love of country, is perhaps the most familiar example) simply have social wholes as their natural objects. We may value our community per se, for the sake of itself, just as we may value our children for the sake of themselves. Wholes may thus have intrinsic value no less problematically than individuals.[13] . . .

The stress upon the value of the biotic community is the distinguishing characteristic of the land ethic and its cardinal strength as an *adequate* environmental ethic. The land ethic directs us to take the welfare of nature—the diversity, stability, and integrity of the biotic community or, to mix metaphors, the health of the land organism—to be the standard of the moral quality, the rightness or wrongness, of our actions. Practically, this means that we should assess the "environmental impact" of any proposed project, whether it be a personal, corporate, or public undertaking, and choose that course of action which will enhance the diversity, integrity, beauty, and stability of the biotic community, the health and well-being of the land organism. Quite obviously, then, environmental problems, from billboards and strip-development to radioactive-waste generation and species extirpation, are directly addressed by the land ethic. It is specifically tailored to be an *adequate* environmental ethic.

The Dangers of an Untempered Holistic Environmental Ethic

But, as with so many things, the cardinal strength of the land ethic is also its cardinal weakness. What are the moral (to say nothing of the economic) costs of the land ethic? Most seriously, it would seem to imply a draconian policy toward the human population, since almost all ecologists and environmentalists agree that, from the perspective of the integrity, diversity, and stability of the biotic community, there are simply too many people and too few redwoods, white pines, wolves, bears, tigers, elephants, whales, and so on. Philosopher William Aiken has recoiled in horror from the land ethic, since in his view it would imply that "massive human diebacks would be good. It is our species' duty to eliminate 90 percent of our numbers."[14] It would also seem to imply a merciless attitude toward nonhuman individual members of the biotic community. Sentient members of overabundant species, like rabbits and deer, may be (as actually presently they are) routinely culled, for the sake of the ecosystems of which they are a part, by hunting or other methods of liquidation. Such considerations have led philosopher Edward Johnson to complain that "we should not let the land ethic distract us from the concrete problems about the treatment of animals which have been the constant motive behind the animal liberation movement."[15] From the perspective of both humanism and its humane extension, the land ethic appears nightmarish in its own peculiar way. It seems more properly the "ethic" of a termitarium or beehive than of anything analogous to a human community. It appears richly to deserve Tom Regan's epithet "environmental fascism."

The Relation of the Land Ethic to Prior Accretions

Despite Leopold's narrative drift away from attention to *members* of the biotic community to the *community per se* and despite some of Leopold's more radical exponents who have confrontationally stressed the holistic dimension of the land ethic, its theoretical foundations yield a subtler, richer, far more complex system of morals than simple environmental holism. The land ethic is the latest step in an evolutionary sequence, according to its own theoretical foundations. Each succeeding step in social-moral evolution—from the savage clan to the family of man—does not cancel or invalidate the earlier stages. Rather, each succeeding stage is layered over the earlier ones, which remain operative.

A graphic image of the evolution of ethics has been suggested by extensionist Peter Singer. Singer suggests we imagine the evolutionary development of ethics to be an "expanding circle."[16] According to this image, as the charmed circle of moral considerability expands to take in more and more beings, its previous boundaries disappear. . . .

A similar but crucially different image of the evolution of ethics has been suggested by Richard Sylvan and Val Plumwood. According to them,

> What emerges is a picture of types of moral obligation as associated with a nest of rings or annular boundary classes. . . . In some cases there is no sharp division between the rings. But there is no single uniform privileged class of items [i.e., rational beings, sentient beings, living beings], no one base class, to which all and only moral principles directly apply.[17]

The evolutionary development of ethics is less well represented by means of Singer's image of an expanding circle, a single ballooning circumference, within which moral principles *apply equally to all* than by means of the image of annular tree rings in which social structures and their correlative ethics are nested in a graded, differential system. That I am now a member of the global human community, and hence have correlative moral obligations to all mankind, does not mean that I am no longer a member of my own family and citizen of my local community and of my country or that I am relieved of the peculiar and special limitations on freedom of action attendant upon these relationships.

The Place of Human Beings in the Land Ethic

Therefore, just as the existence of a global human community with its humanitarian ethic does not submerge and override smaller, more primitive human communities and their moral codes, neither does the newly discovered existence of a global biotic community and its land ethic submerge and override the global human community and its humanitarian ethic. To seriously propose, then, that to preserve the integrity, beauty, and stability of the biotic community we ought summarily to eliminate 90 percent of the current human population is . . . morally skewed. . . .

To agree that the human population should not, in gross and wanton violation of our humanitarian moral code, be immediately reduced by deliberate acts of war or by equally barbaric means does not imply that the human population should not be scaled down, as time goes on, by means and methods that are conscionable from a humanitarian point of view. How obligations across the outermost rings of our nested sociomoral matrix may be weighed and compared is admittedly uncertain—just as uncertain as how one should weigh and compare one's duty, say, to one's family against one's duty to one's country. . . .

The Place of Individual Nonhumans in the Land Ethic

Richard Sylvan and Val Plumwood have developed the view that Leopold briefly suggests, namely, that an ecosystemic ethic primarily provides not rights but *respect* for individual nonhuman members of the biotic community. Al-

though the concept of respect is singular and simple, its practical implications are varied and complex. These thinkers further suggest that American Indian environmental attitudes and values provide a well-developed, rich exemplar of *respectful* participation in the economy of nature, a participation that permits human beings morally to eat and otherwise consumptively to utilize their fellow citizens of the organic society:

> The view that the land, animals, and the natural world should be treated with *respect* was a common one in many hunting-gathering societies. . . . Respect adds a moral dimension to relations with the natural world. . . . The conventional wisdom of Western society tends to offer a false dichotomy of use versus respectful non-use . . . of using animals, for example, in the ways characteristic of large-scale mass-production farming . . . *or* on the other hand of not making use of animals at all. . . . What is left out of this choice is the alternative the Indians . . . recognized . . . of limited and respectful use. . . .[18]

A great deal of controversy has surrounded the hypothesis of an American Indian land ethic. Recent studies, empirically based upon actual cultural materials, have shown beyond reasonable doubt that at least some American Indian cultures did in fact have an ecosystemic or environmental ethic *and* that such an ethic maps conceptually upon the Leopold land ethic.[19] In other words, some American Indian cultures— among them, for example, the Ojibwa of the western Great Lakes—represented the plants and animals of their environment as engaged in *social* and *economic* intercourse with one another and with human beings. And such a social picture of human-environment interaction gave rise to correlative moral attitudes and behavioral restraints. The Ojibwa cultural narratives (myths, stories, and tales), which served as the primary vehicles of enculturation or education, repeatedly stress that animals, plants, and even rocks and rivers (natural entities that Western culture regards as inanimate) are *persons* engaged in reciprocal, mutually beneficial exchange with human beings. A cardinal precept embellished again and again in these narratives is that nonhuman natural entities, both individually and as species, must be treated with respect and restraint. The Ojibwa were primarily a hunting-gathering people, which perforce involved them in killing animals as well as plants for food, clothing, and shelter. But they nevertheless represented the animals and plants of their biotic community as *voluntarily* participating in a mannerized economic exchange with people who, for their part, gave tokens of gratitude and reimbursement and offered guest friendship. . . .

Modern Life in Accordance with an Ecosystemic Environmental Ethic

Of course, most people today do not live by hunting and gathering. Nevertheless, the general ideal provided by American Indian cultures of respectful, restrained, mutually beneficial human use of the environment is certainly applicable in today's context. An ecosystemic environmental ethic does not prohibit human use of the environment; it requires, rather, that that use be subject to two ethical limitations. The first is holistic, the second individualistic.

The first requires that human use of the environment, as nearly as possible, should enhance the diversity, integrity, stability, and beauty of the biotic community. Biologist René Dubos has argued that Western Europe was, prior to the industrial revolution, biologically richer *as a result* of human settlement and cultivation.[20] The creation and cultivation of small fields, hedgerows, and forest edges measurably (objectively and quantitatively) enhanced the diversity and integrity and certainly the beauty of the preindustrial European landscape. Ethnobotanist Gary Nabhan has recently drawn a similar picture of the Papago inhabitation of the Sonoran desert.[21] Human occupation and use of the environment from the perspective of the

quality of the environment as a whole does not *have* to be destructive. On the contrary, it can be, as both hunter-gatherers and yeoman farmers have proved, mutually beneficial.

The second, individualistic ethical limitation on human use of the environment requires that trees cut for shelter or to make fields, animals slain for food or for fur, and so on should be thoughtfully selected, skillfully and humanely dispatched, and carefully used so as to neither waste nor degrade them. The *individual* plant, animal, or even rock or river consumed or transformed by human use deserves to be used respectfully.

Surely we can envision an eminently livable, modern, systemic, *civilized* technological society well adapted to and at peace and in harmony with its organic environment. Human technological civilization can live not merely in peaceful coexistence but in benevolent symbiosis with nature. Is our current *mechanical* technological civilization the only one imaginable? Aren't there alternative technologies? Isn't it possible to envision, for example, a human civilization based upon nonpolluting solar energy for domestic use, manufacturing, and transportation and small-scale, soil-conserving organic agriculture? There would be fewer material *things* and more *services, information,* and opportunity for aesthetic and recreational *activities;* fewer people and more bears; fewer parking lots and more wilderness. I think it is possible. It is a vision shared with individual variations by designer Ian McHarg, biologist René Dubos, poets Wendell Berry and Gary Snyder, and philosophers Holmes Rolston and William Aiken, to mention only a few.

In the meantime, while such an adaptive organic civilization gradually evolves out of our present grotesque mechanical civilization, the most important injunction of ecosystemic ethics remains the one stressed by Leopold—subject, of course, to the humanitarian, humane, and life-respecting qualifications that, as I have just argued, are theoretically consistent with it. We should strive to preserve the diversity, stability, and integrity of the biotic community.

Before ending, it is appropriate to ask what the implications of an ecocentric ethic would be for our daily lives. After all, one value of this ethic, no less than any other, is that it gives meaning to choices that otherwise remain unconscious or arbitrary. If, as I have claimed, an ecocentric ethic is the most practicable environmental ethic, how does it actually inform our real-life choices?

Integrating an ecocentric ethic into our lives would provide new criteria for choices we make everyday in virtually every arena of our lives. Some of these choices are obvious; others, less so.

Most obviously, because a vegetarian diet, more directly and efficiently than a meat-centered diet, conducts solar energy into human bodies, the practice of vegetarianism could not only help reduce human hunger and animal suffering, it would free more land and solar energy for the restoration of natural communities.[22] (Note that eating wild game, respectfully, lawfully, and humanely harvested, would be an exception to the vegetarian implications of ecocentric ethics. Only grain-fed, domestic livestock should in general be avoided.)

Above all, one should try to avoid fast-food beef (McDonald's, Hardee's, and the like) made mostly from the imported carcasses of cattle, not only because consuming such food contributes to the political and economic causes of hunger in the countries from which it is exported, but also because it is produced on lands once covered by rain-forests.[23] Hence, the consumption of such foods not only implicates one (in all probability) in the destructive politics of world hunger and the disrespectful use of animals, it implicates one (almost certainly) in the extinction of endemic species (those specifically adapted to particular rain-forest habitats).

But what we eat is only the most obvious link between our daily choices and the integrity of the biotic community of which we are part. In a multitude of other roles, our choices either contribute to its regeneration or its continued ruin. As *consumers*, do we weigh our purchases according to the environmental consequences of their production? As *students*, do we utilize our learning time to hone our knowledge and sensibilities so as to more effectively live an ecocentric ethic? As *citizens*, of both a nation and a community, do we elect leaders whose policies ignore the need for environmental protection and reparation? As *workers*, do we choose to be employed by corporations whose activities degrade the environment? As *parents and individuals whose opinions necessarily influence others*, do we work to impart to others an understanding of the importance of an ecocentric ethic? As *decisionmakers over resources*—from real estate to other large or small assets—do we assume responsibility for their use? Or do we simply turn a blind eye, allowing others to use them for environmentally destructive ends?

Asking ourselves such questions, we discover that the implications of an ecocentric ethic cannot be reduced to one or even several major life choices. Rather, the contribution of an ecocentric ethic is to be found in the myriad of mundane, even banal decisions we make everyday. A grounding in an ecocentric ethic would thus shape the entire unfolding of one's life.

The second most serious moral issue of our times—second only to our individual and collective responsibility to prevent thermonuclear holocaust—is our responsibility to preserve the biological diversity of the earth. Later, when an appropriately humble, sane, ecocentric civilization comes into being, as I believe it will, its government and citizens will set about rehabilitating this bruised and tattered planet. For their work, they must have as great a library of genetic material as it is possible for us to save. Hence, it must be our immediate goal to prevent further destruction of the biosphere, to save what species we can, and to preserve the biotic diversity and beauty that remain.

NOTES

1. K. S. Shrader-Frechette, *Environmental Ethics*. Pacific Grove, Calif.: Boxwood, 1981, p. 17.

2. Richard Sylvan and Val Plumwood, "Human Chauvinism and Environmental Ethics," in D. Mannison, M. McRobbie, and R. Routley, eds., *Environmental Philosophy*. Canberra, Australia: Australian National University, 1980, p. 131.

3. Cf. Bill Devall, "The Deep Ecology Movement," *Natural Resources Journal* 20 (1980): 299–322, for a comprehensive discussion.

4. Peter Singer, *Animal Liberation: A New Ethics for Our Treatment of Animals*. New York: Avon, 1975.

5. Tom Regan, *The Case for Animal Rights*. Berkeley, Calif.: The University of California Press, 1983.

6. Peter Singer, *Animal Liberation*, pp. 238–239.

7. Cf. Tom Regan, *The Case for Animal Rights*, pp. 359–363; and Peter Singer, "Not for Humans Only: The Place of Nonhumans in Environmental Issues," in K. E. Goodpaster and K. M. Sayre, eds. *Ethics and Problems of the 21st Century*. Notre Dame, Ind.: University of Notre Dame Press, 1979, pp. 191–205.

8. Holmes Rolston III, "Duties to Endangered Species," p. 8. Unpublished paper presented to the Environmental Ethics—New Directions Conference, Oct. 4–6, 1984, at the University of Georgia.

9. Tom Regan, *The Case for Animal Rights*, p. 362.

10. Cf. J. Baird Callicott, "Animal Liberation: A Triangular Affair," *Environmental Ethics* 2 (1980).

11. Aldo Leopold, *A Sand County Almanac*. New York: Ballantine, 1966, p. 239.

12. *Ibid.*, p. 240.

13. Cf. J. Baird Callicott, "Non-anthropocentric Value Theory and Environmental Ethics," *American Philosophical Quarterly* 21 (1984), for a full discussion of intrinsic value for nature and nonhuman natural entities.

14. William Aiken, "Ethical Issues in Agriculture," in Tom Regan, ed., *Earthbound: New Introductory Essays in Environmental Ethics*. New York: Random House, 1984, p. 269.

15. Edward Johnson, "Animal Liberation vs. the Land Ethic," *Environmental Ethics* 3 (1981): 271.

16. Peter Singer, *The Expanding Circle: Ethics and Sociobiology*. New York: Farrar, Straus & Giroux, 1982.

17. Richard Sylvan and Val Plumwood, "Human Chauvinism and Environmental Ethics," p. 107.

18. *Ibid.*, pp. 178–179.

19. Cf. Thomas W. Overholt and J. Baird Callicott, *Clothed-in-Fur and Other Tales: An Introduction to an Ojibwa World View*. Washington, D.C.: University Press of America, 1982; and J. Baird Callicott, "American Indian and Western European Attitudes Toward Nature: An Overview," *Environmental Ethics* 4 (1982): 293–318.

20. Cf. René Dubos, "Franciscan Conservation and Benedictine Stewardship," in D. and E. Spring, eds., *Ecology and Religion in History*. New York: Harper & Row, 1974, pp. 114–136.

21. Gary Nabhan, *The Desert Smells Like Rain*. San Francisco: Northpoint, 1982.

22. Frances Moore Lappé, *Diet for a Small Planet*. New York: Ballantine Books, 1982.

23. Frances Moore Lappé and Joseph Collins, *Food First: Beyond the Myth of Scarcity*. New York: Ballantine Books, 1979.

Review and Discussion Questions

1. What are the practical implications for our day-to-day lives of Callicott's holistic environmental ethic? Do you find these implications acceptable?

2. How would Baxter respond to Callicott's rejection of a humanistic approach? With whom do you agree, and why?

3. Callicott is critical of Singer's position, which he finds less adequate than a "rights" approach. How persuasive do you find his criticism?

4. Assess Callicott's reasons for arguing that extensionism does not provide a satisfactory environmental ethic. How do you think extensionists like Singer and Regan (cited in this essay) would respond?

5. How does Callicott's approach differ from the extensionists' with regard to our treatment of animals? Whose perspective do you find the soundest and most plausible?

6. At the beginning of the essay, Callicott claims that his ethic is more coherent, addresses the moral problems more directly and effectively, and is more practicable than rival environmental ethics. Assess these claims.

Why <u>You</u> Are Committed to the Immorality of Eating Meat

MYLAN ENGEL, JR.

This essay by Mylan Engel, Jr., professor of philosophy at Northern Illinois University, returns to an issue raised by Peter Singer and touched upon by J. Baird Callicott, namely, the morality or immorality of eating meat. Engel's essay appears at the end of this section because he endeavors to develop the ethical case against eating meat and for vegetarianism in a way that is independent of the various philosophical issues disputed by Singer, Machan, Stone, Baxter, and Callicott, for example, whether speciesism is warranted, whether only human beings have rights, whether human beings and animals have comparable value, and whether we should transcend traditional human-centered ethics toward a more bio-centered moral perspective. Engel argues that, given the reality of factory farming and given the fact that eating meat is not nutritionally necessary, various commonplace moral beliefs—beliefs that readers of his essay almost certainly hold—imply that eating meat is immoral. In other words, the things you already believe commit you, on pain of inconsistency, to becoming a vegetarian.

Study Questions

1. What is Engel's basic argumentative strategy and how does it differ from that of Peter Singer?

2. What are the main reasons given by Engel for believing that factory farming is cruel?

3. What are the main ethical beliefs that, according to Engel, imply that we should stop purchasing and consuming meat?

4. What impact does the meat industry have on the environment?

5. What is the main evidence that meat consumption is not necessary for human survival?

Most ARGUMENTS FOR THE MORAL OBLIGATORINESS of vegetarianism take one of two forms. Either they follow Singer's lead and demand equal consideration for animals on utilitarian grounds, or they follow Regan's deontological rights-based approach and insist that most of the animals we routinely consume possess the very same rights-conferring properties that confer rights on humans. While many people have been persuaded to alter their dietary habits on the basis of one of these arguments, most philosophers have not. My experience has been that when confronted with these arguments, meat-loving philosophers often casually dismiss them as follows:

> Singer's preference utilitarianism is irremediably flawed, as is Regan's theory of moral rights. Since Singer's and Regan's arguments for vegetarianism are predicated on flawed ethical theories, their arguments are also flawed. Until someone can provide me with clear moral reasons for not eating meat, I will continue to eat what I please.

A moment's reflection reveals the self-serving sophistry of such a reply. Since no ethical theory to date is immune to objection, one could fashion a similar reply to "justify" or rationalize virtually any behavior. One could "justify" rape as follows: An opponent of rape might appeal to utilitarian, Kantian, or contractarian grounds to establish the immorality of rape. Our fictitious rape-loving philosopher could then point out that all of these ethical theories are flawed and *ipso facto* so too are all the arguments against rape. Our rape proponent might then assert: "Until someone can provide me with clear moral reasons for not committing rape, I will continue to rape whomever I please."

The speciousness of such a "justification" of rape should be obvious. No one who seriously considered the brutality of rape could think that it is somehow justified/permissible *simply because* all current ethical theories are flawed. But such specious reasoning is used to "justify" the equally brutal breeding, confining, mutilating, transporting, killing, and eating of animals all the time. My aim is to block this spurious reply by providing an argument for the immorality of eating meat that does not rest on any particular ethical theory. Rather, it rests on beliefs that you already hold.[1]

Before turning to your beliefs, two prefatory observations are in order. First, unlike other ethical arguments for vegetarianism, my argument is *not* predicated on the wrongness of speciesism,[2] *nor* does it depend on your believing that all animals are equal or that all animals have a right to life. The significance of this can be explained as follows: Some philosophers remain unmoved by Singer's and Regan's arguments for a different reason than the one cited above. These philosophers find that the non-speciesistic implications of Singer's and Regan's arguments just *feel* wrong to them. They sincerely *feel* that humans are more important than nonhumans. Perhaps these feelings are irrational in light of evolutionary theory and our biological kinship with other species, but these feelings are nonetheless real. My argument is neutral with respect to such sentiments. It is compatible with both an anthropocentric and a biocentric worldview. In short, my argument is designed to show that even those of you who are steadfastly committed to valuing humans over nonhumans are nevertheless committed to the immorality of eating meat, given your other beliefs.

Second, ethical arguments are often context-dependent in that they presuppose a specific audience in a certain set of circumstances. Recognizing what that intended audience and context is, and what it is not, can prevent confusions about the scope of the ethical claim being made. My argument is context-dependent in precisely this way. It is not aimed at those relatively few indigenous peoples who, because of the paucity of edible vegetable matter available, must eat meat to survive. Rather, it is directed at people, like you, who live in agriculturally bountiful societies in which a wealth of nutritionally adequate alternatives to meat are readily available. Thus, I intend to show that your beliefs commit you to the view that eating meat is morally wrong for anyone who is in the circumstances in which you typically find yourself and *a fortiori* that it is morally wrong for you to eat meat in these circumstances. Enough by way of preamble, on to your beliefs.

1. The Things You Believe

The beliefs attributed to you herein would normally be considered noncontentious. In most contexts, we would take someone who didn't hold these beliefs to be either morally defective or irrational. Of course, in most contexts, these beliefs are not a threat to enjoying hamburgers, hot dogs, steaks, and ribs; but even with burgers in the balance, you will, I think, readily admit believing the following propositions: (p_1) Other things being equal, a world with less pain and suffering is better than a world with more pain and suffering; and (p_2) A world with less unnecessary suffering is better than a world with more unnecessary suffering.[3] . . . Since you think that unnecessary suffering is an intrinsically bad state of affairs, you no doubt also believe: (p_3) Unnecessary cruelty is wrong and *prima facie* should not be supported or encouraged. You probably believe: (p_4) We ought to take steps to make the world a better place. But even if you reject (p_4) on the grounds that we have no positive duties to benefit, you still think there are negative duties to do no harm, and so you believe: ($p_{4'}$) We ought to do what we reasonably can to avoid making the world a worse place. You also believe: (p_5) A morally good person will take steps to make the world a better place and even stronger steps to avoid making the world a worse place; and (p_6) Even a "minimally decent person"[4] would take steps to help reduce the amount of unnecessary pain and suffering in the world, *if s/he could do so with little effort on her/his part.*

You also have beliefs about yourself. You believe one of the following propositions when the reflexive pronoun is indexed to yourself: (p_7) I am a morally good person; or (p_8) I am at least a minimally decent person. You also believe of yourself: (p_9) I am the sort of person who certainly would take steps to help reduce the amount of pain and suffering in the world, *if I could do so with little effort on my part.* Enough

about you. On to your beliefs about nonhuman animals and our obligations toward them.

You believe: (p_{10}) Many nonhuman animals (certainly all vertebrates) are capable of feeling pain. I do not have to prove (p_{10}). You already believe it, as evidenced by your other beliefs: (p_{11}) Other things being equal, it is morally wrong to cause an animal pain or suffering; and (p_{12}) It is morally wrong and despicable to treat animals inhumanely *for no good reason*. . . . In addition to your beliefs about the wrongness of causing animals unnecessary pain, you also have beliefs about the appropriateness of killing animals, for example, you believe: (p_{13}) We ought to euthanize untreatably injured, suffering animals to put them out of their misery whenever feasible; and (p_{14}) Other things being equal, it is worse to kill a conscious sentient animal than it is to kill a plant. Finally, you believe: (p_{15}) We have a duty to help preserve the environment for future generations (at least for future *human* generations); and consequently, you believe: (p_{16}) One ought to minimize one's contribution toward environmental degradation, *especially in those ways requiring minimal effort on one's part.*

2. Factory Farming and Modern Slaughter: The Cruelty Behind the Cellophane

Before they become someone's dinner, most farm animals raised in the United States are forced to endure intense pain and suffering in "factory farms." Factory farms are intensive confinement facilities where animals are made to live in inhospitable unnatural conditions for the duration of their lives. The first step in intensive farming is early separation of mother and offspring. Chickens are separated from their mothers *before* birth, as they are hatched in incubators and never get to see their mothers; veal calves are removed from their mothers within a few days; and piglets are separated from their mothers two to three weeks after birth. The offspring are then housed in overcrowded confinement facilities. Broiler chickens and turkeys are warehoused in sheds containing anywhere from 10,000–100,000 birds (the poultry industry recommends—but does not require—that each chicken be allotted seven-tenths of a square foot of floor space); veal calves are kept in crates 22" × 54" and are chained at the neck, rendering them unable to move or turn around; pigs are confined in metal crates (which provide 6 square feet of living space) situated on concrete slatted floors with no straw or bedding; and beef cattle are housed in feedlots containing up to 100,000 animals. The inappropriate, unforgiving surfaces on which the animals must stand produce chronic foot and leg injuries. Since they cannot move about, they must stand in their own waste. In these cramped, unsanitary conditions, virtually all of the animals' basic instinctual urges (e.g., to nurse, stretch, move around, root, groom, build nests, rut, establish social orders, select mates, copulate, procreate, and rear offspring) are frustrated, causing boredom and stress in the animals. . . .

The animals react to these inhumane, stressful conditions by developing "stereotypies" (i.e., stress- and boredom-induced, neurotic repetitive behaviors) and other unnatural behaviors including cannibalism. For example, chickens unable to develop a pecking order often try to peck each other to death, and pigs, bored due to forced immobility, routinely bite the tail of the pig caged in front of them. To prevent losses due to cannibalism and aggression, the animals receive preemptive mutilations. To prevent chickens and turkeys from pecking each other to death, the birds are "debeaked" using a scalding hot blade that slices through the highly sensitive horn of the beak leaving blisters in the mouth; and to prevent these birds from scratching each other to death (which the industry refers to as "back ripping"), their toes are amputated using

the same hot knife machine. Other routine mutilations include dubbing (surgical removal of the combs and wattles of male chickens and turkeys), tail docking, branding, dehorning, ear tagging, ear clipping, teeth pulling, castration, and ovariectomy. In the interest of cost efficiency, *all* of these excruciating procedures are performed *without* anaesthesia. *Unanaesthetized* branding, dehorning, ear tagging, ear clipping, and castration are standard procedures on nonintensive family farms, as well.

Lives of frustration and torment finally culminate as the animals are inhumanely loaded onto trucks and shipped long distance to slaughterhouses without food or water and without adequate protection from the elements. Each year millions of animals die or are severely injured as a result of such handling and transportation. For example, in 1998, USDA inspectors condemned 28,500 ducks, 768,300 turkeys, and 37.6 million chickens before they entered the slaughter plant, because they were either dead or severely injured upon arrival. Once inside the slaughterhouse, the animals are hung upside down (pigs, cattle, and sheep are suspended by one hind leg, which often breaks) and are brought via conveyor to the slaughterer who slits their throats and severs their carotid arteries and jugular veins. In *theory*, animals covered by the Federal Humane Slaughter Act are to be rendered unconscious by electric current or by captive bolt pistol (a pneumatic gun that, when aimed properly, renders the animal unconscious by firing an eight-inch pin into the animal's skull). Chickens, turkeys, ducks, and geese are not considered animals under the act and receive no protection at all. In *practice*, the act is not enforced, and as a result, many slaughterhouses elect not to use the captive bolt pistol in the interest of cost efficiency. As for electric shock, it is unlikely that being shocked into unconsciousness is a painless process, based on reports of people who have experienced electroconvulsive therapy. A consequence of the lax enforcement of the Federal

Humane Slaughter Act is that in many cases (and all kosher cases), the animals are fully conscious throughout the entire throat-slitting ordeal. For some, the agony does not even end here. According to Gail Eisnitz, chief investigator for the Humane Farming Association, the killing line speeds are so fast in modern slaughterhouses that animals frequently do not have time to bleed out before reaching the skinners and leggers. As a result, those animals that were unstunned or improperly stunned often have their legs cut off and their skin removed while they are still alive.

These animal rearing and slaughtering techniques are by no means rare: 97% of all poultry are produced in 100,000+ bird operations, 98% of pigs are raised in confinement systems, 59% of the nation's dairy cows are raised in confinement systems, all veal calves are crate-raised by definition, and 74% of beef cattle experience feedlot confinement before slaughter. To see just how many animals suffer the institutionalized cruelties of factory farming, consider the number slaughtered in the United States each year. According to the National Agricultural Statistics Service (NASS), 35.6 million cattle, 1.5 million veal calves, 101.2 million pigs, 3.9 million sheep and lambs, 23.5 million ducks, 273.0 million turkeys, and 7,995.4 million chickens were slaughtered in the United States in 1998. In sum, 8.43 *billion* animals are raised and slaughtered in the United States annually (not counting horses, goats, rabbits, emu, other poultry, or fish). . . . Suffice it to say that no other human activity results in more pain, suffering, frustration, and death than factory farming and animal agribusiness.

3. The Implications of <u>Your</u> Beliefs: Why <u>You</u> Are Committed to the Immorality of Eating Meat

I will now offer an argument for the immorality of eating meat predicated on *your* beliefs (p_1)–(p_{16}). Actually I will offer a family of related ar-

guments, all predicated on different subsets of the set $\{(p_1), (p_2), \ldots, (p_{16})\}$. While you do not have to believe all of (p_1)–(p_{16}) for my argument to succeed, the more of these propositions you believe, the greater *your* commitment to the immorality of eating meat. For convenience, (p_1)–(p_{16}) have been compiled in an appendix at the end of the article.

Your beliefs (p_{10})–(p_{13}) show that you already believe that animals are capable of experiencing intense pain and suffering. I don't have to prove to you that *unanaesthetized* branding, castration, debeaking, tail docking, tooth extraction, and so forth cause animals severe pain. You already believe these procedures to be excruciatingly painful. Consequently, given the husbandry techniques and slaughtering practices documented above, you must admit the fact that: (f_1) Virtually all commercial animal agriculture, *especially* factory farming, causes animals intense pain and suffering and, thus, *greatly increases* the amount of pain and suffering in the world. (f_1) and your belief (p_1) together entail that, other things being equal, the world would be better without animal agriculture and factory farms. It is also a fact that: (f_2) In modern societies the consumption of meat is *in no way necessary* for human survival, and so, the pain and suffering that results from meat production is entirely *unnecessary,* as are all the cruel practices inherent in animal agriculture. Since no one *needs* to eat flesh, all of the inhumane treatment to which farm animals are routinely subjected is done *for no good reason,* and so, your belief that it is morally wrong and despicable to treat animals inhumanely *for no good reason* $[(p_{12})]$ forces you to admit that factory farming and animal agribusiness are morally wrong and despicable. Furthermore, your belief that a world with less unnecessary suffering is better than a world with more unnecessary suffering $[(p_2)]$, together with (f_2), entails that the world would be better if there were less animal agriculture and fewer factory farms, and better still if there were no animal agriculture and no factory farms. Moreover, your belief in (p_3) commits you to the view that factory farming is wrong and *prima facie* ought not be supported or encouraged. When one buys factory farm-raised meat, one *is* supporting factory farms monetarily and thereby encouraging their *unnecessary* cruel practices. The only way to avoid actively supporting factory farms is to stop purchasing their products. . . .

Since, per (p_3), you have a *prima facie* obligation to stop supporting factory farming and animal agriculture, you have a *prima facie* obligation to become a vegetarian. Of course, *prima facie* obligations are overridable. Perhaps they can even be overridden simply by the fact that fulfilling them would be excessively burdensome or require enormous effort and sacrifice on one's part. Perhaps, but this much is clear: When one can fulfill *prima facie* obligation O *with little effort on one's part* and *without thereby failing to perform any other obligation*, then obligation O becomes very stringent indeed.

As for your *prima facie* obligation to stop supporting factory farming, you can easily satisfy it without thereby failing to perform any of your other obligations simply by refraining from eating meat and eating something else instead. For example, you can eat Boca burgers rather than hamburgers, pasta with marinara sauce rather than meat sauce, bean burritos or bean tostadas rather than beef tacos, red beans and rice rather than Cajun fried chicken, barbecued tofu rather than barbecued ribs, moo shoo vegetables rather than moo shoo pork, minestrone rather than chicken soup, hummus-filled whole wheat pitas rather than BLTs, five-bean vegetarian chili rather than chili with ground beef, chick pea salad rather than chicken salad, fruit and whole wheat toast rather than bacon and eggs, scrambled tofu vegetable frittatas rather than ham and cheese omelets, and so forth.[5] These examples underscore the *ease* with which one can avoid consuming flesh, a fact which often seems to elude meat eaters.

From your beliefs (p_1), (p_2), and ($p_{4'}$), it follows that we ought to do what we reasonably can to avoid contributing to the amount of unnecessary suffering in the world. Since one thing we reasonably can do is stop contributing to factory farming with our purchases, it follows that we ought to stop purchasing and consuming meat.

Your other beliefs support the same conclusion. You believe: (p_5) A morally good person will take steps to make the world a better place and even stronger steps to avoid making the world a worse place; and (p_6) Even a "minimally decent person" would take steps to help reduce the amount of unnecessary pain and suffering in the world, *if s/he could do so with little effort on her/his part.* You also believe that you are a morally good person $[(p_7)]$ or at least a minimally decent one $[(p_8)]$. Moreover, you believe that you are the kind of person who would take steps to help reduce the amount of pain and suffering in the world, *if you could do so with little effort on your part* $[(p_9)]$. As shown above, *with minimal effort* you could take steps to help reduce the amount of unnecessary suffering in the world just by eating something other than meat. Accordingly, given (p_6), you ought to refrain from eating flesh. Given (p_9), if you really are the kind of person you think you are, you will quit eating meat, opting for cruelty-free vegetarian fare instead.

Finally, animal agriculture is an extremely wasteful, inefficient, environmentally devastating means of food production. A full discussion of the inefficiencies and environmental degradations associated with animal agriculture is beyond the scope of the present paper, but consider five examples:

(1) Animal agriculture is an extremely energy-intensive method of food production. It takes an average of 28 kcal of fossil energy to produce 1 kcal of animal protein, compared with an average of 3.3 kcal of fossil energy per kcal of grain protein, making animal production

on average more than eight times less energy efficient than grain production.

(2) Animal production is extremely inefficient in its water usage, compared to vegetable and grain production. Producing 1 kg of animal protein requires around 100 times more water than producing 1 kg of plant protein, for example, it takes 500 liters of water to grow 1 kg of potatoes and 900 liters of water to grow 1 kg of wheat, but it requires 100,000 liters of water to produce 1 kg of beef. Hence, agricultural water usage, which currently accounts for 87% of the world's freshwater consumption, could be drastically reduced by a shift toward an entirely plant-based agriculture.

(3) Animal agriculture is also extremely nutrient inefficient. By cycling grains through livestock to produce animal protein, we lose 90% of that grain's protein, 96% of its calories, 100% of its carbohydrates, and 100% of its fiber.

(4) Another negative by-product of the livestock industry is soil erosion. Much of arable land in the United States is devoted to feed crop production. Eighty percent of the corn and 95% of the oats grown in the United States are fed to livestock, and the excessive cultivation of our farmlands needed to produce these crops is responsible for the loss of 7 billion tons of topsoil each year. . . . The United States is losing soil at a rate thirteen times faster than the rate of soil formation.

And (5) animal agriculture creates enormous amounts of hazardous waste in the form of excrement. U.S. livestock produce 250,000 pounds of excrement *per second*, resulting in *1 billion tons* of unrecycled waste per year. According to the U.S. General Accounting Office's Report to the U.S. Senate Committee on Agriculture, Nutrition, and Forestry, animal waste run-off from feedlots and rangeland is a significant factor in water quality, affecting about 72% of impaired rivers and streams, 56% of impaired lake acres, and 43% of impaired estuary miles. . . .

The upshot is this: Animal agriculture is, by far and away, the most resource intensive, inefficient, environmentally harmful and ecologically unsound means of human food production, and consequently, one of the easiest direct actions one can take to help protect the environment and preserve resources for future generations, *one requiring minimal effort*, is to stop eating meat. And so, since you believe that we have a duty to preserve the environment for future generations [(p_{15})], and you believe that one ought to minimize one's contribution toward environmental degradation [(p_{16})], your beliefs commit you to the obligatoriness of becoming vegetarian, since doing so is a simple way to help preserve the environment. . . .

4. Is Meat Consumption Really Unnecessary?

A crucial premise in my argument is: (CP1) The pain and suffering that inevitably results from meat production is entirely *unnecessary*. I defended (CP1) on the grounds that in modern societies meat consumption is *in no way necessary* for human survival [(f_2)]. But (CP1) does not follow from (f_2), since eating meat might be necessary for some reason other than survival. Hence, one might object: "While eating meat is not necessary for survival, it *might* still be necessary for humans to thrive and flourish, in which case (CP1) would be false since the pain and suffering experienced by farm animals would be *necessary* for a significant human benefit."

If meat consumption were *necessary* for humans to flourish, my argument would be seriously compromised, so let us examine the evidence. First, consider the counterexamples. Since world-class athletic competition is one of the most grueling and physically strenuous activities in which humans can engage, one would not expect there to be any highly successful vegetarian athletes or vegetarian world record holders, *if* meat consumption were necessary for humans to thrive and flourish. However, the list of world-class vegetarian athletes is quite long and includes Dave Scott (six-time winner of Hawaii's Ironman Triathlon), Sixto Linares (world-record holder for the 24-hour triathlon), Edwin Moses (400-meter hurdler undefeated in international competition for eight straight years), Paavo Nurmi (20 world records, 9 Olympic medals), Andreas Cahling (1980 Mr. International title in body building), and Ridgely Abele (U.S. Karate Association World Champion), to name a few, which strongly suggests that eating meat is *not* necessary for humans to flourish.

Second, consider the diseases associated with the consumption of meat and animal products—heart disease, cancer, stroke, osteoporosis, diabetes, hypertension, arthritis, and obesity—as documented in numerous, highly regarded studies. Four examples must suffice: (1) The Loma Linda study, involving over 24,000 people, found that lacto-ovo-vegetarian men (who consume eggs and dairy products, but no meat) had a 61% lower coronary heart disease (CHD) mortality rate than California's general population. Pure vegetarian men (who consume no animal products) fared even better: The CHD mortality rate for these males was 86% lower than that of the California general population. (2) The ongoing Framingham heart study has been tracking the daily living and eating habits of thousands of residents of Framingham, Massachusetts, since 1948. Dr. William Castelli, director of the study for the last fifteen years, maintains that based on his research the most heart healthy diet is a *pure* vegetarian diet. . . . [A]ccording to Dr. Castelli . . . "Vegetarians not only outlive the rest of us, they also aren't prey to other degenerative diseases, such as diabetes, strokes, etc., that slow us down and make us chronically ill." (3) The Cornell-Oxford-China Health Project systematically monitored the diet, lifestyle, and disease patterns of 6,500 families from 65 different counties in Mainland China and Taiwan. The data collected in this study has led its director, Dr. T. Colin Campbell, to conclude that 80–90% of all cancers can be controlled or prevented

by a lowfat (10–15% fat) pure vegetarian diet. And (4), the Dean Ornish study demonstrated that *advanced* coronary artery disease could be *reversed* through a combination of stress reduction and an extremely lowfat vegetarian diet (10% fat). . . .

These and countless other studies have led the American Dietetic Association, the leading nutritional organization in the country, to assert:

> Scientific data suggest positive relationships between a vegetarian diet and reduced risk for several chronic degenerative diseases and conditions, including obesity, coronary artery disease, hypertension, diabetes mellitus, and some types of cancer. . . . *It is the position of The American Dietetic Association (ADA) that appropriately planned vegetarian diets are healthful, are nutritionally adequate, and provide health benefits in the prevention and treatment of certain diseases.*

An article in *The Journal of the American Medical Association* concurs, claiming: "A vegetarian diet can prevent 90% of our thrombo-embolic disease and 97% of our coronary occlusions." In light of these findings, the Physicians Committee for Responsible Medicine recommends centering our diets around the following *new* four food groups:

　I. Whole Grains (5+ servings/day)
　II. Vegetables (3+ servings/day)
　III. Fruits (3+ servings/day)
　IV. Legumes (2+ servings/day).

Gone are meat and dairy, the two principal sources of fat and cholesterol in the American diet. The evidence is unequivocal: A vegetarian diet is nutritionally superior to a meat-based diet. One cannot reject my crucial premise—(CP1) The pain and suffering that inevitably results from meat production is entirely *unnecessary*—on the grounds that eating meat is necessary for human flourishing, because it isn't. Rather, eating meat is *detrimental* to human health and well-being. Simply put, eating meat serves no human need that cannot be better met with plant-based foods.

Since all of our nutritional needs can be met and can be met better with plant-based foods than they can with meat and animal-based foods, all of the pain and suffering farm animals are forced to endure to wind up on our dinner plates really is unnecessary. Since purchasing and eating meat does contribute to unnecessary suffering, and since you believe it is wrong to contribute to unnecessary suffering [(p_2)], your beliefs entail that eating meat is wrong.

5. Conclusion

The implications of your beliefs are clear. Given your beliefs, it follows that eating meat is morally wrong. This conclusion was not derived from some highly contentious ethical theory that you can easily reject, but from your own firmly held beliefs. Furthermore, this conclusion follows, regardless of your views on speciesism, animal equality, and animal rights. Even those of you who are staunch speciesists are committed to the immorality of eating meat, given your other beliefs. Consequently, consistency (your own beliefs) demands that you embrace the immorality of eating meat and modify your behavior accordingly.

Appendix

(p_1)   Other things being equal, a world with less pain and suffering is better than a world with more pain and suffering.

(p_2)   A world with less unnecessary suffering is better than a world with more unnecessary suffering.

(p_3)   Unnecessary cruelty is wrong and *prima facie* should not be supported or encouraged.

(p_4)   We ought to take steps to make the world a better place.

(p_4,)   We ought to do what we reasonably can to avoid making the world a worse place.

(p_5)   A morally good person will take steps to make the world a better place and even stronger steps to avoid making the world a worse place.

(p_6)   Even a minimally decent person would take steps to reduce the amount of unnecessary pain and suffering in the world, *if s/he could do so with little effort on her/his part.*

(p_7)   I am a morally good person.

(p_8)   I am at least a minimally decent person.

(p_9)   I am the sort of person who certainly would take steps to help reduce the amount of pain and suffering in the world, *if I could do so with little effort on my part.*

(p_{10})   Many nonhuman animals (certainly all vertebrates) are capable of feeling pain.

(p_{11})   Other things being equal, it is morally wrong to cause an animal pain or suffering.

(p_{12})   It is morally wrong and despicable to treat animals inhumanely for *no good reason.*

(p_{13})   We ought to euthanize untreatably injured, suffering animals to put them out of their misery whenever feasible.

(p_{14})   Other things being equal, it is worse to kill a conscious sentient animal than it is to kill a plant.

(p_{15})   We have a duty to help preserve the environment for future generations (at least for future human generations).

(p_{16})   One ought to minimize one's contribution toward environmental degradation, *especially in those ways requiring minimal effort on one's part.*

NOTES

1. Obviously, if you do not hold these beliefs (or enough of them), my argument will have no force for you, nor is it intended to. It is only aimed at those of you who do hold these widespread commonsense beliefs.

2. *Speciesism* is the widespread view that one's own species is superior to and more valuable than the other species and that, therefore, members of one's own species have the right to dominate members of these other species. While "speciesism" and its cognates are often used pejoratively in the animal rights literature, I use them only descriptively and imply no negative or condescending appraisal of the individual so described.

3. By "*unnecessary* suffering" I mean suffering that serves no greater, outweighing justifying good. If some instance of suffering is required to bring about a greater good (e.g., a painful root canal may

be the only way to save a person's tooth), then that suffering is *not* unnecessary. Thus, in the case of (p_2), no *ceteris paribus* clause is needed, since if other things are *not* equal such that the suffering in question is justified by an overriding, justifying good that can only be achieved by allowing that suffering, then that suffering is *not* necessary.

4. By a "minimally decent person" I mean a person who does the very minimum required by morality and no more. I borrow this terminology from Judith Jarvis Thomson who distinguishes a *good* Samaritan from an *minimally decent* Samaritan. See her "A Defense of Abortion" [reprinted in this volume].

5. It is worth noting that in every case just mentioned the vegetarian option is significantly more nutritious, more healthful, and much lower in fat, saturated fat, and cholesterol than its meat-based counterpart. In fact, none of the vegetarian options listed contain any cholesterol whatsoever.

Review and Discussion Questions

1. Is Engel correct to say that his case for vegetarianism avoids reliance on any controversial ethical theory?

2. Is factory farming cruel and immoral? Is it bad for the environment?

3. Examine carefully each of the seventeen propositions listed in the Appendix. Which are the most important for Engel's argument? Which are the most controversial or debatable? For each of the propositions, state whether you believe it. If you do, how firmly are you committed to it? If you do not believe it, why not?

4. Is the consumption of meat by human beings nutritionally (a) necessary, (b) not necessary but beneficial, (c) neither beneficial nor harmful, or (d) harmful?

5. Are you persuaded by Engel's argument for vegetarianism? If not, why not? Are there arguments against his position that he has overlooked or failed to answer adequately?

6. Assess his argument from the point of view of Tibor Machan and William Baxter. Are they committed to the morality of eating meat?

7

LIBERTY, PATERNALISM, AND FREEDOM OF EXPRESSION

On Liberty

JOHN STUART MILL

The freedom of the individual to choose and to act as he or she sees fit is a fundamental value, cherished by almost everyone, and clearly the upholding of personal liberty shows respect for persons as moral agents and contributes to human happiness. Yet any society must place limits on individual conduct. In the following excerpt from his classic essay *On Liberty*, John Stuart Mill examines one of the most fundamental questions of moral and social philosophy: What are the proper limits to society's power over the individual? Mill's answer is that society may interfere with an individual's actions only to prevent the individual from harming others. In line with this idea, Mill turns first to freedom of thought and expression, vigorously upholding freedom of opinion regardless of whether the viewpoint that the majority wishes to stifle is true or false. Mill then elaborates on his general principle, arguing that society may not compel the individual to do (or not do) something solely because society judges that it would be in the individual's own interest to do it.

Study Questions

1. What is Mill's basic principle, and on what ultimate ethical basis does he say that it rests?

2. Assume that the belief society wishes to suppress is false. Why would suppressing it be wrong, in Mill's view?

3. How does Mill answer the objection that his doctrine is "one of selfish indifference"?

4. What does Mill mean when he writes that "the inconveniences which are strictly

From John Stuart Mill, On Liberty *(1859)*.

inseparable from the unfavorable judgment of others" are the only ones a person should suffer for conduct that affects only himself or herself?

5. From Mill's perspective, why is there an important difference between punishing a person for being drunk and punishing a police officer for being drunk on duty?

6. How does Mill answer the argument that society needs the power to coerce people to take proper care of themselves, in order to bring its weaker members up to ordinary standards of rational conduct?

7. What does Mill see as the strongest argument against public interference in purely personal conduct?

Introductory

THE OBJECT OF THIS ESSAY is to assert one very simple principle, as entitled to govern absolutely the dealings of society with the individual in the way of compulsion and control, whether the means used be physical force in the form of legal penalties or the moral coercion of public opinion. That principle is, that the sole end for which mankind are warranted, individually or collectively, in interfering with the liberty of action of any of their number, is self-protection. That the only purpose for which power can be rightfully exercised over any member of a civilized community, against his will, is to prevent harm to others. His own good, either physical or moral, is not a sufficient warrant. He cannot rightfully be compelled to do or forbear because it will be better for him to do so, because it will make him happier, because, in the opinions of others, to do so would be wise or even right. These are good reasons for remonstrating with him, or reasoning with him, or persuading him, or entreating him, but not for compelling him or visiting him with any evil in case he do otherwise. To justify that, the conduct from which it is desired to deter him must be calculated to produce evil to someone else. The only part of the conduct of anyone, for which he is amenable to society, is that which concerns others. In the part which merely concerns himself, his independence is, of right, absolute. Over himself, over his own body and mind, the individual is sovereign.

It is, perhaps, hardly necessary to say that this doctrine is meant to apply only to human beings in the maturity of their faculties. We are not speaking of children, or of young persons below the age which the law may fix as that of manhood or womanhood. Those who are still in a state to require being taken care of by others, must be protected against their own actions as well as against external injury. For the same reason, we may leave out of consideration those backward states of society in which the race itself may be considered as in its nonage. . . .

It is proper to state that I forego any advantage which could be derived to my argument from the idea of abstract right, as a thing independent of utility. I regard utility as the ultimate appeal on all ethical questions; but it must be utility in the largest sense, grounded on the permanent interests of a man as a progressive being. These interests, I contend, authorize the subjection of individual spontaneity to external control, only in respect to those actions of each which concern the interest of other people. If anyone does an act hurtful to others, there is a *prima facie* case for punishing him, by law, or, where legal penalties are not safely applicable, by general disapprobation. There are also many positive acts for the benefit of others, which he may rightfully be compelled to perform: such as to give evidence in a court of justice; to bear his fair share in the common defense, or in any other joint work necessary to the interest of the society of which he enjoys the protection; and to perform certain acts of individual benefi-cence, such as saving a fellow-creature's life, or interposing to protect the defenseless against ill-usage, things which whenever it is obviously a man's duty to do, he may rightfully be made re-sponsible to society for not doing. A person may cause evil to others not only by his actions but by his inaction, and in either case he is justly ac-countable to them for the injury. . . .

But there is a sphere of action in which soci-ety, as distinguished from the individual, has, if any, only an indirect interest; comprehending all that portion of a person's life and conduct which affects only himself, or if it also affects others, only with their free, voluntary, and undeceived consent and participation. When I say only him-self, I mean directly, and in the first instance; for whatever affects himself, may affect others through himself; and the objection which may be grounded on this contingency, will receive consideration in the sequel. This, then is the ap-propriate region of human liberty. It comprises, *first,* the inward domain of consciousness; de-manding liberty of conscience in the most com-prehensive sense; liberty of thought and feeling; absolute freedom of opinion and sentiment on all subjects, practical or speculative, scientific, moral or theological. The liberty of expressing and publishing opinions may seem to fall under a different principle, since it belongs to that part of the conduct of an individual which concerns other people; but, being almost of as much im-portance as the liberty of thought itself, and rest-ing in great part on the same reasons, is practi-cally inseparable from it. *Secondly,* the principle requires liberty of tastes and pursuits; of framing the plan of our life to suit our own character; of doing as we like, subject to such consequences as may follow: without impediment from our fellow-creatures, so long as what we do does not harm them, even though they should think our conduct foolish, perverse, or wrong. *Thirdly,* from this liberty of each individual, follows the liberty, within the same limits, of combinations among individuals; freedom to unite, for any

purpose not involving harm to others: the per-sons combining being supposed to be of full age, and not forced or deceived.

No society in which these liberties are not, on the whole, respected, is free, whatever may be its form of government; and none is com-pletely free in which they do not exist absolute and unqualified. The only freedom which de-serves the name, is that of pursuing our own good in our own way, as long as we do not at-tempt to deprive others of theirs, or impede their efforts to obtain it. Each is the proper guardian of his own health, whether bodily, or mental and spiritual. Mankind are greater gain-ers by suffering each other to live as seems good to themselves, than by compelling each to live as seems good to the rest. . . .

Of the Liberty of Thought and Discussion

The time, it is to be hoped, is gone by, when any defense would be necessary of the "liberty of the press" as one of the securities against cor-rupt or tyrannical government. No argument, we may suppose, can now be needed against permitting a legislature or an executive, not identified in interest with the people, to pre-scribe opinions to them, and determine what doctrines or what arguments they shall be al-lowed to hear. . . . Let us suppose . . . that the government is entirely at one with the people, and never thinks of exerting any power of coer-cion unless in agreement with what it conceives to be their voice. But I deny the right of the people to exercise such coercion, either by themselves or by their government. The power itself is illegitimate. The best government has no more title to it than the worst. It is as noxious, or more noxious, when exerted in accordance with public opinion than when in opposition to it. If all mankind minus one were of one opin-ion, mankind would be no more justified in si-lencing that one person than he, if he had the power, would be justified in silencing mankind. Were an opinion a personal possession of no value except to the owner, if to be obstructed in the enjoyment of it were simply a private injury, it would make some difference whether the injury was inflicted only on a few persons or on many. But the peculiar evil of silencing the expression of an opinion is that it is robbing the human race, posterity as well as the existing generation—those who dissent from the opinion, still more than those who hold it. If the opinion is right, they are deprived of the opportunity of exchanging error for truth; if wrong, they lose, what is almost as great a benefit, the clearer perception and livelier impression of truth produced by its collision with error.

It is necessary to consider separately these two hypotheses, each of which has a distinct branch of the argument corresponding to it. We can never be sure that the opinion we are endeavoring to stifle is a false opinion; and if we were sure, stifling it would be an evil still.

First, the opinion which it is attempted to suppress by authority may possibly be true. Those who desire to suppress it, of course, deny its truth; but they are not infallible. They have no authority to decide the question for all mankind and exclude every other person from the means of judging. To refuse a hearing to an opinion because they are sure that it is false is to assume that *their* certainty is the same thing as *absolute* certainty. All silencing of discussion is an assumption of infallibility. Its condemnation may be allowed to rest on this common argument, not the worse for being common.

Unfortunately for the good sense of mankind, the fact of their fallibility is far from carrying the weight in their practical judgment which is always allowed to it in theory; for while everyone well knows himself to be fallible, few think it necessary to take any precautions against their own fallibility, or admit the supposition that any opinion of which they feel very certain may be one of the examples of the error to which they acknowledge themselves to be liable. . . .

The objection likely to be made to this argument would probably take some such form as the following. There is no greater assumption of infallibility in forbidding the propagation of error than in any other thing which is done by public authority on its own judgment and responsibility. . . . It is the duty of governments, and of individuals, to form the truest opinions they can; to form them carefully, and never impose them upon others unless they are quite sure of being right. But when they are sure (such reasoners may say), it is not conscientiousness but cowardice to shrink from acting on their opinions and allow doctrines which they honestly think dangerous to the welfare of mankind, either in this life or in another, to be scattered abroad without restraint, because other people, in less enlightened times, have persecuted opinions now believed to be true. . . . There is no such thing as absolute certainty, but there is assurance sufficient for the purposes of human life. We may, and must, assume our opinion to be true for the guidance of our own conduct; and it is assuming no more when we forbid bad men to pervert society by the propagation of opinions which we regard as false and pernicious.

I answer, that it is assuming very much more. There is the greatest difference between presuming an opinion to be true because, with every opportunity for contesting it, it has not been refuted, and assuming its truth for the purpose of not permitting its refutation. Complete liberty of contradicting and disproving our opinion is the very condition which justifies us in assuming its truth for purposes of action; and on no other terms can a being with human faculties have any rational assurance of being right. . . .

Let us now pass to the second division of the argument, and dismissing the supposition that any of the received opinions may be false, let us assume them to be true and examine into the worth of the manner in which they are likely to be held when their truth is not freely and openly canvassed. However unwillingly a person who has a strong opinion may admit the possibility that his opinion may be false, he ought to be moved by the consideration that, however true it may be, if it is not fully, frequently, and fearlessly discussed, it will be held as a dead dogma, not a living truth. . . .

If the cultivation of the understanding consists in one thing more than in another, it is surely in learning the grounds of one's own opinions. Whatever people believe, on subjects on which it is of the first importance to believe rightly, they ought to be able to defend against at least the common objections. . . . He who knows only his own side of the case knows little of that. His reasons may be good, and no one may have been able to refute them. But if he is equally unable to refute the reasons on the opposite side, if he does not so much as know what they are, he has no ground for preferring either opinion. The rational position for him would be suspension of judgment, and unless he contents himself with that, he is either led by authority or adopts, like the generality of the world, the side to which he feels most inclination. Nor is it enough that he should hear the arguments of adversaries from his own teachers, presented as they state them, and accompanied by what they offer as refutations. That is not the way to do justice to the arguments or bring them into real contact with his own mind. He must be able to hear them from persons who actually believe them, who defend them in earnest and do their very utmost for them. He must know them in their most plausible and persuasive form; he must feel the whole force of the difficulty which the true view of the subject has to encounter and dispose of, else he will never really possess himself of the portion of truth which meets and removes that difficulty. . . .

The fact . . . is that not only the grounds of the opinion are forgotten in the absence of discussion, but too often the meaning of the opinion itself. The words which convey it cease to suggest ideas, or suggest only a small portion of those they were originally employed to communicate. Instead of a vivid conception and a living belief, there remain only a few phrases retained

by rote; or, if any part, the shell and husk only of the meanings is retained, the finer essence being lost. The great chapter in human history which this fact occupies and fills cannot be too earnestly studied and meditated on. . . .

We have hitherto considered only two possibilities: that the received opinion may be false, and some other opinion, consequently, true; or that, the received opinion being true, a conflict with the opposite error is essential to a clear apprehension and deep feeling of its truth. But there is a commoner case than either of these: when the conflicting doctrines, instead of being one true and the other false, share the truth between them, and the nonconforming opinion is needed to supply the remainder of the truth of which the received doctrine embodies only a part. Popular opinions, on subjects not palpable to sense, are often true, but seldom or never the whole truth. They are a part of the truth, sometimes a greater, sometimes a smaller part, but exaggerated, distorted, and disjointed from the truths by which they ought to be accompanied and limited. Heretical opinions, on the other hand, are generally some of these suppressed and neglected truths, bursting the bonds which kept them down, and either seeking reconciliation with the truth contained in the common opinion, or fronting it as enemies, and setting themselves up, with similar exclusiveness, as the whole truth. The latter case is hitherto the most frequent, as, in the human mind, one-sidedness has always been the rule, and many-sidedness the exception. . . . Such being the partial character of prevailing opinions, even when resting on a true foundation, every opinion which embodies somewhat of the portion of truth which the common opinion omits ought to be considered precious, with whatever amount of error and confusion that truth may be blended. . . .

We have now recognized the necessity to the mental well-being of mankind (on which all their other well-being depends) of freedom of opinion, and freedom of the expression of opinion, on four distinct grounds, which we will now briefly recapitulate:

First, if any opinion is compelled to silence, that opinion may, for aught we can certainly know, be true. To deny this is to assume our own infallibility.

Secondly, though the silenced opinion be an error, it may, and very commonly does, contain a portion of truth; and since the general or prevailing opinion on any subject is rarely or never the whole truth, it is only by the collision of adverse opinions that the remainder of the truth has any chance of being supplied.

Thirdly, even if the received opinion be not only true, but the whole truth; unless it is suffered to be, and actually is, vigorously and earnestly contested, it will, by most of those who receive it, be held in the manner of a prejudice, with little comprehension or feeling of its rational grounds. And not only this, but, fourthly, the meaning of the doctrine itself will be in danger of being lost or enfeebled, and deprived of its vital effect on the character and conduct: the dogma becoming a mere formal profession, inefficacious for good, but cumbering the ground and preventing the growth of any real and heartfelt conviction from reason or personal experience. . . .

Of the Limits to the Authority of Society over the Individual

. . . As soon as any part of a person's conduct affects prejudicially the interests of others, society has jurisdiction over it, and the question whether the general welfare will or will not be promoted by interfering with it, becomes open to discussion. But there is no room for entertaining any such question when a person's conduct affects the interests of no persons besides himself, or need not affect them unless they like (all the persons concerned being of full age, and the ordinary amount of understanding). In all such cases, there should be perfect freedom, legal and social, to do the action and stand the consequences.

It would be a great misunderstanding of this doctrine to suppose that it is one of selfish indifference, which pretends that human beings have no business with each other's conduct in life, and that they should not concern themselves about the well-doing or well-being of one another, unless their own interest is involved. . . . Human beings owe to each other help to distinguish the better from the worse, and encouragement to choose the former and avoid the latter. They should be forever stimulating each other to increased exercise of their higher faculties, and increased direction of their feelings and aims towards wise instead of foolish, elevating instead of degrading, objects and contemplations. But neither one person, nor any number of persons, is warranted in saying to another human creature of ripe years, that he shall not do with his life for his own benefit what he chooses to do with it. He is the person most interested in his own well-being: the interest which any other person, except in cases of strong personal attachment, can have in it, is trifling, compared with that which he himself has; the interest which society has in him individually (except as to his conduct to others) is fractional, and altogether indirect; while with respect to his own feelings and circumstances, the most ordinary man or woman has means of knowledge immeasurably surpassing those that can be possessed by anyone else. The interference of society to overrule his judgment and purposes in what only regards himself must be grounded on general presumptions; which may be altogether wrong, and even if right, are as likely as not to be misapplied to individual cases, by persons no better acquainted with the circumstances of such cases than those are who look at them merely from without. In this department, therefore, of human affairs, individuality has its proper field of action. In the conduct of human beings towards one another it is necessary that general rules should for the most part be observed, in order that people may know what they have to expect; but in each person's own concerns his individual spontaneity is entitled to free exercise. Considerations to aid his judgment, exhortations to strengthen his will, may be offered to him, even obtruded on him, by others: but he himself is the final judge. All errors which he is likely to commit against advice and warning are far outweighed by the evil of allowing others to constrain him to what they deem his good. . . .

Though doing no wrong to anyone, a person may so act as to compel us to judge him, and feel to him, as a fool, or as a being of an inferior order; and since this judgment and feeling are a fact which he would prefer to avoid, it is doing him a service to warn him of it beforehand, as of any other disagreeable consequence to which he exposes himself. . . . We have a right, also, in various ways, to act upon our unfavorable opinion of anyone, not to the oppression of his individuality, but in the exercise of ours. We are not bound, for example, to seek his society; we have a right to avoid it (though not to parade the avoidance), for we have a right to choose the society most acceptable to us. We have a right, and it may be our duty, to caution others against him, if we think his example or conversation likely to have a pernicious effect on those with whom he associates. We may give others a preference over him in optional good offices, except those which tend to his improvement. In these various modes a person may suffer very severe penalties at the hands of others for faults which directly concern only himself; but he suffers these penalties only in so far as they are the natural and, as it were, the spontaneous consequences of the faults themselves, not because they are purposely inflicted on him for the sake of punishment. . . .

What I contend for is, that the inconveniences which are strictly inseparable from the unfavorable judgment of others, are the only ones to which a person should ever be subjected for that portion of his conduct and character which concerns his own good, but which does not affect the interest of others in their relations with him. Acts injurious to others require a totally different treatment. Encroachment on their rights; infliction on them of any loss or damage not justified by his own rights; falsehood or du-

plicity in dealing with them; unfair or ungenerous use of advantages over them; even selfish abstinence from defending them against injury—these are fit objects of moral reprobation, and, in grave cases, of moral retribution and punishment. And not only these acts, but the dispositions which lead to them, are properly immoral, and fit subjects of disapprobation which may rise to abhorrence. . . .

The distinction here pointed out between the part of a person's life which concerns only himself, and that which concerns others, many persons will refuse to admit. How (it may be asked) can any part of the conduct of a member of society be a matter of indifference to the other members? No person is an entirely isolated being; it is impossible for a person to do anything seriously or permanently hurtful to himself, without mischief reaching at least to his near connections, and often far beyond them. If he injures his property, he does harm to those who directly or indirectly derived support from it, and usually diminishes, by a greater or less amount, the general resources of the community. If he deteriorates his bodily or mental faculties, he not only brings evil upon all who depended on him for any portion of their happiness, but disqualifies himself for rendering the services which he owes to his fellow-creatures generally; perhaps becomes a burden on their affection or benevolence; and if such conduct were very frequent, hardly an offense that is committed would detract more from the general sum of good. Finally, if by his vices or follies a person does no direct harm to others, he is nevertheless (it may be said) injurious by his example; and ought to be compelled to control himself, for the sake of those whom the sight or knowledge of his conduct might corrupt or mislead.

And even (it will be added) if the consequences of misconduct could be confined to the vicious or thoughtless individual, ought society to abandon to their own guidance those who are manifestly unfit for it? If protection against themselves is confessedly due to children and persons under age, is not society equally bound to afford it to persons of mature years who are equally incapable of self-government? If gambling, or drunkenness, or incontinence, or idleness, or uncleanliness, are as injurious to happiness, and as great a hindrance to improvement, as many or most of the acts prohibited by law, why (it may be asked) should not law, so far as is consistent with practicability and social convenience, endeavor to repress these also? And as a supplement to the unavoidable imperfections of law, ought not opinion at least to organize a powerful police against these vices, and visit rigidly with social penalties those who are known to practice them? There is no question here (it may be said) about restricting individuality, or impeding the trial of new and original experiments in living. The only things it is sought to prevent are things which have been tried and condemned from the beginning of the world until now; things which experience has shown not to be useful or suitable to any person's individuality. There must be some length of time and amount of experience after which a moral or prudential truth may be regarded as established: and it is merely desired to prevent generation after generation from falling over the same precipice which has been fatal to their predecessors.

I fully admit that the mischief which a person does to himself may seriously affect, both through their sympathies and their interests, those nearly connected with him and, in a minor degree, society at large. When, by conduct of this sort, a person is led to violate a distinct and assignable obligation to any other person or persons, the case is taken out of the self-regarding class and becomes amenable to moral disapprobation in the proper sense of the term. If, for example, a man, through intemperance or extravagance, becomes unable to pay his debts, or, having undertaken the moral responsibility of a family, becomes from the same cause incapable of supporting or educating them, he is deservedly reprobated, and might be justly punished; but it is for the breach of duty to his family or creditors, not for the extravagance. If the resources which ought to have been devoted to them, had been diverted from them for the most prudent investment, the moral culpability would have been the same. George Barnwell murdered his uncle to get money for his mistress, but if he had done it to set himself up in business he would equally have been hanged. Again, in the frequent case of a man who causes grief to his family by addiction to bad habits, he deserves reproach for his unkindness or ingratitude; but so he may for cultivating habits not in themselves vicious, if they are painful to those with whom he passes his life, or who from personal ties are dependent on him for their comfort. Whoever fails in the consideration generally due to the interests and feelings of others, not being compelled by some more imperative duty, or justified by allowable self-preference, is a subject of moral disapprobation for that failure, but not for the cause of it, nor for the errors, merely personal to himself, which may have remotely led to it. In like manner, when a person disables himself, by conduct purely self-regarding, from the performance of some definite duty incumbent on him to the public, he is guilty of a social offense. No person ought to be punished simply for being drunk; but a soldier or policeman should be punished for being drunk on duty. Whenever, in short, there is a definite damage, or a definite risk of damage, either to an individual or to the public, the case is taken out of the province of liberty and placed in that of morality or law.

But with regard to the merely contingent or, as it may be called, constructive injury which a person causes to society by conduct which neither violates any specific duty to the public, nor occasions perceptible hurt to any assignable individual except himself, the inconvenience is one which society can afford to bear, for the sake of the greater good of human freedom. If grown persons are to be punished for not taking proper care of themselves, I would rather it were for their own sake than under pretense of preventing them from impairing their capacity or rendering to society benefits which society does not pretend it has a right to exact. But I cannot consent to argue the point as if society had no means of bringing its weaker members up to its ordinary standard of rational conduct, except waiting till they do something irrational, and then punishing them, legally or morally, for it. Society has had absolute power over them during all the early portion of their existence; it has had the whole period of childhood and nonage in which to try whether it could make them capable of rational conduct in life. The existing generation is master both of the training and the entire circumstances of the generation to come; it cannot indeed make them perfectly wise and good, because it is itself so lamentably deficient in goodness and wisdom; and its best efforts are not always, in individual cases, its most successful ones; but it is perfectly well able to make the rising generation, as a whole, as good as, and a little better than, itself. If society lets any considerable number of its members grow up mere children, incapable of being acted on by rational consideration of distant motives, society has itself to blame for the consequences. Armed not only with all the powers of education, but with the ascendency which the authority of a received opinion always exercises over the minds who are least fitted to judge for themselves, and aided by the *natural* penalties which cannot be prevented from falling on those who incur the distaste or the contempt of those who know them—let not society pretend that it needs, besides all this, the power to issue commands and enforce obedience in the personal concerns of individuals in which, on all principles of justice and policy, the decision ought to rest with those who are to abide the consequences. . . . With respect to what is said of the necessity of protecting society from the bad example set to others by the vicious or the self-indulgent, it is true that bad example may have a pernicious effect, especially the example of doing wrong to others with impunity to the wrongdoer. But we are now speaking of conduct which,

while it does no wrong to others, is supposed to do great harm to the agent himself; and I do not see how those who believe this can think otherwise than that the example, on the whole, must be more salutary than hurtful, since, if it displays the misconduct, it displays also the painful or degrading consequences which, if the conduct is justly censured, must be supposed to be in all or most cases attendant on it.

But the strongest of all the arguments against the interference of the public with purely personal conduct is that, when it does interfere, the odds are that it interferes wrongly and in the wrong place. On questions of social morality, of duty to others, the opinion of the public, that is, of an overruling majority, though often wrong, is likely to be still oftener right, because on such questions they are only required to judge of their own interests, of the manner in which some mode of conduct, if allowed to be practiced, would affect themselves. But the opinion of a similar majority, imposed as a law on the minority, on questions of self-regarding conduct is quite as likely to be wrong as right, for in these cases public opinion means, at the best, some people's opinion of what is good or bad for other people, while very often it does not even mean that—the public, with the most perfect indifference, passing over the pleasure or convenience of those whose conduct they censure and considering only their own preference. There are many who consider as an injury to themselves any conduct which they have a distaste for, and resent it as an outrage to their feelings; as a religious bigot, when charged with disregarding the religious feelings of others, has been known to retort that they disregard his feelings by persisting in their abominable worship or creed. But there is no parity between the feeling of a person for his own opinion and the feeling of another who is offended at his holding it, no more than between the desire of a thief to take a purse and the desire of the right owner to keep it. And a person's taste is as much his own peculiar concern as his opinion or his purse. It is easy for anyone to imagine an ideal public which leaves the freedom and choice of individuals in all uncertain matters undisturbed and only requires them to abstain from modes of conduct which universal experience has condemned. But where has there been seen a public which set any such limit to its censorship? Or when does the public trouble itself about universal experience? In its interferences with personal conduct it is seldom thinking of anything but the enormity of acting or feeling differently from itself.

Review and Discussion Questions

1. Is no doctrine or opinion so pernicious that it may justifiably be outlawed? Must society tolerate the expression of any opinion? What about those who advocate Nazism, racial oppression, satanism, or the overthrow of the government?

2. Would violent pornography be protected by Mill?

3. In light of Mill's basic principle, assess the legitimacy of laws (a) requiring motorists to wear seat belts and motorcyclists to wear helmets, (b) preventing people from walking naked in public parks, (c) forbidding people to take drugs like cocaine or heroin, or (d) outlawing skateboarding in certain areas.

4. Does Mill satisfactorily answer the criticism that distinguishing between actions that concern only ourselves and actions that affect others is impossible?

5. Has Mill gone too far in restricting the power of society over individual conduct?

6. Some critics of Mill have doubted that he can square his commitment to individual liberty with his underlying utilitarianism. Do you think utilitarianism might sometimes require us to limit individual freedom in ways that *On Liberty* opposes in order to enhance total social welfare?

Paternalism

GERALD DWORKIN

Gerald Dworkin, professor of philosophy at the University of Illinois at Chicago, examines John Stuart Mill's objections to interfering with a person's liberty on paternalistic grounds—that is, in order to promote the person's own good or happiness. Dworkin lists various examples of paternalistic legislation and distinguishes between "pure" and "impure" forms of paternalism. Dworkin argues that Mill implicitly used two types of argument—one utilitarian, the other based on the absolute value of free choice. Utilitarian argument, however, can establish only a presumption but not an absolute prohibition against interference with personal choice. And even the second type of argument allows for certain sorts of paternalism.

From Richard A. Wasserstrom, ed., Morality and the Law. *Copyright © 1971 Wadsworth Publishing Company. Reprinted by permission of the author and the publisher.*

Study Questions

1. What is the difference between "pure" and "impure" paternalism?
2. Why is legislation preventing employees from working more than forty hours per week not necessarily paternalistic?
3. Why, according to Dworkin, does utilitarianism provide a presumption—but not an absolute prohibition—against interference with personal conduct?
4. What justifies parental paternalism, and what limits the exercise of such parental power?
5. What are the two distinct ways in which one can behave in a nonrational fashion?
6. Dworkin argues that rational people would agree to society's imposing restrictions on self-regarding conduct in certain situations. What are three examples?
7. What two principles does he propose in order to limit such paternalistic restrictions?

I TAKE AS MY STARTING POINT the "one very simple principle" proclaimed by Mill in *On Liberty* . . .

> That principle is, that the sole end for which mankind are warranted, individually or collectively, in interfering with the liberty of action of any of their number, is self-protection. That the only purpose for which power can be rightfully exercised over any member of a civilized community, against his will, is to prevent harm to others. He cannot rightfully be compelled to do or forbear because it will be better for him to do so, because it will make him happier, because, in the opinion of others, to do so would be wise, or even right.

This principle is neither "one" nor "very simple." It is at least two principles: one asserting that self-protection or the prevention of harm to others is sometimes a sufficient warrant and the other claiming that the individual's own good is *never* a sufficient warrant for the exercise of compulsion either by the society as a whole or by its individual members. I assume that no one, with the possible exception of extreme pacifists or anarchists, questions the correctness of the first half of the principle. This essay is an examination of the negative claim embodied in Mill's principle—the objection to paternalistic interferences with a man's liberty.

I

By paternalism I shall understand roughly the interference with a person's liberty of action justified by reasons referring exclusively to the welfare, good, happiness, needs, interests or values of the person being coerced. One is always well-advised to illustrate one's definitions by examples but it is not easy to find "pure" examples of paternalistic interferences. For almost any piece of legislation is justified by several different kinds of reasons and even if historically a piece of legislation can be shown to have been introduced for purely paternalistic motives, it may be that advocates of the legislation with an antipaternalistic outlook can find sufficient reasons justifying the legislation without appealing to the reasons which were originally adduced to support it. Thus, for example, it may be that the original legislation requiring motorcyclists to wear safety helmets was introduced for purely paternalistic reasons. But the Rhode Island Supreme Court recently upheld such legislation on the grounds that it was "not persuaded that the legislature is powerless to prohibit individuals from pursuing a course of conduct which could conceivably result in their becoming public charges," thus clearly introducing reasons of a quite different kind. Now I regard this decision as being based on reasoning of a very dubious nature but it illustrates the kind of problem one has in finding examples. The following is a list of the kinds of interferences I have in mind as being paternalistic.

II

1. Laws requiring motorcyclists to wear safety helmets when operating their machines.
2. Laws forbidding persons from swimming at a public beach when lifeguards are not on duty.
3. Laws making suicide a criminal offense.
4. Laws making it illegal for women and children to work at certain types of jobs.
5. Laws regulating certain kinds of sexual conduct, for example, homosexuality among consenting adults in private.
6. Laws regulating the use of certain drugs which may have harmful consequences to the user but do not lead to antisocial conduct.
7. Laws requiring a license to engage in certain professions with those not receiving a license subject to fine or jail sentence if they do engage in the practice.
8. Laws compelling people to spend a specified fraction of their income on the purchase of retirement annuities (Social Security).
9. Laws forbidding various forms of gambling (often justified on the grounds that the poor are more likely to throw away their money on such activities than the rich who can afford to).
10. Laws regulating the maximum rates of interest for loans.
11. Laws against duelling.

In addition to laws which attach criminal or civil penalties to certain kinds of action there are laws, rules, regulations, decrees which make it rather difficult or impossible for people to carry out their plans and which are also justified on paternalistic grounds. Examples of this are:

1. Laws regulating the types of contracts which will be upheld as valid by the courts, for example (an example of Mill's to which I shall return), no man may make a valid contract for perpetual involuntary servitude.
2. Not allowing assumption of risk as a defense to an action based on the violation of a safety statute.
3. Not allowing as a defense to a charge of murder or assault the consent of the victim.
4. Requiring members of certain religious sects to have compulsory blood transfusions. This is made possible by not allowing the patient to have recourse to civil suits for assault and battery and by means of injunctions.
5. Civil commitment procedures when these are specifically justified on the basis of preventing the person being committed from harming himself. The D.C. Hospitalization of the Mentally Ill Act provides for involuntary hospitalization of a person who "is mentally ill, and because of that illness, is likely to injure himself or others if allowed to remain at liberty." The term injure in this context applies to unintentional as well as intentional injuries.

All of my examples are of existing restrictions on the liberty of individuals. Obviously one can think of interferences which have not yet been imposed. Thus one might ban the sale of cigarettes, or require that people wear safety belts in automobiles (as opposed to merely having them installed), enforcing this by not allowing motorists to sue for injuries even when caused by other drivers if the motorist was not wearing a seat belt at the time of the accident. . . .

III

Bearing these examples in mind, let me return to a characterization of paternalism. I said earlier that I meant by the term, roughly, interference with a person's liberty for his own good. But, as some of the examples show, the class of persons whose good is involved is not always identical with the class of persons whose freedom is restricted. Thus, in the case of professional licensing it is the practitioner who is directly interfered with but it is the would-be patient whose interests are presumably being served. Not allowing the consent of the victim to be a defense to certain types of crime primarily affects the would-be aggressor but it is the interests of the willing victim that we are trying to protect. Sometimes a person may fall into both classes as would be the case if we banned the manufacture and sale of cigarettes and a given manufacturer happened to be a smoker as well.

Thus we may first divide paternalistic interferences into "pure" and "impure" cases. In "pure" paternalism the class of persons whose freedom is restricted is identical with the class of persons whose benefit is intended to be promoted by such restrictions. Examples: the making of suicide a crime, requiring passengers in automobiles to wear seat belts, requiring a Christian Scientist to receive a blood transfusion. In the case of "impure" paternalism in trying to protect the welfare of a class of persons we find that the only way to do so will involve restricting the freedom of other persons besides those who are benefitted. Now it might be thought that there are not cases of "impure" paternalism since any such case could always be justified on nonpaternalistic grounds, that is, in terms of preventing harm to others. Thus we might ban cigarette manufacturers from continuing to manufacture their product on the grounds that we are preventing them from causing illness to others in the same way that we prevent other manufacturers from releasing pollutants into the atmosphere, thereby causing

danger to the members of the community. The difference is, however, that in the former but not the latter case the harm is of such a nature that it could be avoided by those individuals affected if they so chose. The incurring of the harm requires, so to speak, the active cooperation of the victim. It would be mistaken theoretically and hypocritical in practice to assert that our interference in such cases is just like our interference in standard cases of protecting others from harm. At the very least someone interfered with in this way can reply that no one is complaining about his activities. It may be that impure paternalism requires arguments or reasons of a stronger kind in order to be justified, since there are persons who are losing a portion of their liberty and they do not even have the solace of having it be done "in their own interest." Of course in some sense, if paternalistic justifications are ever correct, then we are protecting others, we are preventing some from injuring others, but it is important to see the differences between this and the standard case.

Paternalism then will always involve limitations on the liberty of some individuals in their own interest but it may also extend to interferences with the liberty of parties whose interests are not in question.

IV

Finally, by way of some more preliminary analysis, I want to distinguish paternalistic interference with liberty from a related type with which it is often confused. Consider, for example, legislation which forbids employees to work more than, say, forty hours per week. It is sometimes argued that such legislation is paternalistic for if employees desired such a restriction on their hours of work they could agree among themselves to impose it voluntarily. But because they do not the society imposes its own conception of their best interests upon them by the use of coercion. Hence this is paternalism. . . .

There are restrictions which are in the interests of a class of persons taken collectively but are such that the immediate interest of each individual is furthered by his violating the rule when others adhere to it. In such cases the individuals involved may need the use of compulsion to give effect to their collective judgment of their own interest by guaranteeing each individual compliance by the others. In these cases compulsion is not used to achieve some benefit which is not recognized to be a benefit by those concerned, but rather because it is the only feasible means of achieving some benefit which *is* recognized as such by all concerned. This way of viewing matters provides us with another characterization of paternalism in general. Paternalism might be thought of as the use of coercion to achieve a good which is not recognized as such by those persons for whom the good is intended. Again while this formulation captures the heart of the matter—it is surely what Mill is objecting to in *On Liberty*—the matter is not always quite like that. For example, when we force motorcyclists to wear helmets we are trying to promote a good—the protection of the person from injury—which is surely recognized by most of the individuals concerned. It is not that a cyclist doesn't value his bodily integrity; rather, as a supporter of such legislation would put it, he either places, perhaps irrationally, another value or good (freedom from wearing a helmet) above that of physical well-being or, perhaps, while recognizing the danger in the abstract, he either does not fully appreciate it or he underestimates the likelihood of its occurring. But now we are approaching the question of possible justifications of paternalistic measures and the rest of this essay will be devoted to that question.

V

I shall begin for dialectical purposes by discussing Mill's objections to paternalism and then go on to discuss more positive proposals.

An initial feature that strikes one is the absolute nature of Mill's prohibitions against paternalism. It is so unlike the carefully qualified admonitions of Mill and his fellow utilitarians on other moral issues. He speaks of self-protection as the *sole* end warranting coercion, of the individual's own goals as *never* being a sufficient warrant. . . .

Clearly the operative premise here is . . . bolstered by claims about the status of the individual as judge and appraiser of his welfare, interests, needs, etc.:

With respect to his own feelings and circumstances, the most ordinary man or woman has means of knowledge immeasurably surpassing those that can be possessed by any one else.

He is the person most interested in his own well-being: the interest which any other person, except in cases of strong personal attachment, can have in it is trifling, compared to that which he himself has.

These claims are used to support the following generalizations concerning the utility of compulsion for paternalistic purposes:

The interference of society to overrule his judgment and purposes in what only regards himself must be grounded on general presumptions; which may be altogether wrong, and even if right, are as likely as not to be misapplied to individual cases.

But the strongest of all the arguments against the interference of the public with purely personal conduct is that when it does interfere, the odds are that it interferes wrongly and in the wrong place.

All errors which [the individual] is likely to commit against advice and warning are far outweighed by the evil of allowing others to constrain him to what they deem his good.

Performing the utilitarian calculation by balancing the advantages and disadvantages, we find that: "Mankind are greater gainers by suffering each other to live as seems good to themselves, than by compelling each other to live as seems good to the rest.". . .

This is clearly the main channel of Mill's thought and it is one which has been subjected to vigorous attack from the moment it appeared—most often by fellow utilitarians. The link that they have usually seized on is, as Fitzjames Stephen put it in *Liberty, Equality, Fraternity,* the absence of proof that the "mass of adults are so well acquainted with their own interests and so much disposed to pursue them that no compulsion or restraint put upon them by any others for the purpose of promoting their interest can really promote them.". . .

Now it is interesting to note that Mill himself was aware of some of the limitations on the doctrine that the individual is the best judge of his own interests. In his discussion of government intervention in general (even where the intervention does not interfere with liberty but provides alternative institutions to those of the market) after making claims which are parallel to those just discussed, for example, "People understand their own business and their own interests better, and care for them more, than the government does, or can be expected to do," he goes on to an intelligent discussion of the "very large and conspicuous exceptions" to the maxim. . . .

In short, we get a presumption, not an absolute prohibition. The question is why doesn't the argument against paternalism go the same way?

I suggest that the answer lies in seeing that in addition to a purely utilitarian argument Mill uses another as well. . . . When Mill states that "there is a part of the life of every person who has come to years of discretion, within which the individuality of that person ought to reign uncontrolled either by any other person or by the public collectively," he is saying something about what it means to be a person, an autonomous agent. It is because coercing a person for

his own good denies this status as an independent entity that Mill objects to it so strongly and in such absolute terms. To be able to choose is a good that is independent of the wisdom of what is chosen. A man's "mode of laying out his existence is the best, not because it is the best in itself, but because it is his own mode." It is the privilege and proper condition of a human being, arrived at the maturity of his faculties, to use and interpret experience in his own way. . . .

What I have tried to show so far is that there are two strains of argument in Mill—one a straight-forward utilitarian mode of reasoning and one which relies not on the goods which free choice leads to but on the absolute value of the choice itself. The first cannot establish any absolute prohibition but at most a presumption and indeed a fairly weak one given some fairly plausible assumptions about human psychology; the second, while a stronger line of argument, seems to me to allow on its own grounds a wider range of paternalism than might be suspected. I turn now to a consideration of these matters.

VI

We might begin looking for principles governing the acceptable use of paternalistic power in cases where it is generally agreed that it is legitimate. Even Mill intends his principles to be applicable only to mature individuals, not those in what he calls "nonage." What is it that justifies us in interfering with children? The fact that they lack some of the emotional and cognitive capacities required in order to make fully rational decisions. It is an empirical question to just what extent children have an adequate conception of their own present and future interests but there is not much doubt that there are many deficiencies. For example, it is very difficult for a child to defer gratification for any considerable period of time. Given these deficiencies and given the very real and permanent dangers that may befall the child, it becomes not only permissible but even a duty of the parent to restrict the child's freedom in various ways. There is however an important moral limitation on the exercise of such parental power which is provided by the notion of the child eventually coming to see the correctness of his parent's interventions. Parental paternalism may be thought of as a wager by the parent on the child's subsequent recognition of the wisdom of the restrictions. There is an emphasis on what could be called future-oriented consent—on what the child will come to welcome, rather than on what he does welcome. . . .

Let me start by considering a case where the consent is not hypothetical in nature. Under certain conditions it is rational for an individual to agree that others should force him to act in ways which, at the time of action, the individual may not see as desirable. If, for example, a man knows that he is subject to breaking his resolves when temptation is present, he may ask a friend to refuse to entertain his requests at some later stage.

A classical example is given in the Odyssey when Odysseus commands his men to tie him to the mast and refuse all future orders to be set free, because he knows the power of the Sirens to enchant men with their songs. Here we are on relatively sound ground in later refusing Odysseus' request to be set free. He may even claim to have changed his mind but, since it is *just* such changes that he wished to guard against, we are entitled to ignore them.

A process analogous to this may take place on a social rather than individual basis. An electorate may mandate its representatives to pass legislation which when it comes time to "pay the price" may be unpalatable. I may believe that a tax increase is necessary to halt inflation though I may resent the lower pay check each month. However in both this case and that of Odysseus, the measure to be enforced is specifically requested by the party involved and at some point in time there is genuine consent and agreement on the part of those persons whose liberty is infringed. Such is not the case for the paternalistic measures we have been speaking about. What must be involved here is not consent to specific measures but rather consent to a system of government, run by elected representatives, with an understanding that they may act to safeguard our interests in certain limited ways.

I suggest that since we are all aware of our irrational propensities, deficiencies in cognitive and emotional capacities, and avoidable and unavoidable ignorance, it is rational and prudent for us to in effect take out "social insurance policies." We may argue for and against proposed paternalistic measures in terms of what fully rational individuals would accept as forms of protection. Now clearly, since the initial agreement is not about specific measures we are dealing with a more-or-less blank check and therefore there have to be carefully defined limits. What I am looking for are certain kinds of conditions which make it plausible to suppose that rational men could reach agreement to limit their liberty even when other men's interests are not affected. . . .

Let me suggest types of situations in which it seems plausible to suppose that fully rational individuals would agree to having paternalistic restrictions imposed upon them. It is reasonable to suppose that there are "goods" such as health which any person would want to have in order to pursue his own good—no matter how that good is conceived. This is an argument used in connection with compulsory education for children but it seems to me that it can be extended to other goods which have this character. Then one could agree that the attainment of such goods should be promoted even when not recognized to be such, at the moment, by the individuals concerned.

An immediate difficulty arises from the fact that men are always faced with competing goods and that there may be reasons why even a value such as health—or indeed life—may be overridden by competing values. Thus the problem with the Christian Scientist and blood transfusions. It may be more important for him to reject "impure substances" than to go on living. The difficult problem that must be faced is whether one can give sense to the notion of a person irrationally attaching weights to competing values.

Consider a person who knows the statistical data on the probability of being injured when not wearing seat belts in an automobile and knows the types and gravity of the various injuries. He also insists that the inconvenience attached to fastening the belt every time he gets in and out of the car outweighs for him the possible risks to himself. I am inclined in this case to think that such a weighing is irrational. Given his life plans, which we are assuming are those of the average person, his interests and commitments already undertaken, I think it is safe to predict that we can find inconsistencies in his calculations at some point. I am assuming that this is not a man who for some conscious or unconscious reasons is trying to injure himself nor is he a man who just likes to "live dangerously." I am assuming that he is like us in all the relevant respects but just puts an enormously high negative value on inconvenience—one which does not seem comprehensible or reasonable.

It is always possible, of course, to assimilate this person to creatures like myself. I, also, neglect to fasten my seat belt and I concede such behavior is not rational but not because I weigh the inconvenience differently from those who fasten the belts. It is just that having made (roughly) the same calculation as everybody else, I ignore it in my actions. A plausible explanation for this deplorable habit is that although I know in some intellectual sense what the probabilities and risks are I do not fully appreciate them in an emotionally genuine manner.

We have two distinct types of situation in which a man acts in a nonrational fashion. In one case he attaches incorrect weights to some of his values; in the other he neglects to act in accordance with his actual preferences and desires. Clearly there is a stronger and more persuasive argument for paternalism in the latter situation. Here we are really not—by assumption—imposing a good on another person. But why may we not extend our interference to what we might call evaluative delusions? After all, in the case of cognitive delusions we are prepared, often, to act against the expressed will of the person involved. If a man believes that when he jumps out the window he will float upwards—Robert Nozick's example—would not we detain him, forcibly if necessary? The reply will be that this man doesn't wish to be injured and if we could convince him that he is mistaken as to the consequences of his action, he would not wish to perform the action. But part of what is involved in claiming that the man who doesn't fasten his seat belts is attaching an incorrect weight to the inconvenience of fastening them is that if he were to be involved in an accident and severely injured he would look back and admit that the inconvenience wasn't as bad as all that. So there is a sense in which, if I could convince him of the consequences of his action, he also would not wish to continue his present course of action. . . . Let me now consider another factor which comes into play in some of these situations which may make an important difference in our willingness to consent to paternalistic restrictions.

Some of the decisions we make are of such a character that they produce changes which are in one or another way irreversible. Situations are created in which it is difficult or impossible to return to anything like the initial stage at which the decision was made. In particular, some of these changes will make it impossible to continue to make reasoned choices in the future. I am thinking specifically of decisions which involve taking drugs that are physically or psychologically addictive and those which are destructive of one's mental and physical capacities.

I suggest we think of the imposition of paternalistic interferences in situations of this kind as being a kind of insurance policy which we take out against making decisions which are far-reaching, potentially dangerous and irreversible. Each of these factors is important. . . .

A second class of cases concerns decisions which are made under extreme psychological and sociological pressures. I am not thinking here of the making of the decision as being something one is pressured into—for example, a good reason for making duelling illegal is that unless this is done many people might have to manifest their courage and integrity in ways in which they would rather not do so—but rather of decisions, such as that to commit suicide, which are usually made at a point where the individual is not thinking clearly and calmly about the nature of his decision. In addition, of course, this comes under the previous heading of all-too-irrevocable decisions. Now there are practical steps which a society could take if it wanted to decrease the possibility of suicide—for example not paying social security benefits to the survivors or, as religious institutions do, not allowing persons to be buried with the same status as natural deaths. I think we may count these as interferences with the liberty of persons to attempt suicide and the question is whether they are justifiable.

Using my argument schema the question is whether rational individuals would consent to such limitations. I see no reason for them to consent to an absolute prohibition but I do think it is reasonable for them to agree to some kind of enforced waiting period. Since we are all aware of the possibility of temporary states, such as great fear or depression, that are inimical to the making of well-informed and rational decisions, it would be prudent for all of us if there were some kind of institutional arrangement

whereby we were restrained from making a decision which is so irreversible. What this would be like in practice is difficult to envisage and it may be that if no practical arrangements were feasible we would have to conclude that there should be no restriction at all on this kind of action. But we might have a "cooling off" period, in much the same way that we now require couples who file for divorce to go through a waiting period. Or, more far-fetched, we might imagine a Suicide Board composed of a psychologist and another member picked by the applicant. The Board would be required to meet and talk with the person proposing to take his life, though its approval would not be required.

A third class of decisions—these classes are not supposed to be disjoint—involves dangers which are either not sufficiently understood or appreciated correctly by the persons involved. Let me illustrate, using the example of cigarette smoking, a number of possible cases.

1. A man may not know the facts—e.g., smoking between 1 and 2 packs a day shortens life expectancy 6.2 years, the costs and pain of the illness caused by smoking, etc.
2. A man may know the facts, wish to stop smoking, but not have the requisite will-power.
3. A man may know the facts but not have them play the correct role in his calculation because, say, he discounts the danger psychologically since it is remote in time and/or inflates the attractiveness of other consequences of his decision which he regards as beneficial.

In case 1 what is called for is education, the posting of warnings, et cetera. In case 2 there is no theoretical problem. We are not imposing a good on someone who rejects it. We are simply using coercion to enable people to carry out their own goals. (Note: There obviously is a difficulty in that only a subclass of the individuals affected wish to be prevented from doing what they are doing.) In case 3 there is a sense in which we are imposing a good on someone in that given his current appraisal of the facts he doesn't wish to be restricted. But in another sense we are not imposing a good since what is being claimed—and what must be shown or at least argued for—is that an accurate accounting on his part would lead him to reject his current course of action. Now we all know that such cases exist, that we are prone to disregarding dangers that are only possibilities, that immediate pleasures are often magnified and distorted.

If in addition the dangers are severe and far-reaching, we could agree to allow the state a certain degree of power to intervene in such situations. The difficulty is in specifying in advance, even vaguely, the class of cases in which intervention will be legitimate.

A related difficulty is that of drawing a line so that it is not the case that all ultra-hazardous activities are ruled out, for example, mountain-climbing, bull-fighting, sports-car racing, et cetera. There are some risks—even very great ones—which a person is entitled to take with his life.

A good deal depends on the nature of the deprivation—for example, does it prevent the person from engaging in the activity completely or merely limit his participation—and how important to the nature of the activity is the absence of restriction when this is weighed against the role that the activity plays in the life of the person. In the case of automobile seat belts, for example, the restriction is trivial in nature, interferes not at all with the use or enjoyment of the activity, and does, I am assuming, considerably reduce a high risk of serious injury. Whereas, for example, making mountain-climbing illegal completely prevents a person from engaging in an activity which may play an important role in his life and his conception of the person he is.

In general, the easiest cases to handle are those which can be argued about in the terms which Mill thought to be so important—a con-

cern not just for the happiness or welfare, in some broad sense, of the individual but rather a concern for the autonomy and freedom of the person. I suggest that we would be most likely to consent to paternalism in those instances in which it preserves and enhances for the individual his ability to rationally consider and carry out his own decisions.

I have suggested in this essay a number of types of situations in which it seems plausible that rational men would agree to granting the legislative powers of a society the right to impose restrictions on what Mill calls "self-regarding" conduct. However, rational men knowing something about the resources of ignorance, ill-will and stupidity available to the lawmakers of a society—a good case in point is the history of drug legislation in the United States—will be concerned to limit such intervention to a minimum. I suggest in closing two principles designed to achieve this end.

In all cases of paternalistic legislation there must be a heavy and clear burden of proof placed on the authorities to demonstrate the exact nature of the harmful effects (or beneficial consequences) to be avoided (or achieved) and the probability of their occurrence. The burden of proof here is twofold—what lawyers distinguish as the burden of going forward and the burden of persuasion. That the authorities have the burden of going forward means that it is up to them to raise the question and bring forward evidence of the evils to be avoided. Unlike the case of new drugs, where the manufacturer must produce some evidence that the drug has been tested and found not harmful, no citizen has to show with respect to self-regarding conduct that it is not harmful or promotes his best interest. In addition the nature and cogency of the evidence for the harmfulness of the course of action must be set at a high level. To paraphrase a formulation of the burden of proof for criminal proceedings—better ten men ruin themselves than one man be unjustly deprived of liberty.

Finally, I suggest a principle of the least restrictive alternative. If there is an alternative way of accomplishing the desired end without restricting liberty although it may involve great expense, inconvenience, etc., the society must adopt it.

Review and Discussion Questions

1. Do you agree with Dworkin that Mill's argument in *On Liberty* relies on nonutilitarian moral considerations?

2. What are the arguments, paternalistic and nonpaternalistic, for requiring motorcyclists to wear helmets? What is the argument against helmet laws? With which side do you agree?

3. Assess Dworkin's reason for maintaining that paternalistic interference might be justified in the case of certain drugs.

4. Do you think Mill would accept Dworkin's argument that paternalism can be justified in certain cases in order to enhance the individual's ability rationally to weight and carry out his or her own decisions?

Permissible Paternalism: Saving Smokers from Themselves

ROBERT E. GOODIN

Robert E. Goodin, professorial fellow in philosophy at the Australian National University and the author of *No Smoking*, argues that public policy directed toward discouraging smoking is an instance of permissible paternalism. In the eyes of many moral theorists, paternalism conflicts with individual rights because the point of rights is to protect an individual's choices. However, Goodin argues that the conflict between rights and paternalism is not so sharp if the paternalistic intervention is grounded on the person's own interests or values. After examining whether the desire of smokers to continue smoking reflects a preference that is their own and that is also relevant, settled, and "preferred," Goodin argues that there is a strong case for government policies intended to stop people from smoking.

Study Questions

1. What two different accounts of rights does Goodin distinguish? On which account is there a conflict between rights and paternalism? Explain. How does Goodin's approach to smoking attempt to lessen this conflict?

2. Goodin believes that paternalism can only be justified for "big decisions." What does he mean by this?

3. Goodin argues that often the preferences of smokers are neither "relevant" nor "settled." What does he mean by this?

4. How does the concept of "preferred preferences" apply to the case of smoking?

5. Why does Goodin reject the idea that, in framing public policy, we should ignore people's preferences when they have been induced by advertising?

PATERNALISM IS DESPERATELY out of fashion. Nowadays notions of "children's rights" severely limit what even parents may do to their own offspring, in their children's interests but against their will. What public officials may properly do to adult citizens, in their interests but against their will, is presumably even more tightly circumscribed. So the project I have set for myself—carving out a substantial sphere of morally permissible paternalism—might seem simply preposterous in present political and philosophical circumstances.

Here I shall say no more about the paternalism of parents toward their own children. My focus will instead be upon ways in which certain public policies designed to promote people's interests might be morally justifiable even if those people were themselves opposed to such policies.

Neither shall I say much more about notions of rights. But in focusing upon people's interests rather than their rights, I shall arguably be sticking closely to the sorts of concerns that motivate rights theorists. Of course, what it is to have a right is itself philosophically disputed; and on at least one account (the so-called "interest theory") to have a right is nothing more than to have a legally protected interest. But on the rival account (the so-called "choice theory") the whole point of rights is to have a legally protected choice. There, the point of having a right is that your choice in the matter will be respected, even if that choice actually runs contrary to your own best interests.

It is that understanding of rights which leads us to suppose that paternalism and rights are necessarily at odds, and there are strict limits in the extent to which we might reconcile the two positions. Still, there is some substantial scope for compromise between the two positions.

Those theorists who see rights as protecting people's choices rather than promoting their interests would be most at odds with paternalists who were proposing to impose upon people what is judged to be *objectively* good for them. That is to say, they would be most at odds if paternalists were proposing to impose upon people outcomes which are judged to be good for those people, whether or not there were any grounds for that conclusion in those people's own subjective judgments of their own good.

Rights theorists and paternalists would still be at odds, but less at odds, if paternalists refrained from talking about interests in so starkly objective a way. Then, just as rights command respect for people's choices, so too would paternalists be insisting that we respect choices that people themselves have or would have made. The two are not quite the same, to be sure, but they are much more nearly the same than the ordinary contrast between paternalists and rights theorists would seem to suggest.

That is precisely the sort of conciliatory gesture that I shall here be proposing. In paternalistically justifying some course of action on the grounds that it is in someone's interests, I shall always be searching for some warrant in that person's own value judgments for saying that it is in that person's interests.

"Some warrant" is a loose constraint, to be sure. Occasionally will we find genuine cases of what philosophers call "weakness of will": people being possessed of a powerful, conscious present desire to do something that they none-theless just cannot bring themselves to do. Then public policy forcing them to realize their own desire, though arguably paternalistic, is transparently justifiable even in terms of people's own subjective values. More often, though, the subjective value to which we are appealing is one which is present only in an inchoate form, or will only arise later, or can be appreciated only in retrospect.

Paternalism is clearly paternalistic in imposing those more weakly-held subjective values upon people in preference to their more strongly held ones. But, equally clearly, it is less offensively paternalistic thanks to this crucial fact: at least it deals strictly in terms of values that are or will be subjectively present, at some point or another and to some extent or another, in the person concerned.

I. The Scope of Paternalism

When we are talking about public policies (and maybe even when we are talking of private, familial relations), paternalism surely can only be justified for the "big decisions" in people's lives. No one, except possibly parents and perhaps not even they, would propose to stop you from buying candy bars on a whim, under the influence of seductive advertising and at some marginal cost to your dental health.

So far as public policy is concerned, certainly, to be a fitting subject for public paternalism a decision must first of all involve high stakes. Life-and-death issues most conspicuously qualify. But so do those that substantially shape your subsequent life prospects. Decisions to drop out of school or to begin taking drugs involve high stakes of roughly that sort. If the decision is also substantially irreversible—returning to school is unlikely, the drug is addictive—then that further bolsters the case for paternalistic intervention.

The point in both cases is that people would not have a chance to benefit by learning from their mistakes. If the stakes are so high that los-

ing the gamble once will kill you, then there is no opportunity for subsequent learning. Similarly, if the decision is irreversible, you might know better next time but be unable to benefit from your new wisdom.

II. Evaluating Preferences

The case for paternalism, as I have cast it, is that the public officials might better respect your own preferences than you would have done through your own actions. That is to say that public officials are engaged in evaluating your (surface) preferences, judging them according to some standard of your own (deeper) preferences. Public officials should refrain from paternalistic interference, and allow you to act without state interference, only if they are convinced that you are acting on:

- *relevant* preferences;
- *settled* preferences;
- *preferred* preferences; and, perhaps,
- *your own* preferences.

In what follows, I shall consider each of those requirements in turn. My running example will be the problem of smoking and policies to control it. Nothing turns on the peculiarities of that example, though. There are many others like it in relevant respects.

It often helps, in arguments like this, to apply generalities to particular cases. So, in what follows, I shall further focus in on the case of one particular smoker, Rose Cipollone. Her situation is nowise unique—in all the respects that matter here, she might be considered the prototypical smoker. All that makes her case special is that she (or more precisely her heir) was the first to win a court case against the tobacco companies whose products killed her.

In summarizing the evidence presented at that trial, the judge described the facts of the case as follows.

Rose . . . Cipollone . . . began to smoke at age 16 . . . while she was still in high school. She testified that she began to smoke because she saw people smoking in the movies, in advertisements, and looked upon it as something "cool, glamorous and grown-up" to do. She began smoking Chesterfields . . . primarily because of advertising of "pretty girls and movie stars," and because Chesterfields were described . . . as "mild.". . .

Mrs. Cipollone attempted to quit smoking while pregnant with her first child . . . , but even then she would sneak cigarettes. While she was in labor she smoked an entire pack of cigarettes, provided to her at her request by her doctor, and after the birth . . . she resumed smoking. She smoked a minimum of a pack a day and as much as two packs a day.

In 1955, she switched . . . to L&M cigarettes . . . because . . . she believed that the filter would trap whatever was "bad" for her in cigarette smoking. She relied upon advertisements which supported that contention. She . . . switched to Virgina Slims . . . because the cigarettes were glamorous and long, and were associated with beautiful women—and the liberated woman. . . .

Because she developed a smoker's cough and heard reports that smoking caused cancer, she tried to cut down her smoking. These attempts were unsuccessful. . . .

Mrs. Cipollone switched to lower tar and nicotine cigarettes based upon advertising from which she concluded that those cigarettes were safe or safer . . . [and] upon the recommendation of her family physician. In 1981 her cancer was diagnosed, and even though her doctors advised her to stop she was unable to do so. She even told her doctors and her husband that she had quit when she had not, and she continued to smoke until June of 1982 when her lung was removed. Even thereafter she smoked occasionally—in hiding. She stopped smoking in 1983 when her cancer had metastasized and she was diagnosed as fatally ill.

This sad history containing many of the features that I shall be arguing make paternalism most permissible.

Relevant preferences

The case against paternalism consists in the simple proposition that, morally, we ought to respect people's own choices in matters that affect themselves and by-and-large only themselves. But there are many questions we first might legitimately ask about those preferences, without in any way questioning this fundamental principle of respecting people's autonomy.

One is simply whether the preferences in play are genuinely *relevant* to the decision at hand. Often they are not. Laymen often make purely factual mistakes in their means–ends reasoning. They think—or indeed, as in the case of Rose Cipollone, are led by false advertising to suppose—that an activity is safe when it is not. They think that an activity like smoking is glamorous, when the true facts of the matter are that smoking may well cause circulatory problems requiring the distinctly unglamorous amputation of an arm or leg.

When people make purely factual mistakes like that, we might legitimately override their surface preferences (the preference to smoke) in the name of their own deeper preferences (to stay alive and bodily intact). Public policies designed to prevent youngsters from taking up smoking when they want to, or to make it harder (more expensive or inconvenient) for existing smokers to continue smoking when they want to, may be paternalistic in the sense of running contrary to people's own manifest choices in the matter. But this overriding of their choices is grounded in their own deeper preferences, so such paternalism would be minimally offensive from a moral point of view.

Settled preferences

We might ask, further, whether the preferences being manifested are "settled" preferences or whether they are merely transitory phases people are going through. It may be morally permissible to let people commit euthanasia voluntarily, if we are sure they really want to die. But if we think that they may subsequently change their minds, then we have good grounds for supposing that we should stop them.

The same may well be true with smoking policy. While Rose Cipollone herself thought smoking was both glamorous and safe, young sters beginning to smoke today typically know better. But many of them still say that they would prefer a shorter but more glamorous life, and that they are therefore more than happy to accept the risks that smoking entails. Say what they may at age sixteen, though, we cannot help supposing that they will think differently when pigeons eventually come home to roost. The risk-courting preferences of youth are a characteristic product of a peculiarly dare-devil phase that virtually all of them will, like their predecessors, certainly grow out of.

Insofar as people's preferences are not settled—insofar as they choose one option now, yet at some later time may wish that they had chosen another—we have another ground for permissible paternalism. Policy-makers dedicated to respecting people's own choices have, in effect, two of the person's own choices to choose between. How such conflicts should be settled is hard to say. We might weigh the strength or duration of the preferences, how well they fit with the person's other preferences, and so on.

Whatever else we do, though, we clearly ought not privilege one preference over another just because it got there first. Morally, it is permissible for policy-makers to ignore one of a person's present preferences (to smoke, for example) in deference to another that is virtually certain later to emerge (as was Rose Cipollone's wish to live, once she had cancer).

Preferred preferences

A third case for permissible paternalism turns on the observation that people have not only multiple and conflicting preferences but also preferences for preferences. Rose Cipollone wanted to smoke. But, judging from her frequent (albeit failed) attempts to quit, she also wanted *not to want* to smoke.

In this respect, it might be said, Rose Cipollone's history is representative of smokers more generally. The US Surgeon General reports that some 90 percent of regular smokers have tried and failed to quit. That recidivism rate has led the World Health Organization to rank nicotine as an addictive substance on a par with heroin itself.

That classification is richly confirmed by the stories that smokers themselves tell about their failed attempts to quit. Rose Cipollone tried to quit while pregnant, only to end up smoking an entire pack in the delivery room. She tried to quit once her cancer was diagnosed, and once again after her lung was taken out, even then only to end up sneaking an occasional smoke.

In cases like this—where people want to stop some activity, try to stop it but find that they cannot stop—public policy that helps them do so can hardly be said to be paternalistic in any morally offensive respect. It overrides people's preferences, to be sure. But the preferences which it overrides are ones which people themselves wish they did not have.

The preferences which it respects—the preferences to stop smoking (like preferences of reformed alcoholics to stay off drink, or of the obese to lose weight)—are, in contrast, preferences that the people concerned themselves prefer. They would themselves rank those preferences above their own occasional inclinations to backslide. In helping them to implement their own preferred preferences, we are only respecting people's own priorities.

Your own preferences

Finally, before automatically respecting people's choices, we ought to make sure that they are really their *own* choices. We respect people's choices because in that way we manifest respect for them as persons. But if the choices in question were literally someone else's—the results of a post-hypnotic suggestion, for example—then clearly there that logic would provide no reason for our respecting those preferences.

Some people say that the effects of advertising are rather like that. No doubt there is a certain informational content to advertising. But that is not all there is in it. When Rose Cipollone read the tar and nicotine content in advertisements, what she was getting was information. What she was getting when looking at the accompanying pictures of movie stars and glamorous, liberated women was something else altogether.

Using the power of subliminal suggestion, advertising implants preferences in people in a way that largely or wholly by-passes their judgment. Insofar as it does so, the resulting preferences are not authentically that person's own. And those implanted preferences are not entitled to the respect that is rightly reserved for a person's authentic preferences, in consequence.

Such thoughts might lead some to say that we should therefore ignore altogether advertising-induced preferences in framing our public policy. I demur. There is just too much force in the rejoinder that, "Wherever those preferences came from in the first instance, they are mine now." If we want our policies to respect people by (among other things) respecting their preferences, then we will have to respect all of those preferences with which people now associate themselves.

Even admitting the force of that rejoinder, though, there is much that still might be done to curb the preference-shaping activities of, for example, the tobacco industry. Even those who say "they're my preferences now" would presumably have preferred, ahead of time, to make up their own minds in the matter. So there we have a case, couched in terms of people's own (past) preferences, for severely restricting the advertising and promotion of products—especially ones which people will later regret having grown to like, but which they will later be unable to resist.

III. Conclusions

What, in practical policy terms, follows from all that? Well, in the case of smoking, which has served as my running example, we might ban the sale of tobacco altogether or turn it into a drug available only on prescription to registered users. Or, less dramatically, we might make cigarettes difficult and expensive to obtain—especially for youngsters, whose purchases are particularly price-sensitive. We might ban all promotional advertising of tobacco products, designed as it is to attract new users. We might prohibit smoking in all offices, restaurants, and other public places, thus making it harder for smokers to find a place to partake and providing a further inducement for them to quit.

All of those policies would be good for smokers themselves. They would enjoy a longer life expectancy and a higher quality of life if they stopped smoking. But that is to talk the language of interests rather than of rights and choices. In those latter terms, all those policies clearly go against smokers' manifest preferences, in one sense or another. Smokers want to keep smoking. They do not want to pay more or drive further to get their cigarettes. They want to be able to take comfort in advertisements constantly telling them how glamorous their smoking is.

In other more important senses, though, such policies can be justified even in terms of the preferences of smokers themselves. They do not want to die, as a quarter of them eventually will (and ten to fifteen years before their time) of smoking-related diseases; it is only false beliefs or wishful thinking that make smokers think that continued smoking is consistent with that desire not to avoid a premature death. At the moment they may think that the benefits of smoking outweigh the costs, but they will almost certainly revise that view once those costs are eventually sheeted home. The vast majority of smokers would like to stop smoking but, being addicted, find it very hard now to do so.

Like Rose Cipollone, certainly in her dying days and intermittently even from her early adulthood, most smokers themselves would say that they would have been better off never starting. Many even agree that they would welcome anything (like a workplace ban on smoking) that might now make them stop. Given the internally conflicting preferences here in play, smokers also harbor at one and the same time preferences pointing in the opposite direction; that is what might make helping them to stop seem unacceptably paternalistic. But in terms of other of their preferences—and ones that deserve clear precedence, at that—doing so is perfectly well warranted.

Smoking is unusual, perhaps, in presenting a case for permissible paternalism on all four of the fronts here canvassed. Most activities might qualify under only one or two of the headings. However, that may well be enough. My point here is not that paternalism is always permissible but merely that it may always be.

In the discourse of liberal democracies, the charge of paternalism is typically taken to be a knock-down objection to any policy. If I am right, that knee-jerk response is wrong. When confronted with the charge of paternalism, it should always be open to us to say, "Sure, this proposal is paternalistic—but is the paternalism in view permissible or impermissible, good or bad?" More often than not, I think we will find, paternalism might prove perfectly defensible along the lines sketched here.

Further Reading

Goodin, Robert E., "The Ethics of Smoking." *Ethics*, 99 (April 1989), 575–624.
Goodin, Robert E., *No Smoking: The Ethical Issues*, Chicago and London: University of Chicago Press, 1989.

Review and Discussion Questions

1. Goodin believes that public officials should refrain from paternalistic interference with you only if they are convinced that you are acting on relevant preferences, settled preferences, preferred preferences, and preferences that are your own. Do you agree with this principle? Explain why or why not.

2. Goodin argues that smoking presents a case for permissible paternalism on all four of the above points. Assess smoking in terms of each category of preferences.

3. Do cigarette smokers fully understand the risks of smoking? Do they voluntarily assume those risks? How important is cigarette advertising in encouraging people to smoke? Is such advertising manipulative or unfair?

4. Is cigarette smoking (always, sometimes, never) irrational? Explain your answer. Is the answer to this question relevant to the determination of a justifiable smoking policy?

5. How difficult is it to quit smoking? Are most cigarette smokers addicts? How, if at all, is the answer to these questions relevant to the permissibility of paternalistic anti-smoking policies?

6. How would you assess the overall costs and benefits of smoking, both to the individual and to society? Does Goodin overlook the pleasure smokers get from smoking?

7. Would the suppression of cigarette advertising be compatible with our society's commitment to freedom of expression?

8. Is it compatible with Mill's liberty principle for society to undertake to reduce or eliminate smoking? Should society pursue more aggressive policies to discourage or eliminate smoking? If so, what policies? Should over-the-counter cigarette sales be outlawed?

A Drug-Free America—or a Free America?

DAVID BOAZ

David Boaz, executive vice president of the Cato Institute, advocates the legalization of drugs. The "War on Drugs" has failed, he argues, because efforts to restrict the drug trade simply increase the financial incentives for drug dealers. But while drug prohibition has failed to curtail drug use, it has severely limited some fundamental American liberties and violated our fundamental right to live our lives in the way we choose. Unlike many advocates of drug liberalization, however, Boaz rejects the view that addiction is a disease, over which the individual has no control. Instead, he argues that we need to restore traditional notions of individual responsibility.

Study Questions

1. How does prohibition create financial incentives for drug dealers?
2. What are the prohibitionists' arguments against the presumption in favor of individual liberty?
3. What is the "disease concept of addiction"?
4. What evidence does Boaz advance to support the claim that there has been "a flight from individual responsibility" in recent decades?

Introduction: The Drug Problem

HUMAN BEINGS HAVE USED mind-altering substances throughout recorded history. Why? Perhaps because, as one acquaintance put it in a recent conversation, there is a God-shaped void in most people's lives. Perhaps because we fail to love one another as we should. Perhaps because of the social pressure for success. Perhaps because—and this is what really irks the prohibitionists—we enjoy drugs' mind-altering effects.

Though the reasons for drug use are numerous, the governmental response has been singular: almost as long as humans have used drugs, governments have tried to stop them. In the sixteenth century the Egyptian government banned coffee. In the seventeenth century the Czar of Russia and the Sultan of the Ottoman Empire executed tobacco smokers. In the eighteenth century England tried to halt gin consumption and China penalized opium sellers with strangulation.

The drug prohibition experiment most familiar to Americans is the prohibition of alcohol in the 1920s. The period has become notorious for the widespread illegal consumption of alcohol and the resultant crime. Movies such as *Some Like It Hot* typify the popular legend of the era. The failure of Prohibition, however, is not just legendary. Consumption of alcohol probably fell slightly at the beginning of Prohibition but then rose steadily throughout the period. Alcohol became more potent, and there were reportedly more illegal speakeasies than there had been legal saloons. More serious for nondrinkers, the per capita murder rate and the assault-by-firearm rate both rose throughout Prohibition.

Most of the same phenomena are occurring with today's prohibition of marijuana, cocaine, and heroin. Use of these drugs has risen and fallen during the seventy-seven years since Congress passed the Harrison Narcotics Act, with little relationship to the level of enforcement. In the past decade, the decade of the "War on Drugs," use of these drugs seems to have declined, but no faster than the decline in the use of the legal drugs alcohol and tobacco. Over the past twenty years Americans became more health- and fitness-conscious, and use of all drugs seems to have correspondingly decreased. Drug prohibition, however, has not stopped twenty-three million people from trying cocaine and seventy-two million people from trying marijuana. Prohibition also has not stopped the number of heroin users from increasing by one hundred fifty percent and the number of cocaine users from increasing by ten thousand percent. Moreover, prohibition has not kept drugs out of the hands of children: in 1999 fifty-five percent of high school seniors admitted to having tried illicit drugs; eighty-nine percent said it was fairly easy or very easy to obtain marijuana; and forty-four percent said the same about cocaine.

Although drug prohibition has not curtailed drug use, it has severely limited some fundamental American liberties. Programs such as "Zero Tolerance," which advocates seizing a car or boat on the mere allegation of a law enforcement official that the vehicle contains drugs, ignore the constitutional principle that a person is innocent until proven guilty.

In attempting to fashion a solution to "the drug problem," one first needs to define the problem society is trying to solve. If the problem is the age-old human instinct to use mind-altering substances, then the solution might be God, or evolution, or stronger families, or Alco-

holics Anonymous. History suggests, however, that the solution is unlikely to be found in the halls of Congress. If, on the other hand, the problem is the soaring murder rate, the destruction of inner-city communities, the creation of a criminal subculture, and the fear millions of Americans experience on their own streets, then a solution may well be found in Congress—not in the creation of laws but in their repeal.

This article proposes that the repeal of certain laws will force individuals to take responsibility for their actions; the repeal of other laws will provide individuals the right to make important decisions in their lives free from outside interference. Together these changes will create the society in which drugs can, and must, be legalized. Legalization of drugs, in turn, will end the need for the government to make the intrusions into our fundamental rights as it does so often in its War on Drugs.

I. The Futility of Prohibition

A. The War on Drugs

Prohibition of drugs is not the solution to the drug problem. For the past twenty years the United States has waged a "War on Drugs." The goals of this War were simple: prohibit the cultivation or manufacture of drugs, prohibit the import of drugs, and prohibit the use of drugs. As the aforementioned statistics demonstrate, the War has not achieved its goals.

Prohibitionists, however, sometimes claim that the United States has not yet "really fought a drug war." The prohibitionists argue that a "true drug war" would sharply lower drug use. They feel that the government has not fully committed itself to winning this battle. One need only look at the War on Drugs' record, however, to see the commitment:

• Congress passed stricter anti-drug laws in 1984, 1986, 1988, 1994, and 1998. Congress and state legislators steadily increased penalties for drug law violations, mandating jail time even for first offenders, imposing large civil fines, seizing property, denying federal benefits to drug law violators, and evicting tenants from public housing.

- Federal drug war outlays increased by more than 1150% between 1981 and 1999, and the federal government spent more than $75 billion on anti-drug activities during the last five years. Adjusted for inflation, the federal government spends twenty-five times as much on drug law enforcement every year as it spent on Prohibition enforcement throughout the Roaring Twenties.

- Police officers made more than 1.5 million drug law arrests in 1999, about eighty percent of them for drug possession.

- The number of drug busts tripled during the 1980s, and the number of convictions doubled. Arrests continued to rise throughout the 1990s, and the average sentence for drug offenses nearly doubled.

- America's prison population quadrupled between 1981 and 1999, from 344,283 to 1,366,721. More than six million people were on probation, in jail or prison, or on parole at year end 1999—3.1 percent of all U.S. adult residents. On December 31, 1999, state prisons were operating at between one percent and seventeen percent above capacity, while federal prisons were operating at thirty-two percent above capacity. More prisoners are in jail for nonviolent drug law violations than ever before.

- The armed services, Coast Guard, and Civil Air Patrol became more active in the drug fight, providing search and pursuit planes, helicopters, ocean interdiction, and radar. Defense Department spending on the War on Drugs rose from $200 million in 1988 to $800 million in 1990.

- The Central Intelligence Agency (CIA) and National Security Agency began using spy satellites and communications listening technology as part of the drug war. The CIA also designed a special Counter Narcotics Center.

- The federal government forced drug testing upon public employees and required contractors to establish "drug-free" workplaces. Drug testing has also expanded among private companies.

- Seizures of cocaine rose from 2,000 kilograms in 1981 to 120,034 kilograms in 1998.

Despite this enormous effort, drugs are more readily available than ever before. The War on Drugs has failed to achieve its primary goal of diminishing the availability and use of drugs.

B. Prohibition creates financial incentives

One reason for the failure of the War on Drugs is that it ignores the fact that prohibition sets up tremendous financial incentives for drug dealers to supply the demand. Prohibition, at least initially, reduces the supply of the prohibited substance and thus raises the price. In addition, a large risk premium is added onto the price. One has to pay a painter more to paint the Golden Gate Bridge than to paint a house because of the added danger. Similarly, drug dealers demand more money to sell cocaine than to sell alcohol. Those who are willing to accept the risk of arrest or murder will be handsomely—sometimes unbelievably—rewarded.

Drug dealers, therefore, whatever one may think of them morally, are actually profit-seeking entrepreneurs. Drug researcher James Ostrowski points out that "[t]he public has the false impression that drug enforcers are highly innovative, continually devising new schemes to catch drug dealers. Actually, the reverse is true. The dealers, like successful businessmen, are usually one step ahead of the 'competition.'"[1]

New examples of the drug dealers' entrepreneurial skills appear every day. For example, partly because the Supreme Court upheld surveillance flights over private property to look for marijuana fields, marijuana growers have been moving indoors and underground. The

Drug Enforcement Administration seized about 130 indoor marijuana gardens in California in 1989. In 1999 they seized 1,048 gardens, or 87,019 plants.

Overseas exporters have also been showing off their entrepreneurial skills. Some have been sending drugs into the United States in the luggage of children traveling alone, on the assumption that authorities will not suspect children and will go easy on them if they are caught. Others have concealed drugs in anchovy cans, bean-sprout washing machines, fuel tanks, and T-shirts. At least one man surgically implanted a pound of cocaine in his thighs. Some smugglers swallow drugs before getting on international flights. Professor Ethan Nadelmann has explained the spread of overseas exporters as the "push-down/pop-up factor": push down drug production in one country, and it will pop up in another.[2] For example, Nadelmann notes that "Colombian marijuana growers rapidly expanded production following successful eradication efforts in Mexico during the mid-1970s. Today, Mexican growers are rapidly taking advantage of recent Colombian government successes in eradicating marijuana."

Prohibition of drugs creates tremendous profit incentives. In turn, the profit incentives induce drug manufacturers and dealers to creatively stay one step ahead of the drug enforcement officials. The profit incentives show the futility of eradication, interdiction, and enforcement and make one question whether prohibition will ever be successful. . . .

II. Individual Rights

Many of the drug enforcement ideas the prohibitionists suggest trample upon numerous constitutional and natural rights. In any discussion of government policies, it is necessary to examine the effect on natural rights for one simple reason: individuals have rights that governments may not violate. In the Declaration of Independence, Thomas Jefferson defined these rights as life, liberty, and the pursuit of happiness. I argue that these inviolable rights can actually be classified as one fundamental right: individuals have the right to live their lives in any way they choose so long as they do not violate the equal rights of others. To put this idea in the drug context, what right could be more basic, more inherent in human nature, than the right to choose what substances to put in one's own body? Whether it is alcohol, tobacco, laetrile, AZT, saturated fat, or cocaine, this is a decision that the individual should make, not the government. This point seems so obvious to me that it is, to borrow Jefferson's words, self-evident.

The prohibitionists, however, fail to recognize this fundamental freedom. They advance several arguments in an effort to rebut the presumption in favor of liberty. First, they argue, drug users are responsible for the violence of the drug trade and the resulting damage to innocent people. The erstwhile Drug Czar, William Bennett, when asked how his nicotine addiction differed from a drug addiction, responded, "I didn't do any drive-by shootings."[3] Similarly, former First Lady Nancy Reagan said, "The casual user may think when he takes a line of cocaine or smokes a joint in the privacy of his nice condo, listening to his expensive stereo, that he's somehow not bothering anyone. But there is a trail of death and destruction that leads directly to his door. I'm saying that if you're a casual drug user, you are an accomplice to murder."[4]

The comments of both Mr. Bennett and Mrs. Reagan, however, display a remarkable ignorance about the illegal-drug business. Drug use does not cause violence. Alcohol did not cause the violence of the 1920s, Prohibition did. Similarly, drugs do not cause today's soaring murder rates, drug prohibition does. The chain of events is obvious: drug laws reduce the supply and raise the price of drugs. The high price causes addicts to commit crimes to pay for a habit that would be easily affordable if obtaining drugs was legal. The illegality of the business means that business disputes—between customers and suppliers or between rival suppliers—can be settled only through violence, not through the courts. The violence of the business then draws in those who have a propensity—or what economists call a comparative advantage—for violence. When Congress repealed Prohibition, the violence went out of the liquor business. Similarly, when Congress repeals drug prohibition, the heroin and cocaine trade will cease to be violent. As columnist Stephen Chapman put it, "the real accomplices to murder" are those responsible for the laws that make the drug business violent.[5]

Another prohibitionist argument against the right to take drugs is that drug use affects others, such as automobile accident victims and crack babies. With regard to the former, certainly good reasons exist to strictly penalize driving (as well as flying or operating machinery) while under the influence of drugs. It hardly seems appropriate, however, to penalize those who use drugs safely in an attempt to stop the unsafe usage. As for harm to babies, this is a heart-rending problem (though perhaps not as large a problem as is sometimes believed). Again, however, it seems unnecessary and unfair to ban a recreational drug just because it should not be used during pregnancy. Moreover, drug-affected babies have one point in common with driving under the influence: misuse of legal drugs (alcohol, tobacco, codeine, caffeine), as well as illegal drugs, contributes to both problems. Thus, if society wants to ban cocaine and marijuana because of these drugs' potential for misuse, society should logically also ban alcohol, tobacco, and similar legal drugs.

The question of an individual right to use drugs comes down to this: if the government can tell us what we can put into our own bodies, what can it not tell us? What limits on government action are there? We would do well to remember Jefferson's advice: "Was the government to prescribe to us our medicine and diet, our bodies would be in such keeping as our souls are now."[6]

III. The Solution: Re-establish Individual Responsibility

For the past several decades a flight from individual responsibility has taken place in the United States. Intellectuals, often government funded, have concocted a whole array of explanations as to why nothing that happens to us is our own fault. These intellectuals tell us that the poor are not responsible for their poverty, the fat are not responsible for their overeating, the alcoholic are not responsible for their drinking. Any attempt to suggest that people are sometimes responsible for their own failures is denounced as "blaming the victim."

These nonresponsibility attitudes are particularly common in discussions of alcohol, tobacco, and other drugs. Development of these attitudes probably began in the 1930s with the formulation of the classic disease theory of alcoholism. The disease theory holds that alcoholism is a disease that the alcoholic cannot control. People have found it easy to apply the theory of addiction to tobacco, cocaine, heroin, even marijuana. In each case, according to the theory, people get "hooked" and simply cannot control their use. Author Herbert Fingarette, however, stated that "*no* leading research authorities accept the classic disease concept [for alcoholism]."[7] Many scientists, though, believe it is appropriate to mislead the public about the nature of alcoholism in order to induce what they see as the right behavior with regard to alcohol.

In the popular press the addiction theory has spread rapidly. Popular magazines declare everything from sex to shopping to video games an addiction that the addicted person has no power to control. As William Wilbanks said, the phrase "I can't help myself" has become the all-purpose excuse of our time.[8]

The addiction theory has also gained prominence in discussions of illegal drugs. Both prohibitionists and legalizers tend to be enamored of the classic notion of addiction. Prohibitionists say that because people cannot help themselves with respect to addictive drugs, society must threaten them with criminal sanctions to protect them from their own failings. Legalizers offer instead a "medical model": treat drug use as a disease, not a crime. The legalizers urge that the billions of dollars currently spent on drug enforcement be transferred to treatment programs so that government can supply "treatment on demand" for drug addicts.

Despite the popular affection for the addiction theory, numerous commentators denounce the theory. For example, addiction researcher Stanton Peele deplores the effects of telling people that addictive behavior is uncontrollable:

> [O]ne of the best antidotes to addiction is to teach children responsibility and respect for others and to insist on ethical standards for everyone—children, adults, addicts. Crosscultural data indicate, for instance, that when an experience is defined as uncontrollable, many people experience such loss of control and use it to justify their transgressions against society. For example, studies find that the "uncontrollable" consequences of alcohol consumption vary from one society to another, depending upon cultural expectations.[9]

Spreading the disease concept of addiction is not the only way society has undermined the idea of individual responsibility. Some of the other ways have had their greatest impact on America's poorest citizens. For example, author Charles Murray points out that in the 1960s policymakers and opinion molders were seized with the grand idea that poverty could and should be eliminated in the United States.[10] One of the policymakers' first steps was to tell the poor that their poverty was not their own fault. Seeking to eliminate the "stigma" attached to poverty, the policymakers made welfare easier to get. They made it more difficult to throw disruptive or uncooperative students out of school, and they made it more difficult to put criminals in jail. As a result, America ended up with more people on welfare, fewer students learning in the schools, and more crime.

By reducing society's disapproval of people who do not study, do not work, and do not meet their obligations to family and community, the policymakers took away the respectability formerly accorded to those who do study, do work, and do meet their obligations. As Murray wrote, the intelligentsia and the policymakers began treating the poor "in ways that they would never consider treating people they respected."[11]

Recently, Murray has extended his analysis in a penetrating discussion of the drug problem.[12] He cites numerous examples in which the government has taken from people the power to do something about drugs in their own lives. First, in an attempt to prevent school principals from using their power in an arbitrary or racially discriminatory manner, the government has made it very difficult for principals to expel students for disruptive behavior or drug use. Second, legislatures and courts are making it increasingly difficult for employers to dismiss employees: wrongful-discharge suits and federal investigations have replaced the old doctrine of employment at will. Finally, the government has made it more burdensome for landlords to maintain standards in their buildings by taking away the landlords' power to decide—albeit sometimes arbitrarily—to whom to rent and whom to turn away.

Murray proposes solutions designed to give individuals more control over their own lives: school vouchers to allow parents to choose the schools their children will attend, with the schools free to set their own relaxed or zero-tolerance policies toward drugs; freedom for workers and employers to decide on the conditions of employment with regard to drug use without interference from courts and governments; wide discretion for landlords (and tenant committees in public housing) to screen applicants. Murray's basic argument is that "legalization [of drugs will] work in a society where people are held responsible for the consequences of their actions."[13]

. . . Americans might take other steps to restore traditional notions of individual responsibility. Laws regarding drugs should only punish persons who violate the rights of others; private actions should go unpunished. Thus, laws should strictly punish those who drive while under the influence of alcohol or other drugs. Intoxication, moreover, should not be a legal defense against charges of theft, violence, or other rights violations, nor should a claim of "shopping addiction" excuse people from having to pay their debts. Physicians, intellectuals, and religious leaders should recognize that the denial of responsibility has gone too far, and they should begin to stress the moral value of individual responsibility, the self-respect such responsibility brings, and the utilitarian benefits of living in a society in which all persons are held responsible for the consequences of their actions.

Conclusion

Society cannot really make war on drugs, which are just chemical substances. Society can only wage wars against people, in this case people who use and sell drugs. Before America continues a war that has cost many billions of dollars and many thousands of lives—more than eight thousand lives per year even before the skyrocketing murder rates of the late 1980s—Americans should be sure that the benefits exceed the costs. Remarkably, all of the high- ranking officers in the Reagan administration's drug war reported in 1988 that they knew of no studies showing that the benefits of prohibition exceeded the costs.

There is a good reason for the lack of such a study. Prohibition is futile. We cannot win the War on Drugs. We cannot even keep drugs out of our prisons. Thus, we could turn the United States into a police state, and we still would not win the War on Drugs. The costs of prohibition, however, are very real: tens of billions of dollars a year, corruption of law enforcement officials, civil liberties abuses, the destruction of inner-city communities, black-market murders, murders incident to street crime by addicts seeking to pay for their habit, and the growing sense that our major cities are places of uncontrollable violence.

Hundreds, perhaps thousands, of years of history teach us that we will never make our society drug-free. In the futile attempt to do so, however, we may well make our society unfree.

NOTES

1. Ostrowski, "Thinking About Drug Legalization," 121 *Policy Analysis,* May 25, 1989, at 34. . . .

2. Nadelmann, "The Case for Legalization," 92 *Public Interest* 3, 9 (1988). . . .

3. Isikoff, "Bennett Rebuts Drug Legalization Ideas," *Washington Post,* Dec. 12, 1989, at A10, col. 1.

4. Chapman, "Nancy Reagan and the Real Villains in the Drug War," *Chicago Tribune,* March 6, 1988, sec. 4, at 3, col. 1. . . .

5. Chapman, *supra* note 4.

6. T. Jefferson, "Notes on Virginia," in *The Life and Selected Writings of Thomas Jefferson* 187, 275 (1944).

7. H. Fingarette, *Heavy Drinking* at 3 (1988). . . .

8. Wilbanks, "The New Obscenity," 54 *Vital Speeches of the Day* 658, 658–59 (1988).

9. S. Peele, "Control Yourself," *Reason,* Feb. 1990, at 25.

10. C. Murray, *Losing Ground: American Social Policy, 1950–1980* 26–29, 42 (1984). . . .

11. *Id.* at 222.

12. Murray, "How to Win the War on Drugs," *New Republic,* May 21, 1990, at 19, 19–25.

13. *Id.* at 19.

Review and Discussion Questions

1. Is Boaz correct in saying that the war on drugs is futile? How persuasive is the analogy with alcohol prohibition in the 1920s?

2. Do you agree with Boaz that people have a fundamental right to ingest whatever substances they choose?

3. Opponents of drug legalization point to the undeniable social costs of drug abuse and to the enormous harm it causes individuals. Has Boaz effectively addressed these concerns about the dangers of drug abuse?

4. In what ways does Boaz's essay appeal to both utilitarian and nonutilitarian (or Kantian) considerations? Which of Boaz's points do you find the strongest? Which is the weakest?

5. In a previous essay, Gerald Dworkin presented a rationale for paternalistic drug laws that seems to square with the central concerns of John Stuart Mill's *On Liberty*. What is Boaz's view of addiction, and how would he respond to Dworkin's argument?

6. Boaz's point about the financial incentives created by prohibition seems to assume that drug use is price inelastic—that is, that drug users will keep on paying ever higher prices. Presumably, they will pay more because they are addicted to the drugs. But if, in fact, the demand for drugs depends on addiction, is Boaz's focus on individual responsibility undercut?

7. In the previous essay, Robert E. Goodin defended paternalism in the case of smoking by critically examining the character of smokers' preferences. Apply his arguments to the drugs that Boaz wants to legalize. How strong are those arguments, and how might Boaz respond to them?

If He Hollers Let Him Go: Regulating Racist Speech on Campus

CHARLES R. LAWRENCE III

John Stuart Mill's *On Liberty* makes a compelling case for unabridged freedom of expression, and the First Amendment to the U.S. Constitution enshrines free speech as a cardinal value of our political system. In recent years, however, incidents of racially abusive speech on college campuses have instigated a debate over the exact limits of freedom of expression. Some colleges and universities have adopted regulations forbidding racist speech; others have resisted these sorts of regulations, regarding them as a violation of the principle of free expression. Charles R. Lawrence, professor of law at Stanford University, is sensitive to the conflicting values at stake in this debate, but he argues that racist insults—like so-called "fighting words"—are not constitutionally protected. In addition, racist speech reduces the total amount of speech entering the marketplace of ideas. Emphasizing the importance of listening to

From Duke Law Journal, *vol. 1990, no. 2. Copyright © 1990 Charles R. Lawrence III. Reprinted by permission of the author and* Duke Law Journal. *Most footnotes omitted. The full text of this essay appears in Matsuda, Lawrence, et al.,* "Fighting Words": Critical Perspectives on Hate Speech and the First Amendment *(Boulder, Colo.: Westview Press, 1992).*

the victims of racist speech, Lawrence describes the genuine harms that it causes African Americans and other subordinated groups—harms that are too readily over-looked when we decide to tolerate racist speech.

Study Questions

1. What are the "very strong reasons for protecting even racist speech"?

2. What two reasons does Lawrence give to support the view that face-to-face racial insults are undeserving of First Amendment protection?

3. What point does the experience of the gay student, Michael, illuminate?

4. What point is illustrated by the reactions of whites to the racist incident in Wilmington?

5. Why does Lawrence find it misleading to cast the debate in terms of "offensive" speech?

6. How does racist speech distort the marketplace of ideas?

Introduction

IN RECENT YEARS, American campuses have seen a resurgence of racial violence and a corre-sponding rise in the incidence of verbal and symbolic assault and harassment to which blacks and other traditionally subjugated groups are subjected. There is a heated debate in the civil liberties community concerning the proper re-sponse to incidents of racist speech on campus. Strong disagreements have arisen between those individuals who believe that racist speech . . . should be regulated by the university or some public body and those individuals who believe that racist expression should be protected from all public regulation. At the center of the con-troversy is a tension between the constitutional values of free speech and equality. Like the debate over affirmative action in university ad-missions, this issue has divided old allies and re-vealed unrecognized or unacknowledged differ-ences in the experience, perceptions, and values of members of long-standing alliances. It also has caused considerable soul-searching by indi-viduals with long-time commitments to both the cause of political expression and the cause of racial equality.

I write this article from within the cauldron of this controversy. I make no pretense of

dispassion or objectivity, but I do claim a deep commitment to the values that motivate both sides of the debate. As I struggle with the ten-sion between these constitutional values, I par-ticularly appreciate the experience of both be-longing and not belonging that gives to African Americans and other outsider groups a sense of duality. W. E. B. Du Bois—scholar and founder of the National Association for the Advance-ment of Colored People—called the gift and burden inherent to the dual, conflicting heritage of all African Americans their "second-sight."[1]

The "double consciousness" of groups out-side the ethnic mainstream is particularly appar-ent in the context of this controversy. Blacks know and value the protection the first amend-ment affords those of us who must rely upon our voices to petition both government and our neighbors for redress of grievances. Our politi-cal tradition has looked to "the word," to the moral power of ideas, to change a system when neither the power of the vote nor that of the gun are available. This part of us has known the experience of belonging and recognizes our common and inseparable interest in preserving the right of free speech for all. But we also know the experience of the outsider. The Framers ex-cluded us from the protection of the first amendment.* The same Constitution that established rights for others endorsed a story that proclaimed our inferiority. It is a story that remains deeply ingrained in the American psyche.

We see a different world than that which is seen by Americans who do not share this historical experience. We often hear racist speech when our white neighbors are not aware of its presence.†

It is not my purpose to belittle or trivialize the importance of defending unpopular speech against the tyranny of the majority. There are very strong reasons for protecting even racist speech. Perhaps the most important reasons are that it reinforces our society's commitment to the value of tolerance, and that, by shielding racist speech from government regulation, we will be forced to combat it as a community. These reasons for protecting racist speech should not be set aside hastily, and I will not argue that we should be less vigilant in protecting the speech and associational rights of speakers with whom most of us would disagree.

But I am deeply concerned about the role that many civil libertarians have played, or the roles we have failed to play, in the continuing, real-life struggle through which we define the community in which we live. I fear that by framing the debate as we have—as one in which the liberty of free speech is in conflict with the elimination of racism—we have advanced the cause of racial oppression and have placed the bigot on the moral high ground, fanning the rising flames of racism. Above all, I am troubled that we have

not listened to the real victims, that we have shown so little empathy or understanding for their injury, and that we have abandoned those individuals whose race, gender, or sexual orientation provokes others to regard them as second class citizens. These individuals' civil liberties are most directly at stake in the debate. . . .

Racist Speech as the Functional Equivalent of Fighting Words

Much recent debate over the efficacy of regulating racist speech has focused on the efforts by colleges and universities to respond to the burgeoning incidents of racial harassment on their campuses. At Stanford, where I teach, there has been considerable controversy over the questions whether racist and other discriminatory verbal harassment should be regulated and what form that regulation should take. Proponents of regulation have been sensitive to the danger of inhibiting expression, and the current regulation (which was drafted by my colleague Tom Grey) manifests that sensitivity. . . .

This regulation and others like it have been characterized in the press as the work of "thought police," but it does nothing more than prohibit intentional face-to-face insults, a form of speech that is unprotected by the first amendment. When racist speech takes the form of face-to-face insults, catcalls, or other assaultive speech aimed at an individual or small group of persons, then it falls within the "fighting words" exception to first amendment protection.‡ The

---

*In *Dred Scott* v. *Sanford,* 60 U.S. (19 How.) 393 (1857), the Court declared that at the time of the Declaration of Independence, and when the Constitution of the United States was framed and adopted "[blacks] had no rights which the white man was bound to respect." . . .

†*See* Matsuda, "Public Response to Racist Speech: Considering the Victim's Story," 87 *Mich. L. Rev.* 2320 (1989). Matsuda points out that the "mainstream press often ignores these stories [of racist speech and violence], giving rise to the view of racist and anti-Semitic incidents as random and isolated, and the corollary that isolated incidents are inconsequential." *Id.* at 2331.

‡The fighting words doctrine requires that the words be "directed to the person of the hearer." *Cohen* v. *California,* 403 U.S. 15, 20 (1971). This requirement strikes a balance between our concern for protecting the individual from unavoidable personalized attack (one is not given an opportunity to avoid the speech by averting the eyes or leaving the room) and our concern for allowing space for even the most offensive speech in a public forum ("one man's vulgarity is another's lyric," *id.* at 25). I would argue that the face-to-face requirement be expanded in the case of racist verbal assaults to include those words that are intentionally spoken in the presence of members of the denigrated group. . . .

Supreme Court has held that words that "by their very utterance inflict injury or tend to incite an immediate breach of the peace"[2] are not constitutionally protected.

Face-to-face racial insults, like fighting words, are undeserving of first amendment protection for two reasons. The first reason is the immediacy of the injurious impact of racial insults. The experience of being called "nigger," "spic," "Jap," or "kike" is like receiving a slap in the face. The injury is instantaneous. There is neither an opportunity for intermediary reflection on the idea conveyed nor an opportunity for responsive speech. The harm to be avoided is both clear and present. The second reason that racial insults should not fall under protected speech relates to the purpose underlying the first amendment. If the purpose of the first amendment is to foster the greatest amount of speech, then racial insults disserve that purpose. Assaultive racist speech functions as a preemptive strike. The racial invective is experienced as a blow, not a proffered idea, and once the blow is struck, it is unlikely that dialogue will follow. Racial insults are undeserving of first amendment protection because the perpetrator's intention is not to discover truth or initiate dialogue but to injure the victim.

The fighting words doctrine anticipates that the verbal "slap in the face" of insulting words will provoke a violent response with a resulting breach of the peace. When racial insults are hurled at minorities, the response may be silence or flight rather than a fight, but the preemptive effect on further speech is just as complete as with fighting words. Women and minorities often report that they find themselves speechless in the face of discriminatory verbal attacks. This inability to respond is not the result of oversensitivity among these groups, as some individuals who oppose protective regulation have argued. Rather, it is the product of several factors, all of which reveal the non-speech character of the initial preemptive verbal assault. The first factor is that the visceral emotional response to personal attack precludes speech. Attack produces an instinctive, defensive psychological reaction. Fear, rage, shock, and flight all interfere with any reasoned response. Words like "nigger," "kike," and "faggot" produce physical symptoms that temporarily disable the victim, and the perpetrators often use these words with the intention of producing this effect. Many victims do not find words of response until well after the assault when the cowardly assaulter has departed.

A second factor that distinguishes racial insults from protected speech is the preemptive nature of such insults—the words by which to respond to such verbal attacks may never be forthcoming because speech is usually an inadequate response. When one is personally attacked with words that denote one's subhuman status and untouchability, there is little (if anything) that can be said to redress either the emotional or reputational injury. This is particularly true when the message and meaning of the epithet resonates with beliefs widely held in society. This preservation of widespread beliefs is what makes the face-to-face racial attack more likely to preempt speech than are other fighting words. The racist name-caller is accompanied by a cultural chorus of equally demeaning speech and symbols.

The subordinated victim of fighting words also is silenced by her relatively powerless position in society. Because of the significance of power and position, the categorization of racial epithets as "fighting words" provides an inadequate paradigm; instead one must speak of their "functional equivalent." The fighting words doctrine presupposes an encounter between two persons of relatively equal power who have been acculturated to respond to face-to-face insults with violence. The fighting words doctrine is a paradigm based on a white male point of view. In most situations, minorities correctly perceive that a violent response to fighting words will result in a risk to their own life and limb. Since minorities are likely to lose the fight, they are forced to remain silent and submissive. This response is most obvious when women submit to sexually assaultive speech or when the racist name-caller is in a more powerful position—the boss on the job or the mob. . . .

One of my students, a white, gay male, related an experience that is quite instructive in understanding the inadequacy and potential of the fighting words doctrine. In response to my request that students describe how they experienced the injury of racist speech, Michael told a story of being called "faggot" by a man on a subway. His description included all of the speech inhibiting elements I have noted previously. He found himself in a state of semi-shock, nauseous, dizzy, unable to muster the witty, sarcastic, articulate rejoinder he was accustomed to making. He suddenly was aware of the recent spate of gay-bashing in San Francisco, and how many of these had escalated from verbal encounters. Even hours later when the shock receded and his facility with words returned, he realized that any response was inadequate to counter the hundreds of years of societal defamation that one word—"faggot"—carried with it. Like the word "nigger" and unlike the word "liar," it is not sufficient to deny the truth of the word's application, to say, "I am not a faggot." One must deny the truth of the word's meaning, a meaning shouted from the rooftops by the rest of the world a million times a day. Although there are many of us who constantly and in myriad ways seek to counter the lie spoken in the meaning of hateful words like "nigger" and "faggot," it is a nearly impossible burden to bear when one encounters hateful speech face-to-face.

But there was another part of my discussion with Michael that is equally instructive. I asked if he could remember a situation when he had been verbally attacked with reference to his membership in a superordinate group. Had he ever been called a "honkie," a "chauvinist pig," or "mick"? (Michael is from a working class Irish family in Boston.) He said that he had been called some version of all three and that al-

though he found the last one more offensive than the first two, he had not experienced—even in that subordinated role—the same disorienting powerlessness he had experienced when attacked for his membership in the gay community. The question of power, of the context of the power relationships within which speech takes place, must be considered as we decide how best to foster the freest and fullest dialogue within our communities. It is apparent that regulation of face-to-face verbal assault in the manner contemplated by the Stanford provision will make room for more speech than it chills. The provision is clearly within the spirit, if not the letter, of existing first amendment doctrine. . . .

Knowing the Injury and Striking the Balance: Understanding What Is at Stake in Racist Speech Cases

. . . The argument most commonly advanced against the regulation of racist speech goes something like this: We recognize that minority groups suffer pain and injury as the result of racist speech, but we must allow this hatemongering for the benefit of society as a whole. Freedom of speech is the lifeblood of our democratic system. It is a freedom that enables us to persuade others to our point of view. Free speech is especially important for minorities because often it is their only vehicle for rallying support for redress of their grievances. We cannot allow the public regulation of racist invective and vilification because any prohibition precise enough to prevent racist speech would catch in the same net forms of speech that are central to a democratic society. . . .

Understanding the injury inflicted by racist speech

There can be no meaningful discussion about how to reconcile our commitment to equality and our commitment to free speech until we acknowledge that racist speech inflicts real harm and that this harm is far from trivial. I should state that more strongly: To engage in a debate about the first amendment and racist speech without a full understanding of the nature and extent of the harm of racist speech risks making the first amendment an instrument of domination rather than a vehicle of liberation. Not everyone has known the experience of being victimized by racist, misogynist, and homophobic speech, and we do not share equally the burden of the societal harm it inflicts. Often we are too quick to say we have heard the victims' cries when we have not; we are too eager to assure ourselves we have experienced the same injury, and therefore we can make the constitutional balance without danger of mismeasurement. For many of us who have fought for the rights of oppressed minorities, it is difficult to accept that—by underestimating the injury from racist speech—we too might be implicated in the vicious words we would never utter. Until we have eradicated racism and sexism and no longer share in the fruits of those forms of domination, we cannot justly strike the balance over the protest of those who are dominated. My plea is simply that we listen to the victims.

Members of my own family were involved in a recent incident at a private school in Wilmington, Delaware that taught me much about both the nature of the injury racist speech inflicts and the lack of understanding many whites have of that injury.

As a good Quaker school dedicated to a deep commitment to and loving concern for all the members of its community, Wilmington Friends School also had been a haven for white families fleeing the court ordered desegregation of the Wilmington public schools. In recent years, the school strove to meet its commitment to human equality by enrolling a small (but significant) group of minority students and hiring an even smaller number of black faculty and staff. My sister Paula, a gifted, passionate, and dedicated teacher, was the principal of the lower school. Her sons attend the high school. My brother-

in-law, John, teaches geology at the University of Delaware. He is a strong, quiet, loving man, and he is white. My sister's family had moved to Wilmington shouldering the extra burdens and anxieties borne by an interracial family moving to a town where, not long ago, the defamatory message of segregation graced the doors of bathrooms and restaurants. Within a year they had made their place as well-loved and respected members of the community, particularly the school community, where Paula was viewed as a godsend and my nephews had made many good friends.

In May of their second year in Wilmington, an incident occurred that shook the entire school community but was particularly painful to my sister's family and others who found themselves the objects of hateful speech. In a letter to the school community explaining a decision to expel four students, the school's headmaster described the incident as follows:

> On Sunday evening, May 1, four students in the senior class met by prearrangement to paint the soccer kickboard, a flat rectangular structure, approximately 8 ft. by 25 ft., standing in the midst of the Wilmington Friends School playing fields. They worked for approximately one hour under bright moonlight and then went home.
>
> What confronted students and staff the following morning, depicted on the kickboard, were racist and anti-Semitic slogans and, most disturbing of all, threats of violent assault against one clearly identified member of the senior class. The slogans written on the kickboard included "Save the land, join the Klan," and "Down with Jews"; among the drawings were at least twelve hooded Ku Klux Klansmen, Nazi swastikas, and a burning cross. The most frightening and disturbing depictions, however, were those that threatened violence against one of our senior black students. He was drawn, in cartoon figure, identified by his name, and his initials, and by the name of his mother. Directly to the right of his head was a bullet, and farther to the right was a gun with

its barrel directed toward the head. Under the drawing of the student, three Ku Klux Klansmen were depicted, one of whom was saying that the student "dies." Next to the gun was a drawing of a burning cross under which was written "Kill the Tarbaby."

When I visited my sister's family a few days after this incident, the injury they had suffered was evident. The wounds were fresh. My sister, a care-giver by nature and vocation, was clearly in need of care. My nephews were quiet. Their faces betrayed the aftershock of a recently inflicted blow and a newly discovered vulnerability. I knew the pain and scars were no less enduring because the injury had not been physical. And when I talked to my sister, I realized the greatest part of her pain came not from the incident itself but rather from the reaction of white parents who had come to the school in unprecedented numbers to protest the offending students' expulsion. "It was only a prank." "No one was physically attacked." "How can you punish these kids for mere words, mere drawings." Paula's pain was compounded by the failure of these people, with whom she had lived and worked, to recognize that she had been hurt, to understand in even the most limited way the reality of her pain and that of her family.

Many people called the incident "isolated." But black folks know that no racial incident is "isolated" in America. That is what makes the incidents so horrible, so scary. It is the knowledge that they are not the isolated unpopular speech of a dissident few that makes them so frightening. These incidents are manifestations of an ubiquitous and deeply ingrained cultural belief system, an American way of life. Too often in recent months, as I have debated this issue with friends and colleagues, I have heard people speak of the need to protect "offensive" speech. The word offensive is used as if we were speaking of a difference in taste, as if I should learn to be less sensitive to words that "offend" me. I cannot help but believe that those people who speak of offense—those who argue that

this speech must go unchecked—do not understand the great difference between offense and injury: They have not known the injury my sister experienced, have not known the fear, vulnerability, and shame. . . . There is a great difference between the offensiveness of words that you would rather not hear—because they are labeled dirty, impolite, or personally demeaning—and the *injury* inflicted by words that remind the world that you are fair game for physical attack, evoke in you all of the millions of cultural lessons regarding your inferiority that you have so painstakingly repressed, and imprint upon you a badge of servitude and subservience for all the world to see. . . .

The other side of the balance: does the suppression of racial epithets weigh for or against speech?

. . . Blacks and other people of color are . . . skeptical about the absolutist argument that even the most injurious speech must remain unregulated because in an unregulated marketplace of ideas the best ideas will rise to the top and gain acceptance. Our experience tells us the opposite. We have seen too many demagogues elected by appealing to America's racism. We have seen too many good, liberal politicians shy away from the issues that might brand them as too closely allied with us. The American marketplace of ideas was founded with the idea of the racial inferiority of non-whites as one of its chief commodities, and ever since the market opened, racism has remained its most active item in trade.*

But it is not just the prevalence and strength of the idea of racism that makes the unregulated marketplace of ideas an untenable paradigm for those individuals who seek full and equal personhood for all. The real problem is that the

See Lawrence, [39 *Stan. L. Rev.* (1987)], at 330 ("[Racism] is a part of our common historical experience and, therefore, a part of our culture. . . . We attach significance to race even when we are not aware that we are doing so. . . . Racism's universality renders it normal").

idea of the racial inferiority of non-whites infects, skews, and disables the operation of the market (like a computer virus, sick cattle, or diseased wheat). Racism is irrational and often unconscious. Our belief in the inferiority of non-whites trumps good ideas that contend with it in the market, often without our even knowing it. In addition, racism makes the words and ideas of blacks and other despised minorities less saleable, regardless of their intrinsic value, in the marketplace of ideas. It also decreases the total amount of speech that enters the market by coercively silencing members of those groups who are its targets.

Racism is an epidemic infecting the marketplace of ideas and rendering it dysfunctional. Racism is ubiquitous. We are all racists.* Racism is also irrational. Individuals do not embrace or reject racist beliefs as the result of reasoned deliberation. For the most part, we do not recognize the myriad ways in which the racism pervading our history and culture influences our beliefs. In other words, most of our racism is unconscious. . . .

Prejudice that is unconscious or unacknowledged causes even more distortions in the market. When racism operates at a conscious level, opposing ideas may prevail in open competition for the rational or moral sensibilities of the market participant. But when an individual is unaware of his prejudice, neither reason nor moral persuasion will likely succeed.

Racist speech also distorts the marketplace of ideas by muting or devaluing the speech of blacks and other non-whites. An idea that would

* *See* Lawrence, previous note, where he describes America's racist heritage: "Americans share a common historical and cultural heritage in which racism has played and still plays a dominant role. Because of this shared experience, we also inevitably share many ideas, attitudes, and beliefs that attach significance to an individual's race and induce negative feelings and opinions about non-whites. To the extent that this cultural belief system has influenced all of us, we are all racists" (*Id.* at 322).

be embraced by large numbers of individuals if it were offered by a white individual will be rejected or given less credence because its author belongs to a group demeaned and stigmatized by racist beliefs.

An obvious example of this type of devaluation would be the black political candidate whose ideas go unheard or are rejected by white voters, although voters would embrace the same ideas if they were championed by a white candidate. Racial minorities have the same experiences on a daily basis when they endure the microaggression of having their words doubted, or misinterpreted, or assumed to be without evidentiary support, or when their insights are ignored and then appropriated by whites who are assumed to have been the original authority.

Finally, racist speech decreases the total amount of speech that reaches the market. I noted earlier in this article the ways in which racist speech is inextricably linked with racist conduct. The primary purpose and effect of the speech/conduct that constitutes white supremacy is the exclusion of non-whites from full participation in the body politic. Sometimes the speech/conduct of racism is direct and obvious. When the Klan burns a cross on the lawn of a black person who joined the NAACP or exercised his right to move to a formerly all-white neighborhood, the effect of this speech does not result from the persuasive power of an idea operating freely in the market. It is a threat, a threat made in the context of a history of lynchings, beatings, and economic reprisals that made good on earlier threats, a threat that silences a potential speaker. The black student who is subjected to racial epithets is likewise threatened and silenced. Certainly she, like the victim of a cross-burning, may be uncommonly brave or foolhardy and ignore the system of violence in which this abusive speech is only a bit player. But it is more likely that we, as a community, will be denied the benefit of many of her thoughts and ideas. . . .

the Court held that the Texas law was unconstitutional. Delivering the opinion of the Court, Justice Brennan argues that the state cannot "prescribe what shall be orthodox" by punishing symbolic actions like flag burning. The way to preserve the flag's special role in our national life, he argues, is not to punish those who feel differently about this symbol but to persuade them that they are wrong. In their separate dissents, Chief Justice Rehnquist and Justice Stevens reject the idea that the flag is just another symbol, toward which it would be unconstitutional to require minimal respect.

Study Questions

1. According to the state of Texas, what is harmful about burning the flag?
2. What is the "bedrock principle" to which Justice Brennan appeals?
3. Why does Justice Brennan believe that permitting flag burning will strengthen, not weaken, the flag's place in our community?
4. According to Chief Justice Rehnquist, what justifies a governmental prohibition on flag-burning?
5. What is the point of the analogy that Justice Stevens draws to spray-painting a message on the Lincoln Memorial?

JUSTICE BRENNAN *delivered the opinion of the Court:*

After publicly burning an American flag as a means of political protest, Gregory Lee Johnson was convicted of desecrating a flag in violation of Texas law. This case presents the question whether his conviction is consistent with the First Amendment. We hold that it is not.

While the Republican National Convention was taking place in Dallas in 1984, respondent Johnson participated in a political demonstration dubbed the "Republican War Chest Tour." As explained in literature distributed by the demonstrators and in speeches made by them, the purpose of this event was to protest the policies of the Reagan administration and of certain Dallas-based corporations. The demonstrators marched through the Dallas streets, chanting political slogans and stopping at several corporate locations to stage "die-ins" intended to dramatize the consequences of nuclear war. On several occasions they spray-painted the walls of buildings and overturned potted plants, but Johnson himself took no part

in such activities. He did, however, accept an American flag handed to him by a fellow protestor who had taken it from a flag pole outside one of the targeted buildings.

The demonstration ended in front of Dallas City Hall, where Johnson unfurled the American flag, doused it with kerosene, and set it on fire. While the flag burned, the protestors chanted, "America, the red, white, and blue, we spit on you." After the demonstrators dispersed, a witness to the flag-burning collected the flag's remains and buried them in his backyard. No one was physically injured or threatened with injury, though several witnesses testified that they had been seriously offended by the flag-burning.

Of the approximately 100 demonstrators, Johnson alone was charged with a crime. The only criminal offense with which he was charged was the desecration of a venerated object. . . . After a trial, he was convicted, sentenced to one year in prison, and fined $2,000. The Court of Appeals for the Fifth District of Texas at Dallas affirmed Johnson's conviction, . . . but the Texas Court of Criminal Appeals reversed, .

holding that the State could not, consistent with the First Amendment, punish Johnson for burning the flag in these circumstances.

The Court of Criminal Appeals began by recognizing that Johnson's conduct was symbolic speech protected by the First Amendment: "Given the context of an organized demonstration, speeches, slogans, and the distribution of literature, anyone who observed appellant's act would have understood the message that appellant intended to convey. The act for which appellant was convicted was clearly 'speech' contemplated by the First Amendment." To justify Johnson's conviction for engaging in symbolic speech, the State asserted two interests: preserving the flag as a symbol of national unity and preventing breaches of the peace. The Court of Criminal Appeals held that neither interest supported his conviction. . . .

As in *Spence* [a 1974 case on expressive conduct], "[w]e are confronted with a case of prosecution for the expression of an idea through activity," and "[a]ccordingly, we must examine with particular care the interests advanced by [petitioner] to support its prosecution.". . . Johnson was not, we add, prosecuted for the expression of just any idea; he was prosecuted for his expression of dissatisfaction with the policies of this country, expression situated at the core of our First Amendment values. . . .

Moreover, Johnson was prosecuted because he knew that his politically charged expression would cause "serious offense." If he had burned the flag as a means of disposing of it because it was dirty or torn, he would not have been convicted of flag desecration under this Texas law: federal law designates burning as the preferred means of disposing of a flag "when it is in such condition that it is no longer a fitting emblem for display.". . . The Texas law is thus not aimed at protecting the physical integrity of the flag in all circumstances, but is designed instead to protect it only against impairments that would cause serious offense to others. . . .

According to Texas, if one physically treats the flag in a way that would tend to cast doubt

on either the idea that nationhood and national unity are the flag's referents or that national unity actually exists, the message conveyed thereby is a harmful one and therefore may be prohibited.

If there is a bedrock principle underlying the First Amendment, it is that the Government may not prohibit the expression of an idea simply because society finds the idea itself offensive or disagreeable. . . .

We have not recognized an exception to this principle even where our flag has been involved. . . . Justice Jackson described one of our society's defining principles in words deserving of their frequent repetition: "If there is any fixed star in our constitutional constellation, it is that no official, high or petty, can prescribe what shall be orthodox in politics, nationalism, religion, or other matters of opinion or force citizens to confess by word or act their faith therein.". . . If we were to hold that a State may forbid flag-burning wherever it is likely to endanger the flag's symbolic role, but allow it wherever burning a flag promotes that role—as where, for example, a person ceremoniously burns a dirty flag—we would be saying that when it comes to impairing the flag's physical integrity, the flag itself may be used as a symbol—as a substitute for the written or spoken word or a "short cut from mind to mind"— only in one direction. We would be permitting a State to "prescribe what shall be orthodox" by saying that one may burn the flag to convey one's attitude toward it and its referents only if one does not endanger the flag's representation of nationhood and national unity.

We never before have held that the Government may ensure that a symbol be used to express only one view of that symbol or its referents. . . .

We are fortified in today's conclusion by our conviction that forbidding criminal punishment for conduct such as Johnson's will not endanger the special role played by our flag or the feelings it inspires. To paraphrase Justice Holmes, we submit that nobody can suppose that this one gesture of an unknown man will change our Nation's attitude towards its flag. . . . Indeed, Texas' argument that the burning of an American flag "is an act having a high likelihood to cause a breach of the peace," . . . and its statute's implicit assumption that physical mistreatment of the flag will lead to "serious offense," tend to confirm that the flag's special role is not in danger; if it were, no one would riot or take offense because a flag had been burned.

We are tempted to say, in fact, that the flag's deservedly cherished place in our community will be strengthened, not weakened, by our holding today. Our decision is a reaffirmation of the principles of freedom and inclusiveness that the flag best reflects, and of the conviction that our toleration of criticism such as Johnson's is a sign and source of our strength. Indeed, one of the proudest images of our flag, the one immortalized in our own national anthem, is of the bombardment it survived at Fort McHenry. It is the Nation's resilience, not its rigidity, that Texas sees reflected in the flag—and it is that resilience that we reassert today.

The way to preserve the flag's special role is not to punish those who feel differently about these matters. It is to persuade them that they are wrong. "To courageous, self-reliant men, with confidence in the power of free and fearless reasoning applied through the processes of popular government, no danger flowing from speech can be deemed clear and present, unless the incidence of the evil apprehended is so imminent that it may befall before there is opportunity for full discussion. If there be time to expose through discussion the falsehood and fallacies, to avert the evil by the processes of education, the remedy to be applied is more speech, not enforced silence." . . . And, precisely because it is our flag that is involved, one's response to the flag-burner may exploit the uniquely persuasive power of the flag itself. We can imagine no more appropriate response to burning a flag than waving one's own, no better way to counter a flag-burner's message than by saluting the flag that burns, no surer means of

preserving the dignity even of the flag that burned than by—as one witness here did—according its remains a respectful burial. We do not consecrate the flag by punishing its desecration, for in doing so we dilute the freedom that this cherished emblem represents.

Johnson was convicted for engaging in expressive conduct. The State's interest in preventing breaches of the peace does not support his conviction because Johnson's conduct did not threaten to disturb the peace. Nor does the State's interest in preserving the flag as a symbol of nationhood and national unity justify his criminal conviction for engaging in political expression. The judgment of the Texas Court of Criminal Appeals is therefore

Affirmed.

Chief Justice Rehnquist, dissenting:

In holding this Texas statute unconstitutional, the Court ignores Justice Holmes' familiar aphorism that "a page of history is worth a volume of logic." . . . For more than 200 years, the American flag has occupied a unique position as the symbol of our Nation, a uniqueness that justifies a governmental prohibition against flag burning in the way respondent Johnson did here. . . .

In the First and Second World Wars, thousands of our countrymen died on foreign soil fighting for the American cause. At Iwo Jima in the Second World War, United States Marines fought hand-to-hand against thousands of Japanese. By the time the Marines reached the top of Mount Suribachi, they raised a piece of pipe upright and from one end fluttered a flag. That ascent had cost nearly 6,000 American lives. . . .

During the Korean War, the successful amphibious landing of American troops at Inchon was marked by the raising of an American flag within an hour of the event. . . .

The government is simply recognizing as a fact the profound regard for the American flag created by that history when it enacts statutes prohibiting the disrespectful public burning of the flag.

The Court concludes its opinion with a regrettably patronizing civics lecture, presumably addressed to the Members of both Houses of Congress, the members of the 48 state legislatures that enacted prohibitions against flag-burning, and the troops fighting under that flag in Vietnam who objected to its being burned: "The way to preserve the flag's special role is not to punish those who feel differently about these matters. It is to persuade them that they are wrong." . . . The Court's role as the final expositor of the Constitution is well established, but its role as a platonic guardian admonishing those responsible to public opinion as if they were truant school children has no similar place in our system of government. The cry of "no taxation without representation" animated those who revolted against the English Crown to found our Nation—the idea that those who submitted to government should have some say as to what kinds of laws would be passed. Surely one of the high purposes of a democratic society is to legislate against conduct that is regarded as evil and profoundly offensive to the majority of people—whether it be murder, embezzlement, pollution, or flag-burning.

Our Constitution wisely places limits on powers of legislative majorities to act, but the declaration of such limits by this Court "is, at all times, a question of much delicacy, which ought seldom, if ever, to be decided in the affirmative, in a doubtful case." . . . Uncritical extension of constitutional protection to the burning of the flag risks the frustration of the very purpose for which organized governments are instituted. The Court decides that the American flag is just another symbol, about which not only must opinions pro and con be tolerated, but for which the most minimal public respect may not be enjoined. The government may conscript men into the Armed Forces where they must fight and perhaps die for the flag, but the government may not prohibit the public burning of the banner under which they fight. I would uphold the Texas statute as applied in this case.

Justice Stevens, dissenting:

As the Court analyzes this case, it presents the question whether the state of Texas, or indeed the federal government, has the power to prohibit the public desecration of the American flag. The question is unique. In my judgment, rules that apply to a host of other symbols, such as State flags, armbands, or various privately promoted emblems of political or commercial identity are not necessarily controlling. Even if flag-burning could be considered just another species of symbolic speech under the logical application of the rules that the court has developed in its interpretation of the First Amendment in other contexts, this case has an intangible dimension that makes those rules inapplicable.

A country's flag is a symbol of more than "nationhood and national unity." . . . It also signifies the ideas that characterize the society that has chosen that emblem as well as the special history that has animated the growth and power of those ideas. The fleur-de-lis and the tricolor both symbolized "nationhood and national unity," but they had vastly different meanings. The message conveyed by some flags—the swastika, for example—may survive long after it has outlived its usefulness as a symbol of regimented unity in a particular nation.

So it is with the American flag. It is more than a proud symbol of the courage, the determination, and the gifts of nature that transformed 13 fledgling colonies into a world power. It is a symbol of freedom, of equal opportunity, of religious tolerance, and of goodwill for other peoples who share our aspirations. The symbol carries its message to dissidents both at home and abroad who may have no interest at all in our national unity or survival.

The value of the flag as a symbol cannot be measured. Even so, I have no doubt that the interest in preserving that value for the future is both significant and legitimate. Conceivably that value will be enhanced by the Court's conclusion that our national commitment to free expression is so strong that even the United

States as ultimate guarantor of that freedom is without power to prohibit the desecration of its unique symbol. But I am unpersuaded. . . .

The case has nothing to do with "disagreeable ideas." . . . It involves disagreeable conduct that, in my opinion, diminishes the value of an important national asset.

The Court is therefore quite wrong in blandly asserting that respondent "was prosecuted for his expression of dissatisfaction with the policies of this country, expression situated at the core of our First Amendment values." . . . Respondent was prosecuted because of the method he chose to express his dissatisfaction with those policies. Had he chosen to spray paint—or perhaps convey with a motion picture projector—his message of dissatisfaction on the facade of the Lincoln Memorial, there would be no question about the power of the Government to prohibit his means of expression. The prohibition would be supported by the legitimate interest in preserving the quality of an important national asset. Though the asset at stake in this case is intangible, given its unique value, the same interest supports a prohibition on the desecration of the American flag.

The ideas of liberty and equality have been an irresistible force in motivating leaders like Patrick Henry, Susan B. Anthony, and Abraham Lincoln, schoolteachers like Nathan Hale and Booker T. Washington, the Philippine Scouts who fought at Bataan, and the soldiers who scaled the bluff at Omaha Beach. If those ideas are worth fighting for—and our history demonstrates that they are—it cannot be true that the flag that uniquely symbolizes their power is not itself worthy of protection from unnecessary desecration.

I respectfully dissent.

Review and Discussion Questions

1. Does flag-burning involve the expression of an idea? Is this a case about free speech?

2. Is Justice Brennan correct in arguing that to uphold the Texas law would be to "prescribe what shall be orthodox"? Would it really go against our fundamental political and constitutional values for the majority to decide that there is some symbol everyone should respect?

3. Assess Justice Stevens's contention that Johnson was not prosecuted for expressing his ideas but for the method he chose to express them. Is saying that ideas are protected but not the means by which they are expressed compatible with the First Amendment?

4. How persuasive is Justice Stevens's argument that, if the ideas of liberty and equality are worth fighting for, then the flag that symbolizes them is worthy of protection from unnecessary desecration?

5. Should flag-burning be constitutionally protected? Who has the better argument—Justice Brennan or Justices Rehnquist and Stevens? What do you think John Stuart Mill would say?

REPRODUCTION: SURROGACY AND CLONING

Is There Anything Wrong with Surrogate Motherhood? An Ethical Analysis

RUTH MACKLIN

Ruth Macklin is a professor of bioethics at Albert Einstein College of Medicine, New York, and author of *Mortal Choices: Ethical Dilemmas in Modern Medicine,* among other works. In this essay she reviews the emotional responses (both pro and con) that surrogacy arrangements provoke, distinguishes between surrogacy as such and the commercialization of surrogacy arrangements, and explains how the ethical issue is approached from the consequentialist or utilitarian perspective and from the formalist (or nonconsequentialist) perspective. She rejects arguments that surrogacy is intrinsically wrong, that it involves baby selling, or that truly informed consent is impossible. And although she believes that we lack sufficient evidence to judge whether surrogacy as such results in more overall harm than benefits, she argues that *commercialized* surrogacy transactions are ethically flawed and should be prohibited.

Study Questions

1. What different reactions do people have to surrogate motherhood?

2. What are the difficulties with approaching the surrogacy issue from a consequentialist perspective? How does it contrast with a formalist approach?

3. Why does Macklin believe the feminist charge that surrogacy exploits women is paternalistic?

Reprinted from Law, Medicine & Health Care, *vol. 16 (1988), by permission of the American Society of Law & Medicine. Some notes omitted.*

4. Why do some argue that no one is capable of granting truly informed consent to be a surrogate mother?

5. What are Macklin's two arguments against commercial surrogacy?

The Emotional Response

IS THERE ANYTHING ETHICALLY WRONG with surrogate motherhood? Many people confess their inability to articulate their opposition in rational terms, yet they feel uneasy. The practice arouses negative emotions ranging from mild distaste to revulsion. Others say there is nothing wrong, in principle, with surrogate motherhood. It is a way of helping infertile women fulfill a fundamental human longing and, therefore, should be permitted and even facilitated. Many who are not fundamentally opposed to surrogacy nonetheless maintain that the practice ought to be regulated, in order to prevent abuses and to provide a mechanism for resolving conflicts that may develop in particular cases.

Surrogacy arrangements have been condemned by Roman Catholic spokesmen, in a legal brief by a conference of bishops in New Jersey,[1] and by the Vatican in a statement issued by the Pope. . . . Feminists have denounced the practice, using rhetoric rather than argument, with the slogan "woman as vessel." A group of women who agreed to bear children under surrogacy contracts has convened to speak out against such arrangements. A number of them, like Mary Beth Whitehead, the surrogate mother in the Baby M case, were seeking to get their babies back.[2]

Some critics charge that surrogacy exploits women, particularly those from lower economic classes, thus constituting a new form of "slavery." Others contend that it dehumanizes babies, amounting to a new variety of "baby selling." The lawyer for Mary Beth Whitehead argued that surrogacy contracts are "against public policy" and ought to be outlawed, and called the idea of paying surrogate mothers to bear and surrender infants "repulsive and repugnant."[3]

Yet others disagree. Some, consistent with the feminist stance that women should be allowed to control their own bodies, insist that being a surrogate mother is just another reproductive choice, which ought to remain open to women. It is also pointed out that surrogacy fulfills an important biological and emotional need: couples in which the wife is infertile are often desperate to have a child with the father's genetic inheritance, and look to surrogacy as the only way to make this possible. And Noel P. Keane, the Detroit lawyer and founder of the Infertility Center in Manhattan, which arranged the contract between Mary Beth Whitehead and William Stern, Baby M's father, has argued that surrogacy permits "the furtherance of [a couple's] constitutionally protected right to procreation."[4]

The most striking feature of the controversy over surrogacy is the level of emotional response. Few people are neutral on the issue. Newspaper reports of the seven-week Baby M trial remarked on the "many basic emotions" touched by the legal proceedings. An account of legislative hearings on a bill to regulate surrogacy in New York state described the proceedings as "an emotional State Senate committee hearing."[5] Many health professionals and academics confess to having strong feelings against surrogacy, but remain unable to come up with a rational position in defense of their view.

Not long ago, news accounts of a novel surrogacy arrangement stirred even deeper feelings. A forty-eight-year-old South African grandmother, Pat Anthony, served as a surrogate mother for her own daughter's biological infants. Ms. Anthony was implanted with four embryos resulting from ova produced by her daughter and fertilized in vitro with her son-in-law's sperm. . . [and] gave birth to triplets. Re-actions to this story ranged from astonishment to repugnance. The trenchant comment of one biology professor was, "Yuk!"

Understanding Ethical Conflicts

. . . In contrast to reactions stemming from gut feelings, a reasoned approach to the ethics of surrogacy can proceed by using either of two well-known ethical perspectives. The first per-spective examines the good and bad conse-quences of an action or practice as a means of determining its moral rightness or wrongness, while the second tries to determine whether an act or practice is inherently or intrinsically wrong.

According to the first ethical perspective—consequentialism—if the good consequences outweigh the bad, the action or practice is ethi-cally acceptable. If, on the other hand, there is a balance of bad consequences over good ones, then the action or practice is morally wrong. The best-known version of a consequential ethi-cal theory is utilitarianism, but that is only one among several ways of articulating the details of this moral perspective.

Although a consequentialist mode of con-ducting an ethical analysis is basically sound, it is fraught with both theoretical and practical diffi-culties. Not only is it difficult to predict good and bad results; it is also hard to weigh conse-quences, even those that have already come about. Moreover, reasonable people frequently disagree over what should count as good and bad consequences, and how much weight should be assigned to each.

It is worth noting that hundreds of surrogacy arrangements have been successfully completed, with a distinct minority resulting in regrets by the surrogate mother and only a few leading to the sorts of devastating consequences exempli-fied by the Baby M case. If applying the utilitar-ian principle were simply a matter of subtracting the number of individuals who experienced bad consequences from the number of those who experienced good consequences, it would be an easy matter to determine the rightness or wrongness of surrogacy. But a proper applica-tion of the principle is methodologically much more complex. It requires assessing the magni-tude of the good and bad consequences for ev-ery individual affected by the action or practice, a task that is fraught with problems of measure-ment and interpersonal comparisons.

The competing approach to ethics rejects as morally irrelevant the consequences of actions or practices. Sometimes known as formalism, this approach holds that certain actions are wrong because of the very type of action they are. It is the "form" the action takes that makes it right or wrong, not its consequences. Ex-amples include killing innocent human beings, enslaving individuals or groups, the economic or social exploitation of persons or classes, and physical or mental torture. Debates erupt over just which human beings should be considered "innocent"; over whether some living entities, such as fetuses, should be considered human be-ings; and over just what should count as eco-nomic or social exploitation. But such debates do not detract from the respectability of formal-ism as a leading approach to ethics. A notable feature of this perspective is that it generates the morally important concept of rights.

Ethical Analysis

In tackling the broader issue of surrogacy, the first and most fundamental ethical question is whether there is something intrinsically wrong with surrogacy arrangements. Couched in the language of ethical formalism, is this a practice whose very form makes it immoral? Does surrogate motherhood violate some basic ethical principle? Those who believe it does argue that surrogacy ought to be outlawed, not simply regulated. They contend that the prac-

Asking victim groups to pay the price

Whenever we decide that racist hate speech must be tolerated because of the importance of tolerating unpopular speech we ask blacks and other subordinated groups to bear a burden for the good of society—to pay the price for the societal benefit of creating more room for speech. And we assign this burden to them without seeking their advice, or consent. This amounts to white domination, pure and simple. It is taxation without representation. We must be careful that the ease with which we strike the balance against the regulation of racist speech is in no way influenced by the fact the cost will be borne by others. We must be certain that the individuals who pay the price are fairly represented in our deliberation, and that they are heard. . . .

Epilogue

"Enie, menie, minie, mo."

It is recess time at the South Main Street School. It is 1952, and I am nine. Eddie Becker, Muck Makowski, John Thomas, Terry Flynn, Howie Martin, and I are standing in a circle. Right feet thrust forward, the toes of our black, high-top Keds sneakers touching, forming a tight hub of white rubber at the center, our skinny blue-jeaned legs extend like spokes from the hub. Heads bowed, we are intently watching Muck, who is hunkered down on one knee so that he can touch our toes as he calls out the rhyme. We are enthralled and entranced by the drama of this boyhood ritual, this customary pre-game incantation. It is no less important than the game itself.

But my mind is not on the ritual. I have lost track of the count that will determine whose foot must be removed from the hub, who will no longer have a chance to be a captain in this game. I hardly feel Muck's index finger as it presses through the rubber to my toes. My mind is on the rhyme. I am the only black boy in this circle of towheaded prepubescent males. Time stands still for me. My palms are sweaty and I feel a prickly heat at the back of my neck. I know that Muck will not say the word.

"Catch a tiger by the toe."

The heads stay down. No one looks at me. But I know that none of them is picturing the capture of a large striped animal. They are thinking of me, imagining my toe beneath the white rubber of my Keds sneaker—my toe attached to a large, dark, thick lipped, burr-headed American fantasy/nightmare.

"If he hollers let him go."

Tigers don't holler. I wish I could right now.

My parents have told me to ignore this word that is ringing unuttered in my ears. "You must not allow those who speak it to make you feel small or ugly," they say. They are proud, Mississippi-bred black professionals and long time political activists. Oft-wounded veterans of the war against the racist speech/conduct of Jim Crow and his many relations, they have, on countless occasions, answered the bad speech/conduct of racism with the good speech/conduct of their lives—representing the race, being smarter, cleaner and more morally upright than white folk to prove that black folk are equal, are fully human—refuting the lies of the cultural myth that is American racism. "You must know that it is their smallness, their ugliness of which this word speaks," they say.

I am struggling to heed their words, to follow their example, but I feel powerless before this word and its minions. In a moment's time it has made me an other. In an instant it has rebuilt the wall between my friends' humanity and my own, the wall that I have so painstakingly disassembled.

I was good at games, not just a good athlete, but a strategist, a leader. I knew how to make my teammates feel good about themselves so that they played better. It just came naturally to me. I could choose up a team and make them feel like family. When other folks felt good, I felt good too. Being good at games was the main tool I used to knock down the wall I'd found when I came to this white school in this white town. I looked forward to recess because that was when I could do the most damage to the wall. But now this rhyme, this word, had undone all my labors.

"Enie menie minie mo."

I have no memory of who got to be captain or what game we played. I just wished Muck had used "one potato, two potato . . ." We always used that at home.

NOTES

1. W. E. B. Du Bois, *The Souls of Black Folk* 16–17 (1953). . . .

2. *Chaplinsky* v. *New Hampshire,* 315 U.S. 568, 572 (1942).

Review and Discussion Questions

1. Do you believe that universities should have policies that discourage or restrict racist speech? If so, what exactly should the policies be? How far should the university go to prevent speech that may be hurtful? What is the best way to deal with racist speech?

2. Should ethnic jokes be prohibited?

3. To what extent does racist speech fall into the "fighting words" category? Are regulations against face-to-face insults sufficient to prevent the harms that concern Lawrence?

4. Has Lawrence overlooked or failed to address adequately any arguments against the restriction of racist speech on campus?

5. Is Lawrence right in saying that those who advocate tolerance for racist speech do not understand or fail to consider the real injuries it causes? Has Lawrence exaggerated the pain caused by racist speech?

6. Do you think John Stuart Mill would be persuaded by Lawrence's argument?

7. Will restrictions on racist speech encourage or discourage the exchange of ideas on campus?

Texas v. *Johnson*

U.S. SUPREME COURT

After burning the U.S. flag as an act of political protest, Gregory Lee Johnson was convicted of desecrating a flag in violation of Texas law. The case was appealed to the U.S. Supreme Court, which had to decide whether his conviction was consistent with the First Amendment's protection of freedom of speech. By a narrow 5 to 4 vote,

109 S. Ct. 2522 (1989); legal citations omitted.

the Court held that the Texas law was unconstitutional. Delivering the opinion of the Court, Justice Brennan argues that the state cannot "prescribe what shall be orthodox" by punishing symbolic actions like flag burning. The way to preserve the flag's special role in our national life, he argues, is not to punish those who feel differently about this symbol but to persuade them that they are wrong. In their separate dissents, Chief Justice Rehnquist and Justice Stevens reject the idea that the flag is just another symbol, toward which it would be unconstitutional to require minimal respect.

Study Questions

1. According to the state of Texas, what is harmful about burning the flag?
2. What is the "bedrock principle" to which Justice Brennan appeals?
3. Why does Justice Brennan believe that permitting flag burning will strengthen, not weaken, the flag's place in our community?
4. According to Chief Justice Rehnquist, what justifies a governmental prohibition on flag-burning?
5. What is the point of the analogy that Justice Stevens draws to spray-painting a message on the Lincoln Memorial?

J ustice brennan *delivered the opinion of the Court:*

After publicly burning an American flag as a means of political protest, Gregory Lee Johnson was convicted of desecrating a flag in violation of Texas law. This case presents the question whether his conviction is consistent with the First Amendment. We hold that it is not.

While the Republican National Convention was taking place in Dallas in 1984, respondent Johnson participated in a political demonstration dubbed the "Republican War Chest Tour." As explained in literature distributed by the demonstrators and in speeches made by them, the purpose of this event was to protest the policies of the Reagan administration and of certain Dallas-based corporations. The demonstrators marched through the Dallas streets, chanting political slogans and stopping at several corporate locations to stage "die-ins" intended to dramatize the consequences of nuclear war. On several occasions they spray-painted the walls of buildings and overturned potted plants, but Johnson himself took no part

in such activities. He did, however, accept an American flag handed to him by a fellow protestor who had taken it from a flag pole outside one of the targeted buildings.

The demonstration ended in front of Dallas City Hall, where Johnson unfurled the American flag, doused it with kerosene, and set it on fire. While the flag burned, the protestors chanted, "America, the red, white, and blue, we spit on you." After the demonstrators dispersed, a witness to the flag-burning collected the flag's remains and buried them in his backyard. No one was physically injured or threatened with injury, though several witnesses testified that they had been seriously offended by the flag-burning.

Of the approximately 100 demonstrators, Johnson alone was charged with a crime. The only criminal offense with which he was charged was the desecration of a venerated object. . . . After a trial, he was convicted, sentenced to one year in prison, and fined $2,000. The Court of Appeals for the Fifth District of Texas at Dallas affirmed Johnson's conviction, . . . but the Texas Court of Criminal Appeals reversed, . . .

holding that the State could not, consistent with the First Amendment, punish Johnson for burning the flag in these circumstances.

The Court of Criminal Appeals began by recognizing that Johnson's conduct was symbolic speech protected by the First Amendment: "Given the context of an organized demonstration, speeches, slogans, and the distribution of literature, anyone who observed appellant's act would have understood the message that appellant intended to convey. The act for which appellant was convicted was clearly 'speech' contemplated by the First Amendment." To justify Johnson's conviction for engaging in symbolic speech, the State asserted two interests: preserving the flag as a symbol of national unity and preventing breaches of the peace. The Court of Criminal Appeals held that neither interest supported his conviction. . . .

As in *Spence* [a 1974 case on expressive conduct], "[w]e are confronted with a case of prosecution for the expression of an idea through activity," and "[a]ccordingly, we must examine with particular care the interests advanced by [petitioner] to support its prosecution.". . . Johnson was not, we add, prosecuted for the expression of just any idea; he was prosecuted for his expression of dissatisfaction with the policies of this country, expression situated at the core of our First Amendment values. . . .

Moreover, Johnson was prosecuted because he knew that his politically charged expression would cause "serious offense." If he had burned the flag as a means of disposing of it because it was dirty or torn, he would not have been convicted of flag desecration under this Texas law: federal law designates burning as the preferred means of disposing of a flag "when it is in such condition that it is no longer a fitting emblem for display.". . . The Texas law is thus not aimed at protecting the physical integrity of the flag in all circumstances, but is designed instead to protect it only against impairments that would cause serious offense to others. . . .

According to Texas, if one physically treats the flag in a way that would tend to cast doubt on either the idea that nationhood and national unity are the flag's referents or that national unity actually exists, the message conveyed thereby is a harmful one and therefore may be prohibited.

If there is a bedrock principle underlying the First Amendment, it is that the Government may not prohibit the expression of an idea simply because society finds the idea itself offensive or disagreeable. . . .

We have not recognized an exception to this principle even where our flag has been involved. . . . Justice Jackson described one of our society's defining principles in words deserving of their frequent repetition: "If there is any fixed star in our constitutional constellation, it is that no official, high or petty, can prescribe what shall be orthodox in politics, nationalism, religion, or other matters of opinion or force citizens to confess by word or act their faith therein.". . . If we were to hold that a State may forbid flag-burning wherever it is likely to endanger the flag's symbolic role, but allow it wherever burning a flag promotes that role—as where, for example, a person ceremoniously burns a dirty flag—we would be saying that when it comes to impairing the flag's physical integrity, the flag itself may be used as a symbol—as a substitute for the written or spoken word or a "short cut from mind to mind"—only in one direction. We would be permitting a State to "prescribe what shall be orthodox" by saying that one may burn the flag to convey one's attitude toward it and its referents only if one does not endanger the flag's representation of nationhood and national unity.

We never before have held that the Government may ensure that a symbol be used to express only one view of that symbol or its referents. . . .

We are fortified in today's conclusion by our conviction that forbidding criminal punishment for conduct such as Johnson's will not endanger the special role played by our flag or the feelings it inspires. To paraphrase Justice Holmes, we submit that nobody can suppose that this one

gesture of an unknown man will change our Nation's attitude towards its flag. . . . Indeed, Texas' argument that the burning of an American flag "is an act having a high likelihood to cause a breach of the peace," . . . and its statute's implicit assumption that physical mistreatment of the flag will lead to "serious offense," tend to confirm that the flag's special role is not in danger; if it were, no one would riot or take offense because a flag had been burned.

We are tempted to say, in fact, that the flag's deservedly cherished place in our community will be strengthened, not weakened, by our holding today. Our decision is a reaffirmation of the principles of freedom and inclusiveness that the flag best reflects, and of the conviction that our toleration of criticism such as Johnson's is a sign and source of our strength. Indeed, one of the proudest images of our flag, the one immortalized in our own national anthem, is of the bombardment it survived at Fort McHenry. It is the Nation's resilience, not its rigidity, that Texas sees reflected in the flag—and it is that resilience that we reassert today.

The way to preserve the flag's special role is not to punish those who feel differently about these matters. It is to persuade them that they are wrong. "To courageous, self-reliant men, with confidence in the power of free and fearless reasoning applied through the processes of popular government, no danger flowing from speech can be deemed clear and present, unless the incidence of the evil apprehended is so imminent that it may befall before there is opportunity for full discussion. If there be time to expose through discussion the falsehood and fallacies, to avert the evil by the processes of education, the remedy to be applied is more speech, not enforced silence." . . . And, precisely because it is our flag that is involved, one's response to the flag-burner may exploit the uniquely persuasive power of the flag itself. We can imagine no more appropriate response to burning a flag than waving one's own, no better way to counter a flag-burner's message than by saluting the flag that burns, no surer means of

preserving the dignity even of the flag that burned than by—as one witness here did—according its remains a respectful burial. We do not consecrate the flag by punishing its desecration, for in doing so we dilute the freedom that this cherished emblem represents.

Johnson was convicted for engaging in expressive conduct. The State's interest in preventing breaches of the peace does not support his conviction because Johnson's conduct did not threaten to disturb the peace. Nor does the State's interest in preserving the flag as a symbol of nationhood and national unity justify his criminal conviction for engaging in political expression. The judgment of the Texas Court of Criminal Appeals is therefore

Affirmed.

Chief Justice Rehnquist, dissenting:
In holding this Texas statute unconstitutional, the Court ignores Justice Holmes' familiar aphorism that "a page of history is worth a volume of logic." . . . For more than 200 years, the American flag has occupied a unique position as the symbol of our Nation, a uniqueness that justifies a governmental prohibition against flag burning in the way respondent Johnson did here. . . .

In the First and Second World Wars, thousands of our countrymen died on foreign soil fighting for the American cause. At Iwo Jima in the Second World War, United States Marines fought hand-to-hand against thousands of Japanese. By the time the Marines reached the top of Mount Suribachi, they raised a piece of pipe upright and from one end fluttered a flag. That ascent had cost nearly 6,000 American lives. . . .

During the Korean War, the successful amphibious landing of American troops at Inchon was marked by the raising of an American flag within an hour of the event. . . .

The government is simply recognizing as a fact the profound regard for the American flag created by that history when it enacts statutes prohibiting the disrespectful public burning of the flag.

The Court concludes its opinion with a regrettably patronizing civics lecture, presumably addressed to the Members of both Houses of Congress, the members of the 48 state legislatures that enacted prohibitions against flag-burning, and the troops fighting under that flag in Vietnam who objected to its being burned: "The way to preserve the flag's special role is not to punish those who feel differently about these matters. It is to persuade them that they are wrong." . . . The Court's role as the final expositor of the Constitution is well established, but its role as a platonic guardian admonishing those responsible to public opinion as if they were truant school children has no similar place in our system of government. The cry of "no taxation without representation" animated those who revolted against the English Crown to found our Nation—the idea that those who submitted to government should have some say as to what kinds of laws would be passed. Surely one of the high purposes of a democratic society is to legislate against conduct that is regarded as evil and profoundly offensive to the majority of people—whether it be murder, embezzlement, pollution, or flag-burning.

Our Constitution wisely places limits on powers of legislative majorities to act, but the declaration of such limits by this Court "is, at all times, a question of much delicacy, which ought seldom, if ever, to be decided in the affirmative, in a doubtful case." . . . Uncritical extension of constitutional protection to the burning of the flag risks the frustration of the very purpose for which organized governments are instituted. The Court decides that the American flag is just another symbol, about which not only must opinions pro and con be tolerated, but for which the most minimal public respect may not be enjoined. The government may conscript men into the Armed Forces where they must fight and perhaps die for the flag, but the government may not prohibit the public burning of the banner under which they fight. I would uphold the Texas statute as applied in this case.

Justice Stevens, dissenting:

As the Court analyzes this case, it presents the question whether the state of Texas, or indeed the federal government, has the power to prohibit the public desecration of the American flag. The question is unique. In my judgment, rules that apply to a host of other symbols, such as State flags, armbands, or various privately promoted emblems of political or commercial identity are not necessarily controlling. Even if flag-burning could be considered just another species of symbolic speech under the logical application of the rules that the court has developed in its interpretation of the First Amendment in other contexts, this case has an intangible dimension that makes those rules inapplicable.

A country's flag is a symbol of more than "nationhood and national unity." . . . It also signifies the ideas that characterize the society that has chosen that emblem as well as the special history that has animated the growth and power of those ideas. The fleur-de-lis and the tricolor both symbolized "nationhood and national unity," but they had vastly different meanings. The message conveyed by some flags—the swastika, for example—may survive long after it has outlived its usefulness as a symbol of regimented unity in a particular nation.

So it is with the American flag. It is more than a proud symbol of the courage, the determination, and the gifts of nature that transformed 13 fledgling colonies into a world power. It is a symbol of freedom, of equal opportunity, of religious tolerance, and of goodwill for other peoples who share our aspirations. The symbol carries its message to dissidents both at home and abroad who may have no interest at all in our national unity or survival.

The value of the flag as a symbol cannot be measured. Even so, I have no doubt that the interest in preserving that value for the future is both significant and legitimate. Conceivably that value will be enhanced by the Court's conclusion that our national commitment to free expression is so strong that even the United

States as ultimate guarantor of that freedom is without power to prohibit the desecration of its unique symbol. But I am unpersuaded. . . .

The case has nothing to do with "disagreeable ideas." . . . It involves disagreeable conduct that, in my opinion, diminishes the value of an important national asset.

The Court is therefore quite wrong in blandly asserting that respondent "was prosecuted for his expression of dissatisfaction with the policies of this country, expression situated at the core of our First Amendment values." . . . Respondent was prosecuted because of the method he chose to express his dissatisfaction with those policies. Had he chosen to spray paint—or perhaps convey with a motion picture projector—his message of dissatisfaction on the facade of the Lincoln Memorial, there would be no question about the power of the Government to prohibit his means of expression. The prohibition would be supported by the legitimate interest in preserving the quality of an important national asset. Though the asset at stake in this case is intangible, given its unique value, the same interest supports a prohibition on the desecration of the American flag.

The ideas of liberty and equality have been an irresistible force in motivating leaders like Patrick Henry, Susan B. Anthony, and Abraham Lincoln, schoolteachers like Nathan Hale and Booker T. Washington, the Philippine Scouts who fought at Bataan, and the soldiers who scaled the bluff at Omaha Beach. If those ideas are worth fighting for—and our history demonstrates that they are—it cannot be true that the flag that uniquely symbolizes their power is not itself worthy of protection from unnecessary desecration.

I respectfully dissent.

Review and Discussion Questions

1. Does flag-burning involve the expression of an idea? Is this a case about free speech?

2. Is Justice Brennan correct in arguing that to uphold the Texas law would be to "prescribe what shall be orthodox"? Would it really go against our fundamental political and constitutional values for the majority to decide that there is some symbol everyone should respect?

3. Assess Justice Stevens's contention that Johnson was not prosecuted for expressing his ideas but for the method he chose to express them. Is saying that ideas are protected but not the means by which they are expressed compatible with the First Amendment?

4. How persuasive is Justice Stevens's argument that, if the ideas of liberty and equality are worth fighting for, then the flag that symbolizes them is worthy of protection from unnecessary desecration?

5. Should flag-burning be constitutionally protected? Who has the better argument—Justice Brennan or Justices Rehnquist and Stevens? What do you think John Stuart Mill would say?

REPRODUCTION: SURROGACY AND CLONING

Is There Anything Wrong with Surrogate Motherhood? An Ethical Analysis

RUTH MACKLIN

Ruth Macklin is a professor of bioethics at Albert Einstein College of Medicine, New York, and author of *Mortal Choices: Ethical Dilemmas in Modern Medicine,* among other works. In this essay she reviews the emotional responses (both pro and con) that surrogacy arrangements provoke, distinguishes between surrogacy as such and the commercialization of surrogacy arrangements, and explains how the ethical issue is approached from the consequentialist or utilitarian perspective and from the formalist (or nonconsequentialist) perspective. She rejects arguments that surrogacy is intrinsically wrong, that it involves baby selling, or that truly informed consent is impossible. And although she believes that we lack sufficient evidence to judge whether surrogacy as such results in more overall harm than benefits, she argues that *commercialized* surrogacy transactions are ethically flawed and should be prohibited.

Study Questions

1. What different reactions do people have to surrogate motherhood?
2. What are the difficulties with approaching the surrogacy issue from a consequentialist perspective? How does it contrast with a formalist approach?
3. Why does Macklin believe the feminist charge that surrogacy exploits women is paternalistic?

Reprinted from Law, Medicine & Health Care, *vol. 16 (1988), by permission of the American Society of Law & Medicine. Some notes omitted.*

4. Why do some argue that no one is capable of granting truly informed consent to be a surrogate mother?

5. What are Macklin's two arguments against commercial surrogacy?

The Emotional Response

IS THERE ANYTHING ETHICALLY WRONG with surrogate motherhood? Many people confess their inability to articulate their opposition in rational terms, yet they feel uneasy. The practice arouses negative emotions ranging from mild distaste to revulsion. Others say there is nothing wrong, in principle, with surrogate motherhood. It is a way of helping infertile women fulfill a fundamental human longing and, therefore, should be permitted and even facilitated. Many who are not fundamentally opposed to surrogacy nonetheless maintain that the practice ought to be regulated, in order to prevent abuses and to provide a mechanism for resolving conflicts that may develop in particular cases.

Surrogacy arrangements have been condemned by Roman Catholic spokesmen, in a legal brief by a conference of bishops in New Jersey,[1] and by the Vatican in a statement issued by the Pope. . . . Feminists have denounced the practice, using rhetoric rather than argument, with the slogan "woman as vessel." A group of women who agreed to bear children under surrogacy contracts has convened to speak out against such arrangements. A number of them, like Mary Beth Whitehead, the surrogate mother in the Baby M case, were seeking to get their babies back.[2]

Some critics charge that surrogacy exploits women, particularly those from lower economic classes, thus constituting a new form of "slavery." Others contend that it dehumanizes babies, amounting to a new variety of "baby selling." The lawyer for Mary Beth Whitehead argued that surrogacy contracts are "against public policy" and ought to be outlawed, and called the idea of paying surrogate mothers to bear and surrender infants "repulsive and repugnant."[3]

Yet others disagree. Some, consistent with the feminist stance that women should be allowed to control their own bodies, insist that being a surrogate mother is just another reproductive choice, which ought to remain open to women. It is also pointed out that surrogacy fulfills an important biological and emotional need: couples in which the wife is infertile are often desperate to have a child with the father's genetic inheritance, and look to surrogacy as the only way to make this possible. And Noel P. Keane, the Detroit lawyer and founder of the Infertility Center in Manhattan, which arranged the contract between Mary Beth Whitehead and William Stern, Baby M's father, has argued that surrogacy permits "the furtherance of [a couple's] constitutionally protected right to procreation."[4]

The most striking feature of the controversy over surrogacy is the level of emotional response. Few people are neutral on the issue. Newspaper reports of the seven-week Baby M trial remarked on the "many basic emotions" touched by the legal proceedings. An account of legislative hearings on a bill to regulate surrogacy in New York state described the proceedings as "an emotional State Senate committee hearing."[5] Many health professionals and academics confess to having strong feelings against surrogacy, but remain unable to come up with a rational position in defense of their view.

Not long ago, news accounts of a novel surrogacy arrangement stirred even deeper feelings. A forty-eight-year-old South African grandmother, Pat Anthony, served as a surrogate mother for her own daughter's biological infants. Ms. Anthony was implanted with four embryos resulting from ova produced by her daughter and fertilized in vitro with her son-in-

law's sperm. . . [and] gave birth to triplets. Reactions to this story ranged from astonishment to repugnance. The trenchant comment of one biology professor was, "Yuk!"

Understanding Ethical Conflicts

. . . In contrast to reactions stemming from gut feelings, a reasoned approach to the ethics of surrogacy can proceed by using either of two well-known ethical perspectives. The first perspective examines the good and bad consequences of an action or practice as a means of determining its moral rightness or wrongness, while the second tries to determine whether an act or practice is inherently or intrinsically wrong.

According to the first ethical perspective—consequentialism—if the good consequences outweigh the bad, the action or practice is ethically acceptable. If, on the other hand, there is a balance of bad consequences over good ones, then the action or practice is morally wrong. The best-known version of a consequential ethical theory is utilitarianism, but that is only one among several ways of articulating the details of this moral perspective.

Although a consequentialist mode of conducting an ethical analysis is basically sound, it is fraught with both theoretical and practical difficulties. Not only is it difficult to predict good and bad results; it is also hard to weigh consequences, even those that have already come about. Moreover, reasonable people frequently disagree over what should count as good and bad consequences, and how much weight should be assigned to each.

It is worth noting that hundreds of surrogacy arrangements have been successfully completed, with a distinct minority resulting in regrets by the surrogate mother and only a few leading to the sorts of devastating consequences exemplified by the Baby M case. If applying the utilitarian principle were simply a matter of subtracting the number of individuals who experienced bad consequences from the number of those who experienced good consequences, it would be an easy matter to determine the rightness or wrongness of surrogacy. But a proper application of the principle is methodologically much more complex. It requires assessing the magnitude of the good and bad consequences for every individual affected by the action or practice, a task that is fraught with problems of measurement and interpersonal comparisons.

The competing approach to ethics rejects as morally irrelevant the consequences of actions or practices. Sometimes known as formalism, this approach holds that certain actions are wrong because of the very type of action they are. It is the "form" the action takes that makes it right or wrong, not its consequences. Examples include killing innocent human beings, enslaving individuals or groups, the economic or social exploitation of persons or classes, and physical or mental torture. Debates erupt over just which human beings should be considered "innocent"; over whether some living entities, such as fetuses, should be considered human beings; and over just what should count as economic or social exploitation. But such debates do not detract from the respectability of formalism as a leading approach to ethics. A notable feature of this perspective is that it generates the morally important concept of rights.

Ethical Analysis

In tackling the broader issue of surrogacy, the first and most fundamental ethical question is whether there is something intrinsically wrong with surrogacy arrangements. Couched in the language of ethical formalism, is this a practice whose very form makes it immoral? Does surrogate motherhood violate some basic ethical principle? Those who believe it does argue that surrogacy ought to be outlawed, not simply regulated. They contend that the prac-

tice of surrogacy is morally flawed, in principle, and that erecting safeguards cannot erase the fundamental ethical wrong of the practice. Within this category fall the objections of the Roman Catholic church and some feminist groups.

In a brief filed with the New Jersey Supreme Court prior to the appeal in the Baby M case, the New Jersey Catholic Conference, composed of the state's fourteen Roman Catholic bishops, argued that surrogate motherhood "promotes the exploitation of women and infertile couples and the dehumanization of babies." The bishops' brief focused largely (but not entirely) on the commercial aspects of surrogacy. . . . But in trying to determine whether surrogacy is intrinsically immoral, it is necessary to separate the commercial aspects from the practice itself. . . .

The Catholic bishops in New Jersey did not limit their criticism of surrogacy to its commercial aspects. Their brief also referred to the best interests of children born under such arrangements:

> In surrogacy, a child is conceived precisely in order to be abandoned to others and his or her best interests are the last factors to be considered. . . . There is great potential for psychological injury to the child when he realizes that he was born, not of a loving relationship, but from a cold, usually financial relationship.[6]

A similar position is argued by a feminist psychologist, who asserts that "no child wants to live in a womb for hire."[7]

When we begin to contemplate the possible consequences for the child born of surrogacy arrangements, and what is in the child's best interests, a new set of questions arises. Should the child be told, when old enough, the pertinent details about his or her conception and birth? Should the identity of the surrogate mother routinely be disclosed? What if the surrogate mother wants to be known to the child? What if she does not? What if she insists on visitation rights or other ongoing involvement with the child?

Such questions are identical to those that have been posed about adoption and about artificial insemination using the sperm of an anonymous donor. It is instructive that replies to these questions have changed over the years, and that even today there are no settled, universally accepted answers. In fact, some recent proposals mark a radical shift from earlier practices. Some people are now urging that the identity of birth mothers and fathers be disclosed to adoptive parents and, eventually, the child, and that the long-established practice of anonymous donor insemination be eliminated. These suggestions arise partly out of increasing efforts by many adopted children to discover the identity of their biological parents, and also from an assessment of the negative consequences for the children of secrecy surrounding the men who have anonymously donated their sperm for artificial insemination.

As important as these issues are, they are questions that pertain to the consequences of surrogate arrangements. They become pertinent only when the formalist approach to the morality of surrogacy has been rejected, or when it has been determined that the practice does not violate a prohibition against actions of an unacceptable type.

While some critics of surrogate motherhood base their opposition on the best interests of the children or on the motives of the surrogates, others oppose it as exploitative of women. This makes it appear that surrogacy is unethical because of the type of practice it is, namely, a form of exploitation. According to one writer: "When a woman provides womb service, the feminist issue surfaces. Women object to being baby factories or sex objects because it offends their human dignity."[8] And further: "This is going to end up as the final exploitation of women. It is always going to be poor women who have the babies and rich women who get them."[9]

These statements confuse two distinct issues: first, the exploitation of individual women, if that is indeed what really happens in surrogacy arrangements; and second, a form of class exploitation, since poorer women will be the ones serving as surrogates for the more well-to-do. My own view is that these would be sound, principled objections if it were clear that exploitation in some form actually occurs.

The feminist charge that the practice of surrogacy exploits women is paternalistic. It questions women's ability to know their own interests and to enter into a contractual arrangement knowingly and competently. There may well be a coercive aspect to commercial surrogacy, since money—especially a large enough sum—can serve as a coercive inducement to do something a person might not otherwise do voluntarily. But that speaks more to the exploitation of poorer classes of women, which I think is a genuine moral worry, than it does to the exploitation of women generally. Feminists who oppose surrogacy presume to speak for all women. But what they are really saying is that those who elect to enter surrogacy arrangements are incompetent to choose and stand in need of protection.

The charge of "exploitation" contradicts the moral stance that women have the ability and the right to control their own bodies. If that right grants women reproductive freedoms of other sorts, such as the right to abortion or to control the number and spacing of their children, why does it not similarly apply to the informed, voluntary choice to serve as a surrogate? Some feminists draw an analogy with prostitution, another practice believed to constitute exploitation of women. But the chief feminist complaint about prostitution pertains to its commercial aspect, the feature that transforms women's bodies into a commodity. Feminists who see nothing wrong with women engaging in sexual intercourse outside of marriage (in today's terms—as long as they practice safe sex) are inconsistent if they contend that noncommercial surrogacy arrangements are demeaning to women.

Still, it could be argued, to treat one's body as a mere means to the ends of others is degrading.

It could be viewed as a violation of Kant's supreme moral principle, the categorical imperative, which prohibits treating persons merely as a means. But according to that interpretation, other acts and practices typically considered altruistic or even noble would similarly have to be viewed as degrading. A normal, healthy volunteer for biomedical or behavioral research is also acting as a "mere means" to the ends of others—of either the researchers, or future generations, or both. Monetary payments to research subjects would surely have to be outlawed, if it is exploitation to pay people for the use of their bodies or for services that use their bodies. And in the therapeutic context, requests for bone marrow donations would have to be considered suspect.

These analogies serve as a reminder that surrogate motherhood is a biomedical as well as a social practice, as it involves either artificial insemination or embryo transfer, then pregnancy and childbirth. It leads naturally to a consideration of informed consent.

Is informed consent possible?

Although surrogacy arrangements are typically governed by a legal contract, the concept of informed consent is still applicable. Yet it has been argued that no one is capable of granting truly informed consent to be a surrogate mother. This argument contends that even if a woman has already borne children, she cannot know what it is like to have to give them up after birth. In fact, most surrogacy arrangements do require that women who offer to be surrogates already have children. This would seem to meet the objection that surrogate mothers cannot possibly know what it is like to go through pregnancy and childbirth. Yet according to those who say genuine informed consent to be a surrogate mother is impossible, it is the feature of having to give up the child that cannot be known in advance.

There is some merit to that argument. Yet as an argument against the very possibility of informed consent, it is too strong. If it holds for surrogate motherhood, it would seem to apply, as well, to a wide variety of other biomedical treatments and research maneuvers that people have never before experienced. . . . It is unrealistic to maintain that the only way to gain [the necessary] understanding is to have had the actual experience, along with the accompanying feelings.

So, either the meaning of informed consent to become a surrogate mother is the same as that of informed consent to medical treatment, or it is different. If it should be understood in the usual sense, then women should be as capable of granting informed consent to carry a baby to term and then relinquish it as they are to grant consent for removal of a breast when they have breast cancer, or removal of their uterus if they develop a tumor, or for an operation to reduce or enlarge their breasts.

However, if a different, higher standard of informed consent is to be used, then the only women who could qualify would be those who had already undergone the experience of having had a baby and lost it. But that would surely be a bizarre requirement, and probably a cruel one, as well. Having experienced the loss of an infant, such women would be the only ones judged able to consent to enter a surrogacy agreement.

Additional ethical concerns

I believe it is not the element of understanding that poses the problem for the possibility of informed consent but, rather, the element of voluntariness when the arrangement is a commercial one and the surrogate is a person with limited financial assets. A fee of $10,000 paid to a woman of low income may well be an offer she cannot refuse. The remedy for this problem is to pay nothing at all, and to allow surrogacy arrangements only as purely altruistic acts on the part of the surrogate mother.

But is that fair? Is it reasonable? After all, the surrogate mother does have to undergo the in-

convenience of pregnancy, with its possible discomforts, as well as take the time for prenatal visits to the obstetrician, and then undergo the risks and rigors of childbirth. Shouldn't she be paid for her time and inconvenience?

A physician colleague of mine has argued that she should. He said:

> If I wanted to hire a surrogate mother to bear my child, I'd want her to be adequately taken care of financially. I wouldn't want her to have to work at a grueling job. I'd want her to keep from exhausting herself, from being forced to go to work where she may be exposed to environmental hazards to the fetus. In short, I'd want her to be as comfortable and as free from stress as possible during the entire pregnancy.

I find this argument persuasive, but only to a point. For one thing, there is just so much that money can do to alleviate stress. And even if a woman is not exposed to the hazards of toxic fumes in a factory or to a video display terminal in an office, there is no way to eliminate entirely her exposure to potentially damaging substances, and surely no way to protect her from the emotional upset of daily life. It would take more evidence than is now available to conclude that monetary payments to surrogate mothers are likely to decrease the risks of harm to the fetus.

It is true, however, that contracts for surrogate arrangements impose obligations and restrictions on the woman during pregnancy. Most surrogacy contracts include prohibitions against smoking, drinking, and the use of prescription as well as recreational drugs. In the contract signed by Mary Beth Whitehead, the mother of Baby M, clause 15 required her "to adhere to all medical instructions given to her by the inseminating physician as well as her independent obstetrician." She had to agree "not to smoke cigarettes, drink alcoholic beverages, use illegal drugs, or take nonprescription medication or prescribed medications without written consent from her physician." She also had to agree to follow a prenatal medical examination schedule.

These contractual provisions create a different sort of ethical problem: How can it be known whether the surrogate mother is adhering to the restrictions? How can such provisions be enforced? Should monitoring be permitted—for example, screening urine for drug use during pregnancy, installing cigarette smoke detectors in the home or in the car, doing random breathalizer tests for alcohol? These questions might seem far-fetched were it not for the fact that such tests are already in use in some places and for some purposes in our society, and have been recommended in many other settings. Would it be reasonable to require surrogate mothers to give up a substantial amount of privacy for the purpose of detecting violations of the surrogacy contract?

The discussion has now shifted to the provisions of surrogacy contracts, and away from the question with which we began: an ethical assessment of the practice of surrogacy itself. Yet a thorough evaluation of this new reproductive practice requires an examination of relevant public policy concerns.

Surrogacy and Public Policy

A factor that complicates the debate at the policy level is the contention that surrogate motherhood is a form of "baby selling." When the attorney for Mary Beth Whitehead asserted that a contract to be a surrogate mother for money is "against public policy," he was referring to his belief that the contract violated state adoption laws and public policies against the sale of babies.

Once again, this places the assessment of surrogacy in the context of a commercial arrangement. Although I have been urging that the commercial aspects be separated from the social arrangement of surrogacy for the purpose of ethical evaluation, the underlying conceptual question remains: Is this a form of baby selling?

Or should it be considered more like a fee for services rendered? People who express a strong emotional distaste for surrogate motherhood are quick to label it "baby selling." That term has such negative connotations, and the practice is so universally disapproved, that once surrogacy is categorized as a new variety of "baby selling," its rejection is sure to follow quickly. But fairness demands an objective examination of the issue. It is an old trick of argumentation to apply a concept that already carries negative connotations to a different situation, with the aim of persuading listeners that the new situation should, like the old one, be viewed in a negative light.

A Kentucky court, holding that surrogate contracts did not violate public policy, asked how it was possible for a natural father to be accused of buying his own child. My own view on this question is that paying a woman to be a surrogate mother is more like "renting a womb" than it is like buying a baby. Monetary payment is for the woman's inconvenience and possible discomfort, including the risks of any complications of pregnancy. This interpretation can be supported by looking at the features of surrogacy contracts, features that impose certain duties and obligations on the surrogate mother during pregnancy. Also, one proposed law in the state of Michigan contains the provision that the surrogate agreement may not allow for a reduction of payment if the baby is stillborn or born alive but impaired.

But an opposing interpretation is supported by some existing programs and proposed laws. In many surrogacy arrangements, the bulk of the payment is made after birth, and in some cases the surrogate mother does not receive full payment if she miscarries. The law proposed in South Carolina would codify that approach by a provision that the woman will receive no compensation beyond her medical expenses if she miscarries before the fifth month of pregnancy, and will receive only 10 percent of the agreed-upon fee plus medical expenses if she miscarries during or after the fifth month.

Despite my conclusion that contracts for surrogacy should not be considered a form of baby selling, and therefore in violation of laws that prohibit that activity, I believe it is morally wrong to undertake commercial surrogacy transactions. There are two arguments in support of this view.

Two Arguments Against Commercial Surrogacy

The "exploitation" argument

The first argument goes back to an earlier point: There is a risk of richer women exploiting those who are poorer or less advantaged. The magnitude of this danger is probably exaggerated by the opponents of surrogate motherhood. Yet it is surely true that women who are poor, uneducated, or both have fewer options than those who are better off financially. They are more likely to be unemployed, receiving welfare payments, or forced to remain at home caring for their own young children. To offer money to a woman in these circumstances to bear the child of another woman is probably to offer her an undue inducement. It is an offer that may be difficult for a person of little financial means to refuse and would, in that case, be coercive. . . .

The "commodification" argument

The potential for better-off women to exploit those who are less well off is the first argument against commercial surrogacy arrangements. The second is a broader argument that applies to other biomedical concerns as well. Medical and other health services are a special sort of social good, one that should not be subject to the same market forces that govern the sale of pork bellies. The human body, its parts, and its reproductive products are not "mere meat." The

United States Congress wisely enacted a law prohibiting commercial arrangements for procuring and distributing organs for transplantation. There is sufficient evidence of greed, corruption, and duplicity on the part of persons in financial markets, among defense contractors, local and federal officials, and others in the public and private sectors to make us wary of allowing commercial practices to invade and dominate the delivery of health care.

Medical services and other health-related activities should not be treated as commodities. To do so is to feed the coffers of profiteers and enrich brokers and middlemen, people eager to reap personal gain from the misfortunes of others. Commercial arrangements drain monetary resources away from providing medical services and products directly to those in need.

The standard cost of a surrogacy arrangement is a case in point. When Noel P. Keane, the Detroit lawyer, appeared on the TV program "60 Minutes," he reported the breakdown of costs as follows: a one-time fee of $10,000 to the broker; $10,000 to the surrogate mother; and $5,000 for "other costs," for a total of $25,000.

Conclusion

From all of the considerations enumerated here, I conclude that it is not the practice of surrogate motherhood itself that is ethically wrong, rather, its commercialization. This conclusion answers "no" to the question of whether there is something intrinsically unethical about surrogacy. It cannot be seen to violate any fundamental moral principle prohibiting certain types of action. But this conclusion does not yet answer the question of whether, on the whole, the bad consequences of allowing this practice outweigh the good ones. There is not enough evidence at this point for an empirically well-confirmed answer to that question.

But, it will be objected, if commercial surrogacy is prohibited, is that not likely to result in the disappearance of the practice? Who will come forward to serve as surrogate mothers—except for a few women who want to help their own sisters, or daughters, or even mothers, as the case may be?

My reply to this question is simple. The argument that there is nothing inherently unethical about surrogacy is not an argument that surrogacy is a good thing and that, therefore, it ought to be encouraged or promoted. It is simply an argument that noncommercial surrogacy is morally permissible and, therefore, should not be prohibited. If the practice disappears for lack of monetary incentive for women to act as surrogates, so be it. In the absence of evidence or arguments that surrogacy is such a desirable practice that its disappearance would constitute a harm or wrong to society, its loss should not be lamented.

Still, there is sufficient evidence from the Baby M case and that of other surrogate mothers who are seeking to get their babies back to suggest that even noncommercial surrogacy needs to be carefully regulated. Thought should be given to requiring the sort of provisions typical in adoption cases, which permit the birth mother to change her mind during a limited period after the baby is born. That would surely be preferable to lengthy trials, accompanied by the sensational publicity and humiliation that marked the Baby M case.

An ethical analysis of surrogate motherhood should proceed by seeking to determine the probable beneficial and harmful consequences. This requires an ongoing review of evidence as it becomes available. It brings to mind the recommendations of the Ethics Committee of the American Fertility Society. . . . Not only did the committee propose that surrogacy be practiced exclusively as a clinical experiment; it also recommended that clinics involved in surrogacy arrangements publish data about the process and outcomes. Some people might contend that it is too late to reverse social practices already set in motion, but that view is mistaken. Biomedical research involving human subjects was practiced for a long time before regulations and safeguards were introduced. It makes perfectly good sense to do the same for novel reproductive arrangements, in order to provide a scientific basis on which they can be evaluated for the purpose of fashioning public policy.

The argument that surrogacy is a morally flawed activity because of exploitation, dehumanization, or the base motives of the participants does not stand up to critical analysis. The moral flaws are tied to the commercial features of surrogacy, not to the arrangement itself. Although there is nothing ethically wrong, in principle, with surrogate motherhood, if it becomes evident that surrogacy arrangements result in more overall harm than benefits, we shall have to conclude that the practice is morally wrong.

NOTES

1. Joseph Sullivan, "Bishops File Brief Against Surrogate Motherhood," *New York Times,* July 19, 1987, 28.

2. Keith Schneider, "Mothers Urge Ban on Surrogacy as Form of 'Slavery,' " *New York Times,* Sept. 1, 1987.

3. Quoted in "Who's Who in the Fight for Baby M," *New York Times,* April 1, 1987, sec. B2.

4. Quoted in Schneider, supra note 2.

5. James Feron, "Testimony Is Given on Surrogate Bill," *New York Times,* April 11, 1987.

6. Sullivan, supra note 1, at 28.

7. Sidney Callahan, "No Child Wants to Live in a Womb for Hire," *National Catholic Reporter,* Oct. 11, 1985.

8. *Id.*

9. Sidney Callahan, as quoted in Iver Peterson, "Baby M Trial Splits Ranks of Feminists," *New York Times,* Feb. 24, 1987, sec. B1.

Review and Discussion Questions

1. Is surrogate motherhood fairly categorized as "baby selling"?

2. Describe the possible good and bad results of a policy permitting surrogacy arrangements (either commercial or noncommercial) that a consequentialist would have to weigh.

3. Are there plausible nonconsequentialist reasons for believing that noncommercial surrogacy arrangements are wrong?

4. How would a defender of commercial surrogacy transactions defend them against Macklin's two arguments?

5. Explain why you agree or disagree with Macklin's overall position on surrogate motherhood. What is your own view? Do you agree that there are important moral differences between commercial and noncommercial surrogacy?

6. Assess the surrogacy issue from the point of view of John Stuart Mill's *On Liberty*.

Paid Surrogacy: Arguments and Responses

HEIDI MALM

In the previous essay Ruth Macklin argued that, although surrogacy is not intrinsically immoral, commercialized surrogacy is wrong and should be prohibited. In this essay Heidi Malm of Loyola University of Chicago defends paid surrogacy arrangements. She examines and rejects five arguments intended to show that paid surrogacy should be prohibited. She also considers the view that, although paid surrogacy arrangements are morally permissible, they should not be legally enforceable. But even this position she finds problematic.

Study Questions

1. How do the examples involving Francine and Gloria support Malm's argument that surrogate motherhood is not baby selling?

2. What is Malm's argument against the contention that contracted child-bearing arrangements treat the woman's body as an object of commerce?

3. What is the "transferring rights" objection to surrogacy arrangements?

4. What is Malm's concern about the moderate view that contracted child-bearing arrangements should not be legally enforceable?

Reprinted by permission from Public Affairs Quarterly, *vol. 3, no. 2 (April 1989). Copyright © 1989* Public Affairs Quarterly. *Some notes omitted.*

IN A SOCIETY that prizes individual liberty, the burden of proof rests on those who want to prohibit, or otherwise restrict, surrogate motherhood arrangements. This paper examines five arguments intended to show that *paid* surrogacy arrangements ought to be prohibited. The arguments are primarily ethical in nature, as opposed to legal, and deontological as opposed to consequentialist. After finding none of the arguments successful, I consider the view that while paid surrogacy arrangements are morally permissible, they ought not be legally enforceable. I argue that even this view is problematic.

I. Selling Babies

When ruling on the recent Baby "M" case, chief justice Robert N. Wilenz wrote for the New Jersey Supreme Court:

> We find no offense to our present laws where a woman voluntarily and without payment agrees to act as a "surrogate" mother, provided that she is not subject to a binding agreement to surrender her child . . . *this is the sale of a child*, or, at the very least, the sale of a mother's right to her child, the only mitigating factor being that one of the purchasers is the father. Almost every evil that prompted the prohibition of the payment of money in connection with adoption exists here.

This passage contains the central premise of what is perhaps the strongest argument against paid surrogate motherhood arrangements (henceforth called "contracted child-bearing arrangements"),* namely, that the payments made

in these arrangements constitute the buying and selling of a baby. If this is correct, then we have strong moral grounds—Kantian notions of respect for persons (as well as adequate legal grounds—our current laws against baby-selling)—for prohibiting such arrangements. The argument may be stated as follows: (1) It is morally wrong to treat persons (including babies) as objects of commerce. (2) Contracted child-bearing arrangements treat babies as objects of commerce. (3) Therefore, contracted child-bearing arrangements are morally objectionable.

Let us grant the truth of premise (1) (though some might deny even this)[1] and focus our attention on premise (2). Are we committed to viewing the payments made in contracted child-bearing arrangements as payments *for the baby*?[†] A proponent may deny that we are, claiming that the payments are for the woman's services. They are, that is, compensation for the efforts and risks of bearing a child (for example, for not drinking coffee or alcohol for nine months, for not engaging in potentially dangerous activities, for the risks involved in giving birth, for the loss of earnings from other sources, and for the effort it may take to return her body to the condition it was in prior to pregnancy). This is not a patently unreasonable claim. Thus a critic of contracted child-bearing arrangements must provide an argument showing that it is unreasonable, if she is to object to these arrangements on the grounds that they involve the buying and selling of babies.

---

*The term "surrogate mother" is misleading. In typical cases (those not involving embryo transfer) the so-called "surrogate mother" is both the genetic mother of the child and the birth-mother of the child. The only "mother" role she does not (intend to) fulfill is the social one. (Notice, however, that we do not refer to women who relinquish their children for adoption, nor to men who donate sperm for artificial insemination, as "surrogate mothers" and "surrogate

fathers.") The term seems to be rooted in the notion that a woman's proper role in life is to be a child-bearer for a mate. Were that the case, then the woman being paid to bear a child could be viewed as a surrogate for another woman.

Also, although I use the term *"contracted* child-bearing arrangements," my focus is on the permissibility of the arrangements themselves, and not on whether the arrangements should carry the status of legally binding contracts.

[†]For our present purposes, we may treat the purchase of a child, and the purchase of a mother's right to her child, as equivalent. Both, in effect, treat the child as property.

One such argument is suggested in the following passage by Sara Ketchum. She suggests the claim that if the payments made are merely for the woman's services, then the "customers" of contracted child-bearing arrangements may not get what they want, which is custody of the child:

> The "surrogate" or contracting mother is, after all, the mother. In an ordinary custody decision, a genetic father who pays the biological mother of the child to take care of the child does not thereby gain exclusive custody of the child, nor does his financial contribution establish him as the primary caretaker for purposes of determining custody. (Ketchum 1987, p. 3.)

Let us grant that my paying you for your efforts and risks of bearing a child will not *thereby* gain me exclusive custody of the child. This is supported by the case Ketchum cites (in which a father's financial contribution does not establish him as the sole caretaker), and by a case in which the person making the payments is not related to the child (for example, Albert pays Betty to bear a child whose genetic parents would be Betty and Carl). The relevant question is whether it follows from this that the payments made in contracted child-bearing arrangements cannot reasonably be viewed as payments for the woman's services, that they must be for the baby itself (or at least for rights to the baby). To see that it does not, consider the following case:

> Diane and Erick have, respectively, healthy ova and healthy sperm. Diane's uterus, however, has been damaged in a way that prevents her from carrying a child to term. Diane and Erick thus seek the help of Francine, who *is* able to carry a child, and agree to pay her $10,000 to carry to term a conceptus that results from the in vitro fertilization of Diane's ovum with Erick's sperm.

In this case I think it is quite reasonable to maintain that the payments to Francine were payments for her services. If Diane and Erick have custodial rights to the child (and it seems to me that they do), then their rights are a function of their being the child's genetic parents; they did not purchase the rights, nor the baby itself, from Francine. Now consider the following modified version of the above case:

> Diane does not have healthy ova but Gloria does. Gloria donates one of her ova to Diane and Erick, and it is then fertilized, in vitro, with Erick's sperm. The conceptus is implanted in Francine, who is paid $10,000 to carry the child to term.

Again, I think it is quite reasonable to view the payments to Francine as payments for her services. They were not for the baby itself.

The point of these cases is to show that in cases in which the woman bearing the child is not the genetic mother of the child, it is reasonable to view the payments to her as payments for her services. But if it is reasonable in these cases, then it is also reasonable in cases in which the woman bearing the child *is* the genetic mother of the child. For she may be, as did Gloria, donating an ovum (or waiving her claims to custody, as I discuss in section IV), and may be, as did Francine, accepting payments for her efforts and risks of carrying the child to term. Thus even though my paying you for your efforts and risks of bearing a child does not *thereby* gain me exclusive custody of the child (I may gain that custody in other ways), it is nonetheless reasonable to view the payments made in contracted child-bearing arrangements as payments for the woman's services. Given this, we cannot prohibit these arrangements out of hand on the grounds that they involve the buying and selling of babies.

II. Selling Bodies

A second argument against contracted child-bearing arrangements parallels the first. It is captured in the popular notion of "renting a womb" and asserts: To pay a woman to bear a child for another is to treat her body as an object of commerce. But to treat a woman's body as an object of commerce is, as Ketchum argues, to treat her as

> less than an end (or as less than a person). . . . To make a person or a person's body an object of commerce is to treat the person as part of another's domain, particularly if the sale of A to B gives B rights to A or to A's body . . . (Ketchum 1987, p. 9.)

And again:

> . . . treating another person's body as a part of my domain—as among the things I have a rightful claim to—is, if anything is, a denial that there is a person there. (Ketchum 1984, p. 35.)

Let us grant that if contracted child-bearing arrangements do treat women's bodies as objects of commerce—as things that may be bought, sold, or rented—then they ought to be prohibited. The problem with the argument is that it fails to distinguish between (a) my paying you for *you* to use your body in a way that benefits me, and (b) my paying you for *me to* use your body in a way that benefits me. The difference is important, for it determines whether my payments to you give me a right to your body, and thus whether they treat your body as an object of commerce and you as "less than a person." To illustrate the difference, suppose that you own a lawnmower. (I do not mean to suggest that women's bodies are on a par with machines.) If I need to have my lawn mowed then I might (a) pay you for *me* to use your lawnmower to mow my lawn, in which case I can be said to *rent* your lawnmower from you, or (b) pay you for *you* to use your lawnmower to mow my lawn, in which case I do not rent your lawnmower from you but pay you for your services. In the former case I acquire a right to your lawnmower (the right to use it for a limited period of time). In the latter case I do not. The right I have here is at most a right to insist that *you* do with your lawnmower what you said you would. But that is not a right to your lawnmower.

When we apply this distinction to the issue of contracted child-bearing arrangements we see that there is no need to view the payments to the woman as payments that constitute the *rental* of her body. The customer does not acquire a space over which he then has control. He may not paint it blue, keep a coin in it, or do whatever else he pleases as long as he does not cause permanent damage. Instead, the woman is being paid for *her* to use *her* body in a way that benefits him—she is being compensated for her services.* But this does not treat her body as an object of commerce—as something that can be bought, sold, or rented—any more than does my paying a surgeon to perform an operation, a cabby to drive a car, or a model to pose for a drawing. My payments to the surgeon do not give me a right to her arm, make her an object of my domain, nor deny that there is a person there. Indeed, it seems that recognizing that persons can enter into agreements to use their own bodies in ways that benefit others reaffirms their status as persons—as agents—rather than denies it. In short, then, we cannot prohibit contracted child-bearing arrangements on the grounds that they treat women's bodies as commerce and thus treat women as less than persons.

III. Exploitation

A third argument against contracted child-bearing arrangements asserts that the opportunity to be paid for one's services in bearing a

---

*Though I am using the masculine pronoun to refer to the customers of contracted child-bearing arrangements, it is not necessary that a customer be male. A woman with ova but no uterus might have her ovum fertilized with sperm from a sperm bank and pay another woman to carry the child to term. The fact that women may be customers of contracted child-bearing arrangements counsels against our objecting to the arrangements on the grounds that they treat woman as "fungible baby-makers for men whose seed must be carried on." (Margaret Radin (1988, p. 1935) makes the objection within the context of our current gender ideologies.)

child will exploit poor women. They may feel compelled to enter into these arrangements when they would prefer not to do so. Thus we ought to prohibit the arrangements in order to protect poor women from exploitation.

There are four partial responses to this argument which, taken together, seem to me to provide adequate grounds for rejecting the argument. First, there is at least some evidence that the opportunity to be paid for one's services in bearing a child has not in fact, and in general, been exploitive of poor women. Statistics indicate that the "average surrogate mother is white, attended two years of college, married young, and has all the children she and her husband want."[2] These are not the characteristics of the group we envision when we express concerns about protecting the poor from exploitation.*

Second, though the opportunity to be paid for one's services in bearing a child may come to exploit poor women as the arrangements increase in popularity, the same can be said of any opportunity to be paid for one's services. But we do not serve the interests of poor women in general if, in the efforts to protect them from exploitation, we prohibit them the means of escaping poverty.

Third, our concern about exploitation seems to presuppose that the act of bearing a child for another is so detestable, so degrading, that few women would enter into these arrangements were they not forced to do so out of economic necessity. But the statistics mentioned above suggest that this is not the case. Moreover, some women enjoy being pregnant and may view their act as altruistic: They are doing for another what that other cannot do for him or herself, and thereby allowing that other to know the joys (and pains) of raising an offspring.

Finally, if our aim is to protect those women who *do* view bearing a child for another as degrading, but nonetheless feel compelled to do so out of economic necessity, then we can protect those women by putting restrictions on who can *enter into* contracted child-bearing arrangements—we need not prohibit the arrangements entirely. Of course, one might object that such restrictions would be unfair, because they would prohibit poor women from doing something that other women were allowed to do, but that would suggest that the restrictions would be denying the poor women a good, rather than protecting them from a harm, which in turn would suggest that the initial concerns about exploitation were misguided.

IV. Transferring Rights

A fourth argument turns our attention away from the monetary aspect of contracted child-bearing arrangements and towards the nature of parental custodial rights.[†] It can be stated most clearly if we assume that the customer would be the genetic father of the child, and that the woman being paid to bear the child would be the genetic mother. The argument is as follows.

Even if the father does not purchase the mother's custodial right from her, he still must acquire that right if he is to achieve his aim of exclusive custody. But viewing parental custodial rights as something that can be *transferred* from one to another (if not outright sold) presupposes that the custodial relationship between parent and child is a *property* relationship—and that is morally objectionable. On the other hand, if we view parental custodial rights more plausibly as "rights to maintain a relationship,"

---

*It is also worth noting that the offer to bear a child for another (and be compensated for one's efforts and risks in doing so) is not unjustly coercive, in the sense that it does not leave the woman worse off than she would have been had the offer not been made. (For contrast, consider a gunman's "Your money or your life" offer, which does leave the recipient worse off. Robertson (1983, p. 28) develops this point.)

†This argument and the one that follows are applicable to unpaid child-bearing arrangements as well as paid ones. My focus will continue to be on the latter.

then we will be unlikely to think of them as something one can transfer. Ketchum writes:

> We have good reasons for allowing birth-mothers to relinquish their children because otherwise we would be forcing children into the care of people who either do not want them or feel themselves unable to care for them. However, that custody is waivable in this way does not entail that it is saleable or even transferrable. . . . If a mother's right is a right to maintain a relationship, it is implausible to treat it as transferrable; having the option of terminating a relationship with A does not entail having the option of deciding who A will relate to next. (Ketchum 1987, p. 8.)

The suggestion that we view parental custodial rights as rights to maintain a relationship is, I think, a good one. The problem with the argument is that there is nothing in the nature of contracted child-bearing arrangements that requires that custody be transferred rather than waived. In order for one parent to gain exclusive custody of a child, it is not the case that that parent must *acquire* the other parent's parental custodial right, such that he or she now has *two* custodial rights—two rights to maintain a relationship—when before he or she had only one. One parent may obtain exclusive custody of a child merely by the other parent's *waiving* his or her custodial right. The one parent would then have exclusive custody because he or she is then the only parent *with* a custodial right. But his or her right to maintain a relationship has not somehow doubled in size. (This is supported by the fact that a judge is not required to find a parent with exclusive custody *twice* as unfit as a parent who shares custody before she would be justified in removing the child from that parent's care. Indeed, we may think it should be just the reverse.) Thus unless we are willing to assume that the genetic mother of a child is the only parent with a custodial right to the child (an interesting twist on Aristotelian biology), we cannot prohibit contracted childbearing arrangements on the grounds that they require the transfer of parental custodial rights and thus treat children as property.

V. The Needs of Others

The last argument I will address focuses on the needs of persons not principally involved in contracted child-bearing arrangements, namely, children awaiting adoption. Margaret Radin writes:

> There is a danger that unwanted children might remain parentless even if only unpaid surrogacy is allowed, because those seeking children will turn less frequently to adoption. . . . Thus the prohibition of all surrogacy might be grounded on a concern for unwanted children and their chances in life. (Radin 1988, p. 1931.)

Ketchum augments this view by noting that while there may be a shortage of "healthy white infants" available for adoption,

> there are children living in orphanages in third world countries about whom it is hard to believe they would not be better off being adopted by an American couple. . . . It is just possible that they would be more likely to be adopted if contracted motherhood were less available. (Ketchum 1987, p. 13.)

Though I share Radin's and Ketchum's concern for these children, and recognize the need to find homes for them, I have strong reservations about allowing this need to count as grounds for prohibiting contracted child-bearing arrangements. If the need to find homes for hard to place children provides grounds for not allowing an *infertile* couple to have and raise a child genetically related to at least one of them, then it also provides grounds—and just as strong grounds—for not allowing a *fertile* couple to have and raise a child genetically related to at least one of them. Yet few of us would tolerate—much less advocate—a government which could legitimately say to a fertile couple "I am sorry, we cannot allow you to have and raise a child genetically related to at least one of you because there are too many other children who need homes."

VI. Conclusion

I have considered and rejected five arguments in favor of prohibiting contracted child-bearing arrangements. I would like to conclude by raising a concern about the more moderate view that while contracted child-bearing arrangements are morally permissible, they ought not to be legally enforceable.*

Presumably, the grounds in favor of this view are that it would allow persons to enter into contracted child-bearing arrangements while protecting women from the harm of being obliged to waive their custodial right to a child with whom they have bonded. So far so good. Yet if we are to protect the women who *do* bond with the child during pregnancy, without risking harm to those who do not, then the arrangements will have to be cancellable only by the woman. For we would not protect the latter group of women (nor the women in general) were the customers allowed to say, midstream, "I'm sorry, I've changed my mind; you keep the child and I'll keep my money."

Now the concern I have about this view is the picture it paints in which the only interest the man has at stake is his money. It suggests that if the woman cancels the arrangement, then the man keeps his money and everything is *status quo*. But, of course, everything may not be status quo. For if the woman carries the child to

*In other words, while one party ought to be allowed to offer, and another to accept, payments for carrying a child to term, the agreement between the parties ought not to carry the status of a legally binding contract. I suspect that many of the arguments offered in favor of prohibiting contracted child-bearing arrangements are motivated more by a desire to prohibit the *enforcement* of the arrangements than by a desire to prohibit the arrangements entirely. But one way to fulfill the former desire is, of course, to fulfill the latter.

term then the man has in existence a child—a son or daughter—which, given some courts' current presumption against joint custody, and *de facto* presumption in favor of awarding sole custody to the mother, is a child about whom he is not likely to have custody.† This is quite different from never having a child at all. I do not mean to suggest that the interests of the father outweigh those of the mother, but only that when passing legislation we need to be aware that both parties have important non-monetary interests at stake.

NOTES

1. See, for example, Landes and Posner, "The Economics of the Baby Shortage," *Journal of Legal Studies,* vol. 7 (1978), pp. 83–178.

2. Radin, 1988, p. 1930. The statistics are from "Surrogate Motherhood: A Practice That's Still Undergoing Birth Pangs," *Los Angeles Times,* March 22, 1987, sec. 6, at 12, col. 2.

Bibliographic Appendix

Ketchum, Sara, "The Moral Status of the Bodies of Persons," *Social Theory and Practice,* vol. 10 (1984), pp. 25–38.

Ketchum, Sara, "Selling Babies and Selling Bodies: Surrogate Motherhood and the Problem of Commodification." Presented at the Pacific Division Meetings of the American Philosophical Association, Portland Oregon, March 1987.

Landes, Elizabeth, and Richard Posner, "The Economics of the Baby Shortage," *Journal of Legal Studies,* vol. 7 (1978), pp. 83–178.

Radin, Margaret, "Market Inalienability," *Harvard Law Review,* vol. 100 (1988), pp. 1849–1937.

Robertson, John, "Surrogate Mothers: Not So Novel After All," *Hastings Center Report,* vol. 13 (1983), pp. 28–34.

†Given the anger and resentment that is likely to follow a cancelled child-bearing arrangement, it is unlikely that the parents could manage a joint-custody arrangement in a way that would not be injurious to the child. Thus the same may be true even in those states that do not have a presumption against joint custody.

Review and Discussion Questions

1. Review each of the five arguments in favor of prohibiting contracted child-bearing arrangements and assess Malm's replies to each. How persuasive do you find Malm's reasoning?

2. Does paid surrogacy treat the surrogate mother's body as an object of commerce? Does it involve selling a baby?

3. Ruth Macklin maintains that paid surrogacy is exploitative and should be prohibited. Malm argues against this position. With whom do you agree, and why?

4. Has Malm overlooked or failed to deal adequately with any arguments against paid surrogacy?

5. What are the pros and cons of the moderate view that would permit commercial surrogacy but would make the arrangements legally unenforceable?

Is Women's Labor a Commodity?

ELIZABETH S. ANDERSON

Elizabeth S. Anderson, philosophy professor at the University of Michigan, argues that commercial surrogacy constitutes an unconscionable commodification of children and of women's reproductive capacities. She distinguishes between "use" and "respect" as different modes of valuation. Something is a commodity when the market norm of "use" is the mode of valuation proper to it. But persons and some objects are worthy of a higher mode of valuation than use and are not properly regarded as mere commodities. Applying this analysis to paid surrogacy, Anderson argues that treating children as commodities improperly insinuates the norms of commerce into the parental relationship. Furthermore, commercial surrogacy transforms the work of bringing children into the world into a commodity, thereby reducing surrogate mothers from persons worthy of respect to objects of mere use.

Study Questions

1. What is the Kantian critique of slavery, and how does it support Anderson's point about different modes of valuation?

2. Explain how, in Anderson's view, commercial surrogacy substitutes market norms for some of the norms of parental love.

3. What are the three ways in which commercial surrogacy "violates women's claims to respect and consideration"?

From Philosophy & Public Affairs, *vol. 19, no. 1 (Winter 1990). Copyright © 1990 Princeton University Press. Reprinted by permission of Princeton University Press. Some notes omitted.*

4. What is the comparison Anderson draws between surrogacy and the putting-out system of manufacturing?

5. How does the surrogacy industry manipulate the surrogate mother's emotions?

IN THE PAST FEW YEARS the practice of commercial surrogate motherhood has gained notoriety as a method for acquiring children. A commercial surrogate mother is anyone who is paid money to bear a child for other people and terminate her parental rights, so that the others may raise the child as exclusively their own. The growth of commercial surrogacy has raised with new urgency a class of concerns regarding the proper scope of the market. Some critics have objected to commercial surrogacy on the ground that it improperly treats children and women's reproductive capacities as commodities. The prospect of reducing children to consumer durables and women to baby factories surely inspires revulsion. But are there good reasons behind the revulsion? And is this an accurate description of what commercial surrogacy implies? This article offers a theory about what things are properly regarded as commodities, which supports the claim that commercial surrogacy constitutes an unconscionable commodification of children and of women's reproductive capacities.

What Is a Commodity?

The modern market can be characterized in terms of the legal and social norms by which it governs the production, exchange, and enjoyment of commodities. To say that something is properly regarded as a commodity is to claim that the norms of the market are appropriate for regulating its production, exchange, and enjoyment. To the extent that moral principles or ethical ideals preclude the application of market norms to a good, we may say that the good is not a (proper) commodity.

Why should we object to the application of a market norm to the production or distribution of a good? One reason may be that to produce or distribute the good in accordance with the norm is to *fail to value it in an appropriate way.* Consider, for example, a standard Kantian argument against slavery, or the commodification of persons. Slaves are treated in accordance with the market norm that owners may use commodities to satisfy their own interests without regard for the interests of the commodities themselves. To treat a person without regard for her interests is to fail to respect her. But slaves are persons who may not be merely used in this fashion, since as rational beings they possess a dignity which commands respect. In Kantian theory, the problem with slavery is that it treats beings worthy of *respect* as if they were worthy merely of *use.* "Respect" and "use" in this context denote what we may call different *modes of valuation.* We value things and persons in other ways than by respecting and using them. For example, love, admiration, honor, and appreciation constitute distinct modes of valuation. To value a thing or person in a distinctive way involves treating it in accordance with a particular set of norms. For example, courtesy expresses a mode of valuation we may call "civil respect," which differs from Kantian respect in that it calls for obedience to the rules of etiquette rather than to the categorical imperative.

Any ideal of human life includes a conception of how different things and persons should be valued. Let us reserve the term "use" to refer to the mode of valuation proper to commodities, which follows the market norm of treating things solely in accordance with the owner's nonmoral preferences. Then the Kantian argument against commodifying persons can be generalized to apply to many other cases. It can be argued that many objects which are worthy of a higher mode of valuation than use are not properly regarded as mere commodities. Some current arguments against the colorization of classic black-and-white films take this form. Such films have been colorized by their owners in an attempt to enhance their market value by attracting audiences unused to black-and-white cinematography. But some opponents of the practice object that such treatment of the film classics fails to appreciate their aesthetic and historical value. True appreciation of these films would preclude this kind of crass commercial exploitation, which debases their aesthetic qualities in the name of profits. Here the argument rests on the claim that the goods in question are worthy of appreciation, not merely of use.

The ideals which specify how one should value certain things are supported by a conception of human flourishing. Our lives are enriched and elevated by cultivating and exercising the capacity to appreciate art. To fail to do so reflects poorly on ourselves. To fail to value things appropriately is to embody in one's life an inferior conception of human flourishing.

These considerations support a general account of the sorts of things which are appropriately regarded as commodities. Commodities are those things which are properly treated in accordance with the norms of the modern market. We can question the application of market norms to the production, distribution, and enjoyment of a good by appealing to ethical ideals which support arguments that the good should be valued in some other way than use. Arguments of the latter sort claim that to allow certain market norms to govern our treatment of a thing expresses a mode of valuation not worthy of it. If the thing is to be valued appropriately, its production, exchange, and enjoyment must be removed from market norms and embedded in a different set of social relationships.

The Case of Commercial Surrogacy

Let us now consider the practice of commercial surrogate motherhood in the light of this theory of commodities. Surrogate motherhood as a commercial enterprise is based upon contracts involving three parties: the intended father, the broker, and the surrogate mother. The intended father agrees to pay a lawyer to find a suitable surrogate mother and make the requisite medical and legal arrangements for the conception and birth of the child, and for the transfer of legal custody to himself.* The surrogate mother agrees to become impregnated with the intended father's sperm, to carry the resulting child to term, and to relinquish her parental rights to it, transferring custody to the father in return for a fee and medical expenses. Both she and her husband (if she has one) agree not to form a parent-child bond with her child and to do everything necessary to effect the transfer of the child to the intended father. At current market prices, the lawyer arranging the contract can expect to gross $15,000 from the contract, while the surrogate mother can expect a $10,000 fee.

The practice of commercial surrogacy has been defended on four main grounds. First, given the shortage of children available for adoption and the difficulty of qualifying as adoptive parents, it may represent the only hope for some people to be able to raise a family. Commercial surrogacy should be accepted as an effective means for realizing this highly significant good. Second, two fundamental human rights support commercial surrogacy: the right to procreate and freedom of contract. Fully informed autonomous adults should have the right to make whatever arrangements they wish for the use of their bodies and the reproduction of children, so long as the children themselves

*State laws against selling babies prevent the intended father's wife (if he has one) from being a party to the contract.

are not harmed. Third, the labor of the surrogate mother is said to be a labor of love. Her altruistic acts should be permitted and encouraged. Finally, it is argued that commercial surrogacy is no different in its ethical implications from many already accepted practices which separate genetic, gestational, and social parenting, such as artificial insemination by donor, adoption, wet-nursing, and day care. Consistency demands that society accept this new practice as well.

In opposition to these claims, I shall argue that commercial surrogacy does raise new ethical issues, since it represents an invasion of the market into a new sphere of conduct, that of specifically women's labor—that is, the labor of carrying children to term in pregnancy. When women's labor is treated as a commodity, the women who perform it are degraded. Furthermore, commercial surrogacy degrades children by reducing their status to that of commodities. Let us consider each of the goods of concern in surrogate motherhood—the child, and women's reproductive labor—to see how the commercialization of parenthood affects people's regard for them.

Children as Commodities

The most fundamental calling of parents to their children is to love them. Children are to be loved and cherished by their parents, not to be used or manipulated by them for merely personal advantage. Parental love can be understood as a passionate, unconditional commitment to nurture one's child, providing it with the care, affection, and guidance it needs to develop its capacities to maturity. This understanding of the way parents should value their children informs our interpretation of parental rights over their children. Parents' rights over their children are trusts, which they must always exercise for the sake of the child. This is not to deny that parents have their own aspirations in raising children. But the child's interests beyond subsistence are not definable independently of the flourishing of the family, which is the object of specifically parental aspirations. The proper exercise of parental rights includes those acts which promote their shared life as a family, which realize the shared interests of the parents and the child.

The norms of parental love carry implications for the ways other people should treat the relationship between parents and their children. If children are to be loved by their parents, then others should not attempt to compromise the integrity of parental love or work to suppress the emotions supporting the bond between parents and their children. If the rights to children should be understood as trusts, then if those rights are lost or relinquished, the duty of those in charge of transferring custody to others is to consult the best interests of the child.

Commercial surrogacy substitutes market norms for some of the norms of parental love. Most importantly, it requires us to understand parental rights no longer as trusts but as things more like property rights—that is, rights of use and disposal over the things owned. For in this practice the natural mother deliberately conceives a child with the intention of giving it up for material advantage. Her renunciation of parental responsibilities is not done for the child's sake, nor for the sake of fulfilling an interest she shares with the child, but typically for her own sake (and possibly, if "altruism" is a motive, for the intended parents' sakes). She and the couple who pay her to give up her parental rights over her child thus treat her rights as a kind of property right. They thereby treat the child itself as a kind of commodity, which may be properly bought and sold.

Commercial surrogacy insinuates the norms of commerce into the parental relationship in other ways. Whereas parental love is not supposed to be conditioned upon the child having particular characteristics, consumer demand is properly responsive to the characteristics of commodities. So the surrogate industry provides opportunities to adoptive couples to specify the height, I.Q., race, and other attributes of the surrogate mother, in the expectation that these traits will be passed on to the child. Since no industry assigns agents to look after the "interests" of its commodities, no one represents the child's interests in the surrogate industry. The surrogate agency promotes the adoptive parents' interests and not the child's interests where matters of custody are concerned. Finally, as the agent of the adoptive parents, the broker has the task of policing the surrogate (natural) mother's relationship to her child, using persuasion, money, and the threat of a lawsuit to weaken and destroy whatever parental love she may develop for her child.

All of these substitutions of market norms for parental norms represent ways of treating children as commodities which are degrading to them. Degradation occurs when something is treated in accordance with a lower mode of valuation than is proper to it. . . . Since children are valued as mere use-objects by the mother and the surrogate agency when they are sold to others, and by the adoptive parents when they seek to conform the child's genetic makeup to their own wishes, commercial surrogacy degrades children insofar as it treats them as commodities.

. . . Would it be any wonder if a child born of a surrogacy agreement feared resale by parents who have such an attitude? And a child who knew how anxious her parents were that she have the "right" genetic makeup might fear that her parents' love was contingent upon her expression of these characteristics.

The unsold children of surrogate mothers are also harmed by commercial surrogacy. The children of some surrogate mothers have reported their fears that they may be sold like their half-brother or half-sister, and express a sense of loss at being deprived of a sibling. Furthermore, the widespread acceptance of commercial surrogacy

would psychologically threaten all children. For it would change the way children are valued by people (parents and surrogate brokers)—from being loved by their parents and respected by others, to being sometimes used as objects of commercial profit-making.

Proponents of commercial surrogacy have denied that the surrogate industry engages in the sale of children. For it is impossible to sell to someone what is already his own, and the child is already the father's own natural offspring. The payment to the surrogate mother is not for her child, but for her services in carrying it to term. The claim that the parties to the surrogate contract treat children as commodities, however, is based on the way they treat the *mother's* rights over her child. It is irrelevant that the natural father also has some rights over the child; what he pays for is exclusive rights to it. He would not pay her for the "service" of carrying the child to term if she refused to relinquish her parental rights to it. That the mother regards only her labor and not her child as requiring compensation is also irrelevant. No one would argue that the baker does not treat his bread as property just because he sees the income from its sale as compensation for his labor and expenses and not for the bread itself, which he doesn't care to keep.

Defenders of commercial surrogacy have also claimed that it does not differ substantially from other already accepted parental practices. In the institutions of adoption and artificial insemination by donor (AID), it is claimed, we already grant parents the right to dispose of their children. But these practices differ in significant respects from commercial surrogacy. The purpose of adoption is to provide a means for placing children in families when their parents cannot or will not discharge their parental responsibilities. It is not a sphere for the existence of a supposed parental right to dispose of one's children for profit. Even AID does not sanction the sale of fully formed human beings. The semen donor sells only a product of his body, not his child, and does not initiate the act of conception. . . .

Women's Labor as a Commodity

Commercial surrogacy attempts to transform what is specifically women's labor—the work of bringing forth children into the world—into a commodity. It does so by replacing the parental norms which usually govern the practice of gestating children with the economic norms which govern ordinary production processes. The application of commercial norms to women's labor reduces the surrogate mothers from persons worthy of respect and consideration to objects of mere use.

Respect and consideration are two distinct modes of valuation whose norms are violated by the practices of the surrogate industry. To respect a person is to treat her in accordance with principles she rationally accepts—principles consistent with the protection of her autonomy and her rational interests. To treat a person with consideration is to respond with sensitivity to her and to her emotional relations with others, refraining from manipulating or denigrating these for one's own purposes. Given the understanding of respect as a dispassionate, impersonal regard for people's interests, a different ethical concept—consideration—is needed to capture the engaged and sensitive regard we should have for people's emotional relationships. The failure of consideration on the part of the other parties to the surrogacy contract explains the judgment that the contract is not simply disrespectful of the surrogate mother, but callous as well.

The application of economic norms to the sphere of women's labor violates women's claims to respect and consideration in three ways. First, by requiring the surrogate mother to repress whatever parental love she feels for the child, these norms convert women's labor into a form of alienated labor. Second, by manipulating and denying legitimacy to the surrogate mother's evolving perspective on her own pregnancy, the norms of the market degrade her. Third, by taking advantage of the surrogate

mother's noncommercial motivations without offering anything but what the norms of commerce demand in return, these norms leave her open to exploitation. The fact that these problems arise in the attempt to commercialize the labor of bearing children shows that women's labor is not properly regarded as a commodity.

. . . The surrogate industry follows the putting-out system of manufacturing. It provides some of the raw materials of production (the father's sperm) to the surrogate mother, who then engages in production of the child. Although her labor is subject to periodic supervision by her doctors and by the surrogate agency, the agency does not have physical control over the product of her labor as firms using the factory system do. Hence, as in all putting-out systems, the surrogate industry faces the problem of extracting the final product from the mother. This problem is exacerbated by the fact that the social norms surrounding pregnancy are designed to encourage parental love for the child. The surrogate industry addresses this problem by requiring the mother to engage in a form of emotional labor.* In the surrogate contract, she agrees not to form or to attempt to form a parent-child relationship with her offspring. Her labor is alienated, because she must divert it from the end which the social practices of pregnancy rightly promote—an emotional bond with her child. The surrogate contract thus replaces a norm of parenthood, that during pregnancy one create a loving attachment to one's child, with a norm of commercial production, that the producer shall not form any special emotional ties to her product.

The demand to deliberately alienate oneself from one's love for one's own child is a demand which can reasonably and decently be made of no one. Unless we were to remake pregnancy

*One engages in emotional labor when one is paid to express or repress certain emotions. On the concept of emotional labor and its consequences for workers, see Arlie Hochschild, *The Managed Heart* (Berkeley and Los Angeles: University of California Press, 1983).

into a form of drudgery which is only performed for a wage, there is every reason to expect that many women who do sign a surrogate contract will, despite this fact, form a loving attachment to the child they bear. For this is what the social practices surrounding pregnancy encourage. Treating women's labor as just another kind of commercial production process violates the precious emotional ties which the mother may rightly and properly establish with her "product," the child, and thereby violates her claims to consideration.

Commercial surrogacy is also a degrading practice. The surrogate mother, like all persons, has an independent evaluative perspective on her activities and relationships. The realization of her dignity demands that the other parties to the contract acknowledge rather than evade the claims which her independent perspective makes upon them. But the surrogate industry has an interest in suppressing, manipulating, and trivializing her perspective, for there is an ever-present danger that she will see her involvement in her pregnancy from the perspective of a parent rather than from the perspective of a contract laborer. . . .

The treatment and interpretation of surrogate mothers' grief raises the deepest problems of degradation. Most surrogate mothers experience grief upon giving up their children—in 10 percent of cases, seriously enough to require therapy. Their grief is not compensated by the $10,000 fee they receive. Grief is not an intelligible response to a successful deal, but rather reflects the subject's judgment that she has suffered a grave and personal loss. Since not all cases of grief resolve themselves into cases of regret, it may be that some surrogate mothers do not regard their grief, in retrospect, as reflecting an authentic judgment on their part. But in the circumstances of emotional manipulation which pervade the surrogate industry, it is difficult to determine which interpretation of her grief more truly reflects the perspective of the surrogate mother. By insinuating a trivializing interpretation of her emotional responses to the prospect of losing her child, the surrogate agency may be able to manipulate her into accepting her fate without too much fuss, and may even succeed in substituting its interpretation of her emotions for her own. Since she has already signed a contract to perform emotional labor—to express or repress emotions which are dictated by the interests of the surrogate industry—this might not be a difficult task. A considerate treatment of the mothers' grief, on the other hand, would take the evaluative basis of their grief seriously. . . .

The manipulation of the surrogate mother's emotions which is inherent in the surrogate parenting contract also leaves women open to grave forms of exploitation. A kind of exploitation occurs when one party to a transaction is oriented toward the exchange of "gift" values, while the other party operates in accordance with the norms of the market exchange of commodities. Gift values, which include love, gratitude, and appreciation of others, cannot be bought or obtained through piecemeal calculations of individual advantage. Their exchange requires a repudiation of a self-interested attitude, a willingness to give gifts to others without demanding some specific equivalent good in return each time one gives. The surrogate mother often operates according to the norms of gift relationships. The surrogate agency, on the other hand, follows market norms. Its job is to get the best deal for its clients and itself, while leaving the surrogate mother to look after her own interests as best as she can. This situation puts the surrogate agencies in a position to manipulate the surrogate mothers' emotions to gain favorable terms for themselves. For example, agencies screen prospective surrogate mothers for submissiveness, and emphasize to them the importance of the motives of generosity and love. When applicants question some of the terms of the contract, the broker sometimes intimidates them by questioning their character and morality: if they were really generous and loving they would not be so solicitous about their own interests.

Some evidence supports the claim that most surrogate mothers are motivated by emotional needs and vulnerabilities which lead them to view their labor as a form of gift and not a purely commercial exchange. Only 1 percent of applicants to surrogate agencies would become surrogate mothers for money alone; the others have emotional as well as financial reasons for applying. . . .

Many surrogate mothers see pregnancy as a way to feel "adequate," "appreciated," or "special." In other words, these women feel inadequate, unappreciated, or unadmired when they are not pregnant. Lacking the power to achieve some worthwhile status in their own right, they must subordinate themselves to others' definitions of their proper place (as baby factories) in order to get from them the appreciation they need to attain a sense of self-worth. But the sense of self-worth one can attain under such circumstances is precarious and ultimately self-defeating. For example, those who seek gratitude on the part of the adoptive parents and some opportunity to share the joys of seeing their children grow discover all too often that the adoptive parents want nothing to do with them. For while the surrogate mother sees in the arrangement some basis for establishing the personal ties she needs to sustain her emotionally, the adoptive couple sees it as an impersonal commercial contract, one of whose main advantages to them is that all ties between them and the surrogate are ended once the terms of the contract are fulfilled. To them, her presence is a threat to marital unity and a competing object for the child's affections. . . .

The primary distortions which arise from treating women's labor as a commodity—the surrogate mother's alienation from loved ones, her degradation, and her exploitation—stem from a common source. This is the failure to acknowledge and treat appropriately the surrogate mother's emotional engagement with her labor. Her labor is alienated, because she must suppress her emotional ties with her own child, and may be manipulated into reinterpreting these ties in a trivializing way. She is degraded, because her independent ethical perspective is denied, or demoted to the status of a cash sum. She is exploited, because her emotional needs and vulnerabilities are not treated as characteristics which call for consideration, but as factors which may be manipulated to encourage her to make a grave self-sacrifice to the broker's and adoptive couple's advantage. These considerations provide strong grounds for sustaining the claims of women's labor to its "product," the child. The attempt to redefine parenthood so as to strip women of parental claims to the children they bear does violence to their emotional engagement with the project of bringing children into the world.

Review and Discussion Questions

1. Anderson mentions four main defenses of commercial surrogacy before developing her case against it. Assess those four defenses. Do you think Anderson has effectively responded to the points made by Heidi Malm in the previous essay?

2. Do you agree that commercial surrogacy degrades children and that it harms both the "sold" and "unsold" children of the surrogate mother? How would a defender of paid surrogacy respond to Anderson's contentions?

3. Who is right—Ruth Macklin and Malm, or Anderson—about whether paid surrogacy is baby selling?

4. Do you agree with Anderson that the labor of the surrogate mother is alienated? That she is degraded? What if her decision to be a surrogate mother is fully informed and uncoerced?

5. Anderson maintains that the emotions of the surrogate mother are manipulated and that she is exploited. Are such manipulation and exploitation inevitable? If not, are they likely enough to occur that we should prohibit commercial surrogacy?

6. How would Anderson respond to the argument that prohibition of commercial surrogacy is paternalistic and violates John Stuart Mill's liberty principle?

Cloning Human Beings

JOHN A. ROBERTSON

In this essay, John A. Robertson, bioethicist and professor of law at the University of Texas, examines the controversial issue of human cloning. After describing the possible uses and benefits of cloning, he argues that it is sufficiently similar to other reproductive and genetic-selection practices to be permitted. He then goes on to respond to some of the ethical worries that have been expressed about cloning. Robertson rejects calls to ban cloning or research on cloning and instead urges that it be regulated to see that it is done responsibly, to ensure safety and to guarantee informed consent.

Study Questions

1. What are the three situations in which Robertson thinks that couples might choose to reproduce through cloning?

2. In what ways is cloning similar to current reproductive practices? In what ways is it dissimilar?

3. What are the two fears expressed by the National Bioethics Advisory Commission and discussed by Robertson?

4. What regulations or restrictions on cloning does Robertson support?

THE BIRTH OF DOLLY, the sheep cloned from a mammary cell of an adult ewe, has initiated a public debate about human cloning. Although cloning of humans may never be clinically feasible, discussion of the ethical, legal, and social issues raised is important. Cloning is just one of several techniques potentially available to select, control, or alter the genome of offspring.[1-3] The development of such technology poses an important social challenge: how to ensure that the technology is used to enhance, rather than limit, individual freedom and welfare.

From John A. Robertson, "Human Cloning and the Challenge of Regulation," The New England Journal of Medicine, vol. 339, no. 2 (July 9, 1998), pp. 119–122. Copyright © 1998 by the Massachusetts Medical Society. Reprinted by permission. Section titles added.

A key ethical question is whether a responsible couple, interested in rearing healthy offspring biologically related to them, might ethically choose to use cloning (or other genetic-selection techniques) for that purpose. The answer should take into account the benefits sought through the use of the techniques and any potential harm to offspring or to other interests.

I. The Uses of Cloning

The most likely uses of cloning would be far removed from the bizarre or horrific scenarios that initially dominated media coverage.[4] Theoretically, cloning would enable rich or powerful persons to clone themselves several times over, and commercial entrepreneurs might hire women to bear clones of sports or entertainment celebrities to be sold to others to rear. But current reproductive techniques can also be abused, and existing laws against selling children would apply to those created by cloning.

There is no reason to think that the ability to clone humans will cause many people to turn to cloning when other methods of reproduction would enable them to have healthy children. Cloning a human being by somatic-cell nuclear transfer, for example, would require a consenting person as a source of DNA, eggs to be enucleated and then fused with the DNA, a woman who would carry and deliver the child, and a person or couple to raise the child. Given this reality, cloning is most likely to be sought by couples who, because of infertility, a high risk of severe genetic disease, or other factors, cannot or do not wish to conceive a child.

Several plausible scenarios can be imagined. Rather than use sperm, egg, or embryo from anonymous donors, couples who are infertile as a result of gametic insufficiency might choose to clone one of the partners. If the husband were the source of the DNA and the wife provided the egg that received the nuclear transfer and then gestated the fetus, they would have a child biologically related to each of them and would not need to rely on anonymous gamete or embryo donation. Of course, many infertile couples might still prefer gamete or embryo donation or adoption. But there is nothing inherently wrong in wishing to be biologically related to one's children, even when this goal cannot be achieved through sexual reproduction.

A second plausible application would be for a couple at high risk of having offspring with a genetic disease.[5] Couples in this situation must now choose whether to risk the birth of an affected child, to undergo prenatal or preimplantation diagnosis and abortion or the discarding of embryos, to accept gamete donation, to seek adoption, or to remain childless. If cloning were available, however, some couples, in line with prevailing concepts of kinship, family, and parenting, might strongly prefer to clone one of themselves or another family member. Alternatively, if they already had a healthy child, they might choose to use cloning to create a later-born twin of that child. In the more distant future, it is even possible that the child whose DNA was replicated would not have been born healthy but would have been made healthy by gene therapy after birth.

A third application relates to obtaining tissue or organs for transplantation. A child who needed an organ or tissue transplant might lack a medically suitable donor. Couples in this situation have sometimes conceived a child coitally in the hope that he or she would have the correct tissue type to serve, for example, as a bone marrow donor for an older sibling.[6,7] If the child's disease was not genetic, a couple might prefer to clone the affected child to be sure that the tissue would match.

It might eventually be possible to procure suitable tissue or organs by cloning the source DNA only to the point at which stem cells or other material might be obtained for transplantation, thus avoiding the need to bring a child into the world for the sake of obtaining tissue.[8]

Cloning a person's cells up to the embryo stage might provide a source of stem cells or tissue for the person cloned. Cloning might also be used to enable a couple to clone a dead or dying child so as to have that child live on in some closely related form, to obtain sufficient numbers of embryos for transfer and pregnancy, or to eliminate mitochondrial disease.[5]

II. Cloning's Similarity to Current Practices

Most, if not all, of the potential uses of cloning are controversial, usually because of the explicit copying of the genome. As the National Bioethics Advisory Commission noted, in addition to concern about physical safety and eugenics, somatic-cell cloning raises issues of the individuality, autonomy, objectification, and kinship of the resulting children.[5] In other instances, such as the production of embryos to serve as tissue banks, the ethical issue is the sacrifice of embryos created solely for that purpose.

Given the wide leeway now granted couples to use assisted reproduction and prenatal genetic selection in forming families, cloning should not be rejected in all circumstances as unethical or illegitimate. The manipulation of embryos and the use of gamete donors and surrogates are increasingly common. Most fetuses conceived in the United States and Western Europe are now screened for genetic or chromosomal anomalies. Before conception, screening to identify carriers of genetic diseases is widespread.[9] Such practices also deviate from conventional notions of reproduction, kinship, and medical treatment of infertility, yet they are widely accepted.

Despite the similarity of cloning to current practices, however, the dissimilarities should not be overlooked. The aim of most other forms of assisted reproduction is the birth of a child who is a descendant of at least one member of the couple, not an identical twin. Most genetic selection acts negatively to identify and screen out unwanted traits such as genetic disease, not positively to choose or replicate the genome as in somatic-cell cloning.[3] It is not clear, however, why a child's relation to his or her rearing parents must always be that of sexually reproduced descendant when such a relationship is not possible because of infertility or other factors. Indeed, in gamete donation and adoption, although sexual reproduction is involved, a full descendant relation between the child and both rearing parents is lacking. Nor should the difference between negative and positive means of selecting children determine the ethical or social acceptability of cloning or other techniques. In both situations, a deliberate choice is made so that a child is born with one genome rather than another or is not born at all.

Is cloning sufficiently similar to current assisted-reproduction and genetic-selection practices to be treated similarly as a presumptively protected exercise of family or reproductive liberty?[10] Couples who request cloning in the situations I have described are seeking to rear healthy children with whom they will have a genetic or biologic tie, just as couples who conceive their children sexually do. Whether described as "replication" or as "reproduction," the resort to cloning is similar enough in purpose and effects to other reproduction and genetic-selection practices that it should be treated similarly. Therefore, a couple should be free to choose cloning unless there are compelling reasons for thinking that this would create harm that the other procedures would not cause.[10]

III. Fears of Cloning

The concern of the National Bioethics Advisory Commission about the welfare of the clone reflects two types of fear. The first is that a child with the same nuclear DNA as another person, who is thus that person's later-born identical twin, will be so severely harmed by the identity of nuclear DNA between them that it is morally preferable, if not obligatory, that the child not be born at all.[5] In this case the fear is that the later-born twin will lack individuality or the freedom to create his or her own identity because of confusion or expectations caused by having the same DNA as another person.[5,11]

This claim does not withstand the close scrutiny that should precede interference with a couple's freedom to bear and rear biologically related children.[10] Having the same genome as another person is not in itself harmful, as widespread experience with monozygotic twins shows. Being a twin does not deny either twin his or her individuality or freedom, and twins often have a special intimacy or closeness that few non-twin siblings can experience.[12] There is no reason to think that being a later-born identical twin resulting from cloning would change the overall assessment of being a twin.

Differences in mitochondria and the uterine and childhood environment will undercut problems of similarity and minimize the risk of overidentification with the first twin. A clone of Smith may look like Smith, but he or she will not be Smith and will lack many of Smith's phenotypic characteristics. The effects of having similar DNA will also depend on the length of time before the second twin is born, on whether the twins are raised together, on whether they are informed that they are genetic twins, on whether other people are so informed, on the beliefs that the rearing parents have about genetic influence on behavior, and on other factors. Having a previously born twin might in some circumstances also prove to be a source of support or intimacy for the later-born child.

The risk that parents or the child will overly identify the child with the DNA source also seems surmountable. Would the child invariably be expected to match the phenotypic characteristics of the DNA source, thus denying the second twin an "open future" and the freedom to develop his or her own identity?[5,11,13] In response to this question, one must ask whether

couples who choose to clone offspring are more likely to want a child who is a mere replica of the DNA source or a child who is unique and valued for more than his or her genes. Couples may use cloning in order to ensure that the biologic child they rear is healthy, to maintain a family connection in the face of gametic infertility, or to obtain matched tissue for transplantation and yet still be responsibly committed to the welfare of their child, including his or her separate identity and interests and right to develop as he or she chooses.

The second type of fear is that parents who choose their child's genome through somatic-cell cloning will view the child as a commodity or an object to serve their own ends.[5] We do not view children born through coital or assisted reproduction as "mere means" just because people reproduce in order to have company in old age, to fulfill what they see as God's will, to prove their virility, to have heirs, to save a relationship, or to serve other selfish purposes.[14] What counts is how a child is treated after birth. Self-interested motives for having children do not prevent parents from loving children for themselves once they are born.

IV. Conclusion

The use of cloning to form families in the situations I have described, though closely related to current assisted-reproduction and genetic-selection practices, does offer unique variations. The novelty of the relation—cloning in lieu of sperm donation, for example, produces a later-born identical twin raised by the older twin and his spouse—will create special psychological and social challenges. Can these challenges be successfully met, so that cloning produces net good for families and society? Given the largely positive experience with assisted-reproduction techniques that initially appeared frightening, cautious optimism is justified. We should be able to develop procedures and guidelines for cloning that will allow us to obtain its benefits while minimizing its problems and dangers.

In the light of these considerations, I would argue that a ban on privately funded cloning research is unjustified and likely to hamper important types of research.[8] A permanent ban on the cloning of human beings, as advocated by the Council of Europe and proposed in Congress, is also unjustified.[15,16] A more limited ban— whether for 5 years, as proposed by the National Bioethics Advisory Commission and enacted in California, or for 10 years, as in the bill of Senator Dianne Feinstein (D-Calif) and Senator Edward M. Kennedy (D-Mass.) that is now before Congress—is also open to question.[5,17,18] Given the early state of cloning science and the widely shared view that the transfer of cloned embryos to the uterus before the safety and efficacy of the procedure has been established is unethical, few responsible physicians are likely to offer human cloning in the near future.[5] Nor are profit-motivated entrepreneurs, such as Richard Seed, likely to have many customers for their cloning services until the safety of the procedure is demonstrated.[19] A ban on human cloning for a limited period would thus serve largely symbolic purposes. Symbolic legislation, however, often has substantial costs.[20,21] A government-imposed prohibition on privately funded cloning, even for a limited period, should not be enacted unless there is a compelling need. Such a need has not been demonstrated.

Rather than seek to prohibit all uses of human cloning, we should focus our attention on ensuring that cloning is done well. No physician or couple should embark on cloning without careful thought about the novel relational issues and child-rearing responsibilities that will ensue. We need regulations or guidelines to ensure safety and efficacy, fully informed consent and counseling for the couple, the consent of any person who may provide DNA, guarantees of parental rights and duties, and a limit on the number of clones from any single source.[10] It may also be important to restrict cloning to situations where there is a strong likelihood that the couple or individual initiating the procedure will also rear the resulting child. This principle will encourage a stable parenting situation and minimize the chance that cloning entrepreneurs will create clones to be sold to others.[22] As our experience grows, some restrictions on who may serve as a source of DNA for cloning (for example, a ban on cloning one's parents) may also be defensible.[10]

Cloning is important because it is the first of several positive means of genetic selection that may be sought by families seeking to have and rear healthy, biologically related offspring. In the future, mitochondrial transplantation, germ-line gene therapy, genetic enhancement, and other forms of prenatal genetic alteration may be possible.[3,23,24] With each new technique, as with cloning, the key question will be whether it serves important health, reproductive, or family needs and whether its benefits outweigh any likely harm. Cloning illustrates the principle that when legitimate uses of a technique are likely, regulatory policy should avoid prohibition and focus on ensuring that the technique is used responsibly for the good of those directly involved. As genetic knowledge continues to grow, the challenge of regulation will occupy us for some time to come.

REFERENCES

1. Silver, L. M. *Remaking Eden: Cloning and beyond in a brave new world.* New York: Avon Books, 1997.

2. Walters, L., Palmer, J. G. *The ethics of human gene therapy.* New York: Oxford University Press, 1997.

3. Robertson, J. A. "Genetic selection of offspring characteristics." *Boston Univ Law Rev* 1996; 76: 421–82.

4. Begley, S. "Can we clone humans?" *Newsweek.* March 10, 1997: 53–60.

5. *Cloning human beings: Report and recommendations of the National Bioethics Advisory Commission.* Rockville, Md.: National Bioethics Advisory Commission, 1997.

6. Robertson, J. A. *Children of choice: Freedom and the new reproductive technologies.* Princeton, N.J.: Princeton University Press, 1994.

7. Kearney, W., Caplan, A. L. "Parity for the donation of bone marrow: ethical and policy considerations." In Blank, R. H., Bonnicksen, A. L., eds. *Emerging issues in biomedical policy: An annual review.* Vol. 1. New York: Columbia University Press, 1992: 262–85.

8. Kassirer, J. P., Rosenthal, N. A. "Should human cloning research be off limits?" *N Engl J Med* 1998; 38: 905–6.

9. Holtzman, N. A. *Proceed with caution: Predicting genetic risks in the recombinant DNA era.* Baltimore: Johns Hopkins University Press, 1989.

10. Robertson, J. A. "Liberty, identity, and human cloning." *Texas Law Rev* 1998; 77: 1371–456.

11. Davis, D. S. "What's wrong with cloning?" *Jurimetrics* 1997; 38: 83–9.

12. Segal, N. L. "Behavioral aspects of intergenerational human cloning: What twins tell us." *Jurimetrics* 1997; 38: 57–68.

13. Jonas, H. *Philosophical essays: From ancient creed to technological man.* Englewood Cliffs, N.J.: Prentice-Hall, 1974: 161.

14. Heyd, D. *Genethics: Moral issues in the creation of people.* Berkeley: University of California Press, 1992.

15. Council of Europe. Draft additional protocol to the Convention on Human Rights and Biomedicine on the prohibition of cloning human beings with explanatory report and Parliamentary Assembly opinion (adopted September 22, 1997). *XXXVI International Legal Materials* 1415 (1997).

16. *Human Cloning Prohibition Act,* H.R. 923, S. 1601 (March 5, 1997).

17. *Act of Oct. 4, 1997,* ch. 668, 1997 Cal. Legis. Serv. 3790 (West, WESTLAW through 1997 Sess.).

18. *Prohibition on Cloning of Human Beings Act,* S. 1602, 105th Cong. (1998).

19. Stolberg, S. G. "A small spark ignites debate on laws on cloning humans." *New York Times,* January 19, 1998: A1.

20. Gusfield, J. *Symbolic crusades: Status politics and the American temperance movement.* Urbana: University of Illinois Press, 1963.

21. Wolf, S. M. "Ban cloning? Why NBAC is wrong." *Hastings Cent Rep* 1997; 27(5): 12.

22. Wilson, J. Q. "The paradox of cloning." *The Weekly Standard.* May 26, 1997: 23–7.

23. Zhang, J., Grifo, J., Blaszcyk, A., et al. "In vitro maturation of human preovulatory oocytes reconstructed by germinal vesicle transfer." *Fertil Steril* 1997; 68: Suppl:S1. abstract.

24. Bonnicksen, A. L. "Transplanting nuclei between human eggs: implications for germ-line genetics." *Politics and the Life Sciences.* March 1998: 3–10.

Review and Discussion Questions

1. If human cloning were both technologically feasible and legal, would it be a popular procedure? Who would be likely to choose it and why? What reasons, if any, for seeking to clone one's self or a loved one would you consider legitimate? What motives would be morally dubious?

2. Should there be a presumption in favor of cloning on the grounds that people have a right to reproductive freedom? Or should there be a presumption against it on the grounds that it deviates sharply from normal procreation, which is based on sexuality and a human relationship between two persons?

3. Some critics contend that cloning is wrong because it deprives the child of an individual identity. Assess Robertson's response to this challenge. Is cloning harmful to the child in some way?

4. Other critics argue that people who choose their child's genome through somatic-cell cloning will view the child as a commodity. Assess Robertson's response to this objection. Does cloning involve treating the child as a means only, rather than as an end in its own right? Is cloning likely to distort the parent-child relationship? Assess cloning from the perspective of Elizabeth Anderson's essay.

5. The World Health Organization has stated that "cloning for the replication of human individuals" violates the principles of "respect for the dignity of the individual and protection of the security of the human genetic material." Assess this contention.

6. Robertson states that cloning "will create special psychological and social challenges." What do you think these challenges are, and how might they be dealt with?

7. Are there ethical objections to cloning that Robertson has overlooked or failed to address adequately?

8. Should human cloning be banned, permitted but regulated, or left unrestricted? Explain your position. If you agree with Robertson that it should be permitted but regulated, exactly how should it be regulated and why? Assess the restrictions that Robertson mentions.

9

MARRIAGE AND FAMILY OBLIGATIONS

Adultery and Fidelity

MIKE W. MARTIN

In this essay, Mike W. Martin, professor of philosophy at Chapman University, examines the morality of adultery, trying to steer a course between "conventional absolute prohibitions" and "trendy permissiveness." Maintaining that a rule-oriented approach is unsatisfactory, he focuses instead on the moral ideals traditionally associated with marriage, in particular, love, commitment, and trust. Although traditional marriage arrangements are morally optional and couples are free to develop their own particular commitments and understandings, for those who do opt for traditional marriage, a commitment to love implies sexual exclusivity, and sexual fidelity is a virtue because it supports love. However, commitments can change, relationships can deteriorate, and spouses can sometimes fall in love with others, thus complicating the ethics of adultery. Although adultery within traditional marriage is generally immoral, in some circumstances, Martin believes, it may be justified or at least excusable.

Study Questions

1. How does Martin define "adultery"? Do you agree with his definition? What does he mean by "marriage"?

2. How does his approach to the ethics of adultery differ from a "rule-oriented approach"?

3. What are the descriptive and normative senses of "love"?

4. According to Martin, how does sexual exclusivity express and protect love? Why does he want to avoid saying that it is "intrinsically valuable or a feature of all genuine love"?

From the Journal of Social Philosophy, *vol. 25, no. 3 (Winter 1994). Reprinted by permission of the* Journal of Social Philosophy.

5. People can renegotiate their understandings and commitments. But what two difficulties can changing commitments give rise to?

6. Is love-inspired adultery always wrong?

ADULTERY IS MORALLY COMPLEX. . . . Whether as moral judges assessing the character of adulterers or as moral agents confronted with making our own decisions about adultery, we often find ourselves immersed in confusions and ambiguities that are both personally and philosophically troublesome.

I will seek a middle ground between conventional absolute prohibitions and trendy permissiveness. A humanistic perspective should embrace a pluralistic moral outlook that affirms a variety of forms of sexual relationships, including many traditional marriages. It can justify a strong presumption against adultery for individuals who embrace traditional marital ideals.

The ethics of adultery divides into two parts: making commitments and keeping them. The ethics of making commitments centers primarily on commitments to love, where love is a value-guided relationship, and secondarily on the promise of sexual exclusivity (the promise to have sex only with one's spouse) which some couples make in order to support the commitment to love. The ethics of keeping commitments has to do with balancing initial marital commitments against other moral considerations.

Making Commitments

What is adultery? Inspired by the New Testament, some people employ a wide definition that applies to any significant sexual interest in someone besides one's spouse: "You have heard that it was said, 'Do not commit adultery.' But I tell you that anyone who looks at a woman lustfully has already committed adultery with her in his heart."[1] Other people define adultery narrowly to match their particular scruples: for them extramarital genital intercourse may count as adultery, but not oral sex; or falling in love with someone besides one's spouse may count as adultery but not "merely" having sex. Whatever definition we might adopt there will always be borderline cases, if only those created by "brinkmanship"—going as far as possible without having intercourse (e.g., lying naked together in bed).

In this paper, "adultery" refers to married persons having sexual intercourse (of any kind) with someone other then their spouses. I am aware that the word "adultery" is not purely descriptive and evokes a range of emotive connotations. Nevertheless, I use the word without implying that adultery is immoral; that is a topic left open for investigation in specific cases. Like "deception," the world "adultery" raises moral questions about possible misconduct but it does not answer them. By contrast, I will use a wider sense of "marriage" that refers to all monogamous (two-spouse) relationships formally established by legal or religious ceremonies *and* closely analogous moral relationships such as committed relationships between homosexual or heterosexual couples who are not legally married.

A moral understanding of adultery turns on an understanding of morality. If we conceive morality as a set of rules, we will object to adultery insofar as it violates those rules. "Do not commit adultery" is not an irreducible moral principle, but many instances of adultery violate other familiar roles. As Richard Wasserstrom insightfully explained, much adultery violates one or more of these rules: Do not break promises (*viz.*, the wedding vows to abjure outside sex, vows which give one's partner "reasonable expectations" of sexual fidelity); do not deceive (whether by lying, withholding information, or pretending about the affair); do not be unfair (by enjoying outside sex forbidden to one's spouse); and do not cause undeserved harm (to one's spouse who suspects or hears of the affair).[2] Wasserstrom points out that all these rules are *prima facie*: In some situations they are overridden by other moral considerations, thereby justifying some instances of adultery.

Moreover, adultery is not even *prima facie* wrong when spouses have an "open marriage" in which they give each other permission to have extramarital affairs. In this connection Wasserstrom raises questions about the reasonableness of traditional marital promises of sexual exclusivity. Wouldn't it be wiser to break the conventional ties between sex and love, so that the pleasures of adultery can be enjoyed along with those of marriage? Alternatively, should we maintain the connection between sex and love but break the exclusive tie between sexual love and one's spouse, thus tolerating multiple simultaneous loves for one's spouse and for additional partners? No doubt the linking of love, sex, and exclusivity has an *instrumental* role in promoting marriages, but so would the patently unreasonable practices of allowing people to eat decent meals (beyond bread and water) only with their spouses.

In my view, a rule-oriented approach to morality lacks the resources needed to answer the important questions Wasserstrom raises. We need an expanded conception of morality as encompassing ideals and virtues, in particular the moral ideals of love which provide the point of marital commitments and the virtues manifested in pursuing those ideals. The ethics of adultery centers on the moral ideals of and commitments to love—which include ideals of constancy (or faithfulness), honesty, trust, and fairness—that make possible special ways of caring for persons. The ideals are morally optional in that no one is obligated to embrace them. Nevertheless, strong obligations to avoid adultery arise for those couples who embrace the

ideals as a basis for making traditional marital commitments. The primary commitment is to love each other, while the commitment of sexual exclusivity is secondary and supportive. This can be seen by focusing on three ideas that Wasserstrom devotes little attention to: love, commitments to love, and trust.

1. What is *love*? Let us set aside the purely descriptive (value-neutral) senses in which "love" refers to (a) a strong positive attraction or emotion or (b) a complex attitude involving many emotions—not only strong affection, but also excitement, joy, pride, hope, fear, jealousy, anger, and so on. Let us focus instead on the normative (value-laden) sense in which we speak of "true love" or "the real thing." Cogent disputes arise concerning the values defining true love, though ultimately individuals have a wide area of personal discretion in the ideals they pursue in relationships of erotic love.

In its value-laden senses, "love" refers to special ways of valuing persons. As an attitude, love is valuing the beloved, cherishing her or him as unique. Erotic love includes sexual valuing, but the valuing is focused on the person as a unity, not just a body. As a relationship, love is defined by reciprocal attitudes of mutual valuing. The precise nature of this valuing turns on the ideals one accepts, and hence those ideals are part of the very meaning of "love."

2. According to the traditional ideal (or set of ideals) of interest here, marriage is based on a *commitment to love*: "to have and to hold from this day forward, for better for worse, for richer for poorer, in sickness and in health, to love and to cherish, till death us do part." This is not just a commitment to have continuous feelings of strong affection—feelings which are beyond our immediate voluntary control. Instead, it is a commitment to create and sustain a relationship conducive to those feelings, as well as conducive to the happiness and fulfillment of both partners. Spouses assume responsibility for maintaining conditions for mutual caring which in turn foster recurring emotions of deep affection, delight, shared enthusiasm, and joy. The commitment to love is not a promise uttered once during a wedding ceremony; it is an ongoing willingness to assume responsibility for a value-guided relationship.

The commitment to love implies a web of values and virtues. It is a commitment to create a lifelong relationship of deep caring that promises happiness through shared activities (including sexual ones) and through joining interests in mutually supportive ways involving shared decision-making, honesty, trust, emotional intimacy, reciprocity, and (at least in modern versions) fair and equal opportunities for self-expression and personal growth. This traditional ideal shapes how spouses value each other, both symbolically and substantively. Commitments to love throughout a lifetime show that partners value each other as having paramount importance and also value them as a unity, as persons-living-throughout-a-lifetime. Time-limited commitments, such as to remain together only while in college, express at most a limited affirmation of the importance of the other person in one's life.

Valuing each other is manifested in a willingness to make accommodations and sacrifices to support the marriage. For most couples, some of those sacrifices are sexual. The promise of sexual exclusivity is a distinct wedding vow whose supportive status is symbolized by being mentioned in a subordinate clause, "and, forsaking all others, keep thee only unto her/him." Hopefully couples who make the vow of sexual exclusivity are not under romantic illusions that their present sexual preoccupation with each other will magically abolish sexual interests in other people and temptations to have extramarital affairs. They commit themselves to sexual exclusivity as an expression of their love and with the aim of protecting that love.

How does sexual exclusivity express and protect love? In two ways. First, many spouses place adultery at the top of the list of actions which threaten their marriage. They are concerned, often with full justification, that adultery might lead to another love that would damage or destroy their relationship. They fear that the affection, time, attention, and energy (not to mention money) given to an extramarital partner would lessen the resources they devote to sustaining their marriage. They also fear the potential for jealousy to disrupt the relationship. As long as it does not become excessive, jealousy is a healthy reaction of anger, fear, and hurt in response to a perceived loss of an important good. Indeed, if a spouse feels no jealousy whatsoever, the question is raised (though not answered) about the depth of love.

Second, sexual exclusivity is one way to establish the symbolism that "making love" is a singular affirmation of the partner. The love expressed is not just strong affection, but a deep valuing of each other in the ways defined by the ideals embedded in the marriage. Sex is especially well-suited (far more than eating) to express that love because of its extraordinary physical and emotional intimacy, tenderness, and pleasure. The symbolic meaning involved is not sentimental fluff; it makes possible forms of expression that enter into the substance of love.

In our culture sex has no uniform meaning, but couples are free to give it personal meanings. Janet Z. Giele notes two extremes: "On the one hand, the body may be viewed as the most important thing the person has to give, and sexual intercourse therefore becomes the symbol of the deepest and most far-reaching commitment, which is to be strictly limited to one pair-bond. On the other hand, participants may define sexual activity as merely a physical expression that, since it does not importantly envelop the whole personality nor commit the pair beyond the pleasures of the moment, may be regulated more permissively."[3] Between the two extremes lie many variations in the personal symbolism that couples give to sex, and here we are exploring only those variations found in traditional marital vows.

3. *Trust* is present at the time when couples undertake commitments to love, and in turn those commitments provide a framework for sustaining trust. Trust implies but is not reducible to Wasserstrom's "reasonable expectations" about a partner's conduct. Expectations are epistemic attitudes, whereas trust is a moral attitude of relying on others to act responsibly, with goodwill, and (in marriage) with love and support. We have a reasonable expectation that the earth will continue to orbit the sun throughout our lifetime, but no moral relationship of trust is involved. As a way of giving support to others, underwriting their endeavors, and showing the importance of their lives to us, trust and trustworthiness is a key ingredient in caring.

To be sure, trust is not always good. It is valuable when it contributes to valuable relationships, in particular to worthwhile marriages. Marital trust is confidence in and dependence upon a spouse's morally responsible love. As such, it provides a basis for ongoing intimacy and mutual support. It helps spouses undergo the vulnerabilities and risks (emotional, financial, physical) inherent in intimate relationships.

The trust of marital partners is broad-scoped. Spouses trust each other to actively support the marriage and to avoid doing things that might pull them away from it. They trust each other to maintain the conditions for preserving intimacy and mutual happiness. Violating marital trust does more than upset expectations and cause pain. It violates trust, honesty, fairness, caring, and the other moral ideals defining the relationship. It betrays one's spouse. And it betrays one's integrity as someone committed to their ideals.

To sum up, I have avoided Wasserman's narrow preoccupation with the promise of sexual exclusivity. Commitments of sexual exclusivity find their rationale in wider commitments to love each other *if* a couple decides that exclusivity will support their commitments to love *and* where love is understood as a special way to value persons within lasting relationships based on mutual caring, honesty, and trust. Accordingly, marital faithfulness (or constancy) in loving is the primary virtue; sexual fidelity is a supporting virtue. And sexual fidelity must be understood in terms of the particular commitments and understandings that couples establish.

I have also avoided saying that sexual exclusivity is intrinsically valuable or a feature of all genuine love. . . . In my view, the intrinsic good lies in fulfilling love relationships, rather than sexual exclusivity *per se*, thereby recognizing that some couples sustain genuine love without sexual exclusivity. For some couples sexual exclusivity does contribute to the goods found in traditional relationships, but other couples achieve comparable goods through nontraditional relationships, for example open marriages that tolerate outside sex without love. We can recognize the value of traditional relationships while also recognizing the value of alternative relationships, as chosen autonomously by couples.

Keeping Commitments

A complete ethics of keeping commitments of exclusivity would focus on the virtues of responsibility, faithfulness, and self-control. Here, however, I wish to defend Wasserstrom's view that even in traditional relationships the prohibition against adultery is *prima facie*. However strong the presumption against adultery in traditional relationships, it does not yield an exceptionless, all-things-considered judgment about wrong doing and blameworthiness in specific cases. I will discuss four of the many complicating factors. What if partners wish to change their commitments? What happens when love comes to an end? What if one spouse falls in love with an additional partner? And what about the sometimes extraordinary self-affirmation extramarital affairs may bring?

(i) *Changing Commitments.* Some spouses who begin with traditional commitments later revise them. Buoyed by the exuberance of romance, most couples feel confident they will not engage in adultery (much less be among the fifty percent of couples who divorce). Later they may decide to renegotiate the guidelines for their marriage in light of changing attitudes and circumstances, though still within the framework of their commitments to love each other. One study suggests that 90% of couples believe sexual exclusivity to be essential when they marry, but only 60% maintain this belief after several years of marriage (with the changes occurring primarily among those who had at least one affair).

Vita Sackville-West and Harold Nicolson provide an illuminating if unusual example. They married with the usual sexual attraction to each other and for several years were sexually compatible. As that changed, they gave each other permission to pursue extramarital affairs, primarily homosexual ones. Yet their original commitment to love each other remained intact. Indeed, for forty-nine years, until Vita died in 1962, their happy marriage was a model of mutual caring, deep affection, and trust. . . .

Just as we respect the mutual autonomy of couples in forming their initial understanding about their relationship, we should also respect their autonomy in renegotiating that understanding. The account I have offered allows us to distinguish between the primary commitment to love and the secondary commitment of sexual exclusivity. The secondary commitment is made in order to support the primary one, and if a couple agrees that it no longer is needed they are free to revoke it. Renegotiations can also proceed in the reverse directions: Spouses who initially agree on an open marriage may find that allowing extramarital affairs creates unbearable strains on their relationship, leading them to make commitments of exclusivity.

Changing commitments raise two major difficulties. First, couples are sometimes less than explicit about the sexual rules for their relationship. One or both partners may sense that their understandings have changed over the years but fail to engage in discussions that establish explicit new understandings. As a result, one spouse may believe something is acceptable to the other spouse when in fact it is not. . . . Lack of shared understanding generates moral vagueness and ambiguity concerning adultery, whereas periodic forthright communication helps establish clear moral boundaries.

Second, what happens when only one partner wants to renegotiate an original understanding? The mere desire to renegotiate does not constitute a betrayal, nor does it by itself justify adultery if one's spouse refuses to rescind the initial vow of sexual exclusivity. In such cases the original presumption against adultery continues but with an increased risk that the partner wishing to change it may feel adultery is more excusable. Such conflicts may or may not be resolved in a spirit of caring and compromise that enables good relationships to continue. Lacking such resolution, the moral status of adultery may become less clear-cut.

(ii) *Lost Love.* Couples who make traditional commitments sometimes fall out of love, singly or together, or for other reasons find themselves unwilling to continue in a marriage. Sometimes the cause is adultery, and sometimes adultery is a symptom of irresponsibility and poor judgment that erodes the relationship in additional ways. But other times there is little or no fault involved. Lasting love is a creation of responsible conduct *and* luck. No amount of conscientiousness can replace the good fortune of emotional compatibility and conducive circumstances.

In saying that traditional commitments to love are intended to be lifelong, we need not view them as unconditional. Typically they are based on tacit conditions. One condition is embedded in the wedding ceremony in which *mutual* vows are exchanged, namely, that one's spouse will take the marital vows seriously. Others are presupposed as background conditions, for example, that the spouse will not turn into a murderer, rapist, spouse-beater, child-abuser, or psychopathic monster. Usually there are more specific tacit assumptions that evolve before the marriage, for example, that the spouses will support each other's careers. Above all, there is the background hope that with sincere effort the relationship will contribute to the overall happiness of both partners. All these conditions remain largely tacit, as a matter of faith. When that faith proves ill-founded or just unlucky, the ethics of adultery becomes complicated.

As relationships deteriorate, adultery may serve as a transition to new and perhaps better relationships. In an ideal world, marriages would be ended cleanly before new relationships begin. But then, in an ideal world people would be sufficiently prescient not to make traditional commitments that are unlikely to succeed. Contemplating adultery is an occasion for much self-deception, but at least sometimes there may be good reasons for pursuing alternative relationships before officially ending a bad marriage.

(iii) *New Loves.* Some persons claim to (erotically) love both their spouse and an additional lover. They may be mistaken, as they later confess to themselves, but is it impossible to love two (or more) people simultaneously? "Impossible" in what sense?

Perhaps for some people it is a psychological impossibility, but, again, other individuals report a capacity to love more than one person at a time. For many persons it is a practical impossibility, given the demands of time, attention, and affection required in genuine loving. But that would seem to allow that resourceful individuals can finesse (psychologically, logistically, financially, and so forth) multiple simultaneous relationships. I believe that the impossibility is moral and conceptual—*if* one embraces traditional ideals that define marital love as a singular affirmation of one's spouse and *if* a couple establishes sex as a symbolic and substantive way to convey that exclusive love. Obviously people can experience additional romantic attractions

after they make traditional vows, but it is morally impossible for them to actively engage in loving relationships with additional partners without violating the love defined by their initial commitments.

Richard Taylor disagrees in *Having Love Affairs,* a book-length defense of adultery. No doubt this book is helpful for couples planning open marriages, but Taylor concentrates on situations where traditional vows have been made and then searches for ways to minimize the harm to spouses that results from extramarital love affairs.[4] In that regard his book is morally subversive in that it systematically presents only one side of the story. . . .

Bonnie Steinbock affirms an opposite view. She suggests that to fall in love with someone other than one's spouse is already a betrayal: "Sexual infidelity has significance as a sign of a deeper betrayal—falling in love with someone else. It may be objected that we cannot control the way we feel, only the way we behave; that we should not be blamed for falling in love, but only for acting on the feeling. While we may not have direct control over our feelings, however, we are responsible for getting ourselves into situations in which certain feelings naturally arise."[5] I agree that spouses who make traditional vows are responsible for avoiding situations that they know (or should know) foster extramarital love. Nevertheless, deeply committed people occasionally do fall in love with third parties without being blameworthy for getting into situations that spark that love. Experiencing a strong romantic attraction is not by itself an infidelity, and questions of betrayal may arise only when a person moves in the direction of acting on the love in ways that violate commitments to one's spouse.

Having said all this, I know of no argument that absolutely condemns all love-inspired adultery as immoral, all things considered and in all respects, even within traditional relationships. Nonetheless, as I have been concerned to emphasize, there is a serious betrayal of one's spouse. But to say that ends the matter would make the commitment to love one's spouse a moral absolute, with no exceptions whatsoever. Tragic dilemmas overthrow such absolutes, and we need to set aside both sweeping condemnations and wholesale defenses of love-inspired adultery.

To mention just one type of case, when marriages are profoundly unfulfilling, and when constricting circumstances prevent other ways of meeting important needs, there is a serious question whether love-inspired adultery is sometimes justifiable or at least excusable—witness *The Scarlet Letter*, *Anna Karenina*, *Madame Bovary*, *Lady Chatterly's Lover*, and *The Awakening*. Moreover, our deep ambivalence about some cases of love-inspired adultery reflect how there is some good and some bad involved in conduct that we cannot fully justify nor fully condemn.

(iv) *Sex and Self-Esteem.* Extramarital affairs are often grounded in attractions less grand than love. Affection, friendship, or simple respect may be mixed with a desire for exciting sex and the enhanced self-esteem from being found sexually desirable. The sense of risk may add to the pleasure that one is so desirable that a lover will take added risks. Are sex and self-esteem enough to justify violating marital vows? It would seem not. The obligations created through marital commitments are moral requirements, whereas sex and self-esteem pertain to one's self-interest. Doesn't morality trump self-interest?

But things are not so simple. Morality includes rights and responsibilities to ourselves to pursue our happiness and self-fulfillment. Some marriages are sexually frustrating or damaging in other ways to self-respect. Even when marriages are basically fulfilling, more than a few individuals report their extramarital affairs were liberating and transforming, whether or not grounded in love. For example, many women make the following report about their extra-marital affair: "It's given me a whole new way of looking at myself . . . I felt attractive again. I hadn't felt that way in years, really. It made me very, very confident."

In addition, the sense of personal enhancement may have secondary benefits. Occasionally it strengthens marriages, especially after the extramarital affair ends, and some artists report an increase in creative activity. These considerations do not automatically outweigh the dishonesty and betrayal that may be involved in adultery, and full honesty may never be restored when spouses decide against confessing an affair to their partners. But nor are considerations of enhanced self-esteem and its secondary benefits irrelevant.

I have mentioned some possible justifications or excuses for specific instances of adultery after traditional commitments are made. I conclude with a caveat. Specific instances are one thing; general attitudes about adultery are another. Individuals who make traditional commitments and who are fortunate enough to establish fulfilling relationships based on those commitments ought to maintain a general attitude that for them to engage in adultery would be immoral (as well as stupid). The "ought" is stringent, as stringent as the commitment to sexual exclusivity. Rationalizing envisioned adultery with anecdotes about the joys of extramarital sex or statistics about the sometimes beneficial effects of adultery is a form of moral duplicity. It is also inconsistent with the virtues of both sexual fidelity and faithfulness in sustaining commitments to love.

NOTES

1. Matthew 5:27–28, *New International Version*.
2. Richard Wasserstrom, "Is Adultery Immoral?" *Philosophical Forum 5* (1974): 513–528.
3. Janet Z. Giele, as quoted by Philip E. Lampe, "The Many Dimensions of Adultery," in Philip E.

Lampe, ed., *Adultery in the United States* (Amherst, N.Y.: Prometheus Books, 1987), p. 56.

4. Richard Taylor, *Having Love Affairs* (Amherst, N.Y.: Prometheus Books, 1982), pp. 67–68.

5. Bonnie Steinbock, "Adultery," in Alan Soble, ed., *The Philosophy of Sex* (Savage, Md.: Rowman & Littlefield, 1991), p. 192.

Review and Discussion Questions

1. What does Wasserstrom say about adultery? Would you agree that his approach is limited and that Martin's is better?

2. According to Martin, the traditional ideal of marriage is that it is based on a commitment to love. Do you agree? If not, why not? If so, then what, in your view, does a "commitment to love" involve?

3. What is the relation of sexual exclusivity to love? What is the relation of trust to love?

4. What ethical problems are posed by the fact that people's commitments can change over time?

5. Martin believes that adultery inspired by love cannot be absolutely condemned. Why not? Do you agree or disagree?

6. Because marital commitments are moral requirements, they would seem to trump the self-interested reasons for which people usually have affairs (like the pleasure of exciting sex or enhancing one's self-esteem). Yet Martin believes that "things are not so simple." Why not?

7. Assume that a couple has undertaken a traditional commitment to sexual exclusivity. In your view, under what circumstances, if any, would adultery be justified? Under what circumstances, if any, might adultery be excused even if not justified?

Is Divorce Immoral?

LAURENCE D. HOULGATE

In the United States today, almost half of all marriages—many of them involving children—end in divorce. Most of us take this simply as a fact of modern life, and few people criticize parents for divorcing. However, Laurence Houlgate, professor of philosophy at California Polytechnic State University, San Luis Obispo, argues that it is, in general, morally wrong for the parents of small children to divorce. This is because divorce can have very damaging consequences for children. Although "grave cause" may sometimes justify divorce, this is only the case, Houlgate argues, if it would harm the children more for the parents to stay together than it would for them to divorce.

Study Questions

1. What is the Divorce Child-Harm Argument (DCH)? In what way does it parallel arguments against child abuse?

2. How does Houlgate respond to the rejoinder that divorce may be justified if the parents quickly treat any symptoms of emotional harm that their children suffer after the divorce?

3. What two conditions must be satisfied if parents are to take advantage of the "grave cause" loophole to DCH? Why is Houlgate skeptical of the argument that one has no choice but to obtain a divorce in order not to expose one's children to marital discord?

4. How does Houlgate respond to the argument that parents can have legitimate needs and desires that outweigh their obligation not to divorce?

I. Introduction

IN 1929 BERTRAND RUSSELL PUBLISHED *Marriage and Morals,*[1] an extended critique of traditional sexual morality and prevailing moral views about marriage and divorce. The book caused quite a sensation in Britain and the United States, in part because of Russell's suggestion that adultery may not always be wrong and his recommendation that young people contemplating marriage might want to live together for one or two years before solemnizing their relationship. Russell referred to the latter as "trial marriage," and he argued that its encouragement might have the felicitous effect of reducing the chances of marital breakdown and divorce. For this and other mild suggestions Russell was vilified by much of the American press and public.[2]

Forgotten in the commotion surrounding publication of the book was Russell's recommendation regarding divorce between couples who have young children. Russell was concerned about the high rate of divorce in America, which he attributed primarily to "extremely weak" family feeling. He regarded easy divorce "as a transitional stage on the way from the bi-parental to the purely maternal family," and he observed that this is "a stage involving considerable hardship for children, since, in the world as it is, children expect to have two parents and may become attached to their father

before divorce takes place." In characteristically strong language, Russell concluded that "parents who divorce each other, except for grave cause, appear to me to be failing in their parental duty."[3]

There have been significant changes in divorce law in the United States since Russell wrote these words. Every state but South Dakota has adopted some form of "no-fault" divorce rules, making it much easier for persons to divorce than it was when Russell wrote *Marriage and Morals.* Under no-fault laws there is no longer a need to establish grounds in order to obtain a divorce. For example, a woman who wishes to divorce her husband is not required to prove that he is guilty of adultery or cruelty or has committed some other marital fault. It is sufficient to assert that "irreconcilable differences" caused the breakup of the marriage. Second, in many states only *one* of the spouses needs to claim that his or her differences with the other are irreconcilable. Mutual consent is no longer a necessary condition to the granting of a divorce.

Philosophers writing since Russell have had little to say about either the recent changes in divorce law or about the ethics of divorce, neither commenting on whether the new regulations represent moral progress, nor on the question whether it would ever be wrong for someone to seek a divorce. The silence of philosophers about this and other matters related to marriage and family is unfortunate. Divorce is an act that has devastating personal and social consequences[4] for millions of adults and children.[5] If ethics is at least in part about conduct that affects the interests of others, then certainly the impact of divorce on the lives of so many people should qualify it as an act as deserving of the careful attention of the moral philosopher as the acts of punishment, abortion, or euthanasia.

II. The Divorce Child-Harm Argument

One year after the publication of *Marriage and Morals,* fiction writer and essayist Rebecca West echoed Russell's views about the divorce of couples with children in an article for *The London Daily Express.* West wrote that "the divorce of married people with children is nearly always an unspeakable calamity." She gave several reasons for this:

> It is only just being understood, in the light of modern psychological research, how much a child depends for its healthy growth on the presence in the home of both its parents. . . . if a child is deprived of either its father or its mother it feels that it has been cheated out of a right. It cannot be reasoned out of this attitude, for children are illogical, especially where their affections are concerned, to an even greater degree than ourselves. A child who suffers from this resentment suffers much more than grief: he is liable to an obscuring of his vision, to a warping of his character. He may turn against the parent to whom the courts have given him, and regard him or her as responsible for the expulsion of the other from the home. He may try to compensate himself for what he misses by snatching everything else he can get out of life, and become selfish, and even thievish. He may, through yearning for the unattainable parent, get himself into a permanent mood of discontent, which will last his

life long and make him waste every opportunity of love and happiness that comes to him later.[6]

This is a large catalog of psychological and behavioral ills to attribute to a single phenomenon, but Rebecca West thought that there was adequate psychological research to support her claims.[7] Although there was a long period after World War II during which some psychologists argued that "children can survive any family crisis without permanent damage—and grow as human beings in the process,"[8] by the 1980s the earlier research referred to by West was being confirmed. In one long-term study of 131 middle-class children from the San Francisco, California, area, interviews conducted by clinicians at eighteen months, five years, and ten years after their parents' divorce showed that many were doing worse at each of these periods than they were immediately after their parents' separation.[9]

In a twenty-five year follow-up study, 93 of the original 131 children were interviewed.[10] The mean age of the (adult) children was 34.9 years. The researchers also located and interviewed a "comparison group" of 44 adult children from intact families who had grown up alongside the children of divorce.[11] The major findings were that the adult children of divorce had more of their marriages end in divorce than adult children in the comparison group; more of them never married at all; and of those who never married, more of them had never had an intimate relationship. Many more of them were heavy users of alcohol and drugs during high school.[12]

The results of another long-term study of the effects of divorce on children in Great Britain and the United States were published in 1991.[13] Unlike the San Francisco research, this longitudinal study used a large control group. In the British part of the survey, for example, a subsample of children who were in two-parent families during an initial interview at age 7 were followed through the next interview at age 11. At both points in time, parents and teachers independently rated the children's behavior problems,[14] and the children were given reading and mathematics achievement tests. Two hundred thirty-nine children whose parents divorced between these two age intervals were compared to over eleven thousand children whose families remained intact. Although the results were not as dramatic as those reached in the San Francisco study, children whose parents divorced showed more behavior problems and scored lower on the achievement tests at age 11.

Let us assume that there are adequate empirical grounds for the claim that children whose parents divorce while they are young may suffer from either short-term or long-term psychological distress, lowered school achievement scores, and various behavior problems.[15] If this is true, then the following simple argument for the immorality of the divorce of parents with young children seems to apply: (a) Parents have a duty to behave in ways that promote the best interests of their young children. In particular, they ought to refrain from behavior that causes or is likely to cause them harm. (b) Divorce is a type of behavior that harms some young children. Therefore, (c) it is morally wrong for the parents of some young children to divorce.

I call this the Divorce Child-Harm Argument or DCH. DCH is similar in structure to moral arguments used to condemn child abandonment and various forms of child abuse. When we think of child abuse, we usually think of cases in which children have suffered severe physical injury or death as a result of parental behavior. But some child abuse statutes recognize emotional or psychological harm. Thus, the New York Family Court Act defines "impairment of emotional health" as

a state of substantially limited psychological or intellectual functioning in relation to, but not limited to such factors as failure to thrive, con-

trol of aggressiveness or self-destructive impulses, ability to think and reason, or acting out or misbehavior, including incorrigibility, ungovernability or habitual truancy. . . .[16]

If we think that parental behavior that causes or is likely to cause the kind of emotional or psychological harm specified in the preceding statute is morally wrong, and if we think that parents who divorce are likely to cause emotional harm to their children, then it would appear that divorce is wrong for the same reason that these parental behaviors are wrong.

Faced with the conclusion of DCH, there are a number of ways in which the divorced parents of young children might attempt to defend themselves against the charge that it was wrong for them to divorce.

1. First, it may be objected that the preceding analogy between divorce and child abuse is misplaced. Children of divorce may suffer, but their suffering never rises to the minimum level of suffering required by legal standards for determining emotional abuse.

The response to this objection is that DCH does not argue that divorce *is* child abuse. Legal definitions of child abuse and neglect are formulated solely to deal with the problem of the conditions under which the state may justifiably intervene in the family to protect the child. DCH says nothing about state intervention, nor does it recommend any change in the laws regulating divorce. Instead, DCH is an argument about the morality of divorce. It argues that some divorces are wrong *for the same kind of reason* that child abuse is wrong. The reason that some divorces are wrong is that they cause or are likely to cause emotional harm to the children of the divorcing parents. Whether the emotional harm suffered by children whose parents divorce rises to the level of severity required by the child abuse standards of some states is beside the point. The point is whether some children whose parents divorce suffer emotional harm, *not* whether they suffer the kind or amount required by the courts to recognize a child abuse petition for purposes of court-ordered intervention.

2. The second objection to DCH is that so long as parents aggressively treat any symptoms of emotional harm that their children may suffer post-divorce in order to minimize the deleterious effects of the divorce, then they have done nothing wrong by obtaining the divorce. What *would* be wrong would be to ignore the symptoms and to leave them untreated.

This argument has the following structure: It is not wrong to divorce; it is only wrong to divorce and do nothing to minimize its bad effects on children. But consider the following counter-example: so long as I secure medical treatment for my child after I have engaged in risky behavior that resulted in his leg getting broken, then I have done nothing wrong in putting my child at risk. The reason that we resist the conclusion "I have done nothing wrong in putting my child at risk" is that we do not think it justifiable to engage in behavior that puts the lives and health of our children at risk in the first place. This is why we think it morally incumbent on us not to smoke when children are in the house, to put them in restraining seats when we have them in the car with us, and do countless other things to minimize their chances of injury in and out of the home. It is simply not enough to announce that one is prepared to treat a child's injuries after they occur. We demand that parents take steps to prevent the harm *before* it occurs. [17]

3. The third objection to DCH takes advantage of Russell's "loophole," or exception to his general claim (quoted above) that parents who divorce violate their parental duty. Russell's loophole is that the divorce might be justified if it was done for "grave cause." A grave cause exists when it is established that (a) the children will suffer more emotional harm if the marriage of their parents remains intact than they will suf-

fer as a result of their parents' divorce; and (b) during the marriage, the parents could not control those behaviors that caused their children emotional harm. For example, with reference to (b), Russell mentions insanity or alcoholism as possible candidates for grave cause justifications for divorce because the insane or alcoholic parent may be unable to prevent himself from engaging in the abusive behavior toward his spouse that also adversely affects his child.

"Grave cause" is probably the most common of the rationales that parents will offer to justify their divorce. Thus, with reference to condition (a), those who conducted the 1991 longitudinal study mentioned above found that when they took into account such pre-separation characteristics as family dysfunction and marital conflict, the apparent effect of divorce in some cases fell by about half to levels that were no longer significantly different from zero. The authors of the study concluded that "much of the effect of divorce on children can be predicted by conditions that existed well before the separation occurred." One commentator has recently concluded from this that the transition, through divorce, from an intact two-parent family to a single-parent family can no longer be objected to on the grounds that divorce is bad for children.

However, this conclusion follows only if divorce is the only alternative available to the parents. Although a hostile family environment may cause a child to suffer as much or more than he or she would suffer from the divorce, this does not yet establish the existence of a grave cause justifying the divorce. The parents must also prove condition (b); that is, they must show that they could not control the hostile family environment that caused their children to suffer. Russell has the best rejoinder to parents who claim that they had no choice but to obtain a divorce for the sake of their children:

> The husband and wife, if they have any love for their children, will regulate their conduct so as

to give their children the best chance of a happy and healthy development. . . .

[T]o cooperate in rearing children, even after passionate love has decayed, is by no means a superhuman task for sensible people who are capable of natural affections. . . .

[A]s soon as there are children it is the duty of both parties to a marriage to do everything that they can to preserve harmonious relations, even if this requires considerable self-control.[18]

In other words, to say that one had no choice but to obtain a divorce in order not to expose one's children to marital discord is to make the extraordinary assumption that one could not control one's behavior. It is analogous to the contention of a cigarette smoker that he had to abandon his child in order to save her from the physical effects of his second-hand smoke. The point is that we are as capable of controlling the behavior toward our spouse that causes distress in our young children as we are capable of not smoking in their presence. Parents who take seriously their duty to promote the best interests of their children, and who are capable of controlling those aspects of their marital behavior that are harmful to their children, will choose the least detrimental alternative. They will "preserve harmonious relations" during their children's minority.

4. Finally, it may be objected that DCH puts far too much stress on the rights and interests of children, ignoring the legitimate needs of the parents. Surely, it might be said, the desires, projects, and commitments of each parent that give them reasons to divorce in the pursuit of ends that are their own may sometimes outweigh those reasons not to divorce that stem from the special non-contractual obligations that they have to nurture their young children.

To this I can only reply that if it is permissible for parents to divorce for such reasons, then I cannot imagine what it would mean to say that they have obligations to nurture their children. How can one be said to have an *obligation* to nurture her young child if it is permissible for

her to perform an act that risks harming the child for no other reason than that she wants to pursue her own projects? This empties the concept of parental obligation of most of its content. Parents of young children who divorce for no other reason than that they find their marriage unfulfilling and believe that this is justifiable seem to me to be parents who lack an understanding of what it is to have an obligation to their children. They must believe that they can treat their own children as they would treat any other child. In the case of children other than our own, most of us would acknowledge that the effect on these children of what we do counts for something. But even if it is proved to me and my spouse that (e.g.) the children of our next-door neighbor will suffer emotionally as a result of our divorce, we would not think that this puts us under an obligation to cancel or delay our separation. If we did delay it, this would be an act of charity, not a perfect duty of obligation. But with our own children, things are otherwise. Our children exert an "ethical pull" on us that is much stronger than the pull on us of the claims of other children. Making provision for our children's emotional needs becomes a perfect duty within the context of the family, and as such it outweighs our desire to pursue our own projects when this comes into conflict. This is surely a large part of what it means to become a parent.

III. Conclusion

I conclude that Russell is right about the wrongness of many of the divorces of parents who have young children. Such divorces are not justifiable if the reason is similar to one or more of the reasons given by many people who divorce: e.g., "We have grown apart," "We have become different persons than we were when we first married," "We are profoundly unhappy with one another," "We want to pursue a single lifestyle once again," or "I found someone else with whom I would much rather live." For those parents capable of exercising self-control over their negative emotions (e.g. spite, anger, jealousy), none of these reasons rises to the level of a grave cause, and parents who divorce for such reasons are violating their moral duty to their children.

NOTES

1. Bertrand Russell, *Marriage and Morals* (Garden City, New York: Horace Liveright, Inc., 1929).

2. Nine years later, in 1938, Russell was denied a professorial appointment at the College of the City of New York for reasons remarkably similar to those used by the Athenians to justify their conviction of Socrates. In part because of the views expressed in *Marriage and Morals,* concerned New York citizens were afraid that Professor Russell would corrupt the morals of the young people who would attend his lectures.

3. Russell, p. 238.

4. The adverse psychological effects of divorce on children are described in part II. Another deleterious consequence of divorce that some attribute to no-fault divorce laws is economic. Divorced women, and the minor children in their households—90 percent of whom live with their mothers—experience a sharp decline in their standard of living after divorce. See Lenore Weitzman, *The Divorce Revolution: The Unexplored Consequences* (New York: Free Press, 1985). Although 61 percent of women who divorced in the 1980s worked full-time and another 17 percent worked part-time "the husband's average post-divorce per capita income surpassed that of his wife and children overall and in every income group." McLindon, "Separate but Unequal: the Economic Disaster of Divorce for Women and Children," *Family Law Quarterly* 21, no. 3 (1987).

5. In 1988, for example, there were 1,167,000 divorces in the United States, involving 1,044,000 children, at a rate of 16.4 children per 1,000 under the age of 18 years. U.S. Bureau of the Census, *Statistical Abstract of the United States, 1993* (113th edition), Washington, D.C. 1993.

6. Rebecca West, "Divorce," from *The London Daily Express,* 1930.

7. West was probably referring to the research in A. Skolnick and J. Skolnick, eds. *Family in Transition* (Boston: Little, Brown and Co., 1929). In one early study of children of divorced parents between the ages of 6 and 12 half of them showed evidence of a

"consolidation into troubled and conflicted depressive behavior patterns." Their behavior pattern included "continuing depression and low self-esteem, combined with frequent school and peer difficulties" (p. 452).

8. Mel Krantzler, *Creative Divorce: A New Opportunity for Personal Growth* (New York: M. Evans, 1974), p. 191.

9. Judith Wallerstein and Sandra Blakeslee, *Second Chances: Men, Women and Children a Decade After Divorce* (New York: Ticknor and Fields, 1989). Only children who had no previous history of emotional problems were selected for the study. At eighteen months after their parents' divorce, "an unexpectedly large number of children were on a downward course. Their symptoms were worse than before. Their behavior at school was worse. Their peer relationships were worse." At a five-year follow-up, "some were better off than they had been during the failing marriage" (p. xv). But over a third of the whole group of these children "were significantly worse off than before. Clinically depressed, they were not doing well in school or with friends. They had deteriorated to the point that some early disturbances, such as sleep problems, poor learning, or acting out, had become chronic" (p. xvii). At the tenth-year interview, clinicians were astounded to discover that ". . . almost half of the children entered adulthood as worried, underachieving, self-deprecating, and sometimes angry young men and women" (p. 299).

10. Judith Wallerstein, Julia Lewis, and Sandra Blakeslee, *The Unexpected Legacy of Divorce: A 25-year Landmark Study* (New York: Hyperion, 2000).

11. The authors included a comparison group instead of a control group because the former "more accurately describes both its structure and function in this study": "A formal control group is matched to the study group for every possible source of variation except the one in question. As we did not expect to find people who matched our divorced grouping in every way except that their parents had not divorced, we settled on controlling for only those areas we felt were most relevant: age, socioeconomic status of the parents, growing up in the same neighborhoods, and attending the same elementary and high schools." (319).

12. Statistics cited at pp. 329–336.

13. Andrew J. Cherlin, Frank F. Furstenberg, *et al.,* "Longitudinal Studies of Effects of Divorce on Children in Great Britain and the United States," *Science* 252 (7 June 1991), 1386–1389.

14. The behavior problems listed were "temper tantrums, reluctance to go to school, bad dreams,

difficulty sleeping, food fads, poor appetite, difficulty concentrating, bullied by other children, destructive, miserable or tearful, squirmy or fidgety, continually worried, irritable, upset by new situations, twitches or other mannerisms, fights with other children, disobedient at home, and sleepwalking" (*Ibid.*, p. 1397).

15. Children also suffer economic harm as a result of the divorce of their parents. See the data in note 4, above. However, economic loss is the type of post-divorce harm that can be mitigated by the conduct of the parents. For example, if the mother is awarded custody of the children, then the father can offset the economic loss experienced by his former spouse by contributing sufficient funds to insure that the chil-

dren's physical circumstances are not changed by the divorce.

16. N.Y. Family Ct. Act para. 1012 (McKinney Supp. 1974).

17. This does not mean that we should never engage in behavior that risks harm to our children. After all, there is some risk in taking a child out for a walk, a drive in the car, or helping her learn to ski. But we balance such risks against the probable benefit to the child when we make such decisions. When parents divorce for no good reason, there is no predictable benefit to the child that will balance the risk that he or she will suffer emotional harm.

18. Russell, pp. 236–237, and p. 317.

Review and Discussion Questions

1. Is divorce as damaging to children as Houlgate believes? How great is the risk of harm to them? Assess the evidence he provides. In your experience, are the children of divorced parents likely to be less happy or have more problems than other children?

2. Is the Divorce Child-Harm Argument sound? Are its premises true? Do they entail the conclusion? Do you accept the argument, or should it be modified in some way?

3. Do you agree with Houlgate's interpretation of "grave cause"? Are there considerations that would justify divorce that he has overlooked or given insufficient weight to?

4. Houlgate believes that parents who have young children are wrong to divorce simply because they have grown apart, are no longer happy together, or have fallen in love with other people. Do you agree? Does Houlgate ignore the legitimate needs or rights of parents? Does their obligation to their children always take priority over their own happiness? What if the harm to the parents from staying together outweighs the harm of divorce to their children?

5. Should society make divorce more difficult to obtain?

What Do Grown Children Owe Their Parents?

JANE ENGLISH

People generally suppose that grown children owe their parents love and respect, as well as financial and other help, because of the sacrifices their parents made for them. Jane English challenges this notion, arguing that although there are things grown

Reprinted by permission from Onora O'Neill and William Ruddick, eds., Having Children *(New York: Oxford University Press, 1979).*

children ought to do for their parents, the word *owe* is misleading. Rather, the duties of grown children result from the love and friendship they feel for their parents. Where that love and friendship has ended, there is no further filial obligation.

Study Questions

1. How does English use the two versions of the Max and Nina story to make her point that favors create debts?
2. What does English mean when she writes that friendship is characterized by mutuality rather than reciprocity?
3. Why is it inappropriate for the Joneses to say, "We owe the Smiths a dinner"?
4. What two factors determine what children ought to do for their parents?
5. How can the idiom of "owing" your parents be destructive?

WHAT DO GROWN CHILDREN owe their parents? I will contend that the answer is "nothing." Although I agree that there are many things that children *ought* to do for their parents, I will argue that it is inappropriate and misleading to describe them as things "owed." I will maintain that parents' voluntary sacrifices, rather than creating "debts" to be "repaid," tend to create love or "friendship." The duties of grown children are those of friends and result from love between them and their parents, rather than being things owed in repayment for the parents' earlier sacrifices. Thus, I will oppose those philosophers who use the word "owe" whenever a duty or obligation exists. Although the "debt" metaphor is appropriate in some moral circumstances, my argument is that a love relationship is not such a case.

Misunderstandings about the proper relationship between parents and their grown children have resulted from reliance on the "owing" terminology. For instance, we hear parents complain, "You owe it to us to write home (keep up your piano playing, not adopt a hippie lifestyle), because of all we sacrificed for you (paying for piano lessons, sending you to college)." The child is sometimes even heard to reply, "I didn't ask to be born (to be given piano lessons, to be sent to college)." This inappropri-ate idiom of ordinary language tends to obscure, or even to undermine, the love that is the correct ground of filial obligation.

1. Favors Create Debts

There are some cases, other than literal debts, in which talk of "owing," though metaphorical, is apt. New to the neighborhood, Max barely knows his neighbor, Nina, but he asks her if she will take in his mail while he is gone for a month's vacation. She agrees. If, subsequently, Nina asks Max to do the same for her, it seems that Max has a moral obligation to agree (greater than the one he would have had if Nina had not done the same for him), unless for some reason it would be a burden far out of proportion to the one Nina bore for him. I will call this a *favor*: when A, at B's request, bears some burden for B, then B incurs an obligation to reciprocate. Here the metaphor of Max's "owing" Nina is appropriate. It is not literally a debt, of course, nor can Nina pass this IOU on to heirs, demand payment in the form of Max's taking out her garbage, or sue Max. Nonetheless, since Max ought to perform one act of similar nature and amount of sacrifice in return, the term is suggestive. Once he reciprocates, the debt is "discharged"—that is, their obligations revert to the condition they were in before Max's initial request.

Contrast a situation in which Max simply goes on vacation and, to his surprise, finds upon his return that his neighbor has mowed his grass twice weekly in his absence. This is a voluntary sacrifice rather than a favor, and Max has no duty to reciprocate. It would be nice for him to volunteer to do so, but this would be supererogatory on his part. Rather than a favor, Nina's action is a friendly gesture. As a result, she might expect Max to chat over the back fence, help her catch her straying dog, or something similar—she might expect the development of a friendship. But Max would be chatting (or whatever) out of friendship, rather than in repayment for mown grass. If he did not return her gesture, she might feel rebuffed or miffed, but not unjustly treated or indignant, since Max has not failed to perform a duty. Talk of "owing" would be out of place in this case.

It is sometimes difficult to distinguish between favors and non-favors, because friends tend to do favors for each other, and those who exchange favors tend to become friends. But one test is to ask how Max is motivated. Is it "to be nice to Nina" or "because she did x for me"? Favors are frequently performed by total strangers without any friendship developing. Nevertheless, a temporary obligation is created, even if the chance for repayment never arises. For instance, suppose that Oscar and Matilda, total strangers, are waiting in a long checkout line at the supermarket. Oscar, having forgotten the oregano, asks Matilda to watch his cart for a second. She does. If Matilda now asks Oscar to return the favor while she picks up some tomato sauce, he is obliged to agree. Even if she had not watched his cart, it would be inconsiderate of him to refuse, claiming he was too busy reading the magazines. He may have a duty to help others, but he would not "owe" it to her. But if she had done the same for him, he incurs an ad-

ditional obligation to help, and talk of "owing" is apt. It suggests an agreement to perform equal, reciprocal, canceling sacrifices.

2. The Duties of Friendship Versus Debts

The terms "owe" and "repay" are helpful in the case of favors, because the sameness of the amount of sacrifice on the two sides is important; the monetary metaphor suggests equal quantities of sacrifice. But friendship ought to be characterized by *mutuality* rather than reciprocity: friends offer what they can give and accept what they need, without regard for the total amounts of benefits exchanged. And friends are motivated by love rather than by the prospect of repayment. Hence, talk of "owing" is singularly out of place in friendship.

For example, suppose Alfred takes Beatrice out for an expensive dinner and a movie. Beatrice incurs no obligation to "repay" him with a goodnight kiss or a return engagement. If Alfred complains that she "owes" him something, he is operating under the assumption that she should repay a favor, but on the contrary his was a generous gesture done in the hopes of developing a friendship. We hope that he would not want her repayment in the form of sex or attention if this was done to discharge a debt rather than from friendship. Since, if Alfred is prone to reasoning in this way, Beatrice may well decline the invitation or request to pay for her own dinner, his attitude of expecting a "return" on his "investment" could hinder the development of a friendship. Beatrice should return the gesture only if she is motivated by friendship.

Another common misuse of the "owing" idiom occurs when the Smiths have dined at the Joneses' four times, but the Joneses at the Smiths' only once. People often say, "We owe them three dinners." This line of thinking may be appropriate between business acquaintances, but not between friends. After all, the Joneses invited the Smiths not in order to feed them or to be fed in turn, but because of the friendly contact presumably enjoyed by all on such occasions. If the Smiths do not feel friendship toward the Joneses, they can decline future invitations and not invite the Joneses; they owe them nothing. Of course, between friends of equal resources and needs, roughly equal sacrifices (though not necessarily roughly equal dinners) will typically occur. If the sacrifices are highly out of proportion to the resources, the relationship is closer to servility than to friendship.

Another difference between favors and friendship is that after a friendship ends, the duties of friendship end. The party that has sacrificed less owes the other nothing. For instance, suppose Elmer donated a pint of blood that his wife Doris needed during an operation. Years after their divorce, Elmer is in an accident and needs one pint of blood. His new wife, Cora, is also of the same blood type. It seems that Doris not only does not "owe" Elmer blood, but that she should actually refrain from coming forward if Cora has volunteered to donate. To insist on donating not only interferes with the newly-weds' friendship, but it belittles Doris and Elmer's former relationship by suggesting that Elmer gave blood in hopes of favors returned instead of simply out of love for Doris. It is one of the heart-rending features of divorce that it attends to quantity in a relationship previously characterized by mutuality. If Cora could not donate, Doris's obligation is the same as that for any former spouse in need of blood; it is not increased by the fact that Elmer similarly aided her. It *is* affected by the degree to which they are still friends, which in turn may (or may not) have been influenced by Elmer's donation.

In short, unlike the debts created by favors, the duties of friendship do not require equal quantities of sacrifice. Performing equal sacrifices does not cancel the duties of friendship, as it does the debts of favors. Unrequested sacrifices do not themselves create debts, but friends have duties regardless of whether they requested or initiated the friendship. Those who perform favors may be motivated by mutual gain, whereas friends should be motivated by affection. These characteristics of the friendship relation are distorted by talk of "owing."

3. Parents and Children

The relationship between children and their parents should be one of friendship characterized by mutuality rather than one of reciprocal favors. The quantity of parental sacrifice is not relevant in determining what duties the grown child has. The medical assistance grown children ought to offer their ill mothers in old age depends upon the mothers' need, not upon whether they endured a difficult pregnancy, for example. Nor do one's duties to one's parents cease once an equal quantity of sacrifice has been performed, as the phrase "discharging a debt" may lead us to think.

Rather, what children ought to do for their parents (and parents for children) depends upon (1) their respective needs, abilities, and resources and (2) the extent to which there is an ongoing friendship between them. Thus, regardless of the quantity of childhood sacrifices, an able, wealthy child has an obligation to help his needy parents more than does a needy child. To illustrate, suppose sisters Cecile and Dana are equally loved by their parents, even though Cecile was an easy child to care for, seldom ill, while Dana was often sick and caused some trouble as a juvenile delinquent. As adults, Dana is a struggling artist living far away, while Cecile is a wealthy lawyer living nearby. When the parents need visits and financial aid, Cecile has an obligation to bear a higher proportion of these burdens than her sister. This results from her abilities, rather than from the quantities of sacrifice made by the parents earlier.

Sacrifices have an important causal role in creating an ongoing friendship, which may lead us to assume incorrectly that it is the sacrifices that are the source of the obligation. That the source is the friendship instead can be seen by examining cases in which the sacrifices occurred but the friendship, for some reason, did not develop or persist. For example, if a woman gives up her newborn child for adoption, and if no feelings of love ever develop on either side, it seems that the grown child does not have an obligation to "repay" her for her sacrifices in pregnancy. For that matter, if the adopted child has an unimpaired love relationship with the adoptive parents, he or she has the same obligations to help them as a natural child would have.

The filial obligations of grown children are a result of friendship, rather than owed for services rendered. Suppose that Vance married Lola despite his parents' strong wish that he marry within their religion, and that as a result, the parents refuse to speak to him again. As the years pass, the parents are unaware of Vance's problems, his accomplishments, the birth of his children. The love that once existed between them, let us suppose, has been completely destroyed by this event and thirty years of desuetude. At this point, it seems, Vance is under no obligation to pay his parents' medical bills in their old age, beyond his general duty to help those in need. An additional, filial obligation would only arise from whatever love he may still feel for them. It would be irrelevant for his parents to argue, "But look how much we sacrificed for you when you were young," for that sacrifice was not a favor but occurred as part of a friendship which existed at that time but is now, we have supposed, defunct. A more appropriate message would be, "We still love you, and we would like to renew our friendship."

I hope this helps to set the question of what children ought to do for their parents in a new light. The parental argument, "You ought to do x because we did y for you," should be replaced by, "We love you and you will be happier if you

do x," or "We believe you love us, and anyone who loved us would do x." If the parents' sacrifice had been a favor, the child's reply, "I never asked you to do y for me," would have been relevant; to the revised parental remarks, this reply is clearly irrelevant. The child can either do x or dispute one of the parents' claims: by showing that a love relationship does not exist, or that love for someone does not motivate doing x, or that he or she will not be happier doing x.

Seen in this light, parental requests for children to write home, visit, and offer them a reasonable amount of emotional and financial support in life's crises are well founded, so long as a friendship still exists. Love for others does call for caring about and caring for them. Some other parental requests, such as for more sweeping changes in the child's lifestyle or life goals, can be seen to be insupportable, once we shift the justification from debts owed to love. The terminology of favors suggests the reasoning, "Since we paid for your college education, you owe it to us to make a career of engineering, rather than becoming a rock musician." This tends to alienate affection even further, since the tuition payments are depicted as investments for a return rather than done from love, as though the child's life goals could be "bought." Basing the argument on love leads to different reasoning patterns. The suppressed premise, "If A loves B, then A follows B's wishes as to A's life-long career" is simply false. Love does not even dictate that the child adopt the parents' values as to the desirability of alternative life goals. So the parents' strongest available argument here is, "We love you, we are deeply concerned about your happiness, and in the long run you will be happier as an engineer." This makes it clear that an empirical claim is really the subject of the debate.

The function of these examples is to draw out our considered judgments as to the proper relation between parents and their grown children, and to show how poorly they fit the model of favors. What is relevant is the ongoing friendship that exists between parents and children. Although that relationship developed partly as a result of parental sacrifices for the child, the duties that grown children have to their parents result from the friendship rather than from the sacrifices. The idiom of owing favors to one's parents can actually be destructive if it undermines the role of mutuality and leads us to think in terms of quantitative reciprocal favors.

Review and Discussion Questions

1. Is English right in stating that Max owes Nina nothing for mowing his grass?

2. English writes that "friends offer what they can give and accept what they need, without regard for the total amounts of benefits exchanged." How would you respond to a critic who said that this view of friendship was too idealized and unrealistic?

3. Do you agree with English that Vance is under no obligation to pay his parents' medical bills in their old age? Explain why. Would you agree as a general principle that, because we owe our parents nothing, then if we have ceased to be friends with them, we are obligated to do no more for them than we would for any other elderly person? Why or why not? Would it make a difference to your judgment in Vance's case whether it was Vance or his parents who were responsible for ending the relationship between them?

4. Other cultures believe that grown children have strong and continuing obligations to their parents, obligations that are not dependent on the children feeling love for their parents. Accordingly, some critics charge that English's argument reflects a very American point of view. Would you agree, or is such a criticism irrelevant?

Filial Morality

CHRISTINA HOFF SOMMERS

In contrast to Jane English, Christina Hoff Sommers, professor of philosophy at Clark University, argues for a strong notion of filial obligation, an obligation that does not simply rest on mutual friendship. After illustrating with examples the reality of filial duty, she reviews the shifting conceptions philosophers have had of filial obligation. She criticizes both Kantianism and utilitarianism for a commitment to impartiality that has left them unable to deal adequately with special relationships in general and filial obligations in particular. Sommers is also critical of those who reject as inappropriate any talk of duties in this context in favor of an "ethic of care."

Reprinted by permission of the author and publisher from The Journal of Philosophy, *vol. 83, no. 8 (August 1986). Copyright © 1986 The Journal of Philosophy, Inc.*

Study Questions

1. What point is Sommers making with her three examples?
2. What does Sommers mean by the "Jellyby fallacy," and how, in her view, are both utilitarianism and Kantianism guilty of it?
3. What is meant by the "equal pull thesis"? How does it differ from the "thesis of differential pull"? Which one does Sommers advocate?
4. Under what two conditions does "the presumption of a special positive obligation" arise?
5. What is the position of the "sentimentalists," and why does Sommers reject it?

We not only find it hard to say exactly how much a son owes his parents, but we are even reluctant to investigate this.

Henry Sidgwick[1]

WHAT RIGHTS DO PARENTS HAVE to the special attentions of their adult children? Before this century there was no question that a filial relationship defined a natural obligation; philosophers might argue about the nature of filial obligation, but not about its reality. Today, not a few moralists dismiss it as an illusion, or give it secondary derivative status. A. John Simmons[2] expresses "doubts . . . concerning the existence of 'filial' debts," and Michael Slote[3] seeks to show that the idea of filial obedience is an illusion whose source is the false idea that one owes obedience to a divine being. Jeffrey Blustein[4] argues that parents who have done no more than their duty may be owed nothing, and Jane English[5] denies outright that there are any filial obligations not grounded in mutual friendship.

The current tendency to deny or reconstrue filial obligation is related to the more general difficulty that contemporary philosophers have when dealing with the special duties. An account of the special obligations to one's kin, friends, community or country puts considerable strain on moral theories such as Kantianism and utilitarianism, theories that seem better designed for telling us what we should be doing

for everyone impartially than for explaining something like filial obligation. . . . In what follows I shall be arguing for a strong notion of filial obligation, and more generally I shall be making a case for the special moral relations. I first present some anecdotal materials that illustrate the thesis that a filial duty to respect one's parents is not an illusion.

I. The Concrete Dilemmas

I shall be concerned with the filial duties of adult children and more particularly with the duty to honor and respect. I have chosen almost randomly three situations, each illustrating what seems to be censurable failure on the part of adult children to respect their parents or nurturers. It would not be hard to add to these cases, and real life is continually adding to them.

1. An elderly man was interviewed on National Public Radio for a program on old age. This is what he said about his daughter.

> I live in a rooming house. I lost my wife about two years ago and I miss her very much. . . . My little pleasure was to go to my daughter's house in Anaheim and have a Friday night meal. . . . She would make a meal that I would enjoy. . . . So my son-in-law got angry at me one time for a little nothing and ordered me out of the house. That was about eight months ago. . . . I was back once during the day when

he was working. That was about two and a half or three months ago. I stayed for about two hours and left before he came home from work. But I did not enjoy the visit very much. That was the last time I was there to see my daughter.

2. An eighty-two year old woman (call her Miss Tate) spent thirty years working as a live-in housekeeper and baby-sitter for a judge's family in Massachusetts. The judge and his wife left her a small pension which inflation rendered inadequate. After her employers died, she lost contact with the children whom she had virtually brought up. One day Miss Tate arranged for a friend of hers to write to the children (by then middle-aged) telling them that she was sick and would like to see them. They never got around to visiting her or helping her in any way. She died last year without having heard from them.

3. The anthropologist Barbara Meyerhoff did a study of an elderly community in Venice, California.[6] She tells about the disappointment of a group of elders whose children failed to show up at their graduation from an adult education program:

> The graduates, 26 in all, were arranged in rows flanking the head table. They wore their finest clothing bearing blue and white satin ribbons that crossed the breast from shoulder to waist. Most were solemn and flushed with excitement. . . . No one talked openly about the conspicuous absence of the elders' children (87, 104).

I believe it may be granted that the father who had dined once a week with his daughter has a legitimate complaint. And although Miss Tate was duly salaried throughout her long service with the judge's family, it seems clear that the children of that family owe her some special attention and regard for having brought them up. The graduation ceremony is yet another example of wrongful disregard and neglect. Some recent criticisms of traditional conceptions of filial duty (e.g., by Jane English and John Sim-

mons) make much of examples involving unworthy parents. One may agree that exceptional parents can forfeit their moral claims on their children. . . . But I am here concerned with what is owed to the average parent who is neglected or whose wishes are disregarded when they could at some reasonable cost be respected. I assume that such filial disregard is wrong. Although the assumption is dogmatic, it can be defended—though not by any quick maneuver. Filial morality is but one topic in the morality of special relations. The attempt to understand filial morality will lead us to a synoptic look at the moral community as a whole and to an examination of the nature of the rights and obligations that bind its members.

II. Shifting Conceptions

Jeffrey Blustein's *Parents and Children* contains an excellent historical survey of the moral issues in the child-parent relationship. For Aristotle the obligation to serve and obey one's parents is like an obligation to repay a debt. Aquinas too explains the commandment to honor one's parents as "making a return for benefits received."[7] Both Aristotle and Aquinas count life itself as the first and most important gift that the child is given.

With Locke[8] the topic of filial morality changes: the discussion shifts from a concern with the authority and power of the parent to concern with the less formal, less enforceable, right to respect. Hume[9] was emphatic on the subject of filial ingratitude, saying, "Of all the crimes that human creatures are capable, the most horrid and unnatural is ingratitude, especially when it is committed against parents." By Sidgwick's time the special duties are beginning to be seen as problematic: "The question is on what principles . . . we are to determine the nature and extent of the special claims of affection and kind services which arise out of . . . particular relations of human beings" (242). Nevertheless, Sidgwick is still traditional in maintaining that "all are agreed that there are such duties, the nonperformance of which is ground for censure," and he is himself concerned to show how "our common notion of Justice [is] applicable to these no less than to other duties" (243).

If we look at the writings of a contemporary utilitarian such as Peter Singer,[10] we find no talk of justice or duty or rights, and *a fortiori,* no talk of special duties or parental rights. Consider how Singer, applying a version of R. M. Hare's utilitarianism, approaches a case involving filial respect. He imagines himself about to dine with three friends when his father calls saying he is ill and asking him to visit. What shall he do?

> To decide impartially I must sum up the preferences for and against going to dinner with my friends, and those for and against visiting my father. Whatever action satisfies more preferences, adjusted according to the strength of the preferences, that is the action I ought to take (101).

Note that the idea of a special obligation does not enter here. Nor is any weight given to the history of the filial relationship which typically includes some two decades of parental care and nurture. According to Singer, "adding and subtracting preferences in this manner" is the only rational way of reaching ethical judgment.

Utilitarian theory is not very accommodating to the special relations. And it would appear that Bernard Williams is right in finding the same true of Kantianism. According to Williams,[11] Kant's "moral point of view is specially characterized by its impartiality and its indifference to any particular relations to particular persons." In my opinion, giving no special consideration to one's kin commits what might be called the *Jellyby fallacy.* Mrs. Jellyby, a character in Charles Dickens' *Bleak House,*[12] devotes all of her considerable energies to the foreign poor to the complete neglect of her family. She is described as a "pretty diminutive woman with handsome eyes, though they had a curious habit of seeming to look a long way off. As if they

could see nothing nearer than Africa" (52). Dickens clearly intends her as someone whose moral priorities are ludicrously disordered. Yet by some modern lights Mrs. Jellyby could be viewed as a paragon of impartial rectitude. In the next two sections I will try to show what is wrong with an impartialist point of view and suggest a way to repair it.

III. The Moral Domain

By a *moral domain* I mean a domain consisting of what G. J. Warnock[13] calls "moral patients." Equivalently, it consists of beings that have what Robert Nozick[14] calls "ethical pull." A being has *ethical pull* if it is ethically "considerable"; minimally, it is a being that should not be ill treated by a moral agent and whose ill treatment directly wrongs it. The extent of the moral domain is one area of contention (Mill includes animals; Kant does not). The nature of the moral domain is another. But here we find more uniformity. Utilitarians and deontologists are in agreement in conceiving of the moral domain as constituted by beings whose ethical pull is equal on all moral agents. To simplify matters, let us consider a domain consisting only of moral patients that are also moral agents. (For Kant, this is no special stipulation.) Then it is as if we have a gravitational field in which the force of gravitation is not affected by distance and all pairs of objects have the same attraction to one another. Or, if this sort of gravitational field is odd, consider a mutual admiration society no member of which is, intrinsically, more attractive than any other member. In this group, the pull of all is the same. Suppose that Buridan's ass was not standing in the exact middle of the bridge but was closer to one of the bags of feed at either end. We should still say that he was equally attracted to both bags, but also that he naturally would choose the closer one. So too does the utilitarian or Kantian say that the ethical pull of a needy East African and that of a needy relative are the same, but we can more easily act to help the relative. This theory of equal pull but unequal response saves the appearances for impartiality while acknowledging that, in practice, charity often begins and sometimes ends at home.

This is how the principle of impartiality appears in the moral theories of Kant and Mill. Of course their conceptions of ethical pull differ. For the Kantian any being in the kingdom of ends is an embodiment of moral law whose force is uniform and unconditional. For the utilitarian, any being's desires are morally considerable, exerting equal attraction on all moral agents. Thus Kant and Mill, in their different ways, have a common view of the moral domain as a domain of moral patients exerting uniform pull on all moral agents. I shall refer to this as the *equal-pull (EP) thesis*. . . .

IV. Differential Pull

The doctrine of equal ethical pull is a modern development in the history of ethics. It is certainly not attributable to Aristotle or Aquinas, nor, arguably, to Locke. Kant's authority gave it common currency and made it, so to speak, foundational. It is, therefore, important to state that EP is a dogma. Why should it be assumed that ethical pull is constant regardless of circumstance, familiarity, kinship and other special relations? The accepted answer is that EP makes sense of impartiality. The proponent of the special duties must accept this as a challenge: alternative suggestions for moral ontology must show how impartiality can be consistent with differential ethical forces.

I will refer to the rival thesis as the *thesis of differential pull (DP)*. According to the DP thesis, the ethical pull of a moral patient will always partly depend on how the moral patient is related to the moral agent on whom the pull is exerted. Moreover, the "how" of relatedness will be determined in part by the social practices and

institutions in which the agent and patient play their roles. This does not mean that every moral agent will be differently affected, since it may be that different moral agents stand in the same relation to different moral patients. But where the relations differ in certain relevant ways, there the pull will differ. The relevant factors that determine ethical pull are in a broad sense circumstantial, including the particular social arrangements that determine what is expected from the moral agent. How particular circumstances and conventions shape the special duties is a complex question to which we cannot here do justice. We shall, however, approach it from a foundational standpoint which rejects EP and recognizes the crucial role of conventional practice, relationships, and roles in determining the nature and force of moral obligation. The gravitational metaphor may again be suggestive. In DP morality the community of agents and patients is analogous to a gravitational field, where distance counts and forces vary in accordance with local conditions.

V. Filial Duty

. . . The presumption of a special positive obligation arises for a moral agent when two conditions obtain: (1) In a given social arrangement (or practice) there is a specific interaction or transaction between moral agent and patient, such as promising and being promised, nurturing and being nurtured, befriending and being befriended. (2) The interaction in that context gives rise to certain conventional expectations (e.g., that a promise will be kept, that a marital partner will be faithful, that a child will respect the parent). In promising, the content of the obligation is verbally explicit. But this feature is not essential to the formation of other specific duties. In the filial situation, the basic relationship is that of nurtured to nurturer, a type of relationship which is very concrete, intimate, and long-lasting and which is considered to be more morally determining than any other in shaping a variety of rights and obligations.

Here is one of Alasdair MacIntyre's descriptions of the denizens of the moral domain:

> I am brother, cousin, and grandson, member of this household, that village, this tribe. These are not characteristics that belong to human beings accidentally, to be stripped away in order to discover "the real me." They are part of my substance, defining partially at least and sometimes wholly my obligations and my duties.[15]

MacIntyre's description takes Aristotle's dictum that man is a social animal in a sociological direction. A social animal has a specific social role whose prerogatives and obligations characterize a particular kind of person. Being a father or mother is socially as well as biologically descriptive: it not only defines what one is; it also defines who one is and what one owes.

Because it does violence to a social role, a filial breach is more serious than a breach of promise. In the promise the performance is legitimately expected, being, as it were, explicitly made over to the promisee as "his." In the filial situation the expected behavior is implicit, and the failure to perform affects the parent in a direct and personal way. To lose one's entitlements diminishes one as a person. Literature abounds with examples of such diminishment; King Lear is perhaps the paradigm. When Lear first becomes aware of Goneril's defection, he asks his companion: "Who am I?" to which the reply is "A shadow." Causing humiliation is a prime reason why filial neglect is tantamount to active interference. One's sense of dignity varies with temperament. But dignity itself—in the context of an institution like the family—is objective, being inseparable from one's status and role in that context.

The filial duties of adult children include such things as being grateful, loyal, attentive, respectful and deferential to parents (more so than to strangers). Many adult children, of course, are respectful and attentive to their par-

ents out of love, not duty. But, as Melden says: "The fact that, normally, there is love and affection that unites the members of the family . . . in no way undercuts the fact that there is a characteristic distribution of rights and obligations within the family circle."[16]

The mutual understanding created by a promise is simplicity itself when compared with the range of expected behavior that filial respect comprises. What is expected in the case of a promise is clearly specified by the moral agent, but with respect to most other special duties there is little that is verbally explicit. Filial obligation is thus essentially underdetermined, although there are clear cases of what counts as disrespect—as we have seen in our three cases. The complexity and nonspecificity of expected behavior which is written into the domestic arrangements do not affect what the promissory and the filial situation have in common: both may be viewed as particular contexts in which the moral agent must refrain from behavior that interferes with the normal prerogatives of the moral patient. . . .

VI. Grateful Duty

One group of contemporary moral philosophers, whom I shall tendentiously dub *sentimentalists,* has been vocal in pointing out the shortcomings of the mainstream theories in accounting for the morality of the special relations. But they would find my formal and traditional approach equally inadequate. The sentimentalists oppose deontological approaches to the morality of the parent-child relationship, arguing that *duties* of gratitude are paradoxical, that the "owing idiom" distorts the moral ideal of the parent-child relationship, which should be characterized by love and mutual respect. For them, each family relationship is unique, its moral character determined by the idiosyncratic ties of its members. Carol Gilligan[17] has recently distinguished between an "ethic of care" and an "ethic of rights."

The philosophers I have in mind are objecting to the aridity of the "rights perspective" and are urging moral philosophers to attend to the morality of special relations from a "care perspective." The distinction is suggestive, but the two perspectives are not necessarily exclusive. One may recognize one's duty in what one does spontaneously and generously. And just as a Kantian caricature holds one in greater esteem when one does what is right against one's inclination, so the idea of care, responsibility and personal commitment, without formal obligation, is an equally dangerous caricature.

Approaches that oppose care and friendship to rights and obligations can be shown to be sadly inadequate when applied to real-life cases. The following situation described in this letter to Ann Landers is not atypical:

Dear Ann Landers:
We have five children, all overachievers who have studied hard and done well. Two are medical doctors and one is a banker. . . . We are broke from paying off debts for their wedding and their education. . . . We rarely hear from our children. . . . Last week my husband asked our eldest son for some financial help. He was told "File bankruptcy and move into a small apartment." Ann, personal feelings are no longer a factor: it is a matter of survival. Is there any law that says our children must help out?[18]

There are laws in some states that would require that these children provide some minimal support for their indigent parents. But not a few contemporary philosophers could be aptly cited by those who would advocate their repeal. A. John Simmons, Jeffrey Blustein, and Michael Slote, for example, doubt that filial duty is to be understood in terms of special moral debts *owed* to parents. Simmons offers "reasons to believe that [the] particular duty meeting conduct [of parents to children] does not generate an obligation of gratitude on the child" (*op. cit.*, 182). And Blustein opposes what he and Jane English call the "owing idiom" for services parents were

obligated to perform. "If parents have any right to repayment from their children, it can only be for that which was either above and beyond the call of parental duty, or not required by parental duty at all."* (The "overachievers" could not agree more.) Slote finds it "difficult to believe that one has a *duty* to show gratitude for benefits one has not requested" (320). Jane English characterizes filial duty in terms of the duties one good friend owes another. "[A]fter a friendship ends, the duties of friendship end" (354, 356).

Taking a sentimentalist view of gratitude, these philosophers are concerned to remove the taint of onerous duty from what should be a spontaneous and free desire to be considerate of one's parents. One may agree with the sentimentalists that there is something morally unsatisfactory in being considerate of one's parents *merely* out of duty. The mistake lies in thinking that duty and inclination are necessarily at odds. Moreover, the *having* of certain feelings and attitudes may be necessary for carrying out one's duty. Persons who lack feeling for their parents may be morally culpable for that very lack. The sentimentalist objection that this amounts to a paradoxical duty to *feel* (grateful, loyal, etc.) ignores the extent to which people are responsible for their characters; to have failed to develop in oneself the capacity to be considerate of others is to have failed morally, if only because many duties simply cannot be carried out by a cold and unfeeling moral agent. Kant himself speaks of "the universal duty which devolves upon man of so ordering his life as to be fit for the performance of all moral duties."[19] And MacIntyre, who is no Kantian, makes the same point when he says, "moral education is an 'education sentimentale' " (151).

Sentimentalism is not harmlessly false. Its moral perspective on family relationships as spontaneous, voluntary, and duty-free is simply

*Blustein, p. 182. According to Blustein, parents who are financially able are *obligated* to provide educational opportunities for children who are able to benefit from them.

unrealistic. Anthropological observations provide a sounder perspective on filial obligation. Thus Corinne Nydegger[20] warns of the dangers of weakening the formal constraints that ensure that obligations are met: "No society, including our own, relies solely on . . . affection, good will and enlightened self-interest." She notes that the aged in particular "have a vested interest in the social control of obligations" (30).

It should be noted that the sentimentalist is arguing for a morality that is sensitive to special relations and personal commitment; this is in its own way a critique of EP morality. But sentimentalism ignores the extent to which the "care perspective" is itself dependent on a formal sense of what is fitting and morally proper. The ideal relationship cannot be "duty-free," if only because sentimental ties may come unraveled, often leaving one of the parties at a material disadvantage. Sentimentalism then places in a precarious position those who are not (or no longer) the fortunate beneficiaries of sincere personal commitments. If the EP moralist tends to be implausibly abstract and therefore inattentive to the morality of the special relations, the sentimentalist tends to err on the side of excessive narrowness by neglecting the impersonal "institutional" expectations and norms that qualify all special relations.

NOTES

1. *The Methods of Ethics* (New York: Dover, 1966), p. 243.

2. *Moral Principles and Political Obligations* (Princeton, N.J.: University Press, 1979), p. 162.

3. "Obedience and Illusion," in Onora O'Neill and William Ruddick, eds., *Having Children* (New York: Oxford, 1979), pp. 319–325.

4. *Parents and Children: The Ethics of the Family* (New York: Oxford, 1982).

5. "What Do Grown Children Owe Their Parents?" in O'Neill and Ruddick, *op. cit.,* pp. 351–356.

6. *Number Our Days* (New York: Simon & Schuster, 1978).

7. *Summa Theologiae,* vol. 34, R. J. Batten, trans. (New York: Blackfriars, 1975), 2a2ae.

8. John Locke, *Two Treatises of Government,* P. Laslett, ed. (New York: New American Library, 1965), Treatise 1, sec. 100.

9. David Hume, *A Treatise on Human Nature,* Bk. III, p. 1, sec. 1.

10. *The Expanding Circle: Ethics and Sociobiology* (New York: Farrar, Straus & Giroux, 1981).

11. "Persons, Character and Morality," in *Moral Luck* (New York: Cambridge, 1982), p. 2.

12. New York: New American Library, 1964.

13. *The Object of Morality* (London: Methuen, 1971), p. 152.

14. *Philosophical Explanations* (Cambridge, Mass.: Harvard, 1981), p. 451.

15. *After Virtue* (Notre Dame, Ind.: University Press, 1981), p. 32.

16. *Rights and Persons* (Los Angeles: California UP, 1977), p. 67.

17. *In a Different Voice* (Cambridge, Mass.: Harvard, 1983).

18. *The Boston Globe,* Thursday, March 21, 1985.

19. Immanuel Kant, "Proper Self-respect," from *Lectures on Ethics,* Louis Enfield, trans. (New York: Harper & Row, 1963).

20. "Family Ties of the Aged in Cross-cultural Perspective," *The Gerontologist,* XXIII, 1 (1983): 30.

Review and Discussion Questions

1. Sommers argues, against Jane English and others, that we have a strong filial obligation, one that is not simply based on friendship. What is the source of this obligation, and how strong is it?

2. What would English say about the three cases that Sommers presents and about the situation described in the letter to Ann Landers?

3. Do you agree with Sommers that utilitarianism and Kantianism are too committed to impartiality to do justice to special relations and the obligations they create? How could one

reply to Sommers on behalf of these theories? Is "differential pull" more plausible than "equal pull"? Why or why not?

4. Sommers maintains that filial (and other special) obligations are shaped by conventional understandings and expectations. Could English plausibly argue that her position more accurately captures contemporary conventions and expectations than Sommers's does?

5. How persuasive do you find Sommers's critique of the sentimentalists? Do you agree that we should not overlook the importance of duties and obligations in family contexts? What about English's contention that thinking in terms of "owing" can be destructive to one's relationship with parents and friends?

10

SEXUALITY

Pornography, Oppression, and Freedom

HELEN E. LONGINO

After presenting the traditional conception of pornography, Helen E. Longino, professor of philosophy and women's studies at Rice University, offers her own definition. In her view, sexually explicit or erotic material constitutes pornography only if it endorses the degrading or demeaning treatment of women. This is what makes pornography wrong. She argues further that pornography distorts our view of women, reinforces their oppression and exploitation, and encourages violence against them.

Study Questions

1. What does Longino mean by distinguishing "between questions of sexual mores and questions of morality"?

2. What is Longino's definition of pornography? According to her, sexually explicit material is not necessarily pornographic; indeed, not all explicit representations of sexually abusive treatment of women constitute pornography. Explain.

3. In what ways does pornography communicate its endorsement of sexual behavior that demeans women?

4. What does Longino mean when she writes that pornography lies about women and denies their equality to men?

5. Why does she believe that pornography is connected to crimes of violence against women?

Reprinted by permission of the author from "Pornography, Oppression, and Freedom: A Closer Look" in Laura Lederer, ed., Take Back the Night: Women on Pornography *(1980). Some notes omitted.*

I. Introduction

... TRADITIONALLY, PORNOGRAPHY WAS condemned as immoral because it presented sexually explicit material in a manner designed to appeal to "prurient interests" or a "morbid" interest in nudity and sexuality, material which furthermore lacked any redeeming social value and which exceeded "customary limits of candor." While these phrases, taken from a definition of "obscenity" proposed in the 1954 American Law Institute's *Model Penal Code,* require some criteria of application to eliminate vagueness, it seems that what is objectionable is the explicit description or representation of bodily parts or sexual behavior for the purpose of inducing sexual stimulation or pleasure on the part of the reader or viewer. This kind of objection is part of a sexual ethic that subordinates sex to procreation and condemns all sexual interactions outside of legitimated marriage. It is this code which was the primary target of the sexual revolutionaries in the 1960's, and which has given way in many areas to more open standards of sexual behavior.

One of the beneficial results of the sexual revolution has been a growing acceptance of the distinction between questions of sexual mores and questions of morality. This distinction underlies the old slogan, "Make love, not war," and takes harm to others as the defining characteristic of immorality. What is immoral is behavior which causes injury to or violation of another person or people. Such injury may be physical or it may be psychological. To cause pain to another, to lie to another, to hinder another in the exercise of her or his rights, to exploit another, to degrade another, to misrepresent and slander another are instances of immoral behavior. Masturbation or engaging voluntarily in sexual intercourse with another consenting adult of the same or the other sex, as long as neither injury nor violation of either individual or another is involved, is not immoral. Some sexual behavior is morally objectionable, but not because of its sexual character. Thus, adultery is immoral not because it involves sexual intercourse with someone to whom one is not legally married, but because it involves breaking a promise (of sexual and emotional fidelity to one's spouse). Sadistic, abusive, or forced sex is immoral because it injures and violates another.

The detachment of sexual chastity from moral virtue implies that we cannot condemn forms of sexual behavior merely because they strike us as distasteful or subversive of the Protestant work ethic, or because they depart from standards of behavior we have individually adopted. It has thus seemed to imply that no matter how offensive we might find pornography, we must tolerate it in the name of freedom from illegitimate repression. I wish to argue that this is not so, that pornography is immoral because it is harmful to people.

II. What Is Pornography?

I define pornography as *verbal or pictorial explicit representations of sexual behavior that,* in the words of the Commission on Obscenity and Pornography, *have as a distinguishing characteristic "the degrading and demeaning portrayal of the role and status of the human female . . . as a mere sexual object to be exploited and manipulated sexually."*[1] In pornographic books, magazines, and films, women are represented as passive and as slavishly dependent upon men. The role of female characters is limited to the provision of sexual services to men. To the extent that women's sexual pleasure is represented at all, it is subordinated to that of men and is never an end in itself as is the sexual pleasure of men. What pleases women is the use of their bodies to satisfy male desires. While the sexual objectification of women is common to all pornography, women are the recipients of even worse treatment in violent pornography, in which women characters are killed, tortured, gangraped, mutilated, bound, and otherwise abused, as a means of providing sexual stimulation or pleasure to the male characters. It is this development which has attracted the attention of feminists and been the stimulus to an analysis of pornography in general.

Not all sexually explicit material is pornography, nor is all material which contains representations of sexual abuse and degradation pornography.

A representation of a sexual encounter between adult persons which is characterized by mutual respect is, once we have disentangled sexuality and morality, not morally objectionable. Such a representation would be one in which the desires and experiences of each participant were regarded by the other participants as having a validity and a subjective importance equal to those of the individual's own desire and experiences. In such an encounter, each participant acknowledges the other participant's basic human dignity and personhood. Similarly, a representation of a nude human body (in whole or in part) in such a manner that the person shown maintains self-respect—e.g., is not portrayed in a degrading position—would not be morally objectionable. The educational films of the National Sex Forum, as well as a certain amount of erotic literature and art, fall into this category. While some erotic materials are beyond the standards of modesty held by some individuals, they are not for this reason immoral.

A representation of a sexual encounter which is not characterized by mutual respect, in which at least one of the parties is treated in a manner beneath her or his dignity as a human being, is no longer simple erotica. That a representation is of degrading behavior does not in itself, however, make it pornographic. Whether or not it is pornographic is a function of contextual features. Books and films may contain descriptions or representations of a rape in order to explore the consequences of such an assault upon its victim. What is being shown is abusive or degrading behavior which attempts to deny the humanity and dignity of the person assaulted, yet the context surrounding the representation, through its exploration of the consequences of the act, acknowledges and reaffirms her dignity. Such books and films, far from being pornographic, are (or can be) highly moral, and fall into the category of moral realism.

What makes a work a work of pornography, then, is not simply its representation of degrading and abusive sexual encounters, but its implicit, if not explicit, approval and recommendation of sexual behavior that is immoral, i.e., that physically or psychologically violates the personhood of one of the participants. Pornography, then, is verbal or pictorial material which represents or describes sexual behavior that is degrading or abusive to one or more of the participants in *such a way as to endorse the degradation*. The participants so treated in virtually all heterosexual pornography are women or children, so heterosexual pornography is, as a matter of fact, material which endorses sexual behavior that is degrading and/or abusive to women and children. As I use the term "sexual behavior," this includes sexual encounters between persons, behavior which produces sexual stimulation or pleasure for one of the participants, and behavior which is preparatory to or invites sexual activity. Behavior that is degrading or abusive includes physical harm or abuse, and physical or psychological coercion. In addition, behavior which ignores or devalues the real interests, desires, and experiences of one or more participants in any way is degrading. Finally, that a person has chosen or consented to be harmed, abused, or subjected to coercion does not alter the degrading character of such behavior.

Pornography communicates its endorsement of the behavior it represents by various features of the pornographic context: the degradation of the female characters is represented as providing pleasure to the participant males and, even worse, to the participant females, and there is no suggestion that this sort of treatment of others is inappropriate to their status as human beings. These two features are together sufficient to constitute endorsement of the represented behavior. The contextual features which make material pornographic are intrinsic to the material. In addition to these, extrinsic features, such as the purpose for which the material is presented—i.e., the sexual arousal/pleasure/satisfaction of its (mostly) male consumers—or an accompanying text, may reinforce or make explicit the endorsement. Representations which in and of themselves do not show or endorse degrading behavior may be put into a pornographic context by juxtaposition with others that are degrading, or by a text which invites or recommends degrading behavior toward the subject represented. In such a case the whole complex—the series of representations or representations with text—is pornographic.

The distinction I have sketched is one that applies most clearly to sequential material—a verbal or pictorial (filmed) story—which represents an action and provides a temporal context for it. In showing the before and after, a narrator or film-maker has plenty of opportunity to acknowledge the dignity of the person violated or clearly to refuse to do so. It is somewhat more difficult to apply the distinction to single still representations. The contextual features cited above, however, are clearly present in still photographs or pictures that glamorize degradation and sexual violence. Phonograph album covers and advertisements offer some prime examples of such glamorization. Their representations of women in chains (the Ohio Players), or bound by ropes and black and blue (the Rolling Stones) are considered high-quality commercial "art" and glossily prettify the violence they represent. Since the standard function of prettification and glamorization is the communication of desirability, these albums and ads are communicating the desirability of violence against women. Representations of women bound or chained, particularly those of women bound in such a way as to make their breasts, or genital or anal areas vulnerable to any passerby, endorse the scene they represent by the absence of any

indication that this treatment of women is in any way inappropriate.

To summarize: Pornography is not just the explicit representation or description of sexual behavior, nor even the explicit representation or description of sexual behavior which is degrading and/or abusive to women. Rather, it is material that explicitly represents or describes degrading and abusive sexual behavior so as to endorse and/or recommend the behavior as described. The contextual features, moreover, which communicate such endorsement are intrinsic to the material; that is, they are features whose removal or alteration would change the representation or description.

This account of pornography is underlined by the etymology and original meaning of the word "pornography." *The Oxford English Dictionary* defines pornography as "Description of the life, manners, etc. of prostitutes and their patrons [from πορνη (*porne*) meaning "harlot" and γραφειν (*graphein*) meaning "to write"]; hence the expression or suggestion of obscene or unchaste subjects in literature or art."

Let us consider the first part of the definition for a moment. In the transactions between prostitutes and their clients, prostitutes are paid, directly or indirectly, for the use of their bodies by the client for sexual pleasure. Traditionally males have obtained from female prostitutes what they could not or did not wish to get from their wives or women friends, who, because of the character of their relation to the male, must be accorded some measure of human respect. While there are limits to what treatment is seen as appropriate toward women as wives or women friends, the prostitute as prostitute exists to provide sexual pleasure to males. The female characters of contemporary pornography also exist to provide pleasure to males, but in the pornographic context no pretense is made to regard them as parties to a contractual arrangement. Rather, the anonymity of these characters makes each one Everywoman, thus suggesting not only that all women are appropriate subjects for the enactment of the most bizarre and demeaning male sexual fantasies, but also that this is their primary purpose. The recent escalation of violence in pornography—the presentation of scenes of bondage, rape, and torture of women for the sexual stimulation of the male characters or male viewers—while shocking in itself, is from this point of view merely a more vicious extension of a genre whose success depends on treating women in a manner beneath their dignity as human beings.

III. Pornography: Lies and Violence Against Women

What is wrong with pornography, then, is its degrading and dehumanizing portrayal of women (and *not* its sexual content). Pornography, by its very nature, requires that women be subordinate to men and mere instruments for the fulfillment of male fantasies. To accomplish this, pornography must lie. Pornography lies when it says that our sexual life is or ought to be subordinate to the service of men, that our pleasure consists in pleasing men and not ourselves, that we are depraved, that we are fit subjects for rape, bondage, torture, and murder. Pornography lies explicitly about women's sexuality, and through such lies fosters more lies about our humanity, our dignity, and our personhood.

Moreover, since nothing is alleged to justify the treatment of the female characters of pornography save their womanhood, pornography depicts all women as fit objects of violence by virtue of their sex alone. Because it is simply being female that, in the pornographic vision, justifies being violated, the lies of pornography are lies about all women. Each work of pornography is on its own libelous and defamatory, yet gains power through being reinforced by every other pornographic work. The sheer number of pornographic productions expands the moral issue to include not only assessing the morality or immorality of individual works, but also the meaning and force of the mass production of pornography.

The pornographic view of women is thoroughly entrenched in a booming portion of the publishing, film, and recording industries, reaching and affecting not only all who look to such sources for sexual stimulation, but also those of us who are forced into an awareness of it as we peruse magazines at newsstands and record albums in record stores, as we check the entertainment sections of city newspapers, or even as we approach a counter to pay for groceries. It is not necessary to spend a great deal of time reading or viewing pornographic material to absorb its male-centered definition of women. No longer confined within plain brown wrappers, it jumps out from billboards that proclaim "Live X-rated Girls!" or "Angels in Pain" or "Hot and Wild," and from magazine covers displaying a woman's genital area being spread open to the viewer by her own fingers.[2] Thus, even men who do not frequent pornographic shops and movie houses are supported in the sexist objectification of women by their environment. Women, too, are crippled by internalizing as self-images those that are presented to us by pornographers. Isolated from one another and with no source of support for an alternative view of female sexuality, we may not always find the strength to resist a message that dominates the common cultural media.

The entrenchment of pornography in our culture also gives it a significance quite beyond its explicit sexual messages. To suggest, as pornography does, that the primary purpose of women is to provide sexual pleasure to men is to deny that women are independently human or have a status equal to that of men. It is, moreover, to deny our equality at one of the most intimate levels of human experience. This denial is especially powerful in a hierarchical, class society such as ours, in which individuals feel good about themselves by feeling superior to others. Men in our society have a vested interest in maintaining their belief in the inferiority of the female sex, so that no matter how oppressed and exploited by the society in which they live and work, they can feel that they are at least superior to someone or some category of individuals—a woman or women. Pornography, by presenting women as wanton, depraved, and made for the sexual use of men, caters directly to that interest. The very intimate nature of sexuality which makes pornography so corrosive also protects it from explicit public discussion. The consequent lack of any explicit social disavowal of the pornographic image of women enables this image to continue fostering sexist attitudes even as the society publicly proclaims its (as yet timid) commitment to sexual equality.

In addition to finding a connection between the pornographic view of women and the denial to us of our full human rights, women are beginning to connect the consumption of pornography with committing rape and other acts of sexual violence against women. Contrary to the findings of the Commission on Obscenity and Pornography a growing body of research is documenting (1) a correlation between exposure to representations of violence and the committing of violent acts generally, and (2) a correlation between exposure to pornographic materials and the committing of sexually abusive or violent acts against women.[3] While more study is needed to establish precisely what the causal relations are, clearly so-called hard-core pornography is not innocent.

From "snuff" films and miserable magazines in pornographic stores to *Hustler*, to phonograph album covers and advertisements, to *Vogue*, pornography has come to occupy its own niche in the communications and entertainment media and to acquire a quasi-institutional character (signaled by the use of diminutives such as "porn" or "porno" to refer to pornographic material, as though such familiar naming could take the hurt out). Its acceptance by the mass media, whatever the motivation, means a cultural endorsement of its message. As much as the materials themselves, the social tolerance of these de-grading and distorted images of women in such quantities is harmful to us, since it indicates a general willingness to see women in ways incompatible with our fundamental human dignity and thus to justify treating us in those ways. The tolerance of pornographic representations of the rape, bondage, and torture of women helps to create and maintain a climate more tolerant of the actual physical abuse of women. The tendency on the part of the legal system to view the victim of a rape as responsible for the crime against her is but one manifestation of this.

In sum, pornography is injurious to women in at least three distinct ways:

1. Pornography, especially violent pornography, is implicated in the committing of crimes of violence against women.
2. Pornography is the vehicle for the dissemination of a deep and vicious lie about women. It is defamatory and libelous.
3. The diffusion of such a distorted view of women's nature in our society as it exists today supports sexist (i.e., male-centered) attitudes, and thus reinforces the oppression and exploitation of women.

Society's tolerance of pornography, especially pornography on the contemporary massive scale, reinforces each of these modes of injury: By not disavowing the lie, it supports the male-centered myth that women are inferior and subordinate creatures. Thus, it contributes to the maintenance of a climate tolerant of both psychological and physical violence against women. . . .

IV. Conclusion

I have defined pornography in such a way as to distinguish it from erotica and from moral realism, and have argued that it is defamatory and libelous toward women, that it condones crimes against women, and that it invites tolerance of the social, economic, and cultural oppression of women. The production and distribution of pornographic material is thus a social and moral wrong. Contrasting both the current volume of pornographic production and its growing infiltration of the communications media with the status of women in this culture makes clear the necessity for its control. . . .

Appeals for action against pornography are sometimes brushed aside with the claim that such action is a diversion from the primary task of feminists—the elimination of sexism and of sexual inequality. This approach focuses on the enjoyment rather than the manufacture of pornography, and sees it as merely a product of sexism which will disappear when the latter has been overcome and the sexes are socially and economically equal. Pornography cannot be separated from sexism in this way: Sexism is not just a set of attitudes regarding the inferiority of women but the behaviors and social and economic rules that manifest such attitudes. Both the manufacture and distribution of pornography and the enjoyment of it are instances of sexist behavior. The enjoyment of pornography on the part of individuals will presumably decline as such individuals begin to accord women their status as fully human. A cultural climate which tolerates the degrading representation of women is not a climate which facilitates the development of respect for women. Furthermore, the demand for pornography is stimulated not just by the sexism of individuals but by the pornography industry itself. Thus, both as a social phenomenon and in its effect on individuals, pornography, far from being a mere product, nourishes sexism. The campaign against it is an essential component of women's struggle for legal, economic, and social equality, one which requires the support of all feminists.

NOTES

1. *Report of the Commission on Obscenity and Pornography* (New York: Bantam Books, 1979), p. 239. The Commission, of course, concluded that the demeaning content of pornography did not adversely affect male attitudes toward women.

2. This was a full-color magazine cover seen in a rack at the check-out counter of a corner delicatessen.

3. Urie Bronfenbrenner, *Two Worlds of Childhood* (New York: Russell Sage Foundation, 1970); H. J. Eysenck and D. K. B. Nias, *Sex, Violence and the Media* (New York: St. Martin's Press, 1978); and Michael Goldstein, Harold Kant, and John Hartman, *Pornography and Sexual Deviance* (Berkeley: University of California Press, 1973).

Review and Discussion Questions

1. Do you agree with Longino's definition of pornography? Can something be erotic, explicit, and sexually stimulating without being pornographic?

2. When is sexual behavior degrading or demeaning toward women? What does it mean for a book or film to endorse such behavior? Could something be pornographic because it endorses sexual conduct that is demeaning toward men?

3. Explain and assess Longino's contention that pornography is "defamatory and libelous" to women.

4. Longino believes that pornography is connected to violence against women. Do you agree? What reason or evidence supports this belief? If true, what are its implications?

5. Do you agree with Longino that it is necessary to control pornography? If so, how should it be regulated? Should pornography be banned altogether?

Feminism, Moralism, and Pornography

ELLEN WILLIS

In the previous essay, Helen E. Longino attacked pornography from a feminist perspective. In this essay, Ellen Willis, professor of journalism at New York University, challenges the idea that opposition to pornography is a feminist cause. She is critical of attempts to distinguish erotica from pornography, arguing that they rest on an unrealistic view of sexuality. She sees the antipornography movement as problematic from a feminist point of view because it is hostile to lust, refuses to acknowledge that women can enjoy pornography, and has a "goody-goody concept of eroticism."

Study Questions

1. How, in Willis's view, have antipornography feminists attempted to redefine pornography? Why is she critical of attempts to distinguish it from erotica?

2. Why is Willis skeptical of the claim that pornography causes violence against women?

3. Why is Willis critical of the view of sex that has emerged from the antipornography movement? Explain why she believes that the feminist campaign against pornography will not improve the position of women.

4. Why is Willis worried about attempts to ban or censor pornography?

FEMINIST CRITICISM of sexist and misogynist pornography is nothing new; porn is an obvious target insofar as it contributes to larger patterns of oppression—the reduction of the female body to a commodity (the paradigm being prostitution), the sexual intimidation that makes women regard the public streets as enemy territory (the paradigm being rape), sexist images and propaganda in general. But what is happening now is different. By playing games with the English language, antiporn activists are managing to rationalize as feminism a single-issue movement divorced from any larger political context and rooted in conservative moral assumptions that are all the more dangerous for being unacknowledged.

When I first heard there was a group called Women Against Pornography, I twitched. Could I define myself as Against Pornography? Not really. In itself, pornography—which, my dictionary and I agree, means any image or description intended or used to arouse sexual desire—does not strike me as the proper object of a political crusade. As the most cursory observation suggests, there are many varieties of porn, some pernicious, some more or less benign. About the only generalization one can make is that pornography is the return of the repressed, of feelings and fantasies driven underground by a culture that atomizes sexuality, defining love as a noble affair of the heart and mind, lust as a base animal urge centered in unmentionable organs. Prurience—the state of mind I associate with pornography—implies a sense of sex as forbidden, secretive pleasure, isolated from any emotional or social context. I imagine that in utopia, porn would wither away along with the state, heroin, and Coca-Cola. At present, however, the sexual impulses that pornography appeals to are part of virtually everyone's psychology. For obvious political and cultural reasons nearly all porn is sexist in that it is the product of a male imagination and aimed at a male market; women are less likely to be consciously interested in pornography, or to indulge that interest, or to find porn that turns them on. But anyone who thinks women are simply indifferent to pornography has never watched a bunch of adolescent girls pass around a trashy novel. Over the years I've enjoyed various pieces of pornography—some of them of the sleazy Forty-second Street paperback sort—and so have most women I know. Fantasy, after all, is more flexible than reality, and women have learned, as a matter of survival, to be adept at shaping male fantasies to their own purposes. If feminists define pornography, per se, as the enemy, the result will be to make a lot of women ashamed of their sexual feelings and afraid to be honest about them. And the last thing women need is more sexual shame, guilt, and hypocrisy—this time served up as feminism.

So why ignore qualitative distinctions and in effect condemn all pornography as equally bad? WAP organizers answer—or finesse—this question by redefining pornography. They maintain that pornography is not really about sex but about violence against women. Or, in a more colorful formulation, "Pornography is the theory, rape is the practice." Part of the argument is that pornography causes violence; much is made of the fact that Charles Manson and David Berkowitz had porn collections. This is the sort of inverted logic that presumes marijuana to be dangerous because most heroin addicts started with it. It is men's hostility toward women—combined with their power to express

that hostility and for the most part get away with it—that causes sexual violence. Pornography that gives sadistic fantasies concrete shape—and, in today's atmosphere, social legitimacy—may well encourage suggestible men to act them out. But if *Hustler* were to vanish from the shelves tomorrow, I doubt that rape or wife-beating statistics would decline.

Even more problematic is the idea that pornography depicts violence rather than sex. Since porn is by definition overtly sexual, while most of it is not overtly violent, this equation requires some fancy explaining. . . . Robin Morgan and Gloria Steinem . . . distinguish pornography from erotica. According to this argument, erotica (whose etymological root is "eros," or sexual love) expresses an integrated sexuality based on mutual affection and desire between equals; pornography (which comes from another Greek root—"porne," meaning prostitute) reflects a dehumanized sexuality based on male domination and exploitation of women. The distinction sounds promising, but it doesn't hold up. The accepted meaning of erotica is literature or pictures with sexual themes; it may or may not serve the essentially utilitarian function of pornography. Because it is less specific, less suggestive of actual sexual activity, "erotica" is regularly used as a euphemism for "classy porn." Pornography expressed in literary language or expensive photography and consumed by the upper middle class is "erotica"; the cheap stuff, which can't pretend to any purpose but getting people off, is smut. The erotica-versus-porn approach evades the (embarrassing?) question of how porn is *used*. It endorses the portrayal of sex as we might like it to be and condemns the portrayal of sex as it too often is, whether in action or only in fantasy. But if pornography is to arouse, it must appeal to the feelings we have, not those that by some utopian standard we ought to have. Sex in this culture has been so deeply politicized that it is impossible to make clear-cut distinctions between "authentic" sexual impulses and those conditioned by patriarchy. Between, say, *Ulysses* at one end and *Snuff* at the other, erotica/pornography conveys all sorts of mixed messages that elicit complicated and private responses. In practice, attempts to sort out good erotica from bad porn inevitably come down to "What turns me on is erotic; what turns you on is pornographic."

It would be clearer and more logical simply to acknowledge that some sexual images are offensive and some are not. But logic and clarity are irrelevant—or rather, inimical—to the underlying aim of the antiporners, which is to vent the emotions traditionally associated with the word "pornography." . . . There is a social and psychic link between pornography and rape. In terms of patriarchal morality both are expressions of male lust, which is presumed to be innately vicious, and offenses to the putative sexual innocence of "good" women. But feminists supposedly begin with different assumptions—that men's confusion of sexual desire with predatory aggression reflects a sexist system, not male biology; that there are no good (chaste) or bad (lustful) women, just women who are, like men, sexual beings. From this standpoint, to lump pornography with rape is dangerously simplistic. Rape is a violent physical assault. Pornography can be a psychic assault, both in its content and in its public intrusions on our attention, but for women as for men it can also be a source of erotic pleasure. A woman who is raped is a victim; a woman who enjoys pornography (even if that means enjoying a rape fantasy) is in a sense a rebel, insisting on an aspect of her sexuality that has been defined as a male preserve. Insofar as pornography glorifies male supremacy and sexual alienation, it is deeply reactionary. But in rejecting sexual repression and hypocrisy—which have inflicted even more damage on women than on men—it expresses a radical impulse.

That this impulse still needs defending, even among feminists, is evident from the sexual attitudes that have surfaced in the antiporn movement. In the movement's rhetoric pornography is a code word for vicious male lust. To the objection that some women get off on porn, the standard reply is that this only shows how thoroughly women have been brainwashed by male values—though a WAP leaflet goes so far as to suggest that women who claim to like pornography are lying to avoid male opprobrium. (Note the good-girl-versus-bad-girl theme, reappearing as healthy-versus-sick, or honest-versus-devious; for "brainwashed" read "seduced.") And the view of sex that most often emerges from talk about "erotica" is as sentimental and euphemistic as the word itself: lovemaking should be beautiful, romantic, soft, nice, and devoid of messiness, vulgarity, impulses to power, or indeed aggression of any sort. Above all, the emphasis should be on *relationships*, not (yuck) *organs*. This goody-goody concept of eroticism is not feminist but feminine. It is precisely sex as an aggressive, unladylike activity, an expression of violent and unpretty emotion, an exercise of erotic power, and a specifically genital experience that has been taboo for women. Nor are we supposed to admit that we, too, have sadistic impulses, that our sexual fantasies may reflect forbidden urges to turn the tables and get revenge on men. (When a woman is aroused by a rape fantasy, is she perhaps identifying with the rapist as well as the victim?)

. . . Lesbian separatists argue that pornography reflects patriarchal sexual relations; patriarchal sexual relations are based on male power backed by force; ergo, pornography is violent. This dubious syllogism, which could as easily be applied to romantic novels, reduces the whole issue to hopeless mush. If all manifestations of patriarchal sexuality are violent, then opposition to violence cannot explain why pornography (rather than romantic novels) should be singled out as a target. Besides, such reductionism allows women no basis for distinguishing between consensual heterosexuality and rape. . . . To attack pornography, and at the same time equate it with heterosexual sex, is implicitly to condemn not only women who like pornography, but women who sleep with men. This is familiar ground. The argument that straight women collaborate with the enemy has often been, among other things, a relatively polite way of saying that they consort with the beast. . . . Proponents of the separatist line . . . [are] like the modern equivalents of women who, in an era when straightforward prudery was socially acceptable, joined convents to escape men's rude sexual demands. . . . Their revulsion against heterosexuality . . . [serves] as the thinnest of covers for disgust with sex itself. In any case, sanitized feminine sexuality, whether straight or gay, is as limited as the predatory masculine kind and as central to women's oppression; a major function of misogynist pornography is to scare us into embracing it. . . .

Self-righteousness has always been a feminine weapon, a permissible way to make men feel bad. Ironically, it is socially acceptable for women to display fierce aggression in their crusades against male vice, which serve as an outlet for female anger without threatening male power. The temperance movement, which made alcohol the symbol of male violence, did not improve the position of women; substituting porn for demon rum won't work either. One reason it won't is that it bolsters the good girl–bad girl split. Overtly or by implication it isolates women who like porn or "pornographic" sex or who work in the sex industry. WAP has refused to take a position on prostitution, yet its activities—particularly its support for cleaning up Times Square—will affect prostitutes' lives. Prostitution raises its own set of complicated questions. But it is clearly not in women's interest to pit "good" feminists against "bad" whores (or topless dancers, or models for skin magazines).

So far, the issue that has dominated public debate on the antiporn campaign is its potential threat to free speech. Here too the movement's arguments have been full of contradictions. Susan Brownmiller and other WAP organizers claim not to advocate censorship and dismiss the civil liberties issue as a red herring dragged in by men who don't want to face the fact that pornography oppresses women. Yet at the same time, WAP endorses the Supreme Court's contention that obscenity is not protected speech, a doctrine I—and most civil libertarians—regard as a clear infringement of First Amendment rights. Brownmiller insists that the First Amendment was designed to protect political dissent, not expressions of woman-hating violence. But to make such a distinction is to defeat the amendment's purpose, since it implicitly cedes to the government the right to define "political." (Has there ever been a government willing to admit that its opponents are anything more than antisocial troublemakers?) Anyway, it makes no sense to oppose pornography on the grounds that it's sexist propaganda, then turn around and argue that it's not political. Nor will libertarians be reassured by WAP's statement that "we want to change the definition of obscenity so that it focuses on violence, not sex." Whatever their focus, obscenity laws deny the right of free expression to those who transgress official standards of propriety. . . . The basic purpose of obscenity laws is and always has been to reinforce cultural taboos on sexuality and suppress feminism, homosexuality, and other forms of sexual dissidence. No pornographer has ever been punished for being a woman hater, but not too long ago information about female sexuality, contraception, and abortion was assumed to be obscene. In a male supremacist society the only obscenity law that will not be used against women is no law at all.

As an alternative to an outright ban on pornography, Brownmiller and others have advocated restricting its display. There is a plausible case to be made for the idea that antiwoman images displayed so prominently that they are impossible to avoid are coercive, a form of active harassment that oversteps the bounds of free speech. But aside from the evasion involved in simply equating pornography with misogyny or sexual sadism, there are no legal or logical grounds for treating sexist material any differently from (for example) racist or anti-Semitic propaganda; an equitable law would have to prohibit any kind of public defamation. And the very thought of such a sweeping law has to make anyone with an imagination nervous. Could Catholics claim they were being harassed by nasty depictions of the pope? Could Russian refugees argue that the display of Communist literature was a form of psychological torture? Would proabortion material be taken off the shelves on the grounds that it defamed the unborn? I'd rather not find out.

At the moment the First Amendment issue remains hypothetical; the movement has concentrated on raising the issue of pornography through demonstrations and other public actions. This is certainly a legitimate strategy. Still, I find myself more and more disturbed by the tenor of antipornography actions and the sort of consciousness they promote; increasingly their focus has shifted from rational feminist criticism

of specific targets to generalized, demagogic moral outrage. Picketing an antiwoman movie, defacing an exploitative billboard, or boycotting a record company to protest its misogynist album covers conveys one kind of message, mass marches Against Pornography quite another. Similarly, there is a difference between telling the neighborhood news dealer why it pisses us off to have *Penthouse* shoved in our faces and choosing as a prime target every right-thinking politician's symbol of big-city sin, Times Square.

In contrast to the abortion rights movement, which is struggling against a tidal wave of energy from the other direction, the antiporn campaign is respectable. It gets approving press and . . . has begun to attract women whose perspective on other matters is in no way feminist ("I'm anti-abortion," a participant in WAP's march on Times Square told a reporter, "but this is something I can get into"). Despite the insistence of WAP organizers that they support sexual freedom, their line appeals to the antisexual emotions that feed the backlash.

Review and Discussion Questions

1. Longino believes, and Willis denies, that there is a difference between erotica and pornography. With whom do you agree, and why?

2. Do you agree with Willis that women can enjoy pornography? How is this contention relevant to her argument? How might a critic of pornography, like Longino, respond to it?

3. Explain and assess Willis's claim that pornography is "deeply reactionary" and yet "expresses a radical impulse."

4. Would banning pornography violate free speech? What about regulating its display?

5. Longino argues that "the campaign against [pornography] is an essential component of women's struggle for legal, economic, and social equality, one which requires the support of all feminists." Why would Willis reject this proposition? With whom do you agree, and why? Should feminists oppose pornography?

Date Rape: A Feminist Analysis

LOIS PINEAU

Criminal conviction for date rape requires that the sexual encounter was, and was believed by the rapist to be, nonconsensual. But in our culture, resistance by a woman is not necessarily interpreted as a withholding of consent, because our model of sexuality expects women to put up an initial, token resistance before yielding to an insistent male sexuality. Lois Pineau, professor of philosophy at Kansas State University, attacks many of the myths about sexuality that underlie a tolerance of date rape and make its occurrence difficult to prove. She offers a communicative model of sexuality that more accurately captures the mutuality of sexual interaction. Such a model would provide a new criterion for consent that would have important practical implications for solving the problem of date rape.

Study Questions

1. In what way does the law today leave women vulnerable to exploitative tactics by date rapists?

2. Pineau describes in detail a case of date rape. Why is there little chance that the court would interpret this as nonconsensual sex or that, if it did, the man would be found guilty?

3. How does Pineau answer the argument that sexually provocative conduct generates a kind of contract?

4. What is the communicative model of sexuality?

5. What would be the practical results in the courtroom of adopting the communicative model?

D ATE RAPE is nonaggravated sexual assault, nonconsensual sex that does not involve physical injury, or the explicit threat of physical injury. But because it does not involve physical injury, and because physical injury is often the only criterion that is accepted as evidence that the *actus reus** is nonconsensual, what is really sexual assault is often mistaken for seduction. The replacement of the old rape laws with the new laws on sexual assault has done nothing to resolve this problem. . . . The question of whether someone has consented to a sexual encounter is still important, and the criteria for consent continue to be the central concern of discourse on sexual assault. . . .

The following statements by self-confessed date rapists reveal how our lack of a solution for dealing with date rape protects rapists by failing to provide their victims with legal recourse:

*Traditionally, the law defines a crime as having two components: the prohibited act (*actus reus*) committed by the defendant and the prohibited or guilty mental state (*mens rea*) with which it was done.—ED.

From Law and Philosophy 8: 217–243. Copyright © 1989 Kluwer Academic Publishers. Reprinted by permission of Kluwer Academic Publishers.

All of my rapes have been involved in a dating situation where I've been out with a woman I know. . . . I wouldn't take no for an answer. I think it had something to do with my acceptance of rejection. I had low self-esteem and not much self-confidence and when I was rejected for something which I considered to be rightly mine, I became angry and I went ahead anyway. And this was the same in any situation, whether it was rape or it was something else.[1]

When I did date, when I was younger, I would pick up a girl and if she didn't come across I would threaten her or slap her face then tell her she was going to fuck—that was it. But that's because I didn't want to waste time with any come-ons. It took too much time. I wasn't interested because I didn't like them as people anyway, and I just went with them just to get laid. Just to say that I laid them.[2]

There is, at this time, nothing to protect women from this kind of unscrupulous victimization. A woman on a casual date with a virtual stranger has almost no chance of bringing a complaint of sexual assault before the courts. One reason for this is the prevailing criterion for consent. According to this criterion, consent is implied unless some emphatic episodic sign of resistance occurred, and its occurrence can be established. But if no episodic act occurred, or if it did occur, and the defendant claims that it didn't, or if the defendant threatened the plaintiff but won't admit it in court, it is almost impossible to find any evidence that would support the plaintiff's word against the defendant. This difficulty is exacerbated by suspicion on the part of the courts, police, and legal educators that even where an act of resistance occurs, this act should not be interpreted as a withholding of consent, and this suspicion is especially upheld where the accused is a man who is known to the female plaintiff.

In Glanville Williams's classic textbook on criminal law we are warned that where a man is unknown to a woman, she does not consent if she expresses her rejection in the form of an episodic and vigorous act at the "vital moment."

But if the man is known to the woman she must, according to Williams, make use of "all means available to her to repel the man."[3] Williams warns that women often welcome a "mastery advance" and present a token resistance. He quotes Byron's couplet,

> A little still she strove, and much repented
> And whispering "I will ne'er consent"—
> consented

by way of alerting law students to the difficulty of distinguishing real protest from pretence.[4] Thus, while in principle, a firm unambiguous stand, or a healthy show of temper ought to be sufficient, if established, to show nonconsent, in practice the forceful overriding of such a stance is apt to be taken as an indication that the resistance was not seriously intended, and that the seduction had succeeded. The consequence of this is that it is almost impossible to establish the defendant's guilt beyond a reasonable doubt.

Thus, on the one hand, we have a situation in which women are vulnerable to the most exploitive tactics at the hands of men who are known to them. On the other hand, almost nothing will count as evidence of their being assaulted, including their having taken an emphatic stance in withholding their consent. The new laws have done almost nothing to change this situation. Yet clearly, some solution must be sought. Moreover, the road to that solution presents itself clearly enough as a need for a reformulation of the criterion of consent. It is patent that a criterion that collapses whenever the crime itself succeeds will not suffice. . . .

The Problem of the Criterion

The reasoning that underlies the present criterion of consent is entangled in a number of mutually supportive mythologies which see sexual assault as masterful seduction, and silent submission as sexual enjoyment. Because the prevailing ideology has so much informed our conceptualization of sexual interaction, it is extraordinarily difficult for us to distinguish between assault and seduction, submission and enjoyment, or so we imagine. At the same time, this failure to distinguish has given rise to a network of rationalizations that support the conflation of assault with seduction, submission with enjoyment. I therefore want to begin my argument by providing an example which shows both why it is so difficult to make this distinction, and that it exists. Later, I will identify and attempt to unravel the lines of reasoning that reinforce this difficulty.

> The woman I have in mind agrees to see someone because she feels an initial attraction to him and believes that he feels the same way about her. She goes out with him in the hope that there will be mutual enjoyment and in the course of the day or evening an increase of mutual interest. Unfortunately, these hopes of *mutual* and *reciprocal* interest are not realized. We do not know how much interest she has in him by the end of their time together, but whatever her feelings she comes under pressure to have sex with him, and she does not want to have the kind of sex he wants. She may desire to hold hands and kiss, to engage in more intense caresses or in some form of foreplay, or she may not want to be touched. She may have reasons unrelated to desire for not wanting to engage in the kind of sex he is demanding. She may have religious reservations, concerns about pregnancy or disease, a disinclination to be just another conquest. She may be engaged in a seduction program of her own which sees abstaining from sexual activity as a means of building an important emotional bond. She feels she is desirable to him, and she knows, and he knows that he will have sex with her if he can. And while she feels she doesn't owe him anything, and that it is her prerogative to refuse him, this feeling is partly a defensive reaction against a deeply held belief that if he is in need, she should provide. If she buys into the myth of insistent male sexuality she may feel he is suffering from sexual frustration and that she is largely to blame.
>
> We do not know how much he desires her, but we do know that his desire for erotic satisfaction can hardly be separated from his desire

> for conquest. He feels no dating obligation, but has a strong commitment to scoring. He uses the myth of "so hard to control" male desire as a rhetorical tactic, telling her how frustrated she will leave him. He becomes overbearing. She resists, voicing her disinclination. He alternates between telling her how desirable she is and taking a hostile stance, charging her with misleading him, accusing her of wanting him, and being coy, in short of being deceitful, all the time engaging in rather aggressive body contact. It is late at night, she is tired and a bit queasy from too many drinks, and he is reaffirming her suspicion that perhaps she has misled him. She is having trouble disengaging his body from hers, and wishes he would just go away. She does not adopt a strident angry stance, partly because she thinks he is acting normally and does not deserve it, partly because she feels she is partly to blame, and partly because there is always the danger that her anger will make him angry, possibly violent. It seems that the only thing to do, given his aggression, and her queasy fatigue, is to go along with him and get it over with, but this decision is so entangled with the events in process it is hard to know if it is not simply a recognition of what is actually happening. She finds the whole encounter a thoroughly disagreeable experience, but he does not take any notice, and wouldn't have changed course if he had. He congratulates himself on his sexual prowess and is confirmed in his opinion that aggressive tactics pay off. Later she feels that she has been raped, but paradoxically tells herself that she let herself be raped.

The paradoxical feelings of the woman in our example indicate her awareness that what she feels about the incident stands in contradiction to the prevailing cultural assessment of it. She knows that she did not want to have sex with her date. She is not so sure, however, about how much her own desires count, and she is uncertain that she has made her desires clear. Her uncertainty is reinforced by the cultural reading of this incident as an ordinary seduction.

As for us, we assume that the woman did not want to have sex, but just like her, we are unsure whether her mere reluctance, in the presence of high-pressure tactics, constitutes nonconsent. We suspect that submission to an overbearing and insensitive lout is no way to go about attaining sexual enjoyment, and we further suspect that he felt no compunction about providing it, so that on the face of it, from the outside looking in, it looks like a pretty unreasonable proposition for her.

Let us look at this reasoning more closely. Assume that she was not attracted to the kind of sex offered by the sort of person offering it. Then it would be *prima facie* unreasonable for her to agree to have sex, unreasonable, that is, unless she were offered some pay-off for her stoic endurance, money perhaps, or tickets to the opera. The reason is that in sexual matters, agreement is closely connected to attraction. Thus, where the presumption is that she was not attracted, we should at the same time presume that she did not consent. Hence, the burden of proof should be on her alleged assailant to show that she had good reasons for consenting to an unattractive proposition.

This is not, however, the way such situations are interpreted. In the unlikely event that the example I have described should come before the courts, there is little doubt that the law would interpret the woman's eventual acquiescence or "going along with" the sexual encounter as consent. But along with this interpretation would go the implicit understanding that she had consented because when all was said and done, when the "token" resistances to the "masterful advances" had been made, she had wanted to after all. Once the courts have constructed this interpretation, they are then forced to conjure up some horror story of feminine revenge in order to explain why she should bring charges against her "seducer." . . .

Rape Myths

The belief that the natural aggression of men and the natural reluctance of women somehow makes date rape understandable underlies a number of prevalent myths about rape and human sexuality. These beliefs maintain their force partly on account of a logical compulsion exercised by them at an unconscious level. The only way of refuting them effectively is to excavate the logical propositions involved, and to expose their misapplication to the situations to which they have been applied. In what follows, I propose to excavate the logical support for popular attitudes that are tolerant of date rape. These myths are not just popular, however, but often emerge in the arguments of judges who acquit date rapists, and policemen who refuse to lay charges.

The claim that the victim provoked a sexual incident, that "she asked for it," is by far the most common defence given by men who are accused of sexual assault. . . .

Attempts to explain that women have a right to behave in sexually provocative ways without suffering dire consequences still meet with surprisingly tough resistance. Even people who find nothing wrong or sinful with sex itself, in any of its forms, tend to suppose that women must not behave sexually unless they are prepared to carry through on some fuller course of sexual interaction. The logic of this response seems to be that at some point a woman's behaviour commits her to following through on the full course of a sexual encounter as it is defined by her assailant. At some point she has made an agreement, or formed a contract, and once that is done, her contractor is entitled to demand that she satisfy the terms of that contract. Thus, this view about sexual responsibility and desert is supported by other assumptions about contracts and agreement. But we do not normally suppose that casual nonverbal behaviour generates agreements. Nor do we normally grant private persons the right to enforce contracts. What rationale would support our conclusion in this case?

The rationale, I believe, comes in the form of a belief in the especially insistent nature of male sexuality, an insistence which lies at the root of natural male aggression, and which is extremely difficult, perhaps impossible, to contain. At a certain point in the arousal process, it is thought, a man's rational will gives way to the prerogatives of nature. His sexual need can and does reach a point where it is uncontrollable, and his natural masculine aggression kicks in to assure that this need is met. Women, however, are naturally more contained, and so it is their responsibility not to provoke the irrational in the male. If they do go so far as that, they have both failed in their responsibilities, and subjected themselves to the inevitable. One does not go into the lion's cage and expect not to be eaten. Natural feminine reluctance, it is thought, is no protection against a sexually aroused male.

This belief about the normal aggressiveness of male sexuality is complemented by common knowledge about female gender development. Once, women were taught to deny their sexuality and to aspire to ideals of chastity. Things have not changed so much. Women still tend to eschew conquest mentalities in favour of a combination of sex and affection. Insofar as this is thought to be merely a cultural requirement, however, there is an expectation that women will be coy about their sexual desire. The assumption that women both want to indulge sexually, and are inclined to sacrifice this desire for higher ends, gives rise to the myth that they want to be raped. After all, doesn't rape give them the sexual enjoyment they *really* want, at the same time that it relieves them of the responsibility for admitting to and acting upon what they want? And how then can we blame men, who have been socialized to be aggressively seductive precisely for the purpose of overriding female reserve? If we find fault at all, we are inclined to cast our suspicions on the motives of the woman. For it is on her that the contradictory roles of sexual desirer and sexual denier have been placed. Our awareness of the contradiction expected of her makes us suspect her honesty. In the past, she was expected to deny her complicity because of the shame and guilt she felt at having submitted. This expectation persists in many quarters today, and is carried over into a general suspicion about her

character, and the fear that she might make a false accusation out of revenge, or some other low motive. . . .

Dispelling the Myths

. . . The belief that a woman generates some sort of contractual obligation whenever her behaviour is interpreted as seductive is the most indefensible part of the mythology of rape. In law, contracts are not legitimate just because a promise has been made. In particular, the use of pressure tactics to extract agreement is frowned upon. . . .

Even if we assume that a woman has initially agreed to an encounter, her agreement does not automatically make all subsequent sexual activity to which she submits legitimate. If during coitus a woman should experience pain, be suddenly overcome with guilt or fear of pregnancy, or simply lose her initial desire, those are good reasons for her to change her mind. Having changed her mind, neither her partner nor the state has any right to force her to continue. But then if she is forced to continue she is assaulted. Thus, establishing that consent occurred at a particular point during a sexual encounter should not conclusively establish the legitimacy of the encounter. What is needed is a reading of whether she agreed throughout the encounter.

If the "she asked for it" contractual view of sexual interchange has any validity, it is because there is a point at which there is no stopping a sexual encounter, a point at which that encounter becomes the inexorable outcome of the unfolding of natural events. If a sexual encounter is like a slide on which I cannot stop halfway down, it will be relevant whether I enter the slide of my own free will, or am pushed.

But there is no evidence that the entire sexual act is like a slide. While there may be a few seconds in the "plateau" period just prior to orgasm in which people are "swept" away by sexual feelings to the point where we could justifiably understand their lack of heed for the comfort of their partner, the greater part of a sexual encounter comes well within the bounds of morally responsible control of our own actions. Indeed, the available evidence shows that most of the activity involved in sex has to do with building the requisite level of desire, a task that involves the proper use of foreplay, the possibility of which implies control over the form that foreplay will take. Modern sexual therapy assumes that such control is universally accessible, and so far there has been no reason to question that assumption. Sexologists are unanimous, moreover, in holding that mutual sexual enjoyment requires an atmosphere of comfort and communication, a minimum of pressure, and an ongoing check-up on one's partner's state. . . .

In conclusion, there are no grounds for the "she asked for it" defence. Sexually provocative behaviour does not generate sexual contracts. Even where there are sexual agreements, they cannot be legitimately enforced either by the State, or by private right, or by natural prerogative. Secondly, all the evidence suggests that neither women nor men find sexual enjoyment in rape or in any form of noncommunicative sexuality. Thirdly, male sexual desire is containable, and can be subjected to moral and rational control. Fourthly, since there is no reason why women should not be sexually provocative, they do not "deserve" any sex they do not want. This last is a welcome discovery. The taboo on sexual provocativeness in women is a taboo both on sensuality and on teasing. But sensuality is a source of delight, and teasing is playful and inspires wit. What a relief to learn that it is not sexual provocativeness, but its enemies, that constitutes a danger to the world.

Communicative Sexuality: Reinterpreting the Kantian Imperative

The present criterion of consent sets up sexual encounters as contractual events in which sexual aggression is presumed to be consented to unless there is some vigorous act of refusal. As long as we view sexual interaction on a contractual model, the only possibility for finding fault is to point to the presence of such an act. But it is clear that whether or not we can determine such a presence, there is something strongly disagreeable about the sexual aggression described above.

In thinking about sex we must keep in mind its sensual ends, and the facts show that aggressive high-pressure sex contradicts those ends. Consensual sex in dating situations is presumed to aim at mutual enjoyment. It may not always do this, and when it does, it might not always succeed. There is no logical incompatibility between wanting to continue a sexual encounter, and failing to derive sexual pleasure from it.

But it seems to me that there is a presumption in favour of the connection between sex and sexual enjoyment, and that if a man wants to be sure that he is not forcing himself on a woman, he has an obligation either to ensure that the encounter really is mutually enjoyable, or to know the reasons why she would want to continue the encounter in spite of her lack of enjoyment. A closer investigation of the nature of this obligation will enable us to construct a more rational and a more plausible norm of sexual conduct. . . .

The obligation to promote the sexual ends of one's partner implies the obligation to know what those ends are, and also the obligation to know how those ends are attained. Thus, the problem comes down to a problem of epistemic responsibility, the responsibility to know. The solution, in my view, lies in the practice of a communicative sexuality, one which combines the appropriate knowledge of the other with respect for the dialectics of desire.

So let us, for a moment, conceive of sexual interaction on a communicative rather than a contractual model. Let us look at it the way I think it should be looked at, as if it were a proper conversation rather than an offer from the Mafia. . . .

The communicative interaction involved in conversation is concerned with a good deal more than didactic content and argument. Good conversationalists are intuitive, sympathetic, and charitable. Intuition and charity aid the conversationalist in her effort to interpret the words of the other correctly and sympathy enables her to enter into the other's point of view. Her sensitivity alerts her to the tone of the exchange. Has her point been taken good-humouredly or resentfully? Aggressively delivered responses are taken as a sign that *ad hominems* are at work, and that the respondent's self-worth has been called into question. Good conversationalists will know to suspend further discussion until this sense of self-worth has been reestablished. Angry responses, resentful responses, bored responses, even over-enthusiastic responses require that the emotional ground be cleared before the discussion be continued. Often it is better to change the topic, or to come back to it on another day under different circumstances. Good conversationalists do not overwhelm their respondents with a barrage of their own opinions. While they may be persuasive, the forcefulness of their persuasion does not lie in their being overbearing, but rather in their capacity to see the other's point of view, to understand what it depends on, and so to address the essential point, but with tact and clarity.

Just as communicative conversationalists are concerned with more than didactic content, persons engaged in communicative sexuality will be concerned with more than achieving coitus. They will be sensitive to the responses of their partners. They will, like good conversationalists, be intuitive, sympathetic, and charitable. Intuition will help them to interpret their partner's responses; sympathy will enable them to share what their partner is feeling; charity will enable them to care. Communicative sexual partners will not overwhelm each other with the barrage of their own desires. They will treat negative, bored, or angry responses as a sign that the erotic ground needs to be either cleared or abandoned. Their concern with fostering the desire of the other must involve an ongoing state of alertness in interpreting her responses.

Just as a conversationalist's prime concern is for the mutuality of the discussion, a person engaged in communicative sexuality will be most concerned with the mutuality of desire. As such, both will put into practice a regard for their respondent that is guaranteed no place in the contractual language of rights, duties, and consent. The dialectics of both activities reflect the dialectics of desire insofar as each person's interest in continuing is contingent upon the other person wishing to do so too, and each person's interest is as much fueled by the other's interest as it is by her own. . . .

Cultural Presumptions

. . .Traditionally, the decision to date indicates that two people have an initial attraction to each other, that they are disposed to like each other, and look forward to enjoying each other's company. Dating derives its implicit meaning from this tradition. It retains this meaning unless other aims are explicitly stated, and even then it may not be possible to alienate this meaning. It is a rare woman who will not spurn a man who states explicitly, right at the onset, that he wants to go out with her solely on the condition that he have sexual intercourse with her at the end of the evening, and that he has no interest in her company apart from gaining that end, and no concern for mutual satisfaction.

Explicit protest to the contrary aside, the conventions of dating confer on it its social meaning, and this social meaning implies a relationship which is more like friendship than the cutthroat competition of opposing teams. As such, it requires that we do more than stand on our rights with regard to each other. As long as we are operating under the auspices of a dating relationship, it requires that we behave in the mode of friendship and trust. But if a date is more like friendship than a business contract, then clearly respect for the dialectics of desire is incompatible with the sort of sexual pressure that is inclined to end in date rape. And clearly, also, a conquest mentality which exploits a situation of trust and respect for purely selfish ends is morally pernicious. Failure to respect the dialectics of desire when operating under the auspices of friendship and trust is to act in flagrant disregard of the moral requirement to avoid manipulative, coercive, and exploitive behaviour. Respect for the dialectics of desire is *prima facie* inconsistent with the satisfaction of one person at the expense of the other. The proper end of friendship relations is mutual satisfaction. But the requirement of mutuality means that we must take a communicative approach to discovering the ends of the other, and this entails that we respect the dialectics of desire.

But now that we know what communicative sexuality is, and that it is morally required, and that it is the only feasible means to mutual sexual enjoyment, why not take this model as the norm of what is reasonable in sexual interaction? The evidence of sexologists strongly indicates that women whose partners are aggressively uncommunicative have little chance of experiencing sexual pleasure. But it is not reasonable for women to consent to what they have little chance of enjoying. Hence it is not reasonable for women to consent to aggressive noncommunicative sex. Nor can we reasonably suppose that women have consented to sexual encounters which we know and they know they do not find enjoyable. With the communicative model as the norm, the aggressive contractual model should strike us as a model of deviant sexuality, and sexual encounters patterned on that model should strike us as encounters to which *prima facie* no one would reasonably agree. But if acquiescence to an encounter counts as consent only if the acquiescence is reasonable, something to which a reasonable person, in full possession of knowledge relevant to the encounter, would agree, then acquiescence to aggressive noncommunicative sex is not rea-

sonable. Hence, acquiescence under such conditions should not count as consent.

Thus, where communicative sexuality does not occur, we lack the main ground for believing that the sex involved was consensual. Moreover, where a man does not engage in communicative sexuality, he acts either out of reckless disregard, or out of willful ignorance. . . . Thus, the appeal to communicative sexuality as a norm for sexual encounters accomplishes two things. It brings the aggressive sex involved in "date rape" well within the realm of sexual assault, and it locates the guilt of date rapists in the failure to approach sexual relations on a communicative basis.

The Epistemological Implications

Finding a proper criterion for consent is one problem, discovering what really happened, after the event, when the only eyewitnesses give conflicting accounts is another. But while there is no foolproof way of getting the unadulterated truth, it can make a significant difference to the outcome of a prosecution what sort of facts we are seeking. On the old model of aggressive seduction we sought evidence of resistance. But on the new model of communicative sexuality what we want is evidence of an ongoing positive and encouraging response on the part of the plaintiff. This new goal will require quite different tactics on the part of the cross-examiners, and quite different expectations on the part of juries and judges. Where communicative sexuality is taken as the norm, and aggressive sexual tactics as a presumption against consent, the outcome for the example that I described above would be quite different. It would be regarded as sexual assault rather than seduction.

Let us then consider a date rape trial in which a man is cross-examined. He is asked whether he was presuming mutual sexual enjoyment. Suppose he answers in the negative. Then he would have to account for why he persisted in the face of her voiced reluctance. He cannot give as an excuse that he thought she liked it, because he believes that she did not. If he thought that she had consented even though she didn't like it, then it seems to me that the burden of proof would lie with him to say why it was reasonable to think this. Clearly, her initial resistance, her presumed lack of enjoyment, and the pressure tactics involved in getting her to "go along" would not support a reasonable belief in consent, and his persisting in the face of her dissatisfaction would surely cast doubt on the sincerity of his belief in her consent.

But suppose he answers in the affirmative. Then the cross-examiner would not have to rely on the old criteria for non-consent. He would not have to show either that she had resisted him, or that she was in a fearful or intimidated state of mind. Instead he could use a communicative model of sexuality to discover how much respect there had been for the dialectics of desire. Did he ask her what she liked? If she was using contraceptives? If he should? What tone of voice did he use? How did she answer? Did she make any demands? Did she ask for penetration? How was that desire conveyed? Did he ever let up the pressure long enough to see if she was really that interested? Did he ask her which position she preferred? Assuming that the defendant does not perjure himself, he would lack satisfactory answers to these questions. But even where the defendant did lie, a skilled cross-examiner who was willing to go into detail could probably establish easily enough when the interaction had not been communicative. It is extraordinarily difficult to keep up a consistent story when you are not telling the truth.

On the new criterion, the cross-examination focuses on the communicative nature of the ongoing encounter, and the communicative nature of an encounter is much easier to establish than the occurrence of an episodic act of resistance. For one thing, it requires that a fairly long, yet consistent story be told, and this enables us to assess the plausibility of the competing claims in light of a wider collection of relevant data. . . .

The use of a new criterion of communicative sexuality would enable us to introduce a new category of nonaggravated sexual assault which would not necessarily carry a heavy sentence but which would nonetheless provide an effective recourse against "date rape."*

Conclusion

In sum, using communicative sexuality as a model of normal sex has several advantages over the "aggressive-acquiescence" model of seduction. The new model ties the presumption that consensual sex takes place in the expectation of mutual desire much more closely to the facts about how that desire actually functions. Where communicative sex does not occur, this establishes a presumption that there was no consent. The importance of this presumption is that we are able, in criminal proceedings, to shift the burden of proof from the plaintiff, who on the contractual model must show that she resisted or was threatened, to the defendant, who must then give some reason why she should consent after all. The communicative model of sexuality also enables us to give a different conceptual content to the concept of consent. It sees consent as something more like an ongoing cooperation than the one-shot agreement which we are inclined to see it as on the contractual model. Moreover, it does not matter, on the communicative model, whether a woman was sexually provocative, what her reputation is, what went on before the sex began. All that matters is the quality of communication with regard to the sex itself.

But most importantly, the communicative model of normal sexuality gives us a handle on a solution to the problem of date rape. If noncommunicative sexuality establishes a presumption of non-consent, then where there are no

*See sections 520e, Act No. 266, State of Michigan. Sexual assault in the fourth degree is punishable by imprisonment of not more than two years or a fine of not more than $500, or both.

overriding reasons for thinking that consent occurred, we have a criterion for a category of
sexual assault that does not require evidence of
physical violence or threat. If we are serious
about date rape, then the next step is to take
this criterion as objective grounds for establishing that a date rape has occurred. The proper
legislation is the shortest route to establishing
this criterion.

NOTES

1. *Why Men Rape,* Sylvia Levine and Joseph
Loenig, eds. (Toronto: Macmillan, 1980), p. 83.
2. *Ibid.,* p. 77.
3. Williams, *Textbook of Criminal Law* (1983),
p. 238.
4. *Ibid.*

Review and Discussion Questions

1. Is the example that Pineau discusses really a case of date rape? Is it a believable
example? Why does the woman herself have paradoxical and uncertain feelings about what
happened?

2. How does a belief in the natural aggression of men and the natural reluctance of
women make date rape a difficult crime to establish? In your experience, how widespread is
such a belief? Is there any justification for it?

3. How does Pineau's model of communicative sexuality differ from what she sees as the
more traditional model of sexuality? Would you agree that we need to change our thinking
about sexuality? If so, how?

4. Does Pineau's communicative model more accurately reflect the nature of sexuality?
Pineau denies that either women or men find enjoyment in noncommunicative sexuality. Do
you agree? Is sexual seduction compatible with the communicative model?

5. Should the law adopt the communicative model as a basis for determining consent in
date rape or sexual assault cases?

Date Rape: Another Perspective

CAMILLE PAGLIA

In this excerpt from a pair of interviews with *Spin* magazine, Camille Paglia, author
of *Sexual Personae: Art and Decadence from Nefertiti to Emily Dickinson,* contends
that rising concern about date rape reflects a totally abstract, academic view of sexuality, one that refuses to acknowledge the explosive power of male sexuality. Instead
of trying to tame male sexuality and insisting on a risk-free world, women should
acknowledge the uncontrollable and turbulent character of sexuality and assume
responsibility for their actions.

Study Questions

1. What contrast does Paglia draw between elite schools and football schools?
2. What does she mean by a "victim-centered view of the world"?
3. Why does Paglia maintain that women are the dominant sex?
4. Why does Paglia believe that "there is a fundamental prudery about sex" in our attitude toward women who have been raped?
5. Why does Paglia reject the "feminist thing about how we are basically nurturing, benevolent people, and sex is a wonderful thing between two equals"?

PAGLIA: I SEE VERY CLEARLY where this whole date rape thing is coming from. I recognize the language of these smart girls who are entering the media; they are coming from these [Ivy League] schools. They have these stupid, pathetic, completely-removed-from-reality views of things that they've gotten from these academics who are totally off the wall, totally removed. Whereas my views of sex are coming from the fact that I am a football fan and I am a rock fan. Rock and football are revealing something true and permanent and eternal about male energy and sexuality. They are revealing the fact that women, in fact, *like* the idea of a flaunting, strutting, wild masculine energy. . . .

I've been saying that all of this date-rape propaganda has been coming out of the elite schools, where the guys are all these cooperative, literate, introspective, sit-on-their-ass guys, whereas you're not getting it down in these football schools where people accept the fact of the beauty and strength of masculinity. You see these jocks on the campus all the time—they understand what manhood is down there. It's only up here where there is this idea that they can get men on a leash. It's these guys in the Ivy League schools who get used to obeying women. They're sedentary guys. It's ironic that you're getting the biggest bitching about men from the schools where the men are just eunuchs and bookworms.

Spin: That point about primordial male sexuality is also at odds with much contemporary pop psychology. I'm referring to the twelve-step, women-who-love-too-much school of thought, which insists that a woman's attraction to an "untamed" man, as it were, is necessarily a sign of sickness—a sign of a warped emotional life that invariably traces back to childhood, and the attention span of the father. It never considers such an attraction to be a naturally occurring phenomenon—a force of nature. I think the approach to remedying the problem is simplistic, even dangerously so at times.

Paglia: I agree. I'm a Freudian. I like Freud very much, even though I adapt him and add things to him. But his system of analysis is extremely accurate. It's a conflict-based system that allows for paradox. It's also very self-critical and self-analytical. I've watched therapy getting more and more mushy in the last fifteen years in America—it's really disgusting. Instead of being self-analytic and self-critical, it's become what I call coercive compassion. It's disgusting, it's condescending, it's insulting, it's coddling, it keeps everyone in an infantile condition rather than in the adult condition that was postulated as the ultimate goal of Freudian analysis. You were meant to be totally self-aware as a Freudian. Now, it's everyone who will help you, the group will help you. It's awful. It's a return to the '50s conformist model of things. It's this victim-centered view of the world, which is very pernicious. We cannot have a world where everyone is a victim. "I'm this way because my father made me this way. I'm this way because my husband made me this way." Yes, we are indeed formed by traumas that happened to us. But then you must take charge, you must take over, you are responsible. Personal responsibility is at the heart of my system.

But today's system is this whining thing. "Why won't you help me, Mommy and Daddy?" It's like this whole thing with date rape. Girls want to go to fraternity houses, drink eleven tequilas, go off to a guy's room, and then they're wondering, "Gee, what happened?" We of the '60s, we demanded an end to the double standard. We said, "No more parental rules! Get out of our sex lives!" We understood there were risks; we understood that you could go to a place and you could get raped.

Spin: One point that hasn't been made in the whole rape debate is the role of women's [power] over men, sexually. In the case of a rape, a man has to use brute force to obtain something that a woman has—her very sex. So naturally she's weaker physically, and will always be oppressed by him physically. But in that moment when he decides that the only way he can get what he wants from her emotionally, or sexually, or whatever, is to rape her, he is confessing to a weakness that is all-encompassing. She is abused, but he is utterly tragic and pathetic. One is temporary and the other is permanent. I was raped once and it helped me to think of it like that. Not at all to apologize for him, but to focus on my power instead of my helplessness. It was a horrible experience, but it certainly didn't destroy my whole life or my psyche, as much as contemporary wisdom insisted it must have.

Paglia: Right, we *have* what they want. I think woman is the dominant sex. Men have to do all sorts of stuff to prove that they are worthy of a woman's attention.

It's very interesting what you said about the rape, because one of the German magazine reporters who came to talk to me—she's been living in New York for ten years—she came to talk to me about two weeks ago and she told me a very interesting story, very similar to yours. She lives in Brooklyn, and she let this guy in who

she shouldn't have, and she got raped. She said that, because she's a feminist, she'd have to go to counseling now. She said it was awful, that the minute she arrived there, the rape counselors were saying, "You will never recover from this, what's happened to you is so terrible." She said, what the hell, it was a terrible experience, but she was going to pick herself up, and it wasn't that big a deal. The whole system now is designed to make you feel that you are maimed and mutilated forever if something like that happens. She said it made her feel worse. It's absolutely American—it is not European—and the whole system is filled with these clichés about sex. I think there is a fundamental prudery about sex in all this. Rape is one of the risk factors in getting involved with men. It's a risk factor. It's like driving a car. My attitude is, it's like gambling. If you go to Atlantic City—these girls are going to Atlantic City, and when they lose, it's like "Oh Mommy and Daddy, I lost." My answer is stay home and do your nails, if that's the kind of person you are. My '60s attitude is, yes, go for it, take the risk, take the challenge—if you get raped, if you get beat up in a dark alley in a street, it's okay. That was part of the risk of freedom, that's part of what we've demanded as women. Go with it. Pick yourself up, dust yourself off, and go on. We cannot regulate male sexuality. The uncontrollable aspect of male sexuality is part of what makes sex interesting. And yes, it can lead to rape in some situations. What feminists are asking for is for men to be castrated, to make eunuchs out of them. The powerful, uncontrollable force of male sexuality has been censored out of the white middle-class homes. But it's still there in black culture, and in Spanish culture. They have no problem with it.

Spin: In the first part of our interview [published the previous month], the section about rape upset every single woman who read it—in the offices at *Spin* and even at the typesetters. They all seemed to feel that you were defending the rapist.

Paglia: No, that's not it at all. The point is, these white, upper-middle-class feminists believe that a pain-free world is achievable. I'm saying that a pain-free world will be achievable only under totalitarianism. There is no such thing as risk-free anything. In fact, all valuable human things come to us from risk and loss. Therefore we value beauty and youth because they are transient. Part of the sizzle of sex is the danger, the risk of loss of identity in love. That's part of the drama of love. My generation demanded no more overprotection of women. We wanted women to be able to freely choose sex, to freely have all the adventures that men could have. So women began to hike on mountain paths and do all sorts of dangerous things. That's the risk of freedom. If women break their legs on mountain bikes, that's the risk factor. I'm not defending the rapist—I'm defending the freedom to risk rape. I don't want sexual experience to be protected by society. A part of it is that since women are physically weaker than men, in our sexual freedom, women are going to get raped. We should be angry about it, but it's a woman's personal responsibility now, in this age of sexual liberation, to make herself physically fit, so that she can fight off as best she can men's advances. She needs to be alert in her own mind to any potential danger. It's up to the woman to give clear signals of what her wishes are. If she does not want to be out of control of the situation she should not get drunk, she should not be in a private space with a man whom she does not know. Rape does not destroy you forever. It's like getting beaten up. Men get beat up all the time.

Spin: But don't you think that people see a man getting beaten up and a woman getting raped as completely different? Do you think rape should be considered as serious a crime as murder?

Paglia: That's absurd. I dislike anything that treats women as if they are special, frail little creatures. We don't need special protection. Rape is an assault. If it is a totally devastating psychological experience for a woman, then she doesn't have a proper attitude about sex. It's this whole stupid feminist thing about how we are basically nurturing, benevolent people, and sex is a wonderful thing between two equals. With that kind of attitude, then of course rape is going to be a total violation of your entire life, because you have had a stupid, naive, Mary Poppins view of life to begin with. Sex is a turbulent power that we are not in control of; it's a dark force. The sexes are at war with each other. That's part of the excitement and interest of sex. It's the dark realm of the night. When you enter the realm of the night, weird, horrible things can happen there. You can be attacked on a dark street. Does that mean we should never go into dark streets? Part of my excitement as a college student in the '60s was coming out of the very protective '50s. I was wandering those dark streets understanding that not only could I be raped, I could be killed. It's like the gay men going down to the docks and having sex in alleyways and trucks; it's the danger. Feminists have no idea that some women like to flirt with danger because there is a sizzle in it. You know what gets me sick and tired? The battered-woman motif. It's so misinterpreted, the way we have to constantly look at it in terms of male oppression and tyranny, and female victimization. When, in fact, everyone knows throughout the world that many of these working-class relationships where women get beat up often have hot sex. They ask why she won't leave him. Maybe she won't leave him because the sex is very hot. I say we should start looking at the battered-woman motif in terms of sex. If gay men go down to bars and like to get tied up, beaten up, and have their asses whipped, how come we can't allow that a lot of wives like the kind of sex they are getting in these battered-wife relationships? We can't consider that women might have kinky tastes, can we? No, because women are naturally benevolent and nurturing, aren't they? Everything is so damn Mary Poppins and sanitized.

Spin: What do you think is the main quality that women have within them that they aren't using?

Paglia: What women have to realize is their dominance as a sex. That women's sexual powers are enormous. All cultures have seen it. Men know it. Women know it. The only people who don't know it are feminists. Desensualized, de-sexualized, neurotic women. I wouldn't have said this twenty years ago because I was a militant feminist myself. But as the years have gone on I begin to see more and more that the perverse, neurotic psychodrama projected by these women is coming from their own problems with sex.

Review and Discussion Questions

1. What would Paglia say about the case of date rape described by Lois Pineau in the previous essay? Did the woman fail to take personal responsibility? Does Paglia, in your view, take date rape seriously enough? Is she excusing the conduct of date rapists?

2. Paglia argues that, instead of complaining about date rape, women should simply recognize the danger, take the appropriate precautions, and accept the consequences of their free choices. Writers like Pineau believe that date rape reflects something seriously wrong with our society's understanding of sexuality and shows the need for us to change our attitudes and behavior. With whom do you agree, and why?

3. Paglia writes as if aggressive male sexuality is simply a fact of nature, whereas Pineau seems to perceive it more as a cultural product that can be changed. Whose view do you find more accurate?

4. Does Paglia wrongly minimize the seriousness of rape and the harm it does women, or does she have a more realistic view of it?

5. Pineau denies that women find enjoyment in noncommunicative sexuality. Paglia appears to assert the opposite. Who is right, and what are the implications of this disagreement for the problem of date rape?

Homosexuality, Morals, and the Laws of Nature

BURTON M. LEISER

Throughout history, various moralists have condemned homosexuality as immoral, and many societies have outlawed it. In this essay, Burton M. Leiser, professor of philosophy at Pace University, examines and rejects several arguments intended to show that homosexuality is wrong. After challenging Sir Patrick Devlin's contention

From Hugh LaFollette, ed., Ethics in Practice. *Copyright © 1997 Burton M. Leiser. Reprinted by permission of the author.*

that homosexuality is a threat to the common morality that holds society together, Leiser criticizes the claim that homosexuals pose a danger to children as well as the idea that homosexuality is a psychological problem. He then turns to the argument that homosexuality is wrong because homosexuals violate the laws of nature by using their sexual organs in a way that frustrates their procreative purpose. Leiser argues, to the contrary, that it is impossible to violate a descriptive or scientific law of nature and that homosexuality is not unnatural in the sense of being artificial, uncommon, or abnormal. The assumption that any bodily organ has one and only one "proper" or "natural function" is arbitrary and without foundation. Leiser concludes with a discussion of the rights and responsibilities of homosexuals.

Study Questions

1. Why did Sir Patrick Devlin oppose legalizing consensual homosexual conduct? On what ground does Leiser criticize Devlin's position?
2. What is Leiser's reason for rejecting the idea that a homosexual orientation is a psychological "problem"?
3. Why is it impossible to violate a law of nature?
4. How does Leiser respond to the argument that homosexuals violate the principal purpose or function of their sex organs?
5. Why is it implausible to assert that whatever is unnatural is bad?

PHILOSOPHERS AND OTHERS have insisted for centuries that homosexuality is immoral. The Bible proclaims that it is an abomination (e.g., Leviticus 18:22), but in ancient Greece and in some other societies, homosexuality was accepted as a normal form of sexual activity. In our own time, some nations have repealed laws discriminating against homosexuals and others have given legal recognition to homosexual relationships.

Arguments in support of the thesis that homosexual behavior is immoral and ought to be outlawed run the gamut from utilitarian arguments—that homosexuality causes harm to innocent persons or to society as a whole—to those based on the theory that homosexual relations are contrary to the laws of nature. In addition to these attempts to justify an anti-gay stance on philosophical grounds, substantial numbers of people have powerful emotional reactions to the very thought of homosexual relations, while others, relying upon Scripture or

religious tradition as the source of their moral judgments, need no philosophical justifications for their feelings.

This article will critically examine the principal arguments that have been advanced in favor of the proposition that homosexuality is wrong. It will then consider some of the responsibilities that gays and lesbians have in relation to others who may be associated with them, as well as the responsibilities that others have toward gays and lesbians; and finally, some of the moral issues that have arisen as a result of recent attitudes and developments in this area.

I. Devlin's Argument Against Homosexuality

. . . It has . . . been argued that homosexual relations are a threat to the integrity of vital social institutions and are inconsistent with the moral perceptions of ordinary people. In an influential essay he prepared for the British House of Lords long before the AIDS epidemic, Sir Patrick Devlin, one of England's most respected legal experts, responded to a committee that had been charged with recommending legislation on homosexual relations. The committee (known as the Wolfenden Committee) had concluded that consensual sodomy (that is, anal or oral intercourse to which the parties consent—assuming that they are of age and are mentally competent to make such decisions for themselves) should be legalized. Lord Devlin concluded that the committee's conclusion was erroneous, and that the British Parliament should adhere to the traditions of the past, under which homosexual behavior was legally forbidden and violators were subject to severe penalties. The law is not designed solely for the protection of the individual, he said, but for the protection of society. So-called victimless crimes, or crimes to which the "victim" has consented, are criminal nevertheless, for *society as a whole* is the victim in every such case. A murderer who acts with the consent of his victim, or even at the victim's request, is still a murderer, because the purpose of the law is the preservation of "one of the great moral principles upon which society is based, . . . the sanctity of human life." Thus, acts committed in private and with consent, such as dueling, suicide, and incest, may nevertheless be criminal.

The institution of marriage, Devlin argued, is one of the moral foundations of society. Consequently, adultery is not merely a private matter. It is a concern of the public as well, for it strikes at the very heart of the institution of marriage. The same is true of homosexuality, he said, for no society can exist without a shared sense of morals and ethics—common bonds of thought that constitute the glue that holds a society together. A common morality, he argued, is part of the price we pay to live in a civil society, for a society can be as readily destroyed from within, by the destruction of its moral standards, a loosening of its moral bonds, as it can from without. Therefore, he concluded, the suppression of vice is very much the law's business, and it is perfectly reasonable to prohibit homosexual relations.

But what criterion ought to be employed in determining what ought to be the moral standards upon which such legislation should rest? The test of a society's morals, Devlin said, is the standard of the ordinary man in the street. Immorality, he said, is what "every right-minded person is presumed to consider immoral." When ordinary people feel a deep sense of reprobation and disgust, and there is evidence that the practice in question is injurious to society, then, according to Devlin, we have reached the outer limits of toleration, the point at which the practice may be outlawed.

Devlin does not consider the possibility that a society's moral standards, as measured by "the ordinary man" test, might change or that they might differ from place to place, as they clearly do in various regions of the United States. In a very real sense, that "community of ideas" that is fundamental to Devlin's thesis simply does not exist in the vast, multicultural society that stretches across an entire continent and encompasses communities as diverse as Boise, Idaho, Anita, Iowa, New York City, and San Francisco. Nor, for that matter, is it likely to exist in any part of the industrialized world where the government does not impose severe restrictions on movement or the free exchange of ideas. The ordinary person on the streets of the Bronx is likely to have rather different attitudes from his or her counterpart in Charleston, South Carolina, and those differences are likely to be reflected in the persons elected to the state legislature, to Congress, and to the courts. . . .

II. Other Reasons for Condemning Homosexual Behavior

Philosophers, theologians, and social critics have come up with a number of other reasons for condemning homosexuality. None of them, however, seems to hold up under critical analysis. Most, in fact, would apply equally to heterosexuals, if the logic were consistently carried to its ultimate conclusion.

It has been argued, for example, that homosexuals tend to molest children, and that once a young person has been seduced by a gay or lesbian individual, he or she is likely to be initiated irreversibly into that way of life. But the offense being denounced is not homosexuality as such, but pedophilia—having sexual relations with minors. Persons guilty of pedophilia should be strongly denounced and their behavior should remain punishable under criminal statutes. The law has always presumed that minors are not capable of giving meaningful consent to sexual relations with adults, since they are not mature enough or well enough informed to understand the full implications of what they are doing. Criminal sanctions have been imposed upon adults who take advantage of their greater age and authority to seduce youngsters who are under the age of consent, regardless of the alleged willingness of the youngster to participate in such sexual conduct. Thus, an adult who has sexual relations with a 14-year-old may be tried and convicted of statutory rape despite the youngster's express willingness to enter into a sexual liaison with him. There should be no distinction, however, between homosexual and heterosexual relations of this type. Indeed, heterosexuals are guilty of far more acts of pedophilia than homosexuals.

The critics claim that homosexuals are afflicted by such serious psychological problems as feelings of guilt, insecurity, and constant fear of disgrace and ruin, and that homosexuality itself is a psychological problem. There is some truth to this, but as homosexuals "come out of the closet," becoming more open about their sexual preferences, it is becoming less so. One who has openly exposed his or her sexual preferences need no longer fear exposure. One who proudly claims to be a homosexual has conquered much, if not all, of the guilt that he or she might once have felt. The fear of disgrace and ruin is predicated entirely upon the judgment that the critics make: that homosexuals are bad people and that their sexual orientation renders them unfit for a bank loan, for the jobs they hold, or for the homes in which they live. However, if society—or, more specifically, banks, employers, and landlords—abandons its negative judgment on homosexuals and bases individual judgments upon the record of an individual's performance, gays and lesbians would have no more reason to fear exposure or feel insecure than "straight" individuals.

As for homosexual orientation being a psychological "problem," a condition is a problem only when the individual who has it feels that it is one, or when it objectively interferes with the achievement of that individual's goals in life. If homosexuals do not see their sexual preferences as problematic, but (as many evidently do) as liberating, then they are simply not problems, psychological or otherwise. And if those preferences do not interfere with the achievement of a homosexual's goals, except to the extent that society, its institutions, and the individuals who run them stand in the way because of an emotional need to condemn people who are different, then the "problem" is not a psychological one, but a social, political, and legal one that must be addressed as those problems are customarily addressed: through the political process.

The charge that homosexuals are unreliable and are poor security risks is true only if society perceives homosexuality to be evil or imposes criminal or social sanctions on those who are homosexual. A person cannot be blackmailed if the threat is exposure of a trait or practice that is deemed by all concerned to be socially acceptable. The fear that a teacher or scoutmaster might sexually abuse his or her charges is no more and no less rational in the case of a homosexual than it is in the case of a "straight" person. Pedophilia, not homosexuality, is the issue.

Homosexuals who engage in tasteless public displays of affection, cross-dressing, and solicitation or street walking for purposes of prostitution may appropriately be censured, reproached, or, where the offense is particularly egregious, punished. But the same is true of heterosexuals who engage in similarly crude and unseemly behavior in public.

III. Homosexual Behavior and the Law of Nature

By far the most interesting of the reasons offered by philosophers, theologians, and legal thinkers for declaring that homosexuality is wrong is the claim that it is contrary to the laws of nature. Homosexuals, it is said, violate natural law when they misuse their genital organs in ways that frustrate nature's intention that they be employed exclusively for purposes of reproduction. The critics claim that this violation of nature's laws and of God's design deserves the most severe reprobation. Indeed, many of the statutes that criminalize homosexual relations refer to them as the "infamous crime against nature."

Whether they believe that homosexual behavior should be punishable by law or not, many people seem to feel that anal intercourse, for example, is "unnatural." It takes a bit of a jump to infer that because something is *unnatural* or *contrary to the laws of nature,* it is wicked or wrong. A careful analysis of these concepts will reveal that the inference is completely unwarranted. . . .

A simple example of a natural law is Boyle's Law, discovered over three hundred years ago by Robert Boyle. The law states simply that if a given quantity of a gas is kept under constant temperature, its volume will be inversely proportional to the pressure exerted upon it. Thus, an air bubble rising from deep in the ocean to the surface will expand as it rises because the pressure exerted upon it is constantly decreasing as it moves closer to the surface. A helium-filled balloon, lifting from the surface of the earth, will expand as it climbs to ever greater altitudes, because the pressure diminishes as it ascends toward the stratosphere. Eventually, the balloon will burst because the expansion of the gases within it will be greater than the thin skin of the balloon is able to withstand. . . .

Note that at the beginning of the last paragraph, I wrote that Robert Boyle "discovered" the law that was named after him. He did not create it, but through scientific methods of observation and experimentation, he formulated the general rule as to how gases behave under certain conditions.

None of this is remotely like the sort of thing that critics of homosexuality have in mind when they say that it is wrong because it violates the laws of nature. It is simply not possible to violate a law of nature: A gas cannot help but expand when the pressure on it is relieved, and when support is pulled out from under a stone or a person, neither of them can avoid moving toward the center of the earth (what we call "falling"). Since the descriptive laws of nature cannot be violated, it is sheer nonsense to say that homosexual behavior is wrong because it violates such laws.

All is not lost, however, since there are several other senses in which one might interpret the meaning of the claim that "homosexual behavior is wrong because it violates the laws of nature."

What is artificial is unnatural

When we speak of something as being unnatural or not natural, we sometimes mean that it is artificial or synthetic, that it is the product of human artifice. . . .

Homosexual behavior simply cannot be considered unnatural in this sense. There is nothing *artificial* about it. On the contrary, to those who engage in it, it is the most natural thing in the world. Even if it *were* unnatural in this sense, it is difficult to see how that would justify calling it wrong.

The uncommon or abnormal is unnatural

It may be suggested that homosexuality should be condemned because it is "unnatural" in the sense of being uncommon or "abnormal" (i.e., not usual). But this proves no more to the point than the previous suggestions. Many of our most esteemed scientists, artists, musicians, and scholars do things that are quite out of the ordinary, but we don't scorn them for that. Of all the thousands of students who have attended my classes during the years I have been teaching, only one, so far as I can recall, played the harp, and one other played the oboe. Both of them engaged in uncommon or unusual behavior, but the fact that they did so simply set them apart as having unusual interests and uncommon talent. The geniuses like Thomas Alva Edison, Albert Einstein, and Jonas Salk, who gave the world the phonograph and the electric light bulb, the theory of relativity, and a vaccine that has saved millions of people from the ravages of polio, deserve praise rather than condemnation for their extraordinary (i.e., abnormal or uncommon) contributions. If homosexuality is wrong, it cannot be because it is "unnatural" in this sense of the word.

The use of an organ or instrument in a way that is contrary to its principal purpose or function is unnatural

Screwdrivers are admirably suited for their intended function: driving screws; hammers for pounding nails; the eyes for seeing; the teeth for chewing. Abuse of any of these instruments or organs can lead to trouble. One who uses a screwdriver to pound a nail may get hurt, and one who uses his teeth to pry the cap from a beer bottle is likely to end up with less than a full set of teeth. By the same token, it has been suggested that it is inconsistent with the proper function or purpose of one's sex organs to use them for anything but reproduction, that any such use (or abuse) is unnatural, and

that it is therefore wrong and worthy of condemnation. . . .

Because the sex organs are obviously and uniquely designed for the purpose of procreation, it is argued, any use of them for any other purpose is abusive, abnormal, unnatural, and therefore wrong. Masturbation, homosexual relations, and heterosexual intercourse that deliberately frustrates the design of the sex organs are therefore deemed to be perversions that are or ought to be prohibited in any right-thinking society.

But the matter is not so straightforward. Both tools and body organs *can* be used for a multitude of tasks which we ordinarily consider to be perfectly acceptable. Although a screwdriver's original purpose might have been to drive screws, it is not considered a misuse of such a tool, much less a perversion, to use it to pop the cap from a soda bottle or as a wedge or a lever, or for any number of other useful purposes. Teeth seem to be well designed for chewing, to be sure; but they can also be quite attractive, and add considerably to the beauty of a smile or the ferocity of a threatening glare. A person's ears are uniquely adapted for hearing. If a comedian wiggles his ears in order to draw a laugh from his audience, only an utterly humorless crank would accuse him of being perverse and wicked for using his ears to entertain his neighbors when they were designed for hearing.

The sex organs seem to be well suited, not only for reproduction, but also for the production of intense pleasure in oneself and in others. Their being so well suited for that purpose would seem to be utterly inconsistent with calling anyone who uses them merely to produce pleasure, either in himself or in another, while ignoring or frustrating procreation, perverse or wicked simply on the ground that he or she has committed an "unnatural" act. Since sex organs fulfill the function of producing pleasure so admirably, employing them for that purpose scarcely seems to be perverse or wicked on that account alone.

Moreover, it is quite obvious that human sex organs are used to express, in the deepest and most intimate way, the love of one person for another. Even those who most ardently oppose "unfruitful" intercourse concede this point, in practice if not in words, when they permit older married people who are beyond the age of reproduction to have sexual intercourse with one another. Similarly, when a woman is pregnant and thus incapable of becoming pregnant, she and her husband are nevertheless permitted to engage in sexual relations with one another without the slightest thought that what they are doing is perverse or "unnatural" because it is sure to be unfruitful. Under these circumstances, no one thinks that it is perverse or unnatural to engage in sexual relations that one knows will not lead to pregnancy. Sex organs, like other things that we are capable of manipulating, can be put to many uses. In themselves, those uses do not seem to be wicked, perverse, or unnatural, though some may be more common than others, at least in some societies or among some groups within a given society.

The fact that people *are* condemned for using their sex organs for their own pleasure or profit, or for that of others, reveals a great deal about the prejudices and irrational taboos of our society. The assumption that any organ has one and only one "proper" function is indefensible. The identification of such a "proper" or "natural" use when there are others is arbitrary and without foundation in scientific fact. To say that any use of an organ that is contrary to its principal purpose or function is unnatural and therefore evil or depraved proves nothing, for it merely begs the question.

That which is natural is good, and whatever is unnatural is bad

We asked at the beginning what definition of "unnatural" might reasonably lead to the conclusion that homosexual behavior, being unnatural, was therefore evil or wrong. Perhaps this is the key to the solution of our problem. Other senses of the word "unnatural" do not work: some "unnatural" things, such as artificial or synthetic things, are quite good and highly desirable; others, such as the uncommon or "abnormal," may also be good and praiseworthy. In other senses of the word, the unnatural simply cannot exist: the descriptive laws of nature admit of no exceptions. Therefore, nothing can be unnatural if that word is understood to refer to what is contrary to or inconsistent with the laws of nature.

But perhaps there is a sense of the word "unnatural" which simply *means* that which is wrong, perverse, depraved, or wicked. Then if homosexuality is unnatural, it would logically follow that it is wrong, perverse, depraved, or wicked!

But this is not very helpful, for it explains nothing at all. This is what it amounts to:

> Whatever is unnatural is, by definition, wicked, wrong, perverse, and depraved. Now, why is homosexuality wicked, wrong, perverse, and depraved? Because it is unnatural.

Now let's substitute the *definition* of "unnatural" for the *word* "unnatural" in this sentence: **Homosexuality is wicked, wrong, perverse, and depraved because it is *unnatural*.** And we come up with the result: **Homosexuality is wicked, wrong, perverse, and depraved because it is *wicked, wrong, perverse, and depraved*.**

What is the end result? A tautology—a sentence that is true by definition, but is completely worthless since it communicates no information about anything whatever. In other words, if "unnatural" means wicked, wrong, perverse, and depraved, then it provides no support whatever for the argument that homosexuality is wicked, wrong, perverse, and depraved *because* it is unnatural. The argument is question-begging, and should be completely unconvincing to anyone who is at all familiar with elementary logic.

IV. Is Homosexuality Immoral?

Upon careful analysis, we have seen that those arguments that are advanced most often with the intention of supporting the thesis that homosexuality is wrong simply do not hold up. We have not established that *no* valid argument exists to support that thesis. But a diligent search of the literature fails to discover one.

For some people, the fact that the Bible expresses very strong disapproval of homosexuality is sufficient to establish the fact that it is wicked. For them, no further argument is needed. Others are so disgusted by what they consider to be gross practices, more or less on the same level as bestiality or the consumption of rats or insects, that no intellectual arguments are likely to overcome their powerful emotional reactions. But such reasons are not philosophical, and are not likely to persuade anyone who chooses to base her moral judgments on reason rather than on ancient authority or pure emotionalism.

Despite the weight of tradition, the burden is on those who advocate the ostracism of homosexuals to demonstrate that there are cogent reasons for so punishing human beings whose only crime, if it is one, is to engage in the only form of love-making that they feel capable of. Nor is there any intellectually acceptable justification for the imposition of civil or criminal sanctions against gays and lesbians, or depriving them of the benefits of legal privileges that are available to people whose sexual inclinations are more in accordance with the views of most other people—such privileges as the right to inherit, to enjoy tax relief that is open to married couples, and perhaps to adopt children. (I say "perhaps" because further considerations may be relevant to that policy issue.) Some adult gays and lesbians have adopted their lovers, with their lovers' consent, in order to establish a kind of family relationship that would be recognized by the law. That they have had to resort to this rather strange use of adoption laws is an unfortunate consequence of the law's refusal to recognize long-term, stable relationships between them.

Legislatures have generally refused to change the law to make it more favorable to homosexual relationships because many legislators and their constituents view homosexuality as immoral and are unwilling to confer legal recognition upon it.

V. Homosexuals: Rights and Responsibilities

The moral issues surrounding homosexuality are not exhausted, however, by this discussion. Even if our communities recognize the rights of gays and lesbians to pursue their way of life without legal interference, there remain exceedingly delicate questions of the relations of gays and lesbians with their families and associates, and the moral dimensions of some of those relationships. Since none of the philosophical arguments against homosexuality holds up under critical analysis, it would seem to be reasonable to conclude that there remains no cogent justification for discriminating against homosexuals, either legally or in social relations. At the same time, however, it is reasonable to expect homosexuals to behave responsibly toward others, including those who—for whatever reason—find their way of life unacceptable.

Gays and lesbians who have demonstrated in St. Patrick's Cathedral in New York City, for example, disrupting services by raucous chanting designed to draw attention to their displeasure with the Church's policies toward people with their orientation, seem to have overstepped the bounds of decency and propriety. The gay and lesbian organization "Act Up" has mounted numerous rowdy demonstrations and marches, protesting what its participants see as injustices perpetrated against homosexuals. Far from winning sympathy for their cause, such incidents are likely to drive potential supporters away. But there is a larger question of the moral propriety of their behavior.

The American legal tradition exempts religious institutions from governmental control. The public policy behind this tradition derives from the theory that private associations should be free to determine their own policies, so long as they do not seriously jeopardize the fundamental rights of others. That principle implies that religious institutions, and other private associations, should be free to change their ancient strictures against homosexuality if their leaders choose to do so; but that they ought also to be free to *refuse* to abandon those practices and restrictions, as they see fit. Neither the First Amendment nor liberal views on free speech sanction the disruption of religious services, however worthy the cause. Nor do they authorize gays and lesbians to appoint themselves as censors to delete Biblical passages that unequivocally condemn homosexuality, however hurtful those passages might be. . . .

Many gays and lesbians, having been hurt by others, may have become callous toward persons who do not share their views on sexuality. Intent on pursuing their own inclinations—perhaps with justification—they may fail to realize how much hurt they cause to others in the process. No doubt it can be extremely painful for the traditional parents of a gay person to accept the strange (to them) way of life that their son or daughter has adopted. The natural desire of the gay son or daughter to be accepted by his or her parents should, one would think, be accompanied by an understanding of the difficulty the parents must have in accepting what must seem to them to be an outrageous, immoral way of life.

On the other hand, it is difficult to think of anything more cruel and heartless than the utter abandonment of a dying AIDS victim by his or her family because of self-righteousness religious zealotry, or disapproval of homosexuality. Too many victims of that awful disease have withered, suffered, and died with no one to comfort them but their lovers, who are often weakened by the same affliction. Those who should be closest to them—their fathers and mothers, brothers and sisters—may be so preoccupied with nursing their own anger, their hurts, and their grievances that they have lost the capacity to be understanding or compassionate toward those to whom they have the closest possible biological connections. In some ways, this is one of the most grievous moral afflictions of our time. If there were a law of nature, one might wish that it would teach us, if not incline us, to care for our sons and daughters, despite our disagreements with them over matters that touch us deeply, particularly when they are suffering. Some have, indeed, responded to that call in heroic measure. But all too many have not.

Like every real human problem, the issues surrounding homosexual relations are complex and fraught with deep emotions. Philosophers may be able to shed some light on the arguments, but in the final analysis, only compassion and good will on all sides will lead to the kind of understanding and acceptance that may ultimately lead to a resolution of the most painful of them.

Review and Discussion Questions

1. Devlin argued that private acts between consenting adults may rightly be criminalized if they violate the ordinary person's sense of morality. Examine his reasoning from the perspective of Mill's liberty principle.

2. Is there any sense in which homosexuality is unnatural? Explain why or why not. Does something's being abnormal or unusual ever have any ethical relevance?

3. What explains our society's traditional disapproval of homosexuality? Why do so many people believe it to be wrong or disgusting?

4. Are there moral arguments against homosexuality that Leiser has overlooked or failed to do justice to? What should be society's attitude and public policy toward homosexuality? Is discrimination against homosexuals always wrong?

5. Leiser appears to suggest that gays and lesbians are wrong to demonstrate against religious groups that view homosexuality as immoral. Do you agree? Explain why or why not.

6. Should homosexuals be permitted to marry?

Is It Wrong to Discriminate on the Basis of Homosexuality?

JEFF JORDAN

Jeff Jordan, professor of philosophy at the University of Delaware, argues that in some situations—in particular, with respect to marriage—it is morally permissible to discriminate against homosexuals. In our society, conflicting views about the morality of homosexuality have led to what Jordan calls a "public dilemma," that is, a moral impasse with public policy implications. Although the state is sometimes justified in declaring that one side of a public dilemma is correct (as it did in the case of slavery), in general the state should strive to be neutral between the disputing parties and to resolve a public dilemma by an accommodation that gives as much as possible to those on both sides of the issue. Although the state should tolerate private homosexual acts, to sanction same-sex marriages would be for it to take sides in the dispute over the morality of homosexuality. Doing so would be wrong, Jordan argues, because it would fail to respect the moral and religious integrity of opponents of homosexuality.

Study Questions

1. What does Jordan mean by "discrimination"? What is the "parity thesis"? What is the "difference thesis"?

2. Why, in Jordan's view, does the argument presented in section 2 fail to prove the parity thesis?

3. What does Jordan mean by a "public dilemma," and what are the two ways in which such a dilemma can be resolved? How is the distinction between the public realm and the private realm relevant to the accommodation that Jordan recommends with regard to the public dilemma over homosexuality?

4. What is the argument from conflicting claims and what are the two objections to it that Jordan addresses?

5. What is the point of the "no-exit argument"?

Reprinted by permission from the Journal of Social Philosophy, *vol. 30, no. 1 (Spring 1995). Copyright ©* 1995 Journal of Social Philosophy. *Some notes omitted.*

Much like the issue of abortion in the early 1970s, the issue of homosexuality has exploded to the forefront of social discussion. Is homosexual sex on a moral par with heterosexual sex? Or is homosexuality in some way morally inferior? Is it wrong to discriminate against homosexuals—to treat homosexuals in less favorable ways than one does heterosexuals? Or is some discrimination against homosexuals morally justified? These questions are the focus of this essay.

In what follows, I argue that there are situations in which it is morally permissible to discriminate against homosexuals because of their homosexuality. That is, there are some morally relevant differences between heterosexuality and homosexuality which, in some instances, permit a difference in treatment. The issue of marriage provides a good example. While it is clear that heterosexual unions merit the state recognition known as marriage, along with all the attendant advantages—spousal insurance coverage, inheritance rights, ready eligibility of adoption—it is far from clear that homosexual couples ought to be accorded that state recognition.

The argument of this essay makes no claim about the moral status of homosexuality per se. Briefly put, it is the argument of this essay that the moral impasse generated by conflicting views concerning homosexuality, and the public policy ramifications of those conflicting views, justify the claim that it is morally permissible, in certain circumstances, to discriminate against homosexuals.

1. The Issue

The relevant issue is this: does homosexuality have the same moral status as heterosexuality? Put differently, since there are no occasions in which it is morally permissible to treat heterosexuals unfavorably, whether because they are heterosexual or because of heterosexual acts, are there occasions in which it is morally permissible to treat homosexuals unfavorably, whether because they are homosexuals or because of homosexual acts?

A negative answer to the above can be termed the "parity thesis." The parity thesis contends that *homosexuality has the same moral status as heterosexuality.* If the parity thesis is correct, then it would be immoral to discriminate against homosexuals because of their homosexuality. An affirmative answer can be termed the "difference thesis" and contends that there are morally relevant differences between heterosexuality and homosexuality which justify a difference in moral status and treatment between homosexuals and heterosexuals. The difference thesis entails that *there are situations in which it is morally permissible to discriminate against homosexuals.*

It is perhaps needless to point out that the difference thesis follows as long as there is at least one occasion in which it is morally permissible to discriminate against homosexuals. If the parity thesis were true, then on no occasion would a difference in treatment between heterosexuals and homosexuals ever be justified. The difference thesis does not, even if true, justify discriminatory actions on every occasion. Nonetheless, even though the scope of the difference thesis is relatively modest, it is, if true, a significant principle which has not only theoretical import but important practical consequences as well.

A word should be said about the notion of discrimination. To discriminate against X means treating X in an unfavorable way. The word "discrimination" is not a synonym for "morally unjustifiable treatment." Some discrimination is morally unjustifiable; some is not. For example, we discriminate against convicted felons in that they are disenfranchised. This legal discrimination is morally permissible even though it involves treating one person unfavorably different from how other persons are treated. The difference thesis entails that there are circumstances in which it is morally permissible to discriminate against homosexuals.

2. An Argument for the Parity Thesis

. . . Perhaps the strongest reason to hold that the parity thesis is true is something like the following:

1. Homosexual acts between consenting adults harm no one. And,
2. respecting persons' privacy and choices in harmless sexual matters maximizes individual freedom. And,
3. individual freedom should be maximized. But,
4. discrimination against homosexuals, because of their homosexuality, diminishes individual freedom since it ignores personal choice and privacy. So,
5. the toleration of homosexuality rather than discriminating against homosexuals is the preferable option since it would maximize individual freedom. Therefore,
6. the parity thesis is more plausible than the difference thesis.

Premise (2) is unimpeachable: if an act is harmless and if there are persons who want to do it and who choose to do it, then it seems clear that respecting the choices of those people would tend to maximize their freedom. Step (3) is also beyond reproach: since freedom is arguably a great good and since there does not appear to be any ceiling on the amount of individual freedom—no "too much of a good thing"—(3) appears to be true. . . .

If premise (1) is understood to apply only to acts done in private, then it would appear to be true. The same goes for (4): discrimination against homosexuals for acts done in private would result in a diminishing of freedom. So (1)–(4) would lend support to (5) only if we understand (1)–(4) to refer to acts done in pri-

vate. Hence, (5) must be understood as referring to private acts; and, as a consequence, (6) also must be read as referring only to acts done in private.

With regard to acts which involve only willing adult participants, there may be no morally relevant difference between homosexuality and heterosexuality. In other words, acts done in private. However, acts done in public add a new ingredient to the mix; an ingredient which has moral consequence. Consequently, the argument (1)–(6) fails in supporting the parity thesis. The argument (1)–(6) may show that there are some circumstances in which the moral status of homosexuality and heterosexuality are the same, but it gives us no reason for thinking that this result holds for all circumstances.

3. Moral Impasses and Public Dilemmas

Suppose one person believes that X is morally wrong, while another believes that X is morally permissible. The two people, let's stipulate, are not involved in a semantical quibble; they hold genuinely conflicting beliefs regarding the moral status of X. If the first person is correct, then the second person is wrong; and, of course, if the second person is right, then the first must be wrong. This situation of conflicting claims is what we will call an "impasse." Impasses arise out of moral disputes. Since the conflicting parties in an impasse take contrary views, the conflicting views cannot all be true, nor can they all be false.[1] Moral impasses may concern matters only of a personal nature, but moral impasses can involve public policy. An impasse is likely to have public policy ramifications if large numbers of people hold the conflicting views, and the conflict involves matters which are fundamental to a person's moral identity (and, hence, from a practical point of view, are probably irresolvable) and it involves acts done in public. Since not every impasse has public policy ramifications, one can mark off "public dilemma" as a special case of moral impasses: those moral impasses that have public policy consequences. Public dilemmas, then, are impasses located in the public square. Since they have public policy ramifications and since they arise from impasses, one side or another of the dispute will have its views implemented as public policy. Because of the public policy ramifications, and also because social order is sometimes threatened by the volatile parties involved in the impasse, the state has a role to play in resolving a public dilemma.

A public dilemma can be actively resolved in two ways.[2] The first is when the government allies itself with one side of the impasse and, by state coercion and sanction, declares that side of the impasse the correct side. The American Civil War was an example of this: the federal government forcibly ended slavery by aligning itself with the Abolitionist side of the impasse. Prohibition is another example. The 18th Amendment and the Volstead Act allied the state with the Temperance side of the impasse. State mandated affirmative action programs provide a modern example of this. This kind of resolution of a public dilemma we can call a "resolution by declaration." The first of the examples cited above indicates that declarations can be morally proper, the right thing to do. The second example, however, indicates that declarations are not always morally proper. The state does not always take the side of the morally correct; nor is it always clear which side is the correct one.

The second way of actively resolving a public dilemma is that of accommodation. An accommodation in this context means resolving the public dilemma in a way that gives as much as possible to all sides of the impasse. A resolution by accommodation involves staking out some middle ground in a dispute and placing public policy in that location. The middle ground location of a resolution via accommodation is a virtue since it entails that there are no absolute victors and no absolute losers. The middle ground

is reached in order to resolve the public dilemma in a way which respects the relevant views of the conflicting parties and which maintains social order. The Federal Fair Housing Act and, perhaps, the current status of abortion (legal but with restrictions) provide examples of actual resolutions via accommodation.[3]

In general, governments should be, at least as far as possible, neutral with regard to the disputing parties in a public dilemma. Unless there is some overriding reason why the state should take sides in a public dilemma—the protection of innocent life, or abolishing slavery, for instance—the state should be neutral, because no matter which side of the public dilemma the state takes, the other side will be the recipient of unequal treatment by the state. A state which is partial and takes sides in moral disputes via declaration, when there is no overriding reason why it should, is tyrannical. Overriding reasons involve, typically, the protection of generally recognized rights. In the case of slavery, the right to liberty; in the case of protecting innocent life, the right involved is the negative right to life. If a public dilemma must be actively resolved, the state should do so (in the absence of an overriding reason) via accommodation and not declaration since the latter entails that a sizable number of people would be forced to live under a government which "legitimizes" and does not just tolerate activities which they find immoral. Resolution via declaration is appropriate only if there is an overriding reason for the state to throw its weight behind one side in a public dilemma.

Is moral rightness an overriding reason for a resolution via declaration? What better reason might there be for a resolution by declaration than that it is the right thing to do? Unless one is prepared to endorse a view that is called "legal moralism"—that immorality alone is a sufficient reason for the state to curtail individual liberty—then one had best hold that moral rightness alone is not an overriding reason. Since some immoral acts neither harm nor offend nor violate another's rights, it seems clear enough that too much liberty would be lost if legal moralism were adopted as public policy.

Though we do not have a definite rule for determining *a priori* which moral impasses genuinely constitute public dilemmas, we can proceed via a case by case method. For example, many people hold that cigarette smoking is harmful and, on that basis, is properly suppressible. Others disagree. Is this a public dilemma? Probably not. Whether someone engages in an imprudent action is, as long as it involves no unwilling participants, a private matter and does not, on that account, constitute a public dilemma. What about abortion? Is abortion a public dilemma? Unlike cigarette smoking, abortion is a public dilemma. This is clear from the adamant and even violent contrary positions involved in the impasse. Abortion is an issue which forces itself into the public square. So, it is clear that, even though we lack a rule which filters through moral impasses designating some as public dilemmas, not every impasse constitutes a public dilemma.

4. Conflicting Claims on Homosexuality

The theistic tradition, Judaism and Christianity and Islam, has a clear and deeply entrenched position on homosexual acts: they are prohibited. . . . As a consequence, many contemporary theistic adherents of the theistic tradition . . . hold that homosexual behavior is sinful. Though God loves the homosexual, these folk say, God hates the sinful behavior. To say that act X is a sin entails that X is morally wrong, not necessarily because it is harmful or offensive, but because X violates God's will. So, the claim that homosexuality is sinful entails the claim that it is also morally wrong. And, it is clear, many people adopt the difference thesis just because of their religious views: because the Bible or the Koran holds that homosexuality is wrong, they too hold that view.

Well, what should we make of these observations? We do not, for one thing, have to base our moral conclusions on those views, if for no other reason than not every one is a theist. If one does not adopt the religion-based moral view, one must still respect those who do; they cannot just be dismissed out of hand. And, significantly, this situation yields a reason for thinking that the difference thesis is probably true. Because many religious people sincerely believe homosexual acts to be morally wrong and many others believe that homosexual acts are not morally wrong, there results a public dilemma.

The existence of this public dilemma gives us reason for thinking that the difference thesis is true. It is only via the difference thesis and not the parity thesis, that an accommodation can be reached. Here again, the private/public distinction will come into play.

To see this, take as an example the issue of homosexual marriages. A same-sex marriage would be a public matter. For the government to sanction same-sex marriages—to grant the recognition and reciprocal benefits which attach to marriage—would ally the government with one side of the public dilemma and against the adherents of religion-based moralities. This is especially true given that, historically, no government has sanctioned same-sex marriages. The status quo has been no same-sex marriages. If the state were to change its practice now, it would be clear that the state has taken sides in the impasse. Given the history, for a state to sanction a same-sex marriage now would not be a neutral act.

Of course, some would respond here that by not sanctioning same-sex marriages the state is, and historically has been, taking sides to the detriment of homosexuals. There is some truth in this claim. But one must be careful here. The respective resolutions of this issue—whether the state should recognize and sanction same-sex marriages—do not have symmetrical implications. The asymmetry of this issue is a function of the private/public distinction and the fact that marriage is a public matter. If the state sanctions same-sex marriages, then there is no accommodation available. In that event, the religion-based morality proponents are faced with a public, state sanctioned matter which they find seriously immoral. This would be an example of a resolution via declaration. On the other hand, if the state does not sanction same-sex marriages, there is an accommodation available: in the public realm the state sides with the religion-based moral view, but the state can tolerate private homosexual acts. That is, since homosexual acts are not essentially public acts, they can be, and historically have been, performed in private. The state, by not sanctioning same-sex marriages is acting in the public realm, but it can leave the private realm to personal choice.

5. The Argument from Conflicting Claims

It was suggested in the previous section that the public dilemma concerning homosexuality, and in particular whether states should sanction same-sex marriages, generates an argument in support of the difference thesis. The argument, again using same-sex marriages as the particular case, is as follows:

7. There are conflicting claims regarding whether the state should sanction same-sex marriages. And,
8. this controversy constitutes a public dilemma. And,
9. there is an accommodation possible if the state does not recognize same-sex marriages. And,
10. there is no accommodation possible if the state does sanction same-sex marriages. And,
11. there is no overriding reason for a resolution via declaration. Hence,
12. the state ought not sanction same-sex marriages. And,

13. the state ought to sanction heterosexual marriages. So,
14. there is at least one morally relevant case in which discrimination against homosexuals, because of their homosexuality, is morally permissible. Therefore,
15. the difference thesis is true.

Since proposition (14) is logically equivalent to the difference thesis, then, if (7)–(14) are sound, proposition (15) certainly follows.

Premises (7) and (8) are uncontroversial. Premises (9) and (10) are based on the asymmetry that results from the public nature of marriage. Proposition (11) is based on our earlier analysis of the argument (1)–(6). Since the strongest argument in support of the parity thesis fails, we have reason to think that there is no overriding reason why the state ought to resolve the public dilemma via declaration in favor of same-sex marriages. We have reason, in other words, to think that (11) is true.

Proposition (12) is based on the conjunction of (7)–(11) and the principle that, in the absence of an overriding reason for state intervention via declaration, resolution by accommodation is the preferable route. Proposition (13) is just trivially true. So, given the moral difference mentioned in (12) and (13), proposition (14) logically follows.

6. Two Objections Considered

The first objection to the argument from conflicting claims would contend that it is unsound because a similar sort of argument would permit discrimination against some practice which, though perhaps controversial at some earlier time, is now widely thought to be morally permissible. Take mixed-race marriages, for example. The opponent of the argument from conflicting claims could argue that a similar argument would warrant prohibition against mixed-race marriages. If it does, we would have good reason to reject (7)–(14) as unsound.

There are three responses to this objection. The first response denies that the issue of mixed-race marriages is in fact a public dilemma. It may have been so at one time, but it does not seem to generate much, if any, controversy today. Hence, the objection is based upon a faulty analogy.

The second response grants for the sake of the argument that the issue of mixed-race marriages generates a public dilemma. But the second response points out that there is a relevant difference between mixed-race marriages and same-sex marriages that allows for a resolution by declaration in the one case but not the other. As evident from the earlier analysis of the argument in support of (1)–(6), there is reason to think that there is no overriding reason for a resolution by declaration in support of the parity thesis. On the other hand, it is a settled matter that state protection from racial discrimination is a reason sufficient for a resolution via declaration. Hence, the two cases are only apparently similar, and, in reality, they are crucially different. They are quite different because, clearly enough, if mixed-race marriages do generate a public dilemma, the state should use resolution by declaration in support of such marriages. The same cannot be said for same-sex marriages.

One should note that the second response to the objection does not beg the question against the proponent of the parity thesis. Though the second response denies that race and sexuality are strict analogues, it does so for a defensible and independent reason: it is a settled matter that race is not a sufficient reason for disparate treatment; but, as we have seen from the analysis of (1)–(6), there is no overriding reason to think the same about sexuality.

The third response to the first objection is that the grounds of objection differ in the respective cases: one concerns racial identity; the other concerns behavior thought to be morally problematic. A same-sex marriage would involve behavior which many people find morally objectionable; a mixed-race marriage is objectionable to some, not because of the participants' behavior, but because of the racial identity of the participants. It is the race of the marriage partners which some find of primary complaint concerning mixed-race marriages. With same sex marriages, however, it is the behavior which is primarily objectionable. To see this latter point, one should note that . . . the kind of sexual acts that are likely involved in a same-sex marriage are objectionable to some, regardless of whether done by homosexuals or heterosexuals. So again, there is reason to reject the analogy between same-sex marriages and mixed-race marriages. Racial identity is an immutable trait and a complaint about mixed-race marriages necessarily involves, then, a complaint about an immutable trait. Sexual behavior is not an immutable trait and it is possible to object to same-sex marriages based on the behavior which would be involved in such marriages. Put succinctly, the third response could be formulated as follows: objections to mixed-race marriages necessarily involve objections over status, while objections to same-sex marriages could involve objections over behavior. Therefore, the two cases are not analogues since there is a significant modal difference in the ground of the objection.

The second objection to the argument from conflicting claims can be stated so: if homosexuality is biologically based—if it is inborn[4]—then how can discrimination ever be justified? If it is not a matter of choice, homosexuality is an immutable trait which is, as a consequence, morally permissible. Just as it would be absurd to hold someone morally culpable for being of a certain race, likewise it would be absurd to hold someone morally culpable for being a homosexual. Consequently, according to this objection, the argument from conflicting claims "legitimizes" unjustifiable discrimination.

But this second objection is not cogent, primarily because it ignores an important distinction. No one could plausibly hold that homosexuals act by some sort of biological compulsion. If there is a biological component involved in sexual identity, it would incline but it would not compel. Just because one naturally (without any choice) has certain dispositions, is not in itself a morally cogent reason for acting upon that disposition. Most people are naturally selfish, but it clearly does not follow that selfishness is in any way permissible on that account. Even if it is true that one has a predisposition to do X as a matter of biology and not as a matter of choice, it does not follow that doing X is morally permissible. . . . The reason that the appeal to biology is specious is that it ignores the important distinction between being a homosexual and homosexual acts. One is status; the other is behavior. Even if one has the status naturally, it does not follow that the behavior is morally permissible, nor that others have a duty to tolerate the behavior.

But, while moral permissibility does not necessarily follow if homosexuality should turn out to be biologically based, what does follow is this: in the absence of a good reason to discriminate between homosexuals and heterosexuals, then, assuming that homosexuality is inborn, one ought not discriminate between them. If a certain phenomenon X is natural in the sense of being involuntary and nonpathological, and if there is no good reason to hold that X is morally problematic, then that is reason enough to think that X is morally permissible. In the absence of a good reason to repress X, one should tolerate it since, as per supposition, it is largely nonvoluntary. The argument from conflicting claims, however, provides a good reason which overrides this presumption.

7. A Second Argument for the Difference Thesis

A second argument for the difference thesis, similar to the argument from conflicting claims, is what might be called the "no-exit argument." This argument is based on the principle that:

(A): No just government can coerce a citizen into violating a deeply held moral belief or religious belief.

Is (A) plausible? It seems to be since the prospect of a citizen being coerced by the state into a practice which she finds profoundly immoral appears to be a clear example of an injustice. Principle (A), conjoined with there being a public dilemma arising over the issue of same-sex marriages, leads to the observation that if the state were to sanction same-sex marriages, then persons who have profound religious or moral objections to such unions would be legally mandated to violate their beliefs since there does not appear to be any feasible "exit right" possible with regard to state sanctioned marriage. An exit right is an exemption from some legally mandated practice, granted to a person or group, the purpose of which is to protect the religious or moral integrity of that person or group. Prominent examples of exit rights include conscientious objection and military service, home-schooling of the young because of some religious concern, and property used for religious purposes being free from taxation.

It is important to note that marriage is a public matter in the sense that, for instance, if one is an employer who provides health care benefits to the spouses of employees, one must provide those benefits to any employee who is married. Since there is no exit right possible in this case, one would be coerced, by force of law, into subsidizing a practice one finds morally or religiously objectionable.

In the absence of an exit right, and if (A) is plausible, then the state cannot morally force persons to violate deeply held beliefs that are moral or religious in nature. In particular, the state morally could not sanction same-sex marriages since this would result in coercing some into violating a deeply held religious conviction.

8. A Conclusion

It is important to note that neither the argument from conflicting claims nor the no-exit argument licenses wholesale discrimination against homosexuals. What they do show is that some discrimination against homosexuals, in this case refusal to sanction same-sex marriages, is not only legally permissible but also morally permissible. The discrimination is a way of resolving a public policy dilemma that accommodates, to an extent, each side of the impasse and, further, protects the religious and moral integrity of a good number of people. In short, the arguments show us that there are occasions in which it is morally permissible to discriminate on the basis of homosexuality.

NOTES

1. Perhaps it would be better to term the disputing positions "contradictory" views rather than "contrary" views.

2. Resolutions can also be passive in the sense of the state doing nothing. If the state does nothing to resolve the public dilemma, it stands pat with the status quo, and the public dilemma is resolved gradually by sociological changes (changes in mores and in beliefs).

3. The Federal Fair Housing Act prohibits discrimination in housing on the basis of race, religion, and sex. But it does not apply to the rental of rooms in single-family houses, or to a building of five units or less if the owner lives in one of the units. See 42 U.S.C. Section 3603.

4. There is some interesting recent research which, though still tentative, strongly suggests that homosexuality is, at least in part, biologically based. See Simon LeVay, *The Sexual Brain* (Cambridge, MA: MIT Press, 1993), pp. 120–122; and J. M. Bailey & R. C. Pillard, "A Genetic Study of Male Sexual Orientation," *Archives of General Psychiatry* 48 (1991): 1089–1096; and C. Burr, "Homosexuality and Biology," *The Atlantic* 271/3 (March, 1993): 64; and D. Hamer, S. Hu, V. Magnuson, N. Hu, A. Pattatucci, "A Linkage Between DNA Markers on the X Chromosome and Male Sexual Orientation," *Science* 261 (16 July 1993): 321–327; and see the summary of this article by Robert Pool, "Evidence for Homosexuality Gene," *Science* 261 (16 July 1993): 291–292.

Review and Discussion Questions

1. Assess the argument for the parity thesis that Jordan criticizes in section 2. Is his criticism persuasive, or is the argument stronger than he acknowledges?

2. Jordan grants that in some cases the government should take sides in a public dilemma. In your view, what distinguishes these cases from cases in which the government should remain neutral? Is homosexuality a public dilemma? If so, is it a dilemma with respect to which the government should strive to remain neutral?

3. Critics of the conflicting-claims argument contend that it would entail that the government could rightly prohibit mixed-race marriages. How persuasive are Jordan's three responses to this objection?

4. Some people argue that if homosexuality is biologically based, then it is wrong to discriminate against homosexuals. Are Jordan's reasons for rejecting this argument sound?

5. Jordan's no-exit argument contends that "if the state were to sanction same-sex marriages, then persons who have profound religious or moral objections to such unions would be legally mandated to violate their beliefs. . . ." Assess this contention.

6. In the previous essay, Burton Leiser maintains that there are no respectable arguments for the conclusion that homosexuality is wrong and that people who condemn it do so on the basis of emotion or religious authority, not reason. If Leiser is correct, what are the implications, if any, of this fact for Jordan's argument?

7. Examine the issue of gay marriage from the perspective of Mill's liberty principle.

AFFIRMATIVE ACTION

One Way to Understand and Defend Programs of Preferential Treatment

RICHARD A. WASSERSTROM

In this essay, Richard A. Wasserstrom, professor of philosophy at the University of California, Santa Cruz, defends programs that take race into account when considering an individual for admission, a job, or a promotion. By introducing blacks into careers and institutional positions from which they have been historically excluded, Wasserstrom argues, such programs help make society less racially oppressive and more just. He defends programs of preferential treatment against the charge that they violate the rights of individuals or treat them unfairly.

Study Questions

1. What is the point of Wasserstrom's thought experiment about choosing to be black or white?
2. In what ways, according to Wasserstrom, do affirmative action programs help to break down the existing system of racial disadvantage and oppression?
3. How does Wasserstrom answer the objection that, if it was wrong to take race into account in the past, then it is wrong to do so now?
4. Why is the arbitrariness of relying on an irrelevant characteristic not the main thing wrong with either slavery or racial segregation and discrimination?
5. How does Wasserstrom respond to the argument that one should take into account only an individual's qualifications when considering him or her for a job, for promotion, or for acceptance into a university?

From The Moral Foundations of Civil Rights *by Robert K. Fullinwider and Claudia Mills, eds. (Savage, Md.: Rowman and Littlefield Publishers, 1986). Reprinted by permission of the publisher. Section titles added.*

PROGRAMS OF PREFERENTIAL TREATMENT make relevant the race or sex of individuals in the sense that the race or sex of an applicant for admission, a job, or a promotion constitutes a relevant, although not a decisive, reason for preferring that applicant over others. In my discussion of these programs I will consider only preferential treatment programs concerned with preferring a person who is black over one who is white, but what I have to say will be illustrative of a way to approach and assess comparable programs in which members of other ethnic or minority groups, or women, are concerned.

My thesis is a twofold one. First, such programs can very plausibly be seen to be good programs for us to have in our society today because they help to make the social conditions of life less racially oppressive and thereby more just, and because they help to distribute important social goods and opportunities more equally and fairly. Second, these programs can be seen to help to realize these desirable aims without themselves being in any substantial respect unjust—without, that is, taking an impermissible characteristic into account, violating persons' rights, failing to give individuals what they deserve, or treating them in some other way that is unfair.

I. The Case for Programs of Preferential Treatment

The positive case for such programs begins with the following claim about our own society: we are still living in a society in which a person's race, his or her blackness rather than whiteness, is a socially significant and important category. Race is not, in our culture, like eye color. Eye color is an irrelevant category in that eye color is not an important social or cultural fact about individuals; nothing of substance turns on what eye color they have. To be black rather than white is not like that at all. To be black is to be

at a disadvantage in terms of most of the measures of success or satisfaction—be they economic, vocational, political, or social. To see, in a very crude and rough way, that this is so one could conduct a thought experiment. If one wanted to imagine maximizing one's chances of being satisfied with one's employment or career, politically powerful rather than powerless, secure from arbitrary treatment within the social institutions, reasonably well off economically, and able to pursue one's own goals and develop one's own talents in ways that would be satisfying to oneself, and if one could choose whether to be born either white or black, wouldn't one choose to be born white rather than black?

If this claim about the existing social reality of race is correct, then two further claims seem plausible. The first is that there is in place what can correctly be described as a system of racial oppression. It is a racial system in that the positions of political, economic, and social power and advantage are concentrated and maintained largely in the hands of those who are white rather than black. It is an oppressive one in that some of these inequalities in social burdens and lessened opportunities are unjust because of the nature of the disadvantages themselves—they are among those that no one ought fairly be required to confront or combat in any decent society. And it is an oppressive one in that others of these inequalities are tied to race in contexts and ways that make such a connection itself manifestly unfair and unjust. But the primary and fundamental character of the oppression is in what results from these and related features and is not reducible to them. The oppression has to do, first, with the *systemic nature* of the unequal and maldistributed array of social benefits, opportunities, and burdens, and it has to do, as well, with *how* things are linked together to constitute an interlocking, mutually reinforcing system of social benefits and burdens, ideology, and the like which, when tied to race as they are, make it a system of *racial* disadvantage and oppression—and, for all of these reasons, a decidedly and distinctly unjust one.

Now, if this be granted, the next claim is that even if it is assumed that the intentions and motivations of those occupying positions of relative power and opportunity are wholly benign and proper with respect to the pursuit of the wrongful perpetuation of any unjust racial oppression toward blacks, it is likely that the system will perpetuate itself unless blacks come to occupy substantially more of the positions within the major social institutions than they have occupied in the past and now do. Thus, to have it occur that blacks do come to occupy more of these positions of power, authority, and the like is *a* way, if not *the* way, to bring about the weakening, if not the destruction, of that interlocking system of social practices, structures, and ideology that still plays a major if not fundamental role in preventing persons who are black from being able to live the kinds of lives that all persons ought to be able to live—lives free from the burdens of an existing, racially oppressive system.

If this is so, then the case for programs of preferential treatment can be seen to rest upon the truth of the claim that they are designed specifically to accomplish this end, and upon the truth of the claim that they do accomplish it. They do succeed in introducing more blacks into the kinds of vocations, careers, institutional positions, and the like than would have been present if these programs had not been in place. In this respect there is, I believe, little question but that the programs have worked and do work to produce, for example, black judges and lawyers where few if any existed before, and to produce, more generally, black employees in businesses and in places within the other major structures and hierarchies where few if any were present before. And this can be seen to be especially important and desirable because changes of this sort in the racial composition of these institutions have mutually reinforcing consequences that can reasonably be thought to play an important role in bringing about the dismantling of the existing system of racial disadvantage and oppression.

They do so, first, by creating role models for other black persons to identify with and thereby come to see as realizable in their own lives. They do so, second, by bringing members of this historically excluded and oppressed group into relationships of equality of power, authority, and status with members of the dominant group. This is important because when relationships of this kind are nonexistent or extremely infrequent, as they are in the system of racial oppression, the system tends most easily and regularly to sustain itself. Third, changes in the racial composition of the major social institutions work, as well, to make it possible for blacks, with their often different and distinctive but no less correct views of the nature of the complex social world in which we all live, to participate in such things as the shaping of academic programs and disciplines and to participate in the definition, focus, and direction of significant social, legal, economic, and related institutional policies, and in deliberations and debates concerning their supporting justifications. And they do so, finally, by making it more likely that there will be the more immediate and meaningful provision of important services and benefits to other members of that group who have up until now been denied fair and appropriate access to them.

Thus, the primary claim in support of these programs is that, in what they do and how they work, they can be seen to play a substantial role in weakening the system of racial oppression that is still in place and that makes a person's blackness have the kind of pervasively deleterious social meaning and significance that it ought not. The aim of these programs is to eliminate this system and to produce a society in which race will cease to matter in this way; and on this view of things it may be superficially paradoxical but is, nonetheless, more deeply plausible to believe that such can be significantly accomplished by taking race into account in the way these programs do.

What should be apparent is that, in some large measure, there are empirical claims involved here, and to the degree to which there are, disagreements about the justifiability of preferential treatment programs can be located and settled by attending to their truth or falsity. Thus, if such programs produce or exacerbate racial hostility, or if they lead to a reduced rather than an enhanced sense of self-respect on the part of blacks, then these are matters that count against the overall case for these programs. But I do not, myself, think the case against them can be rested very easily upon such grounds, and I do not think that, when it is, the evidence is very convincing and the arguments very plausible. Nor are such programs typically opposed on grounds of this sort. Instead, the main ground of principled opposition has to do with what is thought to be fundamentally wrong with them: with the fact that they are unjust, inconsistent with important ideals and principles, and violative of persons' basic rights. In what follows, I will seek very briefly to indicate why this is not so and how my way of understanding and justifying these programs can help to bring these matters, too, into a different and more proper focus.

II. Responses to Objections

The first argument that is both common and close to the core of the cluster of objections to these programs is this: if it was wrong to take race into account when blacks were the objects of racial policies of exclusion, then it is wrong to take race into account when the objects of the policies differ only in their race. Simple considerations of intellectual consistency—of what it means to have had a good reason for condemning those social policies and practices—require that what was a good reason then be a good reason now.

The right way to answer this objection is, I think, to agree that the practices of racial exclu-sion that were an integral part of the fabric of our culture, and which still are, to some degree, were and are pernicious. Yet, one can grant this and also believe that the kinds of racial preferences and quotas that are a part of contemporary preferential treatment programs are commendable and right. There is no inconsistency involved in holding both views. The reason why depends upon a further analysis of the social realities. A fundamental feature of programs that discriminated against blacks was that these programs were a part of a larger social universe in which the network of social institutions concentrated power, authority, and goods in the hands of white individuals. This same social universe contained a complex ideology that buttressed this network of institutions and at the same time received support from it. Practices that prevented or limited the access of blacks to the desirable social institutions, places, and benefits were, therefore, wrong both because of their direct consequences on the individuals most affected by them, and because the system of racial superiority that was constituted by these institutions and practices was an immoral one, in that it severely and unjustifiably restricted the capacities, autonomy, and happiness of those who were members of the less favored category.

Whatever may be wrong with today's programs of preferential treatment, even those with quotas, it should be clear that the evil, if any, is simply not the same. Blacks do not constitute the dominant social group. Nor is the prevailing ideological conception of who is a fully developed member of the moral and social community one of an individual who is black rather than white. Programs that give a preference to blacks do not add to an already comparatively overabundant supply of resources and opportunities at the disposal of members of the dominant racial group in the way in which exclusionary practices of the past added to the already overabundant supply of resources and opportunities at the disposal of whites. Thus, if preferential treatment programs are to be condemned or abandoned, it cannot be either because they seek to perpetuate an unjust society in which the desirable options for living are husbanded by and for those who already have the most, or because they realize and maintain a morally corrupt ideal of distinct grades of political, social, and moral superiority and inferiority—in this case grades or classes of superiority and inferiority tied to and determined by one's race.

A related objection that fares no better, I believe, has to do with the identification of what exactly was wrong, say, with the system of racial discrimination in the South, or with what is wrong with any system of racial discrimination. One very common way to think about the wrongness of racial discrimination is to see the essential wrongness as consisting in the use of an irrelevant characteristic, namely race, to allocate social benefits and burdens of various sorts, for, given this irrelevance, individuals end up being treated in an arbitrary manner. On this view, the chief defect of the system of racial segregation and discrimination that we had and still have is to be located in its systemic capriciousness. Hence, on this view, what is wrong and unjust about any practice or act of taking any individual's race into account is the irrational and arbitrary character of the interest in and concern with race.

I am far less certain that that is the central flaw at all—especially with our own historical system of racial segregation and discrimination. Consider, for instance, the most hideous of the practices, human slavery. The primary thing that was wrong, I think, with that institution was not that the particular individuals who were assigned the place of slaves were assigned there arbitrarily by virtue of an irrelevant characteristic, i.e., their race. Rather, the fundamental thing that was and is wrong with slavery is the practice itself—the fact that some human beings were able to own other human beings—and all that goes with the acceptance of that practice and that conception of permissible interpersonal relationships. A comparable criticism can be made of many of the other discrete practices and institutions that comprised the system of racial discrimination even after human slavery was abolished.

The fundamental wrongness in taking race into account in this way has to do, perhaps, with arbitrariness, but it is the special arbitrariness attendant upon using race in the constitution and maintenance of any system of oppression so as to make that system a system of racial oppression. The irrationality, arbitrariness, and deep injustice of taking race into account cannot, I think, be isolated or severed from the place of a racial criterion in the very constitution of that system which becomes both a system of *oppression* and a system of *racist* oppression in and through the regular systematic use of that criterion. Whatever may be said about the appropriateness of regarding race as relevant in other contexts, the arbitrariness of taking race into account has a special and distinctive bite of injustice when race becomes the basis for fixing persons' unequal positions, opportunities, and status in this kind of systemically pervasive fashion. When viewed in the light of existing social realities and in the light of this conception of the wrongness of a racially oppressive system, the central consideration is that contemporary programs of preferential treatment, even when viewed as a system of programs, cannot plausibly be construed in either their design or effects as consigning whites to the kind of oppressed status systematically bestowed upon blacks by the dominant social institutions.

A third very common objection is that, when used in programs of preferential treatment, race is too broad a category for programs designed to promote, in a legitimate way in our present society, conditions of fair equality of opportunity and full equality with respect to political and social status. The objection presupposes that whatever the appropriate or relevant characteristic, it is not race. Instead, almost always it is taken to be disadvantaged socio-economic status.

This objection, too, helps to bring into focus the mistaken conception of the social realities upon which a number of the central objections to preferential treatment programs depend. While socio-economic status unquestionably affects in deep and pervasive ways the kinds of lives persons can and will be able to fashion and live, it is, I think, only a kind of implausible, vulgar Marxism, or socio-economic reductionism of some other type, that ultimately underlies the view that, in our society, socio-economic status is the sole, or even the primary, locus of systemic oppression. Given my analysis of the social realities, blackness is as much a primary locus of oppression as is socio-economic status. And if so, it is implausible to insist, as this objection does, that socio-economic status is central while race is not. Race is just the appropriate characteristic to make directly relevant if the aim is to alter the existing system of racial oppression and inequality, or otherwise to mitigate its effects. Socio-economic status is an indirect, imperfect, unduly narrow, and overly broad category with which to deal with the phenomena of *racial* oppression and disadvantage, in precisely the same way in which race is an indirect, imperfect, unduly narrow, and overly broad category to take on the phenomena of *socio-economic* oppression and disadvantage.

The final objection I wish to introduce concerns the claim that these programs are wrong because they take race into account rather than taking into account the only thing that does and should matter: an individual's qualifications. And qualifications, it is further claimed, have nothing whatsoever to do with race. Here, I can mention only very briefly some of the key issues that seem to me to be at stake in understanding and assessing such an objection.

First, it is important to establish what the argument is for making selections solely on the basis of who is the most qualified among the applicants, candidates, and the like. One such argument for the exclusive relevance of qualifications—although it is seldom stated explicitly—is that the most qualified persons should always be selected for a place or position because the tasks

or activities connected with that place or position will then be done in the most economical and efficient manner. Now, there is nothing wrong in principle with an argument based upon the good results that will be produced by a social practice of selection based solely upon the qualifications of the applicant. But there is a serious problem that many opponents of preferential treatment programs must confront. The nature and magnitude of their problem is apparent if their objection to my way of justifying these programs is that any appeal to good and bad results is the wrong *kind* of justification to offer. For if that is the basis of their objection, then it is simply inconsistent for them to rest their case for an exclusive preoccupation with qualifications upon a wholly analogous appeal to the good results alleged to follow upon such a practice. In any event, what is central is that this reason for attending only to qualifications fails to shift inquiry to that different kind of analysis having to do with justice that was originally claimed to be decisive.

Second, given the theses offered earlier concerning how the increased presence of blacks in the positions of the major social institutions changes the workings of those institutions, it is anything but obvious why a person's blackness cannot or should not appropriately be taken into account as one of the characteristics which, in any number of contexts, genuinely should count as an aspect of one's qualifications for many positions or places at this time in our social life. And preferential treatment programs can, therefore, often be plausibly construed as making just the judgment that a person's blackness is indeed one of the relevant characteristics helping to establish his or her overall qualifications.

Third, even if this way of looking at qualifications is rejected, a further question must still be addressed with respect to any or all of the characteristics of the more familiar sort that are thought to be the ones that legitimately establish who is the most qualified for a position: is the person who possesses these characteristics, and who is, hence, the most qualified, to be selected because that is what he or she deserves, or for some other reason? If persons do truly deserve to be selected by virtue of the possession of the characteristics that make them the most qualified, then to fail to select them is to treat them unjustly. But I am skeptical that a connection of the right sort can be established between being the most qualified in this sense and deserving to be selected. The confusion that so often arises in thinking about this issue comes about, I think, because of a failure to distinguish two very different ways in which the linkage between qualifications and desert might be thought to be a sound one.

The first way is this. If there is a system of selection in place with rules and criteria that specify how to determine who is the most qualified and therefore is to be selected, then there is, of course, a sense in which the most qualified, as defined by those criteria, do deserve to be selected by virtue of their relationship to those rules and criteria. But this sense of desert is a surface one, and any resulting desert claim is very weak because it derives its force and significance wholly from the existing criteria and rules for selection. In this same sense, once preferential treatment programs are established and in place, as many now are, these new programs can also be understood to establish alternative grounds and criteria for selection; as such, they stand on the same footing as more conventional systems of qualification and selection. In the identical manner, therefore, these new programs also give rise to surface claims of desert, founded now upon the respect in which those who best satisfy those criteria have a claim that they deserve to be selected because that is what the rules of these programs provide should happen.

What this suggests, I believe, is that the real and difficult question about the possible linkage between qualifications and desert has to be sought elsewhere, for that question has to do with whether those who possess certain characteristics deserve, in virtue of their possession of those characteristics, to have a selection procedure in place which makes selections turn on the possession of those characteristics. If they do, then those who possess those characteristics do deserve in a deep, nonsurface way to be selected because of their qualifications. But now the problem is that being the best at something, or being the most able in respect to some task or role, does not, by itself at least, seem readily convertible into a claim about what such persons thereby genuinely deserve in virtue of things such as these being true of them. Perhaps a theory of desert of the right sort can be developed and adequately defended to show how and why those who are most able deserve (in a deep sense) selection criteria that will make them deserving of selection (in a surface sense); however, given the difficulty of connecting in any uniform way the mere possession of abilities with things that the possessor can claim any credit or responsibility for, and given the alternative plausibility of claims of desert founded upon attributes such as effort or need, the intellectual task at hand is a formidable one, and one that opponents of preferential treatment programs have not yet, I think, succeeded in coming to terms with in a convincing fashion.

Nonetheless, as was suggested earlier, there may be good reasons of other sorts for being interested in persons' qualifications—reasons which have to do, for example, with how well a predefined job or role will be performed and with the relative importance of having it done as well as possible. These reasons point directly to the good that will be promoted by selecting the most able. Still, a concern for having some predetermined job or role performed *only* by the person who will be *the best* at performing it is something that itself must be defended, given the good that is otherwise done by programs of preferential treatment (construed, as they must be within this objection, as programs which make race a relevant, but non-qualification-related criterion for selection). And the plausibility of that exclusive concern with performance will vary greatly with the position and its context. Sometimes this concern will be of decisive, or virtually decisive, importance; when it legitimately is, preferential treatment of the sort I have been defending should play a very minor or even nonexistent role in the selections to be made. But in many contexts, and most of them are the ones in which preferential treatment programs operate, no such exclusive concern seems defensible. In the case of admission to college or professional school, of selection to a faculty, or of selection for training or employment, the good that is secured in selecting the most

qualified person, in this restricted sense, is at most only one of the goods to be realized and balanced against those other, quite substantial ones whose realization depends upon the implementation of such programs. In sum, therefore, preferential treatment programs are presumptively justifiable insofar as they work to dismantle the system of racial oppression that is still in place, although it should not be; and their justifiability is rendered more secure once it can be seen, as I think it should be, that they are not unjust either in themselves or as constitutive elements of any larger system of racial oppression.

Review and Discussion Questions

1. Is Wasserstrom correct to describe our social system as one of racial oppression? What would count as evidence for or against this claim?

2. To what extent can Wasserstrom's positive argument for preferential treatment be applied to other minorities? To women?

3. Does Wasserstrom dismiss too quickly the possibility that the programs he defends will exacerbate racial hostility or reduce rather than enhance blacks' sense of self-respect? How great a danger are these possibilities? To what extent do they undermine the good results of affirmative action? How would you evaluate programs of preferential treatment from a utilitarian point of view?

4. Are defenders of affirmative action guilty of inconsistency in opposing earlier discrimination on the basis of race while advocating programs of preferential treatment now? Do you agree with Wasserstrom that there are some basic and relevant differences between the historic discrimination that blacks have suffered and preferential treatment on the grounds of race today?

5. Some argue that, if we give preferential treatment at all, we should focus on disadvantaged socioeconomic status rather than race. Is Wasserstrom right to reject this position? How would Wasserstrom respond to the argument that African Americans from well-off families should not be given preferential treatment?

6. Does it make sense to say that race can be a relevant job qualification? Explain why or why not. Many people believe that the best-qualified person *deserves* the job. Wasserstrom challenges the linkage between qualifications and desert. Do you find his reasoning persuasive?

The Case Against Affirmative Action

LOUIS P. POJMAN

After distinguishing between modest and strong affirmative action, Louis P. Pojman, professor of philosophy at the U.S. Military Academy at West Point, argues that strong affirmative action is not morally justified. He first challenges five arguments often advanced in defense of strong affirmative action, namely, that it: (1) supplies a need for role models; (2) compensates blacks for injuries they have suffered; (3) only removes an advantage that white males unjustly enjoy; (4) is necessary for diversity; and (5) is not unjust because the better qualified person, who is passed over, does not have a right to the job or position in question. Professor Pojman then presses two arguments *against* affirmative action: it requires discrimination against white males and violates the principle of merit.

Study Questions

1. What is the difference between modest affirmative action and strong affirmative action? What does Pojman mean when he contends that strong affirmative action implies that "two wrongs make a right"?
2. What is Pojman's response to the role-models argument?
3. Why does Pojman reject the compensation argument?
4. What is the point of the "no one deserves his talents" argument?
5. What is the relevance of the chart on page 388 to Pojman's argument?
6. What are the two pillars that support the case for meritocracy?

HARDLY A WEEK GOES BY but that the subject of affirmative action does not come up. Whether in the form of preferential hiring, non-traditional casting, quotas, "goals and time-tables," minority scholarships, race-norming, reverse discrimination, or employment of members of underutilized groups, this issue confronts us as a terribly perplexing problem . . . .

Let us agree that despite the evidences of a booming economy, the poor are suffering grievously, with children being born into desperate material and psychological poverty, for whom the ideal of "equal opportunity for all" is a cruel joke. Many feel that the federal government has abandoned its guarantee to provide the minimum necessities for each American, so that the pace of this tragedy seems to be worsening daily. Add to this the fact that in our country African Americans have a legacy of slavery and unjust discrimination to contend with, and we have the makings of an inferno, and, perhaps, in the worst-case scenario, the downfall of a nation. What is the answer to our national problem? Is it increased welfare? More job training? More support for education? Required licensing of parents to have children? Negative income tax?

More support for families or for mothers with small children? All of these have merit and should be part of the national debate. But, my thesis is, however tragic the situation may be (and we may disagree on just how tragic it is), one policy is *not* a legitimate part of the solution and that is *reverse, unjust discrimination* against young white males. Strong affirmative action, which implicitly advocates reverse discrimination, while, no doubt, well intentioned, is morally heinous, asserting, by implication, that *two wrongs make a right*.

The *two wrongs make a right* thesis goes like this: Because *some* whites once enslaved some blacks, the descendants of those slaves, some of whom may now enjoy high incomes and social status, have a right to opportunities and offices over better qualified whites who had nothing to do with either slavery or the oppression of blacks, and who may even have suffered hardship comparable to that of poor blacks. In addition, strong affirmative action creates a new hierarchy of the oppressed: Blacks get primary preferential treatment, women second, Native Americans third, Hispanics fourth, handicapped fifth, and Asians sixth and so on until white males, no matter how needy or well qualified, must accept the leftovers. Naturally, combinations of oppressed classes (e.g., a one-eyed, black Hispanic female) trump all single classifications. The equal protection clause of the Fourteenth Amendment becomes reinterpreted as "Equal protection for all equals, but some equals are more equal than others."

When I speak about civil rights or affirmative action, people usually ask for my credentials. What have I done to end racism and sexism? Briefly, I began working for racial integration in my teens, quixotically fighting windmills in trying to integrate my all-white town of Cicero, Illinois in the 1950s. I went into Chicago's black ghetto every Sunday and Monday after school to work with poor children, tutoring them and organizing activities. I was a civil rights activist. When I entered the ministry in the early 1960s I

was selected by a predominantly black congregation in the Bedford-Stuyvesant neighborhood of Brooklyn as its minister. There my wife and I served for about four years until I went back to graduate school. Our children were born in this community: Paul and Ruth Freedom, named in hopes that we could create a world where all children, regardless of race or class, could grow up with equal opportunity for a fulfilled life. I engaged in nonviolent civil rights demonstrations, led workshops on racial integration, was a member of the Congress of Racial Equality, and was even arrested for my activities. I was also a Black Studies student in graduate school, writing my master's thesis on "A Philosophy of Negro Culture." My goals have not changed over the years, but I have been chastened by the harsh realities of life. I still strive to promote equal opportunity and to eliminate unjust discrimination. The irony is that I have gone from being a radical liberal to being a conservative without changing a single basic idea! For equal opportunity, once the hallmark of liberalism, is now sneered at by many modern liberals as a conservative fantasy. Such are the ironies of history.

Before analyzing arguments concerning affirmative action, I must define my terms.

By *modest affirmative action* I mean policies that will increase the opportunities of disadvantaged people to attain social goods and offices. It includes the dismantling of segregated institutions, widespread advertisement to groups not previously represented in certain privileged positions, special scholarships for the disadvantaged classes (e.g., the poor, regardless of race or gender), and even using diversity or underrepresentation of groups or history of past discrimination as a tiebreaker when candidates for these goods and offices are relatively equal. The goal of *modest affirmative action* is equal opportunity to compete, not equal results. There is no more moral requirement to guarantee that 12 percent of professors are black than to guarantee that 85 percent of the players in the National Basketball Association are white.

By *strong affirmative action* I mean preferential treatment on the basis of race, ethnicity, or gender (or some other morally irrelevant criterion), discriminating in favor of underrepresented groups against overrepresented groups, aiming at roughly equal results. *Strong affirmative action* is reverse discrimination. It says it is right to do wrong to correct a wrong. It is the policy that is currently being promoted under the name of *affirmative action,* so I will use that term or "AA" for short throughout this essay to stand for this version of affirmative action. I will not argue for or against the principle of *modest affirmative action.* Indeed, I think it has some moral weight. *Strong affirmative action* has none, or so I will argue.

In what follows I will mainly concentrate on affirmative action policies with regard to race, but the arguments can be extended to cover ethnicity and gender. I think that if a case for affirmative action can be made it will be as a corrective to racial oppression. I will examine [seven] arguments regarding affirmative action. The first [five] will be *negative,* attempting to show that the best arguments for affirmative action fail. The last [two] will be *positive* arguments for policies opposing affirmative action.

I. A Critique of Arguments for Affirmative Action

1. The need for role models

This argument is straightforward. We all need role models, and it helps to know that others like us can be successful. We learn and are encouraged to strive for excellence by emulating our heroes and "our kind of people" who have succeeded.

In the first place it's not clear that role models of one's own racial or sexual type are necessary (let alone sufficient) for success. One of my heroes was Gandhi, an Indian Hindu; another was my grade school science teacher, Miss DeVoe; and another Martin Luther King, behind whom I marched in civil rights demonstrations. More important than having role models of one's "own type" is having genuinely good people, of whatever race or gender, to emulate. Our common humanity should be a sufficient basis for us to see the possibility of success in people of virtue and merit. To yield to the demand, however tempting it may be to do so, for "role-models-just-like-us" is to treat people like means, not ends. It is to elevate morally irrelevant particularity over relevant traits, such as ability and integrity. We don't need people exactly like us to find inspiration. As Steve Allen once quipped, "If I had to follow a role model exactly, I would have become a nun."

Furthermore, even if it helps people with low self-esteem to gain encouragement from seeing others of their particular kind in successful positions, it is doubtful whether this need is a sufficient reason to justify preferential hiring or reverse discrimination. What good is a role model who is inferior to other professors or physicians or business personnel? The best way to create role models is not to promote people because of race or gender but because they are the best qualified for the job. It is the violation of this fact that is largely responsible for the widespread whisper in the medical field (at least in New York), "Never go to a black physician under 40" (referring to the fact that AA has affected the medical system during the past twenty years). Fight the feeling how I will, I cannot help wondering on seeing a black or a woman in a position of honor, "Is she in this position because she merits it or because of affirmative action?" Where affirmative action is the policy, the "figment of pigment" creates a stigma of undeservedness, whether or not it is deserved.

2. The compensation argument

The argument goes like this: Blacks have been wronged and severely harmed by whites. Therefore white society should compensate blacks for the injury caused them. Reverse discrimination in terms of preferential hiring, contracts, and scholarships is a fitting way to compensate for the past wrongs.

This argument actually involves a distorted notion of compensation. Normally, we think of compensation as owed by a specific person A to another person B whom A has wronged in a specific way C. For example, if I have stolen your car and used it for a period of time to make business profits that would have gone to you, it is not enough that I return your car. I must pay you an amount reflecting your loss and my ability to pay. If I have made only $5,000 and have only $10,000 in assets, it would not be possible for you to collect $20,000 in damages—even though that is the amount of loss you have incurred.

Sometimes compensation is extended to groups of people who have been unjustly harmed by the greater society. For example, the U.S. government has compensated the Japanese Americans who were imprisoned during the Second World War, and the West German government has paid reparations to the survivors of Nazi concentration camps. But here a specific people have been identified who were wronged in an identifiable way by the government of the nation in question.

On the face of it, demands by blacks for compensation do not fit the usual pattern. Perhaps Southern states with Jim Crow laws could be accused of unjustly harming blacks, but it is hard to see that the U.S. government was involved in doing so. Much of the harm done to blacks was the result of private discrimination, not state action. So the Germany/U.S. analogy doesn't hold. Furthermore, it is not clear that all blacks were harmed in the same way or whether some were *unjustly* harmed or harmed more than poor whites and others (e.g., short people). Finally, even if identifiable blacks were harmed by identifiable social practices, it is not clear that most forms of affirmative action are appropriate to restore the situation. The usual practice of a financial payment seems more appropriate than giving a high-level job to someone unqualified or only minimally qualified, who, speculatively, might have been better qualified had he not been subject to racial discrimination. If John is the star tailback of our college team with a promising professional future, and I accidentally (but culpably) drive my pickup truck over his legs, and so cripple him, John may be due compensation, but he is not due the tailback spot on the football team.

Still, there may be something intuitively compelling about compensating members of an oppressed group who are minimally qualified. Suppose that the Hatfields and the McCoys are enemy clans and some youths from the Hatfields go over and steal diamonds and gold from the McCoys, distributing it within the Hatfield economy. Even though we do not know which Hatfield youths did the stealing, we would want to restore the wealth, as far as possible, to the McCoys. One way might be to tax the Hatfields, but another might be to give preferential treatment in terms of scholarships and training programs and hiring to the McCoys.

This is perhaps the strongest argument for affirmative action, and it may well justify some weaker versions of AA, but it is doubtful whether it is sufficient to justify strong versions with quotas and goals and timetables in skilled positions. There are at least two reasons for this. First, we have no way of knowing how many people of any given group would have achieved some given level of competence had the world been different. . . . Secondly, the normal criterion of competence is a strong prima facie consideration when the most important positions are at stake. There are two reasons for this: (1) Society has given people expectations that if they attain certain levels of excellence they will be awarded appropriately, and (2) filling the most important positions with the best qualified is the best way to insure efficiency in job-related areas and in society in general. These reasons are not absolutes. They can be overridden. But there is a strong presumption in their favor so that a burden of proof rests with those who would override them.

At this point we get into the problem of whether innocent nonblacks should have to pay a penalty in terms of preferential hiring of blacks. We turn to that argument.

3. The argument for compensation from those who innocently benefited from past injustice

Young white males, as innocent beneficiaries of unjust discrimination of blacks and women, have no grounds for complaint when society seeks to level the tilted field. They may be innocent of oppressing blacks, other minorities, and women, but they have unjustly benefited from that oppression or discrimination. So it is perfectly proper that less-qualified women and blacks be hired before them.

The operative principle is: He who knowingly and willingly benefits from a wrong must help pay for the wrong. Judith Jarvis Thomson puts it this way: "Many [white males] have been direct beneficiaries of policies which have downgraded blacks and women . . . and even those who did not directly benefit . . . had, at any rate, the advantage in the competition which comes of the confidence in one's full membership [in the community], and of one's right being recognized as a matter of course."[1] That is, white males obtain advantages in self-respect and self-confidence deriving from a racist/sexist system that denies the same to blacks and women.

Here is my response to this argument: As I noted in the previous section, compensation is normally individual and specific. If A harms B regarding x, B has a right to compensation from A in regard to x. If A steals B's car and wrecks it, A has an obligation to compensate B for the stolen car, but A's son has no obligation to compensate B. Furthermore, if A dies or disappears, B has no moral right to claim that society compensate him for the stolen car—though if he has insurance, he can make such a claim to the insurance company. Sometimes a wrong cannot

be compensated, and we just have to make the best of an imperfect world.

Suppose my parents, divining that I would grow up to have an unsurpassable desire to be a basketball player, bought an expensive growth hormone for me. Unfortunately, a neighbor stole it and gave it to little Michael, who gained the extra 18 inches—my 18 inches—and shot up to an enviable 6 feet 10 inches. Michael, better known as Michael Jordan, would have been a runt like me but for his luck. As it is he profited from the injustice and excelled in basketball, as I would have done had I had my proper dose.

Do I have a right to the millions of dollars that Jordan made as a professional basketball player—the unjustly innocent beneficiary of my growth hormone? I have a right to something from the neighbor who stole the hormone, and it might be kind of Jordan to give me free tickets to the Bulls' basketball games, and perhaps I should be remembered in his will. As far as I can see, however, he does not *owe* me anything, either legally or morally.

Suppose further that Michael Jordan and I are in high school together and we are both qualified to play basketball, only he is far better than I. Do I deserve to start in his position because I would have been as good as he is had someone not cheated me as a child? Again, I think not. But if being the lucky beneficiary of wrongdoing does not entail that Jordan (or the coach) owes me anything in regard to basketball, why should it be a reason to engage in preferential hiring in academic positions or highly coveted jobs? If minimal qualifications are not adequate to override excellence in basketball, even when the minimality is a consequence of wrongdoing, why should they be adequate in other areas?

4. The diversity argument

It is important that we learn to live in a pluralistic world, learning to get along with those of other races and cultures, so we should have fully integrated schools and employment situations. Diversity is an important symbol and educative device. Thus preferential treatment is warranted to perform this role in society.

But, again, while we can admit the value of diversity, it hardly seems adequate to override considerations of merit and efficiency. *Diversity for diversity's sake is moral promiscuity,* since it obfuscates rational distinctions, undermines treating individuals as ends, treating them, instead as mere means (to the goals of social engineering), and, furthermore, unless those hired are highly qualified, the diversity factor threatens to become a fetish. At least at the higher levels of business and the professions, *competence* far outweighs considerations of diversity. I do not care whether the group of surgeons operating on me reflect racial or gender balance, but I do care that they are highly qualified. Neither do most football or basketball fans care whether their team reflects ethnic and gender diversity, but whether their team has the best combination of players available. And likewise with airplane pilots, military leaders, business executives, and, may I say it, teachers and university professors. Moreover, there are other ways of learning about other cultures besides engaging in reverse discrimination.

5. The "no one deserves his talents" argument against meritocracy

According to this argument, the competent do not deserve their intelligence, their superior character, their industriousness, or their discipline; therefore they have no right to the best positions in society. Hence it is not unjust to give these positions to less (but still minimally) qualified blacks and women. In one form this argument holds that since no one deserves anything, society may use any criteria it pleases to distribute goods. The criterion most often designated is social utility. Versions of this argument are found in the writings of John Arthur, John Rawls, Bernard Boxill, Michael Kinsley, Ronald Dworkin, and Richard Wasserstrom.

Rawls writes, "No one deserves his place in the distribution of native endowments, any more than one deserves one's initial starting place in society. The assertion that a man deserves the superior character that enables him to make the effort to cultivate his abilities is equally problematic; for his character depends in large part upon fortunate family and social circumstances for which he can claim no credit. The notion of desert seems not to apply to these cases."[2] Michael Kinsley is even more adamant:

> Opponents of affirmative action are hung up on a distinction that seems more profoundly irrelevant: treating individuals versus treating groups. What is the moral difference between dispensing favors to people on their "merits" as individuals and passing out society's benefits on the basis of group identification?
>
> Group identifications like race and sex are, of course, immutable. They have nothing to do with a person's moral worth. But the same is true of most of what comes under the label "merit." The tools you need for getting ahead in a meritocratic society—not all of them but most: talent, education, instilled cultural values such as ambition—are distributed just as arbitrarily as skin color. They are fate. The notion that people somehow "deserve" the advantages of these characteristics in a way they don't "deserve" the advantage of their race is powerful, but illogical.[3]

It will help to enumerate the argument's steps:

1. Society may award jobs and positions as it sees fit as long as individuals have no claim to these positions.
2. To have a claim to something means that one has earned it or deserves it.
3. But no one has earned or deserves his intelligence, talent, education, or cultural values, which produce superior qualifications.
4. If a person does not deserve what produces something, he does not deserve its products.
5. Therefore, better qualified people do not deserve their qualifications.

6. Therefore, society may override their qualifications in awarding jobs and positions as it sees fit (for social utility or to compensate for previous wrongs).

So it is permissible if a minimally qualified black or woman is admitted to law or medical school ahead of a white male with excellent credentials, or if a less qualified person from an "under-utilized" group gets a professorship ahead of an eminently better-qualified white male. Sufficiency and underutilization together outweigh excellence.

My response: Premise 4 is false. To see this, reflect that just because I do not deserve the money that I have been given as a gift (for instance) does not mean that I am not entitled to what I get with that money. If you and I both get a gift of $100 and I bury mine in the sand for five years while you invest yours wisely and double its value at the end of five years, I cannot complain that you should split the increase 50/50 since neither of us deserved the original gift. If we accept the notion of responsibility at all, we must hold that persons deserve the fruits of their labor and conscious choices. Of course, we might want to distinguish moral from legal desert and argue that, morally speaking, effort is more important than outcome, whereas, legally speaking, outcome may be more important. Nevertheless, there are good reasons in terms of efficiency, motivation, and rough justice for holding a strong prima facie principle of giving scarce high positions to those most competent.

The attack on moral desert is perhaps the most radical move that egalitarians like Rawls and company have made against meritocracy, and the ramifications of their attack are far reaching. Here are some implications: Since I do not deserve my two good eyes or two good kidneys, the social engineers may take one of each from me to give to those needing an eye or a kidney—even if they have damaged their organs by their own voluntary actions. Since no one deserves anything, we do not deserve pay for our labors or praise for a job well done or first prize in the race we win. The notion of moral responsibility vanishes in a system of leveling.

But there is no good reason to accept the argument against desert. We do act freely and, as such, we are responsible for our actions. We deserve the fruits of our labor, reward for our noble feats and punishment for our misbehavior.

We have considered [five] arguments for affirmative action and have found no compelling case for Strong AA and only one plausible argument (a version of the compensation argument) for Modest AA. We must now turn to the arguments against affirmative action to see whether they fare any better.

II. Arguments Against Affirmative Action

6. Affirmative action requires discrimination against a different group

Modest AA weakly discriminates against new minorities, mostly innocent young white males, and Strong AA strongly discriminates against these new minorities. As I argued in section I.3, this discrimination is unwarranted, since, even if some compensation to blacks were indicated, it would be unfair to make innocent white males bear the whole brunt of the payments. Recently I had the following experience. I knew a brilliant philosopher, with outstanding publications in first-level journals, who was having difficulty getting a tenure-track position. For the first time in my life I offered to make a phone call on his behalf to a university to which he had applied. When I got the Chair of the Search Committee, he offered that the committee was under instructions from the administration to hire a woman or a black. They had one of each on their short list, so they weren't even considering the applications of white males. At my urging he retrieved my friend's file and said, "This fellow looks far superior to the two candidates we're interviewing, but there's nothing I can do about it." Cases like this come to my attention regularly. In fact, it is poor white youth who have become the new pariahs on the job market. The children of the wealthy have no trouble getting into the best private grammar schools and, on the basis of superior early education, into the best universities, graduate schools, managerial and professional positions. Affirmative action simply shifts injustice, setting blacks, Hispanics, Native Americans, Asians, and women against young white males, especially ethnic and poor white males. It makes no more sense to discriminate in favor of a rich black or a female who had the opportunity of the best family and education available against a poor white, than it does to discriminate in favor of white males against blacks or women. It does little to rectify the goal of providing equal opportunity to all.

At the end of his essay supporting affirmative action, Albert Mosley points out that other groups besides blacks have been benefited by affirmative action: "women, the disabled, the elderly."[4] He's correct in including the elderly, for through powerful lobbies such as the AARP, they do get special benefits including medicare and may sue on the grounds of being discriminated against due to *Ageism,* prejudice against older people. Might this not be a reason to reconsider affirmative action? Consider the sheer rough percentages of those who qualify for affirmative action programs.

Group	Percentage
1. Women	52%
2. Blacks	12%
3. Hispanics	8%
4. Native Americans	2%
5. Asians	4%
6. Physically disabled	10%
7. Welfare recipients	6%
8. The elderly	30%
9. Italians (in New York City)	3%
Totals	127%

Recently, it has been proposed that homosexuals be included in oppressed groups deserving affirmative action.[5] At Northeastern University in 1996 the faculty governing body voted to grant homosexuals affirmative action status at this university. How many more percentage points would this add? Several authors have advocated putting all poor people on the list.[6] And if we took handicaps seriously would we not add ugly people, obese people, and, especially, short people, for which there is ample evidence of discrimination? How about left-handed people—they can't play shortstop or third base and have to put up with a right-handedly biased world. The only group not on the list is white males. Are they, especially healthy, middle-class, young white males, becoming the new "oppressed class"? Should we add them to our list?

If our goal is the creation of a society where everyone has a fair chance, then it would be better to concentrate on support for families and early education and decide the matter of university admissions and job hiring on the basis of traditional standards of competence....

7. An argument from the principle of merit

Traditionally, we have believed that the highest positions in society should be awarded to those who are best qualified. The Koran states that "A ruler who appoints any man to an office, when there is in his dominion another man better qualified for it, sins against God and against the State." Rewarding excellence both seems just to the individuals in the competition and makes for efficiency. Note that one of the most successful acts of racial integration, the Brooklyn Dodgers' recruitment of Jackie Robinson in the late 1940s, was done in just this way, according to merit. If Robinson had been brought into the major leagues as a mediocre player or had batted .200 he would have been scorned and sent back to the minors where he belonged.

As I mentioned earlier, merit is not an absolute value, but there are strong prima facie reasons for awarding positions on its basis, and it should enjoy a weighty presumption in our social practices.

. . . We generally want high achievers to have the best positions, the best-qualified candidate to win the political office, the most brilliant and competent scientist to be chosen for the most challenging research project, the best qualified pilots to become commercial pilots, only the best soldiers to become generals. Only when little is at stake do we weaken the standards and content ourselves with sufficiency (rather than excellence)—there are plenty of jobs where "sufficiency" rather than excellence is required. Perhaps we have even come to feel that medicine or law or university professorships are so routine that they can be performed by minimally qualified people, in which case AA has a place.

Note! No one is calling for quotas or proportional representation of *underutilized* groups in the National Basketball Association where blacks make up 80 percent of the players. But, surely, if merit and merit alone reigns in sports, should it not be valued at least as much in education and industry?

The case for meritocracy has two pillars. One pillar is a deontological argument that holds that we ought to treat people as ends and not merely means. By giving people what they deserve as *individuals,* rather than as members of *groups,* we show respect for their inherent worth. If you and I take a test, and you get 95 percent of the answers correct and I get only 50 percent correct, it would be unfair to you to give both of us the same grade, say an A, and even more unfair to give me a higher grade, say A+ over your B+. Although I have heard cases where teachers have been instructed to "race-norm" in grading (giving blacks and Hispanics higher grades for the same numerical scores), most proponents of affirmative action stop short of advocating such a practice. But, I would ask them, what's really the difference between taking the overall average of a white and a black and "race-norming" it? If teachers shouldn't do it, why should administrators?

The second pillar for meritocracy is utilitarian. In the end, we will be better off by honoring excellence. We want the best leaders, teachers, policemen, physicians, generals, lawyers, and airplane pilots that we can possibly produce in society. So our program should be to promote equal opportunity, as much as is feasible in a free market economy, and reward people according to their individual merit.

Conclusion

Let me sum up my discussion. The goal of the civil rights movement and of moral people everywhere has been justice for all, including equal opportunity. The question is: How best to get there. Civil rights legislation removed the legal barriers, opening the way toward equal opportunity, but it did not tackle the deeper causes that produce differential results. Modest affirmative action aims at encouraging minorities in striving for the highest positions without unduly jeopardizing the rights of majorities. The problem of Modest AA is that it easily slides into Strong AA where quotas, "goals and timetables," "equal results,"—in a word—reverse discrimination prevails and is forced onto groups, thus promoting mediocrity, inefficiency, and resentment. Furthermore, affirmative action aims at the higher levels of society—universities and skilled jobs—but if we want to improve our society, the best way to do it is to concentrate on families, children, early education, and the like, so all are prepared to avail themselves of opportunity. Affirmative action, on the one hand, is too much, too soon and on the other hand, too little, too late.

NOTES

1. Judith Jarvis Thomson, "Preferential Hiring" in Marshall Cohen, Thomas Nagel and Thomas Scanlon, eds., *Equality and Preferential Treatment* (Princeton: Princeton University Press, 1977).
2. John Rawls, *A Theory of Justice* (Harvard University Press, 1971), p. 104; see Bernard Boxill, "The Morality of Preferential Hiring," *Philosophy and Public Affairs,* vol. 7:3 (1983).
3. Michael Kinsley, "Equal Lack of Opportunity," *Harper's* (June 1983).

4. Albert Mosley, "Affirmative Action: Pro" in Albert Mosley and Nicholas Capaldi, *Affirmative Action: Social Justice or Unfair Preference?* (Lanham, Md.: Rowman & Littlefield, 1997), p. 53.

5. J. Sartorelli, "The Nature of Affirmative Action, Anti-Gay Oppression, and the Alleviation of En-

during Harm," *Journal of Applied Philosophy,* vol. 11, no. 2 (1997).

6. For example, Iddo Landau, "Are You Entitled to Affirmative Action?" *Journal of Applied Philosophy,* vol. 11, no. 2 (1997) and Richard Kahlenberg "Class Not Race," *The New Republic* (April 3, 1995).

Review and Discussion Questions

1. Explain each of the five arguments for affirmative action that Pojman criticizes. How effective are his criticisms? Are there plausible rejoinders to any of his criticisms?

2. Are there arguments for affirmative action that Pojman has overlooked or failed to do justice to?

3. Pojman gives two arguments against affirmative action. How might a defender of affirmative action respond to each of them?

4. Pojman seems to assume that we live in a basically meritocratic society in which—if it were not for affirmative action—people would be rewarded strictly according to their merit and ability. Is this assumption sound?

5. Pojman believes in equal opportunity, but can there be meaningful equality of opportunity for African Americans without affirmative action? If Wasserstrom is right that our society is racially oppressive, what are the implications of this fact for Pojman's arguments?

6. Is it possible to eliminate the socioeconomic disparities between blacks and whites without some form of affirmative action? If so, how?

7. Wasserstrom concedes that affirmative action might exacerbate racial hostility, but he appears confident that the social benefits outweigh the costs. Pojman believes that affirmative action does more harm than good. Who is right about this issue? Is it a purely factual dispute? How could it be resolved?

A Case for Race-Consciousness

T. ALEXANDER ALEINIKOFF

Color blindness with regard to race is widely affirmed as a fundamental moral and social ideal. In the past, the principle of color blindness underlay legal strategies to eliminate racial segregation and discrimination. Today, many critics of affirmative action reject it because it violates the principle of color blindness. In this essay, Professor T. Alexander Aleinikoff of the University of Michigan School of Law criticizes the principle of color blindness and defends the legitimacy of racially conscious programs. He argues that color blindness actually supports racial domination and that programs premised on it can do little to influence social consciousness and end racism.

Study Questions

1. Besides affirmative action, what sort of racially conscious programs does Aleinikoff have in mind?
2. What point does Aleinikoff make using the example of IQ tests?
3. What's the difference between "strong colorblindness" and "weak colorblindness"?
4. What does Clifford Geertz mean by "local knowledge"?
5. Why is the viewpoint of subordinated groups likely to differ from that of the dominant majority?
6. How does Aleinikoff respond to the criticism that affirmative action reinforces racism?

I WANT, IN THIS ARTICLE, to consider and critique "colorblindness.". . .

Specifically, I will argue that we are not currently a colorblind society, and that race has a deep social significance that continues to disadvantage blacks and other Americans of color. While the legal strategy of colorblindness achieved great victories in the past, it has now become an impediment in the struggle to end racial inequality. At the base of racial injustice is a set of assumptions—a way of understanding the world—that so characterizes blacks as to make persistent inequality seem largely untroubling. A remedial regime predicated on colorblindness will have little influence at this deep level of social and legal consciousness because it cannot adequately challenge white attitudes or recognize a role for black self-definition. In the pages ahead I will explain and justify this somewhat paradoxical claim that a norm of colorblindness supports racial domination. I will conclude that in order to make progress in ending racial oppression and racism, our political and moral discourse must move from colorblindness to color-consciousness, from antidiscrimination to racial justice.

I. Colorblindness and Race-Consciousness: Clarifying the Categories

. . . In the colorblind world, race is an arbitrary factor—one upon which it is doubly unfair to allocate benefits and impose burdens: one's race is neither voluntarily assumed nor capable of change. For nearly all purposes, it is maintained, the race of a person tells us nothing about an individual's capabilities and certainly nothing about her moral worth. Race-consciousness, from this perspective, is disfavored because it assigns a value to what should be a meaningless variable. To categorize on the basis of race is to miss the individual.

Adhering to a strategy of colorblindness does not make race a prohibited classification. Violations of the colorblind principle cannot be recognized and remedied without "noticing" the race of the harmed individual or racial group. But, to be true to the model, race-conscious measures must be limited to identified instances of past discrimination.

The debate over colorblindness and race-consciousness has usually appeared in the cases and literature discussing programs that give preferences in employment or other opportunities to nonwhites. In now familiar terms, advocates of colorblindness characterize affirmative action programs as unjustifiably altering meritocratic standards and requiring a distribution of social goods that reflects the proportionate representation of minority groups in the population as a whole.

The presuppositions of supporters of affirmative action may be closer to those of their opponents than is usually recognized. Many advocate "goals" of rough proportional representation upon the claim that since race is, or ought to be, an irrelevant factor in the distribution of the good in question, deviation from proportionate shares is the result either of present discrimination or the continuing effects of past discrimination. That is, the justification for affirmative action programs is usually stated in terms of remedying past and present violations of the colorblind principle. What separates most of the participants in the debate is not so much the goal of colorblindness, but rather differing views about the cause of current inequality and of the efficacy of race-blind or race-conscious remedies in reaching a colorblind future.[1]

In this article, I will use the term "race-consciousness" to apply to more than just "affirmative action" programs intended to help bring about a colorblind world or remedy past discrimination. There are many other situations in which race *qua* race might be seen as relevant to the pursuit of a legitimate and important governmental goal. These include: ensuring the presence of persons of color on juries; taking race into account in allocating radio and television licenses; seeking nonwhites to fill positions in social service agencies that deal largely with minority populations; requiring voting rules and districts that improve the chances of electing minority representatives; fostering integration by adopting race-based school assignment plans and housing programs; taking measures to integrate police forces; adding the works of minority authors to the "literary canon" taught to

college students; and giving weight to the race of applicants for teaching positions in higher education. In each of these situations, the race-consciousness of the program may be justified in other than remedial (and colorblind) terms.

II. The Difference That Race Makes

We live in a world of racial inequality. In almost every important category, blacks as a group are worse off than whites. Compared to whites, blacks have higher rates of unemployment, lower family incomes, lower life expectancy, higher rates of infant mortality, higher rates of crime victimization, and higher rates of teenage pregnancies and single-parent households. Blacks are less likely to go to college, and those who matriculate are less likely to graduate. Blacks are underrepresented in the professions, in the academy, and in the national government.[2]

Of course there has been progress. Comparing the situation of blacks half a century ago to their situation today shows a difference that is startling, and even encouraging, although the last decade evidences a slowing progress and some backsliding. But when the comparison is made between whites and blacks today, it is impossible to ignore the deep and widening difference that race makes.[3]

To say that race makes a difference means more than simply identifying material disadvantages facing people of color in contemporary America. It also recognizes that race may have an influence on how members of society understand their worlds and each other, and how such understandings may serve to perpetuate racial inequalities in our society. The next two sections pursue these psychological and cultural claims.

A. Race and cognition

Race matters. Race is among the first things that one notices about another individual. To be born black is to know an unchangeable fact about oneself that matters every day. "[I]n my life," wrote W. E. B. Du Bois in his autobiography *Dusk of Dawn*, "the chief fact has been race—not so much scientific race, as that deep conviction of myriads of men that congenital differences among the main masses of human beings absolutely condition the individual destiny of every member of a group."[4] To be born white is to be free from confronting one's race on a daily, personal, interaction-by-interaction basis. Being white, it has been said, means not having to think about it. Understandably, white people have a hard time recognizing this difference.* Most blacks have to overcome, when meeting whites, a set of assumptions older than this nation about one's abilities, one's marriageability, one's sexual desires, and one's morality. Most whites, when they are being honest with themselves, know that these racial understandings are part of their consciousness.

Race matters with respect to the people we choose to spend time with or marry, the neighborhoods in which we choose to live, the houses of worship we join, our choice of schools for our children, the people for whom we vote, and the people we allow the state to execute. We make guesses about the race of telephone callers we do not know and about persons accused of crimes. While not every decision we make necessarily has a racial component, when race is present it almost invariably influences our judgments. We are intensely—even if subconsciously—race-conscious.

It is common to speak of racial attitudes as being based on "stereotypes"—an incorrect or unthinking generalization applied indiscriminately to individuals simply on the basis of group membership. From this perspective, stereotypes can be overcome by supplying more information about an individual or the group to which that individual belongs.

But this explanation fails to recognize race-consciousness as an entrenched structure of thought that affects how we organize and process information. Social science research suggests that stereotypes serve as powerful heuristics, supplying explanations for events even when evidence supporting nonstereotypical explanations exists, and leading us to interpret situations and actions differently when the race of the actors varies. It is often more likely that our mental schema will influence how we understand new information than it is that the new information will alter our mental schema.

A troubling example can be found in *Larry P. by Lucille P. v. Riles,*[5] a case challenging the use of IQ tests that disproportionately assigned black children to special classes for the "educable mentally retarded." In discussing the expert testimony presented on the adequacy of the tests, the court of appeals observed:

> Since the 1920's it has been generally known that black persons perform less well than white persons on the standardized intelligence tests. IQ tests had been standardized so that they yielded no bias because of sex. For example, when sample tests yielded different scores for boys and girls, the testing experts assumed such differences were unacceptable and modified the tests so that the curve in the standardization sample for boys and girls was identical. No such modification on racial grounds has ever been tried by the testing companies.[6]

The testing companies received two sets of data and chose to act on just one. Their assumptions made one set of data "surprising" and the other "expected" or "natural."

Because cognitive racial categories predispose us to select information that conforms to existing categories and to process information in such a way that it will fit into those categories, they are self-justifying and self-reinforcing. And because we adopt racial categories more through a process of cultural absorption than rational construction, we are likely to be unaware of the role that the categories play in the way we perceive the world. . . .

This deeply imbedded race-consciousness has a distressing effect on discourse between

---

*Much as men have a difficult time understanding the routine and ever-present fears that women have for their physical safety.

the races. In many ways, whites and blacks talk past each other. The stories that African-Americans tell about America—stories of racism and exclusion, brutality and mendacity—simply do not ring true to the white mind. Whites have not been trained to hear it, and to credit such accounts would be to ask whites to give up too much of what they "know" about the world. It would also argue in favor of social programs and an alteration in power relations that would fundamentally change the status quo. White versions of substantial progress on racial attitudes are also likely to ring hollow for many blacks. One might see an equality of missed communication here. But there is actually a great inequality because it is the white version that becomes the "official story" in the dominant culture.

B. The power of definition

In our society, race has not been a benign mode of classification. The designation of one's race has had a double function, both defining social categories and assigning characteristics to members of those categories. The predominant power of social and cultural definition has, from the start, been exercised by and for whites.

The theme of invisibility that permeates black literature portrays white erasure of black attempts at self-definition. Listen to Audre Lorde:

> . . . I can recall without counting
> eyes
> cancelling me out
> like an unpleasant appointment
> postage due
> stamped in yellow red purple
> any color
> except Black[7]

Blacks are "invisible" not in the sense that whites do not see them; they are "invisible" in the sense that whites see primarily what a white dominant culture has trained them to see. In a curious yet powerful way, whites create and reflect a cultural understanding of blackness that requires little contribution from blacks. The dominant and dominating story excludes or ignores black representations of blackness not out of vindictiveness or animus but because the black stories simply do not register. Robert Berkhofer's description of the process by which whites understand American Indians applies here: "preconception became conception and conception became fact."[8]. . .

Continued white ignorance of blacks and lack of contact in daily life makes white understandings of race difficult to alter.* Whites are only dimly aware of how blacks live or what it means to be black in America. Despite attempts to bring African-American history into the classroom, most whites do not understand the role of black slavery in the economic development of the United States, nor are they familiar with major trends in black political and social thought, or even the contributions of Frederick Douglass, W. E. B. Du Bois, and Malcolm X. Absence of knowledge is compounded by physical and social segregation. Blacks and whites rarely get to know each other in neighborhoods, schools, or churches; and interracial friendships remain surprisingly rare. As a result, most of what a white person in America knows about blacks is likely to have been learned from white family, friends, or the white-dominated media.

That the white-created image of African-Americans should remain largely unchallenged by black conceptions is troubling not only because the white version reflects stereotypes, myths, and half-truths, but also because of the role the white definition plays in explaining the

---

*This is not to say that simply putting white and black folks together will end discrimination. As social science studies have suggested, such contacts may actually increase prejudice unless the contact occurs under particular conditions—such as when there are superordinate goals or institutional support in the form of superordinate norms and sanctions. For a review of the "contact" literature, see Amir, "The Role of Intergroup Contact in Change of Prejudice and Ethnic Relations," in *Towards the Elimination of Racism* 245, 245–308 (P. A. Katz ed. 1976).

historical treatment and current condition of blacks. Given strong incentives to absolve whites and blame blacks for existing social and economic inequalities, the white story about blacks has never been flattering. As Kimberle Crenshaw has powerfully argued, when the white image of blacks is combined with other American stories—such as equality of opportunity—it becomes "difficult for whites to see the Black situation as illegitimate or unnecessary." It works this way:

> Believing both that Blacks are inferior and that the economy impartially rewards the superior over the inferior, whites see that most Blacks are indeed worse off than whites are, which reinforces their sense that the market is operating "fairly and impartially"; those who should logically be on the bottom are on the bottom. This strengthening of whites' belief in the system in turn reinforces their beliefs that Blacks are *indeed* inferior. After all, equal opportunity *is* the rule, and the market *is* an impartial judge; if Blacks are on the bottom, it must reflect their relative inferiority.[9]

In sum, racial inequality has many faces. Social and economic statistics paint a clear and distressing picture of the differences among racial groups. Yet other inequalities are less obvious, based on nearly inaccessible and usually unchallenged assumptions that hide power and explain away domination. The next section examines alternative legal responses to this complex web of inequalities based on race. . . .

III. From Colorblindness to Race-Consciousness

Colorblindness may seem to be a sensible strategy in a world in which race has unjustly mattered for so long. Yet the claim that colorblindness today is the most efficacious route to colorblindness tomorrow has always been controversial. Justice Blackmun's paradoxical aphorism in *Bakke* reflects the usual counterclaim:

"In order to get beyond racism, we must first take account of race. There is no other way. And in order to treat some persons equally, we must treat them differently."[10] . . .

The claim I wish to press here is different from Blackmun's familiar stance in the affirmative action debate. I will argue in this section that a legal norm of colorblindness will not end race-consciousness; rather, it will simply make the unfortunate aspects and consequences of race-consciousness less accessible and thus less alterable. Furthermore, colorblind strategies are likely to deny or fail to appreciate the contribution that race-consciousness can make in creating new cultural narratives that would support serious efforts aimed at achieving racial justice.

Before these claims can be made, however, two varieties of colorblindness should be distinguished. The first, which I will call "strong colorblindness," argues that race should truly be an irrelevant, virtually unnoticed, human characteristic. Richard Wasserstrom has described this "assimilationist ideal":

> [A] nonracist society would be one in which the race of an individual would be the functional equivalent of the eye color of individuals in our society today. In our society no basic political rights and obligations are determined on the basis of eye color. No important institutional benefits and burdens are connected with eye color. Indeed, except for the mildest sort of aesthetic preferences, a person would be thought odd who even made private, social decisions by taking eye color into account.[11]

The second type, "weak colorblindness," would not outlaw all recognition of race, but would condemn the use of race as a basis for the distribution of scarce resources or opportunities and the imposition of burdens. Under "weak colorblindness," race might function like ethnicity: an attribute that could have significance for group members, and one that society as a whole could recognize, but not one upon which legal distinctions could be based. Furthermore, individuals would be able to choose how important a role race would play in their associations and identifications, but their race would not be used by others to limit their opportunities or define their identities. Thus, college courses on "African-American literature" might well be permissible under a weak colorblindness regime, but such a regime would not tolerate allocating places in the class based on race or allowing race to be used as a factor in the choice of an instructor. In the sections that follow, I will argue that strong colorblindness is impossible and undesirable, and that weak colorblindness—although perhaps able to be implemented as a legal strategy—is an inadequate response to current manifestations of racial inequality.

A. Masking race-consciousness

It is apparently important, as a matter of widespread cultural practice, for whites to assert that they are strongly colorblind, in the sense that they do not notice or act on the basis of race. One can see this at work in such statements as: "I judge each person as an individual." Of course, it cannot be that whites do not notice the race of others. Perhaps what is being said is that the speaker does not begin her evaluation with any preconceived notions. But this too is difficult to believe, given the deep and implicit ways in which our minds are color-coded. To be truly colorblind in this way, as David Strauss has shown, requires color-consciousness: one must notice race in order to tell oneself not to trigger the usual mental processes that take race into account.

The denial of race-consciousness occasioned by the desire to be strongly colorblind is described in a recent study of a desegregated junior high school by psychologist Janet Schofield. She reports that teachers, apparently concerned that acknowledging racial awareness would be viewed as a sign of prejudice, claimed not to notice the race of their students. In pursuit of colorblindness, teachers rarely used the words

"white" or "black," and avoided racial topics and identifications in class.[12]

This act of denial is troubling not only because it distorts reality, but also because it will make less accessible the ways in which color-consciousness influences our understanding of the world and of others. Strong colorblindness will perpetuate the white image of blacks by rendering irrelevant the kind of race-based discussion and data necessary for a serious critique of white definitions. Schofield's study documents how teachers' desires to act in a colorblind fashion harmed the educational experience by ignoring or denying race when it would have been appropriate to notice it:

> [One] teacher included George Washington Carver on a list of great Americans from which students could pick individuals to learn about but specifically decided not to mention he was black for fear of raising racial issues. In the best of all worlds, there would be no need to make such mention, because children would have no preconceptions that famous people are generally white. However, in a school where one white child was surprised to learn from a member of our research team that Martin Luther King was black, not white[!], it would seem reasonable to argue that highlighting the accomplishments of black Americans and making sure that students do not assume famous figures are white is a reasonable practice.[13]

Certainly such conduct creates possibilities for serious miscommunication. There is significant evidence of cultural differences between whites and blacks. . . . When white teachers, unaware of such differences, ask questions in a way that conforms to white middle-class practice, they unwittingly disadvantage black school children.

But the problem runs deeper than the level of miscommunication. Whites believe that they can act in a colorblind fashion merely by acting as they always have. Colorblindness puts the burden on blacks to change; to receive "equal" treatment, they must be seen by whites as "white."* Hence, the "compliment" that some whites pay to blacks: "I don't think of you as black." Colorblindness is, in essence, not the absence of color, but rather monochromatism: whites can be colorblind when there is only one race—when blacks become white.

B. Local knowledge: race-consciousness as cultural critique

Strong colorblindness, I have argued, is unlikely to produce the result it promises—a world in which race does not matter. In this section, I want to make the case for race-consciousness more direct by focusing on the benefits of race-consciousness in undermining and shifting deep cultural assumptions and ultimately, perhaps, making progress in overcoming racism. In presenting these claims, I hope also to undermine the case for weak colorblindness. To be effective, strategies for attacking racism may well demand affirmative race-conscious governmental policies. Clifford Geertz, in a collection of his essays entitled *Local Knowledge,* has stated that:

> To see ourselves as others see us can be eye-opening. To see others as sharing a nature with ourselves is the merest decency. But it is from the far more difficult achievement of seeing ourselves amongst others, as a local example of the forms human life has locally taken, a case among cases, a world among worlds, that the largeness of mind, without which objectivity is self-congratulation and tolerance a sham, comes.[14]

Colorblindness operates at Geertz's level of "merest decency." It begins and ends with the observation that there is something, under the skin, common to all human beings. . . . But Geertz clearly seeks more than this; he would reorient the usual hierarchical relationship between dominant and subordinate cultures by rotating the axis through its center point, making the vertical horizontal. This shift requires two related transformations: the first is to appreciate the contingency, the nonuniversalism of one's own culture—to view it as an example of "local knowledge"; the second is to recognize and credit the "local knowledges" of other groups. Of course, these two efforts are related. By valorizing the dominated, one is likely to cast doubts on the dominant group's characterizations or definition of the dominated group, which, in turn, tells us something new about the dominant group as well.

My claim outlined in the pages that follow is that race-consciousness can aid in these cultural transformations. . . .

Rotating the axis helps us to be open to other accounts and perspectives, and in doing so it reminds us of the fictional or constructed nature of "local knowledges"—including our own. Once white Americans shed the false assumption that "they know all they need to know" about African-Americans, they will begin to learn as much about themselves as about others. . . .

"[T]he quickest way to bring the reason of the world face to face [with white racism]," Du Bois wrote, "is to listen to the complaint of those human beings today who are suffering most from white attitudes, from white habits, from the conscious and unconscious wrongs which white folk are today inflicting on their victims."[15]. . . Since dominant groups are not the direct victims of their acts toward dominated groups, they may underestimate the burdens suffered by the dominated groups. This problem is compounded if dominant and dominated groups inhabit separate geographical and social spaces, so that the extent and harms of

---

*James Baldwin commented on the "tone of warm congratulation with which so many [white] liberals address their Negro equals. It is the Negro, of course, who is presumed to have become equal—an achievement that not only proves the comforting fact that perseverance has no color but also overwhelmingly corroborates the white man's sense of his own value." J. Baldwin, *The Fire Next Time* 127 (1962).

domination remain largely hidden from the dominant groups. . . .

Finally, recognizing race validates the lives and experiences of those who have been burdened because of their race. White racism has made "blackness" a relevant category in our society. Yet colorblindness seeks to deny the continued social significance of the category, to tell blacks that they are no different from whites, even though blacks as blacks are persistently made to feel that difference. Color-consciousness allows for recognition of the distinct and difficult difference that race has made; it facilitates white awareness of the efforts of African-Americans to describe and examine that difference. This is not simply the telling of a story of oppression. Color-consciousness makes blacks subjects and not objects, undermining the durability of white definitions of "blackness." It permits recognition of the strength and adaptive power of a black community able to survive slavery and oppression; and it acknowledges the contributions of black culture—not simply as windows on "the race question" but as distinct (if varied) voices and traditions, worthy of study in their own right. . . .

C. Weak colorblindness and its costs

It is common for advocates of affirmative action to point out that a legal strategy dedicated to "equality of opportunity" is likely to replicate deeply imbedded inequalities. The familiar metaphor is of a race between two runners, one of whom starts many yards back from the starting line, or is encumbered by ankle weights. Color-conscious policies are said to remove the advantage that has for several centuries been granted to whites. The simplicity of this argument should not disguise its soundness or moral power. Unfortunately, however, affirmative action programs based on the objective of overcoming past societal discrimination are deemed to run afoul of the Court's model of weak colorblindness.[16] To the extent race-conscious policies help ameliorate material disadvantage due to societal discrimination, the negative injunction of weak colorblindness imposes heavy costs.

Beyond this familiar terrain in the affirmative action debate, there are other advantages to race-conscious programs that also call into question the adequacy of weak colorblindness. As Justice Stevens has noted, there are a number of situations in which it seems eminently reasonable for government decision makers to take race into account. For example:

> in a city with a recent history of racial unrest, the superintendent of police might reasonably conclude that an integrated police force could develop a better relationship with the community and thereby do a more effective job of maintaining law and order than a force composed only of white officers.[17]

Similar claims could be made about integrated civil service and school administrations. That situations exist that could benefit from race-conscious policies should hardly be surprising, given the prominent role that race has played in allocating benefits and burdens throughout American history. . . . To the extent that weak colorblindness makes these forms of race-consciousness problematic, it is simply near-sighted social policy. . . .

Universities need more than African-American literature classes; they need a diversity of students in all literature classes, and not simply to show white students that students of color can perform as well as white students, but also to help all students become more self-conscious of the underlying assumptions with which they approach the world. To be sure, there are risks. Given the power of imbedded ways of thinking, new information may simply be "processed" in accordance with pre-existing views; or, white students may make the error of assuming that comments by black students express "the" black perspective. But to students and faculty open to a Geertzian moment, the intellectual rewards are enormous.

D. An objection to race-consciousness

. . . [An] objection . . . that figures prominently in the attack on affirmative action is that race-consciousness is self-defeating to the extent that it reinforces rather than undermines racism. Affirmative action, it is argued, may have this effect because it inevitably creates the impression of a lowering of standards in order to benefit minorities. Furthermore, as Shelby Steele argues, the "implication of inferiority in racial preferences" has a demoralizing effect on blacks, contributing to "an enlargement of self doubt."[18]

One response is that we ought to run this claim by those who have been the victims of racism. Despite assertions by whites that race-conscious programs "stigmatize" beneficiaries, blacks remain overwhelmingly in favor of affirmative action. Would we not expect blacks to be the first to recognize such harms and therefore to oppose affirmative action if it produced serious stigmatic injury? It might be argued, however, that individual blacks are willing to participate in affirmative action programs because of the direct benefits they receive, yet those blacks who are not beneficiaries suffer the stigmatic harm without the compensating gains. But, again, one would expect that if this were the case, then blacks as a class would oppose affirmative action since the vast majority of blacks are not beneficiaries of affirmative action. Furthermore, Randall Kennedy provides a convincing argument that affirmative action, on balance, is more likely to reduce stigma than to impose it:

> It is unrealistic to think . . . that affirmative action causes most white disparagement of the abilities of blacks. Such disparagement, buttressed for decades by the rigid exclusion of blacks from educational and employment opportunities, is precisely what engendered the explosive crisis to which affirmative action is a response. . . . In the end, the uncertain extent to which affirmative action diminishes the accomplishments of blacks must be balanced

against the stigmatization that occurs when blacks are virtually absent from important institutions in the society.[19]

Confident measures of the costs and benefits of affirmative action do not exist. Given the material gains afforded minorities by race-conscious programs and the fact that these gains are likely, as Kennedy notes, to counteract "conventional stereotypes about the place of the Negro,"[20] I would put the burden of proof on those who claim that affirmative action contributes more to racism than it diminishes racism. Significantly, the case for race-consciousness suggested here would affect the evaluation of the costs and benefits because it would count as one of the benefits—as colorblindness cannot—the gains to white society of increased association with minorities and greater awareness of nondominant cultures. . . .

IV. From Antidiscrimination to Racial Justice

Discussion about the appropriateness of race-conscious measures is but the doctrinal manifestation of a broader debate regarding the animating principle of race discrimination law. The strategy of colorblindness follows from an understanding of discrimination law that views the use of racial classifications as morally and politically objectionable. In contrast, support for broad race-conscious policies is usually imbedded in a description of race discrimination law as aimed at ending the second-class citizenship of African-Americans and other subordinated minorities. . . .

Starting fresh, it appears obvious that an anti-discrimination model that sees the use of racial classifications as the central problem to be addressed ill fits this society's current racial situation. There is no symmetry in either the use of racial classifications or the experiences of different racial groups. To see the problem of race discrimination as the problem of using racial criteria is to wrench legal theory out of social reality.* . . .

The choice among race discrimination law principles is, in the deepest sense, moral and political. Arrayed on the side of the antidiscrimination-as-colorblindness model is the knowledge of the terrible wrongs that color-consciousness has wrought in our history, the ending of legal segregation effectuated by colorblindness, an ideology of individualism that stresses evaluation and rewards based on individual effort and personal characteristics over which a person has control, and the antagonisms that race-based preferences may breed. These, of course, are not trivial arguments, which suggests why colorblindness has had such significant appeal.

But the claim that race should be ignored would be far more persuasive if the difference that race had made in the past had been overcome. What cannot be denied—even if it is often ignored—is that blacks, as a class, have never attained economic or social equality with whites. . . .

There are strong reasons for continuing the struggle to fulfill the initial goals of race discrimination law. Whether phrased as "anti-caste," "anti-group disadvantage," or "anti-subjugation," the task remains where it began: the ending of second class status of an historically oppressed group and the achieving of racial justice.

There are two interrelated aspects to this agenda for race discrimination law. The first supports programs that would produce material improvements in the lives of black people: programs promoting jobs, medical care, and decent housing. Such programs, it should be noted, need not be race-based. A "racial justice" perspective need not entail explicitly race-conscious policies. It seems clear, however, that a racial justice perspective is friendly to race-conscious policies directed at overcoming the effects of past and present societal discrimination. . . . Set-aside programs . . . are modest examples of the kind of state intervention that is needed.

The second aspect of a racial justice perspective is an attack on the set of beliefs that makes existing inequalities untroubling. What must be addressed is not just old-fashioned racism, but also the deeply ingrained mental structures that categorize and define race to the disadvantage of blacks and other nonwhite groups. As suggested above, altering the image of blacks in the white mind requires paying attention to, and crediting, black voices, and to refashioning institutions in ways that will allow those voices to be heard. Here race-conscious programs may be crucial. . . .

V. Conclusion: Toward an Inclusive American Story

In the current political and social climate, a call for color-consciousness poses real risks. For several centuries of American history, noticing race provided the basis for a caste system that institutionalized second-class status for people of color. It was precisely this oppressive use of race that colorblindness sought to overcome. Furthermore, central to white opposition to affirmative action is the belief that blacks have attained equality of opportunity, and therefore any assistance directed to minorities qua minorities affords them an undeserved benefit and an unfair advantage. . . .

[But] race-neutral strategies simply postpone our society's inevitable rendezvous with its history of racism. Constant liminal and subliminal messages of the difference that race makes take their toll—no matter what justificatory rhetoric enshrouds official governmental action—and will ultimately breed a powerful claim of enough-is-enough. Such a call can take the

* To its advocates, colorblindness remains an instrumental strategy for achieving racial justice. I do not mean to imply that supporters of colorblindness have no regard for the real-world consequences of their theoretical positions.

form of a national commitment to end racial injustice, or it can take the form of "by any means necessary" in the minds and hands of the victims of discrimination who know that color-blindness is a descriptive lie and a normative mistake.

Race-conscious programs alone will not end racism. At best, they represent a small step toward changing social relations and structures of thought and perception. What is needed is direct, self-conscious scrutiny of the way we think and of the assumptions about race that each of us holds and upon which we act. Attention to black constructions of reality can provide a counterbalance to the white construction of blacks in the white mind. . . .

Blacks as blacks have had a unique history in this country. It is a history that whites and blacks confront every day and will continue to confront into the indefinite future. In pretending to ignore race, this society denies itself the self-knowledge that is demanded for eradicating racism and achieving racial justice.

NOTES

1. See *Regents of the Univ. of Cal.* v. *Bakke*, 438 U.S. 265, 407 (1978) (Blackmun, J., dissenting). ("In order to get beyond racism, we must first take account of race. There is no other way.")

2. See *A Common Destiny: Blacks & American Society* 3–32 (G. Jaynes & R. Williams, Jr. eds. 1989). . . .

3. For data to support the assertions in the preceding two paragraphs, see id. at 122–23, 278, 280–81, 293, 295, 302–03, 399, 416–17, 465, 524, 530.

4. W. E. B. Du Bois, *Dusk of Dawn* 139 (1940).

5. 793 F. 2d 969 (9th Cir. 1984).

6. Id. at 975–76; see generally S. Gould, *The Mismeasure of Man* (1981).

7. A. Lorde, "To the Poet Who Happens to Be Black and the Black Poet Who Happens to Be a Woman," in *Our Dead Behind Us* 6–7 (1986).

8. R. Berkhofer, *The White Man's Indian* 71 (1978).

9. Crenshaw, ["Race, Reform, and Retrenchment," 101 *Harv. L. Rev.* 1331], at 1380 (footnote omitted).

10. *Regents of Univ. of Cal.* v. *Bakke*, 438 U.S. 265, 407 (1978) (Blackmun, J., dissenting).

11. R. Wasserstrom, *Philosophy and Social Issues* 24 (1980). . . .

12. Schofield, "Causes and Consequences of the Colorblind Perspective," in *Prejudice, Discrimination, and Racism* (J. Dovidio & S. Gaertner eds., 1986) at 231.

13. Id. at 249.

14. C. Geertz, *Local Knowledge: Further Essays in Interpretive Anthropology* 16 (1983).

15. W. E. B. Du Bois, supra note [4], at 172.

16. See, e.g., *City of Richmond* v. *J. A. Croson Co.*, 109 S. Ct. 706, 720–23 (1989); *Wygant* v. *Jackson Bd. of Educ.*, 476 U.S. 267, 277–78, 293–94 (1986). . . .

17. *Wygant*, 476 U.S. at 314 (Stevens, J., dissenting).

18. S. Steele, *The Content of Our Character* 116–17 (1990).

19. Kennedy, "Persuasion and Distrust: A Comment on the Affirmative Action Debate," 99 *Harv. L. Rev.* 1327, 1331 (1986) (footnotes omitted).

20. Id.

Review and Discussion Questions

1. What do you see as the strong and weak points of color blindness, in comparison with race consciousness, as a principle underlying social policy?

2. Aleinikoff writes that whites and blacks tend to talk past one another and that whites have little understanding of the black experience. Would you agree or disagree? What evidence is there for and against what Aleinikoff says?

3. "If the goal is to make our society fairer and less racially divided, then adopting racially conscious policies will only make things worse—it's like fighting fire with fire." Explain why you agree or disagree with this statement.

4. Aleinikoff writes that "race-neutral strategies simply postpone our society's inevitable rendezvous with its history of racism." What does this statement mean? Do you agree with it?

5. Are there some programs, institutions, and situations in which race consciousness is necessary and others in which color blindness would be more appropriate? Give examples. Should race be a consideration in university admission? Why or why not?

City of Richmond v. *Croson*

U.S. SUPREME COURT

In this case, the U.S. Supreme Court found unconstitutional Richmond's requirement that contractors who wanted city construction contracts must subcontract at least 30 percent of the dollar amount of their contracts to "minority business enterprises." The majority of the court, in an opinion delivered by Justice O'Connor, held that past evidence of racial discrimination in the construction industry was insufficient to justify Richmond's racially conscious program and that the program therefore violated the Fourteenth Amendment's guarantee of "equal protection of the laws." In a vigorous dissent from the majority opinion, Justice Marshall upheld Richmond's minority set-aside program.

Study Questions

1. What exactly was the Richmond plan?
2. What did proponents of the plan say on its behalf?
3. On what grounds did the plan's opponents criticize it?
4. Why does Justice O'Connor argue that "the sorry history of both private and public discrimination . . . cannot [by itself] justify a rigid racial quota in the awarding of public contracts"?
5. What, in Justice O'Connor's view, would be the bad effects of upholding the Richmond plan?
6. On what grounds does Justice Marshall criticize the majority's decision?

JUSTICE O'CONNOR *announced the judgment of the Court:*

On April 11, 1983, the Richmond City Council adopted the Minority Business Utilization Plan (the Plan). The Plan required prime contractors to whom the city awarded construction contracts to subcontract at least 30% of the dollar amount of the contract to one or more Minority

109 S. Ct. 706 (1989); legal citations omitted.

Business Enterprises (MBEs). . . . The 30% set-aside did not apply to city contracts awarded to minority-owned prime contractors. . . .

The Plan defined an MBE as "[a] business at least fifty-one (51) percent of which is owned and controlled . . . by minority group members.". . . "Minority group members" were defined as "[c]itizens of the United States who are Blacks, Spanish-speaking, Orientals, Indians, Eskimos, or Aleuts.". . . There was no geographic limit to the Plan; an otherwise qualified MBE from anywhere in the United States could avail itself of the 30% set-aside. The Plan declared that it was "remedial" in nature, and enacted "for the purpose of promoting wider participation by minority business enterprises in the construction of public projects.". . . The Plan expired on June 30, 1988, and was in effect for approximately five years. . . .

The Plan authorized the Director of the Department of General Services to promulgate rules which "shall allow waivers in those individual situations where a contractor can prove to the satisfaction of the director that the requirements herein cannot be achieved." . . . To this end, the Director promulgated Contract Clauses, Minority Business Utilization Plan. . . . Section D of these rules provided:

> No partial or complete waiver of the foregoing [30% set-aside] requirement shall be granted by the city other than in exceptional circumstances. To justify a waiver, it must be shown that every feasible attempt has been made to comply, and it must be demonstrated that sufficient, relevant, qualified Minority Business Enterprises . . . are unavailable or unwilling to participate in the contract to enable meeting the 30% MBE goal. . . .

The Director also promulgated "purchasing procedures" to be followed in the letting of city contracts in accordance with the Plan. . . . Bidders on city construction contracts were provided with a "Minority Business Utilization Plan Commitment Form.". . . Within 10 days

of the opening of the bids, the lowest otherwise responsive bidder was required to submit a commitment form naming the MBEs to be used on the contract and the percentage of the total contract price awarded to the minority firm or firms. The prime contractor's commitment form or request for a waiver of the 30% set-aside was then referred to the city Human Relations Commission (HRC). The HRC verified that the MBEs named in the commitment form were in fact minority owned, and then either approved the commitment form or made a recommendation regarding the prime contractor's request for a partial or complete waiver of the 30% set-aside. . . .

The Plan was adopted by the Richmond City Council after a public hearing. . . . Seven members of the public spoke to the merits of the ordinance: five were in opposition, two in favor. Proponents of the set-aside provision relied on a study which indicated that, while the general population of Richmond was 50% black, only 0.67% of the city's prime construction contracts had been awarded to minority businesses in the 5-year period from 1978 to 1983. It was also established that a variety of contractors' associations, whose representatives appeared in opposition to the ordinance, had virtually no minority businesses within their membership. . . . The city's legal counsel indicated his view that the ordinance was constitutional under this Court's decision in *Fullilove* v. *Klutznick*. . . . Councilperson Marsh, a proponent of the ordinance, made the following statement:

> There is some information, however, that I want to make sure that we put in the record. I have been practicing law in this community since 1961, and I am familiar with the practices in the construction industry in this area, in the State, and around the nation. And I can say without equivocation, that the general conduct of the construction industry in this area, and the State, and around the nation, is one in which race discrimination and exclusion on the basis of race is widespread. . . .

There was no direct evidence of race discrimination on the part of the city in letting contracts or any evidence that the city's prime contractors had discriminated against minority-owned subcontractors. . . .

Opponents of the ordinance questioned both its wisdom and its legality. They argued that a disparity between minorities in the population of Richmond and the number of prime contracts awarded to MBEs had little probative value in establishing discrimination in the construction industry. . . . Representatives of various contractors' associations questioned whether there were enough MBEs in the Richmond area to satisfy the 30% set-aside requirement. . . . Mr. Murphy noted that only 4.7% of all construction firms in the United States were minority owned and that 41% of these were located in California, New York, Illinois, Florida, and Hawaii. He predicted that the ordinance would thus lead to a windfall for the few minority firms in Richmond. . . . Councilperson Gillespie indicated his concern that many local labor jobs, held by both blacks and whites, would be lost because the ordinance put no geographic limit on the MBEs eligible for the 30% set-aside. . . . Some of the representatives of the local contractors' organizations indicated that they did not discriminate on the basis of race and were in fact actively seeking out minority members. . . .

Appellant argues that it is attempting to remedy various forms of past discrimination that are alleged to be responsible for the small number of minority businesses in the local contracting industry. Among these the city cites the exclusion of blacks from skilled construction trade unions and training programs. This past discrimination has prevented them "from following the traditional path from laborer to entrepreneur.". . . The city also lists a host of nonracial factors which would seem to face a member of any racial group attempting to establish a new business enterprise, such as deficiencies in working capital, inability to meet bonding requirements, unfamiliarity with bidding procedures, and disability caused by an inadequate track record. . . .

While there is no doubt that the sorry history of both private and public discrimination in this country has contributed to a lack of opportunities for black entrepreneurs, this observation, standing alone, cannot justify a rigid racial quota in the awarding of public contracts in Richmond, Virginia. Like the claim that discrimination in primary and secondary schooling justifies a rigid racial preference in medical school admissions, an amorphous claim that there has been past discrimination in a particular industry cannot justify the use of an unyielding racial quota.

It is sheer speculation how many minority firms there would be in Richmond absent past societal discrimination, just as it was sheer speculation how many minority medical students would have been admitted to the medical school at Davis absent past discrimination in educational opportunities. Defining these sorts of injuries as "identified discrimination" would give local governments license to create a patchwork of racial preferences based on statistical generalizations about any particular field of endeavor.

These defects are readily apparent in this case. The 30% quota cannot in any realistic sense be tied to any injury suffered by anyone. The District Court relied upon five predicate "facts" in reaching its conclusion that there was an adequate basis for the 30% quota: (1) the ordinance declares itself to be remedial; (2) several proponents of the measure stated their views that there had been past discrimination in the construction industry; (3) minority businesses received 0.67% of prime contracts from the city while minorities constituted 50% of the city's population; (4) there were very few minority contractors in local and state contractors' associations; and (5) in 1977, Congress made a determination that the effects of past discrimination had stifled minority participation in the construction industry nationally. . . .

None of these "findings," singly or together, provide the city of Richmond with a "strong basis in evidence for its conclusion that remedial action was necessary.". . . There is nothing approaching a prima facie case of a constitutional or statutory violation by *anyone* in the Richmond construction industry. . . .

The District Court accorded great weight to the fact that the city council designated the Plan as "remedial." But the mere recitation of a "benign" or legitimate purpose for a racial classification is entitled to little or no weight. . . . Racial classifications are suspect, and that means that simple legislative assurances of good intention cannot suffice.

The District Court also relied on the highly conclusionary statement of a proponent of the Plan that there was racial discrimination in the construction industry "in this area, and the State, and around the nation.". . . It also noted that the city manager had related his view that racial discrimination still plagued the construction industry in his home city of Pittsburgh. . . . These statements are of little probative value in establishing identified discrimination in the Richmond construction industry. The fact-finding process of legislative bodies is generally entitled to a presumption of regularity and deferential review by the judiciary. . . . But when a legislative body chooses to employ a suspect classification, it cannot rest upon a generalized assertion as to the classification's relevance to its goals. . . . A governmental actor cannot render race a legitimate proxy for a particular condition merely by declaring that the condition exists. . . . The history of racial classifications in this country suggests that blind judicial deference to legislative or executive pronouncements of necessity has no place in equal protection analysis. . . .

Reliance on the disparity between the number of prime contracts awarded to minority firms and the minority population of the city of Richmond is similarly misplaced. There is no doubt that "[w]here gross statistical disparities can be shown, they alone in a proper case may constitute prima facie proof of a pattern or practice of discrimination" under Title VII. . . . But it is equally clear that "[w]hen special qualifica-

tions are required to fill particular jobs, comparisons to the general population (rather than to the smaller group of individuals who possess the necessary qualifications) may have little probative value.". . .

In the employment context, we have recognized that for certain entry level positions or positions requiring minimal training, statistical comparisons of the racial composition of an employer's workforce to the racial composition of the relevant population may be probative of a pattern of discrimination. . . . But where special qualifications are necessary, the relevant statistical pool for purposes of demonstrating discriminatory exclusion must be the number of minorities qualified to undertake the particular task.

In this case, the city does not even know how many MBEs in the relevant market are qualified to undertake prime or subcontracting work in public construction projects. . . . Nor does the city know what percentage of total city construction dollars minority firms now receive as subcontractors on prime contracts let by the city. . . .

In sum, none of the evidence presented by the city points to any identified discrimination in the Richmond construction industry. We, therefore, hold that the city has failed to demonstrate a compelling interest in apportioning public contracting opportunities on the basis of race. To accept Richmond's claim that past societal discrimination alone can serve as the basis for rigid racial preferences would be to open the door to competing claims for "remedial relief" for every disadvantaged group. The dream of a Nation of equal citizens in a society where race is irrelevant to personal opportunity and achievement would be lost in a mosaic of shifting preferences based on inherently unmeasurable claims of past wrongs. "Courts would be asked to evaluate the extent of the prejudice and consequent harm suffered by various minority groups. Those whose societal injury is thought to exceed some arbitrary level of tolerability then would be entitled to preferential classifications.". . . We think such a result would be contrary to both the letter and spirit of a constitutional provision whose central command is equality.

Justice Marshall, dissenting:

It is a welcome symbol of racial progress when the former capital of the Confederacy acts forthrightly to confront the effects of racial discrimination in its midst. In my view, nothing in the Constitution can be construed to prevent Richmond, Virginia, from allocating a portion of its contracting dollars for businesses owned or controlled by members of minority groups. Indeed, Richmond's set-aside program is indistinguishable in all meaningful respects from—and in fact was patterned upon—the federal set-aside plan which this Court upheld in *Fullilove* v. *Klutznick*. . . .

A majority of this Court holds today, however, that the Equal Protection Clause of the Fourteenth Amendment blocks Richmond's initiative. The essence of the majority's position is that Richmond has failed to catalogue adequate findings to prove that past discrimination has impeded minorities from joining or participating fully in Richmond's construction contracting industry. I find deep irony in second-guessing Richmond's judgment on this point. As much as any municipality in the United States, Richmond knows what racial discrimination is; a century of decisions by this and other federal courts has richly documented the city's disgraceful history of public and private racial discrimination. In any event, the Richmond City Council *has* supported its determination that minorities have been wrongly excluded from local construction contracting. Its proof includes statistics showing that minority-owned businesses have received virtually no city contracting dollars and rarely if ever belonged to area trade associations; testimony by municipal officials that discrimination has been widespread in the local construction industry; and the same exhaustive and widely publicized federal studies relied on in *Fullilove*, studies which showed that pervasive discrimination in the Nation's tight-knit construction industry had operated to exclude minorities from public contracting. These are precisely the types of statistical and testimonial evidence which, until today, this Court had credited in cases approving of race-conscious measures designed to remedy past discrimination.

More fundamentally, today's decision marks a deliberate and giant step backward in this Court's affirmative action jurisprudence. Cynical of one municipality's attempt to redress the effects of past racial discrimination in a particular industry, the majority launches a grapeshot attack on race-conscious remedies in general. The majority's unnecessary pronouncements will inevitably discourage or prevent governmental entities, particularly States and localities, from acting to rectify the scourge of past discrimination. This is the harsh reality of the majority's decision, but it is not the Constitution's command.

Review and Discussion Questions

1. If you had been a member of the Richmond City Council, would you have voted for its Minority Business Utilization Plan? What are the pros and cons of such programs? Do they have good consequences? Do they infringe on anyone's moral rights?

2. In what ways does Justice O'Connor's opinion reflect what T. Alexander Aleinikoff calls "the Court's model of weak colorblindness"?

3. Do you believe that there was sufficient evidence of racial discrimination to justify the city's plan? Who is right about this evidence—Justice O'Connor or Justice Marshall?

4. Justice O'Connor and the majority of the Court seem to believe that some specific, identifiable individuals must have been discriminated against before race-conscious measures can be adopted. Do you agree that affirmative action measures must meet this standard?

5. What measures could Richmond have taken that would have increased opportunities for minority businesses but would not have involved racial quotas? Could the city have taken any color-blind measures to help minority businesses?

12

CRIME AND PUNISHMENT

Handguns and Violent Crime

NICHOLAS DIXON

Today Americans are more worried about violent crime than ever before. In this essay, Nicholas Dixon, professor of philosophy at Alma College in Alma, Michigan, makes a utilitarian case for banning handguns. Basing his argument on international comparisons and on the correlation over recent decades between the number of handguns and the number of homicides in the United States, Dixon contends that a high rate of handgun ownership is one of the causes of our high rate of homicide and that banning handguns is likely to reduce the overall rate of violent crime. He criticizes the Brady Bill as inadequate and responds to both utilitarian and rights-based objections to a ban on handguns.

Study Questions

1. How does our rate of handgun ownership and handgun homicide compare with that of other countries? What do the statistics about handgun ownership in the U.S. and our homicide rates over the last four decades reveal?

2. How does Dixon respond to the objection that other factors besides the ownership of handguns affect the homicide rate? Why does he believe that a reduction in handgun ownership is likely to lower the overall rate of violent crime?

3. What does the Brady Bill require, and on what grounds does Dixon criticize it?

4. What is "substitution theory" and what is Dixon's criticism of it? How does he respond to the argument that a ban on handguns would actually increase violent crime by denying peaceful citizens the use of handguns in self-defense?

5. How does Dixon respond to the argument that banning handguns would violate people's rights by restricting their freedom?

Reprinted from Nicholas Dixon, "Handguns, Violent Crime, and Self-Defense," The International Journal of Applied Philosophy, *Vol. 13:2 (Fall 1999), pp. 239–260 by permission of the Editor. Some notes omitted.*

OVER THE LAST TWENTY YEARS, philosophers have written extensively on such public policy issues as abortion, euthanasia, and the death penalty. I believe that the debate over handgun control in the United States should be added to this list. My goal in this paper is twofold. First, I want to persuade applied ethicists that handgun control is worthy of their attention. Second, drawing in part on data and arguments that I have published elsewhere,[1] I will argue that an outright handgun ban is the best policy.

A. The Initial Case for Restricting Handguns

The following table compares handgun ownership and handgun homicide rates per 100,000 people in selected countries. The left-hand column is an estimate of handgun ownership rates in 1991, roughly the midpoint of the time span under investigation, based on FBI projections and on independent inquiries to the police departments in each country. The handgun homicide rates are calculated from data provided by Handgun Control, Inc., which obtained the information from each country's police department.[2]

The first stage of my argument is to contend that these data are most plausibly explained by a causal relationship between handgun ownership and handgun homicide rates. First, the method of concomitant variation supports this causal assertion, based on the perfect coincidence between the rank orderings in terms of handgun ownership and average handgun homicide rates.[3] Second, and more important, in view of the vast disparity between the United States and all of the other countries in terms of both handgun ownership and handgun homicide, the method of difference supports the claim that the United States' extremely high handgun ownership rate is a cause of its extremely high handgun homicide rate.[4] To complete this stage of my causal argument, and to minimize the likelihood that the correlations I cite are purely coincidental, I need a causal theory to explain how the causation that I assert works. My theory is based on common sense: Handguns are necessary for handgun homicides, so a higher ownership rate is likely to lead to a higher homicide rate. Simplistic though my causal theory is, I suggest that the correlations I have produced are so striking that the burden of proof is on those who would deny my causal argument.

I do not claim that the handgun ownership rate is the only determinant of homicide and other violent crimes committed with handguns. Two societies may have identical handgun ownership rates yet very different rates of violent crime, both with and without handguns. Economic and racial inequities, unemployment, and

	Handgun Ownership Per 100,000	Handgun Homicide Rate Per 100,000							
		1980	1983	1985	1988	1990	1992	1996	Average
U.S.A.	22,696	4.60	3.60	3.23	3.56	4.22	5.28	3.75	4.03
Israel	3,716	0.50	N/A	0.39	0.54	N/A	N/A	N/A	0.48
Sweden	3,700	0.22	0.08	N/A	0.23	0.16	0.43	N/A	0.22
Canada	2,301	0.03	0.02	0.02	0.03	0.26	0.50	0.41	0.18
Australia	1,596	0.02	0.06	0.03	0.07	0.06	0.08	0.08	0.06
U.K.	837	0.01	0.01	0.01	0.01	0.04	0.06	0.05	0.03

countless historical and cultural factors are doubtless also important causal factors. I claim only that the handgun ownership rate is one important determinant of handgun violence rates.

Opponents of handgun prohibition could concede that handgun ownership is causally connected with handgun homicide, while denying that it has any relationship with overall homicide rates. The vital second step in my causal argument, then, is showing that a reduction in handgun homicide and violence in the United States would reduce its overall rate of homicide and other violent crime. Note that I do not assert that a reduction in the handgun violence rate in other countries will substantially reduce their overall rate of violent crime. Handgun ownership and crime in most other countries is so low as to have a negligible impact on their overall crime rate.

I offer two arguments as to why a reduction in handgun violence in the United States will substantially decrease its overall level of violent crime. First, a huge number and a substantial percentage of its homicides and other violent crimes are committed with handguns. Since 1970, over 50% of homicides in this country have been committed with handguns, standing at 53% in 1997.[5] In the United States in 1997, 39.7% of its 497,950 robberies and 20% of its 1,022,492 aggravated assaults involved firearms.[6] Handguns are used in over 80% of firearms-related robberies[7] and 86% of firearms-related aggravated assaults.[8] Second, because of their lethality, cheapness, ease of use, and small size (and hence ease of concealability), handguns are uniquely suited to homicide and other violent crimes. The importance of concealability of weapons for use in crime was reinforced by a study of crime weapons seized by the police done by the Bureau of Alcohol, Tobacco, and Firearms: "Seventy-one percent, or 7,538 of the handguns submitted for tracing, had a barrel length of 3 inches or less. Sixty-one percent, or 6,476, had a caliber of .32 or less. Since both of these factors relate to the size of the weapon,

these figures indicate that concealability is an overriding factor in selecting a handgun for use in crime."[9]

The connection between handgun ownership and the overall homicide rate is further confirmed by a comparison of the number of handguns and the overall homicide rate in the United States in the last four decades.

	Number of Handguns	Handguns Per 100,000	Homicides Per 100,000
1950	12 million	7,931	4.6
1960	16 million	8,924	5.1
1970	27 million	13,281	7.8
1980	48 million	21,192	10.2
1990	66 million	26,358	9.4[10]

From 1950 until 1970, the increase in the handgun ownership rate was matched by a steady increase in the overall homicide rate. Since the early 1970s, the annual homicide rate has become relatively stable, deviating very little from the 8 to 10 per 100,000 range. The likely reason why the homicide rate has not risen appreciably since the early 1970s, even though the handgun ownership rate has continued to rise, is that the United States has become "saturated" with sufficient handguns to supply potential murderers.

I now summarize my main argument. First, the extremely high handgun ownership rate in the United States is a major cause of its high rate of homicides and other violent crimes committed with handguns. A reduction in its handgun ownership rate is therefore likely to reduce its rate of handgun violence. Second, because of the high percentage of violent crimes currently committed in the United States with handguns, and because of the special effectiveness of handguns in committing violent crimes, a reduction in the rate of handgun violence is likely to reduce its overall rate of violent crime. In the next section I argue that an outright ban on handguns is the only realistic way to effect such a reduction.[11]

B. Why the Brady Bill Doesn't Go Far Enough

Arguments such as the foregoing may have played a role in the final passage by Congress of a version of the Brady Bill at the end of 1993. The bill imposes a waiting period of a few days, during which a "background check" is conducted, before a handgun can be purchased. Those found to have criminal records or a history of mental illness will be denied legal access to handguns. It is a "targeted" ban, designed to keep handguns out of the hands of those who are allegedly most likely to abuse them. It is hailed as a compromise that will reduce handgun violence, while respecting law-abiding citizens' right to bear arms. In reality, the one benefit of the Brady Bill is that it may have moved this country slightly closer to considering meaningful handgun control. In itself, the Brady Bill is likely to have little effect in reducing handgun crime.

The only people whose legal access to handguns will be ended will be those who have been convicted of felonies and those with documented mental illness. While opponents of handgun prohibition point out that a high percentage of murders are committed by people with prior arrest records, they estimate that only 25% of murderers have felony convictions. Seventy-five percent of murderers, then, will be unaffected by the Brady Bill. Moreover, lawbreakers who have thus far eluded conviction will be untouched by the Bill, as will those who will buy handguns in order to begin a career of violent crime. This is to say nothing of previously law-abiding handgun owners who lose their temper and use the weapon to kill or maim after arguments.

The situation is even worse for supporters of the Brady Bill when we turn to illegal access to handguns. Its supporters are vulnerable to an objection often raised against a general handgun prohibition. The objection is that only law-abiding citizens are likely to obey a general handgun ban, while felons are likely to keep the handguns they already own, and have continued access to handguns by theft and illegal transfers. The result of a general handgun ban, then, is alleged to be the disarmament of peaceful citizens, while violent types will maintain or even increase their possession of handguns. However, this argument is more damaging as an objection to a targeted ban, such as the Brady Bill, than it is to my proposal for a general handgun ban.

This is because the bill will do nothing to restrict wrongdoers' access to handguns through the illegal channels that already exist: theft and illegal transfers. Felons will be able to get friends with "clean" records to "buy" for them, with no more difficulty than is currently experienced by teenagers in search of alcohol. Handgun "brokers" have already begun to legally purchase large amounts of handguns, which they then illegally sell on the streets to customers with criminal records. The Brady Bill will allow unlimited access (except a few days' wait) to unlimited numbers of handguns for the vast majority of people. Since on average well over two million new handguns have been made available for sale in the United States every year since 1980,[12] there is every reason to believe that the U.S. arsenal of privately owned handguns, which will remain subject to theft and illegal transfer, will continue to grow rapidly.

In contrast, the outright ban that I propose will immediately stem this influx of handguns, which is especially important in view of the fact that a disproportionate number of handgun crimes are committed with new handguns.[13] The pool of sixty-six million handguns already in private hands or available for sale can be gradually reduced by voluntary return by their owners, with the aid of amnesty and buyback schemes, and by police seizure of weapons from felons. Of course, a handgun ban will never be completely effective in removing all sixty-six million handguns from circulation, but "a handgun ban does not need to be perfectly effective to lead to a major decrease in handgun violence."[14]

The Brady Bill is inadequate, then, because it will allow continued legal access to handguns to the majority of future violent criminals, and because it will allow the pool of handguns available for theft and illegal transfer to grow ever larger.

C. Utilitarian Objections to Handgun Prohibition

I present my argument that a handgun ban will reduce violent crime in the United States as an empirical hypothesis supported by striking correlations between handgun ownership and handgun homicide rates, and by a simple, intuitively plausible causal theory. Replies thus far given to my argument for handgun prohibition make the elementary error of treating it and other arguments for prohibition as if they were advanced as deductively valid. These replies consist of thought experiments or conjectures showing how handgun prohibition may conceivably fail to reduce violent crime. While this is indeed sufficient to show that my argument is not deductively valid (a point that I readily concede), it does nothing to undermine my actual claim: Handgun prohibition will probably reduce violent crime. To refute my actual claim, opponents need to show that it is probably false, not just that it may be false.

Both steps of my argument have been contested. I begin with the second step, in which I claim that a reduction in handgun violence in this country will reduce overall violent crime. The most common response is what I call "substitution theory": If handguns are banned, criminals will simply turn to even more lethal long guns and other weapons, with no net reduction in the amount of violent crime. Kates and Benenson argue that if only 30% of potential murderers were to "upgrade" to long guns (rifles and shotguns) in the event of a handgun ban, while the other 70% "downgraded" to knives, there would still be a "substantial in-

crease" in homicide.[15] Based on the results of prisoner surveys, Gary Kleck asserts that an even higher rate of substitution of more lethal guns is likely to occur.[16]

The problem with these arguments for substitution theory is the flimsy nature of their empirical support. First, the responses of prisoners to surveys scarcely establish Kleck's intuitively implausible prediction of widespread use of bulky, long guns in crime. Second, Kates and Benenson calculated their 30% "threshold" (which is widely cited in the anti–gun control literature) by comparing the relative lethality of long gun and handgun wounds, without considering the fact that it is far easier to inflict wounds in the first place with small, concealable handguns. Given the fact that substitution theory is advanced by opponents of handgun prohibition in order to deny the intuitively plausible view that a reduction in handgun violence will result in a reduction in overall violence, the burden of proof is on its proponents to provide much better support for it. The weakness of substitution theory is especially damaging for those opponents of handgun prohibition who concede that a ban would reduce the level of handgun violence.

Further presumptive evidence against substitution theory is provided by the fact that the U.S. overall homicide rate is substantially higher than that of the comparison countries. In fact, it is higher, in most cases by several hundred percent, than that of all the other seventeen countries in a recent study. If substitution of other, more lethal weapons were likely to occur in the United States, then we would expect these other countries with low handgun ownership rates to have high non-handgun homicide rates to "compensate" for their low handgun homicide rates; but they do not.

I turn next to the first stage of my argument, in which I claim that a handgun ban would reduce the amount of handgun violence in the United States. The usual strategy of opponents is to argue that the extremely high rate of handgun violence in the United States is attributable to factors unrelated to its high handgun ownership rate. The weakness of most such arguments is that they give little or no analysis of these alleged factors. The unsupported assertion that there may be causes of handgun violence unrelated to handgun ownership rates fails for two reasons to undercut my argument. First, as explained above, showing the bare logical possibility that my causal hypothesis is false does nothing to undercut it. Second, since I claim only that the high handgun ownership rate is one of the causes of our rampant handgun violence rate, the existence of other causes in no way weakens my argument. If anything, the existence of multiple causes of handgun violence makes the striking international correlation between ownership and homicide rates even harder to dismiss as a coincidence. . . .

The strongest objection to handgun prohibition is the claim that it would cause an increase in violent crime by denying peaceful citizens the use of handguns in defense of self and property. Any benefits of a handgun ban have to be weighed against a possible reduction in the defensive use of handguns.

The first weakness of this objection is once again the flimsy nature of the empirical evidence adduced in its support. The sole evidence for the effectiveness and the frequency of the defensive uses of handguns is provided by highly suspect surveys of prisoners and gun owners, and a conjecture that the number of justified self-defensive homicides is underreported by the FBI. Second, the argument that the use of handguns in self-defense causes a net decrease in violent crime is further weakened by the fact that a substantial percentage of the very violent crimes that handgun ownership is supposed to prevent are themselves committed with handguns. Rather than acquiescing in an endless spiral of increasingly heavily armed aggressors and victims, we would do better to strive for a society in which neither aggressors nor victims have handguns. Third, underlying the self-defense argument against handgun prohibition may be

the fear that it would leave ordinary law-abiding citizens helpless against gun-wielding predators. In reality, however, this distinction between peaceful handgun owners and predators is suspect. Even a handgun purchased for purely defensive purposes may be used offensively, since we are all capable of heated arguments that can easily turn lethal when a handgun is available. In about one half of all murders, the victim is a relative or acquaintance of the murderer, and about one third of murders result from arguments, which are hardly circumstances that apply only to predators. A recent study directly supports my claim that the risk of offensive abuses of handguns outweighs their defensive utility: "Despite the widely held belief that guns are effective for protection, our results suggest that they actually pose a substantial threat to members of the household."[17]

The comparative international data cited above also counts against the hypothesis that handgun ownership reduces violence because of the defensive use of handguns. The more handguns that are owned in a given country, we may assume, the more times they will be used defensively and, according to the hypothesis we are considering, the less violent crimes will occur. But the data indicates the direct opposite: the higher the handgun ownership rate, the higher the handgun homicide rate. In particular, the United States, which far outstrips its rivals in handgun ownership, is also the clear leader in terms of both the handgun and overall homicide rate. . . .

D. Utilitarianism, Handgun Prohibition, and Individual Rights

The objections discussed in the previous section did not challenge the utilitarian framework in which my argument is expressed, and I need to pause to consider rights-based objections to handgun prohibition. The U.S. legal system does not regard the prevention of violence as an absolute value. We provide defendants with an extensive array of rights, with the result that some people are acquitted even though they committed the violent act of which they are accused. This indicates that we regard protecting individual rights as an important constraint on the utilitarian goal of reducing violent crime. How do these objections affect my utilitarian argument for banning handguns?

A general defense of utilitarianism is both beyond the scope of a paper in applied ethics and unnecessary in order to defend my proposal. My strategy in responding to these objections will be to show that handgun prohibition does not violate individual moral rights, so that the overwhelming utilitarian arguments for prohibition prevail.

Handgun prohibition undeniably restricts people's freedom. They are prevented from owning handguns, which they may desire for target shooting, collectors' items, or self-defense. However, the right to life and bodily integrity of innocent victims of handgun violence—which, if my main thesis is sound, are constantly endangered by the prevalence of handguns—is arguably far stronger than any rights that are allegedly violated by banning handguns. Gun collectors would remain free to own other types of firearms, and handguns would still be available for enthusiasts at government-run shooting ranges. The most substantial freedom that would be curtailed by my proposal, and the one to which I devote the rest of this section, is the use of handguns in self-defense; but my arguments in the last section showed that defensive uses of handguns are heavily outweighed by offensive abuses. Of what moral force is an alleged right to defend ourselves with handguns if (1) exercising this "right" endangers rather than protects gun owners, and (2) the widespread handgun ownership necessary for the exercise of this freedom causes the death or wounding of thousands of innocent people, violating their unquestioned right to life and bodily integrity?

Now opponents of prohibition could adopt an "absolutist" stance, and insist that central to

the very meaning of the concept of a right is that it cannot be "trumped" by rival moral considerations. According to this view, my right to defend myself with a handgun is inviolable, regardless of the pernicious consequences that my exercise of this right may have for the rest of society (and, indeed, for myself). However, the implausibility of such an absolutist approach is glaring.

First, we cannot sidestep conflicts of rights by simply declaring one of the rival rights to be absolute. For instance, we cannot solve the abortion debate by a fiat that the fetus's (or the pregnant woman's) rights are inviolable. Instead, arguments are needed to explain why one right takes precedence over another. Thus opponents of handgun prohibition need to explain exactly why my right to defend myself with a handgun outweighs the rights of innocent victims of the violent crimes that occur as a result of widespread ownership of handguns.

Second, while my right to defend myself against harm arguably is absolute, in the sense that I may always respond to aggression, it is not unconditional. . . . The right to use violence in self-defense is qualified by such requirements as necessity and proportionality. The general right to self-defense does not entail the right to use any particular method that I happen to desire. Thus arguments, and not just a bare assertion, are needed to support the claim that we have a right to use handguns in self-defense. The view that enshrines the use of handguns in self-defense as a right simply because some people desire to do so—i.e., that the right to self-defense is unlimited—is easily reduced to absurdity. Paranoid anti-government survivalist militias doubtless believe that possessing huge arsenals of automatic weapons and explosives (and quite likely, if they could get their hands on them, nuclear weapons) is necessary to protect themselves against the constant threat of governmental tyranny. Unless we are willing to accept the consequence that militia members would indeed have the right to own such weaponry, we need a more substantial argument for the right to own handguns for defensive purposes than the mere fact that some people desire to do so. . . .

Handgun prohibition is based on the least controversial ground for restricting freedom: preventing harm to others. Even the most innocuous laws—for instance, those prohibiting people from driving at speeds over 100 mph, privately owning anti-tank weapons or nuclear warheads, or making child pornography—restrict people's freedom, on the ground that these activities pose an unacceptable risk or certainty of harm to others. These familiar examples show that, just as we do not regard preventing harm to others as an absolute value, and are prepared to tolerate some such harm in order to preserve individual rights, neither do we regard protecting individual freedom as sacrosanct. We restrict freedom without violating rights when doing so will prevent substantial harm to others, while imposing minimal restraints on people's behavior. Handgun prohibition falls well within this familiar rationale. . . .

E. Conclusion: Is Handgun Prohibition Realistic?

The most common response that I have encountered to my proposal to ban handguns is that it is too "idealistic." Those who give this response may grant my contention that eradicating handguns would reduce violent crime without violating individual rights, but they insist that handgun prohibition is not a practical goal in the United States. Underlying this skepticism is the belief that we cannot realistically expect the U.S. Congress to pass legislation to ban handguns, and that, even if such a ban were passed, it would be unenforceable.

I have already addressed the issue of enforceability above in section B. While no legislation will ever completely rid the country of handguns, a federal ban would immediately halt the current legal sale of over two million new handguns per year, while voluntary buyback programs and the seizure of weapons used in crime will gradually reduce the arsenal of handguns in private hands. And this reduction will, in turn, reduce the level of violent crime.

As for whether handgun prohibition legislation could be enacted in the first place, the recent passage of precisely such a measure in the United Kingdom, in response to the Dunblaine massacre, shows that it can actually be done. The only way to maintain the view that handgun prohibition is impossible to enact in the United States is to insist that the socio-political realities unique to this country make it so. These realities include the powerful influence of the gun lobby in Congress, the long tradition of gun ownership, and the fervent belief held by a significant minority that owning a handgun is necessary for self-protection.

Little doubt exists that such factors do indeed make the passage of a handgun ban in the United States currently unattainable. However, to count this as a refutation of my position is to adopt a truly disturbing view about the role of applied ethics. We surely need to distinguish between prescribing what we should do—this is the appropriate role for applied ethicists—and, on the other hand, predicting what Congress actually will do, which falls instead into the province of political science. The question of what we should do is prior to the question of what is currently attainable. Compromise and accommodation to practical realities should only be discussed after we have first determined what would be the fair and just thing to do.

NOTES

1. Nicholas Dixon, "Why We Should Ban Handguns in the United States," *Saint Louis University Public Law Review* 12:2 (1993), pp. 243–283; and "Perilous Protection: A Reply to Kopel," *Ibid,* pp. 361–391.

2. For more detail on the derivation of many of these statistics, see Nicholas Dixon, "Why We Should

Ban Handguns in the United States," pp. 248–250, and "Perilous Protection: A Reply to Kopel," pp. 372–373.

3. When the amount or rate of the effect E (in this case, handgun homicide) varies according to the amount or rate of antecedent factor X (handgun ownership), the method of concomitant variation indicates that X is probably a cause of E.

4. When the effect E (in this case, an extremely high handgun homicide rate) occurs in the presence of antecedent factor X (an extremely high handgun ownership rate) but not in its absence, the method of difference indicates that X is probably a cause of E.

5. *Uniform Crime Reports for the United States 1970–97* (Washington, D.C.: Federal Bureau of Investigations, U.S. Department of Justice, 1971–98).

6. *Uniform Crime Reports* 1997, pp. 31, 34.

7. Franklin E. Zimring, "Firearms, Violence and Public Policy," *Scientific American*, November 1991, p. 50.

8. This statistic, which comes from 1967, is cited by Franklin E. Zimring and Gordon Hawkins, *The Citizen's Guide to Gun Control* (New York: Macmillan, 1987), p. 38.

9. "Project Identification: A Study of Handguns Used in Crime" (Department of Treasury, May 1976), p. 2.

10. Handgun ownership numbers are based on the Bureau of Alcohol, Tobacco, and Firearms data on the number of handguns available for sale in the United States since 1899. See "Civilian Firearms—Domestic Production, Importation, Exportation, and Availability for Sale," BATF document, 1991. Overall United States homicide rates are taken from *Uniform Crime Reports*, 1950, 1960, 1970, 1980, and 1990.

11. For detail on the exceptions I propose to handgun prohibition, see "Why We Should Ban Handguns," pp. 244–247.

12. "Civilian Firearms—Domestic Production, Importation, Exportation, and Availability for Sale," BATF document.

13. Studies have shown that over half the handguns used in crime were first purchased from retailers within five years of the crime. See Zimring and Hawkins, *The Citizen's Guide to Gun Control*, pp. 39–41. See also Robert J. Spitzer, *The Politics of Gun Control* (Chatham, NJ: Chatham House Publishers, Inc., 1995), p. 80.

14. Nicholas Dixon, "Perilous Protection: A Reply to Kopel," p. 379.

15. See, e.g., Don B. Kates, Jr. and Mark K. Benenson, "Handgun Prohibition and Homicide: A Plausible Theory Meets the Intractable Facts," in Kates (ed.), *Restricting Handguns: The Liberal Skeptics Speak Out* (North River Press, 1979), p. 111.

16. Kleck, "Policy Lessons from Recent Gun Control Research," *Law and Contemporary Problems* 49.

17. Arthur Kellermann et al, "Gun Ownership as a Risk Factor for Homicide in the Home," *New England Journal of Medicine* 329:15 (1993), p. 1090.

Review and Discussion Questions

1. How persuasive do you find the statistics that Dixon presents? Do they establish a strong case for restricting handguns? How important a cause of our high rate of violent crime is handgun ownership?

2. Are you persuaded that reducing the number of handguns would reduce the amount of violent crime? Which would be best—a complete ban on handguns, tighter restrictions without a general ban, or no restrictions at all?

3. Assess the argument that handguns reduce crime by enabling citizens to defend themselves. What about the argument that, if handguns are banned, then criminals will simply use other weapons, with results that are just as bad?

4. The Second Amendment states: "A well regulated Militia, being necessary to the security of a free State, the right of the people to keep and bear Arms, shall not be infringed." Do individuals have either a moral or political right to own handguns?

5. Dixon believes that a handgun ban is a defensible restriction of people's liberty. Do you agree? Assess the banning of handguns from the perspective of Mill's *On Liberty*.

The False Promise of Gun Control

DANIEL D. POLSBY

Rejecting the proposition that handguns cause violence, Daniel D. Polsby, professor of law at Northwestern University, argues that gun-control laws do not work, that their effects are counterproductive, and that they divert attention from the roots of our crime problem. For certain people, criminal conduct is a rational occupational choice, and gun-control laws are unlikely to keep guns out of their hands. Given this and given the limits on what we can expect the police to do, citizens need firearms to protect themselves.

Study Questions

1. Unlike some other opponents of gun control, Polsby does not appeal to the Second Amendment. Explain why not.

2. What is the point of Polsby's discussion of the "demand curve" for guns? What evidence does he provide that firearms do not increase violence and crime?

3. What is the "futility theorem"? What practical problems would a prohibition on handguns face?

4. What does Polsby see as the "most important reason for criminal behavior"? Will more prisons and more police diminish the crime rate?

D URING THE 1960s and 1970s the robbery rate in the United States increased sixfold, and the murder rate doubled; the rate of handgun ownership nearly doubled in that period as well. Handguns and criminal violence grew together apace, and national opinion leaders did not fail to remark on the coincidence.

It has become a bipartisan article of faith that more handguns cause more violence. . . .

Alas, however well accepted, the conventional wisdom about guns and violence is mistaken. Guns don't increase national rates of crime and violence—but the continued proliferation of gun-control laws almost certainly does. Current rates of crime and violence are a bit below the peaks of the late 1970s, but because of a slight oncoming bulge in the at-risk population of males aged fifteen to thirty-four, the crime rate will soon worsen. The rising generation of criminals will have no more difficulty than their elders did in obtaining the tools of their trade. Growing violence will lead to calls for laws still more severe. Each fresh round of legislation will be followed by renewed frustration.

Gun-control laws don't work. What is worse, they act perversely. While legitimate users of firearms encounter intense regulation, scrutiny, and bureaucratic control, illicit markets easily adapt to whatever difficulties a free society throws in their way. Also, efforts to curtail the supply of firearms inflict collateral damage on freedom and privacy interests that have long been considered central to American public life. Thanks to the seemingly never-ending war on drugs and long experience attempting to suppress prostitution and pornography, we know a great deal about how illicit markets function and how costly to the public attempts to control them can be. It is essential that we make use of this experience in coming to grips with gun control.

The thousands of gun-control laws in the United States are of two general types. The older kind sought to regulate how, where, and by whom firearms could be carried. More recent laws have sought to make it more costly to buy, sell, or use firearms (or certain classes of firearms, such as assault rifles, Saturday-night specials, and so on) by imposing fees, special taxes, or surtaxes on them. The Brady bill is of both types: it has a background-check provision, and its five-day waiting period amounts to a "time tax" on acquiring handguns. All such laws can be called scarcity-inducing, because they seek to raise the cost of buying firearms, as figured in terms of money, time, nuisance, or stigmatization. . . .

Opponents of gun control have traditionally wrapped their arguments in the Second Amendment to the Constitution. Indeed, most modern scholarship affirms that so far as the drafters of the Bill of Rights were concerned, the right to bear arms was to be enjoyed by everyone, not just a militia, and that one of the principal justifications for an armed populace was to secure the tranquillity and good order of the community. But most people are not dedicated antiquitarians, and would not be impressed by the argument "I admit that my behavior is very dangerous to public safety, but the Second Amendment says I have a right to do it anyway." That would be a case for repealing the Second Amendment, not respecting it.

Fighting the Demand Curve

Everyone knows that possessing a handgun makes it easier to intimidate, wound, or kill someone. But the implication of this point for social policy has not been so well understood. It is easy to count the bodies of those who have been killed or wounded with guns, but not easy to count the people who have avoided harm because they had access to weapons. Think about uniformed police officers, who carry handguns in plain view not in order to kill people but simply to daunt potential attackers. And it works. Criminals generally do not single out police officers for opportunistic attack. Though officers can expect to draw their guns from time to time, few even in big-city departments will actually fire a shot (except in target practice) in the course of a year. This observation points to an important truth: people who are armed make comparatively unattractive victims. A criminal might not know if any one civilian is armed, but if it becomes known that a large number of civilians do carry weapons, criminals will become warier. . . .

In order to predict who will comply with gun-control laws, we should remember that guns are economic goods that are traded in markets. Consumers' interest in them varies. For religious, moral, aesthetic, or practical reasons, some people would refuse to buy firearms at any price. Other people willingly pay very high prices for them.

Handguns, so often the subject of gun-control laws, are desirable for one purpose—to allow a person tactically to dominate a hostile transaction with another person. The value of a weapon to a given person is a function of two factors: how much he or she wants to dominate a confrontation if one occurs, and how likely it is that he or she will actually be in a situation calling for a gun.

Dominating a transaction simply means getting what one wants without being hurt. Where people differ is in how likely it is that they will be involved in a situation in which a gun will be valuable. Someone who *intends* to engage in a transaction involving a gun—a criminal, for example—is obviously in the best possible position to predict that likelihood. Criminals should therefore be willing to pay more for a weapon than most other people would. Professors, politicians, and newspaper editors are, as a group, at very low risk of being involved in such transactions, and they thus systematically underrate the value of defensive handguns. (Correlative, perhaps, is their uncritical readiness to accept studies that debunk the utility of firearms for self-defense.) The class of people we wish to deprive of guns, then, is the very class with the most inelastic demand for them—criminals—whereas the people most likely to comply with gun-control laws don't value guns in the first place.

Do Guns Drive Up Crime Rates?

Which premise is true—that guns increase crime or that the fear of crime causes people to obtain guns? . . .

If firearms increased violence and crime, then rates of spousal homicide would have skyrocketed, because the stock of privately owned handguns has increased rapidly since the mid-1960s. But according to an authoritative study of spousal homicide in the *American Journal of Public Health,* by James Mercy and Linda Saltzman, rates of spousal homicide in the years 1976 to 1985 fell. If firearms increased violence and crime, the crime rate should have increased throughout the 1980s, while the national stock of privately owned handguns increased by more than a million units in every year of the decade. It did not. Nor should the rates of violence and crime in Switzerland, New Zealand, and Israel be as low as they are, since the number of firearms per civilian household is comparable to that in the United States. Conversely, gun-controlled Mexico and South Africa should be islands of peace instead of having murder rates more than twice as high as those here. The determinants of crime and law-abidingness are, of course, complex matters, which are not fully understood and certainly not explicable in terms of a country's laws. But gun-control enthusiasts, who have made capital out of the low murder rate in England, which is largely disarmed, simply ignore the counterexamples that don't fit their theory.

If firearms increased violence and crime, Florida's murder rate should not have been falling since the introduction, seven years ago, of a law that makes it easier for ordinary citizens to get permits to carry concealed handguns. Yet the murder rate has remained the same or fallen every year since the law was enacted, and it is now lower than the national murder rate (which has been rising). As of last November 183,561 permits had been issued, and only seventeen of the permits had been revoked because the holder was involved in a firearms offense. It would be precipitate to claim that the new law has "caused" the murder rate to subside. Yet here is a situation that doesn't fit the hypothesis that weapons increase violence.

If firearms increased violence and crime, programs of induced scarcity would suppress violence and crime. But—another anomaly—they don't. Why not? A theorem, which we could call the futility theorem, explains why gun-control laws must either be ineffectual or in the long term actually provoke more violence and crime. Any theorem depends on both observable fact and assumption. An assumption that can be made with confidence is that the higher the number of victims a criminal assumes to be armed, the higher will be the risk—the price—of assaulting them. By definition, gun-control laws should make weapons scarcer and thus more expensive. By our prior reasoning about demand among various types of consumers, after the laws are enacted criminals should be better armed, compared with noncriminals, than they were before. Of course, plenty of noncriminals will remain armed. But even if many noncriminals will pay as high a price as criminals will to obtain firearms, a larger number will not.

Criminals will thus still take the same gamble they already take in assaulting a victim who might or might not be armed. But they may appreciate that the laws have given them a freer field, and that crime still pays—pays even better, in fact, than before. What will happen to the rate of violence? Only a relatively few gun-mediated transactions—currently, five percent of armed robberies committed with firearms—result in someone's actually being shot (the statistics are not broken down into encounters between armed assailants and unarmed victims, and encounters in which both parties are armed). It seems reasonable to fear that if the number of such transactions were to increase because criminals thought they faced fewer deterrents, there would be a corresponding increase in shootings. Conversely, if gun-mediated transactions declined—if criminals initiated fewer of them because they feared encountering an armed victim or an armed good Samaritan—the number of shootings would go down. The magnitude of these effects is, admittedly, uncertain. Yet it is hard to doubt the general tendency of a change in the law that imposes legal burdens on buying guns. The futility theorem suggests that gun-control laws, if effective at all, would unfavorably affect the rate of violent crime. . . .

Are there empirical studies that can serve to help us choose between the futility theorem and the hypothesis that guns increase violence? Unfortunately, no: the best studies of the effects of gun-control laws are quite inconclusive. Our statistical tools are too weak to allow us to identify an effect clearly enough to persuade an open-minded skeptic. But it is precisely when we are dealing with undetectable statistical effects that we have to be certain we are using the best models available of human behavior.

Sealing the Border

Handguns are not legally for sale in the city of Chicago, and have not been since April of 1982. Rifles, shotguns, and ammunition are available, but only to people who possess an Illinois Firearm Owner's Identification card. It takes up to a month to get this card, which involves a background check. Even if one has a FOID card there is a waiting period for the delivery of a gun. In few places in America is it as difficult to get a firearm legally as in the city of Chicago.

Yet there are hundreds of thousands of unregistered guns in the city, and new ones arriving all the time. It is not difficult to get handguns—even legally. Chicago residents with FOID cards merely go to gun shops in the suburbs. Trying to establish a city as an island of prohibition in a sea of legal firearms seems an impossible project.

Is a state large enough to be an effective island, then? Suppose Illinois adopted Chicago's handgun ban. Same problem again. Some people could just get guns elsewhere: Indiana actually borders the city, and Wisconsin is only forty miles away. . . .

Even if many states outlawed sales of handguns, then, they would continue to be available, albeit at a somewhat higher price, reflecting the increased legal risk of selling them. Mindful of the way markets work to undermine their efforts, gun-control proponents press for federal regulation of firearms, because they believe that only Congress wields the authority to frustrate the interstate movement of firearms.

Why, though, would one think that federal policing of illegal firearms would be better than local policing? The logic of that argument is far from clear. Cities, after all, are comparatively small places. Washington, D.C., for example, has an area of less than 45,000 acres. Yet local officers have had little luck repressing the illegal firearms trade there. Why should federal officers do any better watching the United States' 12,000 miles of coastline and millions of square miles of interior? Criminals should be able to frustrate federal police forces just as well as they can local ones. Ten years of increasingly stringent federal efforts to abate cocaine trafficking, for example, have not succeeded in raising the street price of the drug. . . .

In firearms regulation, translating theory into practice will continue to be difficult, at least if the objective is to lessen the practical availability of firearms to people who might abuse them. On the demand side, for defending oneself against predation there is no substitute for a firearm. Criminals, at least, can switch to varieties of law-breaking in which a gun confers little or no advantage (burglary, smash-and-grab), but people who are afraid of confrontations with criminals, whether rationally or (as an accountant might reckon it) irrationally, will be very highly motivated to acquire firearms. Long after the marijuana and cocaine wars of this century have been forgotten, people's demand for personal security and for the tools they believe provide it will remain strong.

On the supply side, firearms transactions can be consummated behind closed doors. Firearms buyers, unlike those who use drugs, pornography, or prostitution, need not recurrently expose themselves to legal jeopardy. One trip to the marketplace is enough to arm oneself for life. This could justify a consumer's taking even greater precautions to avoid apprehension, which would translate into even steeper enforcement costs for the police. . . .

Seeing that local firearms restrictions are easily defeated, gun-control proponents have latched onto national controls as a way of finally making gun control something more than a gesture. But the same forces that have defeated local regulation will defeat further national regulation. Imposing higher costs on weapons ownership will, of course, slow down the weapons trade to some extent. But planning to slow it down in such a way as to drive down crime and violence, or to prevent motivated purchasers from finding ample supplies of guns and ammunition, is an escape from reality. And like many another such, it entails a morning after.

Administering Prohibition

. . . Unless people are prepared to surrender their guns voluntarily, how can the U.S. government confiscate an appreciable fraction of our country's nearly 200 million privately owned firearms? We know that it is possible to set up weapons-free zones in certain locations—commercial airports and many courthouses and,

lately, some troubled big-city high schools and housing projects. The sacrifices of privacy and convenience, and the costs of paying guards, have been thought worth the (perceived) gain in security. No doubt it would be possible, though it would probably not be easy, to make weapons-free zones of shopping centers, department stores, movie theaters, ball parks. But it is not obvious how one would cordon off the whole of an open society.

Voluntary programs have been ineffectual. From time to time community-action groups or police departments have sponsored "turn in your gun" days, which are nearly always disappointing. Sometimes the government offers to buy guns at some price. . . . If the price offered exceeds that at which a gun can be bought on the street, one can expect to see plans of this kind yield some sort of harvest—as indeed they have. But it is implausible that these schemes will actually result in a less-dangerous population. Government programs to buy up surplus cheese cause more cheese to be produced without affecting the availability of cheese to people who want to buy it. So it is with guns.

One could extend the concept of intermittent roadblocks of the sort approved by the Supreme Court for discouraging drunk driving. Metal detectors could be positioned on every street corner, or ambulatory metal-detector squads could check people randomly, or hidden magnetometers could be installed around towns, to detect concealed weapons. As for firearms kept in homes (about half of American households), warrantless searches might be rationalized on the well-established theory that probable cause is not required when authorities are trying to correct dangers to public safety rather than searching for evidence of a crime. . . .

Ignoring the Ultimate Sources of Crime and Violence

The American experience with prohibition has been that black marketeers—often professional criminals—move in to profit when legal markets are closed down or disturbed. In order to combat them, new laws and law-enforcement techniques are developed, which are circumvented almost as soon as they are put in place. New and yet more stringent laws are enacted, and greater sacrifices of civil liberties and privacy demanded and submitted to. But in this case the problem, crime and violence, will not go away, because guns and ammunition (which, of course, won't go away either) do not cause it. One cannot expect people to quit seeking new weapons as long as the tactical advantages of weapons are seen to outweigh the costs imposed by prohibition. Nor can one expect large numbers of people to surrender firearms they already own. The only way to make people give up their guns is to create a world in which guns are perceived as having little value. This world will come into being when criminals choose not to use guns because the penalties for being caught with them are too great, and when ordinary citizens don't think they need firearms because they aren't afraid of criminals anymore.

Neither of these eventualities seems very likely without substantial departures in law-enforcement policy. Politicians' nostrums—increasing the punishment for crime, slapping a few more death-penalty provisions into the code—are taken seriously by few students of the crime problem. The existing penalties for predatory crimes are quite severe enough. The problem is that they are rarely meted out in the real world. The penalties formally published by the code are in practice steeply discounted, and criminals recognize that the judicial and penal systems cannot function without bargaining in the vast majority of cases. . . .

The problem is not simply that criminals pay little attention to the punishments in the books. Nor is it even that they also know that for the majority of crimes, their chances of being arrested are small. The most important reason for criminal behavior is this: the income that offenders can earn in the world of crime, as compared with the world of work, all too often makes crime appear to be the better choice.

. . . More prisons means that fewer violent offenders will have to be released early in order to make space for new arrivals; perhaps fewer plea bargains will have to be struck—all to the good. Yet a moment's reflection should make clear that one more criminal locked up does not necessarily mean one less criminal on the street. The situation is very like one that conservationists and hunters have always understood. Populations of game animals readily recover from hunting seasons but not from loss of habitat. Mean streets, when there are few legitimate entry-level opportunities for young men, are a criminal habitat, so to speak, in the social ecology of modern American cities. Cull however much one will, the habitat will be reoccupied promptly after its previous occupant is sent away. So social science has found.

Similarly, whereas increasing the number of police officers cannot hurt, and may well increase people's subjective feelings of security, there is little evidence to suggest that doing so will diminish the rate of crime. . . .

Communities must, in short, organize more effectively to protect themselves against predators. No doubt this means encouraging properly qualified private citizens to possess and carry firearms legally. It is not morally tenable—nor, for that matter, is it even practical—to insist that police officers, few of whom are at a risk remotely as great as are the residents of many city neighborhoods, retain a monopoly on legal firearms. It is needless to fear giving honest men and women the training and equipment to make it possible for them to take back their own streets.

Over the long run, however, there is no substitute for addressing the root causes of crime—bad education and lack of job opportunities and the disintegration of families. Root causes are much out of fashion nowadays as explanations of criminal behavior, but fashionable or not, they are fundamental. *The root cause of crime is that for certain people, predation is a rational occupational choice.* Conventional crime-control measures, which by stiffening punishments or raising the probability of arrest aim to make crime pay less, cannot consistently affect the behavior of people who believe that their alternatives to crime will pay virtually nothing. Young men who did not learn basic literacy and numeracy skills before dropping out of their wretched public schools may not [be] . . . worth hiring at the minimum wage. . . . Their legitimate opportunities, always precarious in a society where race and class still matter, often diminish to the point of being for all intents and purposes absent. . . .

The solution to the problem of crime lies in improving the chances of young men. Easier said than done, to be sure. No one has yet proposed a convincing program for checking all the dislocating forces that government assistance can set in motion. One relatively straightforward change would be reform of the educational system. Nothing guarantees prudent behavior like a sense of the future, and with average skills in reading, writing, and math, young people can realistically look forward to constructive employment and the straight life that steady work makes possible.

But firearms are nowhere near the root of the problem of violence. As long as people come in unlike sizes, shapes, ages, and temperaments, as long as they diverge in their taste for risk and their willingness and capacity to prey on other people or to defend themselves from predation, and above all as long as some people have little or nothing to lose by spending their lives in crime, dispositions to violence will persist.

This is what makes the case for the right to bear arms, not the Second Amendment. It is foolish to let anything ride on hopes for effective gun control. As long as crime pays as well as it does, we will have plenty of it, and honest folk must choose between being victims and defending themselves.

Review and Discussion Questions

1. Polsby argues that handguns do not increase violence and crime. Nicholas Dixon argues the opposite. Compare and assess their reasoning. Who is right? What evidence would it take to settle this issue?

2. Do you agree with Polsby that banning handguns will not reduce crime and violence and make us safer? Explain why or why not.

3. Assess Polsby's argument that gun-control laws will be unable to stem the flow of guns. Is he right that banning handguns would be futile and counterproductive? How might Nicholas Dixon respond to Polsby?

4. Polsby asserts that firearms are not the root cause of crime and violence. What is? Polsby suggests that an armed citizenry is the best prevention against crime and that "honest folk must choose between being victims and defending themselves [with guns]." Do you agree? Is he right that police and prisons can do little to control crime? Would crime be reduced if more citizens went armed? Would this be a good thing?

5. Do proponents of gun control like Dixon and opponents like Polsby disagree only about certain factual matters or are there also philosophical or ethical differences between them?

6. Dixon advocates a total ban on the private ownership of handguns. Polsby appears to be against any gun-control laws at all. Are there alternatives between these two extremes that might reduce crime and violence in our society?

Juvenile Curfews and Gang Violence: Exiled on Main Street

EDITORS, *HARVARD LAW REVIEW*

In recent years, gang violence has reached epidemic proportions, terrorizing communities and killing our young people. One response has been juvenile curfews that bar youths below a given age from city streets after certain hours. This essay from the *Harvard Law Review* assesses the pros and cons of such curfews from three different theoretical perspectives: civil libertarianism, communitarianism, and critical race theory.

Study Questions

1. What factors do the authors see as promoting gang activity, and what measures have governments and communities taken against gang violence?

2. What was the effect of the juvenile curfew in Hartford? What are the pros and cons of juvenile curfews in general?

3. What is the focus of civil libertarianism with respect to curfews? Why do the authors believe that its defense of freedom is incomplete?

4. Why would communitarians tend to favor juvenile curfews more than civil libertarians do?

5. Why is critical race theory skeptical of curfews? Explain what the authors have in mind when they write that the theory "does not seem to accommodate comfortably the potential benefits that curfews provide."

WE HAVE BECOME NUMB to the statistics and perhaps even to the images: schools with metal detectors, drive-by shootings, crack houses, broken homes, nearly one in four Black men between the ages of twenty and twenty-nine in prison or on parole on any given day. Together they paint a much-publicized picture of crisis in urban America. Central to that picture is the particular problem of street gangs and gang violence.

Gangs are in part a product of urban decay. Many young people who grow up without economic opportunity and in struggling families and communities turn to gangs for a sense of belonging, a source of respect and support. Families may be dysfunctional or merely too strained by economic pressures to provide better guidance. Gangs can provide an outlet for youthful energy in neighborhoods that lack more constructive activities. Lack of conventional economic opportunity creates an incentive to look elsewhere for income. Concerns about the physical risk of a gang lifestyle may diminish in the face of stronger feelings about the hopelessness of the future. The result of these converging forces is that youth gangs in cities across America war against each other and force unfortunate neighbors to dive for cover. The desperation of inner-city life fosters gang membership, and the violence and crime that accompany gang activity in turn further urban decline.

Communities under fire have begun searching for ways to fight back against gang violence. One prevalent response has been to impose juvenile curfews, which bar youths below a certain age from city streets after established hours and prescribe various criminal penalties for violations. These curfews bring some order and safety to a community and its inhabitants. By requiring parental supervision of children, curfews also target the deeper social causes of the violence.

The use of curfews, however, has sparked vigorous debate about both the legality and the effectiveness of curfew measures. Curfews require individuals and families to sacrifice some of their freedom and to alter their lifestyles. Groups like the American Civil Liberties Union have been highly critical of the restrictive measures and have challenged some juvenile curfews in court. Yet many citizens seem willing to pay the price. As one commentator remarked, people "[a]re willing to trade . . . abstract personal freedom for a very real sense of enhanced personal safety." . . . This Note explains and evaluates curfews through three . . . conceptual lenses: civil libertarianism, communitarianism, and critical race theory. In theory and in practice, juvenile curfews offer only a marginal response to the problem of gang violence. In different ways, civil libertarianism, communitarianism, and critical race theories all point to the conclusion that, ultimately, curfews should be coupled with more comprehensive policies to address the ingrained social causes of gang violence. . . .

I. Communities Struggling to Respond: The Rise of Juvenile Curfews

In response to the problem of gang violence, governments and communities have launched an onslaught of measures that have varied in their effectiveness. Police have employed stop and search policies, road blocks, and special gang profiles designed to target suspected gang members. Prosecutors have creatively used existing and new legislation to find grounds for trial, including application of the Racketeer Influenced Corrupt Organizations Act (RICO) to gangs, parental liability for the actions of children, enforcement of new anti-gang statutes like California's Street Terrorism Enforcement and Protection Act, and prosecution of gangs as public nuisances. New legislation provides for stiffer sentences, and judges enjoin gang activities. Policymakers also seek longer-term social solutions through special education and job programs, counseling, alternative recreational activities, and official attempts to cooperate and negotiate with gangs. Efforts to improve employment, housing, and health conditions complement gang-specific measures.

Juvenile curfews fall into an intermediate category of measures that regulate "legitimate" conduct that is seen as related to criminal gang activity. In addition to curfews, public schools have banned gang clothing, and towns have passed tailored anti-loitering ordinances. Curfews and these other measures lie between traditional law enforcement and longer-term efforts to address the underlying social decay that spurs gang formation.

Juvenile curfews have been one remarkably prevalent policy chosen by cities across the country. New curfews have been enacted and existing curfews revived in Detroit, Los Angeles, Milwaukee, Philadelphia, Newark, Atlanta, Buffalo, Miami, Phoenix, and Little Rock. San Francisco, New Orleans, and Birmingham have witnessed a recent rise in pro-curfew sentiment. Washington, D.C. enacted a curfew that was struck down in the courts, but a new curfew in Dallas survived a legal challenge. Each city's curfew varies in its particulars. Each covers different age groups, restricts different hours, applies different sanctions, and permits different exceptions to the curfew. Understanding how juvenile curfews work in at least one city is essential to a textured assessment of their benefits and drawbacks.

A. One example: Hartford, Connecticut

In Hartford, Connecticut, the two largest youth gangs have been at war for years. Violence peaked in the summer of 1993, when the Latin Kings and Los Solidos gangs escalated their attacks and murdered rival gang members and shot innocent bystanders. In the hardest hit neighborhoods, many residents were afraid to leave their homes or to let their children out of the house unattended. On September 8, 1993, the Hartford city council instructed police to begin enforcing a citywide curfew that banned youths under fifteen years of age from city streets after nine o'clock at night. Eight days later, the City Council unanimously voted to raise the curfew age to include all youths under the age of eighteen. Minors caught violating the ordinance are to be returned to their parents, who are then subject to a ninety-dollar fine or jail. The measure generally seems to have reduced the violence and brought some quiet to Hartford's neighborhoods. As one resident explained, "It's almost like a police state, which I like."

The relative peace, however, has cost community life and individual freedom. A police officer called one Hartford neighborhood "a ghost town." A reporter described the city streets as "virtually deserted." Residents—particularly young Hispanic males who match police profiles of gang members—suffer frequent police stops and questioning. The Connecticut Civil Liberties Union (CCLU) has expressed concern that the curfew and police actions may violate the federal Constitution. Nevertheless, even some CCLU board members believe that the emergency situation justifies the curfew. Most residents seem willing to trade some personal freedom for a measure of security and relative peace. As a neighborhood organizer explained, "A lot of these folks . . . talking about civil liberties, et cetera, don't live here, and if they want to have no curfew in their neighborhoods, that's fine. . . . [I]n this community, the people who live here should have a right to determine how they want to live."

B. The policy debate

The immediate purpose of curfews in Hartford and other cities is to keep juveniles off the streets, both for their own safety and to prevent the loitering associated with gangs and gang delinquency. Curfews give police an added weapon to detain suspicious youth and preempt potentially criminal activity. Although children who are not in gangs might have to alter their behavior to comply with the curfew, proponents of the curfew argue that the concession is not too great given that most curfew ordinances do not apply if the juvenile is traveling with a parent, commuting to or from work, or attending organized activities. Curfew supporters emphasize the potential increase in public safety that can result. Besides making the streets safe for the public, community confidence and morale can be boosted by demonstrating that something is being done about the community's problems. A ceasefire in gang fighting might even allow community redevelopment efforts to begin.

Critics of the curfew counter that juvenile curfews require innocent children and their families to rearrange their daily lives and to sacrifice a measure of personal freedom even if the curfews allow for reasonable exceptions. The more a curfew's hours are extended, its age groups broadened, and its exceptions limited, the more it disrupts legitimate activities. Curfew enforcement also diverts scarce police and administrative resources from more serious criminal activity. Despite the expenditures, those intent on breaking the law may not even be deterred by a curfew, either because of the curfew ordinance's limited sanctions or a general indifference on the part of targeted youths to threats of criminal punishment. Also, increased police stops and questioning performed during investigations of possible curfew violations might further strain tenuous citizen/police relations. More seriously, selective enforcement of a curfew could present a very real danger of discrimination, particularly against the many innocent young minority males who match overly inclusive gang-member profiles that are based primarily on race. . . .

II. Applying Theory to Practice: Rethinking Curfews

A reassessment of curfews from a broader theoretical perspective can inform the complex policy dispute and suggest how curfews might achieve the goals of Hartford and like-situated communities. Civil libertarianism, communitarianism, and critical race theory all offer insights into the purpose—and potential problems—of curfews. In turn, an application of the theories to a concrete social problem reveals some of the powers and deficiencies of the theories themselves.

A. Civil libertarianism

Civil libertarianism focuses on individual freedom and threats to that freedom from the potentially oppressive power of the state. The civil libertarian is particularly wary of utilitarian tradeoffs that sacrifice important individual liberties in the name of the public interest or the greater good. Personal freedom can be defended from officials and transient local majorities by defining a sphere of liberty and a set of concomitant rights that, at least presumptively, cannot be abridged. Courts then police political action and uphold those rights through interpretation of the Constitution and judicial review. Particular care should be exercised to ensure that the rights of vulnerable minority groups not be abridged.

Civil libertarianism provides an apt warning of the ways that curfews endanger personal freedom. Spurred by the gang crisis and enacted in the name of the general welfare, curfews restrict free movement and limit the choices available to young people and their families. . . . Curfews put citizens under the watchful eye of the police, who, in enforcing a curfew, monitor the public activity of juveniles and perceived juveniles, as well as oversee parents and the owners of public establishments. In addition, police could abuse the added power and discretion that a curfew provides them to burden randomly chosen individuals or to discriminate systematically against certain groups. . . .

Although the civil libertarian focus protects individuals from state oppression, it remains an incomplete defense of freedom. Civil libertarianism's primary emphasis on erecting barriers to state action offers no guidance for evaluating the potential for curfews to increase the freedom that all individuals can effectively enjoy as a result of revived community life. Because it views curfews primarily as a threat, civil libertarianism is ill-suited to judge how a curfew can serve as a constructive response to the gang problem.

Civil libertarianism's emphasis on liberty also understates other ways that curfews imperil civil equality. That is, curfews seem to disadvantage racial minorities in particular ways even if the curfews preserve the liberty interests of the larger community. To explore these concerns, curfews must be analyzed through theoretical lenses more attuned to issues of community and of social relations.

B. Communitarianism

Communitarianism shifts attention from the relationship between the individual and the state to the relationships between individuals themselves and challenges civil libertarianism's failure to consider the communal aspects of people's lives. To promote these important social bonds in the service of a refined conception of freedom, communitarians . . . stress the need to enforce civic responsibility through law and politics and to counter our current obsession with atomistic and falsely perceived "absolute" rights. Other communitarians . . . remain focused on rights, but deploy rights to ensure full civic participation in public discourse rather than to safeguard individuals in isolated and pre-defined private spheres. At base, communitarians believe that the self is at least partially constituted through social interaction. The challenge for communitarianism is to enable the pursuit of public ends given the lack of a unitary community or moral consensus.

Although some communitarians would emphasize the particular importance of individual participation in collective self-governance, the process of social interaction can occur at many levels. Through confronting each others' views in constructive interchange, individuals become enlightened and communities are able to forge and to pursue collective ends.

At first blush, communitarianism would seem to endorse juvenile curfews. Given the reality of ongoing urban warfare, a law that sacrifices a small measure of individual rights might allow individuals greater effective enjoyment of the freedoms civil libertarians so adamantly champion. Victims of gang violence might even be given a right to enjoy a measure of safety on their streets and in their homes. Curfews enable communities to respond in a constructive fashion to the gang problem by establishing norms of acceptable juvenile behavior and by encouraging parental supervision of children.

Even if curfews enhance public safety, however, they seem to harm community life in other ways. Curfews diminish the vibrancy of neighborhood life by prohibiting youths from being in public spaces at certain times and by directing police to patrol city streets and to stop and question those perceived to be in violation of the curfew. The development of juveniles into members of the community might be stunted. Reliance on curfews and other law enforcement solutions to combat gangs might also dull a community's perceived need to enact other policies and to take additional actions to eliminate gangs or the conditions that breed gangs.

Gang violence itself, however, already stifles much community life. A community-centered analysis, then, suggests that the risks and shortcomings of juvenile curfews must be confronted to preserve the potential benefits of curfews. The danger that a community's capacity to respond to gangs will be dulled, for example, can be reduced if communities themselves deliberate and choose whether to impose a curfew. Curfews nevertheless remain limited solutions. Although curfews might produce a ceasefire in gang fighting and permit community activities that were not previously possible, curfews themselves do not directly spur community organization. To rejuvenate community life, then, curfews must be coupled with other programs and efforts.

. . . Ultimately, communitarianism cannot point to a definitive judgment on whether curfews are good or bad, but it provides a set of criteria by which to evaluate curfews, criteria that civil libertarianism seems to lack.

Communitarianism seems less helpful in fully identifying the dangers curfews present to individuals and even to social life. First, an overly simplistic emphasis on community and the need to promote public safety in the face of the gang crisis can lead to excessive infringements on individual freedoms or insufficient consideration of the interests or preferences of politically weak minority groups. No guarantee exists that a given community will reach consensus on the merits of a curfew, even after extensive discussion, so some individuals' rights might always be infringed. . . .

C. Critical race theory

Critical race theory underscores the fundamental role of race in social relations and how the dynamic of racial inequality informs and is affected by social and legal policy. Racism is a central fact of American existence and shapes how individuals and groups experience the law and in particular the criminal law. The law remains constructed by dominant groups, and racial stereotypes and discriminatory motives often infect the formulation and enforcement of the law.

The protection of civil liberties or formal rights may not be able to remedy racial inequality; if everyone is given equal rights in an unequal system, the resulting outcome will be predetermined. Yet rights can advance minority interests when situated in a considered consciousness about race. Once reconceived, rights are compatible with efforts to advance racial communities and racial identity. Community-centered theories must be similarly reconceived. They have tended to pay inadequate attention to the problems of entrenched racial inequality; the ideal of community deliberation has failed to give weight to the exclusion of blacks and other minorities from the conception of community. Theories that accommodate an understanding of the needs of minority communities can advance those communities' interests.

Viewed through the lens of critical race theory, the initial choice to impose curfews and to devote special energy to cracking down on gangs appears motivated by racial bias or stereotypes. Like civil libertarians, critical race scholars are skeptical of efforts to justify repressive law enforcement measures by pointing to high crime rates. . . .

Once curfews are imposed, the burden falls disproportionately on minority individuals and communities. Police resources are concentrated and curfews most stringently enforced in neighborhoods with large minority populations because that is where gang activity is often highest. Minority youths, who often match race-based police profiles of gang members, are detained and singled out for harassment. Even if minority neighborhoods are made safer by curfew measures, the use of curfews may reinforce deeply held stereotypes of minorities as criminals or as morally inferior and in need of special supervision.

Critical race theory offers more than just a heightened sense of the downside of juvenile curfews, however. A sharpened sensitivity to the relationship between the gang problem, community responses, and the dynamic of racial and social inequality emphasizes that curfews should not be just another effort to criminalize the symptoms of deeper social problems. Evidence suggests that using curfews as part of a law enforcement "war model" against gangs oversimplifies the issues and is not effective in reducing crime. A more complete solution should recognize that there are understandable reasons for delinquent behavior in an oppressed minority population.

. . . [However] critical race theory does not seem to accommodate comfortably the potential benefits that curfews promise—the enhancement of the personal safety of minority citizens and communities. Critical race theory underscores the acute dangers that curfews pose to racial equality but is less apt to recognize how curfews might improve the quality of life for many people. . . . Curfews might disproportionately benefit those who are disproportionately burdened. Critical race theory broadens our understanding of curfews but leaves us with a tension between the racially discriminatory impulses and consequences that underlie curfews and the benefits that curfews promise to minority communities.

III. Conclusion

Civil libertarianism, communitarianism, and critical race theory highlight the complex mix of benefits and costs that curfews present. Together, these theories reveal that curfews can be of marginal benefit in helping embattled neighborhoods rebound. As suggested in particular by communitarianism, curfews can enhance public safety and facilitate community organization. Such a conclusion may be consistent with the analysis of critical race theory scholars who emphasize the need to develop minority communities.

The benefits curfews promise should not be reaped, however, without vigilance to the dangers they present. Civil libertarianism in particular accents the threat posed by overly re-strictive curfews and the need for vigorous judi-cial review of curfew legislation to ensure that curfews are justified by a genuine gang crisis. The warning of civil libertarianism is refined by the lessons of critical race theory—curfews may be overtly or covertly motivated by racial bias and may also contribute to destructive racial stereotyping. These apprehensions can be less-ened but not eliminated if the push to impose curfews comes from minority communities themselves. . . .

The application of diverse theoretical para-digms to the issue of curfews illustrates that it is too simplistic to say that curfews are good or bad; curfews present both possibilities and perils and should be considered as one option in an array of short- and long-term strategies. Con-structive programs that rebuild support struc-tures for young people growing up in urban centers, more than the quick fix of curfews, can enable both individual and community self-determination and avoid an inevitably unsatis-factory balancing of individual and community interests. Curfews, if chosen, should be part of a comprehensive response to the social and eco-nomic ills that beset urban areas and must not become an end in themselves.

Review and Discussion Questions

1. Why do young people join gangs? In your opinion, why are gangs associated with violence? Is the problem of gang violence exaggerated?

2. What can and should be done to reduce gang violence? Are juvenile curfews a good idea? Explain why or why not. What are the strongest arguments for and against curfews? If you support curfews, what age should be set?

3. Do curfews violate the rights of young people? Are they unfair to juveniles who are not in gangs? Are curfews justified on utilitarian grounds? Assess curfews from the point of view of John Stuart Mill's *On Liberty*.

4. Are juvenile curfews good or bad for a community? Can the needs of a community override the rights or interests of young people? Do curfews discourage gang membership or gang violence?

5. What does critical race theory have to say about curfews? How important is race to the issue of gangs?

6. Which of the three theoretical perspectives provides the most useful approach to the question of curfews? How do you think the question should be approached?

Punishment and the Criminal Justice System

WILLIAM H. SHAW

When we punish people, we do to them something that it is normally wrong to do to other people: We restrict their liberty, take away their property, harm them physically, or even deprive them of their lives. On what basis then, if any, can punishment be morally justified? In this excerpt from his book *Contemporary Ethics: Taking Account of Utilitarianism*, William H. Shaw presents the utilitarian approach to punishment and to criminal justice. He explains how deterrence works and argues against retributivist theories of punishment. He concludes by addressing the criticism that a utilitarian approach to punishment might require us to punish an innocent person if doing so maximized overall social benefit.

Study Questions

1. According to Shaw, what is the point of criminal law? By contrast, what do "minimalists" believe? What do "maximalists" believe?
2. According to the utilitarian theory, under what circumstances is punishment justified?
3. In what three ways can punishment affect the future conduct of the criminal? How does it affect the conduct of others?
4. What is Mill's point about the death penalty?
5. What does a utilitarian approach to punishment imply about the severity of punishment?
6. What is the retributivist view of punishment, and how does it differ from the utilitarian approach?
7. Explain the "hanging the innocent man" objection to utilitarianism.

A WORLD OF PERFECTLY MORAL AGENTS could do without a criminal justice system with its police, judges, and prisons, for there would be no wrongdoers to catch and punish. Laws, or at least public rules and regulations of some kind, would probably be needed to coordinate people's actions and direct them in mutually beneficial ways. However, any violations of those laws or rules would be inadvertent or unintentional, the result of accident, error, miscalculation, or minor negligence, rather than malicious intent, gross recklessness, or criminal design.

Unfortunately, we live in a different world. Society needs criminal laws not only to steer the conduct of morally motivated people in socially useful directions, but also, among other things, to restrain those with weaker internal moral inhibitions from injuring others. Society also needs an apparatus to enforce those laws.

Although the details of a welfare-maximizing criminal code do not concern us here, it seems beyond debate that utilitarianism firmly underwrites the core provisions of traditional criminal law. For people's lives to go well, they must be

Reprinted from Contemporary Ethics: Taking Account of Utilitarianism *(Oxford and Malden, Mass.: Blackwell, 1999). Reprinted by permission.*

protected from extortion, battery, and rape, their homes secured from trespass, burglary, and vandalism, and their possessions preserved from theft, embezzlement, and malicious destruction. Not only do such crimes directly harm people, but the fear and insecurity they provoke diminish people's well-being and the quality of their lives. An efficient and effective system of criminal justice is not valuable for its own sake, nor generally speaking does it directly enhance individual well-being. Rather, by making possible a civilized and secure social existence, it facilitates our obtaining various social and material goods that are central to our lives going well.

That the point of criminal law is to promote our collective welfare may seem obvious, but there are those who would deny it. On the one hand, minimalists believe that the purpose of criminal laws is more modest: not to enhance general welfare, but only to secure respect for people's rights. On the other hand, maximalists believe that the function of criminal law is broader: to root out and punish immoral conduct. [Elsewhere this book] argues that utilitarianism takes rights seriously (and, in fact, provides the soundest theoretical account of them), but nevertheless the theory approaches criminal justice with broader goals than just the protection of rights. Not all crimes violate people's rights. Indeed, utilitarianism can justify criminalizing conduct that is not otherwise wrongful (parking one's car on the sidewalk) or that in a particular instance risks little harm to others (the carrying of a loaded firearm by an experienced but nonviolent marksman) if the gains from doing so outweigh the costs. However, contrary to the maximalists, even when conduct is clearly wrong—for example, callously inducing an emotionally distressed person to commit suicide—utilitarian considerations may argue against criminalizing it. The criminal justice apparatus is a blunt instrument, and bringing it to bear on some types of wrongful conduct will prove too costly and intrusive. Whether a certain kind of conduct is right or wrong is one is-

sue. Whether the state should outlaw the conduct and punish those guilty of it is an entirely separate matter.

Utilitarianism makes sense of the core content of criminal law and certain basic and familiar legal doctrines. Among these are the following principles: that laws be public; that they not be applied retroactively; that necessity or self-defense can sometimes justify conduct that would otherwise be criminal; that certain considerations are exculpatory, such as a mistake of fact or the insanity of the defendant; and that various mitigating factors may reduce the seriousness of the crime, as when one person kills another, not with premeditation, but impulsively or in the heat of passion. Putting the legal details aside, the point is that utilitarianism provides solid grounds for these and a number of other well-established principles of criminal law.

The Utilitarian Approach to Punishment

Punishment is the flip side of the criminal law: "If you can't do the time," the saying goes, "don't do the crime." Because of this, we tend to take its moral legitimacy for granted. Yet our practice of punishment is disquieting, and not just because one can question the effectiveness of existing penal institutions. Even under the best of circumstances, whenever we punish people, we are doing to them something that it is normally wrong to do to people. We restrict their liberty, take away their property, harm them physically, or even deprive them of their lives. On what basis, if any, can punishment be justified?

The utilitarian answer is straightforward. Punishment is justified if and only if (1) the pain and suffering (or, more broadly, the loss of welfare) to those who are punished is outweighed by the benefits of punishment and (2) those benefits cannot be achieved with less suffering or at a lower cost to those punished. On the basis of this formula, utilitarians have something to say not only about the considerations that support the practice of punishment in general, but also about what sort of conduct should be criminalized and about the appropriateness of particular punishments for specific types of crimes. However, before we pursue these matters further, bear in mind that punishment is an after the fact response to antisocial behavior. Utilitarians, like other social theorists and reformers, will be concerned not only with society's response to criminals, but also with understanding and confronting the social and psychological circumstances that conduce to crime.

As an institutional practice, the punishment of lawbreakers benefits society as a whole by reducing the amount of criminal activity. It does this in several ways. To begin with, punishment can affect the future conduct of the criminal who has been caught, along three different avenues. First, if it involves incarceration, exile, or execution, punishment removes the delinquent from society and physically prevents him from committing any other crimes for the duration of his sentence. Second, punishing the miscreant can teach him a lesson and discourage him from violating the law in the future. Having been punished once, the ex-convict will be reluctant to risk being punished again and will therefore be more likely than he was before to abstain from illicit conduct. Third, punishment can sometimes reform or rehabilitate the criminal, making him a better person—someone who is motivated less by the threat of punishment than by the desire to be a law-abiding and productive citizen.

It is important to be clear about two things. First, the issue for utilitarians is not whether we can identify the specific benefits of punishing a given individual for a particular crime. That is usually impossible. Rather, the issue is the benefits that come from the general practice of punishing those who violate the law. Second, utilitarianism does not claim that our system of punishment, as it actually functions in the United States, succeeds in rehabilitating very many convicted criminals or in discouraging them from future wrongdoing. The evidence that it does so is slight, and many suspect that prisons, as they exist today, only harden inmates and reinforce a criminal orientation toward life.[1] To the extent that our system of punishment fails to rehabilitate the criminal or deter him from future misconduct, the less likely it is to be justified on utilitarian grounds.

Punishing a lawbreaker not only discourages him from future crimes, it can also deter other potential wrongdoers from committing the same crime. This deterrent effect is an extremely important part of the rationale for punishment and is often singled out as if it were the one and only utilitarian reason for punishment. Deterrence reflects the sad fact that sanctions are necessary to give some people an incentive to obey the law. For example, car theft causes inconvenience, distress, and financial loss to its victims, and the specter of it spreads insecurity and worry. Although the thief profits from his larceny, there is an overall loss of welfare. Other things being equal, the less car theft there is, the better off society as a whole will be. For this reason we have laws against taking a motor vehicle without its owner's permission. Nevertheless, there are those who will be tempted to do just that, for fun or profit. Unless we make it a practice to attempt to catch and then punish car thieves, no potential thief has an incentive to refrain from stealing cars. Thus, punishment not only dissuades the criminal who is caught from breaking the law again, but it also deters those people who would otherwise be tempted to do the crime if doing so brought no risk of punishment.

To be sure, the threat of criminal punishment is not what deters most people from criminal activity. They refrain from stealing, not because they fear punishment, but because they believe that theft is wrong and are strongly disposed not to do it. Abolishing the laws against car theft would be unlikely to cause most people to try their hand at stealing cars. Although the risk of punishment is not what prevents moral people from doing wrong, punishment may nevertheless be one factor in their moral education. It may be a component of a socialization process that has shaped their moral character so that they are strongly averse to robbing, injuring, or killing other people. Punishing a wrongdoer teaches a moral lesson to others. When society punishes someone for a crime, it sends a vivid, forceful, and public message that it rejects certain conduct, and that message can profoundly influence the norms that people absorb. The revulsion that law-abiding people feel toward serious crime and their aversion to engaging in it themselves may derive in part from the vivid association of crime with punishment.

Discussions of punishment often overlook this important utilitarian consideration, but John Stuart Mill saw it clearly. Writing about the death penalty, he refers to the "efficacy of a punishment which acts principally through the imagination . . . by the impression it makes on those who are still innocent." It does this "by the horror with which it surrounds the first promptings of guilt [and] the restraining influence it exercises over the beginning of the thought, which, if indulged, would become a temptation."[2] Mill's argument illuminates an important feature of punishment in general, but it is far from conclusive with respect to whether execution or life imprisonment (or some other punishment) is the most effective response to murder. Some writers believe that capital punishment teaches the enormity of murder more effectively than any other punishment.[3] Others believe that execution should go the way of torture: progress in civilization is characterized by our refusing to inflict horrible punishments even on wicked people.[4] In this view, killing criminals sends the wrong moral message. This dispute turns on controversial matters of social psychology and moral development. Although these elude simple answer, they are of crucial importance for anyone approaching capital punishment from a utilitarian perspective.

Understanding Deterrence

Most people are moral, and except in situations of unusual temptation, the prospect of punishment does not deter them from crime because their consciences already restrain them. On the other hand, some people are hotheaded or imprudent, lack the self-control of normal adults, or are prone to irrational or self-destructive behavior. The prospect of punishment may deter such people only weakly or not at all. For any given type of crime, however, there will be some people who will be deterred by the risk of punishment. Their number will vary with the likelihood and severity of the punishment in question.

Thus, as we have seen, a policy of punishing car thieves is justified because it discourages people from stealing cars who would otherwise be tempted to do so. The cost to the convicted thieves is outweighed by the greater benefit to society of a lower level of car theft. For utilitarians, however, not only must the benefits of reducing car theft be greater than the cost of enforcement and punishment, but we must be unable to achieve those benefits at a lower cost. Because utilitarians want to increase *net* welfare as much as possible, they consider both the costs and the benefits of any policy or practice. For instance, if speeding were a capital crime, far fewer drivers would violate the speed limit, and we would all be a little safer on the road. But clearly the benefit to society of increased compliance with this traffic law would be outweighed by the harm done to the executed drivers and their loved ones and by the worry and insecurity that knowledge of such draconian punishment would cause drivers in general.

If the deterrent effect of two punishments is the same, then, all other things being equal, utilitarianism requires us to choose the less severe punishment. If imprisoning burglars for two years deters potential burglars as effectively as a policy of imprisoning them for three years, then one can justify the harsher sentencing policy only if it provides some non-deterrent benefit. This issue is central to the debate over capital punishment. Does execution prevent homicide more effectively than life imprisonment? In other words, can we reasonably expect the threat of capital punishment to lower the rate of murder? If it does, then executing murderers will save innocent lives, and that fact would provide a compelling utilitarian argument for capital punishment. On the other hand, if executing murderers deters potential killers no more effectively than life imprisonment does, then capital punishment would be difficult to justify on utilitarian grounds (assuming, as most people do, that it is worse to be executed than to spend one's life in prison). From a utilitarian perspective, it cannot be right to increase the harm done to wrongdoers if this brings no offsetting benefit to them or to the rest of society.

If no crime ever went unresolved and unpunished, then relatively mild penalties would suffice to deter wrongdoers. For instance, if every burglary were solved and every burglar captured, even a clement punishment would eliminate any gains to the burglar and make committing the crime pointless. Not all crimes are solved, however, and a calculating criminal might reasonably believe, let's suppose, that there is only a one out of twenty chance that he will be caught and convicted for stealing a car. If so, the punishment for car theft must be at least twenty times more costly to the thief than his gain from stealing the car. This is because the rational car thief will discount the disutility of being punished by the likelihood of capture and conviction. If few car thieves are ever caught, very severe punishments may be needed to deter car theft. Of course, real life is complicated, and thieves do not always rationally calculate the costs and benefits of the crimes they contemplate. Nevertheless, the simple but often neglected point holds that deterrence is a function of both the severity of the punishment and the likelihood of its being inflicted.

In fact, we know surprisingly little about the comparative deterrent effect of different punishments, and some commentators doubt that putting criminals in prison achieves anything that could not be accomplished by less harsh means, such as monetary fines, community service, house arrest with electronic monitoring, intermittent incarceration (on weekends, for instance), or half-way houses with close supervision.[5] Utilitarians will consider and perhaps experiment with these and other alternatives to conventional punishment. They are not wedded to the status quo but, rather, favor whatever system of criminal justice and whatever forms and mechanisms of punishment produce the greatest expected net benefit for society as a whole. Determining this is no easy matter, and utilitarian reformers will doubtless proceed in an incremental fashion, basing their recommendations on the best available empirical data and on whatever insights psychology, social theory, and scientific criminology can provide.

Against Retributivism

Retributivists advance the non-utilitarian thesis that punishment is justified because it is the morally appropriate response to wrongdoing. It is right and fitting that wrongdoers be punished. Having done evil, they should be paid back for what they have done; they deserve to suffer. Retributivists urge that whereas utilitarianism concerns itself with the future effects of punishment, punishment is properly backward looking. It looks to the past, to what people deserve because of what they have done. Just as someone can merit praise or reward for doing something well, so a person can deserve blame or punishment for doing wrong. No further justification, in terms of social benefit or anything else, is called for. Staunch retributivists believe that it is right to punish wrongdoers even if doing so has no positive social benefits whatsoever.

Retributivism enjoys some commonsense appeal, but it is debatable whether desert is the independent moral variable retributivists take it to be. Given an established practice, or within the context of certain rules, people can appropriately be said to deserve the reward or penalties they incur. A prizefighter can deserve to be judged the winner of a heavyweight bout; a basketball player can deserve to be thrown out of the game for an egregious foul. Likewise, assuming that the laws are reasonable and people are aware of them, we can say that, having broken the "rules of the game" by assaulting someone, stealing a purse, or embezzling money, a person can deserve to be punished. Utilitarians have no problem with this way of talking. However, they will insist that desert is always relative to some institutional framework or to some system of rules, norms, or established expectations, which system is itself subject to consequentialist assessment. In their view, desert is not an antecedent or free-standing moral factor capable of showing what laws we should have in the first place, which transgressions we should punish, or what penalties we should mete out.

Likewise, utilitarians can accommodate the point (urged by a number of philosophers) that punishment is justified on grounds of fair play. Criminals take advantage of law-abiding citizens by breaking rules that those citizens have adhered to. In this way, they attempt to benefit themselves unfairly at the expense of others. Society therefore has a right to punish criminals, these philosophers argue, to restore an equitable distribution of benefits and burdens. Although utilitarians do not center their analysis of punishment on the idea of fair play, the underlying point is perfectly compatible with a utilitarian approach. Those who adhere to rules that others get away with breaking may come to feel resentful or aggrieved, especially if obeying the rules requires an effort on their part or if the rule breakers injure their interests. A failure to punish lawbreakers can jeopardize the allegiance of the law abiding. From a utilitarian perspec-

tive, this point highlights another positive social effect of punishment. Like desert, however, the idea of fair play is parasitic on existing institutional arrangements; it does not tell us what conduct should be criminalized, what type of punishment is the appropriate response, or how severe that punishment should be.

Retributivists would dispute this. They affirm, not just that criminals deserve to be punished, but also that they deserve to be punished in proportion to the evil they have done; the worse the crime, the harsher the punishment should be. This is a sensible precept, to be sure, and it is one that utilitarians can easily endorse. Unfortunately, the principle that the severity of the punishment should correspond to the gravity of the deed provides little practical guidance. Some retributivists embrace the ancient tenet of "an eye for an eye," at least in the case of murder. The thought that those who kill deserve to die has to be modified, of course, if it is to accommodate different degrees of murder (first degree, second degree, manslaughter, etc.) or to determine the appropriate punishment for attempted murder. Some people who think that they agree with "an eye for an eye" implicitly assume that execution has a greater deterrent effect than life imprisonment. If they came to believe otherwise, then they might cease to believe that the death penalty is a moral imperative. They would almost certainly cease to believe this if they thought that capital punishment actually increased the murder rate (because, say, state-sponsored executions cause some impressionable citizens to become less averse to killing people in other circumstances).

Some retributivists fear that a utilitarian approach to punishment will lead us to let criminals off too easily, not punishing them as fully as they deserve. Kant, for instance, firmly believed in capital punishment and was vexed by the thought that utilitarian reasoning might induce us to refrain from executing murderers.[6] There is, however, no more substantial ground for this belief than for its opposite, that utilitarians will punish criminals too harshly. For instance, one might contend that if a certain kind of crime is very difficult to detect, then a utilitarian society might have to punish the few violators it catches more severely than they deserve. Or suppose that someone who commits a crime has himself been wronged or abused or received less than a fair share of society's resources; one might argue that the criminal is more sinned against than sinning and thus does not deserve the punishment that utilitarianism might authorize. The fact that some retributivists allege that a utilitarian approach to punishment is too harsh whereas others allege that it is too lenient highlights a weakness of retributivism. It provides no agreed upon framework from which questions of punishment can be systematically addressed. In practice, retributivists fall back on their sometimes conflicting intuitions about what criminals deserve or don't deserve under different circumstances.

The criminal justice system of any advanced society comprises several complex institutions and practices. Utilitarians seek to shape these institutions and practices so as to direct and modify people's behavior in welfare-enhancing directions. By contrast, for retributivists the prime or perhaps only point of these institutions is to see that people get what they morally deserve. But assessing people's desert is problematic.[7] Moreover, retributivists have relatively little interest in the impact that these institutions have on social well-being (for instance, their effect on the overall level of crime and anti-social behavior). This stance seems, at best, misguided.

Hanging the Innocent Man

Retributivists contend that utilitarianism ignores considerations of desert and argue that, as a result, the theory could conceivably require us to punish an innocent person if doing so maximized overall social benefit. To illustrate their point, they ask us to imagine a sheriff in a small town where a heinous, racially inflammatory crime has been committed.[8] The local community is restless and upset, demanding that the culprit be caught and punished. Unless this happens soon, there will be (the sheriff knows) violent rioting resulting in several deaths and much future bitterness. The sheriff has a suspect in custody but learns that he is innocent. Nevertheless, the sheriff could plausibly frame the suspect for the crime. If he does, then the potential riot will be averted, public faith in law enforcement renewed, and widespread fear and anxiety replaced by a sense of safety and security. The retributivist contends, then, that if the sheriff is a utilitarian, he should frame the innocent man and see him hanged because it is better than one man dies than that a riot occurs with multiple deaths. (To make his argument tighter, the critic might stipulate further imaginary details. The true criminal confesses his crime to the sheriff immediately before dying. Unfortunately, there is no other evidence of his guilt, and he is so well regarded and the circumstances so strange that nobody would be likely to believe the sheriff's report.)

To this line of argument, utilitarians respond that the imagined case is too fanciful to take seriously and that the same is true of any other story that one might concoct in an effort to show the utility of executing an innocent person. The example assumes as certainties what are only extremely risky possibilities. For one thing, the sheriff cannot know with confidence what he is supposed to know. He cannot be sure that proceeding honestly and setting the innocent man free really would have dire consequences, nor can he safely assume that no one will ever figure out what he has done. And if the truth ever leaked out, the results would be extremely bad.

Furthermore, the example rests on a naive view of human psychology and institutional life. It clearly promotes long-run utility for the rule of law to prevail and for people working in the criminal justice system to follow established professional standards. Yet we are to suppose that somehow the sheriff (and perhaps others) could decide to break the law this one time and yet on all other occasions be firmly committed to acting legally and professionally. Yet if the sheriff believes that he is right to fabricate evidence when he knows an accused person is innocent, he will surely be tempted to invent evidence against people he firmly believes to be guilty. This is something it would be madness to encourage.

There is another and deeper point here as well. Judicial punishment is part of a larger criminal justice system, and it is the rules and practices of that system that utilitarianism seeks to assess and possibly reform. As a number of writers have stressed, one must distinguish between justifying a practice or institution and justifying conduct within that practice or institution.[9] With regard to the former, there are conclusive utilitarian objections to a legal (or quasilegal) system that instructs or permits its officials to frame innocent people whenever those officials deem it necessary for the benefit of society. The potential for abuse is so great that the contention that utilitarians would favor and attempt to design such a system is preposterous.

Assume that we have a democratic society with a morally defensible criminal justice system in place. Once the legislature has decided what the punishment is for a particular crime, then it follows that although judges may have some discretion in the sentencing of individual lawbreakers (taking into account, for instance, age or prior convictions), their role is essentially to determine legal guilt or innocence and to assign a reasonable and appropriate penalty (within a predetermined range). It is not to calculate what precise social benefit, if any, will come from sentencing this particular person to jail. By analogy, in baseball the umpire's job is to call balls and strikes, rather than to determine on utilitarian grounds whether a particular batter should be allowed extra swings.

Retributivists contend that utilitarianism fails to give moral weight to the fact that criminals deserve to be punished. Utilitarianism is forward looking, they say, whereas punishment properly looks back to what the criminal has done. But we can now see that this contention is simplistic. In assessing different systems of punishment, utilitarians do, to be sure, approach the whole issue in terms of benefits and costs. If they approve of a particular system, it will be on forward-looking grounds. However, a judge within that system looks backward and attempts to determine what the accused person did and whether it fits the legally established criteria of the crime in question. Likewise, other officials will have specific institutional roles to play. For them to ignore both the rules of the system and their own institutional duties whenever they think that doing so is best would have very poor long-term results. Rather, utilitarians will want officials to stick to established institutional procedures and perform their assigned roles as well as possible.

NOTES

1. C. L. Ten, *Crime, Guilt, and Punishment* (Oxford: Oxford University Press, 1987), pp. 8–13.

2. "Capital Punishment," in John Stuart Mill, *Public and Parliamentary Speeches* (*Collected Works of John Stuart Mill*, vol. XXVIII). J. M. Robson and B. L. Kinzer, eds. (Toronto: University of Toronto Press, 1988), p. 269.

3. Steve Goldberg, "On Capital Punishment," *Ethics*, vol. 85, no. 1 (October 1974), pp. 67–79.

4. Jeffrey H. Reiman, "Justice, Civilization, and the Death Penalty" [reproduced later in this volume].

5. Richard B. Brandt, *Facts, Values, and Morality* (Cambridge: Cambridge University Press, 1996), p. 258.

6. Immanuel Kant, *Practical Philosophy* (Cambridge Edition of the Works of Immanuel Kant), ed. M. J. Gregor (Cambridge: Cambridge University Press, 1996), p. 473.

7. If incompatabilists or hard determinists are correct that our actions are determined and therefore we are not responsible for them, then retributivists will have a problem making sense of talk of moral desert.

Their position assumes either that we have free will or that our normal ideas about responsibility are compatible with the truth of determinism. Utilitarianism, by contrast, is neutral with respect to the debate over free will, determinism, and responsibility.

8. This much-discussed example originated in H. J. McCloskey, "An Examination of Restricted Utilitarianism," *Philosophical Review*, vol. 66, no. 4 (October 1957), pp. 466–485.

9. John Rawls, "Two Concepts of Rules," *Philosophical Review*, vol. 64, no. 1 (January 1955), pp. 3–32. Mill, Austin, and others anticipated this distinction.

Review and Discussion Questions

1. What factors are relevant to the issue of whether a particular punishment is an effective deterrent? Besides deterrence, what other considerations might a utilitarian take into account in determining whether a particular punishment, or a particular system of criminal justice, is justified?

2. Do you think our system of criminal punishment as it actually exists today is justifiable on utilitarian grounds? Is it justifiable on retributivist grounds? Should our system of punishment be reformed in some way?

3. Explain and contrast the retributivist and utilitarian approaches to punishment. Which approach do you find the most attractive?

4. Explain Shaw's response to the "hanging the innocent man" objection. Do you find it convincing? Explain why or why not. Are there objections to the utilitarian approach to punishment that Shaw has ignored or failed to do justice to?

5. Assess capital punishment from a utilitarian point of view. Assess it from a retributivist point of view.

The Ultimate Punishment: A Defense

ERNEST VAN DEN HAAG

A long-time defender of capital punishment, Ernest van den Haag, formerly John M. Olin Professor of Jurisprudence and Public Policy at Fordham University, states the case for the death penalty in this essay and answers various criticisms of it. Van den Haag believes in the deterrent effect of the death penalty, and he also maintains that retribution supplies an independent moral justification of it. Critics of capital punishment contend that it is administered in a discriminatory or capricious way. Van den Haag replies that such discrimination is not inherent in capital punishment and that

Reprinted by permission from Harvard Law Review *99 (1986). Copyright © 1986 by Harvard Law Review. Some notes omitted.*

neither its maldistribution nor the fact that innocent people have been executed would justify abolishing it. He concludes by responding to the argument that the death penalty is excessive and degrading.

Study Questions

1. Van den Haag writes that "justice is independent of distributional inequalities." How is this point relevant to his defense of capital punishment?

2. Why does van den Haag believe that the death penalty has a greater deterrent effect than imprisonment?

3. Why does van den Haag believe that "the death penalty cannot be unjust to the guilty criminal"?

4. How does van den Haag respond to the charge that the death penalty is excessive and degrading?

IN AN AVERAGE YEAR about 20,000 homicides occur in the United States. Fewer than 300 convicted murderers are sentenced to death. But because no more than thirty murderers have been executed in any recent year, most convicts sentenced to death are likely to die of old age. Nonetheless, the death penalty looms large in discussions: it raises important moral questions independent of the number of executions.

The death penalty is our harshest punishment.* It is irrevocable: it ends the existence of those punished, instead of temporarily imprisoning them. Further, although not intended to cause physical pain, execution is the only corporal punishment still applied to adults.[1] These singular characteristics contribute to the perennial, impassioned controversy about capital punishment.

---

*Some writers, for example, Cesare Bonesana Marchese di Beccaria, have thought that life imprisonment is more severe. *See* C. Beccaria, *Dei Delitti e Delle Pene* 62–70 (1764). More recently, Jacques Barzun has expressed this view. *See* Barzun, "In Favor of Capital Punishment," in *The Death Penalty in America* 154 (H. Bedau ed. 1964). However, the overwhelming majority of both abolitionists and of convicts under death sentence prefer life imprisonment to execution.

I. Distribution

Consideration of the justice, morality, or usefulness of capital punishment is often conflated with objections to its alleged discriminatory or capricious distribution among the guilty. Wrongly so. If capital punishment is immoral *in se,* no distribution among the guilty could make it moral. If capital punishment is moral, no distribution would make it immoral. Improper distribution cannot affect the quality of what is distributed, be it punishments or rewards. Discriminatory or capricious distribution thus could not justify abolition of the death penalty. Further, maldistribution inheres no more in capital punishment than in any other punishment.

Maldistribution between the guilty and the innocent is, by definition, unjust. But the injustice does not lie in the nature of the punishment. Because of the finality of the death penalty, the most grievous maldistribution occurs when it is imposed upon the innocent. However, the frequent allegations of discrimination and capriciousness refer to maldistribution among the guilty and not to the punishment of the innocent.

Maldistribution of any punishment among those who deserve it is irrelevant to its justice or morality. Even if poor or black convicts guilty of capital offenses suffer capital punishment, and other convicts equally guilty of the same crimes do not, a more equal distribution, however desirable, would merely be more equal. It would not be more just to the convicts under sentence of death.

Punishments are imposed on persons, not on racial or economic groups. Guilt is personal. The only relevant question is: does the person to be executed deserve the punishment? Whether or not others who deserved the same punishment, whatever their economic or racial group, have avoided execution is irrelevant. If they have, the guilt of the executed convicts would not be diminished, nor would their punishment be less deserved. To put the issue starkly, if the death penalty were imposed on guilty blacks, but not on guilty whites, or, if it were imposed by a lottery among the guilty, this irrationally discriminatory or capricious distribution would neither make the penalty unjust, nor cause anyone to be unjustly punished, despite the undue impunity bestowed on others.*

Equality, in short, seems morally less important than justice. And justice is independent of distributional inequalities. The ideal of equal justice demands that justice be equally distributed, not that it be replaced by equality. Justice requires that as many of the guilty as possible be punished, regardless of whether others have avoided punishment. To let these others escape

the deserved punishment does not do justice to them, or to society. But it is not unjust to those who could not escape.

These moral considerations are not meant to deny that irrational discrimination, or capriciousness, would be inconsistent with constitutional requirements. But I am satisfied that the Supreme Court has in fact provided for adherence to the constitutional requirement of equality as much as is possible. Some inequality is indeed unavoidable as a practical matter in any system.† But, *ultra posse nemo obligatur.* (Nobody is bound beyond ability.)

Recent data reveal little direct racial discrimination in the sentencing of those arrested and convicted of murder.[2] The abrogation of the death penalty for rape has eliminated a major source of racial discrimination. Concededly, some discrimination based on the race of murder victims may exist; yet, this discrimination affects criminal victimizers in an unexpected way. Murderers of whites are thought more likely to be executed than murderers of blacks. Black victims, then, are less fully vindicated than white ones. However, because most black murderers kill blacks, black murderers are spared the death penalty more often than are white murderers. They fare better than most white murderers.‡ The motivation behind unequal distribution of the death penalty may well have been to discriminate against blacks, but the result has favored them. Maldistribution is thus a straw man for empirical as well as analytical reasons.

---

*Justice Douglas, concurring in *Furman* v. *Georgia,* 408 U.S. 238 (1972), wrote that "a law which . . . reaches that [discriminatory] result in practice has no more sanctity than a law which in terms provides the same." . . . Indeed, a law legislating this result "in terms" would be inconsistent with the "equal protection of the laws" provided by the fourteenth amendment, as would the discriminatory result reached in practice. But that result could be changed by changing the distributional practice. Thus, Justice Douglas notwithstanding, a discriminatory result does not make the death penalty unconstitutional, unless the penalty ineluctably must produce that result to an unconstitutional degree.

†The ideal of equality, unlike the ideal of retributive justice (which can be approximated separately in each instance), is clearly unattainable unless all guilty persons are apprehended, and thereafter tried, convicted and sentenced by the same court, at the same time. Unequal justice is the best we can do; it is still better than the injustice, equal or unequal, which occurs if, for the sake of equality, we deliberately allow some who could be punished to escape.

‡It barely need be said that any discrimination *against* (for example, black murderers of whites) must also be discrimination *for* (for example, black murderers of blacks).

II. Miscarriages of Justice

In a recent survey Professors Hugo Adam Bedau and Michael Radelet found that 7000 persons were executed in the United States between 1900 and 1985 and that 25 were innocent of capital crimes.[3] Among the innocents they list Sacco and Vanzetti as well as Ethel and Julius Rosenberg. Although their data may be questionable, I do not doubt that, over a long enough period, miscarriages of justice will occur even in capital cases.

Despite precautions, nearly all human activities, such as trucking, lighting, or construction, cost the lives of some innocent bystanders. We do not give up these activities, because the advantages, moral or material, outweigh the unintended losses. Analogously, for those who think the death penalty just, miscarriages of justice are offset by the moral benefits and the usefulness of doing justice. For those who think the death penalty unjust even when it does not miscarry, miscarriages can hardly be decisive.

III. Deterrence

Despite much recent work, there has been no conclusive statistical demonstration that the death penalty is a better deterrent than are alternative punishments.[4] However, deterrence is less than decisive for either side. Most abolitionists acknowledge that they would continue to favor abolition even if the death penalty were shown to deter more murders than alternatives could deter. Abolitionists appear to value the life of a convicted murderer or, at least, his nonexecution, more highly than they value the lives of the innocent victims who might be spared by deterring prospective murderers.

Deterrence is not altogether decisive for me either. I would favor retention of the death penalty as retribution even if it were shown that the threat of execution could not deter prospective murderers not already deterred by the threat of imprisonment.* Still, I believe the death penalty, because of its finality, is more feared than imprisonment, and deters some prospective murderers not deterred by the threat of imprisonment. Sparing the lives of even a few prospective victims by deterring their murderers is more important than preserving the lives of convicted murderers because of the possibility, or even the probability, that executing them would not deter others. Whereas the lives of the victims who might be saved are valuable, that of the murderer has only negative value, because of his crime. Surely the criminal law is meant to protect the lives of potential victims in preference to those of actual murderers.

Murder rates are determined by many factors; neither the severity nor the probability of the threatened sanction is always decisive. However, for the long run, I share the view of Sir James Fitzjames Stephen: "Some men, probably, abstain from murder because they fear that if they committed murder they would be hanged. Hundreds of thousands abstain from it because they regard it with horror. One great reason why they regard it with horror is that murderers are hanged."[5] Penal sanctions are useful in the long run for the formation of the internal restraints so necessary to control crime. The severity and finality of the death penalty is appropriate to the seriousness and the finality of murder.†

---

*If executions were shown to increase the murder rate in the long run, I would favor abolition. Sparing the innocent victims who would be spared, *ex hypothesi,* by the nonexecution of murderers would be more important to me than the execution, however just, of murderers. But although there is a lively discussion of the subject, no serious evidence exists to support the hypothesis that executions produce a higher murder rate. . . .

†*Weems* v. *United States,* 217 U.S. 349 (1910), suggests that penalties be proportionate to the seriousness of the crime—a common theme of the criminal law. Murder, therefore, demands more than life imprisonment, if, as I believe, it is a more serious crime than other crimes punished by life imprisonment. In modern times, our sensibility re-

IV. Incidental Issues: Cost, Relative Suffering, Brutalization

Many nondecisive issues are associated with capital punishment. Some believe that the monetary cost of appealing a capital sentence is excessive.[6] Yet most comparisons of the cost of life imprisonment with the cost of execution, apart from their dubious relevance, are flawed at least by the implied assumption that life prisoners will generate no judicial costs during their imprisonment. At any rate, the actual monetary costs are trumped by the importance of doing justice.

Others insist that a person sentenced to death suffers more than his victim suffered, and that this (excess) suffering is undue according to the *lex talionis* (rule of retaliation).[7] We cannot know whether the murderer on death row suffers more than his victim suffered; however, unlike the murderer, the victim deserved none of the suffering inflicted. Further, the limitations of the *lex talionis* were meant to restrain private vengeance, not the social retribution that has taken its place. Punishment—regardless of the motivation—is not intended to revenge, offset, or compensate for the victim's suffering, or to be measured by it. Punishment is to vindicate the law and the social order undermined by the crime. This is why a kidnapper's penal confinement is not limited to the period for which he imprisoned his victim; nor is a burglar's confinement meant merely to offset the suffering or the harm he caused his victim; nor is it meant only to offset the advantage he gained.*

Another argument heard at least since Beccaria is that, by killing a murderer, we encourage, endorse, or legitimize unlawful killing. Yet, although all punishments are meant to be unpleasant, it is seldom argued that they legitimize the unlawful imposition of identical unpleasantness. Imprisonment is not thought to legitimize kidnapping; neither are fines thought to legitimize robbery. The difference between murder and execution, or between kidnapping and imprisonment, is that the first is unlawful and undeserved, the second a lawful and deserved punishment for an unlawful act. The physical similarities of the punishment to the crime are irrelevant. The relevant difference is not physical, but social.†

V. Justice, Excess, Degradation

We threaten punishments in order to deter crime. We impose them not only to make the threats credible but also as retribution (justice) for the crimes that were not deterred. Threats and punishments are necessary to deter and deterrence is a sufficient practical justification for them. Retribution is an independent moral justification.[8] Although penalties can be unwise, repulsive, or inappropriate, and those punished can be pitiable, in a sense the infliction of legal punishment on a guilty person cannot be unjust. By committing the crime, the criminal volunteered to assume the risk of receiving a

---

quires that the range of punishments be narrower than the range of crimes—but not so narrow as to exclude the death penalty.

*Thus restitution (a civil liability) cannot satisfy the punitive purpose of penal sanctions, whether the purpose be retributive or deterrent.

†Some abolitionists challenge: if the death penalty is just and serves as a deterrent, why not televise executions? The answer is simple. The death even of a murderer, however well-deserved, should not serve as public entertainment. It so served in earlier centuries. But in this respect our sensibility has changed for the better, I believe. Further, television unavoidably would trivialize executions, wedged in, as they would be, between game shows, situation comedies, and the like. Finally, because televised executions would focus on the physical aspects of the punishment, rather than the nature of the crime and the suffering of the victim, a televised execution would present the murderer as the victim of the state. Far from communicating the moral significance of the execution, television would shift the focus to the pitiable fear of the murderer. We no longer place in cages those sentenced to imprisonment to expose them to public view. Why should we so expose those sentenced to execution?

legal punishment that he could have avoided by not committing the crime. The punishment he suffers is the punishment he voluntarily risked suffering and, therefore, it is no more unjust to him than any other event for which one knowingly volunteers to assume the risk. Thus, the death penalty cannot be unjust to the guilty criminal.*

There remain, however, two moral objections. The penalty may be regarded as always excessive as retribution and always morally degrading. To regard the death penalty as always excessive, one must believe that no crime—no matter how heinous—could possibly justify capital punishment. Such a belief can be neither corroborated nor refuted; it is an article of faith.

Alternatively, or concurrently, one may believe that everybody, the murderer no less than the victim, has an imprescriptible (natural?) right to life. The law therefore should not deprive anyone of life. I share Jeremy Bentham's view that any such "natural and imprescriptible rights" are "nonsense upon stilts."†

*An explicit threat of punitive action is necessary to the justification of any legal punishment: *nulla poena sine lege* (no punishment without [preexisting] law). To be sufficiently justified, the threat must in turn have a rational and legitimate purpose. "Your money or your life" does not qualify; nor does the threat of an unjust law; nor, finally, does a threat that is altogether disproportionate to the importance of its purpose. In short, preannouncement legitimizes the threatened punishment only if the threat is warranted. But this leaves a very wide range of justified threats. Furthermore, the punished person is aware of the penalty for his actions and thus volunteers to take the risk even of an unjust punishment. His victim, however, did not volunteer to risk anything. The question whether any self-inflicted injury—such as a legal punishment—ever can be unjust to a person who knowingly risked it is a matter that requires more analysis than is possible here.

† *The Works of Jeremy Bentham* 105 (J. Bowring ed. 1972). However, I would be more polite about prescriptible natural rights, which Bentham described as "simple nonsense." *Id.* (It does not matter whether natural rights are called "moral" or "human" rights as they currently are by most writers.)

Justice Brennan has insisted that the death penalty is "uncivilized," "inhuman," inconsistent with "human dignity" and with "the sanctity of life,"[9] that it "treats members of the human race as nonhumans, as objects to be toyed with and discarded,"[10] that it is "uniquely degrading to human dignity"[11] and "by its very nature, [involves] a denial of the executed person's humanity."[12] Justice Brennan does not say why he thinks execution "uncivilized." Hitherto most civilizations have had the death penalty, although it has been discarded in Western Europe, where it is currently unfashionable probably because of its abuse by totalitarian regimes.

By "degrading," Justice Brennan seems to mean that execution degrades the executed convicts. Yet philosophers, such as Immanuel Kant and G. W. F. Hegel, have insisted that, when deserved, execution, far from degrading the executed convict, affirms his humanity by affirming his rationality and his responsibility for his actions. They thought that execution, when deserved, is required for the sake of the convict's dignity. (Does not life imprisonment violate human dignity more than execution, by keeping alive a prisoner deprived of all autonomy?)[13]

Common sense indicates that it cannot be death—our common fate—that is inhuman. Therefore, Justice Brennan must mean that death degrades when it comes not as a natural or accidental event, but as a deliberate social imposition. The murderer learns through his punishment that his fellow men have found him unworthy of living; that because he has murdered, he is being expelled from the community of the living. This degradation is self-inflicted. By murdering, the murderer has so dehumanized himself that he cannot remain among the living. The social recognition of his self-degradation is the punitive essence of execution. To believe, as Justice Brennan appears to, that the degradation is inflicted by the execution reverses the direction of causality.

Execution of those who have committed heinous murders may deter only one murder per year. If it does, it seems quite warranted. It is also the only fitting retribution for murder I can think of.

NOTES

1. For a discussion of the sources of opposition to corporal punishment, see E. van den Haag, *Punishing Criminals* 196–206 (1975).

2. *See* Bureau of Justice Statistics, U.S. Dept. of Justice, Bulletin No. NCJ-98, 399, *Capital Punishment 1984*, at 9 (1985); Johnson, "The Executioner's Bias," *Nat'l Rev.*, Nov. 15, 1985, at 44.

3. Bedau & Radelet, "Miscarriages of Justice in Potentially Capital Cases," (1st draft, Oct. 1985) (on file at Harvard Law School Library).

4. For a sample of conflicting views on the subject, see Baldus & Cole, "A Comparison of the Work of Thorsten Sellin and Isaac Ehrlich on the Deterrent Effect of Capital Punishment," 85 *Yale L. J.* 170 (1975); Bowers & Pierce, "Deterrence or Brutalization: What Is the Effect of Executions?," 26 *Crime & Delinq.* 453 (1980); Bowers & Pierce, "The Illusion of Deterrence in Isaac Ehrlich's Research on Capital Punishment," 85 *Yale L. J.* 187 (1975); Ehrlich, "Fear of Deterrence: A Critical Evaluation of the 'Report of the Panel on Research on Deterrent and Incapacitative Effects,'" 6 *J. Legal Stud.* 293 (1977); Ehrlich, "The Deterrent Effect of Capital Punishment: A Question of Life and Death," 65 *Am. Econ. Rev.* 397, 415–16 (1975); Ehrlich & Gibbons, "On the Measurement of the Deterrent Effect of Capital Punishment and the Theory of Deterrence," 6 *J. Legal Stud.* 35 (1977).

5. H. Gross, *A Theory of Criminal Justice* 489 (1979) (attributing this passage to Sir James Fitzjames Stephen).

6. *Cf.* Kaplan, "Administering Capital Punishment," 36 *U. Fla. L. Rev.* 177, 178, 190–91 (1984) (noting the high cost of appealing a capital sentence).

7. For an example of this view, see A. Camus, *Reflections on the Guillotine* 24–30 (1959). On the limitations allegedly imposed by the *lex talionis*, see Reiman, "Justice, Civilization, and the Death Penalty: Answering van den Haag," 14 *Phil. & Pub. Aff.* 115, 119–34 (1985).

8. *See* van den Haag, "Punishment as a Device for Controlling the Crime Rate," 33 *Rutgers L. Rev.* 706, 719 (1981) (explaining why the desire for retribution, although independent, would have to be satisfied even if deterrence were the only purpose of punishment).

9. *The Death Penalty in America* 256–63 (H. Bedau ed., 3d ed. 1982) quoting *Furman v. Georgia*, 408 U.S. 238, 286, 305 (1972) (Brennan, J., concurring).

10. *Id.* at 272–73; *see also Gregg v. Georgia*, 428 U.S. 153, 230 (1976) (Brennan, J., dissenting).

11. *Furman v. Georgia*, 408 U.S. 238, 291 (1972) (Brennan, J., concurring).

12. *Id.* at 290.

13. *See* Barzun, *supra* [footnote p. 440], *passim*.

Review and Discussion Questions

1. Suppose, as many people believe, that murderers who are black or poor are more likely to be executed than other murderers. How would this situation affect your assessment of capital punishment?

2. How satisfactory do you find van den Haag's response to the fact, so troubling to critics of capital punishment, that over the years a number of innocent people have been executed?

3. Van den Haag believes that the death penalty is a better deterrent than alternative punishments, even though no statistical evidence supports this proposition. Do you agree? Explain why or why not.

4. Critics argue that the death penalty should be abandoned if it cannot clearly be shown to be a better deterrent than imprisonment. Van den Haag, on the other hand, contends that the death penalty should be maintained even if it is not a more effective deterrent. Which position is right?

5. Has van den Haag ignored or failed to answer adequately any arguments against capital punishment?

Justice, Civilization, and the Death Penalty

JEFFREY H. REIMAN

Jeffrey H. Reiman, professor of philosophy at American University in Washington, D.C., argues for the abolition of capital punishment. Although Reiman believes on retributive grounds that the death penalty is a just punishment for murder, he argues that, simply because something is deserved, it does not follow that it should be done. Torturers, for example, may deserve to be tortured, but it would be incompatible with the advance of civilization for society to punish them in this way. Likewise, Reiman contends, capital punishment is too horrible to do even to those who deserve it—unless execution were clearly proven a better deterrent to murder than life imprisonment, which he argues it has not been.

Study Questions

1. What's the difference between the *lex talionis* and "proportional retributivism"? How is there an affinity between the *lex talionis* and the Golden Rule?

2. How do the Hegelian and Kantian approaches to punishment lead to the "retributivist principle" and, thus, to the *lex talionis*?

3. Even if the *lex talionis* is just, Reiman argues, the question of what punishment we should administer is not settled. Why not?

4. According to Reiman, in what ways is execution analogous to torture?

5. What is Ernest van den Haag's commonsense argument for the deterrent value of the death penalty? What four reasons does Reiman give for doubting van den Haag's argument?

O<small>N THE ISSUE OF CAPITAL PUNISHMENT,</small> there is as clear a clash of moral intuitions as we are likely to see. Some (now a majority of Americans) feel deeply that justice requires payment in kind and thus that murderers should die; and others (once, but no longer, nearly a majority of Americans) feel deeply that the state ought not be in the business of putting people to death. Arguments for either side that do not do justice to the intuitions of the other are unlikely to persuade anyone not already convinced.

And, since, as I shall suggest, there is truth on both sides, such arguments are easily refutable, leaving us with nothing but conflicting intuitions and no guidance from reason in distinguishing the better from the worse. In this context, I shall try to make an argument for the abolition of the death penalty that does justice to the intuitions on both sides. I shall sketch out a conception of retributive justice that accounts for the justice of executing murderers, and then I shall argue that *though the death penalty is a*

From Philosophy & Public Affairs, *vol. 14, no. 2 (Spring 1985). Copyright © 1985 by Princeton University Press. Reprinted by permission of Princeton University Press. Some notes omitted.*

just punishment for murder, abolition of the death penalty is part of the civilizing mission of modern states. . . .

I. Just Deserts and Just Punishments

In my view, the death penalty is a just punishment for murder because the *lex talionis,* an eye for an eye, and so on, is just, although, as I shall suggest at the end of this section, it can only be rightly applied when its implied preconditions are satisfied. The *lex talionis* is a version of retributivism. Retributivism—as the word itself suggests—is the doctrine that the offender should be *paid back* with suffering he deserves because of the evil he has done, and the *lex talionis* asserts that injury equivalent to that he imposed is what the offender deserves. But the *lex talionis* is not the only version of retributivism. Another, which I shall call "proportional retributivism," holds that what retribution requires is not equality of injury between crimes and punishments, but "fit" or proportionality, such that the worst crime is punished with the society's worst penalty, and so on, though the society's worst punishment need not duplicate the injury of the worst crime.* Later, I shall try to show how a form of proportional retributivism is compatible with acknowledging the justice of the *lex talionis.* Indeed, since I shall

* "The most extreme form of retributivism is the law of retaliation: 'an eye for an eye' " (Stanley I. Benn, "Punishment," *The Encyclopedia of Philosophy* 7, ed. Paul Edwards [New York: Macmillan, 1967], p. 32). Hugo Bedau writes: "retributive justice need not be thought to consist of *lex talionis.* One may reject that principle as too crude and still embrace the retributive principle that the severity of punishments should be graded according to the gravity of the offense" (Hugo Bedau, "Capital Punishment," in *Matters of Life and Death,* ed. Tom Regan [New York: Random House, 1980], p. 177). See also, Andrew von Hirsch, "Doing Justice: The Principle of Commensurate Deserts," and Hyman Gross, "Proportional Punishment and Justifiable Sentences," in *Sentencing,* eds. H. Gross and A. von Hirsch (New York: Oxford University Press, 1981), pp. 243–56 and 272–83, respectively.

defend the justice of the *lex talionis,* I take such compatibility as a necessary condition of the validity of any form of retributivism.

There is nothing self-evident about the justice of the *lex talionis* nor, for that matter, of retributivism.† The standard problem confronting those who would justify retributivism is that of overcoming the suspicion that it does no more than sanctify the victim's desire to hurt the offender back. Since serving that desire amounts to hurting the offender simply for the satisfaction that the victim derives from seeing the offender suffer, and since deriving satisfaction from the suffering of others seems primitive, the policy of imposing suffering on the offender for no other purpose than giving satisfaction to his victim seems primitive as well. Consequently, defending retributivism requires showing that the suffering imposed on the wrongdoer has some worthy point beyond the satisfaction of victims. In what follows, I shall try to identify a proposition—which I call the *retributivist principle*—that I take to be the nerve of retributivism. I think this principle accounts for the justice of the *lex talionis* and indicates the point of the suffering demanded by retributivism. . . .

I think that we can see the justice of the *lex talionis* by focusing on the striking affinity between it and the *golden rule.* The *golden rule* mandates "Do unto others as you would have others do unto you," while the *lex talionis* counsels "Do unto others as they have done unto you." It would not be too far-fetched to say that the *lex talionis* is the law enforcement arm of the golden rule, at least in the sense that if people were actually treated as they treated others, then everyone would necessarily follow the golden rule because then people could only willingly act toward others as they were willing to have others act toward them. This is not to suggest that the

† Stanley Benn writes: "to say 'it is fitting' or 'justice demands' that the guilty should suffer is only to affirm that punishment is right, not to give grounds for thinking so" (Benn, "Punishment," p. 30).

lex talionis follows from the golden rule, but rather that the two share a common moral inspiration: the equality of persons. Treating others as you *would* have them treat you means treating others as equal to you, because adopting the golden rule as one's guiding principle implies that one counts the suffering of others to be as great a calamity as one's own suffering, that one counts one's right to impose suffering on others as no greater than their right to impose suffering on one, and so on. This leads to the *lex talionis* by two approaches [the "Hegelian" and the "Kantian"] that start from different points and converge. . . .

The "Hegelian" and "Kantian" approaches arrive at the same destination from opposite sides. The "Hegelian" approach starts from the victim's equality with the criminal, and infers from it the victim's right to do to the criminal what the criminal has done to the victim. The "Kantian" approach starts from the criminal's rationality, and infers from it the criminal's authorization of the victim's right to do to the criminal what the criminal has done to the victim. Taken together, these approaches support the following proposition: The equality and rationality of persons implies that an offender deserves and his victim has the right to impose suffering on the offender equal to that which he imposed on the victim. This is the proposition I call the *retributivist principle,* and I shall assume henceforth that it is true. This principle provides that the *lex talionis* is the criminal's just desert and the victim's (or as his representative, the state's) right. Moreover, the principle also indicates the point of retributive punishment, namely, it affirms the equality and rationality of persons, victims and offenders alike.* And the point of this affirmation is, like any moral affir-

mation, to make a statement, to the criminal, to impress upon him his equality with his victim (which earns him a like fate) and his rationality (by which his actions are held to authorize his fate), and to the society, so that recognition of the equality and rationality of persons becomes a visible part of our shared moral environment that none can ignore in justifying their actions to one another. . . .

The truth of the retributivist principle establishes the justice of the *lex talionis,* but, since it establishes this as a right of the victim rather than a duty, it does not settle the question of whether or to what extent the victim or the state should exercise this right and exact the *lex talionis.* This is a separate moral question because strict adherence to the *lex talionis* amounts to allowing criminals, even the most barbaric of them, to dictate our punishing behavior. It seems certain that there are at least some crimes, such as rape or torture, that we ought not try to match. And this is not merely a matter of imposing an alternative punishment that produces an equivalent amount of suffering, as, say, some number of years in prison that might "add up" to the harm caused by a rapist or a torturer. Even if no amount of time in prison would add up to the harm caused by a torturer, it still seems that we ought not torture him even if this were the only way of making him suffer as much as he has made his victim suffer. Or, consider someone who has committed several murders in cold blood. On the *lex talionis,* it would seem that such a criminal might justly be brought to within an inch of death and then revived (or to within a moment of execution and then reprieved) as many times as he has killed (minus one), and then finally executed. But surely this is a degree of cruelty that would be monstrous.[†] . . .

---

* Herbert Morris defends retributivism on parallel grounds. See his "Persons and Punishment," *The Monist* 52, no. 4 (October 1968): 475–501. Isn't what Morris calls "the right to be treated as a person" essentially the right of a rational being to be treated only as he has authorized, implicitly or explicitly, by his own free choices?

[†]Bedau writes: "Where criminals set the limits of just methods of punishment, as they will do if we attempt to give exact and literal implementation to *lex talionis,* society will find itself descending to the cruelties and savagery that criminals employ. But society would be deliberately authorizing

I suspect that it will be widely agreed that the state ought not administer punishments of the sort described above even if required by the letter of the *lex talionis,* and thus, even granting the justice of *lex talionis,* there are occasions on which it is morally appropriate to diverge from its requirements. . . .

This way of understanding just punishment enables us to formulate proportional retributivism so that it is compatible with acknowledging the justice of the *lex talionis:* If we take the *lex talionis* as spelling out the offender's just deserts, and if other moral considerations require us to refrain from matching the injury caused by the offender while still allowing us to punish justly, then surely we impose just punishment if we impose the closest morally acceptable approximation to the *lex talionis.* Proportional retributivism, then, in requiring that the worst crime be punished by the society's worst punishment and so on, could be understood as translating the offender's just desert into its nearest equivalent in the society's table of morally acceptable punishments. Then the two versions of retributivism (*lex talionis* and proportional) are related in that the first states what just punishment would be if nothing but the offender's just desert mattered, and the second locates just punishment at the meeting point of the offender's just deserts and the society's moral scruples. And since this second version only modifies the requirements of the *lex talionis* in light of other moral considerations, it is compatible with believing that the *lex talionis* spells out the offender's just deserts, much in the way that modifying the obligations of promisers in light of other moral considerations is compatible with believing in the binding nature of promises. . . .

such acts, in the cool light of reason, and not (as is often true of vicious criminals) impulsively or in hatred and anger or with an insane or unbalanced mind. Moral restraints, in short, prohibit us from trying to make executions perfectly retributive" (Bedau, "Capital Punishment," p. 176).

II. Civilization, Pain, and Justice

As I have already suggested, from the fact that something is justly deserved, it does not automatically follow that it should be done, since there may be other moral reasons for not doing it such that, all told, the weight of moral reasons swings the balance against proceeding. The same argument that I have given for the justice of the death penalty for murderers proves the justice of beating assaulters, raping rapists, and torturing torturers. Nonetheless, I believe, and suspect that most would agree, that it would not be right for us to beat assaulters, rape rapists, or torture torturers, *even though it were their just deserts*—and even if this were the only way to make them suffer as much as they had made their victims suffer. Calling for the abolition of the death penalty, though it be just, then, amounts to urging that as a society we place execution in the same category of sanction as beating, raping, and torturing, and treat it as something it would also not be right for us to do to offenders, *even if it were their just deserts.* . . .

Progress in civilization is characterized by a lower tolerance for one's own pain and that suffered by others. And this is appropriate, since, via growth in knowledge, civilization brings increased power to prevent or reduce pain and, via growth in the ability to communicate and interact with more and more people, civilization extends the circle of people with whom we empathize.* If civilization is characterized by lower tolerance for our own pain and that of others,

*Van den Haag writes that our ancestors "were not as repulsed by physical pain as we are. The change has to do not with our greater smartness or moral superiority but with a new outlook pioneered by the French and American revolutions [namely, the assertion of human equality and with it 'universal identification'], and by such mundane things as the invention of anesthetics, which make pain much less of an everyday experience" (Ernest van den Haag and John P. Conrad, *The Death Penalty: A Debate* [New York: Plenum Press, 1983], p. 215; cf. van den Haag's *Punishing Criminals* [New York: Basic Books, 1975], pp. 196–206).

then publicly refusing to do horrible things to our fellows both signals the level of our civilization *and, by our example, continues the work of civilizing.* And this gesture is all the more powerful if we refuse to do horrible things to those who deserve them. I contend then that the more things we are able to include in this category, the more civilized we are and the more civiliz*ing.* Thus we gain from including torture in this category, and if execution is especially horrible, we gain still more by including it. . . .

I accept that if some horrible punishment is necessary to deter equally or more horrible acts, then we may have to impose the punishment. Thus my claim is that reduction in the horrible things we do to our fellows is an advance in civilization *as long as our lives are not thereby made more dangerous,* and that it is only then that we are called upon to extend that reduction as part of the work of civilization. Assuming then, for the moment, that we suffer no increased danger by refraining from doing horrible things to our fellows when they justly deserve them, . . . such refraining to do what is just is not doing what is unjust. . . . Otherwise, it would be unjust to refrain from torturing torturers, raping rapists, or beating assaulters. . . .

To complete the argument, however, I must show that execution is horrible enough to warrant its inclusion alongside torture. Against this it will be said that execution is not especially horrible since it only hastens a fate that is inevitable for us. I think that this view overlooks important differences in the manner in which people reach their inevitable ends. I contend that execution is especially horrible, and it is so in a way similar to (though not identical with) the way in which torture is especially horrible. I believe we view torture as especially awful because of two of its features, which also characterize execution: intense pain and the spectacle of one human being completely subject to the power of another. . . .

In addition to the spectacle of subjugation, execution, even by physically painless means, is also characterized by a special and intense psychological pain that distinguishes it from the loss of life that awaits us all. Interesting in this regard is the fact that although we are not terribly squeamish about the loss of life itself, allowing it in war, self-defense, as a necessary cost of progress, and so on, we are, as the extraordinary hesitance of our courts testifies, quite reluctant to execute. I think this is because execution involves the most psychologically painful features of deaths. We normally regard death from human causes as worse than death from natural causes, since a humanly caused shortening of life lacks the consolation of unavoidability. And we normally regard death whose coming is foreseen by its victim as worse than sudden death, because a foreseen death adds to the loss of life the terrible consciousness of that impending loss.* As a humanly caused death whose advent is foreseen by its victim, an execution combines the worst of both.

Thus far, by analogy with torture, I have argued that execution should be avoided because of how horrible it is to the one executed. But there are reasons of another sort that follow from the analogy with torture. Torture is to be avoided not only because of what it says about *what* we are willing to do to our fellows, but also because of what it says about *us* who are willing to do it. To torture someone is an awful spectacle not only because of the intensity of pain imposed, but because of what is required to be able to impose such pain on one's fellows. The tortured body cringes, using its full exertion to escape the pain imposed upon it—it literally begs for relief with its muscles as it does with its cries. To torture someone is to demon-

*This is no doubt partly due to modern skepticism about an afterlife. Earlier peoples regarded a foreseen death as a blessing allowing time to make one's peace with God. Writing of the early Middle Ages, Phillippe Aries says, "In this world that was so familiar with death, sudden death was a vile and ugly death; it was frightening; it seemed a strange and monstrous thing that nobody dared talk about" (Phillippe Aries, *The Hour of Our Death* [New York: Vintage, 1982], p. 11).

strate a capacity to resist this begging, and that in turn demonstrates a kind of hardheartedness that a society ought not parade.

And this is true not only of torture, but of all severe corporal punishment. Indeed, I think this constitutes part of the answer to the puzzling question of why we refrain from punishments like whipping, even when the alternative (some months in jail versus some lashes) seems more costly to the offender. Imprisonment is painful to be sure, but it is a reflective pain, one that comes with comparing what is to what might have been, and that can be temporarily ignored by thinking about other things. But physical pain has an urgency that holds body and mind in a fierce grip. . . .

By placing execution alongside torture in the category of things we will not do to our fellow human beings even when they deserve them, we broadcast the message that totally subjugating a person to the power of others *and* confronting him with the advent of his own humanly administered demise is too horrible to be done by civilized human beings to their fellows even when they have earned it: too horrible to do, and too horrible to be capable of doing. And I contend that broadcasting this message loud and clear would in the long run contribute to the general detestation of murder and be, to the extent to which it worked itself into the hearts and minds of the populace, a deterrent. In short, refusing to execute murderers though they deserve it both reflects and continues the taming of the human species that we call civilization. Thus, I take it that the abolition of the death penalty, though it is a just punishment for murder, is part of the civilizing mission of modern states.

III. Civilization, Safety, and Deterrence

Earlier I said that judging a practice too horrible to do even to those who deserve it does not exclude the possibility that it could be justified if necessary to avoid even worse consequences. Thus, were the death penalty clearly proven a better deterrent to the murder of innocent people than life in prison, we might have to admit that we had not yet reached a level of civilization at which we could protect ourselves without imposing this horrible fate on murderers, and thus we might have to grant the necessity of instituting the death penalty.* But this is far from proven. The available research by no means clearly indicates that the death penalty reduces the incidence of homicide more than life imprisonment does. . . .

Conceding that it has not been proven that the death penalty deters more murders than life imprisonment, van den Haag has argued that neither has it been proven that the death penalty does *not* deter more murders, and thus we must follow common sense which teaches that the higher the cost of something, the fewer people will choose it, and therefore at least some potential murderers who would not be deterred by life imprisonment will be deterred by the death penalty. Van den Haag writes:

> . . . our experience shows that the greater the threatened penalty, the more it deters.
> . . . Life in prison is still life, however unpleasant. In contrast, the death penalty does not just threaten to make life unpleasant—it threatens to take life altogether. This difference is perceived by those affected. We find that when they have the choice between life in prison and execution, 99% of all prisoners under sentence of death prefer life in prison. . . .
> From this unquestioned fact a reasonable conclusion can be drawn in favor of the supe-

---

*I say "might" here to avoid the sticky question of just how effective a deterrent the death penalty would have to be to justify overcoming our scruples about executing. It is here that the other considerations often urged against capital punishment—discrimination, irrevocability, the possibility of mistake, and so on—would play a role. Omitting such qualifications, however, my position might crudely be stated as follows: *Just desert limits what a civilized society may do to deter crime, and deterrence limits what a civilized society may do to give criminals their just deserts.*

rior deterrent effect of the death penalty. Those who have the choice in practice . . . fear death more than they fear life in prison. . . . If they do, it follows that the threat of the death penalty, all other things equal, is likely to deter more than the threat of life in prison. One is most deterred by what one fears most. From which it follows that whatever statistics fail, or do not fail, to show, the death penalty is likely to be more deterrent than any other. [pp. 68–69]

Those of us who recognize how common-sensical it was, and still is, to believe that the sun moves around the earth, will be less willing than Professor van den Haag to follow common sense here, especially when it comes to doing something awful to our fellows. Moreover, there are good reasons for doubting common sense on this matter. Here are four:

1. From the fact that one penalty is more feared than another, it does not follow that the more feared penalty will deter more than the less feared, unless we know that the less feared penalty is not fearful enough to deter everyone who can be deterred—and this is just what we don't know with regard to the death penalty. Though I fear the death penalty more than life in prison, I can't think of any act that the death penalty would deter me from that an equal likelihood of spending my life in prison wouldn't deter me from as well. Since it seems to me that whoever would be deterred by a given likelihood of death would be deterred by an *equal* likelihood of life behind bars, I suspect that the common-sense argument only seems plausible because we evaluate it unconsciously assuming that potential criminals will face larger likelihoods of death sentences than of life sentences. If the likelihoods were equal, it seems to me that where life imprisonment was improbable enough to make it too distant a possibility to worry much about, a similar low probability of death would have the same effect. After all, we are undeterred by small likelihoods of death ev-

ery time we walk the streets. And if life imprisonment were sufficiently probable to pose a real deterrent threat, it would pose as much of a deterrent threat as death. And this is just what most of the research we have on the comparative deterrent impact of execution versus life imprisonment suggests.

2. In light of the fact that roughly 500 to 700 suspected felons are killed by the police in the line of duty every year, and the fact that the number of privately owned guns in America is substantially larger than the number of households in America, it must be granted that anyone contemplating committing a crime *already* faces a substantial risk of ending up dead as a result. It's hard to see why anyone *who is not already deterred by this* would be deterred by the addition of the more distant risk of death after apprehension, conviction, and appeal. Indeed, this suggests that people consider risks in a much cruder way than van den Haag's appeal to common sense suggests—which should be evident to anyone who contemplates how few people use seatbelts (14% of drivers, on some estimates), when it is widely known that wearing them can spell the difference between life (outside prison) and death.

3. Van den Haag has maintained that deterrence doesn't work only by means of cost-benefit calculations made by potential criminals. It works also by the lesson about the wrongfulness of murder that is slowly learned in a society that subjects murderers to the ultimate punishment (p. 63). But if I am correct in claiming that the refusal to execute even those who deserve it has a civilizing effect, then the refusal to execute also teaches a lesson about the wrongfulness of murder. My claim here is admittedly speculative, but no more so than van den Haag's to the contrary. And my view has the added virtue of accounting for the failure of research to show an increased deterrent effect from executions *without having to deny the plau-*

sibility of van den Haag's common-sense argument that at least some additional potential murderers will be deterred by the prospect of the death penalty. If there is a deterrent effect from *not executing*, then it is understandable that while executions will deter some murderers, this effect will be balanced out by the weakening of the deterrent effect of not executing, such that no net reduction in murders will result.* And this, by the way, also disposes of van den Haag's argument that, in the absence of knowledge one way or the other on the deterrent effect of executions, we should execute murderers rather than risk the lives of innocent people whose murders might have been deterred if we had. If there is a deterrent effect of not executing, it follows that we risk innocent lives either way. And if this is so, it seems that the only reasonable course of action is to refrain from imposing what we know is a horrible fate.†

4. Those who still think that van den Haag's common-sense argument for executing murderers is valid will find that the argument proves more than they bargained for. Van den Haag maintains that, in the absence of conclusive evidence on the relative deterrent impact of the death penalty versus life imprisonment, we must follow common sense and assume that if one punishment is more fearful than another, it will deter some potential criminals not deterred by the less fearful punishment. Since people sentenced to death will almost universally try to get their sentences changed to life in prison, it follows that death is more fearful than life imprisonment, and thus that it will deter some additional murderers. Consequently, we should institute the death penalty to save the lives these additional murderers would have taken. But, since people sentenced to be tortured to death would surely try to get their sentences changed to simple execution, the same argument proves that death-by-torture will deter still more potential murderers. Consequently, we should institute death-by-torture to save the lives these additional murderers would have taken. Anyone who accepts van den Haag's argument is then confronted with a dilemma: Until we have conclusive evidence that capital punishment is a greater deterrent to murder than life imprisonment, he must grant *either* that we should not follow common sense and not impose the death

---

*A related claim has been made by those who defend the so-called brutalization hypothesis by presenting evidence to show that murders *increase* following an execution. See, for example, William J. Bowers and Glenn L. Pierce, "Deterrence or Brutalization: What Is the Effect of Executions?" *Crime & Delinquency* 26, no. 4 (October 1980): 453–84. They conclude that each execution gives rise to two additional homicides in the month following and that these are real additions, not just a change in timing of the homicides (ibid., p. 481). My claim, it should be noted, is not identical to this, since, as I indicate in the text, what I call "the deterrence effect of not executing" is not something whose impact is to be seen immediately following executions but over the long haul, and, further, my claim is compatible with finding no net increase in murders due to executions. Nonetheless, should the brutalization hypothesis be borne out by further studies, it would certainly lend support to the notion that there is a deterrent effect of not executing.

†Van den Haag writes: "If we were quite ignorant about the marginal deterrent effects of execution, we would have to choose—like it or not—between the certainty of the convicted murderer's death by execution and the likelihood of the survival of future victims of other murderers on the one hand, and on the other his certain survival and the likelihood of the death of new victims. I'd rather execute a man convicted of having murdered others than put the lives of innocents at risk. I find it hard to understand the opposite

choice" (p. 69). Conway was able to counter this argument earlier by pointing out that the research on the marginal deterrent effects of execution was not *inconclusive* in the sense of *tending to point both ways*, but rather in the sense of *giving us no reason to believe that capital punishment saves more lives than life imprisonment*. He could then answer van den Haag by saying that the choice is not between risking the lives of murderers and risking the lives of innocents, but between killing a murderer with no reason to believe lives will be saved and sparing a murderer with no reason to believe lives will be lost (Conway, "Capital Punishment and Deterrence," [*Philosophy & Public Affairs* 3, no. 4], pp. 442–43). This, of course, makes the choice to spare the murderer more understandable than van den Haag allows. . . .

penalty; *or* we should follow common sense and torture murderers to death. In short, either we must abolish the electric chair or reinstitute the rack. Surely, this is the *reductio ad absurdum* of van den Haag's common-sense argument.

Conclusion

I believe that, taken together, these arguments prove that we should abolish the death penalty though it is a just punishment for murder.

Review and Discussion Questions

1. Is the *lex talionis* an acceptable principle of justice? Explain. How compelling do you find the Hegelian and Kantian cases for the retributivist principle? How would a utilitarian assess this principle?

2. Can something be a just punishment and yet be wrong? Why or why not?

3. Why has modern society stopped using torture and severe corporal punishments? Should execution be placed in the category of things we do not do to our fellow human beings even when they deserve them? Is abolition of the death penalty a sign of increased civilization?

4. Van den Haag upholds, and Reiman challenges, the deterrent value of capital punishment. With whom do you side and why? Is this an issue about which reasonable people can reach agreement? Suppose the deterrent value of the death penalty remains in dispute and the evidence inconclusive. What are the implications for the morality of capital punishment? Do proponents of capital punishment have an obligation to prove that it has deterrent value, or is the burden on critics of the death penalty to show that it is not effective?

13

ECONOMIC JUSTICE

Rich and Poor

PETER SINGER

After reviewing the seriousness and extensiveness of world poverty, Professor Peter Singer argues that we have a duty to provide far more aid to those in need than we now give. The principle to which he appeals is one that, he argues, we already implicitly acknowledge in everyday life. Singer answers several objections to his position: that we have an obligation to take care of our own poor first, that his argument ignores property rights, and that we should simply write off certain countries as "hopeless" and allow famine, disease, and natural disaster to reduce their populations.

Study Questions

1. What is the difference between absolute and relative poverty?
2. What is the key moral premise in Singer's argument for an obligation to assist? What is the analogy he uses to support it?
3. What is Singer's response to the position that we should take care of our own poor before aiding people overseas?
4. Why does Singer object to an individualistic theory of property rights?
5. What is triage? What is the point of Garrett Hardin's lifeboat analogy?

Some Facts About Poverty

. . . CONSIDER THESE FACTS: by the most cautious estimates, 400 million people lack the calories, protein, vitamins and minerals needed to sustain their bodies and minds in a healthy state. Millions are constantly hungry; others suffer from deficiency diseases and from infections they would be able to resist on a better diet.

Children are the worst affected. According to one study, 14 million children under five die every year from the combined effects of malnutrition and infection. In some districts half the children born can be expected to die before their fifth birthday.

Nor is lack of food the only hardship of the poor. To give a broader picture, Robert McNamara, when president of the World Bank, suggested the term "absolute poverty." The poverty we are familiar with in industrialised nations is relative poverty—meaning that some citizens are poor, relative to the wealth enjoyed by their neighbours. People living in relative poverty in Australia might be quite comfortably off by comparison with pensioners in Britain, and British pensioners are not poor in comparison with the poverty that exists in Mali or Ethiopia. Absolute poverty, on the other hand, is poverty by any standard. In McNamara's words:

> Poverty at the absolute level . . . is life at the very margin of existence. The absolute poor are severely deprived human beings struggling to survive in a set of squalid and degraded circumstances almost beyond the power of our sophisticated imaginations and privileged circumstances to conceive.

> Compared to those fortunate enough to live in developed countries, individuals in the poorest nations have:

> An infant mortality rate eight times higher
> A life expectancy one-third lower
> An adult literacy rate 60 per cent less
> A nutritional level, for one out of every two in the population, below acceptable standards;
> And for millions of infants, less protein than is sufficient to permit optimum development of the brain.

McNamara has summed up absolute poverty as "a condition of life so characterised by malnutrition, illiteracy, disease, squalid surroundings, high infant mortality and low life expectancy as to be beneath any reasonable definition of human decency." . . .

Death and disease apart, absolute poverty remains a miserable condition of life, with inadequate food, shelter, clothing, sanitation, health services and education. The Worldwatch Institute estimates that as many as 1.2 billion people—or 23 percent of the world's population—live in absolute poverty. For the purposes of this estimate, absolute poverty is defined as "the lack of sufficient income in cash or kind to meet the most basic biological needs for food, clothing, and shelter." Absolute poverty is probably the principal cause of human misery today. . . .

The problem is not that the world cannot produce enough to feed and shelter its people. People in the poor countries consume, on average, 180 kilos of grain a year, while North Americans average around 900 kilos. The difference is caused by the fact that in the rich countries we feed most of our grain to animals, converting it into meat, milk, and eggs. Because this is a highly inefficient process, people in rich countries are responsible for the consumption of far more food than those in poor countries who eat few animal products. If we stopped feeding animals on grains and soybeans, the amount of food saved would—if distributed to those who need it—be more than enough to end hunger throughout the world.

These facts about animal food do not mean that we can easily solve the world food problem by cutting down on animal products, but they show that the problem is essentially one of distribution rather than production. The world does produce enough food. Moreover, the poorer nations themselves could produce far more if they made more use of improved agricultural techniques.

So why are people hungry? Poor people cannot afford to buy grain grown by farmers in the richer nations. Poor farmers cannot afford to buy improved seeds, or fertilisers, or the machinery needed for drilling wells and pumping water. Only by transferring some of the wealth of the rich nations to the poor can the situation be changed.

That this wealth exists is clear. Against the picture of absolute poverty that McNamara has painted, one might pose a picture of "absolute affluence." Those who are absolutely affluent are not necessarily affluent by comparison with their neighbours, but they are affluent by any reasonable definition of human needs. This means that they have more income than they need to provide themselves adequately with all the basic necessities of life. After buying (either directly or through their taxes) food, shelter, clothing, basic health services, and education, the absolutely affluent are still able to spend money on luxuries. The absolutely affluent choose their food for the pleasures of the palate, not to stop hunger; they buy new clothes to look good, not to keep warm; they move house to be in a better neighborhood or have a play-room for the children, not to keep out the rain; and after all this there is still money to spend on stereo systems, video-cameras, and overseas holidays.

At this stage I am making no ethical judgments about absolute affluence, merely pointing out that it exists. Its defining characteristic is a significant amount of income above the level necessary to provide for the basic human needs of oneself and one's dependents. By this standard, the majority of citizens of Western Europe, North America, Japan, Australia, New Zealand, and the oil-rich Middle Eastern states are all absolutely affluent. To quote McNamara once more:

> The average citizen of a developed country enjoys wealth beyond the wildest dreams of the one billion people in countries with per capita incomes under $200.

These, therefore, are the countries—and individuals—who have wealth that they could, without threatening their own basic welfare, transfer to the absolutely poor.

At present, very little is being transferred. Only Sweden, the Netherlands, Norway, and some of the oil-exporting Arab states have reached the modest target, set by the United Nations, of 0.7 per cent of gross national product (GNP). Britain gives 0.31 per cent of its GNP in official development assistance and a small additional amount in unofficial aid from voluntary organisations. The total comes to about £2 per month per person, and compares with 5.5 per cent of GNP spent on alcohol, and 3 per cent on tobacco. Other, even wealthier nations, give little more: Germany gives 0.41 per cent and Japan 0.32 per cent. The United States gives a mere 0.15 per cent of its GNP. . . .

The Obligation to Assist

The argument for an obligation to assist

The path from the library at my university to the humanities lecture theatre passes a shallow ornamental pond. Suppose that on my way to give a lecture I notice that a small child has fallen in and is in danger of drowning. Would anyone deny that I ought to wade in and pull the child out? This will mean getting my clothes muddy and either cancelling my lecture or delaying it until I can find something dry to change into; but compared with the avoidable death of a child this is insignificant.

A plausible principle that would support the judgment that I ought to pull the child out is this: if it is in our power to prevent something very bad from happening, without thereby sacrificing anything of comparable moral significance, we ought to do it. This principle seems uncontroversial. It will obviously win the assent of consequentialists; but non-consequentialists should accept it too, because the injunction to prevent what is bad applies only when nothing comparably significant is at stake. Thus the principle cannot lead to the kinds of actions of which non-consequentialists strongly disapprove—serious violations of individual rights, injustice, broken promises, and so on. If non-consequentialists regard any of these as comparable in moral significance to the bad thing that is to be prevented, they will automatically regard the principle as not applying in those cases in which the bad thing can only be prevented by violating rights, doing injustice, breaking promises, or whatever else is at stake. Most non-consequentialists hold that we ought to prevent what is bad and promote what is good. Their dispute with consequentialists lies in their insistence that this is not the sole ultimate ethical principle: that it is an ethical principle is not denied by any plausible ethical theory.

Nevertheless the uncontroversial appearance of the principle that we ought to prevent what is bad when we can do so without sacrificing anything of comparable moral significance is deceptive. If it were taken seriously and acted upon, our lives and our world would be fundamentally changed. For the principle applies, not just to rare situations in which one can save a child from a pond, but to the everyday situation in which we can assist those living in absolute poverty. In saying this I assume that absolute poverty, with its hunger and malnutrition, lack of shelter, illiteracy, disease, high infant mortality, and low life expectancy, is a bad thing. And I assume that it is within the power of the affluent to reduce absolute poverty, without sacrificing anything of comparable moral significance. If these two assumptions and the principle we have been discussing are correct, we have an obligation to help those in absolute poverty that is no less strong than our obligation to rescue a drowning child from a pond. Not to help would be wrong, whether or not it is intrinsically equivalent to killing. Helping is not, as conventionally thought, a charitable act that it is praiseworthy to do, but not wrong to omit; it is something that everyone ought to do.

This is the argument for an obligation to assist. Set out more formally, it would look like this.

First premise: If we can prevent something bad without sacrificing anything of comparable significance, we ought to do it.
Second premise: Absolute poverty is bad.

Third premise: There is some absolute poverty we can prevent without sacrificing anything of comparable moral significance.
Conclusion: We ought to prevent some absolute poverty.

The first premise is the substantive moral premise on which the argument rests, and I have tried to show that it can be accepted by people who hold a variety of ethical positions.

The second premise is unlikely to be challenged. Absolute poverty is, as McNamara put it, "beneath any reasonable definition of human decency" and it would be hard to find a plausible ethical view that did not regard it as a bad thing.

The third premise is more controversial, even though it is cautiously framed. It claims only that some absolute poverty can be prevented without the sacrifice of anything of comparable moral significance. It thus avoids the objection that any aid I can give is just "drops in the ocean" for the point is not whether my personal contribution will make any noticeable impression on world poverty as a whole (of course it won't) but whether it will prevent some poverty. This is all the argument needs to sustain its conclusion, since the second premise says that any absolute poverty is bad, and not merely the total amount of absolute poverty. If without sacrificing anything of comparable moral significance we can provide just one family with the means to raise itself out of absolute poverty, the third premise is vindicated.

I have left the notion of moral significance unexamined in order to show that the argument does not depend on any specific values or ethical principles. I think the third premise is true for most people living in industrialised nations, on any defensible view of what is morally significant. Our affluence means that we have income we can dispose of without giving up the basic necessities of life, and we can use this income to reduce absolute poverty. Just how much we will think ourselves obliged to give up will depend on what we consider to be of comparable moral significance to the poverty we could prevent: stylish clothes, expensive dinners, a sophisticated stereo system, overseas holidays, a (second?) car, a larger house, private schools for our children, and so on. For a utilitarian, none of these is likely to be of comparable significance to the reduction of absolute poverty; and those who are not utilitarians surely must, if they subscribe to the principle of universalisability, accept that at least some of these things are of far less moral significance than the absolute poverty that could be prevented by the money they cost. So the third premise seems to be true on any plausible ethical view—although the precise amount of absolute poverty that can be prevented before anything of moral significance is sacrificed will vary according to the ethical view one accepts.

Objections to the argument

Taking Care of Our Own. Anyone who has worked to increase overseas aid will have come across the argument that we should look after those near us, our families, and then the poor in our own country, before we think about poverty in distant places.

No doubt we do instinctively prefer to help those who are close to us. Few could stand by and watch a child drown; many can ignore a famine in Africa. But the question is not what we usually do, but what we ought to do, and it is difficult to see any sound moral justification for the view that distance, or community membership, makes a crucial difference to our obligations.

Consider, for instance, racial affinities. Should people of European origin help poor Europeans before helping poor Africans? Most of us would reject such a suggestion out of hand: . . . people's need for food has nothing to do with their race, and if Africans need food more than Europeans, it would be a violation of the principle of equal consideration to give preference to Europeans.

The same point applies to citizenship or nationhood. Every affluent nation has some relatively poor citizens, but absolute poverty is limited largely to the poor nations. Those living on the streets of Calcutta, or in the drought-prone Sahel region of Africa, are experiencing poverty unknown in the West. Under these circumstances it would be wrong to decide that only those fortunate enough to be citizens of our own community will share our abundance.

We feel obligations of kinship more strongly than those of citizenship. Which parents could give away their last bowl of rice if their own children were starving? To do so would seem unnatural, contrary to our nature as biologically evolved beings—although whether it would be wrong is another question altogether. In any case, we are not faced with that situation, but with one in which our own children are well-fed, well-clothed, well-educated, and would now like new bikes, a stereo set, or their own car. In these circumstances any special obligations we might have to our children have been fulfilled, and the needs of strangers make a stronger claim upon us.

The element of truth in the view that we should first take care of our own, lies in the advantage of a recognised system of responsibilities. When families and local communities look after their own poorer members, ties of affection and personal relationships achieve ends that would otherwise require a large, impersonal bureaucracy. Hence it would be absurd to propose that from now on we all regard ourselves as equally responsible for the welfare of everyone in the world; but the argument for an obligation to assist does not propose that. It applies only when some are in absolute poverty, and others can help without sacrificing anything of comparable moral significance. To allow one's own kin to sink into absolute poverty would be to sacrifice something of comparable significance; and before that point had been reached, the breakdown of the system of family and community responsibility would be a factor to weigh the balance in favour of a small degree of preference for family and community. This small degree of preference is, however, decisively outweighed by existing discrepancies in wealth and property.

Property Rights. Do people have a right to private property, a right that contradicts the view that they are under an obligation to give some of their wealth away to those in absolute poverty? According to some theories of rights (for instance, Robert Nozick's), provided one has acquired one's property without the use of unjust means like force and fraud, one may be entitled to enormous wealth while others starve. This individualistic conception of rights is in contrast to other views, like the early Christian doctrine to be found in the works of Thomas Aquinas, which holds that since property exists for the satisfaction of human needs, "whatever a man has in superabundance is owed, of natural right, to the poor for their sustenance." A socialist would also, of course, see wealth as belonging to the community rather than the individual, while utilitarians, whether socialist or not, would be prepared to override property rights to prevent great evils.

Does the argument for an obligation to assist others therefore presuppose one of these other theories of property rights, and not an individualistic theory like Nozick's? Not necessarily. A theory of property rights can insist on our *right* to retain wealth without pronouncing on whether the rich *ought* to give to the poor. Nozick, for example, rejects the use of compulsory means like taxation to redistribute income, but suggests that we can achieve the ends we deem morally desirable by voluntary means. So Nozick would reject the claim that rich people have an "obligation" to give to the poor, in so far as this implies that the poor have a right to our aid, but might accept that giving is something we ought to do and failing to give, though within one's rights, is wrong—for there is more to an ethical life than respecting the rights of others.

The argument for an obligation to assist can survive, with only minor modifications, even if we accept an individualistic theory of property rights. In any case, however, I do not think we should accept such a theory. It leaves too much to chance to be an acceptable ethical view. For instance, those whose forefathers happened to inhabit some sandy wastes around the Persian Gulf are now fabulously wealthy, because oil lay under those sands; while those whose forefathers settled on better land south of the Sahara live in absolute poverty, because of drought and bad harvests. Can this distribution be acceptable from an impartial point of view? If we imagine ourselves about to begin life as a citizen of either Bahrein or Chad—but we do not know which—would we accept the principle that citizens of Bahrein are under no obligation to assist people living in Chad?

Population and the Ethics of Triage. Perhaps the most serious objection to the argument that we have an obligation to assist is that since the major cause of absolute poverty is overpopulation, helping those now in poverty will only ensure that yet more people are born to live in poverty in the future.

In its most extreme form, this objection is taken to show that we should adopt a policy of "triage." The term comes from medical policies adopted in wartime. With too few doctors to cope with all the casualties, the wounded were divided into three categories: those who would probably survive without medical assistance, those who might survive if they received assistance, but otherwise probably would not, and those who even with medical assistance probably would not survive. Only those in the middle category were given medical assistance. The idea, of course, was to use limited medical resources as effectively as possible. For those in the first category, medical treatment was not strictly necessary; for those in the third category, it was likely to be useless. It has been suggested that we should apply the same policies to countries, according to their prospects of becoming self-sustaining. We would not aid countries that even without our help will soon be able to feed their populations. We would not aid countries that, even with our help, will not be able to limit their population to a level they can feed. We would aid those countries where our help might make the difference between success and failure in bringing food and population into balance.

Advocates of this theory are understandably reluctant to give a complete list of the countries they would place into the "hopeless" category; Bangladesh has been cited as an example, and so have some of the countries of the Sahel region of Africa. Adopting the policy of triage would, then, mean cutting off assistance to these countries and allowing famine, disease, and natural disasters to reduce the population of those countries to the level at which they can provide adequately for all.

In support of this view Garrett Hardin has offered a metaphor: we in the rich nations are like the occupants of a crowded lifeboat adrift in a sea full of drowning people. If we try to save the drowning by bringing them aboard, our boat will be overloaded and we shall all drown. Since it is better that some survive than none, we should leave the others to drown. In the world today, according to Hardin, "lifeboat ethics" apply. The rich should leave the poor to starve, for otherwise the poor will drag the rich down with them. . . .

Anyone whose initial reaction to triage was not one of repugnance would be an unpleasant sort of person. Yet initial reactions based on strong feelings are not always reliable guides. Advocates of triage are rightly concerned with the long-term consequences of our actions. They say that helping the poor and starving now merely ensures more poor and starving in the future. When our capacity to help is finally unable to cope—as one day it must be—the suffering will be greater than it would be if we

stopped helping now. If this is correct, there is nothing we can do to prevent absolute starvation and poverty, in the long run, and so we have no obligation to assist. Nor does it seem reasonable to hold that under these circumstances people have a right to our assistance. If we do accept such a right, irrespective of the consequences, we are saying that, in Hardin's metaphor, we should continue to haul the drowning into our lifeboat until the boat sinks and we all drown.

If triage is to be rejected it must be tackled on its own ground, within the framework of consequentialist ethics. Here it is vulnerable. Any consequentialist ethics must take probability of outcome into account. A course of action that will certainly produce some benefit is to be preferred to an alternative course that may lead to a slightly larger benefit, but is equally likely to result in no benefit at all. Only if the greater magnitude of the uncertain benefit outweighs its uncertainty should we choose it. Better one certain unit of benefit than a 10 per cent chance of five units; but better a 50 per cent chance of three units than a single certain unit. The same principle applies when we are trying to avoid evils.

The policy of triage involves a certain, very great evil: population control by famine and disease. Tens of millions would die slowly. Hundreds of millions would continue to live in absolute poverty, at the very margin of existence. Against this prospect, advocates of the policy place a possible evil that is greater still: the same process of famine and disease, taking place in, say, fifty years' time, when the world's population may be three times its present level, and the number who will die from famine, or struggle on in absolute poverty, will be that much greater. The question is: how probable is this forecast that continued assistance now will lead to greater disasters in the future?

Forecasts of population growth are notoriously fallible, and theories about the factors that affect it remain speculative. One theory, at least as plausible as any other, is that countries pass through a "demographic transition" as their standard of living rises. When people are very poor and have no access to modern medicine their fertility is high, but population is kept in check by high death rates. The introduction of sanitation, modern medical techniques, and other improvements reduces the death rate, but initially has little effect on the birth-rate. Then population grows rapidly. Some poor countries, especially in sub-Saharan Africa, are now in this phase. If standards of living continue to rise, however, couples begin to realise that to have the same number of children surviving to maturity as in the past, they do not need to give birth to as many children as their parents did. The need for children to provide economic support in old age diminishes. Improved education and the emancipation and employment of women also reduce the birth-rate, and so population growth begins to level off. Most rich nations have reached this stage, and their populations are growing only very slowly, if at all.

If this theory is right, there is an alternative to the disasters accepted as inevitable by supporters of triage. We can assist poor countries to raise the living standards of the poorest members of their population. We can encourage the governments of these countries to enact land reform measures, improve education, and liberate women from a purely child-bearing role. We can also help other countries to make contraception and sterilisation widely available. There is a fair chance that these measures will hasten the onset of the demographic transition and bring population growth down to a manageable level. According to United Nations estimates, in 1965 the average woman in the third world gave birth to six children, and only 8 per cent were using some form of contraception; by 1991 the average number of children had dropped to just below four, and more than half the women in the third world were taking contraceptive measures. Notable successes in encouraging the use of contraception had oc-

curred in Thailand, Indonesia, Mexico, Colombia, Brazil, and Bangladesh. This achievement reflected a relatively low expenditure in developing countries—considering the size and significance of the problem—of $3 billion annually, with only 20 per cent of this sum coming from developed nations. So expenditure in this area seems likely to be highly cost-effective. Success cannot be guaranteed; but the evidence suggests that we can reduce population growth by improving economic security and education, and making contraceptives more widely available. This prospect makes triage ethically unacceptable. We cannot allow millions to die from starvation and disease when there is a reasonable probability that population can be brought under control without such horrors.

Population growth is therefore not a reason against giving overseas aid, although it should make us think about the kind of aid to give. Instead of food handouts, it may be better to give aid that leads to a slowing of population growth. This may mean agricultural assistance for the rural poor, or assistance with education, or the provision of contraceptive services. Whatever kind of aid proves most effective in specific circumstances, the obligation to assist is not reduced.

One awkward question remains. What should we do about a poor and already overpopulated country that, for religious or nationalistic reasons, restricts the use of contraceptives and refuses to slow its population growth? Should we nevertheless offer development assistance? Or should we make our offer conditional on effective steps being taken to reduce the birth-rate? To the latter course, some would object that putting conditions on aid is an attempt to impose our own ideas on independent sovereign nations. So it is—but is this imposition unjustifiable? If the argument for an obligation to assist is sound, we have an obligation to reduce absolute poverty; but we have no obligation to make sacrifices that, to the best of our knowledge, have no prospect of reducing poverty in the long run. Hence we have no obligation to assist countries whose governments have policies that will make our aid ineffective. This could be very harsh on poor citizens of these countries—for they may have no say in the government's policies—but we will help more people in the long run by using our resources where they are most effective. (The same principles may apply, incidentally, to countries that refuse to take other steps that could make assistance effective—like refusing to reform systems of land holding that impose intolerable burdens on poor tenant farmers.)

Review and Discussion Questions

1. Are any people in the United States in absolute, as opposed to relative, poverty?

2. Why do governments and individuals in affluent countries do so little to aid people in absolute poverty overseas?

3. Review each of the premises in Singer's argument. Are they as uncontroversial as he thinks? How large a sacrifice do you think Singer's principle would require of us? What is "of comparable moral significance" to the reduction of absolute poverty?

4. Singer rejects an individualistic conception of property rights, but he also thinks that, even if we accept such a conception, it does not necessarily undermine his position. Assess Singer's reasoning on both of these points.

5. Hardin and Singer disagree about the long-term consequences of giving aid. Whose position do you find the most plausible?

6. Do you see any possible objections to Singer's argument that he has overlooked or failed to answer satisfactorily? Do you agree with him that helping people in absolute poverty is not just charity, but a moral obligation?

World Hunger and the Extent of Our Positive Duties

ROBERT N. VAN WYK

Drawing his inspiration from Kant, Robert N. Van Wyk, professor of philosophy at the University of Pittsburgh, rejects Peter Singer's implicitly utilitarian approach to world hunger. Instead, Van Wyk argues that wealthy countries may owe reparations to poorer countries and that individuals have a duty to do their fair share to alleviate hunger and distress (although their personal ideals may lead them to do more than their fair share).

Reprinted by permission from "Perspectives on World Hunger and the Extent of Our Positive Duties," Public Affairs Quarterly, *vol. 2, no. 2 (April 1988). Copyright © 1988* Public Affairs Quarterly. *Some notes omitted.*

Study Questions

1. What is Peter Singer's ethical approach to world hunger and what questions or problems does Van Wyk raise concerning it?

2. What is Robert Nozick's position and what shortcomings does Van Wyk see in it?

3. What is the point of the example about Bengal?

4. What is Van Wyk's "fair share" position, and how is it a middle way between Singer and Nozick? How does it address the "overload problem"?

A MORAL PROBLEM that faces institutions —especially governments, as well as individuals, is the question of the extent of the duty to prevent harm to other people, and/or benefit them. This is not an academic problem but one that stares us in the face through the eyes of starving and malnourished people, and in particular, children. Estimates of the number of severely malnourished people in the world have ranged from seventy million, to 460 million, to one billion. What duties do individuals have to help?

I. Utilitarian/Consequentialist Approaches

A. The views of Peter Singer and Garrett Hardin

According to some moral theories the very fact of widespread hunger imposes a duty on each person to do whatever he or she is capable of doing to accomplish whatever is necessary to see to it that all people have enough to eat. Peter Singer, a utilitarian, writes:

> I begin with the assumption that suffering and death from lack of food, shelter, and medical care are bad. . . . My next point is this: if it is in our power to prevent something bad from happening without thereby sacrificing anything of comparable moral importance, we ought, morally, to do it.[1]

Does this mean that governments of prosperous countries ought to call upon their citizens to sacrifice enough of the luxuries of life to pay taxes that will be used to see to it that everyone in the world has the basic necessities of life? Suppose that governments do not do this. Suppose I give a considerable amount to famine relief but the need remains great because many others have not given. Is this case parallel to the following one to which Singer compares it? I have saved the life of one drowning person. There is still another person who needs to be saved. Other people could have saved the second person while I was saving the first but no one did. Even though I have saved one, and even though other people have failed in their duty to try to save the other, it would seem reasonable to claim that I have a duty to try to do so. Would I similarly have a duty to keep on giving more to aid the hungry regardless of the personal sacrifice involved? Many objections raised against giving sacrificially have to do with whether certain kinds of assistance really do much good. But such objections do not really affect the question of how much one should sacrifice to help others, but only have to do with the best way of using what is given (for example, for food assistance, development assistance, family planning, encouraging political change, supporting education, and so on). But if we reach the conclusion that we have a duty to do all we can, just as in the case of the drowning people, we are faced with the problem . . . of being overwhelmed with obligations in a way that expands the area of moral duty to the point of obliterating both the area of the morally indifferent and the area of the morally supererogatory.

There are, however, other considerations. What are the long range consequences of keeping people alive? "Neo-malthusians" and "crisis environmentalists" argue that population growth is outstripping food production and also leading both to the depletion of the world's natural resources and the pollution of the environment, so that the more people who are saved the more misery there will be in the long run. Garrett Hardin compares rich nations to lifeboats and the poor of the world to drowning people trying to get into the lifeboats. To allow them in would be to risk sinking the lifeboats and so to risk bringing disaster on everyone. The high rate of population growth among the poor nations insures that even if there is enough room at the moment, eventually the lifeboats will be swamped.[2] The lifeboat ethic is an application of what Hardin calls the logic of the commons. If a pasture is held as common property each herdsman is tempted to overgraze it for the sake of short-term profits. Even the individual who wants to preserve the land for the future has no reason to stop as long as there are others who will continue to overgraze it. Similarly, if we regard the food production of the world as a "commons" to which everyone is entitled we undermine any incentive among the poor of the world to increase production and limit population growth. The increasing population will continually reduce the amount available for each individual while at the same time increasing pollution and putting other strains on the environment.[3] So Hardin writes that "for posterity's sake we should never send food to any population that is beyond the realistic carrying capacity of its land."[4] This view that certain countries should be left to have "massive diebacks of population,"[5] while others should perhaps be helped, has been called "triage."

B. Questions about these approaches

One way of responding to Hardin's argument is to raise questions about the choice of metaphors and their applicability. Why speak of lifeboats rather than of luxury liners? Why should the Asian or African people be compared to the "sheep" who are the greatest threat to the commons when the average American uses up thirty times the amount of the earth's resources as does the average Asian or African,[6] and when the developed nations import more protein from the developing nations than they export to them?[7] How are the lifeboat metaphors applicable when apart from special famine conditions almost every country in the world has the resources necessary to feed its people if they were used primarily for that purpose?

The focus here, however, will be on moral theory. In spite of their very different conclusions, Singer and Hardin both presuppose a utilitarian position that says that what we ought to do depends completely on the anticipated consequences of our choices. . . .

II. Hunger, Respect for Persons, and Negative Duties

Many philosophers, especially those emphasizing the stringency of negative duties, subscribe to Kant's principle of respect for persons, whether or not they are supporters of Kant's moral philosophy taken as a whole. Robert Nozick uses the principle of respect for persons to defend absolute duties to do no harm while at the same time denying the existence of any duties to benefit others. Kant himself, however, maintained that we have imperfect duties to help others. One might still claim that government may not collect taxes for the sake of aiding others, since one ought not to force people (taxpayers) to fulfill imperfect duties when doing so violates the perfect duty to respect the right of citizens to use their resources as they themselves choose to do so. Kant himself did not reach such a conclusion, but Nozick does, arguing that since "individuals are ends and not merely means; they may not be sacrificed, or used for the achieving of other ends without their consent."[8]

Nozick's views can be attacked at many points. Even if they were correct, however, it would not follow that governments would have no right to tax citizens to aid people in distress. This is because individuals, corporations (to which individuals are related as stockholders and employees), and governments would still have duties not to harm, and thus also duties to take corrective action in response to past harms. So wealthy countries and their citizens could still have many responsibilities of compensatory justice with respect to the world's poor. Some countries face poverty because their economies are heavily dependent on a single export material or crop (for example, copper in Chile), the prices of which are subject to great fluctuations. If the original situation, or the subsequent fluctuations, were brought about by policies of wealthy nations or their corporations, then suffering does not just happen but is caused by the actions of people in developed nations. If corporations can strangle economies of developing nations and choose to do so if they do not get special tax advantages, or unfairly advantageous contracts, then poverty and hunger are harms caused by the decisions of the wealthy.[9] If, furthermore, government officials are bribed to keep taxes down, as was done in Honduras by the banana companies, then poverty is directly caused by human actions. If a developed nation overthrows the government of a poor nation which tries to correct some past injustice (as was done when the C.I.A. helped overthrow the democratically elected government of Guatemala in 1954 in order to protect the interests of the United Fruit Company), then poverty is a harm caused by human actions. The decisions of the Soviet Union to import large amounts of grain from the United States during the Nixon administration led to a dramatic and unexpected rise in the price of grain on the world market, which in turn caused hunger. Americans' use of energy at twice the rate of Western Europeans must raise energy prices for the poor. Dramatic price increases by oil exporting nations no doubt meant that people went without petroleum-based fertilizers, or energy to transport food or pump water for irrigation, and so led to additional people

dying of hunger. When petroleum prices fall the poverty of people in some oil-exporting countries is aggravated because of the difficulty their governments have financing their debts—debts which were acquired partially due to the encouragement of the banks in the wealthy countries.

What duties do the wealthy countries have to the poor and hungry of the world? The first duty is not to harm them. While seldom are the hungry intentionally killed, they are often killed in the same way that someone is killed by a reckless driver who just does not take into consideration what his actions might do to other vulnerable human beings, and there is no doubt that reckless drivers are to be held accountable for what they do.[10] In some cases it may be morally justifiable to endanger the lives of people in order to work toward some desirable goal, as it may be morally justifiable to risk people's lives in order to rush a critically ill person to the hospital. But a person who is speeding for good reason, or who benefits from that speeding, is not thereby relieved of responsibility for someone who is thereby injured, for otherwise the endangered or harmed would be treated only as means to the ends of others. Similarly, those who make or benefit from economic and political decisions are not relieved of responsibility for those who are thereby harmed or endangered. So even if we were to accept the view that no individual or government has any duty to aid those in distress simply because they are in distress, there would still be few people of more than adequate means in the real world who would not have an obligation to aid those in need. As Onora Nell writes:

> Only if we knew that we were not part of any system of activities causing unjustifiable deaths could we have no duties to support policies which seek to avoid such deaths. Modern economic causal chains are so complex that it is likely that only those who are economically isolated and self-sufficient could know that they are part of no such system of activities.[11]

With respect to compensating those who have been harmed we do not have to be part of the causal chain that causes harm in order to have an obligation to those who still bear the effects of past harm. If *A* stole *B*'s money yesterday and gave the money to *C* today, *C* obviously has a duty to return it. While in some cases mentioned above decisions were made by companies, individuals and governments still were beneficiaries of such decisions through lower prices and increased tax revenue. Furthermore, it would not make any difference if *A* stole *B*'s money before *C* was born. Consider the following case:

> Bengal (today's Bangladesh and the West Bengal state of India), the first territory the British conquered in Asia, was a prosperous province with highly developed centers of manufacturing and trade, and an economy as advanced as any prior to the industrial revolution. The British reduced Bengal to poverty through plunder, heavy land taxes and trade restrictions that barred competitive Indian goods from England, but gave British goods free entry into India. India's late Prime Minister Nehru commented bitterly, "Bengal can take pride in the fact that she helped greatly in giving birth to the Industrial Revolution in England."[12]

Those who benefited from the Industrial Revolution in England, including those alive today, would still have duties to aid Bengal, just as those who inherited a fortune partially based on stolen money have a duty to return what was stolen, with interest, even though they themselves are in no way guilty of the theft. So it is with most citizens of the industrialized West with respect to the poor of some parts of the world. However, in the light of the complexity of both the causal chains of harm and the causal chains of benefit, we are again faced with a great deal of uncertainty as to the allocation of responsibility for correcting for past injustices.

III. Hunger, Positive Duties, and the Idea of a Fair Share

So there is no doubt that a Kantian ethic would include duties of reparation for harms done to people in the past and that this would be a basis

of obligations to aid many of the underdeveloped countries in the world today, even though it would be difficult to specify the extent of obligation. But is there a duty to help those in severe need even if the causes of the need are not due to any past injustice or are unknown, as may also be true about parts of the world today? Kant does not always treat duties to aid others as fully binding, but whether or not, as one Kantian argues, "it is impermissible not to promote the well-being of others,"[13] it can be argued that it is impermissible not to relieve others in distress and provide them with the basic necessities of life, for this is to fail to treat them as having any value as ends in themselves. . . .

To what extent do individuals and nations have a duty to relieve those in distress? Is there a middle way between Singer and Nozick? Perhaps the following line of reasoning would provide a guideline. An estimate can be made of what resources would be needed to feed the hungry, bring about political and economic change, promote development, limit population growth, and to do whatever is necessary to see that all people have a minimally decent standard of living (or that their basic rights are met). Some formula based on ability to help could determine what a fair share would be for each citizen of a developed country to contribute to the needs of those in distress in that country and to that country's share of helping the people of other nations. To the extent that nations adopt this procedure and make it part of their tax structure a person could fulfill the duty of doing her share by paying her taxes. The ideal would be for nations to do this so that the responsibilities would be carried out and the burden would be distributed fairly. To the extent that nations have not done this (and it is unlikely that any have) what duties do citizens have to contribute through private or religious agencies? . . . In the absence of adequate government action each individual could still make some sort of estimate of what a fair share would be and give that amount (or what remains of that amount after taking into consideration that part of her taxes that are used for appropriate purposes) through private or religious agencies. I am claiming that it is a strict duty or duty of perfect obligation for an individual to give at least her fair share, according to some plausible formula, toward seeing that all human beings are treated as ends in themselves, which involves seeing that they have the basic necessities of life in so far as that can depend on the actions of others. This conclusion can also be supported by a generalization argument. If everyone contributed at least a fair share the subsistence rights of human beings would cease to be violated (since that would be one of the criteria for deciding on a fair share). There is a problem about the applicability of generalization arguments where the efforts of one individual accomplishes nothing if most other people do not also do their fair share. (It is, for example, probably pointless to be the only person who refrains from taking a short cut across the grass; the grass will not grow.) In such cases the failure of some to fulfill their duties may relieve others of theirs. The duty to contribute to the cause of combatting hunger, however, is not of this sort, since one individual's contributions still accomplish some good whether or not other people are giving their fair share.

On the other hand there is the problem of whether the failure of some people to fulfill their duties increases the duties of others. If many are not giving a fair share, does the individual who is already giving a fair share have a duty to give more? The example of the two drowning people suggests that the individual who has done his fair share does have a duty to do more. But there is a major difference between the two cases. Saving people from drowning, in so far as the chances of losing one's own life are not great, is something that takes a minimal amount of time out of the rescuer's life and does not threaten his ability to live a life of pursuing goals he sets for himself. A similar duty to keep on giving of one's resources, even after one has done his fair share, would threaten to eclipse everything else a person might choose to do with his life, for ex-

ample, develop his talents, raise a family, send his children to college, and so on; so that that person would become nothing but a means to meeting the needs of others. The idea of a strict duty to do at least one's fair share seems to avoid the problem of overload (unless the total need is overwhelming) and draws a line at a plausible point somewhere between doing nothing and sacrificing one's whole life to the cause of relieving the distress of others. . . . Of course a person might choose to make the rescuing of those in distress her special vocation, and it may be noble for her to do so, but to claim that if the needs of others are great enough she has a duty to surrender any choice about the direction of her own life is to claim that a person has a duty to be purely the means to meeting the needs of others, and so in fact a duty to love others not as oneself, but instead of oneself. On the other hand, not to recognize a duty to give a fair share is to indicate that one believes either that it is not important that the needs of those in distress should be met (perhaps because they do not have subsistence rights) or that others should do more than their fair share. . . .

IV. Considerations Beyond a Fair Share

If redistribution of wealth were in fact the major need of the most vulnerable in the world, and if in fact government foreign aid programs could be modified so that they could be trusted to meet that need, then . . . I would claim that for the sake of fairness both to those in need and those willing to help, it would be better if everyone did his or her fair share and it would be legitimate to coerce people through the tax system to do so. In the absence of such taxation and in the absence of any official calculation of such a share, individuals generally do not have the information on which to assess their own fair share, and if they did they would probably tend to underestimate it. What most people tend to think of as their fair share depends much less on any informed calculation than on what they think their neighbors, fellow citizens, or fellow church members, are contributing, consoling themselves with the thought that it cannot really be their duty to do more than others. But since most people who do something probably tend to think that they are doing more with respect to their resources than others, the idea of a duty to do a fair share is in danger of succumbing to a downward pressure to require less and less. If the vulnerable are to be protected then perhaps doing one's fair share to meet their needs is not the only duty. Rather there must also be a duty to put upward pressure on the prevailing idea of a fair share. This can be done only by those who do considerably more than what is perceived of as a fair share, and often more than an actual fair share. This is embodied in Christian ethics in the ideal of being a light to witness to a higher and more demanding way of life and in the ideal of being the salt of the earth that preserves it from decay, perhaps primarily the decay brought about by downward pressure on prevailing standards.[14] Probably a secular counterpart to these ideals would be accepted by others.

There are doubts about whether redistribution of wealth is the major need, as opposed to various changes in policies, including trade policies. There are also grave doubts concerning the degree to which government aid in the past has really benefited the most vulnerable and about its prospects of doing so in the future. That raises the possibility that the major duty individuals have is that of exerting pressure on government to make sure that policies do protect the vulnerable. . . . Giving one's fair share to help those in need accomplishes some good whether or not others are cooperating by doing their share. In the matter of influencing legislation an insufficient number of people doing their fair share (with respect to all who might participate in the effort) may accomplish nothing. Does the failure of enough others to do their fair share release one from one's duty to work for change (as it may release one from the

duty not to walk on the grass)? If so, the vulnerable are left without protection. Or does such a failure impose a duty on others to do as much as possible (as in the case of saving drowning people), so that we could again be faced with the problem of overload? . . . Perhaps there is no precise answer to the question of just how much more money or effort than prevailing standards require one "ought" to devote to the cause here being considered, since this may be a matter of living up to an ideal rather than fulfilling a perfect duty to a specific individual, or a perfect duty of doing a fair share. Even in the absence of any way of determining what a fair share might be one can attempt to live by this ideal by doing significantly more than the society as a whole generally thinks is required. . . .

V. Postscript: Additional Kantian Reflections on Duties to Others

There are still a number of things to be taken into consideration. Kant says that a person should "not push the expenditure of his means in beneficence . . . to the point where he would finally need the beneficence of others."[15] That could be regarded as treating others as a means to one's own end of trying to achieve some kind of sainthood. Secondly, help should not be given in a manner or to an extent that reduces the ability of the person (or group) that is helped to be self-reliant and self-determining. It is doubtful whether the wealthy have ever given too much help to the poor, but they have sometimes (perhaps frequently) given in a manner which made the recipients more dependent in the long run, for example, in a way that reduced the incentives of local farmers to increase production. Thirdly, according to Kant, every effort must be made to "carefully avoid any appearance of intending to obligate the other person, lest he (the giver) not render a true benefit, inasmuch as by his act he expresses that he wants to lay an obligation upon the receiver."[16] Presumably nations such as the United States can and do give aid for ulterior purposes, such as to get rid of agricultural surpluses, help farm prices, gain political influence, or to stimulate markets and/or a favorable climate of investment for U.S. companies, but then citizens of these nations ought not congratulate themselves on their generosity (as Americans often do). Such acts are not acts of beneficence and from Kant's point of view they have no moral worth since they are not done for the sake of duty, nor are they done from other motives that might be regarded as being other than morally neutral.

Fourthly, there are conditions under which it could be argued that a wealthy country has the right to refuse to give aid, other than emergency disaster aid, if it is not something that is owed as reparations. Suppose that achieving the goal of advancing the self-sufficiency and self-determination of a nation depends in part on the receiving nation's own effort to make necessary changes such as redistributing land, bringing population growth under control, and so on. It could be argued that if the receiving nation fails to make a good-faith effort to bring about these changes, and if it then asks for additional aid, the developed country may legitimately claim that it is being used, and its people are being used, solely as means to the ends of the underdeveloped country or its people. The major problem with using this line of argument is that the people who are facing hunger may have little to say about the decisions of their government. That problem, however, does not prevent the aid-giving country from legitimately making demands for reform in advance, from doing what it can to see to it that they are carried out, and from threatening sanctions other than those that would increase the deprivation of hungry people. Perhaps it has seldom, if ever, happened that a developed nation has given enough non-military aid to an underdeveloped nation to be in a position to dictate what steps the receiving nation should take to improve the ability of its people to be self-sufficient; or perhaps it has been in the interest of the political

strategy, military effort, or business investment of the developed nations not to demand that specific remedial steps be taken on the part of the receiving country; but it would seem to be legitimate to make such demands.

NOTES

1. Peter Singer, "Famine, Affluence, and Morality," *Philosophy and Public Affairs,* vol. 1 (1972), p. 231.

2. Garrett Hardin, "Lifeboat Ethics: The Case Against Helping the Poor," *Psychology Today,* vol. 8 (1974), pp. 38–43, 123–126.

3. Garrett Hardin, "The Tragedy of the Commons," *Science,* vol. 102 (1968), pp. 1243–1248.

4. Garrett Hardin, "Carrying Capacity as an Ethical Concept," in George R. Lucas and Thomas W. Ogletree (eds.), *Lifeboat Ethics: The Moral Dilemmas of World Hunger* (New York: Harper and Row, 1976), p. 131.

5. Part of the title of an article by Garrett Hardin, "Another Face of Bioethics: The Case for Massive 'Diebacks' of Population," *Modern Medicine,* vol. 65 (March 1, 1975).

6. Paul Verghese, "Muddled Metaphors," in Lucas and Ogletree, *op. cit.,* p. 152. While changes in cattle production and eating habits may have brought some changes, at one time it was estimated that the average American citizen consumed 1,850 pounds of grain a year directly and through meat production, compared to 400 pounds in poor countries. . . . It was also estimated that the United States used as much energy for its air-conditioners as the billion people of China used for all purposes and that the United States wasted as much energy as Japan used.

7. U.N.'s *Handbook of International Trade and Development Statistics,* 1972; and U.N.'s *Monthly Bulletin of Statistics,* July 1975 and Feb. 1976; both cited by Ronald J. Sidor, *Rich Christians in an Age of Hunger* (Downers Grove, Ill.: Inter-varsity Press, 1977), p. 154; U.S. Bureau of the Census, *Statistical Abstract of the U.S.,* 1976, pp. 818, 820, cited by Sidor, p. 156. Protein is imported in the form of oilseed, oilseed products, and fish meal while grain is exported.

8. Robert Nozick, *Anarchy, State, and Utopia* (New York: Basic Books, Inc., 1974), p. 31

9. As occurred in Panama, Honduras, and Costa Rica at the hands of the fruit and banana import companies, United Brands, Castle and Cooke, and Del Monte.

10. There are, of course, still problems with the moral relevance of different sorts of causal relation-

ships between past actions and harm to others. Have Western nations incurred special obligations to do something about poverty and hunger because they encouraged population growth by providing medicine and sanitation without dealing with the birth rate? If advantages to some countries and disadvantages to others are a byproduct of chance conditions and the operation of the free market system, do those who have benefited from these conditions have duties to those who were harmed? (For example, in 1968 it cost Brazil 45 bags of coffee to buy one U.S. jeep as compared to 14 in 1954. [Pierre Ghedo, *Why Is the Third World Poor?* (Maryknoll, N.Y.: Orbis Books, 1973), p. 64.])

11. Onora Nell, "Lifeboat Earth," *Philosophy and Public Affairs,* vol. 4 (1975), p. 286.

12. Arthur Simon, *Bread for the World* (New York: Paulist Press, 1975), p. 41.

13. Alan Donagan, *Theory of Morality* (Chicago: University of Chicago Press, 1977), p. 85.

14. See *Matthew* 5:6, 13–18, 20, 46–48.

15. Immanuel Kant, *Metaphysics of Morals,* tr. by John Ladd (Indianapolis: Bobbs-Merrill Co., 1965), p. 118 (454).

16. *Ibid.* (453).

Review and Discussion Questions

1. Should the moral problem of world hunger be approached from a utilitarian/consequentialist perspective? What is Kantian about Van Wyk's ethical orientation? How does his approach differ from Singer's?

2. Robert Nozick uses Kant's principle of moral respect to defend his own position. What is Nozick's position, and is it true to Kant's moral philosophy?

3. Can a country today owe reparation to another country because of wrongs done in the past?

4. Assess Van Wyk's claim that we have a strict duty to do our fair share to alleviate hunger. What does this imply in practice? What exactly is our fair share? What if others are not doing their fair share?

5. Van Wyk writes that we also have "a duty to put upward pressure on the prevailing idea of a fair share." What does this statement mean, and what are its implications? Should one do more than his or her fair share? Would a morally good person do so?

6. When, if ever, does a wealthy country have a right to refuse to aid a poorer country?

Property and Global Justice

RICHARD T. DE GEORGE

The question of who properly owns the resources of the world is frequently raised. In this essay, Richard T. De George, professor of philosophy at the University of Kansas, distinguishes two basic answers. De George is critical of both and argues that the issue is not really one of property or ownership but rather of basic human

Reprinted by permission from Philosophy in Context, *vol. 15. Copyright © 1985 Cleveland State University. Some section titles added.*

rights. All persons deserve and are entitled to what is necessary for living in dignity, and this right takes precedence over property rights. Although global justice is based on the rights of individuals, nations can claim an indirect right to development. De George explains what this right involves and examines some of the obstacles to achieving global justice.

Study Questions

1. What are the two conflicting moral intuitions many people have when considering the question of who rightly owns the natural resources of the world?

2. What is the "status quo" view, and what are its implications?

3. What does De George see as the strengths and weaknesses of the "universal ownership" view?

4. What are the different types of justice that De George distinguishes? What does he mean when he writes that there is no distributive justice on a global level but that there is a sense in which there should be?

5. According to De George, what basic rights do people have? What does he mean by a "right to access"?

6. On what prior obligation of the individual does the positive obligation of others to satisfy his or her basic rights depend?

7. What three things are involved in a nation's claiming a right to development?

8. How is national sovereignty an obstacle to global justice?

WHO PROPERLY OWNS the resources of the world? The question is being increasingly raised and stridently answered. Yet, despite the question's simple appearance, it is a complex one to which no easy answer is both appropriate and possible.

The question of who rightly owns the natural resources of the world is sometimes considered a question about property. The moral intuitions of many people facing the question in this form are ambivalent. On the one hand, the natural resources of most of the world have been divided up and nations and individuals seem to hold legitimate claims to what they have. On the other hand, the resources of the world can be said to belong to everyone; the world is mankind's to use, and it seems appropriate that all mankind benefit from its riches. Both intuitions have a certain amount of force to them, and articulate spokesmen have defended them. Can the two intuitions be reconciled, or can the

force of each at least be given its due? I shall argue that these intuitions can be reconciled if we interpret the original question not as one about property, but as a question of rights and of equal access to the resources of the world.

The Status Quo View of Resources

The first intuition is embodied in the common-sense view that the resources of the world have already been divided up. Governments, corporations, and individuals own them. It is futile to inquire about the original allocation of resources or to deny the reality of present ownership. However resources are defined, property comes into existence only in society and always in a certain socio-economic system. The world is divided into countries, each of which makes territorial claims. Most of these are not challenged by others, even though a few areas and borders are in dispute. Each of the countries has within it some government and some economic order. Ownership means different things in different societies, and claims and rights are treated differently in different countries. In some, individuals or groups are allowed to own land, minerals, factories; in others only the government owns these. In all systems, however, some food and some goods are produced and distributed; some services are available and enjoyed. Each system has a mechanism for deciding when the ownership rights it recognizes have been violated, and procedures for deciding how to allocate them when there is a dispute. Justice, according to this view, means abiding by the rules and procedures governing those within the system. This is usually equated with legality.

Thus, the oil in the Soviet Union belongs to the Soviet Union, the oil in the United States belongs to the United States, the oil in Arabia belongs to Arabia, and the oil in Mexico belongs to Mexico. In each of these countries, the oil may be further divided and the legal property rights assigned. In all the countries individuals wishing gasoline for a car must pay for it. Any attempt to claim that Mexico's oil does not belong to Mexico but to all the people of the earth would be met with immediate, fierce, and legitimate resistance. For according to the rules by which Mexico and the whole rest of the world abide, the oil is Mexico's.

The question of ownership, allocation, and use of natural resources on a global scale does not, as the Marxist asserts, hinge on private versus social ownership. Rich countries include some that are socialist as well as so-called capitalist ones, just as the poor countries include both. The Soviet Union has and claims the oil in the Soviet Union in the same way that the United States claims the oil in the United States. Chad, which has no oil, has a recognized claim on neither Soviet nor American oil. The legitimacy of any claim it may have is not dependent on the presence or absence of private property, nor on the presence or absence of social property. Nor is

the issue of the allocation of goods and resources primarily an issue of power, although it is frequently put in that mode. If power were truly in the hands of the people of either the United States or the Soviet Union, it is not clear that the approach of either to the Third World countries or of the Third World countries to them would be different from what it is now.

The status quo view resists any property claims by resource-poor countries on the resources of other countries.

The Universal Ownership View

The status quo view is attacked, however, by those who claim that the present division of the world's resources is unjust. The distribution of resources is arbitrary. Some countries have very few while others have a great many. The second intuition with which we started now comes into play. From a moral point of view the natural distribution can be taken as the starting point; but it must be corrected. Originally the goods of the earth belonged in common to all, and all people retain a claim on the earth's resources despite arbitrary divisions and allocations that some people have introduced.

What does it mean, however, to say that the resources of the earth belong to everyone? In one sense something can belong to everyone if each person has a right to its use and no one has a right to exclude anyone else from its use. Thus a public park might be said to belong to all the people. Anyone who wants can use the park as a park. But there are limits on the use one can make of it; and the obligation to maintain it must somehow be assigned.

A second sense in which all land, resources, and productive property may belong to everyone is the sense in which each has the equal right to appropriate and use, and in the process consume, the item in question. If everyone in a society owns the wheat grown in that country, then everyone has a claim on an equal or fair share of the grain. The grain does not belong to the farmers who grow it or to the people who process it or to those who distribute it. It belongs to all and all are entitled to a fair, and other things being the same, an equal share. This would also be true of the mineral resources of a land.

Yet it would be a vacuous right or type of ownership if the iron in the ground belonged to everyone and this meant that everyone had the right to go to where it is, dig it up, and use it. Most people do not live near iron deposits, and do not need iron ore. What they need and want are products made from iron. Their ownership of the iron in the ground, to be effective, must mean a right or claim on that iron such that they eventually get the iron products they need. In practice this will mean that some people will have the right and obligation to mine the ore, to smelt it, to process it, to turn it into goods. At each stage only certain people will have the right to access and to work on the material. It is unlikely that anyone who wished, anywhere along the line, could take what he wanted because everything belongs to everyone. One reason is that since there is scarcity, although everything may belong to everyone in the society, it must be apportioned so that each gets his fair share. To allow anyone to take anything at any time would interfere with the fair allocation. In this sense, saying that everything belongs to everyone means that each of us has a certain claim on a certain portion of what is available.

Clearly if we are to have a society of any complexity, there will have to be rules and regulations about allocation, production, work, and the distribution of goods. How allocation, production, and distribution are to be carried out in a society in which all property is socially owned is far from clear, since thus far socially owned property has been more or less equal to government-owned property. Whether on a large scale there is any alternative, such as true social ownership without government, is at best problematic. But even if it were achieved, individuals would still have different bundles of rights with respect to different goods.

Defenders of the universal ownership view have no clear plan for world-wide redistribution; but they defend the need for this redistribution nonetheless. They argue that national sovereignty stands in the way of a world-wide just distribution of natural resources. Hence, sovereignty is to this extent morally arbitrary and should be superseded. The argument, even if it could be made out, is not soon to be accepted by the people of any country today—rich or poor. Nor is it clear what would replace national sovereignty and how a just allocation of natural resources would be accomplished without sovereign states.

Justice and the Contending Intuitions

Each of the positions characterized by the conflicting intuitions contains a view of property and a view of justice. The strength of the first intuition stems from its correct description of the existing division of the resources of the world, the existence of sovereign states, and the allocation of property rights within each of them. Just as the notion of what property is depends on the bundle of rights recognized within a society, so the notion of what constitutes justice with respect to property depends on the structures of a given society. The weakness of the position is that its notions hinge on the status quo of each nation; because it is difficult to extrapolate from these to any global notion of property or justice does not mean any such view is nonsense. The strength of the universal ownership view is its moral insight that natural resources are distributed by nature arbitrarily and that such arbitrariness does not morally justify ownership claims. There *is* a sense in which the world and its resources belong to everyone. The weakness of the position is that in the concrete it is difficult to give much meaning to the universal ownership claims, and in today's world there is no agreed upon sense of justice on a global scale that can be used as a basis for reallocation.

The conflict of these two intuitions necessitates a closer look at both justice and property claims if we are to find a way out of the dilemma they pose.

Justice can be defined initially, following Aristotle, as giving each person his due. What constitutes one's due may be decided in many ways. If we speak of justice within a system, as the status quo position does, justice is in part determined by the rules of the society, which make certain kinds of transactions possible. If the rules set up a system whereby one pays for goods, then it is just to give someone the equivalent value for the goods received. Justice in this sense is similar to property in that it exists within a given system at a specific time and place.

Yet we can say of some systems that they are unjust. Thus we can say slavery is unjust because it deprives human beings of the freedom and dignity they are due as human beings. Whether or not ancient slavery could be justified, at the present time slavery cannot be justified. Within the slave system some transactions were considered fair or just and one might even speak of the just or fair price for a given slave.

Since it is possible to make some judgments about systems or societies irrespective of the social system from which we speak, it may be possible to make global judgments of justice.

Commutative justice governs transactions between individuals within a society, and transactions between individuals or groups of different societies, as well as international trade. Commutative justice consists of two sides freely trading equals for equals. Injustice consists either of one side's forcing an exchange or of trading unequals. One form of such injustice is exploitation, which might be practiced either within a society or by one society or people on another.

Compensatory justice consists in making compensation for a previous harm or injustice. Thus the victims of exploitation deserve compensation for the harm they have suffered. This is true within a society as well as between societies.

Both of these types of justice are compatible with the status quo and with the existence of nation states. Both can be applied internationally. Neither is directly pertinent to the question of who properly owns the resources of the world. That question falls under the domain of distributive justice.

Distributive justice in its most commonly used sense consists of a government or society distributing in some fair way benefits and burdens to its members. It is because its members are united by common bonds, social structures, culture, and government that within a society both benefits and burdens are distributed. Different societies, which distribute benefits and burdens in different ways through a variety of background institutions, might each realize distributive justice to a rather high degree. The distribution in contemporary societies is typically governed by law and administered by government.

While commutative and compensatory justice operate both within and between societies (we can call the latter international justice), distributive justice to the extent that it requires global background distributive institutions does not operate on a global scale because there are insufficient background institutions and no distribution mechanism for distributing benefits and burdens on a global scale. Under the present division of the world into nation states, the status quo view correctly says that there is no distributive justice on a global level—nor is there any global distributive injustice—since the conditions for any redistribution are lacking. This is a descriptive statement. Yet there is a sense in which we can say that just as burdens and benefits are distributed within a society, so they *should* be distributed globally. In that sense we can say there should be global distributive justice. This is very close to the claim that the resources of the world by right belong to everyone. Yet there are important differences.

The Right to Universal Access

Although the natural distribution of resources is arbitrary, from a moral point of view what is done with the resources is not arbitrary. The riches of the earth should be used for the benefit of all. This is a correct insight of the universal ownership view. But the heart of the dispute between rich and poor countries does not hinge on the ownership of land or resources, even though it is sometimes couched in those terms. Ownership and property claims obscure rather than clarify what is really at issue. The question to whom the resources of the world properly belong, as it is frequently posed today, is a rhetorical question. The question is not really about property but about human rights.

Each just society should recognize the fundamental respect due to human beings as members of the society and their fundamental equality as moral beings. All persons deserve and are entitled to what is necessary for living in dignity. Their basic entitlements are the right to life, the right to respect, the right to satisfy their basic needs, and the right to access to what is necessary to develop their potentialities. These rights are not maximal ideals but minimal entitlements. Fulfillment of these basic rights is compatible with different societies being at different stages of development and enjoying different standards of living.

These basic rights, moreover, take precedence over property rights, however defined or specified. The reason is that the right to life and minimal sustenance at the human level are more fundamental than property.

What I have a right to, and what all others have the right to, is what is necessary for subsistence and for as much beyond that as fair structures allow me and them access. Members of underdeveloped countries have a right to the same as I do. Their structures do not presently allow them as much access. It would be pointless, however, to claim that they each had a right to as much oil as I do, even if they have no need or use for oil. They have a right to access when

they have need. This point is often distorted into a claim that those of us with present needs are immoral if we use oil in certain ways, because by our using it now we will deprive others from using it when they have sufficiently developed to have needs similar to ours.

The claim is confused because it assumes that each person has a certain permanent claim on natural resources, rather than on the right to a certain level of life and equality of access. Acknowledging that the waste of unrenewable natural resources is immoral is consistent with the legitimacy of some people using more than others because of their real present needs, even if those needs are at a higher level than those of other people.

No one should seriously hold that each person has the right to a certain amount of land or of oil and that, as the population of the globe increases, the amount of land or of oil to which we are each entitled diminishes accordingly. Basically the moral concern of most people expressed in the intuition of universal ownership is properly translated into a claim that either all should have equal or that all should have an adequate standard of living. That latter claim, rather than a specific claim about ownership, whether it be private or social, is the fundamental one.

Against whom does one appropriately exercise these basic rights? In an abstract sense one exercises them against all other human beings. In a negative sense this means that no one should be kept from taking the means necessary to preserve his life and developing his capacities. But this negative sense is not enough in a society of scarcity. Does anyone in a positive sense have the obligation to implement those basic rights for others? This positive, as opposed to negative, obligation, depends first of all on the fulfillment by the right-holder of the prior obligation to work if he is capable of doing so, to take care of himself, to expend his energy to learn, and so on. Positive obligations of others arise to the extent that the right-holder's own initiatives are inadequate because of the lack of resources, skill, energy, or other necessary factors.

The individual person properly exercises his basic rights first against members of his own society. It is with them that he has the closest social relations, it is with them that he can most readily share benefits and burdens. The obligation to help those in need in a society falls on the other members of the society. These obligations might be met individually or within a family or social unit; usually in organized societies today other general obligations of mutual aid are structured through government.

Just as individuals, who through no fault of their own are unable to secure the means of satisfying their basic needs, have a claim on their fellow citizens, mediated through government, so, if their fellow citizens and government cannot satisfy their basic needs, the individuals have a claim on other people. Just as the individual has a stronger claim on those with whom he forms a closer community than on the larger community, so on the global level one's claim would fall first on those other peoples with whom one has closer ties and, if they are unable to help, then on those further removed who are able to help. Rights that all human beings have *qua* human beings may thus impose obligations on other human beings in foreign lands.

The same foundation for distributive justice on the national level exists on the global level. But the implementation on the global level encounters many difficulties.

When one's society can satisfy its citizens' right to food and the wherewithal for development but does not, the claim of individuals to outside help becomes an individual one on the part of the citizens; it is not the claim of one society or nation on another. As individual, however, the claim is not addressed to other nations as such, and can only be vaguely addressed to other individuals. Their response is limited in many ways—by lack of knowledge, by lack of wherewithal to make the needed goods available, and perhaps by the state structure itself, which often precludes individuals from dealing directly with other individuals. Other mediating groups may or may not be successful.

If we consider the legitimate government of a nation as an actor on the global stage, its main function on the dominant view is *internal* to the nation. Externally it represents the collective body, interacts with other governments, and protects and promotes the interests of its people individually and collectively. It is not established by the people of one nation primarily to help people of other nations. What a government can appropriately do for people of other lands with its resources, natural or monetary, obtained through taxation or derived directly from production, is limited. One can give away one's own money or goods if one chooses. One cannot give away the money and goods of others in the same manner. Such money and goods can be used to fulfill obligations but not, without proper consent, to be charitable. A government uses public monies appropriately to fulfill its own obligations and the obligations of those it represents. This includes seeing to the welfare of all within its jurisdiction. However, the American welfare system does not extend to those in other countries; nor do similar systems in other countries apply to the population of the United States. A government's obligation with respect to other people or peoples is to do them no unjustifiable harm. Its positive obligations to them, if it has any, are a function of the obligations of its members to help others. If the people within a country have the obligation to help foreign people, they may use the mechanism of government and taxes to fulfill that obligation. The government then acts for the people to fulfill the people's (individual or collective) obligation, not its own. If a country owns the productive resources within its borders, then it may allocate a certain amount to fulfill the obligation of its people to others in need.

A Nation's Right to Development

We have already noted that the question to whom the resources of the world properly belong is a rhetorical one. As such it is sometimes used as a means of asserting a nation's right to development, where development means modern industrialization. It is then used to ground claims of one nation against others.

The basis for global justice is the basic right of individuals. Nations are not individuals, and hence nations do not have the same rights as human persons—if nations have rights at all. Human beings have the right to self-development. But the development of human beings is not identical with the industrial development of a nation. The development of a nation is not the same as the development of all the individuals in it, nor even of many of the individuals in it. Although the development of a nation may necessitate having individuals who are developed in certain ways and to a requisite degree, its development is not necessarily the same as their development. However, to the extent that a nation must develop in order to allow and enable its people to develop, it can claim the indirect right to development, based on the human rights of its citizens. A nation has no moral right on this account to develop at the expense of its people; nor does any group within a nation have the right to develop at the expense of other groups.

Nations have no right to continuance, much less to development, simply because they happen to have been established.

What is being claimed in claiming the right of a nation to develop? First, by the right to develop is meant the freedom to develop, that is, the right to be allowed to develop and not be prevented from developing by other nations. Although nations are not human persons, the right to develop as they wish without being kept from their development by other nations is a right easily defended if the nation is seen as the collection of people within it. Each nation legitimately exercises this right providing it does not violate a similar right of other nations and providing it does not violate the rights of the persons who make it up. This claim raises no special problems and is generally acknowledged

in principle, if not always in fact, by proponents even of the status quo view.

Second, the claim to development may be a claim of one nation to receive from those nations that have them the wealth and resources that the first country needs in order to develop as it wishes. This will clearly conflict with the right those others will claim to what they have justly (according to their society's legal system) appropriated, produced, or in other ways obtained. What nations can morally demand is equal access to what they need to develop.

The developed nations do not deny the right of all nations to equal access, and they have in fact developed institutions, e.g., the International Monetary Fund and the World Bank, that assist nations in their development through capital loans. These are funded by developed nations. As the undeveloped nations develop and their people achieve higher standards of living they increase the market for more and more goods. The development of the less developed countries is thus in the interest of the more developed countries. The universal access view insists both on the right of access and the concomitant right to aid from developed nations. What is now done in the name of self-interest or charity should be recognized as a right. As with persons, more can be expected in the way of self-help from nations with more than from nations with less.

The third component of the claim to development is the right to the knowledge—technological, scientific, social, and organizational—necessary for development. Since knowledge is not used up by consumption and is infinitely shareable, it does not fall prey to the tragedy of the commons. All can cultivate it freely and fully without using it up or destroying it. Sharing knowledge necessary for development with underdeveloped countries is among the easiest and most fruitful ways of helping them to help themselves. The moral obligation to make such knowledge available in useful ways to them is greater than the obligation to supply resource-poor countries with material resources. This is because those with such knowledge can do so at less cost to themselves.

Although knowledge is the key to development for underdeveloped countries, they also need capital to finance the substructure—the needed roads, railroads, telephone lines, schools, hospitals, electric power plants and lines, and so on—and the development of home industries. Adam Smith spoke of the wealth of nations. There is also the wealth of the world as a whole. Just as knowledge was not developed by any one person or people and belongs to all mankind, so there is a sense in which the wealth of nations is not the result only of individual enterprise and work, but the result of the contributions of mankind as a whole. Each nation has some claim on that general world wealth.

Conclusion

Global justice forms a basis for poor countries in the name of their citizens to demand aid from rich countries, acting as mediators for their citizens. The demands of distributive justice on the global level, however, are much weaker than the demands of distributive justice that take place within a given society. On the national level distributive justice does not end with simply fulfilling minimal needs and providing equal access. The reason for the difference is that within a society social structures make possible the sharing of both burdens and benefits through organized and accepted social institutions. The members of a society are related in many more ways than are the people of the world.

Even on this minimalist level global justice is difficult—sometimes impossible—to implement even where the will to do so is present because of the lack of global background institutions. In cases of short-term famine and natural disasters there are mechanisms through which the International Red Cross and UN agencies help the stricken country and people with aid; but such agencies are dependent on good will and charity and there is no effective mechanism for proportioning the amount of aid each country should give or of assessing each country its fair share. In cases of chronic malnutrition and severe deprivation of natural resources the situation is even worse.

National sovereignty is one of the central factors preventing the implementation of global justice. The developed nations refuse to recognize any superior international body that has the right to tax them for purposes of redistribution to other countries and to those suffering severe deprivation of their basic needs. Underdeveloped nations are just as reluctant as developed nations to give up their sovereignty and, as recipients of aid, they are reluctant to allow outsiders to dictate how such aid is to be used. This they consider an incursion into their internal affairs.

If we assume that in the present day more harm than good is achieved by attempting forcibly to violate national sovereignty even to achieve the good of helping those in need, the problems associated with implementing global justice are multiplied.

The demands of global justice are actual moral demands on people today. The immediate responsibility of those able to do so, individually and collectively, is not only to respond to them as best they can but also creatively and generously to work towards developing the necessary global implementing organizations and apparatus. Even if people do so, the result will be less than the full global justice possible if all mankind were a single unified society. Nonetheless even if the possibility of developing such a society in the near future is slim, the demands of global justice on at least the minimal level are actual and present. Responding to them is a present actual moral demand that should be widely articulated and met, rather than, as is too often the case, either ignored or denied.

Review and Discussion Questions

1. Should the status quo view of resources be rejected on the ground that the distribution of the world's resources is arbitrary? Does the fact that you have acquired something without having done anything to deserve it imply that you have acquired it arbitrarily? Does it imply that you are not entitled to it or that it is unjust for you to have it?

2. Do you agree with De George that the question of who owns the world's resources is not really an issue of property rights or ownership?

3. De George writes that he and everyone else have a right to "what is necessary for subsistence and for as much beyond that as fair structures allow me and them access." What exactly does this mean? Do you agree that we have such a right? If so, what is its basis?

4. Is De George correct in saying that the basic rights take precedence over property rights? How could this claim be defended? What implications does it have for our conduct?

5. Do you agree that individuals have a claim for the basic necessities of life not only against their own government but against other countries as well?

6. Some philosophers would maintain that, although there can be justice (or injustice) within a country, it makes no sense to speak of global justice (or injustice) because there is no international government tying the world's people together as one society. How would you respond to this position?

7. Can developing nations claim a moral right to economic aid and development assistance from the more developed countries? How much, and what sort of, assistance are developed nations required to give? De George argues that distributive justice demands more on a national level than it does on an international level. If you agree with this view, explain what it means in practical terms.

Welfare and Social Justice

JOHN ISBISTER

The previous essays in this section focus on world poverty and hunger and on issues of global justice, but what does morality require with respect to the less fortunate in our own society? In this essay, John Isbister, professor of economics at the University of California, Santa Cruz, examines the U.S. welfare system. He argues not only that children and working people should be guaranteed a decent living, but also that even those who are voluntarily unemployed should be guaranteed sufficient income to raise them out of poverty. He criticizes the welfare reforms of the 1990s as unjust and proposes replacing the current system with a negative income tax.

Reprinted from John Isbister, "Welfare," in Capitalism and Justice: Envisioning Social and Economic Fairness *(Bloomfield, Conn. Kumarian Press, Inc., 2001), 112–125. Copyright © 2001 Kumarian Press. Some notes omitted.*

Study Questions

1. According to Isbister, why does justice require that rich countries eliminate poverty? What is special about the situation of children?

2. On what grounds does Isbister support welfare even for those who are voluntarily poor? What is Elster's objection to Isbister's position?

3. What were the main changes brought about by reform of the welfare laws in the 1990s?

4. On what grounds does Isbister reject the claim that a democratically elected government can impose whatever conditions it wants on recipients of financial assistance?

5. What is the "doctrine of moral hazard"?

6. Why does Isbister believe that the new welfare system is unjust?

7. Describe the three variants of a negative income system discussed by Isbister.

THE GREATEST INJUSTICE of unregulated, free-market capitalism is that it provides for only some of the people and excludes others. Some get rich, some do reasonably well, and others are left in poverty by the market. Consequently, governments of advanced capitalist countries intervene—in different ways and to different extents—to rescue those for whom the market system does not provide.

The United States Census Bureau estimates that in 1999, 17 percent of the population fell below the poverty line, set at just under $20,000 for a family of four. The poverty rates in the other advanced capitalist countries are at most half the American rate, and in many countries they are far lower than half. Robert M. Solow, citing studies by L. Kenworthy, has shown that the high poverty rate in the United States is the consequence not of anything unusual about American labor markets but rather of a welfare system that does much less to support poor people than do the welfare systems in comparable countries. "What really distinguishes the U.S.," he writes, "is the equanimity with which the majority contemplates the poverty of a minority."[1] . . .

Any assessment of the welfare system is complicated by the fact that there are many different reasons for poverty. Some adults are poor even though they are working for pay part or full time; their wages are insufficient to pull them above the poverty line. Others are in the labor force but unemployed; they are willing and able to work but they cannot find a job. Still others are unable or unwilling to work. In this latter group are found the elderly, the sick, and the physically and mentally disabled, people who simply cannot work, as well as single parents of young children.

One overwhelming fact stands out among all the descriptive facts about poverty, a fact that can guide us through the conflicts of justice and give us a clue to the best sort of welfare programs: all categories of poor adults, no matter what the reasons for their poverty, have children. Children in the United States are twice as likely to be poor as adults. The children are victims of poverty, not its creators. Their parents may or may not be responsible for the poverty in which they live—no doubt some parents are and some are not, some to a greater extent and some to a lesser extent—but not a single child is responsible for her poverty. We can say with certainty, therefore, that programs that punish parents for their alleged irresponsibility do an injustice to their innocent dependent children, none of whom deserve to be impoverished.

Is Poverty Permissible?

The first question is whether it is permissible to have poor people at all in an affluent country. According to the Gospel of Matthew, Jesus said, "For ye have the poor always with you," but first-century Palestine was not a rich society by today's standards, at least in material terms. Jesus' words may still be applicable in today's poor countries, but in a country like the United States where the average family income is close to $90,000,* it is not a requirement of nature that some families subsist on less than $20,000. Poverty could be eliminated simply by taxing those who are better off and transferring enough income to the poor to raise them above the poverty line.

It is difficult to argue against the proposition that since poverty could be eliminated in rich countries, justice requires that it be eliminated. The norms of equality and freedom demand it, and efficiency does not stand in its way. At the very least, . . . equality means equality of opportunity, and equality of opportunity is not available to children who are born into poverty. They lack the opportunities for intellectual and physical development that more affluent children have, and they find it harder to compete as adults. The true meaning of freedom . . . is that people have both the means and the absence of restrictions to pursue their goals. Poverty denies people the means to pursue their goals and therefore restricts their freedom. . . .

There is no excuse for working people to be in poverty. The minimum wage should be sufficient to raise a working person to the poverty level, rather than to just half that level, as it is now. Better programs than currently exist should be available to help people upgrade their skills and be more productive. Community development programs of all sorts can bring businesses and jobs to low-income neighborhoods. Simi-

larly, the unemployed should not fall into poverty. They are looking for work, and it is not their fault that jobs are lacking. Neither should people be poor who are out of the labor force through no fault of their own, whether they are elderly or disabled or responsible for the care of young children or for some other reason. They are equally worthy as everyone else and therefore deserve some of society's bounty, and furthermore their children deserve the chance to start life on an even footing. There is no moral case that is even slightly plausible for allowing such people to live in poverty is an affluent country.

The tricky moral question comes with the voluntarily unemployed.

The Voluntarily Unemployed

Philippe Van Parijs asks whether surfers should be fed.[2] Do people who could work and voluntarily choose not to, for any reason at all, perhaps because they are lazy, have the right to be supported by the income-earning taxpayers? . . .

People who have followed the acrimonious debate over welfare may reasonably object to posing such a question, because it seems to malign poor people as undeserving parasites who have chosen to live off others. My purpose is the opposite. It is well documented that most poor people want to support themselves and get out of poverty.[3] Among those who appear not to want to do so are many who are psychologically incapable of sustained work, so their poverty is not really voluntary. Under the current welfare system, it is not clear that an able-bodied person who voluntarily chose a life of poverty could qualify for any welfare support at all. The current welfare system is, however, terribly unjust; later in this chapter I will propose reforms that would lift every person in the country out of poverty, irrespective of his or her motivations. Even though the proposed new welfare system would contain incentives to work, still I expect that under its provisions some people would

---

*This is the mean family income. Elsewhere Isbister states that the median family income is approximately $45,000. —Ed.

choose not to work but to live off a grant that would leave them just at the margin of poverty. Unless this can be morally justified, the case for completely eliminating poverty collapses.

Under a welfare system such as I will propose, the voluntary poor would no doubt be a varied group. They might be Van Parijs's surfers; they might be contemplatives, scholars, artists, or wanderers. They might work hard at tasks that produced no income, or they might take it easy. They might hope to earn an income by their activities—like Vincent Van Gogh, creating a masterpiece every day but finding no market for his work—or they might be consciously disengaged from income-producing work. What they did with their time might be useful to other people, or not. They might move in and out of income-earning work. Would they have the right to an income sufficient to raise them out of poverty? Another way to put the question is this. Since they would need some income in order to survive, would they have the right to pursue their non-income-producing goals, or would they be forced into income-producing work that they preferred not to do?

Many people would argue that if they can work for pay they must and that any exemption from work constitutes exploitation of the taxpayers. Political scientist John Elster writes, "People who chose to work for an income . . . would have to pay higher taxes in order to support those who took the other option. They would think, correctly in my opinion, that they were being exploited by the other group."[4]

Against this is the argument from freedom. We have the right to pursue our goals and to have the means that are necessary to pursue them. If our goal is art or contemplation, we have the right to pursue our goal just as much as does the person whose goal is to be an investment banker. This cannot be an absolute right, and in this respect the right to pursue the goal of not working for pay is the same as most other freedoms, few of which are absolute. This particular freedom depends upon the existence of

enough total income that the support of a few non-earners is not overly burdensome. It depends upon the number of voluntary non-earners being relatively small and their demands for subsistence being relatively low. It is a right that can be met more easily in the United States or Switzerland than in India or Zimbabwe. Surely it is a good thing, however, not a bad thing, to allow people to pursue the goals they really wish to pursue and not force them into a cookie-cutter life for which they have neither desire nor perhaps aptitude. . . .

The poverty cutoff is a good state-supported income for such people. It is low enough to keep the burden on the taxpayers from being onerous and to ensure that people not be attracted to this lifestyle just for the money. It is high enough that people can survive on it and pursue at least some of their goals.

Elster finds this sort of argument unpersuasive. He is less concerned with the freedom of the surfers and the scholars than with the freedom of the taxpayers. Just because people prefer work to nonwork, he says, is no reason to tax them for support of the nonworkers. "They might well prefer the forty-hour week over the fifty-hour week they had to work because of the high taxes imposed on them by those who chose to live on the grant. Hence the argument from freedom of choice fails, because the workers would be forced by the nonworkers to work harder than they wished."[5]

Elster's is a serious objection. It is not as extreme as the objection to taxation made by libertarians like Robert Nozick, who deny that there is any reason for the state to take away people's legitimately earned income without their individual consent. Elster simply argues that the freedom of people to pursue a life of nonpaid work or leisure conflicts with the freedom of working folk to pursue their goals, and he chooses the latter over the former. He is not alone.

He is wrong in this choice, however. Of course people who work for pay find that their life choices are constrained by the fact that they have to pay taxes. Taxation restricts our individual freedom. Virtually no working person has to change his or her way of life fundamentally because of taxes, however. Taxes limit our choices, but they do not eliminate them. The failure to provide a minimum income to a contemplative, however, is likely to make that entire way of life unattainable. The sorts of restrictions on our freedom imposed by taxes are significantly less severe, it seems obvious to me, than the dictate that one cannot pursue one's life goal. If taxes had to be so high as to be confiscatory, that would be an unacceptable violation of people's freedom to be secure in their property. If the transfer payment were so high as to attract a large number of otherwise working people to the nonworking life, the criterion of efficiency would be violated. Where overall national income is high enough, however, and the transfer payment fairly low, justice requires that even voluntary nonworkers receive financial support from the state.

If even voluntary nonworkers deserve support, there is no question but that the involuntary poor, the great majority, should be rescued from poverty.

Welfare Reform of the 1990s

Prior to the 1990s, most poor people in the United States qualified for some financial support—although usually not enough to raise them above the poverty line—simply because of their low income. Depending upon the category into which they fell, their grant might be higher or lower; for example, people with dependent children typically received more than people without. In either case, however, the welfare support continued for as long as the person remained in poverty. In the 1990s a new philosophy was imposed, first in several states and then nationally with the passage of the Parental Responsibility and Work Opportunity Act in 1996.

Among other provisions, the law replaced the old AFDC (Aid to Families with Dependent Children) with the new TANF (Temporary Assistance to Needy Families):

- The entitlement of poor people to support was replaced by block grants, limited to a certain amount of money, to the states. If and when the grants run out, the people who depend upon them may be out of luck, since the states are not required to make additional expenditures.

- Welfare recipients can be required by the states to work for pay or to enroll in a training program, as a condition of support. They must work after two years on assistance.

- Support is limited to a lifetime maximum of five years, and this period may be shortened by the states. A recipient who has not successfully made the transition to self-sufficiency can be cut off.

The federal law is supplemented by welfare-to-work laws in the states, plus individual county plans. Taken together, it has been a controversial shift in policy, reversing decades of movement in the opposite direction. As it happened, it coincided with a significant decline in the number of people receiving welfare payments. The reasons for this decline are not clear. They may include an improving economy that offered more opportunities to the previously unemployed, and they may also include the success of the new approach in encouraging people to make themselves employable. Critics worry, however, that the decline in welfare rolls may partly be an indication of people being denied welfare support without having yet developed the skills to take care of themselves. Administrative data in most states do not reveal whether people who leave welfare are better off or if they are leaving welfare for work. A survey of New York State residents dropped form welfare under the new law found that only 29 percent had found employment—when employment was defined as earning at least $100 over three months. Other studies have found better results, but this may be because they added together people who voluntarily left welfare because they found a job with those who were involuntarily dropped.

The new time-limited welfare philosophy grew out of a concern that the previous approach to welfare had failed. The old approach had created, it was alleged, a dependent class of people who were encouraged to be unproductive because they were supported by the state. The new approach would require them to become productive, and this would have benefits both for the taxpayers and for the poor people themselves. The taxpayers would be relieved of much of their burden, and the previously poor would have the satisfaction of entering mainstream society.

The Injustice of the New Welfare System

The state does not have the moral right to impose the conditions on welfare recipients that it currently does, conditions relating to marital status, work requirements, and time limits.

It might be claimed that a democratically elected government has the right to impose these sorts of conditions, in return for offering financial support. To reason by analogy, if you pay money to the launderer, you have every right to impose conditions on him: you expect him to starch these shirts, leave those shirts unstarched, patch a rip in your jacket, and have everything washed and ironed by Wednesday morning. No one's rights or freedoms are violated by such an understanding. Why then is it not justified for the state to impose any condition a majority of the people want on welfare recipients?

The difference between the two cases is that you have no obligation to give money to the launderer, whereas people with means have an obligation to poor people. No one would criticize you if you washed your own shirts or if you took your laundry to a different establishment. You have a purely voluntary contract with the launderer: if you do not want to take your shirts to him you do not have to, and if he does not want to wash them he does not have to.

The obligation of middle-class and rich people to the poor is not like this commercial relationship. I do not owe the launderer anything unless he washes my shirts, but I owe poor people at least enough support that they not be destitute. The poor are owed support not because of the services they provide to the nonpoor but because they are human beings of equal moral standing with the nonpoor, human beings who share the same social space. The state does not, therefore, have an unconditional moral right to impose conditions on welfare recipients. It may impose some conditions, but the conditions should be defensible in terms of justice.

The conditions imposed on welfare recipients in the 1990s moved away from justice, not toward it. The first thing to say about them is that they severely restrict the freedom of the recipients. Most importantly, single mothers who would prefer to work in the home with even their very young children or babies have lost this right. They must be out of the house, either working for pay or getting trained. . . . The law will allow women to stay at home only if they are living with their husband or the father of their children. Authorities are entitled to the most personal of information pertaining to sexual habits, in order to identify absent fathers and collect child-support payments. These conditions are demeaning, and they violate the norms of privacy.

Liberty is not the only component of justice, however. Can the new approach to welfare be justified on efficiency grounds? This is how it is usually defended, as a kind of tough-love approach that gets recipients off their duffs and into the world of work so that they can be self-sufficient. It may well have this effect for some poor people, but it does not for others. The issue of efficiency is complex. The most obvious rejoinder for people who think the new system is efficient is to point out that it is based on the bizarre assumption that the raising of young children is not work. The truth is that child care is demanding and that it is just about the most valuable work that exists in our society. For the most part it is not paid work, but that is irrelevant to its true value. It is hard to think of anything more important than giving children a good foundation in life, but this is foreclosed by the new laws.

Beyond this obvious point, economic theory provides two conflicting perspectives on the relationship of efficiency to the welfare system. The first is that individuals know best what is best for them; the second is that insurance creates what is called a "moral hazard." The individuals-know-best doctrine leads to an argument against the imposition of any conditions on welfare recipients. . . . Efficiency . . . means getting the best out of a given set of resources: not the most, in a crude sense of accumulation, but the best. Who is better situated to decide what is best for a person than that person herself? If she is facing the difficult decision to work outside the home or to stay with her young children, is it likely that a social worker or a bureaucrat or a legislator can make the decision better than she can? This is what the current welfare reform assumes, and it is a patronizing assumption. If the conditions imposed by the state are different from the choices the poor person would have made herself, the doctrine of individuals-know-best tells us that the result will be inefficient.

The doctrine of moral hazard, however, gives one pause. The doctrine asserts that the existence of insurance is likely to induce people to make decisions that may be in their own self-interest but that are harmful to society as a whole, decisions they would not make in the absence of insurance. If you have fire insurance on your house, for example, you may be careless with matches, since you will not bear the cost of a fire. There is a real social cost to your house burning down, however, a cost that will be paid by all the purchasers of fire insurance in the form of higher premiums. If you have health insurance, you may go to the doctor more often than is really necessary, since the visits are free to you. They are not free to society, however, and we all pay for excessive medical use through higher health insurance premiums.

Does the welfare system, which can be thought of as insurance protecting against the possibility of being poor, create a moral hazard? It may. Even though the benefits are very low, some people may be induced into staying dependent, not becoming self-sufficient even though they could. This is the reason that the Congress decided to abandon the old entitlement approach to welfare and replace it with the personally intrusive, time-limited, workfare system. The new system can be thought of as an attempt to eliminate the moral hazard attendant upon welfare payments.

We must be careful, though. Just because we are likely safe in thinking that some people fall into the moral-hazard trap, it does not follow that every welfare recipient under the old system became dependent or even that most did. At the time of the debate over welfare reform, a pervasive image existed of the slothful, unmotivated, excessively fecund poor single mother, but no actual evidence existed that the image was accurate for a large number of people. . . .

Some people may be helped by the new system, in the sense of being forced to become self-sufficient when they could have done so all along but were discouraged or demoralized. It is clear, however, that others are hurt, because they are not able to measure up to the demands of the new system and will eventually be dropped from the welfare rolls.

The report card on the new system is therefore this: without question it violates people's freedom to choose their marital arrangements and to choose between caring for children or working outside the home. In terms of efficiency, it may help some become more efficient, but it hurts others by denying them the ability to make choices that they are competent to make. In terms of equality, it certainly harms those—and their children—who are unable in the long run to get a job. Overall, the welfare reform of the 1990s earns a failing grade: it is unjust.

A Welfare System Based on Justice

A way exists to preserve the positive effect of the new system, namely, encouragement of some people to develop labor market skills, while avoiding the negative effects—the facts that it leaves some people still in poverty and worse off than they were before and that it severely limits the freedom of choice of the recipients. It is a system that has sometimes been called the negative income tax.[6] It can be structured in such a way as to meet the goals of pulling everyone out of poverty, giving people an incentive to work and preserving basic freedoms. The current earned-income tax credit goes a small distance in the direction of the negative income tax.

A normal income tax takes money away from people, the amount of the tax depending upon the person's income. A negative income tax gives money to people, the amount of the grant depending upon the person's income. Just as the normal income tax is adjusted by deductions—for example, people can claim deductions for their children and thereby reduce their tax liability—in the same way the negative income tax can be adjusted according to the number of dependents and perhaps other factors. Given these adjustments, the amount of the grant depends only on the person's adjusted income, not upon such factors as marital status, presence of a man in the house, length of time in poverty, participation in training programs, or success in finding a job. In the same way that taxpayers now file a form documenting their income and paying taxes that are based on that income, under the negative income tax poor people would file a form documenting their income and receiving a grant on that basis.

The first and most obvious advantage of the negative income tax over the current or previous welfare system is that it increases the recipients' freedom. They would be free to marry or not to marry, to stay home with the children or not, to get a job or not, to stay in a grant-receiving status for a long time or not. The amount of their grant would be affected by such choices, because the choices would affect their incomes, but their options would not be foreclosed to them by the law. On grounds of liberty, the negative income tax is easily preferable.

The more difficult questions about the negative income tax have to do with equality and efficiency, and here the devil is in the details. The precise terms of the negative income tax make a big difference. Suppose the tax is structured in such a way as to eliminate poverty and nothing more. With zero earned income over the year, a person receives a grant of $20,000. With $10,000 earned income, the grant is $10,000, and with $20,000 earned income, the grant is zero. Above an earned income of $20,000, people begin to pay positive taxes. The consequence is that poverty is eliminated. People who would otherwise be poor are raised to the poverty line. It sounds good, and from the perspective of equality, it certainly is good. It is bad for efficiency, however, since it contains a strong incentive not to work. A negative income tax structured this way has a 100 percent, confiscatory marginal tax rate. Think about a person earning nothing and contemplating whether to get a job and start earning money. Why should she do such a think when she knows that, until she reaches an income of $20,000, her grant will be reduced by a dollar for every dollar she earns? Her take-home income will be $20,000, no matter how much she works.

The problem can be solved, although not easily. Suppose the negative income tax is set up in the following way. A person earning nothing receives a grant of $10,000. For every dollar he earns above zero, his grant is cut back by 50 cents. So, for example, if he earns $10,000, his grant is cut back from $10,000 to $5,000, and he nets $15,000. When he earns $20,000, the poverty line, his grant is cut back by the full $10,000, and he breaks even. This system solves the efficiency problem. The marginal tax rate is just 50 percent, not 100 percent. People get to keep 50 cents out of every extra dollar they earn, so they have an incentive to work. The problem with this second scheme is that it is not very good for equality. In fact, it raises no one out of poverty. It puts money in the hands of the poor, but the gap between their earnings and the poverty line is cut only in half, not completely.

So far, it seems, the negative income tax is good for freedom, but it contains an inherent conflict between equality and efficiency. A solution to this conflict exists, a solution that most observers have rejected out of hand, but which I think makes sense. Why not set the base income at $20,000, the poverty line, rather than $10,000, and impose something like a 50 percent marginal tax rate on all earned income? Here is how it would work. A person earning nothing would get a grant of $20,000, sufficient to pull her out of poverty. With $10,000 earned income, the grant would be cut back to $15,000, for a net income of $25,000. With earned income of $20,000, the grant would be cut back to $10,000, for a net income of $30,000, and so forth. At an earned income of $40,000, the grant would be eliminated completely, and beyond that level people would pay positive taxes. This scheme would resolve both our problems. It would be good for equality, because it would raise everyone out of poverty. It would be good for efficiency, because people could keep half of every extra dollar they earned.

One may usefully compare this scheme with the current philosophy of time-limited welfare. Both embody incentives to get people off welfare and into the labor market, but the negative income tax uses the carrot while the time-limited scheme uses the stick. The difference is dramatic for those who do not or cannot respond to the stick. With the negative income tax, they are as-

sured of a basic income that will keep them out of poverty, while in the time-limited scheme they are left penniless.

The third variant of the negative income tax is, however, very expensive, imposing a heavier burden on the taxpayers than the first two. In the first two, all the transfer payments from the government go to poor people, while people earning more than the poverty-level income begin to pay taxes at a moderate rate. In the third variant, people earning an income up to twice the poverty level receive a subsidy from the taxpayers. The overall distribution of the disbursed funds depends upon the number of people at each income level, but it is easily possible that more money will be transferred to the nonpoor than to the poor. Since so much money would have to be transferred, the positive tax rates on people earning more than $40,000 would have to be significantly higher than in the first two schemes.

One of the ways of understanding why the third variant is so expensive is to see that it is equivalent to what has sometimes been called the unconditional basic income, the basic grant or the demogrant.[7] The basic grant is a flat subsidy, the same amount of money paid to everyone regardless of their earned income. It is untaxed, but all earned income is taxed heavily in order to pay for the grant. The third variant can therefore be thought of as a basic grant of $20,000, with earned income between zero and $40,000 taxed at a 50 percent rate and earned income above that level taxed perhaps at a higher rate.

Neither the negative income tax nor the basic grant is in use in any country, but the structure of both programs reveals the problems and contradictions inherent in most programs of transfers to the poor. The American system of welfare subsidies, while more complex than the negative income tax, faces the same contradictions. If a welfare program is restricted to grants to the poor, it can honor the virtue of equality while violating efficiency (like the first scheme) or it can honor efficiency while violating equality (like the second). If a welfare program is to honor both, in the way that the third scheme does, it will transfer significant resources to the nonpoor and will impose a much higher burden on the taxpayers.

It is important, therefore, to decide whether something like the third plan can be justified. Most analysts of welfare programs have concluded that it is completely out of the question; they think it impossible because it imposes too high a tax burden and unjustified because it transfers resources to the nonpoor. I, on the other hand, think it is exactly what justice calls for. From the perspective of justice, the fact that it does not focus only on the poor is a merit. It narrows the dispersal of take-home incomes in the entire population and hence moves the population closer to a just overall income distribution. . . . All earning less than $40,000 receive some sort of subsidy, helping to push them toward the middle range of incomes. . . . The taxes necessary to finance this transfer are high but not confiscatory. They allow high-income earners to retain some of their incomes, as freedom requires, but they can be structured in such a way as to reduce high incomes significantly and hence reduce the overall dispersion of incomes.

Among these various possibilities, therefore, the third is the best. It eliminates poverty and compresses the range of incomes in the society, while retaining incentives to work and allowing people to keep a portion of their earnings. It is certainly better than the time-limited approach to welfare, an approach that is designed to allow people to fall between the cracks and remain desperately poor.

NOTES

1. Robert M. Solow, "Welfare: The Cheapest Country," *New York Review of Books* 47 (March 23, 2000): 20–23.
2. Philippe Van Parijs, "Why Surfers Should Be Fed: The Liberal Case for an Unconditional Basic Income," *Philosophy and Public Affairs* 20 (1991): 101–31.
3. Robert M. Solow has collected evidence to support this statement in *Work and Welfare* (Princeton, N.J.: Princeton University Press, 1998).
4. Jon Elster, *Solomonic Judgements: Studies in the Limitations of Rationality* (Cambridge: Cambridge University Press, 1989), 215.
5. Elster, *Solomonic Judgements*, 216.
6. The negative income tax was proposed by Milton Friedman in 1962 and has received wide discussion since that time. See Milton Friedman, *Capitalism and Freedom* (Chicago: University of Chicago Press, 1962).
7. Van Parijs, "Why Surfers Should Be Fed," and Philippe Van Parijs, *Real Freedom for All: What (If Anything) Can Justify Capitalism?* (Oxford: Clarendon Press, 1995). For a proposal showing how the basic grant would work in practice, see S. Lerner, C. M. A. Clark, and W. R. Needham, *Basic Income: Economic Security for All Canadians* (Toronto: Between the Lines, 1999).

Review and Discussion Questions

1. Do you agree that justice requires rich countries to eliminate poverty? Explain why or why not. If they are required to eliminate poverty, how should they do it?
2. State and critically assess the arguments for and against the proposition that justice requires us to support those who would rather surf than work. Do you agree that we have an obligation to preserve the voluntarily unemployed from poverty? If we do, how much support should they receive?
3. Assess the welfare reforms discussed by Isbister. Did they make the welfare system fairer? Did they make it more efficient? Do you agree with Isbister that "overall, the welfare

reform of the 1990s earns a failing grade"? Are there considerations in favor of the present welfare system that he has overlooked or failed to do justice to?

4. Would a negative income tax be better—in particular, with respect to freedom, equality, and efficiency—than the present welfare system? Which of the three negative income tax systems discussed by Isbister would be best?

Is Inheritance Justified?

D. W. HASLETT

Many people support inheritance and believe it to be just because they believe it is an essential and necessary feature of capitalism. After reviewing some facts about wealth distribution and inheritance in the United States today, D. W. Haslett, a philosophy professor at the University of Delaware, argues against this view. He contends not only that inheritance is not essential to capitalism but that it is inconsistent with the fundamental values underlying capitalism. In particular, inheritance violates the capitalistic ideals of "distribution according to productivity," "equal opportunity," and "freedom." Haslett maintains, accordingly, that the practice of inheritance as it exists today should be abolished.

Study Questions

1. Do inheritance taxes do much to reduce inequalities in the distribution of wealth today?

2. How does inheritance contravene the ideal of distribution according to productivity?

3. Why does equal opportunity promote productivity and a more just distribution of income?

4. What is the difference between freedom in the narrow sense and freedom in the broad sense?

5. How would abolishing inheritance enhance freedom in the broad sense?

6. What exactly is Haslett's proposal for abolishing inheritance, and what are the three exceptions to it?

7. How does Haslett respond to the objection that without inheritance people will lose their incentive to work hard?

From Philosophy and Public Affairs, *vol. 15, no. 2 (Spring 1986). Copyright © 1986 by Princeton University Press. Reprinted by permission of Princeton University Press. Some notes omitted, and some section titles added.*

I. Background Information

FAMILY INCOME IN THE UNITED STATES today is not distributed very evenly. The top fifth of American families receives 57.3 percent of all family income, while the bottom fifth receives only 7.2 percent.

But, for obvious reasons, a family's financial well-being does not depend upon its income nearly as much as it does upon its wealth, just as the strength of an army does not depend upon how many people joined it during the year as much as it does upon how many people are in it altogether. So if we really want to know how unevenly economic well-being is distributed in the United States today, we must look at the distribution not of income, but of wealth.

Although—quite surprisingly—the government does not regularly collect information on the distribution of wealth, it has occasionally done so. The results are startling. One to two percent of American families own from around 20 to 30 percent of the (net) family wealth in the United States; 5 to 10 percent own from around 40 to 60 percent. The top fifth owns almost 80 percent of the wealth, while the bottom fifth owns only 0.2 percent. So while the top fifth has, as we saw, about eight times the income of the bottom fifth, it has about 400 times the wealth. Whether deliberately or not, by regularly gathering monumental amounts of information on the distribution of income, but not on the distribution of wealth, the government succeeds in directing attention away from how enormously unequal the distribution of wealth is, and directing it instead upon the less unequal distribution of income. But two things are clear: wealth is distributed far more unequally in the United States today than is income, and this inequality in the distribution of wealth is enormous. These are the first two things to keep in mind throughout our discussion of inheritance.

The next thing to keep in mind is that, although estate and gift taxes in the United States are supposed to redistribute wealth, and thereby lessen this inequality, they do not do so. Before 1981 estates were taxed, on an average, at a rate of only 0.2 percent—0.8 percent for estates over $500,000—hardly an amount sufficient to cause any significant redistribution of wealth. And, incredibly, the Economic Recovery Act of 1981 *lowered* estate and gift taxes.

Of course the top rate at which estates and gifts are *allegedly* taxed is far greater than the 0.2 percent rate, on the average, at which they are *really* taxed. Prior to 1981, the top rate was 70 percent, which in 1981 was lowered to 50 percent. Because of this relatively high top rate, the average person is led to believe that estate and gift taxes succeed in breaking up the huge financial empires of the very rich, thereby distributing wealth more evenly. What the average person fails to realize is that what the government takes with one hand, through high nominal rates, it gives back with the other hand, through loopholes in the law. . . . Indeed, as George Cooper shows, estate and gift taxes can, with the help of a good attorney, be avoided so easily they amount to little more than "voluntary" taxes.[1] As such, it is not surprising that, contrary to popular opinion, these taxes do virtually nothing to reduce the vast inequality in the distribution of wealth that exists today.

Once we know that estate and gift taxes do virtually nothing to reduce this vast inequality, what I am about to say next should come as no surprise. This vast inequality in the distribution of wealth is (according to the best estimates) due at least as much to inheritance as to any other factor. Once again, because of the surprising lack of information about these matters, the extent to which this inequality is due to inheritance is not known exactly. One estimate, based upon a series of articles appearing in *Fortune* magazine, is that 50 percent of the large fortunes in the United States were derived basically from inheritance. But by far the most careful and thorough study of this matter to date is that of John A. Brittain. Brittain shows that the estimate based upon the

Fortune articles actually is too low;[2] that a more accurate estimate of the amount contributed by inheritance to the wealth of "ultra-rich" males is 67 percent.[3] In any case, it is clear that, in the United States today, inheritance plays a large role indeed in perpetuating a vastly unequal distribution of wealth. This is the final thing to keep in mind throughout the discussion which follows.

II. Inheritance and Capitalism

Capitalism (roughly speaking) is an economic system where (1) what to produce, and in what quantities, is determined essentially by supply and demand—that is, by people's "dollar votes"—rather than by central planning, and (2) capital goods are, for the most part, privately owned. In the minds of many today, capitalism goes hand in hand with the practice of inheritance; capitalism without inheritance, they would say, is absurd. But, if I am right, the exact opposite is closer to the truth. Since, as I shall try to show in this section, the practice of inheritance is incompatible with basic values or ideals that underlie capitalism, what is absurd, if anything, is capitalism *with* inheritance. . . .

I do not try to show here that the ideals underlying capitalism are worthy of support; I only try to show that inheritance is contrary to these ideals. And if it is, then from this it follows that, *if* these ideals are worthy of support (as, incidentally, I think they are), then we have prima facie reason for concluding that inheritance is unjustified. What then are these ideals? For an answer, we can do no better than turn to one of capitalism's most eloquent and uncompromising defenders: Milton Friedman.

Distribution according to productivity

The point of any economic system is, of course, to produce goods and services. But, as Friedman tells us, society cannot very well *compel* people to be productive and, even if it could,

out of respect for personal freedom, probably it should not do so. Therefore, he concludes, in order to get people to be productive, society needs instead to *entice* them to produce, and the most effective way of enticing people to produce is to distribute income and wealth according to productivity. Thus we arrive at the first ideal underlying capitalism: "To each according to what he and the instruments he owns produces."[4]

Obviously, inheritance contravenes this ideal. For certain purposes, this ideal would require further interpretation; we would need to know more about what was meant by "productivity." For our purposes, no further clarification is necessary. According to *any* reasonable interpretation of "productivity," the wealth people get through inheritance has nothing to do with their productivity. And one need not be an adherent of this ideal of distribution to be moved by the apparent injustice of one person working eight hours a day all his life at a miserable job, and accumulating nothing, while another person does little more all his life than enjoy his parents' wealth, and inherits a fortune.

Equal opportunity

But for people to be productive it is necessary not just that they be *motivated* to be productive, but that they have the *opportunity* to be productive. This brings us to the second ideal underlying capitalism: equal opportunity—that is, equal opportunity for all to pursue, successfully, the occupation of their choice. According to capitalist ethic, it is OK if, in the economic game, there are winners and losers, provided everyone has an "equal start." As Friedman puts it, the ideal of equality compatible with capitalism is not equality of outcome, which would *discourage* people from realizing their full productive potential, but equality of opportunity, which *encourages* people to do so.[5]

Naturally this ideal, like the others we are considering, neither could, nor should, be realized fully; to do so would require, among other things, no less than abolishing the family and engaging in extensive genetic engineering. But the fact that this ideal cannot and should not be realized fully in no way detracts from its importance. Not only is equal opportunity itself an elementary requirement of justice but, significantly, progress in realizing this ideal could bring with it progress in at least two other crucial areas as well: those of productivity and income distribution. First, the closer we come to equal opportunity for all, the more people there will be who, as a result of increased opportunity, will come to realize their productive potential. And, of course, the more people there are who come to realize their productive potential, the greater overall productivity will be. Second, the closer we come to equal opportunity for all, the more people there will be with an excellent opportunity to become something other than an ordinary worker, to become a professional or an entrepreneur of sorts. And the more people there are with an excellent opportunity to become something other than an ordinary worker, the more people there will be who in fact become something other than an ordinary worker or, in other words, the less people there will be available for doing ordinary work. As elementary economic theory tells us, with a decrease in the supply of something comes an increase in the demand for it, and with an increase in the demand for it comes an increase in the price paid for it. An increase in the price paid for it would, in this case, mean an increase in the income of the ordinary worker vis-à-vis that of the professional and the entrepreneur, which, surely, would be a step in the direction of income being distributed more justly.

And here I mean "more justly" even according to the ideals of capitalism itself. As we have seen, the capitalist ideal of distributive justice is "to each according to his or her productivity." But, under capitalism, we can say a person's income from some occupation reflects his or her productivity only to the extent there are no unnecessary limitations upon people's opportunity to pursue, successfully, this occupation—and by

"unnecessary limitations" I mean ones that either *cannot* or (because doing so would cause more harm than good) *should not* be removed. According to the law of supply and demand, the more limited the supply of people in some occupation, then (assuming a healthy demand to begin with) the higher will be the income of those pursuing the occupation. Now if the limited supply of people in some high-paying occupation . . . is the result of unnecessary limitations upon people's opportunity to pursue that occupation, then the scarcity is an "artificial" one, and the high pay can by no means be said to reflect productivity. The remedy is to remove these limitations; in other words, to increase equality of opportunity. To what extent the relative scarcity of professions and entrepreneurs in capitalist countries today is due to natural scarcity, and to what extent to artificial scarcity, no one really knows. I strongly suspect, however, that a dramatic increase in equality of opportunity will reveal that the scarcity is far more artificial than most professionals and entrepreneurs today care to think—*far* more artificial. . . .

That inheritance violates the (crucial) second ideal of capitalism, equal opportunity, is, once again, obvious. Wealth *is* opportunity, and inheritance distributes it very unevenly indeed. Wealth is opportunity for realizing one's potential, for a career, for success, for income. There are few, if any, desirable occupations that great wealth does not, in one way or another, increase—sometimes dramatically—one's chances of being able to pursue, and to pursue successfully. And to the extent that one's success is to be measured in terms of one's income, nothing else, neither intelligence, nor education, nor skills, provides a more secure opportunity for "success" than does wealth. Say one inherits a million dollars. All one then need do is purchase long-term bonds yielding a guaranteed interest of 10 percent and (presto!) one has a yearly income of $100,000, an income far greater than anyone who toils eight hours a day in a factory will probably ever have. If working in the factory pays, relatively, so little, then why, it might be asked, do not all these workers become big-time investors themselves? The answer is that they are, their entire lives, barred from doing so by a lack of initial capital which others, through inheritance, are simply handed. With inheritance, the old adage is only too true: "The rich get richer, and the poor get poorer." Without inheritance, the vast fortunes in America today, these enormous concentrations of economic power, would be broken up, allowing wealth, and therefore opportunity, to become distributed far more evenly.

Freedom

But so far I have not mentioned what many, including no doubt Friedman himself, consider to be the most important ideal underlying capitalism: that of liberty, or, in other words, freedom. This ideal, however, takes different forms. One form it takes for Friedman is that of being able to engage in economic transactions free from governmental or other types of human coercion. The rationale for this conception of freedom—let us call it freedom in the "narrow" sense—is clear. As Friedman explains it, assuming only that people are informed about what is good for them, this form of freedom guarantees that ". . . no exchange will take place unless both parties benefit from it."[6] If at least the parties themselves benefit from the transaction, and it does not harm anyone, then, it is fair to say, the transaction has been socially valuable. So people with freedom of exchange will, in doing what is in their own best interests, generally be doing what is socially valuable as well. In other words, with this form of freedom, the fabled "invisible hand" actually works.

All of this is a great oversimplification. For one thing, a transaction that benefits both parties may have side effects, such as pollution, which harm others and, therefore, the transaction may not be socially valuable after all. So freedom, in the narrow sense, should certainly not be absolute. But the fact that freedom, in

this sense, should not be absolute does not prevent it from serving as a useful ideal. . . .

There are [those] whose conception of freedom is that of not being subject to any governmental coercion (or other forms of human coercion) for any purposes whatsoever—a conception sometimes referred to as "negative" freedom. It is true that governmental (or other) coercion for purposes of enforcing the abolition of inheritance violates this ideal, but then, of course, so does any such coercion for purposes of *maintaining* inheritance. So this "anticoercion" ideal . . . neither supports nor opposes the practice of inheritance, and therefore this conception of freedom need not concern us further here. . . .

A very popular variation of the anticoercion conception of freedom is one where freedom is, once again, the absence of all governmental (or other human) coercion, *except for any coercion necessary for enforcing our fundamental rights.* Prominent among our fundamental rights, most of those who espouse such a conception of freedom will tell us, is our right to property. So whether this conception of freedom supports the practice of inheritance depends entirely upon whether our "right to property" should be viewed as incorporating the practice of inheritance. But whether our right to property should be viewed as incorporating the practice of inheritance is just another way of stating the very point at issue in this investigation. . . . Consequently, this popular conception of freedom cannot be used here in support of the practice of inheritance without begging the question.

But there is still another conception of freedom espoused by many: that which we might call freedom in the "broad" sense. According to this conception of freedom, to be free means to have the ability, or the opportunity, to do what one wants. For example, according to this conception of freedom, rich people are, other things being equal, freer than poor people, since their wealth provides them with opportunities to do things that the poor can only dream about. . . .

Let us now see whether inheritance and freedom are inconsistent. Consider, first, freedom in the narrow sense. Although inheritance may not be inconsistent with this ideal, neither is the *abolishment* of inheritance. This ideal forbids governmental interference with free exchanges between people; it does not necessarily forbid governmental interference with *gifts* or *bequests* (which, of course, are not *exchanges*). Remember, Friedman's rationale for this ideal is, as we saw, that free exchange promotes the "invisible hand"; that is, it promotes the healthy functioning of supply and demand, which is at the very heart of capitalism. Supply and demand hardly require gifts, as opposed to exchanges, in order to function well.

If anything, gifts and bequests, and the enormous concentrations of economic power resulting from them, hinder the healthy functioning of supply and demand. First of all, gifts and bequests, and the enormous concentrations of economic power resulting from them, create such great differences in people's "dollar votes" that the economy's demand curves do not accurately reflect the needs of the population as a whole, but are distorted in favor of the "votes" of the rich. And inheritance hinders the healthy functioning of supply and demand even more, perhaps, by interfering with supply. As we have seen, inheritance (which, as I am using the term, encompasses large gifts) is responsible for some starting out in life with a vast advantage over others; it is, in other words, a major source of unequal opportunity. As we have also seen, the further we are from equal opportunity, the less people there will be who come to realize their productive potential. And, of course, the less people there are who come to realize their productive potential, the less overall productivity there will be or, in other words, the less healthy will be the economy's *supply* curves. So, while inheritance may not be *literally* inconsistent with freedom in the narrow sense, it does, by hindering indirectly both supply and demand, appear to be inconsistent with the "spirit" of this ideal. . . .

So we may conclude that, at best, inheritance receives no support from freedom in the narrow sense. But it remains for us to consider whether inheritance receives any support from the other relevant ideal of freedom, an ideal many, including myself, would consider to be the more fundamental of the two: freedom in the broad sense—being able to do, or having the opportunity to do, what one wants. So we must now ask whether, everything considered, there is more overall opportunity throughout the country for people to do what they want with inheritance, or without it.

On the one hand, without inheritance people are no longer free to leave their fortunes to whomever they want and, of course, those who otherwise would have received these fortunes are, without them, less free to do what they want also.

But to offset these losses in freedom are at least the following gains in freedom. First, as is well known, wealth has, generally speaking, a diminishing marginal utility. What this means is that, generally speaking, the more wealth one already has, the less urgent are the needs which any given increment of wealth will go to satisfy and, therefore, the less utility the additional wealth will have for one. This, in turn, means that the more evenly wealth is distributed, the more overall utility it will have.* And since we may assume that, generally speaking, the more utility some amount of wealth has for someone, the more freedom in the broad sense it allows that person to enjoy, we may conclude that the more evenly wealth is distributed, the more overall freedom to which it will give rise. Now assuming that abolishing inheritance would not lessen *overall* wealth . . . and that it would indeed distribute wealth more evenly, it follows

---

* The more evenly wealth is distributed, the more overall utility it will have since any wealth that "goes" from the rich to the poor, thereby making the distribution more even, will (given the diminishing marginal utility of wealth) have more utility for these poor than it would have had for the rich, thus increasing overall utility.

that, by abolishing inheritance, there would be some gain in freedom in the broad sense attributable to the diminishing marginal utility of wealth. Next, abolishing inheritance would also increase freedom by increasing equality of opportunity. Certainly those who do not start life having inherited significant funds (through either gift or bequest) start life, relative to those who do, with what amounts to a significant handicap. Abolishing inheritance, and thereby starting everyone at a more equal level, would obviously leave those who otherwise would have suffered this handicap (which would be the great majority of people) more free in the broad sense.

I, for one, believe these gains in freedom—that is, those attributable to the diminishing marginal utility of wealth and more equality of opportunity—would *more* than offset the loss in freedom resulting from the inability to give one's fortune to whom one wants. Abolishing inheritance is, I suggest, analogous to abolishing discrimination against blacks in restaurants and other commercial establishments. By abolishing discrimination, the owners of these establishments lose the freedom to choose the skin color of the people they do business with, but the gain in freedom for blacks is obviously greater and more significant than this loss. Likewise, by abolishing inheritance the gain in freedom for the poor is greater and more significant than the loss in freedom for the rich. So to the list of ideals that inheritance is inconsistent with, we can, if I am right, add freedom in the broad sense.

To recapitulate: three ideals that underlie capitalism are "distribution according to productivity," "equal opportunity," and "freedom," the latter being, for our purposes, subject to either a narrow or a broad interpretation. I do not claim these are the *only* ideals that may be said to underlie capitalism; I do claim, however, that they are among the most important. Inheritance is inconsistent with both "distribution according to productivity," and "equal opportunity." Perhaps it is not, strictly speaking, inconsistent with the ideal of freedom in the narrow sense, but neither is the abolishment of inheritance.

On the other hand, it probably *is* inconsistent with what many would take to be the more fundamental of the two relevant ideals of freedom: freedom in the broad sense. Since these are among the most important ideals that underlie capitalism, I conclude that inheritance not only is not essential to capitalism, but is probably inconsistent with it. . . .

III. A Proposal for Abolishing Inheritance

First, my proposal for abolishing inheritance includes the abolishment of all large gifts as well—gifts of the sort, that is, which might serve as alternatives to bequests. Obviously, if such gifts were not abolished as well, any law abolishing inheritance could be avoided all too easily.

Of course we would not want to abolish along with these large gifts such harmless gifts as ordinary birthday and Christmas presents. This, however, raises the problem of where to draw the line. I do not know the best solution to this problem. The amount that current law allows a person to give each year tax free ($10,000) is too large a figure at which to draw the line for purposes of a law abolishing inheritance. We might experiment with drawing the line, in part at least, by means of the distinction between, on the one hand, consumer goods that can be expected to be, within ten years, either consumed or worth less than half their current value and, on the other hand, all other goods. We can be more lenient in allowing gifts of goods falling within the former category since, as they are consumed or quickly lose their value, they cannot, themselves, become part of a large, unearned fortune. The same can be said about gifts of services. But we need not pursue these technicalities further here. The general point is simply that, so as to avoid an obvious loophole, gifts (other than ordinary birthday presents, etc.) are to be abolished along with bequests.

Next, according to my proposal, a person's estate would pass to the government, to be used for the general welfare. If, however, the government were to take over people's property upon their death then, obviously, after just a few generations the government would own virtually everything—which would certainly not be very compatible with capitalism. Since this proposal for abolishing inheritance *is* supposed to be compatible with capitalism, it must therefore include a requirement that the government sell on the open market, to the highest bidder, any real property, including any shares in a corporation, that it receives from anyone's estate, and that it do so within a certain period of time, within, say, one year from the decedent's death. This requirement is, however, to be subject to one qualification: any person specified by the decedent in his will shall be given a chance to *buy* any property specified by the decedent in his will before it is put on the market (a qualification designed to alleviate slightly the family heirloom/business/farm problem discussed elsewhere). The price to be paid by this person shall be whatever the property is worth (as determined by governmental appraisers, subject to appeal) and any credit terms shall be rather lenient (perhaps 10 percent down, with the balance, plus interest, due over the next 30 years).

Finally, the abolishment of inheritance proposed here is to be subject to three important exceptions. First, there shall be no limitations at all upon the amount a person can leave to his or her spouse. A marriage, it seems to me, should be viewed as a joint venture in which both members, whether or not one stays home tending to children while the other earns money, have an *equally* important role to play; and neither, therefore, should be deprived of enjoying fully any of the material rewards of this venture by having them taken away at the spouse's death. And unlimited inheritance between spouses eliminates one serious objection to abolishing inheritance: namely, that it is not right for a person suddenly to be deprived, not only of his or her spouse, but also of most of the wealth upon which he or she has come to depend—especially in those cases where the spouse has, for the sake

of the marriage, given up, once and for all, any realistic prospects of a career.

The second exception to be built into this proposal is one for children who are orphaned, and any other people who have been genuinely dependent upon the decedent, such as any who are mentally incompetent, or too elderly to have any significant earning power of their own. A person shall be able to leave funds (perhaps in the form of a trust) sufficient to take care of such dependents. These funds should be used only for the dependent's living expenses, which would include any educational or institutional expenses no matter how much. They should not, of course, be used to provide children with a "nest egg" of the sort others are prohibited from leaving their children. And at a certain age, say twenty-one (if the child's formal education has been completed), or upon removal of whatever disability has caused dependency, the funds should cease. This exception eliminates another objection to abolishing inheritance—the objection that it would leave orphaned children, and other dependents, without the support they needed.

The third and final exception to be built into this proposal is one for charitable organizations—ones created not for purposes of making a profit, but for charitable, religious, scientific, or educational purposes. And, in order to prevent these organizations from eventually controlling the economy, they must, generally, be under the same constraint as is the government with respect to any real property they are given, such as an operating factory: they must, generally, sell it on the open market within a year. . . .

IV. An Objection

We turn next to what is, I suppose, the most common objection to abolishing inheritance: the objection that, if people were not allowed to leave their wealth to their children, they would lose their incentive to continue working hard, and national productivity would therefore fall. In spite of the popularity of this objection, all the available evidence seems to indicate the contrary. For example, people who do not intend to have children, and therefore are obviously not motivated by the desire to leave their children a fortune, do not seem to work any less hard than anyone else. And evidence of a more technical nature leads to the same conclusion: people, typically, do not need to be motivated by a desire to leave their children (or someone else) great wealth in order to be motivated to work hard.[7]

Common sense tells us the same thing. The prospect of being able to leave one's fortune to one's children is, no doubt, for some people one factor motivating them to be productive. But even for these people, this is only *one* factor; there are usually other factors motivating them as well, and motivating them to such an extent that, even if inheritance were abolished, their productivity would be unaffected. Take, for example, professional athletes. If inheritance were abolished, would they try any less hard to win? I doubt it. For one thing, abolishing inheritance would not, in any way, affect the amount of money they would be able to earn for use during their lives. So they would still have the prospect of a large income to motivate them. But there is something else which motivates them to do their best that is, I think, even more important, and is not dependent on money: the desire to win or, in other words, to achieve that which entitles them to the respect of their colleagues, the general public, and themselves. Because of the desire to win, amateur athletes compete just as fiercely as professionals. Abolishing inherit-

ance would in no way affect this reason for doing one's best either. Athletes would still have the prospect of winning to motivate them. Businessmen, doctors, lawyers, engineers, artists, researchers—in general, those who contribute most to society—are not, with respect to what in the most general sense motivates them, really very different from professional athletes. Without inheritance, these people would still be motivated by the prospect of a sizable income for themselves and, probably even more so, by the prospect of "winning"; that is, by the prospect of achieving, or continuing to achieve, that which entitles them to the respect of their colleagues, the general public, and themselves.

NOTES

1. George A. Cooper, *A Voluntary Tax? New Perspectives on Sophisticated Estate Tax Avoidance* (Washington, D.C.: Brookings Institution, 1979).

2. John A. Brittain, *Inheritance and the Inequality of National Wealth* (Washington, D.C.: Brookings Institution, 1978), pp. 14–16.

3. *Ibid.,* p. 99.

4. Milton Friedman, *Capitalism & Freedom* (Chicago: University of Chicago Press, 1962), pp. 161–162.

5. Milton & Rose Friedman, *Freedom to Choose* (New York: Harcourt Brace Jovanovich, 1979), pp. 131–140. . . .

6. Friedman, *Capitalism & Freedom,* p. 13.

7. See, for example, D. C. McClelland, *The Achieving Society* (Princeton: Van Nostrand, 1961), pp. 234–235; and Seymour Fiekowsky, *On the Economic Effects of Death Taxation in the United States* (unpublished doctoral dissertation, Harvard University, 1959), pp. 370–371.

Review and Discussion Questions

1. Has Haslett correctly identified the fundamental ideals underlying capitalism? Would you agree that inheritance is contrary to capitalism's fundamental values?

2. Do you agree that inheritance violates the principle of equality of opportunity and that abolishing it would promote productivity and a distribution of income that is fairer even by capitalist standards?

3. Explain and assess Haslett's argument that abolishing inheritance would not violate capitalism's commitment to freedom in the narrow sense and would actually enhance people's freedom in the broad sense.

4. How feasible do you find Haslett's proposal for abolishing inheritance? Would you modify it in any way?

5. Has Haslett overlooked any arguments in favor of inheritance? How would a utilitarian look at Haslett's proposal? Would abolishing inheritance violate anyone's moral rights?

14

CONCLUDING ESSAY

Can Higher Education Foster Higher Morals?

DEREK BOK

When any college course draws to an end, it is natural to reflect on what you have learned from it. In a philosophy class, it is natural to reflect not only on what you have learned but also on the deeper and longer-term value, if any, of your having studied the particular issues that you did. In particular, people often question the purpose, relevance, and value of studying ethics at the college or university level. After all, are not students already moral, and if not, isn't it too late to do anything about their morality? In this essay Derek Bok, former president of Harvard University, explains why the teaching of ethics has been controversial and upholds the offering of courses in applied ethics as part of a comprehensive program in moral education. In addition to offering ethics courses, universities need to discuss codes of conduct with students and administer them fairly; they need to set high standards in dealing with moral issues on campus and to encourage programs of community service; and they should be alert to the moral messages contained in the countless institutional signals sent to students.

Study Questions

1. Why are people concerned today about the university's impact on students' ethical standards?
2. On what grounds have neoconservatives attacked university courses on ethics?
3. How did Socrates' approach differ from the traditional Athenian way of teaching ethics and civic responsibility? How did Aristotle's approach contrast with that of Socrates?
4. How does Bok respond to the objection that courses on ethics and moral reasoning have no effect on behavior?

Reprinted by permission of the author from Business and Society Review *66 (Summer 1988).*

5. What is wrong with the way most universities treat the rules governing student conduct?

6. How does the atmosphere of the university encourage administrators and faculty to adhere to ethical standards?

As PEOPLE EVERYWHERE worry about our ethical standards, universities are bound to come under scrutiny. Almost every public servant, business executive, attorney, physician—indeed, virtually all leaders in every walk of life—enter our colleges and professional schools and remain there for several formative years. Other institutions in society also play an important role in the development of young people—especially families, schools, and communities of faith. But only a minority of children now grow up in a two-parent family, and the time they spend with adults of any kind has been dropping steadily for several decades. Schools are often preoccupied with problems of racial integration, political intervention, drugs, and strikes while suffering the effects of a long-term decline in the status of teachers. Religious institutions no longer seem as able as they once were to impart basic values to the young. In these circumstances, universities need to think hard about what they can do in the face of what many perceive as a widespread decline in ethical standards.

Such evidence as we have about the values of college students only heightens these concerns. Several studies have found that undergraduates are growing less altruistic and more preoccupied with self-serving goals. In polls of entering freshmen over the past fifteen to twenty years, the values that have risen most are the desire to be "very well off financially," to gain personal recognition, and to "have administrative responsibility for the work of others." The goal that has plummeted furthest is the desire to find "a meaningful philosophy of life," while other values that have fallen include the desire to keep up-to-date in political affairs, to participate in community action programs, and to help clean up the environment. Further studies suggest that the number of college students who admit to having cheated in class has risen appreciably over the past thirty years.

Amid these trends, how confident are we that universities are graduating executives "well prepared to lead in the general management of people and organizations in the service of society"? How certain can we be that our professional schools are preparing lawyers "ready to aid in the shaping of those wise restraints that make us free" or public officials able "to offer leadership in the quest for enlightened public policy"? In their quest to fulfill these goals, what *can* universities do and what *should* they do to help students to achieve higher ethical standards? As we will discover, these questions have provoked a curious debate in which neither side seems to hear what the other is saying.

Awkward Discussions

While courses on ethics have made their way into the curriculum, enthusiasm has burned more brightly among alumni than within the university. In the professional schools particularly, there is little talk of ethical issues outside the classroom except with close friends. Granted, no one is against discussing these topics, but many feel awkward in doing so. Some believe that such talk will seem soft and sentimental in an atmosphere that appears to value intellectual toughness and close analysis. Others worry that they will be thought to be pompous and overbearing. At bottom, many may harbor a secret fear that once they start discussing ethical issues openly, they will reach conclusions that force them into troubling reassessments of their life and future career.

Able instructors teaching elective courses can usually overcome such reticence and provoke a lively interest in their classes. But the rest of the faculty tend to regard these offerings with tepid interest or outright skepticism. Only rarely is instruction in ethics made a part of the required curriculum. Instead, courses in applied ethics, if they exist at all, are elective and taken only by a minority of the student body. . . .

Skeptical Faculty

Faculty members have several reasons for being skeptical. A decade ago there was concern that applied ethics was a soft subject that would fall into the hands of ideologues bent on forcing their views on students. These fears have receded with experience. A more troublesome problem, however, is the dearth of well-trained faculty to offer instruction, especially in professional schools. Courses in professional ethics are difficult to teach because they call for preparation in two entirely different subjects: moral philosophy (or a related discipline) and some area of practical application, such as government, law, business, or medicine. Since no established program in a university combines training in both fields, instructors typically have to teach themselves an important part of what they need to know. Such preparation can often be inadequate, causing instruction to be irritatingly superficial or theoretical.

The obstacles within the academy pale beside the objections from another quarter. Prominent neoconservatives have vociferously attacked the new ethics courses on several grounds. These critics claim that teachers of practical ethics are so anxious to be tolerant of differing ethical systems and creeds that they lead students to believe that all moral views are entitled to equal respect. Neoconservatives also deplore the constant assurances by instructors that they will not

engage in indoctrination, even to the point of refusing to endorse such basic virtues as honesty and keeping one's word. Finally, teachers of applied ethics are attacked for emphasizing difficult moral dilemmas that seem to have no convincing solution, thus leaving the impression that all questions of morality are unanswerable. Because of these shortcomings, critics claim that courses in practical ethics, at best, will confuse students, reinforce their ethical relativism, and fail to improve their standards of behavior. At worst, it is said, participants will emerge from such classes more cynical about ethics and cleverer at thinking up plausible arguments for any course of conduct they wish to follow.

Secretary of Education William Bennett voiced these concerns with customary verve when he stated: "Where are our colleges and universities, on the issue of their responsibility to foster moral discernment in their students? With the exception of a relatively few places—mostly religious or military institutions—higher education is silent." When asked about efforts such as the moral reasoning courses in the core curriculum, he replied: "That's about [moral] dilemmas, lifeboat stuff. I don't mean theory. I meant getting drugs off campus." Alas, the debate was never squarely joined, nor has it been in other forums. Bennett and his supporters seem bent on caricaturing the new courses without understanding what the instructors are actually doing. Proponents of applied ethics, on the other hand, have failed to answer Bennett's charge to look beyond the classroom and consider aspects of most education apart from courses on ethical issues.

Viable Program

The current controversy over the teaching of ethics echoes a dispute dating back at least to ancient Greece. In fifth-century Athens, two schools of thought emerged on how to carry out the critical task of teaching ethics and civic responsibility. The traditional view relied on exhorting the young to do the proper thing and punishing them when they failed. The newer way, urged by Socrates, sought to teach people to know the good by provoking them to think about fundamental moral aims and dilemmas. Socrates argued that those who had not learned to reason about such questions could not apply their principles to the shifting circumstances they would face in later life. In this he was surely correct. Yet Socrates sometimes talked as if knowledge alone would suffice to ensure virtuous action. He did not stress the value of early habituation, positive example, and obedience to rules in giving students the desire and self-discipline to live up to their beliefs and to respect the basic norms of behavior essential to civilized communities. For this neglect he was savagely attacked. It fell to Aristotle to see the wisdom of combining both traditions to help young people acquire not merely an ability to think clearly about ethical problems but the desire and will to put their conclusions into practice.

In the contemporary university, as in ancient Greece, the key question is how to combine education in moral reasoning with a broader effort to teach by habit, example, and exhortation. The ability to reason is essential to help us make our way through all the confusing dilemmas and conflicting arguments that abound in an era when society's consensus on issues of value has disintegrated under the weight of cultural diversity, self-serving rationalization, technological change, and other complexities of modern life. But moral reasoning alone may not be enough to cause us to behave morally. How, then, can a university go further and help students to develop the desire and the will to adhere to moral precepts without resorting to forms of indoctrination inimical to the academy?

The very question will make many people uneasy. The history of higher education is studded with efforts to develop character that in retrospect seem quaint, ineffective, or downright objectionable. More often than not, such endeavors have degenerated into crude attempts to impose particular doctrines or petty rules of behavior. Nevertheless, moral education is too important to discard merely because of past failures. Besides, universities cannot avoid the task whether or not they relish the responsibility. Like it or not, they will affect the moral development of their students by the ways in which they administer their rules of conduct, by the standard they achieve in dealing with ethical issues confronting the institution, by the manner in which they counsel their students and coach their athletic teams. The only question is whether they choose to proceed deliberately and with forethought. Let us consider, then, how an institution could construct a program to help its students to enhance not only their capacity to perceive moral issues and to think about them clearly, but their ability to put their ethical beliefs into practice. Having described what such a program might look like, we can then ask whether the attempt is worth making.

Early Steps

The first weeks that students spend at a university are often critical in shaping their attitudes toward the institution and their expectations of what they will take away from their experience. Never again are they likely to be so attentive to what the institution says or so open to advice about what aspirations and values matter most. As a result, colleges that are concerned about moral education will need to emphasize this aspect of the undergraduate experience at the very outset in catalogues and welcoming speeches. . . .

Although the traditional liberal arts curriculum may not automatically provide an adequate moral education, it undoubtedly helps in many ways to develop ethical awareness and moral reasoning. The study of literature can awaken one's conscience by making more vivid the predicament of others. Traditional courses in ethics can provide a philosophical foundation for thinking precisely about moral issues. Studying the social sciences can help students to understand the causes and effects of various policies and practices and thus appreciate their moral significance more precisely. Indeed, almost any well-taught course can strengthen the capacity to think more carefully about intellectual problems, including ethical issues. Together, these experiences help to explain why several studies have found that young people continue to develop their powers of moral reasoning as long as they remain in school or at the university and usually cease to do so when their formal education comes to an end.

Ethics and Humanism

Yet by themselves, traditional courses in the liberal arts do not go far enough. Neither history nor the classics have yielded a sufficiently compelling normative vision to justify the hopes of a Jowett or a Burckhardt that studying these subjects would enable students to learn how to lead a virtuous life. Humanistic disciplines have become too preoccupied with other concerns to give close attention to ethical questions, and most professors in these fields do not feel competent to teach such material. Besides, courses in the liberal arts are deliberately nonvocational and hence are unlikely to consider the complicated moral dilemmas that arise within the professions.

Moral Dilemmas

These are the gaps that the new courses in applied and professional ethics seek to fill. Properly taught, they can yield important benefits. By studying problems that commonly arise in personal and professional life, students will be more likely to perceive moral dilemmas they would otherwise ignore. By finding that these dilemmas raise issues that are susceptible to careful reasoning and argument, students will be less inclined, not more, to believe that every ethical view is entitled to tolerance and respect. By learning to analyze moral issues more rigorously, students will realize that often such problems *do* have reasonably clear solutions, given basic ethical premises that almost all human beings share.

Skeptics will reply that courses in moral reasoning have no effect on *behavior*, but this criticism seems overdrawn. To be sure, no instruction can suffice to turn a scoundrel into a virtuous human being. But most young people arrive at the university with decent instincts and a genuine concern for others. For them, courses that foster an ability to detect ethical issues more perceptively, to think about them more carefully, to understand more clearly the reasons for acting morally seem likely not only to train their minds but to have a positive effect on their behavior as well.

In view of these benefits, there is ample reason to encourage students to take classes devoted to ethical dilemmas arising in their personal or professional lives. The question then arises whether to offer special courses on this subject or to include material on ethical dilemmas in regular courses where such issues arise naturally out of the material. Both alternatives have merit. It is undoubtedly important, at least in professional schools, to encourage faculty members in a variety of courses to discuss ethical issues arising naturally from the subject matter in their classes. Only a comprehensive effort of this kind will make the point that ethics is not simply a specialized topic confined to a separate world but a subject that is relevant to all aspects of professional life. At the same time, without courses specifically devoted to moral problems, there will be no one to teach the subject in depth, no one to carry on sustained writing in the field, no one to whom other faculty members can turn for advice on how to deal with ethical questions arising in their own courses.

Under such conditions, efforts to insert ethical issues into the regular curriculum will almost certainly wither. A wise faculty, therefore, will seek to provide *both* special courses in applied ethics *and* opportunities to discuss moral problems as they emerge in other subjects throughout the curriculum.

Rules of Conduct

Even the staunchest advocates of applied ethics courses would admit that their effects on behavior are limited and uncertain. Hence, universities need to consider extending their efforts beyond the classroom. An obvious step in this direction is to have rules that prohibit lying, cheating, stealing, violent behavior, interference with free expression, or other acts that violate fundamental norms. Such rules not only protect the rights of everyone in the community, they also signal the importance of basic moral obligations and strengthen habits of ethical behavior.

But students do not learn to put ethical precepts into practice by rules and punishments alone. This much seems evident from looking at the disobedience that accompanied the stern campus discipline of the nineteenth century. If rules are truly to educate and not merely to coerce, campus officials must bear further principles in mind.

Although universities no longer stand *in loco parentis* toward their students, their purpose is always to teach and to explain. Hence, those who administer discipline should enact rules only where they have a persuasive justification and should publish the reasons for each requirement whenever the rationale is not clear. This point seems obvious, yet it is frequently overlooked. For example, even though I have regularly presided over faculty meetings that have approved student regulations, only recently did I realize how many rules are stated summarily even when they seem to call for explanation. It is not immediately obvious why "recognized

organizations must maintain their local autonomy," or why "no organizations shall be allowed to appear on a commercially sponsored radio or television program," or why "no student resident in a university dormitory may operate a business out of his or her room."

Bereft of reasons that connect the rules with underlying ethical principles, such regulations can evoke a legalistic attitude in which only published rules are obeyed and students object to being punished for any conduct that is not expressly prohibited. Worse yet, as more and more prohibitions accumulate, many of them are not enforced at all by campus authorities. Not only does this permit an arbitrary use of power, but it undermines the importance of rules and makes them an object of cynicism and derision.

Even when regulations *are* discussed, the explanation can be formalistic and inadequate. This is especially true in the case of prohibitions on the use of alcohol and drugs. Too often the official literature fails to explain why using these substances is wrong. Instead, there is a tendency to concentrate on warning students of the legal consequences. Thus, the standard letter to Harvard students on the subject of drugs begins with the sentence: "Attached is a summary of the laws that deal with illicit drugs in the Commonwealth of Massachusetts." A letter to students on drinking begins: "If you serve alcohol to friends under 21, you are opening yourself to arrest, fine and imprisonment."

Such statements are not irrelevant, of course; students need to be warned. What is lacking is a serious effort to explain why such rules exist by pointing out, for example, that almost all acts of violence on campus are linked to alcohol and that teenage drinking produce[s] an inordinate number of traffic fatalities. . . . Such explanations will doubtless provoke the retort that drinking wine or sherry at a Master's reception could not possibly result in highway deaths or violent brawls. But this reply itself can be an occasion for more extended discussion of why people should not decide for themselves in what way and under what circumstances to obey legitimate laws. Such discussions may not be easy or brief. Without them, however, a university can leave the impression that laws against alcohol and drugs are merely arbitrary requirements placed on young people by hypocritical and uncaring elders.

Fair Administration

A second requirement, which hardly needs explanation, is that regulations must be administered fairly and consistently with penalties sufficient to make the rules credible. Most campuses satisfy this standard most of the time. But some rules, such as prohibitions against drinking alcohol or smoking marijuana, are often not enforced by proctors who object to the law or do not wish to become unpopular by reporting violations. Violations of a political nature, such as harassing speakers or occupying buildings, frequently result in only token penalties as long as no violence is done to persons or property. Still other rules are rarely invoked against certain privileged persons, a practice that has become more common as universities find themselves in strenuous competition for money, visibility, and prestige. It is rivalry of this sort that accounts for the willingness of some universities to overlook the petty corruptions of big-time athletic coaches or to tolerate famous professors who spend unconscionable amounts of time away from their campus duties.

On other occasions, faculty members or administrators will seek to camouflage embarrassing incidents to avoid adverse publicity. Few institutions are free of such lapses. Some years ago, for example, local newspapers recounted the extraordinary tale of a resident in one of our teaching hospitals who had sexually assaulted several patients. Rather than discipline the culprit or insist on appropriate psychiatric treatment, those in charge first arranged for him to leave quietly and then sent letters of recommen-

dation to other hospitals, without mentioning the circumstances of his departure. Needless to say, the lesson conveyed by this episode could hardly have been worse.

A final aim in maintaining discipline should be to involve students in the process of devising and administering rules. The more responsibility students can assume, the more likely they are to understand the reasons for regulations and to gain a stake in implementing them successfully. For example, no system for maintaining the right to speak on campus is likely to work well without building a strong grass-roots consensus based on thorough understanding of the reasons for valuing free expression.

In addition to discussing rules, students can also assist in their administration. Most institutions include students as members of judicial bodies at least for some types of offenses. An even more extensive form of student participation occurs in schools with honor codes. At Haverford, for example, undergraduates not only vote each year on whether to renew their code but take responsibility for educating freshmen about the system, sit on judicial boards to consider violations, and pledge to report classmates if they observe them cheating.

Acquiring Concern

Moral responsibility cannot develop through rules and penalties alone. It must grow out of a genuine concern for others and a desire to respect their legitimate interests. The best way of acquiring such concern is to experience situations in which one can appreciate the effects of one's actions on others and understand how one's own interests are affected in return. Education does not automatically provide enough of these experiences. Often, students pursue their studies alone in competition with their peers for the grades that will give them entry to the best graduate schools and the choicest careers. Without more, such an environment can drive people apart rather than enhance their sense of responsibility to others. This danger can be countered by extracurricular activities that bring the participants into collaborative or communal relationships—especially if someone with experience is available to offer advice and counsel when ethical challenges arise.

In graduate and professional schools, on the other hand, such activities are less numerous and the curriculum may not offer many opportunities for properly supervised collaboration. When I was dean of Harvard Law School, the faculty actually refused to allow eight students to collaborate in writing a third-year project because it was impossible to grade each student's individual contribution. Rather than discourage such initiatives, professional school faculties need to build cooperative work into the educational program and foster adequately supervised group activities of a quasi-professional nature outside the curriculum.

Among these activities, community service programs are especially valuable because they offer such a vivid opportunity to perceive the needs of others while feeling the satisfaction of helping people less fortunate than themselves. Such programs are all the more important today in light of the fifteen-year trend among college students toward valuing self-centered aspirations at the expense of more altruistic goals. To encourage these activities, universities should encourage them publicly, offer seed money to help them get started, and assist their administration and supervision. Professional schools might even offer further incentives by giving positive weight to applications from students who have devoted substantial time and effort to endeavors of this kind. . . .

Institutional Environment

Despite its anarchic, irreverent qualities, the atmosphere of the university helps in important ways to cause administrators and faculty members to adhere to ethical standards. Campus debate can clarify moral choices and improve the

quality of official decisions. Prevailing scholarly values emphasizing accuracy and meticulousness reinforce high standards of intellectual honesty. In an environment that relies on personal influence rather than formal power, presidents, deans, and professors all have to behave ethically in order to gain respect. . . .

The examples universities set through their official policies are but a few of the innumerable messages bearing ethical content that pass through the campus community. Coaches periodically grapple with moral issues in full view of their players as they strive to resolve conflicts between winning and playing by the rules. Financial aid officers must cope with students who misrepresent their family assets. Proctors have to respond to petty acts of discrimination against black students, women, or homosexuals. In the way they treat individual students and staff, professors signal whether important personalities need have concern for others or whether one can get ahead with little regard for anyone save oneself. By the questions asked, even application forms suggest the importance professional schools attach to matters of character as opposed to matters of intellect.

In seeking to create an ethical environment, universities must try to make these implicit messages affirm rather than undermine basic moral values. Yet those in authority act with much less power than leaders of many other organizations possess. The strong commitment to academic freedom precludes them from trying to influence the views of faculty members even if a professor utters bizarre ethical opinions or openly disparages moral values. . . . Moreover, universities have largely abandoned the attempt to pick professors on the basis of their moral character. However sincere their concern for ethical standards, therefore, universities must proceed with little control over the adults who have the greatest influence on the lives of students.

Fortunately, most faculty members do set high standards of probity, conscientiousness, and service to others. Moreover, a university can emphasize character in appointing other adult figures who touch the lives of students in important ways: deans and other administrators, athletic coaches, faculty heads of student residences, and many more.

Of course, situations will arise in which faculty members or administrators behave in improper ways. But one can learn from bad examples as well as good ones. Indeed, a morally perfect environment might be a poor preparation for the real world. What is truly destructive, therefore, is not the fact that immoral acts occur but the willingness of an administration to overlook them. This is a matter that does lie within the university's control. Even the tenets of academic freedom do not prevent an administration from holding the faculty to appropriate rules regarding sexual harassment, conflicts of interest, excessive consulting, and other forms of misconduct. . . .

Program Reconsidered

These, then, are the elements of a comprehensive program of moral education: offering courses in applied ethics at the college and professional school level, discussing rules of conduct with students and administering them fairly, building programs of community service, striving for a high ethical standard in dealing with moral issues facing the university, and finally, being more alert to the countless signals that institutions send to students so that these messages will support rather than undermine basic norms.

But will these efforts do any good? A university is only one institution among many that affect students' lives. It offers an experience late in youth when ideas and values are more developed and students less open to adult advice than in earlier years. It competes with television, motion pictures, and the tumult of an outside world replete with scandals and lurid exposés. With its commitment to intellectual freedom and diversity, a university even lacks the power to bring a

consistent, coordinated influence to bear on those who live and work within its walls.

Despite these limitations, the years of college and professional school still represent an important stage in the development of most young people. In graduate schools of law, business, medicine, and the like, students form a sense of what kind of a professional they wish to be— what skills and attitudes matter most and how they can adapt their values to the special circumstances and challenges of their calling. In college, freshmen arrive, free from family influence, to think about their lives in new and different ways. As many observers have noted, this experience frequently leads students to discard a simple moral code they have previously acquired in favor of a new set of values. These values are often the product of considerable thought and introspection and are typically built upon some notion of the reciprocal obligations human beings need to observe toward one another in order to form a viable community. In Carol Gilligan's words, "Moral development in the college years thus centers on the shift from moral ideology to ethical responsibility."

As students search to define their ethical responsibilities, the university can play an important role. Its usefulness comes in part from the capacity to instill a greater respect for facts and a greater ability to reason carefully about complicated problems. Equally valuable is its diverse community populated by students and faculty with many different backgrounds and points of view. Such an environment teaches tolerance, a respect for differing values, a recognition of the complexity of human problems. In so doing, it prepares students well for the real world and helps a perceptive person to acquire a moral understanding far richer and more firmly rooted in the intricacies of modern life than simpler dogmas nurtured in more homogeneous, more carefully controlled environments.

These advantages, however, are not sufficient to ensure a sound moral education. Indeed, they carry substantial risks that need to be countered by a serious effort on the part of the university. Precisely because its community is so diverse, set in a society so divided and confused over its values, a university that pays little attention to moral development may find that many of its students grow bewildered, convinced that ethical dilemmas are simply matters of personal opinion beyond external judgement or careful analysis.

Nothing could be more unfortunate or more unnecessary. Although moral issues sometimes lack convincing answers, that is often not the case. Besides, universities should be the last institutions to discourage a belief in the value of reasoned argument and carefully considered evidence in analyzing even the hardest human problems. And universities should be among the first to reaffirm the importance of basic values, such as honesty, promise keeping, free expression, and nonviolence, for these are not only principles essential to civilized society, they are values on which all learning and discovery ultimately depend. There is nothing odd or inappropriate, therefore, for a university to make these values the foundation for a serious program to help students develop a strong set of moral standards.

Review and Discussion Questions

1. How much can the university contribute to an individual's moral education? How much has your university experience contributed to your moral development? How much has this course contributed?

2. What do you see as the benefits of studying ethics? Are there drawbacks? Should a course in applied ethics be required of all students?

3. Some might argue that students are either moral or they are not. If they are, they don't need an ethics course; if they are not, then the college years are too late. Either way, studying ethics won't do students any good. How would you respond to this argument?

4. Are the rules of conduct at your college or university discussed and examined in the way Bok recommends?

5. Do you agree with Bok that the university should encourage community service programs?

FOR FURTHER READING

Ethical Theory

Christina Hoff Sommers, ed., *Right and Wrong: Basic Readings in Ethics* (New York: Harcourt Brace Jovanovich, 1986) and Mark Timmons, ed., *Conduct and Character: Readings in Moral Theory,* 3rd ed. (Belmont, Calif.: Wadsworth, 1999) contain important, accessible essays on Kantianism, utilitarianism, relativism, egoism, and other topics. Tom L. Beauchamp, *Philosophical Ethics,* 2nd ed. (New York: McGraw-Hill, 1991) is an excellent introduction to ethics, combining text and readings on the nature of morality, on classical ethical theories, and on rights, liberty, and justice. Peter Singer, ed., *A Companion to Ethics* (Cambridge, Mass.: Blackwell, 1991) is a comprehensive reference work with survey essays by many individual authors on both theoretical and applied issues. William H. Shaw, *Contemporary Ethics: Taking Account of Utilitarianism* (Oxford: Blackwell, 1999) sympathetically examines the utilitarian approach to ethics. Three large collections of more difficult essays on a variety of theoretical topics in ethics that have engaged contemporary philosophers are George Sher, ed., *Moral Philosophy: Selected Readings,* 2nd ed. (New York: Harcourt Brace Jovanovich, 1998), Louis P. Pojman, ed., *Ethical Theory: Classical and Contemporary Readings,* 3rd ed. (Belmont, Calif.: Wadsworth, 1998), and Thomas L. Carson and Paul K. Moser, eds., *Morality and the Good Life* (New York: Oxford University Press, 1997).

Suicide, Euthanasia, and Abortion

The following four collections are a good place to start; they contain intelligent but accessible essays on both sides of these controversial issues, along with further references: John Donnelly, ed., *Suicide: Right or Wrong?* (Buffalo, N.Y.: Prometheus, 1990); Robert M. Baird and Stuart E. Rosenbaum, eds., *Euthanasia: The Moral Issues* (Buffalo, N.Y.: Prometheus, 1989) and *The Ethics of Abortion: Pro-Life vs. Pro-Choice,* rev. ed. (Buffalo, N.Y.: Prometheus, 1993); Joel Feinberg, ed., *The Problem of Abortion,* 2nd ed. (Belmont, Calif.: Wadsworth, 1984). L. W. Sumner defends a moderate position on abortion from a basically utilitarian perspective in *Abortion and Moral Theory* (Princeton, N.J.: Princeton University Press, 1981), as does D. W. Haslett in "On Life, Death, and Abortion," *Utilitas,* vol. 8., no. 2 (July 1996). Essays by Jeffrey Reiman and Don Marquis debate the morality of abortion in the *Journal of Social Philosophy,* vol. 27, no. 3 (Winter 1996); vol. 29, no. 1 (Spring 1998); and vol. 29, no. 2 (Fall 1998).

Animals and Environmental Ethics

Peter Singer, *Animal Liberation,* 2nd ed. (New York: Random House, 1990) is a seminal work advocating a radical change in our treatment of animals. Harlan B. Miller and William H. Williams, eds., *Ethics and Animals* (Clifton, N.J.: Humana Press, 1983) and Peter Singer and Tom Regan, eds., *Animal Rights and Human Obligations,* 2nd ed. (Englewood Cliffs, N.J.: Prentice-Hall, 1989) both contain good philosophical essays that debate our obligations to animals. *The Monist,* vol. 70, no. 1 (January 1989) focuses on "animal rights," with several essays discussing Tom Regan's influential book *The Case for Animal Rights* (Berkeley: University of California Press, 1983). David Paterson and Richard D. Ryder, eds., *Animals' Rights—a Symposium* (London: Centaur Press, 1979) and Peter Singer, ed., *In Defence of Animals* (Oxford: Blackwell, 1985) are interesting and readable collections of essays favorable to animal rights, with contributions from a number of leading animal-rights activists. R. G. Frey ably defends meat eating in *Rights, Killing, and Suffering* (Oxford: Blackwell, 1983). Robert M. Baird and Stuart E. Rosenbaum, eds., *Animal Experimentation: The Moral Issues* (Buffalo, N.Y.: Prometheus, 1991) offers accessible essays, both pro and con.

On environmental ethics, the following two collections are a good place to begin: Tom Regan, ed., *Earthbound: Introductory Essays in Environmental Ethics* (Prospect Heights, Ill.: Waveland, 1984) and Donald VanDeVeer and Christine Pierce, eds., *People, Penguins, and Plastic Trees,* 2nd ed. (Belmont, Calif.: Wadsworth, 1995). Robin Attfield, *The Ethics of Environmental Concern,* 2nd ed. (New York: Columbia University Press, 1991) is a solid introduction to the subject, and the journal *Environmental Ethics* is a good source of more advanced work in the field.

Liberty, Paternalism, and Freedom of Expression

Richard A. Wasserstrom, ed., *Morality and the Law* (Belmont, Calif.: Wadsworth, 1971) contains some classic essays on John Stuart Mill's principle and the legal enforcement of morality. Also recommended are Robert M. Baird and Stuart E. Rosenbaum, eds., *Morality and the Law* (Buffalo, N.Y.: Prometheus, 1988) and—for rather more advanced reading—Rolf Sartorius, ed., *Paternalism* (Minneapolis: University of Minnesota Press, 1983). C. L. Ten, *Mill on Liberty* (Oxford: Oxford University Press, 1980) and John C. Rees, *John Stuart Mill's* On Liberty (Oxford: Oxford University Press, 1985) are very good for further scholarly study of Mill's classic essay. Daniel Shapiro, "Smoking Tobacco: Irrationality, Addiction, and Paternalism,"

Public Affairs Quarterly, vol. 8, no. 2 (April 1994) is a response to Robert E. Goodin's book *No Smoking.* Fred Berger, ed., *Freedom of Expression* (Belmont, Calif.: Wadsworth, 1980) is a good source of some important essays on the topic. On free speech and racial harassment, with special reference to Stanford University's policy, see Thomas C. Grey, "Civil Rights Versus Civil Liberties: The Case of Discriminatory Verbal Harassment," *Social Philosophy & Policy,* vol. 8, no. 2 (Spring 1991).

Reproduction, Marriage, and Family Obligations

John A. Robertson, "Surrogate Mothers: Not So Novel After All," and Herbert T. Krimmel, "The Case Against Surrogate Parenting," *Hastings Center Report* (October 1983) are widely cited. Among more recent work, Sara Ann Ketchum, "Selling Babies and Selling Bodies," *Hypatia,* vol. 4, no. 3 (Fall 1989) (with a reply by Heidi Malm) and Michele M. Moody-Adams, "On Surrogacy: Morality, Markets, and Motherhood," *Public Affairs Quarterly,* vol. 5, no. 2 (April 1991) are worth consulting. Margaret Radin, "Market Inalienability," *Harvard Law Review* 100 (June 1987) is not easy for introductory students, but it has had a significant influence on recent critics of surrogacy. Both Debra Satz, "Markets in Women's Reproductive Labor," and Richard J. Arneson, "Commodification and Commercial Surrogacy," *Philosophy & Public Affairs,* vol. 21, no. 2 (Spring 1992) respond to Elizabeth Anderson. Glenn McGee criticizes cloning in "Parenting in an Era of Genetics," *Hastings Center Report,* vol. 27, no. 2 (1997) while John Harris defends it in "'Goodbye Dolly?' The Ethics of Human Cloning," *Journal of Medical Ethics,* vol. 23 (1997).

Richard Wasserstrom, "Is Adultery Immoral?" *Philosophical Forum,* vol. 5 (1974) is a classic. James Rachels's "Morality, Parents, and Children," in George Graham and Hugh LaFollette, eds. *Person to Person* (Philadelphia: Temple University Press, 1989) addresses the relationship between moral impartiality and the special concern we feel for our children.

Sexuality

Susan Dwyer, ed., *The Problem of Pornography* (Belmont, Calif.: Wadsworth, 1995), and David Copp and Susan Wendel, eds., *Pornography and Censorship* (Buffalo, N.Y.: Prometheus, 1983) are very useful collections, as are Robert M. Baird and Katherine M. Baird, eds., *Homosexuality* (Buffalo, N.Y.: Prometheus, 1995) and Robert M. Baird and Stuart E. Rosenbaum, eds., *Same-Sex Marriage* (Buffalo, N.Y.: Prometheus, 1997). Chapter 4 of John Arthur, *The Unfinished Constitution* (Belmont, Calif.: Wadsworth, 1989), is a clear and engaging discussion of the constitutional issues surrounding obscenity and pornography, including recent feminist efforts to outlaw pornography. In Leslie Francis, ed., *Date Rape* (University Park, Penn.: Penn State Press, 1996), several writers critically assess Lois Pineau's analysis; see in particular, Catharine Pierce Wells, "Date Rape and the Law: Another Feminist View." David Boonin responds to Jeff Jordan's argument in "Same-Sex Marriage and the Argument from Public Disagreement," *Journal of Social Philosophy,* vol. 30, no. 2 (Summer 1999).

Affirmative Action

Steven M. Cahn, ed., *The Affirmative Action Debate* (New York: Routledge, 1995), Marshall Cohen, Thomas Nagel, and Thomas Scanlon, eds., *Equality and Preferential Treatment* (Princeton, N.J.: Princeton University Press, 1977), and *Social Philosophy & Policy*, vol. 5, no. 1 (Autumn 1987), "Equal Opportunity," and vol. 8, no. 2 (Spring 1991), "Reassessing Civil Rights," provide useful selections of philosophical essays both for and against affirmative action. Gertude Ezorsky, *Racism and Justice: The Case for Affirmative Action* (Ithaca, N.Y.: Cornell University Press, 1991) is a short, clear defense. In "The Spoils of Victimhood," *The New Yorker* (March 27, 1995), Michael Kinsley analyzes the politics behind the backlash against affirmative action. For a good but challenging critique of the diversity argument for affirmative action, see George Sher, "Diversity," *Philosophy & Public Affairs*, vol. 28, no. 2 (Spring 1999).

Crime and Punishment

For essays both for and against gun control, see Lee Nisbet, ed., *The Gun Control Debate: You Decide* (Buffalo, N.Y.: Prometheus, 1990). Hugh LaFollette, "Gun Control," *Ethics*, vol. 110, no. 2 (January 2000), provides a cool, thoughtful discussion of this controversial topic. Also useful is Todd C. Hughes and Lester H. Hunt, "The Liberal Basis of the Right to Bear Arms," *Public Affairs Quarterly*, vol. 14, no. 1 (January 2000).

  Hugo Adam Bedau is a long-time critic of the death penalty. His "Capital Punishment" in Tom Regan, ed., *Matters of Life and Death* (New York: Random House, 1980) is a very useful introduction; also recommended is his book *Death Is Different: Studies in the Morality, Law, and Politics of Capital Punishment* (Boston: Northeastern University Press, 1987). Ernest van den Haag and John P. Conrad debate capital punishment in *The Death Penalty: A Debate* (New York: Plenum, 1983). Tom Sorell, *Moral Theory and Capital Punishment* (Oxford: Blackwell, 1988) draws the links between normative theory and the debate over capital punishment in a clear and accessible way. Some influential essays on both capital punishment and the justification of punishment in general are reprinted in Robert M. Baird and Stuart E. Rosenbaum, eds., *Punishment and the Death Penalty* (Buffalo, N.Y.: Prometheus, 1995).

Economic Justice

John Arthur and William H. Shaw, eds., *Justice and Economic Distribution*, 2nd ed. (Englewood Cliffs, N.J.: Prentice-Hall, 1991) contains representative extracts from the major contemporary theories of justice along with recent essays discussing the topic. Will Kymlicka, *Contemporary Political Philosophy* (Oxford: Oxford University Press, 1990) covers today's major schools of political thought and their competing views of justice and community. On world hunger, Will Aiken and Hugh LaFollette, eds., *World Hunger and Morality*, 2nd ed. (Englewood Cliffs, N.J.: Prentice-Hall,

1996), Nigel Dower, *World Hunger—Challenge and Response* (York, England: Ebor Press, 1983), and Henry Shue, *Basic Rights: Subsistence, Affluence, and U.S. Foreign Policy* (Princeton, N.J.: Princeton University Press, 1980) are all recommended. Jean Drèze and Amartya Sen, *Hunger and Public Action* (Oxford: Oxford University Press, 1989) brings economic theory and empirical data to bear on the analysis of world hunger. For more of Peter Singer's thinking, see his essay "The Singer Solution," *New York Times Magazine* (September 5, 1999). Mark L. Ascher, "Curtailing Inherited Wealth," *Michigan Law Review* (October 1990) is a long, extensively documented critique of our inheritance system. For further development of Haslett's views, see his essay "Distributive Justice and Inheritance," in Guido Erreygers and Toon Vandevelde, eds., *Is Inheritance Legitimate? Ethical and Economic Aspects of Wealth Transfers* (Heidelberg: Springer, 1997).